Penman of the Founding

THE PATRIOTIC AMERICAN FARMER.
J-N D-K-NS——N Esqr. BARRISTER at LAW:
Who with Attic Eloquence and Roman Spirit hath Asserted,
The Liberties of the BRITISH Colonies in America.

'Tis nobly done, to Stem Taxations Rage,
And raise, the thoughts of a degen'rate Age,
For Happiness, and Joy, from Freedom Spring;
But Life in Bondage, is a worthless Thing.

Printed for & Sold by R. Bell. Bookseller

Penman of the Founding

A Biography of John Dickinson

JANE E. CALVERT

OXFORD
UNIVERSITY PRESS

Oxford University Press is a department of the University of Oxford. It furthers
the University's objective of excellence in research, scholarship, and education
by publishing worldwide. Oxford is a registered trade mark of Oxford University
Press in the UK and certain other countries.

Published in the United States of America by Oxford University Press
198 Madison Avenue, New York, NY 10016, United States of America.

Library of Congress Cataloging-in-Publication Data
Names: Calvert, Jane E., 1970– author.
Title: Penman of the founding : a biography of John Dickinson / Jane E. Calvert.
Other titles: Biography of John Dickinson
Description: New York, NY : Oxford University Press, [2024] | Includes index.
Identifiers: LCCN 2024006342 (print) | LCCN 2024006343 (ebook) |
ISBN 9780197541692 (hardback) | ISBN 9780197541715 (epub)
Subjects: LCSH: Dickinson, John, 1732–1808. |
Statesmen—United States—Biography. | United States. Continental Congress—Biography. |
United States—Politics and government—1775–1783. |
Founding Fathers of the United States—Biography. | Quakers—Pennsylvania—Biography.
Classification: LCC E302.6.D5 C357 2024 (print) | LCC E302.6.D5 (ebook) |
DDC 973.3092 [B]—dc23/eng/20240209
LC record available at https://lccn.loc.gov/2024006342
LC ebook record available at https://lccn.loc.gov/2024006343

DOI: 10.1093/oso/9780197541692.001.0001

Printed by Sheridan Books, Inc., United States of America

Contents

Acknowledgments

This biography was over twenty years in the making; yet it is also that much premature and more than two hundred years overdue. One might consider that it was begun at a 2002 Liberty Fund conference on Dickinson in Philadelphia. Unbeknownst to me at the time, Librarian James Green at the Library Company of Philadelphia (LCP) had recommended me to the organizers, as I had a chapter on Dickinson planned for my doctoral dissertation. Excited to attend and learn more about this elusive figure, I was shocked when Kenneth Bowling, editor at the First Federal Congress Project, introduced me as the "Dickinson expert" of the group. To be sure, that label said much more about the poor state of Dickinson scholarship than my abilities or knowledge. There I also met historian Paul Rahe, who, along with Ken, became a mentor and friend, and historian Lance Banning, whose position I would assume at the University of Kentucky only five years later after his untimely death. There I floated my nascent ideas about Dickinson and the Quaker influences on his politics. I seem to recall that they fell flat. Nevertheless, although I didn't realize it at the time, I was launched as a Dickinson scholar.

This book is the final third of a trilogy of projects that comprised my scholarly research agenda. The first element is *Quaker Constitutionalism and the Political Thought of John Dickinson* (Cambridge 2009), the first exposition of Dickinson's political theory as it grew out of Quakerism. The second element is the necessary prequel to the biography, *The Complete Writings and Selected Correspondence of John Dickinson* (University of Delaware Press, 2020–). To create this, in 2010 I founded the John Dickinson Writings Project (JDP). To date, the JDP has produced three of an estimated twelve volumes of his papers, only scratching the surface of his life's work.

In the acknowledgments of any respectable Founder biography, one will find generous expressions of gratitude to the editors of the documentary editions on which the author depended. The papers of Benjamin Franklin, George Washington, Thomas Jefferson, and others present the biographer with tidy packages of information in the form of clean and orderly documents that have been explicated and contextualized with meticulous annotations. The biographer must only peruse the pages and pluck the materials to craft the narrative. There certainly must be additional research to weave the tale, but the foundational work is already done. A main reason why no full and accurate biography of Dickinson has been produced until now is because, unlike every other major Founder, his complete papers had never been collected and published. Volume One of the *Writings* and the epilogue of this biography tell the story.

That this biography is appearing in 2024 instead of 2044 is due to Governor John Carney of Delaware. From a desire to educate the citizens of Delaware about Dickinson, he asked me to prioritize the biography over my other two jobs—teaching college history courses and working on the JDP. To free me from these duties, the Delaware legislature granted me funds to pay the University of Kentucky (UK) to release me from most teaching responsibilities and so the JDP could hire a managing editor in my place. The legislature obliged, and the department of state administered the grant to UK.

The other funder was the Public Scholars program at the National Endowment for the Humanities. I am grateful to historians Nancy Isenberg and the late, great Gary Nash, who recommended me for the award. In addition to allowing me to buy out my remaining courses and write full time, the NEH's flexibility with deadlines during the time of COVID-19 was a significant relief.

Producing this study was one of the most grueling exercises of my career. Writing began in earnest in March 2020, just as lockdown started. Like university faculty around the world, I was ousted from my office, separated from my books, and denied access to the archives and scholarly community, all essential tools for writing a book. My husband, away from home in the second year of his medical residency, was seeing COVID patients. My elderly mother with a heart condition resided with me. My colleagues were all struggling with remote teaching. In this fraught isolation, I flailed in an unfamiliar genre with mostly raw sources. Because the JDP had not yet published a single volume, it was (and still is) mainly a few hundred gigabytes of minimally processed materials—namely thousands of digital images of Dickinson's inscrutable drafts and some first-pass transcriptions—and no scholarly apparatus to contextualize the documents, many of which lack even a date or title. But this was still more than the two other Dickinson biographers had possessed. I am thus deeply appreciative of those who have worked on the project over the years to help me begin processing the documents. My debts to them, the JDP partners and funders, and those in the documentary editing community are expressed in the volumes.

Archivists and institutional support staff have been critical to the success of the JDP and thus this biography. Among the archivists, six stand out: Connie King of the LCP, Sarah Heim, formerly of the Historical Society of Pennsylvania (HSP) and now at University of Pennsylvania's Kislak Center, Steve Smith of the HSP, Margaret Dunham Raubacher at the Delaware Public Archives, and Leslie White and Barnaby Bryan of the Middle Temple. Without their vast knowledge of the collections they steward and their infinite patience filling my endless requests, my research on Dickinson would be partial at best. Similarly, for many years, staff at UK aided the JDP. Particularly, grants officer Mary Boulton helped me submit immensely complicated and stressful grant proposals to federal agencies and never let on that she noticed my innumeracy. And without IT Infrastructure Director Jon Milby ensuring that my staff, collaborators, and I had access to digital files and databases, there could hardly have been a project at all.

Before lockdown, members of the Early American Seminar that met in Frankfort, Kentucky, coordinated by historian Brad Wood, provided helpful feedback on the prologue, as did friend and scholar A.J. Aiséirithe. Writing in isolation during lockdown was hard; writing in an unfamiliar genre with partial sources and a tight deadline was panic-inducing. There were, however, instances of reassurance. Literary scholars Charlotte Gordon and Gretchen Gerzina offered much-appreciated advice and encouragement. Fellow historians and aspiring biographers Amy Speckart and Ben Lyons formed a little support group with me. Their feedback on the writing and other difficulties was invaluable. Other constants have been John Sweeney and the Friends of the John Dickinson Mansion, not to mention the staff at the Dickinson Plantation itself, especially Gloria Henry, who has been with me since the beginning, and also Vertie Lee and Anne Fenimore. I am grateful to those such as Randy Flood and Liz Covart, a new breed of historian with a knack for reaching the general public through digital media, who took an interest in my work and publicized it. Thanks also goes to many hosts for speaking engagements over the years who gave me the opportunity to refine my thoughts and gauge the interest of public audiences in Dickinson.

When I returned to the classroom, over several semesters I taught a Founders biography course in which game upper-level and honors undergraduates served as guinea pigs, slogging diligently through early drafts and offering suggestions about what worked and what didn't. I am especially appreciative of those students who chose to write their reviews on the Dickinson manuscript. It was a challenging enough assignment without also having the author present. But Tabitha Charter, James Vowels, and Stephen Lumpp each rose admirably to the occasion. Special mention goes to Abigail Mortell, who suffered through the earliest version, when it was little better than a two-hundred-pound toddler bellowing for attention and taking hostages. Evidence of the apparent Stockholm Syndrome she developed as a result is that she is currently an excellent full-time Assistant Editor at the JDP.

Growing out of the JDP was the John Dickinson Symposium that took place in Philadelphia in October 2022. Sponsored by the American Philosophical Society, the HSP, the LCP, the McNeil Center for Early American Studies, and the Omohundro Institute for Early American History and Culture, this event was the first of its kind for Dickinson. Scholars with early access to the JDP files produced ground-breaking essays that gave me fresh scholarly perspectives on Dickinson. Kevin Bendesky, Rebecca Brannon, Charlotte Crane, Charles Fithian, Jon Kershner, Nathan Kozuskanich, Jelte Olthof, and Helena Yoo, while presenting on very different topics, including criminal jurisprudence, aging, taxation, the military, and Indian diplomacy, offered analyses that expanded, complemented, and affirmed my sense of Dickinson as a thinker and actor. This enlarged sense, in turn, informed and clarified my narrative of Dickinson's life

I feel very fortunate to have connected with professionals in various fields who facilitated this journey. To reduce the bloated first draft chapters, I hired developmental editor Rio Hartwell. He not only demonstrated skillfully how they could be pared down while preserving their essence, discussions with him rekindled my excitement and confidence. My agent, Giles Anderson, guided me well at each turn and helped me land with editor Timothy Bent at OUP who, from our first discussion, impressed me by explaining to me why this biography was unique and important. With unfailing graciousness, he guided me towards best practices. Like the NEH, Tim understood well the trials authors faced during COVID, and, without blinking, cheerfully granted me an extension that allowed me to write the book I wanted to write. When the two other massive bureaucracies involved with this project conspired to compel speed over quality, Giles Anderson, and JDP volunteer Chris Koelbl, Michael Poliakoff, and Jack and Helen Rakove offered support and perspective. I was especially glad to have attorney Edwin H. Clark in my corner, whose Dickinsonian strategizing allowed me to resist their pressure.

I am privileged to have gained the support of scholars who, to me in my early career, seemed hardly more accessible than distant stars. In my very first conference presentation on Dickinson, it seemed unbelievable that Pauline Maier was in the audience and engaging with me in discussion of his political thought. We had worked together only briefly when she passed away much too soon. I was fortunate to receive enthusiastic remarks from Al Young while a fellow at the Newberry Library. Peter Mancall kindly helped me publish one of my earliest essays on Dickinson while I was a fellow at the Huntington Library. Losing the ever-affirmative Gary Nash was a blow. When he and wife, Cindy, welcomed me into their home, I showed up in my Dickinson t-shirt to find Gary in his Thomas Paine t-shirt. We puzzled together on Dickinson's work, and I lament that he isn't here to check my conclusions. Another great loss was friend and colleague Richard Bernstein, who, himself a noted biographer, always had helpful and encouraging advice about "the Founding guys." I learned an immense amount from teaching his biographies of Jefferson and Adams many times, and I would have valued more conversations with him before he left us so unexpectedly. I can only hope they both would have approved of my efforts. I thank former colleague Ron Formisano, who meant well when he took me aside right after I received tenure and told me that working on Dickinson would ruin my career. A week later, when I received my first NEH Scholarly Editions grant for the JDP, he happily reversed his advice. I thank Mark Noll for advising me to resist temptations to become distracted by other topics of research, and Jack Rakove for his constant encouragement in all things Dickinson. After the manuscript was mostly finished in the spring of 2023, the moment was appropriately marked with another Liberty Fund conference, though not one focused exclusively on Dickinson. When discussion leader Gordon Wood turned to me to explain the significance of the *Farmer's Letters*, he gave me one of the highlights of my career. That time, I was ready. Readers familiar with Wood's work will see his influence everywhere in this study with the ideas of republicanism, virtue, and disinterested civic engagement.

I have leaned on friends, colleagues, and family over these years. My mother, Jenifer Patterson, was always ready to read drafts and listen supportively. She and cousin Thomas Hutchinson kindly read a draft, as did Nate Kozuskanich, who has been my constant friend and colleague through more trials than we could have imagined when we met at the LCP more than twenty years ago. My uncle, Fred Calvert, an author himself, provided much-needed early encouragement. New and old friends and colleagues, in close touch or not, were there for me at one time or another: Kim and Haley Antonelli, Matthew Catron, Jonathan Clark, Steve Davis, Renata Howard DeWees, Lisa Diller, Caroline Evarts, Abigail Firey, Tom Hamm, Chris Koelbl, Connie King, Wynn and Anne Silvers Lee, Laura Myers, Jonel Priddy, Sarah Pugach, Dan Riches, Jess Roney, the late L.D. Shank III, Nona Martin Storr, Mark Summers, Tammy Whitlock, and Barbara Zierfuß. Of everyone, however, it is my husband, Eric Kiltinen, to whom I am most indebted. After enduring my incessant prattle about Dickinson for almost twenty-five years, he still had the patience, interest, and stamina at the end of this process to provide the most incisive and challenging editing of these pages. His many queries and our long discussions led me to add depth and accuracy that would have otherwise been lacking. His observations helped me see Dickinson more clearly than ever before.

In the end, I did what I could with the time and resources available. The result is far from perfect, but I hope that one day, when the JDP has finished its work, this biography will have served Dickinson well enough to inspire someone to write a better one.

JANE E. CALVERT
March 2024

Chronology of the Life of John Dickinson
with Major Committee Assignments and Selected Publications

1731

Nov. 4 (old calendar): Samuel Dickinson (b. 1689) married Mary Cadwalader (b. 1700)

1732

Nov. 13 (**Nov. 2**, old calendar): John Dickinson born at Crosia-doré in Talbot Co., Md.

1734

Oct. 4 (old calendar): Brother Thomas born (died young)

1739

April 5 (old calendar): Brother Philemon born

1741

Jan. 18 (old calendar): Samuel Dickinson moved family to Kent Co. estate Poplar Hall near Dover, Del.

1740s

Tutored by James Orr and William Killen

1750–53

Read law in Phila. in the office of king's attorney John Moland

1753

Passed the bar in Pa.
Oct. 15: Sailed for London to study at the Middle Temple, Inns of Court
Dec. 15: Arrival in England

1754

Jan. 23: For his health, moved with Robert Goldsborough to the village of Clapham outside London

Jan. 25: First attended court (Court of the King's Bench)

Feb. 23: Returned to London from Clapham

March 22: First met Pa. governor Thomas Penn

April 18–May 20: General elections in London

May 3: Bonded to dine in Commons at the Middle Temple

May 28: French and Indian War began in America

Summer: Visited St. Albans in Herfordshire and Chatham and Rochester in Kent Co.; toured the HMS *Somerset* at Sheerness on the Isle of Sheppey

Oct.: Visited Oxford University and Blenheim Palace in Oxfordshire

Nov. 10: Attended birthday party for George II at St. James's Palace

1755

Jan: For his health, moved to Kingston outside London with Robert Goldsborough

End of October: Returned to London

1756

Feb. 26: Attended hearings of Pa. petitions before the Board of Trade at Whitehall Palace

May 17: Declaration of war against France began the Seven Years' War

June 4: Six Quakers abdicated their seats in Pa. Assembly, beginning "Reformation" of Quakerism

October: Four more Quakers abdicated seats in Pa. Assembly

1757

Feb. 8: Called to the bar

March 14: Middle Temple barrister certificate issued

Returned to Poplar Hall
Began law practice in Phila.

1758

Jan. 17–25: Represented Rev. William Smith in libel trial by the Pa. Assembly

1759

Aug. 10: Elected member of the Young Junto in Phila.

Oct. 1: Elected to Del. Assembly as representative from Kent Co.

1760

July 6: Father, Samuel Dickinson, died

Oct. 1: Elected to the Del. Assembly; chosen speaker of the House

1761
Served in Del. Assembly

1762
May 14: Elected to Pa. Assembly in special election as representative from Phila. Co.
Oct. 1: Elected to Pa. Assembly in regular election
Jan. 11: Took seat in Pa. Assembly; served on 12 committees

1763
Feb. 10: Treaty of Paris ended French and Indian War and Seven Years' War
March: Elected a director of the Library Company of Philadelphia
Oct. 1: Elected to Pa. Assembly; served on 16 committees
Dec. 14 & 27: Paxton Riots

1764
June: Assisted in defense of the Moravian Indian Renatus in his murder trial;
    Renatus acquitted
June 29: Published *A Speech, Delivered in the House of Assembly*
July: Published *To the King's Most Excellent Majesty*
July 19: Published "A Protest against a Resolution of the Assembly"
Sept.: Published *A Receipt to Make a Speech*
Sept. 24: Published *A Reply to a Piece Called the Speech of Joseph Galloway*
Oct. 1: Elected to the Pa. Assembly; served on 10 committees
Published "Last Tuesday Morning . . . "
Oct. 26: Published *A Protest Presented to the House of Assembly*

1765
Spring: Donated £6.10 to Pa. Hospital
Sept. 10: Appointed to committee to draft instructions from Pa. Assembly to the
    delegates of the Stamp Act Congress
Sept. 11: Appointed delegate to the Stamp Act Congress
Sept. 20: Wrote Resolutions of the Pa. Assembly on the Stamp Act
Oct. 7–c. 20: Served as delegate to the Stamp Act Congress; drafted the Declaration
    of Rights of the Stamp Act Congress and Petition to the King from the Stamp Act
    Congress
Nov. 1: Stamp Act went into effect
Nov.: Published "Friends and Countrymen"
Dec. 7: Published *The Late Regulations Respecting the British Colonies*

1766
Jan. 10: Donated pay from service in the Assembly to widows and orphans of
    Presbyterian ministers
March 18: Stamp Act repealed; Declaratory Act passed

May: Published *An Address to the Committee of Correspondence in Barbados* as "A North-American"
Oct. 29: Founding member of the Gloucester Fox Hunting Club

1767
Fall: Donated £25 to the Pa. Hospital
Nov. 30: Townshend Acts went into effect
Dec. 3: Began publication of the 12 "Letters from a Farmer in Pennsylvania" serially in newspapers

1768
Feb. 11: Mass. Assembly issued circular letter in response to the "Farmer's Letters"
Feb. 18: Last "Farmer's Letter" published
April–July: Published "The Centinel," nos. 6, 7, 8, & 16 serially in newspapers
April 16: Named honorary member of the Society of Fort St. Davids
April 25: Published *An Address Read at a Meeting of Merchants to Consider Non-Importation*
July 7: Published "The Liberty Song"
July 16: Published *To the Public* as "Pacificus"
July 22: Published *A Copy of a Letter from a Gentleman in Virginia*
Jan. 19: Elected member of American Philosophical Society

1769
Sept. 29: Awarded an honorary degree from College of New Jersey (later Princeton)

1770
March 5: Townshend Acts repealed except for tea tax; Boston "Massacre"
July 19: Married Mary (Polly) Norris (MND; b. July 17, 1740); moved to Fairhill, the Norris estate in Phila.
Oct. 1: Elected to Pa. Assembly (against his wishes)
Oct. 17: Took seat in Assembly; served on 6 committees

1771
Donated to the Overseers of the Poor
March 17: Honorary member of Friendly Sons of St. Patrick for charitable works for Irish immigrants
Sept. 2: Declined to stand for election to Assembly
Dec. 10: First child, daughter Sarah (Sally; SND), born (d. 1855)

1772
June 10: Burning of the *Gaspée* off the coast of R.I.
Oct. 1: Candidate for Assembly (against his wishes); not elected

1773

Jan.: R.I. Assembly requested advice from JD for how to handle *Gaspée* affair

April 28: Invited to join the Sons of St. Tammany for charitable works

Nov. 3: Published "Extract of a Letter [on the Tea Tax]"

Nov. 27: Published *A Letter from the Country, to a Gentleman in Philadelphia* as "Rusticus"

Dec. 16: Boston Tea Party

1774

March 31: The first Coercive (Intolerable) Acts passed

May 7: Second child, daughter Mary, born

May–June: Published "Letters to the Inhabitants of the British Colonies" serially in the newspapers

May 20: Meeting at City Tavern; appointed to the Pa. Committee of Correspondence ("The Nineteen")

June 10: Proposed convention-committee system to organize resistance to Great Britain

June 18: Appointed to the Pa. committee of Forty-Three

July 4: Appointed to committee to draft instructions for Pa. delegates to the First Continental Congress

July 15: Led Convention in Phila. to prepare for Congress

July 21: Offered by the Convention as delegate to Congress; rejected by Assembly

Sept.: Published instructions to Pa. delegates to Congress along with *An Essay on the Constitutional Power of Great Britain*

Oct. 1: Elected to Pa. Assembly; served on 15 committees

Oct. 15: Added as a delegate from Pa. to the First Continental Congress

Oct. 17: Took seat in the First Continental Congress

Oct. 18–26: In Congress, drafted the Bill of Rights and List of Grievances

Oct. 20: In Congress, signed the Articles of Association

Oct. 21: In Congress, JD's draft of *To the Inhabitants of the Colonies* adopted

Wrote *A Letter to the Inhabitants of the Province of Quebec*

Added to committee drafting a petition to the king; wrote the Petition to the King

Dec. 5. Appointed to the Pa. Committee of Inspection and Observation ("The Sixty-Six")

Dec. 15: In Assembly, appointed delegate to the Second Continental Congress

1775

Feb. 19: In Congress, appointed to the Secret Committee of Correspondence

April 19: Battles of Lexington and Concord

April-May: The Sixty-Six began organizing military force; JD raised the First Philadelphia Battalion of Associators and was commissioned as colonel

May 3: In Assembly, appointed to committee to prepare response to Lord North's offer of accommodation; wrote response rejecting offer

May 5: Daughter, Mary, died

May 10: Second Continental Congress met

June 3: In Congress, appointed to committee to draft a petition to the king

June 26: In Congress, appointed to committee to prepare the militia for defense of America Added to the committee to prepare a declaration to be read to American troops

June 17: The Battle of Bunker Hill

June 30: In Assembly, appointed to a Committee of Safety to call Associators into service

July 5: Congress approved JD's draft of the Second Petition to the King (Olive Branch Petition; issued July 8)

July 6: Congress approved JD's draft of the Declaration on the Causes and Necessity of Taking Up Arms

July 24: John Adams wrote letter with "piddling genius" remark that was intercepted and published by the British

Aug. 23: George III declared the colonies in rebellion

Sept. 1: George III refused to receive Olive Branch Petition

Sept. 19: In Congress, appointed to a secret committee on importing arms and powder

Oct. 1: Elected to Pa. Assembly; served on 15 committees

Oct. 19: In Assembly, appointed to the Committee of Safety

Oct. 24: Took seat in Assembly; added to the Committee of Correspondence

Oct. 31: Colonists learned that the king refused to receive the Olive Branch Petition

Nov. 3: In Assembly, appointed delegate to Congress

Nov. 7: In Assembly, wrote instructions disallowing Pa. delegates to vote for independence (approved Nov. 9)

Nov. 8: In Assembly, wrote *Rules and Regulations for the Better Government of the Military Association in Pennsylvania*

Nov. 29: In Congress, appointed to committee to correspond with friends of America in Great Britain and elsewhere

Dec.: In Congress, appointed to Secret Committee of Correspondence

Dec. 4: In Congress, appointed to committee to confer with the Assembly of N.J.

Dec. 5: Gave speech in N.J. Assembly against their negotiating separately with Great Britain

1776

Jan. 10: Colonists learned that George III withdrew protection from the colonies; *Common Sense* published

Jan. 23–28: Attended Pa. Convention

Jan. 24: In Congress, appointed to committee to draft an address to the inhabitants of the colonies

Feb. 12: Prepared to lead his battalion of Associators to New York to meet the British

March 22: Mother, Mary Cadwalader Dickinson, died near Trenton, N.J.

May 10: John Adams motioned in Congress that all colonial governments unfriendly to independence be replaced

May 15: May 10 resolution on replacing colonial governments passed in Congress with preamble specifying oaths to be taken

May 20: Philadelphia radicals met and denounced the Assembly's November 1775 instructions to the delegates to Congress

May 24: In Assembly, appointed to committee to draft resolutions rendering naturalization, oaths, and affirmations unnecessary in Pa.

June 5: In Assembly, appointed to committee to write instructions to delegates to Congress allowing them to vote for independence (approved June 8)

June 7: Richard Henry Lee motioned in Congress for independence

June 11: In Congress, appointed to committee to draft a model treaty; wrote an early draft

June 12: In Congress, appointed to committee to draft the Articles of Confederation; wrote first draft

June 13: Final meeting of Assembly under the 1701 Charter of Privileges

July 1: Delivered speech in Congress against the Declaration of Independence

July 2: In Congress, abstained from vote on independence

July 10: Joined battalion at Elizabethtown, N.J., as part of the Flying Camp

July 27: Published *An Essay on a Frame of Government for Pennsylvania*

Aug. 27–30: Americans defeated at the Battle of Long Island

Aug. Donated some of his pay as colonel to the wives and children of Associators and the remainder for the use of the poor

Sept. 1: Returned to Phila. with battalion

Sept. 30: Resigned commission in Pa. militia

Nov. 5: Elected to Pa. Assembly

Nov. 7: Elected delegate to Congress from Del. (declined)

Nov. 27: Proposed amending the Pa. constitution; after proposal was rejected, abdicated seat in Assembly

Dec. 10: Fled Phila. with family ahead of British invasion

1777

Jan. 14: Confronted Pa. Council of Safety about false accusations of treason

Jan.: Council of Safety seized JD's house on Chestnut St., Phila., and converted it to a hospital

May 12: Manumitted all his enslaved persons conditionally

Summer: Served as private in Del. militia

Sept. 26: Received commission as brigadier general in Del. militia (did not act on it)

Oct. 30: Dickinson family escaped Phila., joined JD at Poplar Hall

Nov. 22: Fairhill (Phila.) burned by the British

Dec. 19: Resigned commission in Del. militia

1778

May 9: Named by Del. House to committee for stating an account of expenditures (appointment declined)

June 29: Affirmed fidelity to the State of Del.

Aug. 19: Third child, son John, born

Sept. 2: Son, John, died

1779

Feb. 1: Appointed by the Del. Assembly to serve in the Continental Congress

April 23: Took seat in Congress; served on 24 committees

May 5: Signed Articles of Confederation

May 21: In Congress, published "To the Inhabitants of the United States"

July 5: Fourth child, a son, stillborn

Nov. 18: Received leave of absence

Dec. 22: Appointed delegate to Congress from Del.

1780

April 12: Declined appointment as delegate to the Continental Congress from Del.

Nov. 28: Elected to the Del. Assembly for New Castle Co. in special election

1781

Aug. 10: Poplar Hall plundered by Loyalists

Sept. 21: Manumitted some enslaved persons unconditionally

Oct. 20: Elected to Del. Executive Council

Oct. 25: Took seat in Council; served on 3 committees

Nov. 6: Elected president of Del. for a term of 3 years (served 1)

Nov. 13: Assumed presidency of Del.

1782

Spring: Published *For the Use of the Militia of the Delaware State, an Abstract of the Regulations for the Order and Discipline of the Troops of the United States*

Sept. 25: Donated £100 to the College of N.J. (Princeton)

Nov. 7: Elected president of the Supreme Executive Council of Pa.

Dec.–Jan. 1783: Attacked by "Valerius" serially in the newspapers; published response Served as *ex officio* member and president of the board of trustees of the University of Pennsylvania (to 1785)

1783

Jan. 14: Resigned as president of Del.

Feb.: Prevented secession of "Westsylvania"

June 21–24: Prevented Mutiny of 1783; Congress departed Phila.

Sept. 9: Dickinson College founded by Benjamin Rush; JD donated 600 acres and books; served as president of the board of trustees

Oct. 15: Elected honorary member of the Society of the Cincinnati
Nov. 6: Fifth child, daughter Maria, born (died 1860)
Nov. 7: Reelected president of the Supreme Executive Council of Pa.

1784
Spring: Halted armed conflict in the Wyoming Valley
Spring-Summer: Dealt with Marbois-Longchamps Affair
Nov. 3: Reelected president of the Supreme Executive Council of Pa.

1785
Fall: Refused to issue warrant of execution for Aaron Doan
Oct.: Established permanent residence in Wilmington, Del.

1786
Feb.: JD's bill for the abolition of slavery presented to Del. Assembly (failed)
May 11: Manumitted remaining enslaved persons unconditionally
June 16: Appointed delegate from Del. to the Annapolis Convention
Sept. 11–14: Served as chairman of the Annapolis Convention; wrote *The Report of the Annapolis Convention*

1787
Feb. 3: Declined to serve as delegate to the Confederation Congress from Del.
Feb. 21: Congress read and approved JD's letter from the Annapolis Convention proposing a Federal Convention
March: Proposed founding a Quaker boarding school in Chester Co. (future Westtown School)
Donated seed funds of £14 annually to found the Society for Alleviating the Miseries of Public Prisons
May 12: Published *Fragments on the Confederation of the American States*
May 29: Took seat in the Federal Convention
June 7: Offered plan for proportional representation in one branch of the legislature and equal representation in the other using the solar system metaphor
Aug. 18: Appointed to Committee of Assumption of State Debts
Aug. 22: Appointed to Committee of Slave Trade
Aug. 31: Appointed to Committee of Postponed Parts
Sept. 13: Appointed to Committee of Economy, Frugality and Manufactures
Sept. 15: Last day at Convention; departed early because of illness
Sept. 17: George Read signed the Constitution for JD by proxy
Dec. 7: Del. the first state to ratify Constitution
Dec.: Donated his pay of £559 from service to Del. since 1779 to charitable causes

1788
April–May: Published the first 9 "Fabius Letters" advocating ratification of the US Constitution serially in the newspapers

Feb. 2: Appointed judge in the Del. Court of Errors and Appeals
June: Charter member of the Library Company of Wilmington

1791

Oct. 10: Resigned as judge in the Del. Court of Errors and Appeals
Nov. 29–Dec. 31: Attended Del. constitutional convention
Dec. 7: Elected president of the Del. convention

1792

May 29–June 27: Attended Del. constitutional convention
June 21: Preemptively declined to stand for governor's office
Aug.: Donated £50 to the Medical Society of the State of Delaware
Sept. 15: Put forth as candidate for senator from Del.
Oct. 15: Elected to Del. Senate

1793

Jan. 7: Took seat in Del. Senate; served on 7 committees
Jan. 19: Nominated by the Del. General Assembly as candidate for US Senate (not
   elected)
June 19: Resigned seat in the Del. Senate Donated $160 to Presbyterians in
   Dover, Del.

1794

Donated funds to found the Wilmington Academy (Del.) for the education of poor
   children

1795

June 10: Deeded land to the Quakers to found Westtown School (Pa.)
Aug. 5: Led Wilmington, Del., protest against the Jay Treaty; published memorial to
   Pres. Washington

1796

Jan.: Deeded land worth $1,460.62 to the Methodists
Deeded land to found the Brandywine Academy (Del.) for millworkers' children
Oct. 13: Published *A Fragment* on the education of youth

1797

Jan. 2: Published "Ode, on France"
April 12–May 30: Published a second set of "Fabius Letters" in support of France
   serially in the newspapers

1798

Jan.: Published *A Caution; or, Reflections on the Present Contest between France and Great-Britain*

Feb 19: Published "Ode, on the French Revolution"

1799

May 6: Westtown School opened

1800

Asked to run for Congress (declined)

1801

Deeded land to Merion Friends Meeting

Asked to run for governor of Del. (declined)

1802

Jan.: Wrote legislation pertaining to inheritances for Del. (did not pass)

April 15: Published *The Political Writings of John Dickinson, Esq.*

1803

Feb.: Published *An Address on the Past, Present and Eventual Relations of the United States to France* as "Anticipation"

March: Deeded land to the Philadelphia Society for the Establishment and Support of Charity Schools

July 23: Wife, Mary Norris Dickinson, died, age 63

1804

Paid for education of Thomas Mason

Began urging the U.S. Senate to pass law against trade with Haiti

March: Poplar Hall burnt down

1805

March 30: Donated 150 bushels of corn to people of Kent Co., Del., after crop failure

Aug. 9: Donated land for the Claymont School, New Castle Co., Del.

1807

Oct.: Nominated by Del. Republicans for election to Congress (not elected)

1808

Feb. 14: Died, aged 75; buried at Wilmington Friends Meeting burial ground

Abbreviations and Short Titles

AFC	*Adams Family Correspondence.* ed. H. L. Butterfield et al. 14 vols. Cambridge: Belknap Press of Harvard University Press, 1963–.
ALP	Arthur Lee Papers, Houghton Library, Harvard College, Cambridge, MA
ANBO	*American National Biography Online*
APS	American Philosophical Society, Philadelphia, PA
Coxe	Coxe Family Papers, Historical Society of Pennsylvania, Philadelphia, PA
CTP	Charles Thomson Papers, Library of Congress, Washington, DC
DCA	Dickinson College Archives and Special Collections, Carlisle, PA
DHRC	*Documentary History of the Ratification of the Constitution, Commentaries on the Constitution: Public and Private: Volume 17: April 1–May 9, 1788.* ed. John P. Kaminski et al. Madison: University of Wisconsin Society Press, 1995.
DHS	Delaware Historical Society, Wilmington, DE
DJA	*The Diary and Autobiography of John Adams.* ed. L. H. Butterfield et al. 4 vols. Cambridge: The Belknap Press of Harvard University Press, 1962.
DNL	Deborah Norris Logan
DPA	Delaware Public Archives, Dover, DE
EGF	Elizabeth Graeme Fergusson
EDA	Esther Duke Archives, Westtown School, West Chester, PA
Emmet	Thomas Addis Emmet Collection, New York Public Library, New York, NY
Etting	Frank M. Etting Collection, Historical Society of Pennsylvania, Philadelphia, PA
Farrand	*The Records of the Federal Convention of 1787.* ed. Max Farrand. 4 vols. New Haven: Yale University Press, 1911.
FHL	Friends Historical Library, Swarthmore College, Swarthmore, PA
FJ	*Freeman's Journal* (Philadelphia)
Force	*American Archives, Fourth Series: Containing a Documentary History of the English Colonies in North America.* ed. Peter Force. 6 vols. Washington, DC: M. St. Clair Clarke and Peter Force, 1837–1846.
Gilbert	William Kent Gilbert Collection, Library of Congress, Washington, DC

Gratz	Simon Gratz Autograph Collection, Historical Society of Pennsylvania, Philadelphia, PA
GW Papers	Papers of George Washington, Library of Congress, Washington, DC
HL	Houghton Library, Harvard College, Cambridge, MA
HSP	Historical Society of Pennsylvania, Philadelphia. PA
JBL	James Bringhurst Letters, Friends Historical Library, Swarthmore College, Swarthmore, PA
JCC	*Journals of the Continental Congress, 1774–1789.* ed. Worthington C. Ford et al. 34 vols. Washington, DC: Government Printing Office, 1904–1937.
JD	John Dickinson
JDP	John Dickinson Papers, Library Company of Philadelphia
LBR	*Letters of Benjamin Rush.* ed. Lyman H. Butterfield. 2 vols. Princeton: Princeton University Press, 1951.
LCP	Library Company of Philadelphia, Philadelphia. PA
LDC	*Letters of Delegates to Congress, 1774–1789* ed. Paul H. Smith et al. 26 vols. Washington, DC: Library of Congress, 1976–2000.
LOC	Library of Congress, Washington, DC
Logan	Logan Family Collection, Historical Society of Pennsylvania, Philadelphia, PA
LSD	*Laws of the State of Delaware.* 2 vols. New Castle: S. and J. Adams, 1797.
MCD	Mary Cadwalader Dickinson
MCDS	*Minutes of the Council of the Delaware State, From 1776 to 1792.* Dover DE: James Kirk & Son, 1886.
MDL	Maria Dickinson Logan Collection, Historical Society of Pennsylvania, Philadelphia, PA
Memoir	Deborah Norris Logan et al., *Memoir of Dr. George Logan of Stenton.* Philadelphia: The Historical Society of Pennsylvania, 1899.
Mf.	Microfilm from the DeValinger Dickinson Project, Historical Society of Pennsylvania, Philadelphia, PA
MHS	Massachusetts Historical Society, Boston, MA.
MND	Mary ("Polly") Norris Dickinson
MPCP	*Minutes of the Provincial Council of Pennsylvania: From Its Organization to the Termination of the Revolution.* ed. Samuel Hazard. Harrisburg: J. Severns, 1851–1853.
MSEC	*Minutes of the Supreme Executive Council of Pennsylvania.* 16 vols. Harrisburg: T. Fenn & Co., 1852–1853.
N-YHS	New-York Historical Society, New York, NY
NYPL	New York Public Library, New York, NY
OBP	Owen Biddle Papers, Esther Duke Archives, Westtown School, West Chester, PA

PA   *Pennsylvania Archives*. First Series. ed. Samuel Hazard et al.
              Harrisburg, PA: Joseph Severn & Co., 1852–1856.
PAH   *The Papers of Alexander Hamilton*. ed. Harold C. Syrett et al. 27 vols.
              New York: Columbia University Press, 1961–1987.
PBF   *The Papers of Benjamin Franklin*. ed. Leonard W. Larabee et al. 44
              vols. New Haven: Yale University Press, 1959–.
PC   *Pennsylvania Chronicle*
PEP   *Pennsylvania Evening-Post*
PG   *Pennsylvania Gazette*
PGW   *The Papers of George Washington*. ed. W. W. Abbot, Philander D.
              Chase, Dorothy Twohig et al. Charlottesville, VA: University of
              Virginia Press, 1983–.
PJ   *Pennsylvania Journal*
PJA   *The Papers of John Adams*. ed. Robert J. Taylor, et al. 19 vols.
              Cambridge: The Belknap Press of Harvard University Press,
              1977–2018.
PM   *Pennsylvania Mercury*
PMHB   *Pennsylvania Magazine of History and Biography*
Poulson's   *Poulson's American Daily Advertiser* (Philadelphia)
PP   *Pennsylvania Packet*
PTJ   *The Papers of Thomas Jefferson* ed. Julian P. Boyd et al. Princeton:
              Princeton University Press, 1950–.
PUL   Princeton University Library, Princeton, NJ
RHLP   Richard Henry Lee Papers, American Philosophical Society,
              Philadelphia, PA
Rockwood   Rockwood Collection, University of Delaware Special Collections,
              Newark, DE
RRL   Robert R. Logan Collection, Historical Society of Pennsylvania,
              Philadelphia, PA
RSR   Richard S. Rodney Collection, Delaware Historical Society,
              Wilmington, DE*SALP*
              Statutes at Large of Pennsylvania. ed. James T. Mitchell et al. 17 vols.
              Harrisburg: C. M. Busch, 1896–1915.
SCP   *The Susquehannah Company Papers*. ed. Julian P. Boyd et al., 11
              vols. Ithaca: Cornell University Press for Wyoming Historical &
              Geological Society [1962–1971].
SD   Samuel Dickinson
SMC   Small Manuscript Collection, Delaware Public Archives, Dover, DE
SMP   Samuel Miller Papers, Princeton University Library, Princeton, NJ
SND   Sally Norris Dickinson
TJ Papers   Thomas Jefferson Papers, Library of Congress, Washington, DC
TMP   Thomas McKean Papers, Historical Society of Pennsylvania,
              Philadelphia, PA

UDSC   University of Delaware, Special Collections, Newark, DE

Votes ([year])   *Votes and Proceedings of the House of Representatives of the Province of Pennsylvania.* Philadelphia: B. Franklin et al., 1730–75; Henry Miller, 1777.

WJD   *The Complete Writings and Selected Correspondence of John Dickinson.* ed. Jane E. Calvert et al. Newark: University of Delaware Press, 2020–.

WMQ   *William & Mary Quarterly*

Introduction

"A Wheel to effect the general Good": Understanding John Dickinson's Pivotal Role at the Founding

In Signers' Hall at the National Constitution Center in Philadelphia, the statue of John Dickinson stands alone in a corner, hand pensively on chin, apart from the action of the Federal Convention. The clear message is that Dickinson was too reserved, or perhaps too timid, to engage. He appears to be modeled on the Roman general Fabius, called "the delayer" for his caution in battle. This is how Americans think of Dickinson—if they think of him. Alternatively, they might imagine him in the manner of the musical *1776*, strutting across a stage, ever to the right, never to the left, with ruffles aflutter, singing jubilantly about his conservatism. There he at least possesses the virtue of energy. Or they could imagine him as HBO's pale, sweaty, scowling disbeliever in the American cause, opposite a stalwart John Adams. But none of these images of him is accurate.

For more than two hundred years, John Dickinson has suffered from an image problem that no one in his day would have thought possible. Known for the better part of his life by his most popular pen name, the Pennsylvania Farmer, if there were a single individual who could be credited with bringing the United States of America into being, it would be Dickinson. Of course, such a claim for any one man would be absurd, but most Americans today, including many historians, would probably name Washington, Jefferson, or Franklin in that role without hesitation. But that myth would be no more accurate than Dickinson's withdrawn form at the Constitution Center.

In fact, Dickinson was America's first celebrity and internationally recognized spokesman for the American resistance to Britain. The world knew and admired Dickinson's name, or at least his pen name, well before they learned to idolize either Franklin or Washington. In his service in the national congresses and as a private citizen, he wrote more for the American cause than any other person, leading one scholar to designate him "the Penman of the Revolution."[1] But that, too, is a romantic misnomer, both too much and not enough.

In the first instance, Dickinson didn't want the Revolution and wrote against it. At this point, memories of grade-school history classes surface, and Dickinson's present anonymity seems to make sense. Ah yes! He was the one who refused to sign the Declaration of Independence. True enough; he also refused to vote on it. Dickinson voluntarily and knowingly sacrificed his celebrity status, believing not only that he was doing what was best for his country but also that he would be compensated for whatever fame he lost during his lifetime by grateful posterity. Although he was glad to be wrong about independence, he never regretted his decision, based as it was on conscience. Nor did he attempt to hide his decision or insert himself into a past event where he did not belong. He had no need.

This was because, in the second instance, he was much more than simply an author. The only leading Founder present and active in America at every phase of the Revolution, from the Stamp Act crisis through the ratification of the Constitution, he held more public offices than any other figure, from revolutionary committees to the presidency of two states, for a while simultaneously. He had more extensive and varied military service than any leading Founder, not just raising and leading a battalion as a colonel and drafting military policy, but also enlisting as a private and serving as commander in chief. At each stage, he produced documents that guided his countrymen in their efforts. In assuming these roles and as a private citizen, he, more than any other leading figure, attempted to put into practice the most famous principles of the Declaration of Independence as we interpret it today: that all *people* are created equal and deserve protection of their rights.

Dickinson's contribution to the Founding of the country was exceptional. But a robust curriculum vitae does not tell us about the man, who he was, or what motivated him. One of the most highly educated men in America and, as one contemporary put it, "one of the most accomplished scholars that our country has produced," Dickinson was a lover of literature and poetry, a devotee of science, and a voracious student of the law.[2] He was driven by an unyielding sense of virtue and patriotism to work for the good of his country. Although he was one of the wealthiest men in America, he refused to follow the prescribed social norms of hierarchy or allow his privilege to excuse him from his duty to those less fortunate. On the contrary, his privilege dictated a greater obligation. Dickinson was a tireless champion for the underdog, be it a poor widow or a beleaguered colony. His were the politics of conscience, a civics lesson to future generations to stand on principle without regard for self or party. His thirty-plus years of public service were a testament to his boundless faith in the American people, as were his attempts to educate ordinary Americans about their rights and draw them into the national dialogue on important matters of state. He took on causes others avoided due to another unique attribute—his Quakerism, although he was not a Quaker.[3] His conviction that each individual, including himself, was a "wheel" contributing to the public happiness contrasted with other thinkers of the age—Alexander Pope, Adam Smith, even Thomas Paine—who feared disruption to the mechanisms of government.[4] Instead, Dickinson sought it and encouraged it in others.

Dickinson himself chose the pen name "Fabius" to advocate ratification of the Constitution. Forgotten is Fabius's genius, his innovative strategies, now considered the advent of guerrilla warfare, that allowed him to defeat Hannibal in the Second Punic War with minimal loss of life. He was respected by Hannibal and revered by the Romans, who knew he had saved their republic during the worst crisis in their history. Dickinson's strategy throughout his career was Fabian. In every forum he entered—the courtroom, the state house, the battlefield—he was the chess master, controlling the unruly pieces, sometimes sacrificing the lesser for the greater—including himself for America—and never losing sight of victory: saving the republic.

Such encomia are not to suggest that Dickinson was without faults. His passion for education knew no bounds and caused him to transgress into didacticism as he played teacher to those around him. Although juries and law clerks undoubtedly found him helpful, his fiancée and political opponents certainly did not. His studied circumspection in public office, though appreciated by some, enraged more forward spirits impatient for action. His studied inflexibility in matters of virtue, conscience, and patriotism, though admirable to an extent, may have been his Achilles heel, at times exasperating even his closest friends, earning him steadfast enemies in every phase of his life and perhaps costing him his rightful legacy. His determination to take unpopular and highly visible stances made him a target like no other. But all the sources reveal that he came by his faults honestly in his attempts to do good.

In seeking to understand Dickinson and his legacy, the nautical metaphor of the "trimmer" is useful. The term can have negative or positive connotations. It can refer to the person who trims the sails on a ship to go with the prevailing winds—in other words, the justly despised political opportunist. Or it can refer to the person who shifts the ballast in the hold to prevent the ship (of state) from capsizing or sailing off course by listing too far to the right or left. Dickinson was the latter type. Here, something of an optical illusion occurs. While the trimmer stays true to the final destination—in this case, the preservation of American liberties—his shifting of the ballast appears to favor one side or the other. Moreover, because he is powerful, all parties desire his weight on their side. Assuming this role came at a price. As a seventeenth-century author described it, "the poor *Trimmer* hath all the Powder spent on him alone. . . . [T]here is no danger now to the state . . . but from the Beast called a *Trimmer*."[5] Though some of the powder was spent on Dickinson during his lifetime, much more has been used since. Dickinson accepted the former with grace; the latter, however, was unimaginable.

In 1785, the painter Robert Edge Pine wrote to Dickinson for permission to include the Pennsylvania Farmer in his painting of the signing of the Declaration of Independence. Dickinson declined with an explanation. "The Truth is," he reminded Pine, "that I opposed the making the Declaration of Independence at the Time when it was made. I cannot be guilty of so false an Ambition, as to seek for any Share in the Fame of that Council." This was just one moment, just one patriotic decision in a life devoted to public service. Dickinson was therefore sanguine about the one thing that haunted every Founder's dreams: his legacy. "Enough it will be for Me," he explained, "that my Name be remembered by Posterity, if it is acknowledged, that I cheerfully staked every thing dear to Me upon the Fate of my Country, & that no Measure however contrary to my Sentiments, no Treatment however unmerited, could, in the deepest Gloom of our Affairs, change that Determination."[6]

There is much more to Dickinson than that one moment. To distill his life down in such a way is to fail in our civic duty to understand our own history and give Dickinson the acknowledgment that he both expected and deserved. The following pages, the first complete biography of Dickinson, aim to set things aright.

A Note on the Text

In using quotes from the historical actors, I have left the eighteenth-century spellings and capitalization, but to make them more readable, I have taken some liberties. While staying true to the sense of the passages, I have silently expanded abbreviations, supplied missing words, added punctuation, and made other minor adjustments to aid in clarity and to preserve the flow of the prose. For those interested in discovering the original source, the citations point the way.

Prologue

"The most distinguished of patriots": The Congress of the United States Remembers John Dickinson, February 1808

Hutchins's *Almanac* predicted snow for Washington, DC, on Monday, the twenty-second day of February 1808.[1] Situated on the banks of the Potomac River, the young Federal City experienced unpleasant winters. It was vulnerable to damp and biting winds off the Atlantic, which met little resistance as they swept in over a landscape denuded of trees. Houses of brick and wood seemed placed at random, and there were few buildings large enough to deflect the blasts. Winter also meant mud. Wide boulevards that would one day be lined with Roman columns and punctuated by marble monuments were now rivers of thick muck that sucked the shoes off horses' hooves, with the occasional tree trunk to break the wheel of a struggling carriage. Neither the fledging government nor private citizens would pay to pave and light the streets.

The scene was hardly what one would expect for the capital of a large and growing nation of more than seven million people—or perhaps it was precisely what one should expect of the new seat of government for the United States. Compared to its European counterparts, Washington was primitive, but it had grandiose visions of its future.[2]

The District of Columbia had not yet lived up to hopes that it would be a thriving manufacturing and commercial center. But it was beginning to bustle. As attorneys and apothecaries, looking more like farmers, stepped from offices and shops that looked like sheds and hovels, they braced themselves against the wind. Merchants, brewers, innkeepers, and journeyman laborers, along with many slaves, slogged through the darkening streets. Politicians in weathered coats huddled in half-built chambers and advocated for their separate states against the federal power. In and out of doors, all went about their businesses of hawking, concocting, hauling, and fabricating the things that nourished the young city and nation.

Although visitors from Philadelphia and London complained of Washington's desolation—one could hardly find a decent milliner, after all—it was the very potential for growth and prosperity that worried some of them. Those devoted to the classical republican ideology that animated the Founding of the nation a quarter of a century earlier suspected monarchical conspiracies in every marble column proposed and every magnificent edifice sketched. Cries of "taxation without representation" were loud in the District, which was denied its vote. President Jefferson, however, was determined to stifle any talk of moving the seat of government away from the South. Immediately upon taking office in 1801, he had hastened the construction of federal buildings in order to sink the roots of the town deeper into the banks of the Potomac. Now, in 1808, nearing the end of Jefferson's term of office, the buildings for the State and War Departments had been erected, barracks had been constructed for the Marine Corps, the Navy Yard was outfitted, and the executive mansion was furnished. Although the federal government at that time consisted of only 131 employees, the expansion promised, eventually, to match line for line Pierre L'Enfant's complex plan for the city, with its crisscrossing grid and wagon wheels design. One might justly accuse the surveyor of the city, Andrew Ellicott, of forsaking his Quaker simplicity when he helped realize L'Enfant's elaborate vision.

For all the construction, talk of moving the seat of the federal government hadn't completely disappeared. This very February, James Sloan, Federalist representative from New Jersey, had called for the removal of the capital back to Philadelphia. But it was the last of such calls. The city was beginning to prosper, if slowly. The number of boarding houses and banks had multiplied, and construction on Eastern Market, for fresh produce, was complete. St. Patrick's Roman Catholic Church and the Episcopalian Christ Church had been consecrated, and Baptist, Methodist, and Quaker meetings had sprung up, signifying a lively religious presence. The first toll bridge over the Potomac River to Arlington, Virginia, home to the nation's busiest slave market, had just been authorized. Manufacturing was still only a cottage industry, but there were ventures afoot for textile companies. New canals facilitated a brisk trade in corn, tobacco, whiskey, and flour.

At the heart of it all, the partially constructed Capitol sat upon what had been known as Jenkins's Hill and was in 1808 a gigantic mound of mud. The enslaved workers who clambered in the scaffolding did not have far to travel: they were housed in pens scattered throughout the city, including near the Capitol, so that members of Congress might studiously debate their own freedoms while manacled men and women were driven under their windows in the raw winter air. The Senate chamber, completed first, was partially heated and warm enough to conduct the business of the day. The less-august body of Representatives still squatted in its partially finished chamber on the south side of the building. Members might have longed for the days when they were encamped in "The Oven," a temporary appendage off the north wing.

The business before the Senate this February day was mostly ordinary. Resolutions and bills of varied import were read, considered, and debated. Of weightiest concern was a resolution submitted by the Pennsylvania legislature for an amendment to the third article of the Constitution that would give Congress more power over the judiciary. A committee would consider it, but it did not look likely to pass. More material issues pressed as well. As Americans pushed westward, the body deliberated on a bill addressing how best to use and distribute the vast new territory the United States now possessed from the Louisiana Purchase. The senators agreed that it should be read for the third time, with amendments. Tensions with Britain were growing over trade and the impressment of American sailors; a bill to prohibit the importation of certain British merchandise was now pending. Everyone was aware of the balancing act necessary to avoid a second war against Britain. And there was the ever-present question of loyalty to what seemed to some an unstable American polity. Senators debated a bill on the punishment of treason. Nothing, however, would be decided today, except for one issue—not of policy but of patriotism.

It was nearly time to adjourn, but the senators remained seated as they awaited the last order of business. The chamber grew quiet and expectant; all of Washington had heard the news of February 14. On February 19 in the House of Representatives, John W. Eppes, a Democratic-Republican from Virginia, had made a motion: because the House was impressed with "a full sense of the eminent services rendered to his country, in the most arduous times, by the late John Dickinson," they resolved to wear black crepe armbands for one month "in testimony of the national gratitude and reverence towards the memory of that illustrious patriot."[3]

Now the Senate would follow the House.[4] Samuel White, a member of the Federalist Party from Delaware, rose to speak. He looked to Senate President George Clinton and began:

> Mr. President: It is with much pain and regret, sir, that I rise to announce to the Senate the irreparable loss our country has sustained in the death of one of her worthiest citizens and the most distinguished of patriots. Time has measured and told the days of another venerable sage of the Revolution. JOHN DICKINSON, the illustrious contemporary and friend of Washington and Franklin, is now no more—

White paused to let his words settle in the chamber. "His head and his heart," he continued, "devoted to the service and love of his country, till his locks were bleached by the frosts of more than seventy winters, have now descended in silence to the grave. No humble eulogy of mine shall attempt to approach his exalted merit."

Although many of those present were only infants when Dickinson's influence was greatest, they were well aware of his contributions and sacrifices that had helped bring the nation to this thriving point. They had grown up hearing about "the Pennsylvania Farmer." He had taught Americans about their liberties and how to think of themselves as one people and had wielded his pen in the service of the new nation more often and to greater effect than any other person. Significantly, he had delayed the Declaration of Independence just long enough to allow Americans to become minimally prepared for war and statehood.

"The happiness of his fellow-citizens was his only aim," White continued, "and upon the grateful hearts of his countrymen is indelibly engraven the dearest memento of his wisdom and his worth. Those who shared his personal acquaintance will never forget his private virtues—"[5]

Tall and trim, with a prominent nose that gave him a genteel air, suitable to his station in life as one of America's foremost lawyers, landowners, and statesmen, John Dickinson was, according to Debby Logan, wife of Pennsylvania senator George Logan, "graceful, polite and affable to all, and in the most endearing manner kind to the afflicted and unfortunate." Some thought he embodied the very notion of being a gentleman—a "beau ideal." One of the few colonials trained at the Middle Temple in London's Inns of Court, Dickinson became wealthy from his law practice and as the largest landholder in the Delaware Valley, with nearly ten thousand acres. This land he rented out for farming, which allowed him to accept cases pro bono for the defense of the innocent, the injured, and the poor. In retirement, where other leaders such as George Washington devoted their time and wealth to aggrandizing their own legacies through improving their estates, Dickinson directed his efforts to charity and social welfare projects. Communities received land and funds for meeting houses, poor children were given schools, and towns received libraries. He took on causes most ignored, founding the first prison reform society and becoming an abolitionist.[6]

Despite his considerable fortune and stature, Dickinson's conduct reflected Quaker plainness and republican frugality. Though not formally a member of the Religious Society of Friends, he shared many of their beliefs and "peculiar" practices. He was what Friends called a "fellow traveler." The fabric of his suits was of the best sort but plain, without embellishments or ruffles. He wore no wig in affectation of British aristocracy. His manners were likewise unostentatious: elegant but with no assumption of superiority over any man—or woman. Some found him overly reserved, but generally he was cheerful and ready to engage in lively conversation over a glass of wine—when temperance did not forbid it. In his conversation, he used the Quakers' plain speech, "Will thee take another glass, friend?"

Although Philadelphia was where he had conducted much of his business, he preferred the peace he found at his childhood home outside Dover in the State of Delaware. It was to Poplar Hall that he would retreat when he needed respite from the tumultuous world, to lose himself in his books and fields. There he would take exercise on horseback, wonder at nature's changes from season to season, share drink and wit in the Golden Fleece Tavern, and indulge in private dialogues with long-dead sages—Cicero, Plutarch, Machiavelli, and Bacon.[7] He was a scholar of history, and these authors were alive to him.

Dickinson's friendships, his "dear connections" with the living, were likewise long and deep, some enduring through decades and surviving political turmoil.[8] Among his closest friends and allies was the renowned doctor, religious thinker, and educator Benjamin Rush. Others included Delaware politicians Thomas McKean, George Read, and Caesar Rodney; secretary of Congress Charles Thomson; and his cousin and physician to George Washington, Dr. John Jones. In his later years, he was friend and mentor to Pennsylvania politicians George Logan and Tench Coxe; United States Attorney General Caesar A. Rodney, nephew of his old friend; and the Presbyterian minister Samuel Miller. Over the years he counted several prominent women as friends: Philadelphia writer Elizabeth Graeme Fergusson; Quaker poet, physician, and landowner Susanna Wright; British historian Catharine Macaulay; and Mercy Otis Warren of Massachusetts, whose plays and poems had stirred rebellion against Great Britain.

In his family, he found inspiration and solace. Dickinson had revered his father, Samuel, a wealthy planter and respected judge, who died just as his son's political career began in 1760. He adored his mother, Mary, with whom he shared everything, from politics to his personal aspirations and failings. His older half-sister, Elizabeth, died when he was young, and he had grown apart from his older half-brother, Henry. He loved his younger brother, Philemon, despite their political differences. But as Dickinson grew older, he turned increasingly to his more like-minded Quaker kin by marriage, the Pemberton brothers, with whom he united in causes to improve the world. Unusually, his innermost circle consisted of female relatives, strong-willed, literary-minded Quaker women: his mother, Mary Cadwalader Dickinson; his wife, Mary Norris Dickinson (called Polly), and her cousins Hannah Harrison and Hannah Griffitts, the latter a poet; his two daughters, Sally and Maria; his aunt by marriage, Mary Parker Norris; and his cousin by marriage, Deborah Norris Logan, the historian. He turned to these powerful personalities for both religious and political advice and for refuge from the often-brutal political world. Polly was Dickinson's cherished helpmeet and soul mate.

Dickinson's solid fidelity to his friends and family was nearly matched by his animosity towards his enemies. Although he had many political adversaries, there were only a few to whom he returned the same ire that was dealt him. In 1764, he almost came to blows with Joseph Galloway, an attorney who later led the Loyalist cause, on the steps of the Pennsylvania State House. Another antagonist was Benjamin Franklin, whom Dickinson bested in a constitutional dispute in the Assembly. Senator White's assertion of a friendship between Dickinson and Franklin was, in fact, wishful thinking; the state of their relationship can be gauged by what was *not* said—the two prominent Pennsylvanian and American politicians exchanged not a word of personal correspondence throughout the entirety of their long and active lives. But the man who remained Dickinson's inveterate "enemy" for much of his life was John Adams. Their vastly different political priorities and styles, not to mention personalities, quickly turned them against one another even before America declared independence. It is arguably Adams who is most responsible for Dickinson's present-day obscurity.

These animosities were exceptions, because for Dickinson, a political opponent did not have to be a personal enemy. He disagreed profoundly with the politics and policies of Washington and Alexander Hamilton, who, like Adams, were Federalists—champions of the elites and manufacturing.

Dickinson was aligned with Democratic-Republicans, advocates of ordinary farmers. He thought Washington a middling military commander and a poor president, and he hated Hamilton's seeming affinity for monarchy. Yet he respected both men and extended his friendship, support, and sympathy when the occasion arose. Where possible, Dickinson sought commonalities among his fellow Americans rather than divisions. During the political battles that wracked the early Republic, he proclaimed, with Thomas Jefferson, "We are all republicans: we are all federalists."[9]

At first impression, given all this, Dickinson might have seemed an unlikely leader of a colony-wide resistance movement. At first glance, he didn't look the part. His pale complexion betrayed the ailments he suffered throughout his life—headaches, fevers, chest and back pain—symptoms not of a sickly constitution but of overwork. But his frequent physical incapacity belied an abiding passion for the public good that gleamed in his eyes when he spoke of politics or religion. Debby Logan found that his demeanor "impressed an holy awe upon those that heard him," and his desire to do good drove him to accomplishments beyond the talents of even more robust men. This passion was Dickinson's animating force, but it was also something he struggled to restrain and to channel towards virtue in his own life and in the life of the country. Usually he succeeded.[10]

To the younger members of the Senate at that 1808 session, those who had not known Dickinson personally, he was a legend. Beginning with the Stamp Act in 1765, he had been the foremost leader of the resistance to Britain; the internationally renowned author of *Letters from a Farmer in Pennsylvania* (1767–1768), which was the best-selling and most discussed pamphlet in pre-Revolutionary America; and the author of more seminal congressional papers and patriotic pamphlets than any other individual. Historians later called him "the Penman of the Revolution." His 1768 "Liberty Song," America's first patriotic song, was sung in taverns from Boston to Charleston.

> COME, join Hand in Hand, brave AMERICANS all,
> And rouse your bold Hearts at fair LIBERTY's Call;
> No *tyrannous Acts* shall suppress your *just Claim*,
> Or stain with *Dishonour* AMERICA's Name.
>> In FREEDOM we're born, and in FREEDOM we'll live,
>> Our Purses are ready,
>> Steady, Friends, Steady,
>> Not as SLAVES but as FREEMEN our Money we'll give.

Glasses were raised across the colonies to the "Patriotic Farmer." Many agreed with Debby Logan that he was "master of the most commanding & persuasive eloquence."[11] He continued to write for the general public, touching on every major issue and controversy of the Founding era and many of the early Republic.[12] "Volumes from his pen," proclaimed Senator White, "that do honor to the age, that will be read and admired as long as the love of science and freedom shall be cherished, record his inflexible patriotism; and the liberties of this country, which he contributed so essentially in establishing, will I hope long, very long indeed, sir, continue to be the proud and unshaken monument of his fame."

Even John Adams had to admit that "Mr. Dickinson was primus inter pares"—first among equals, though in typical Adams style, he meant this as a backhanded compliment, the equals here being "aristocrats."[13] Before 1776, few equaled Dickinson in reputation, and none surpassed him in influence. Individuals toasted him as the "American Cicero"; colonial legislatures sought his counsel; Congress looked to him for direction; and the British considered him, as green-eyed Adams put it, the "ruler of America."[14] Taverns and ships were named after him, and less patriotic spirits attacked his admirers for their devotion to the "divine Farmer." Still, tributes continued to pour in from all corners of British North America and across the Atlantic. It was generally understood that Dickinson was the man who was most responsible for bringing about the Revolution.

History is the story of unintended consequences. The senators gathered in 1808 knew that Dickinson's life was complicated. There were reasons he had such determined enemies. At the height of his power and influence, after leading America in her most strenuous and effective resistance, Dickinson refused to vote on or sign the Declaration of Independence. Revolution was not what he intended, only resistance. Convinced that it was not what was best for America at that moment, his "inflexible" patriotism and sense of virtue was held against him.[15] Despite the fact that he then took up arms for the American cause as one of the few members of Congress to command a battalion and, later, the only one to enlist as a private, a few vocal opponents targeted him. To these men, however, Dickinson's not signing the Declaration was less important than his stalwart opposition to the radical Pennsylvania constitution of 1776, which was inspired by the extreme democracy of Franklin and Thomas Paine. Dickinson believed that it privileged mob rule over rule of law and jeopardized dissenters' rights, and he had led opposition to it—a fact not forgotten after the war was won. For most Americans, however, his continued service to the country demonstrated his loyalty. After independence was declared, in addition to serving in the military, he was a member of Congress, president of Delaware and Pennsylvania, chairman of the Annapolis Convention, an active member of the Federal Convention, president of the Delaware constitutional convention, an honorary member of the Society of the Cincinnati, and author of more pamphlets on national affairs.

The senators assembled in February 1808 pondered Dickinson's legacy, admiring him and his service regardless of party. The Revolution was so recently behind them that they understood the complexity of declaring independence. Few questioned what confounded later Americans—his stance against it. Some could not fathom a gentleman who would sacrifice reputation and power for principle or conscience. Had he only acquiesced, they mused, there is little doubt who would have written the Declaration and been the first president of the United States.

President Jefferson himself was unequivocal about what Dickinson had accomplished. When informed by one of Dickinson's physicians, Dr. Joseph Bringhurst, of Dickinson's passing, he replied, "A more estimable man, or truer patriot, could not have left us. Among the first of the advocates for the rights of his country when assailed by Great Britain," wrote Jefferson,

> he continued to the last the orthodox advocate of the true principles of our new government: and his name will be consecrated in history as one of the great worthies of the revolution. We ought to be grateful for having been permitted to retain the benefit of his counsel to so good an old age; still, the moment of losing it, whenever it arrives, must be a moment of deep-felt regret.[16]

Now in the fading light of this February day, Senator White's reticence to eulogize must have prompted his colleagues to consider the life of the man who, more than most, was responsible for their presence there.

1

"Nursd in the Arms of Liberty"

Growing Up in Early America, 1732–1753

Early November on the Eastern Shore of Maryland is a fine time of year. The breezes off the Chesapeake Bay are sufficiently cool to turn the leaves vibrant but still mild enough to give hope for an Indian summer. In the eighteenth century, fishermen could catch blue crab for a few more weeks; enslaved people, indentured servants, and farmers sowed the winter wheat; and women poured candles to see them through the impending winter. Although planters had long grown tobacco here, by 1732, the year John Dickinson was born, grains were more profitable as tobacco prices stagnated.[1] Public tobacco houses still dotted the landscape, and the acrid smell of the drying weed seeped from black barns and mingled with the pungent scent of the bay.

On the tobacco plantation called Crosia-doré in Talbot County lived a Quaker couple, Samuel and Mary Dickinson (Figs. 1 and 2). At forty-three, Samuel was one of the wealthiest men in the colony. His father had migrated from Virginia in 1659 to establish Crosia-doré, meaning "cross of gold," where Samuel was born in 1689. It was a fine two-story, five-bay brick estate surrounded by stately trees and pungent boxwood. Situated on the Choptank River, it was ideally placed for easy transport of his cash crop, tobacco. The elegant staircase and wainscoting within suggested the country seats of the English aristocracy that Maryland planters sought to emulate.[2]

Samuel Dickinson was a shrewd businessman with an eye for a bargain. As tobacco planters struggled with fluctuating prices and lost their land, he snapped up their properties, until eventually he owned a number of substantial plantations. In addition to his Maryland holdings, he also possessed thirteen hundred acres in the neighboring colony of Pennsylvania. His family had accumulated hundreds of acres in the Three Lower Counties of New Castle, Kent, and Sussex on the Delaware River, mostly in Kent County, where Samuel planned to move his family. The volatility of the market, along with the strife it had caused in Maryland politics, meant prospects for wheat were better than those for tobacco.

The Three Lower Counties would also be a calmer political environment than either Maryland or Pennsylvania proper. Although still owned by the Penn family and technically part of Pennsylvania, since 1701 the Three Lower Counties had functioned like a separate colony from Pennsylvania. More religiously and ethnically diverse than their parent colony, they shared the same governor but had separate legislatures and court systems. They were thus insulated from the ongoing factional strife in the Quaker-dominated Pennsylvania Assembly.

Recent years had been difficult for Samuel personally. A wave of illness in 1729 had taken his wife of nineteen years, Judith Troth, as well as their daughters Rebecah, seven, and Rachell, four. Also that year, their eldest son, William, twenty-one, had met the same fate as his younger brothers, Samuel, fourteen, and Walter, sixteen, who had died of smallpox while in London for their educations.[3] What good, Samuel must have wondered, was having the means to send one's sons abroad if the cost was so high? Another daughter had died in infancy in 1725. Of the couple's nine children, only two, Henry, fifteen, and Elizabeth, eleven, survived.[4]

After Judith's death, Samuel needed a helpmeet and a mother for the children, so he began searching for a new wife. As a third-generation Quaker, he looked among his brethren. The Quaker community in the region was both extensive and tight-knit. Word spread of Samuel's situation, and soon a likely bride presented herself. Born in Marion, Pennsylvania, Mary Cadwalader descended from Welsh Quakers. In 1705, her industrious and devout father, a schoolteacher named John Cadwalader, had moved his family to Philadelphia, then a provincial town of a few thousand residents. After receiving an inheritance, Cadwalader retired from teaching and became a successful merchant.[5] He joined the upper echelons of Pennsylvania society, working as a tax collector and a judge for the Court for the Trial of Negroes—whose penalties for crimes were markedly harsher than for whites—and serving as a five-term assemblyman.[6] Mary's younger brother, Thomas, was on his way to becoming a well-regarded physician (Fig. 3), and her sister, Hannah, at eighteen, was just of marriageable age.

Mary was a handsome woman with a strong will that showed in her countenance. With wavy brown hair modestly tucked into a delicate linen cap and blue eyes that sparkled with intelligence and humor, Mary exuded self-possession. Described as "a distinguished woman, of fine understanding and graceful manner," by the age of thirty it looked as though she might not wed.[7] Mary was unconcerned. For Quaker women, spinsterhood was an acceptable condition. She was defined not by her status as someone's wife but by her faith and virtue. But Samuel Dickinson was a good match in intellect, temperament, and worldly standing, and they married in Philadelphia on November 4, 1731. A year later and far from the city, Mary found her life drastically altered; she was the mistress of a large plantation, the stepmother of two adolescent children, and an expectant mother.

Johney Dickinson, as his family called him, was born on November 2, 1732.[8] At first glance, the Maryland world he entered appeared quiet and rural, a backwater compared to Philadelphia, with its active business community, raucous Quaker politics, and budding intellectual and cultural institutions. Philadelphia was gaining a reputation around the Atlantic World as a center of urban enlightenment. By contrast, on the Eastern Shore of Maryland, the plantations were little worlds unto themselves, spread at a distance, with the planter elite in relative isolation from one another. Life in Maryland was structured as its original Catholic proprietors, the Calvert family, had envisioned in 1632, not progressive but reminiscent of a feudal system of lords, manors, and peasants. Lacking landed titles, American colonials could never truly replicate the English aristocracy they so admired, yet the fortunate few nevertheless fancied themselves a gentry class, with all the associated rights, liberties, and privileges.[9]

Any parity between American colonials and their aspirant peers in England in the eighteenth century depended on a foundation of inequality. It was understood that by divine decree all things in the cosmos were ordered hierarchically into a single, harmonious Great Chain of Being, stretching from the greatest to the least, from the Divine Author to the smallest pebble. Everyone, everything, had its place and its associated duties to those above and below. Some exercised rights, while others were meant only to serve. It was the duty of the lower sorts and slaves to work; it was the obligation of the upper sorts, with their learning and virtue, to care for, protect, and speak for them. It was everyone's duty to obey God. But some—upstarts, radicals, and libertines—heard divine whispers of *liberty* and *equality* growing louder in their consciences.

Early eighteenth-century Maryland was changing rapidly, with a few fortunes rising and many others falling. As the colonial population proliferated, men such as Samuel Dickinson grew in stature, while others tumbled downwards with the price of tobacco. After the bursting in 1720 of the so-called South Sea Bubble, a massive stock market crash that destroyed lives and fortunes, the imperial mercantile economy had resumed the expansion begun at the end of the Glorious Revolution of 1688. The stability offered by the new constitutional monarchy under William and Mary created a boom in cottage industry, the manufacturing of all manner of products. The colonies fulfilled their duty to the mother country by exporting raw goods, such as lumber, furs, and cotton, which were returned to them in the form of finished products, such as china, hats, textiles, and books. Because they were now produced in greater quantities, these goods were, for the first time, affordable for ordinary colonists. Items that had once seemed extravagant luxuries—tea services, looking glasses, and kid gloves—were now necessities, undermining the once reliable distinctions between the elites and those who aspired to be.[10]

The anxious planters of the southern colonies became obsessed with the pursuit of wealth as a means to reaffirm social distinctions. They looked to increase the output of labor-intensive tobacco cultivation. At first, indentured servants and poor white tenant farmers performed the labor, but they were not enough, and planters turned increasingly to a cheaper alternative: slavery. Whereas an indentured servant would eventually leave or die in debt to his master, an enslaved person was a one-time purchase that could also reproduce. As the population of Maryland expanded in the late-seventeenth and early eighteenth centuries, enslaved people accounted for nearly half of the growth. Like other colonies to the south, Maryland planters did not merely replicate British hierarchy and inequality; they intensified and brutalized it.

Although Quakers were less susceptible than most to the rampant consumerism of the age, their mantra being that possessions should be "of the best sort, but plain," Samuel Dickinson and his family still followed the pattern in Chesapeake planter society of amassing land, wealth, tenants, and slaves. Yet despite being born and bred in Maryland, Samuel Dickinson did not fit comfortably there. Although Quakers were no longer beaten, whipped, and driven from the province, as they had once been, they were discriminated against in other ways. In 1718, the colony passed legislation requiring an oath for office holding. Non-Quakers believed that invoking God in an oath supposedly guaranteed truthfulness.[11] Because Quakers followed Matthew 5:34–37 and refused to swear, they were thus excluded from all public service. Mary Dickinson was no more at home, being accustomed to the religious liberty of her native Pennsylvania written into its uniquely Quaker constitution. Unable to serve in any public office in his native colony, her husband shared her sentiments.

Each First Day, as Quakers called Sunday, Samuel and Mary made the ten-mile trek north to a crossroads called Trappe, where they worshipped at Third Haven Friends Meeting.[12] Founded in 1684, the meeting house was starkly plain. The unpainted wood of the walls and benches, unadorned by carving or embellishment, furthered the worshipper's purpose—to go inwards and seek God's light in her conscience. The trepidation at having her sins revealed by the Divine Light might cause her to quake with fear. Movable panels sequestered the sexes to conduct their own particular business with appropriate discretion. No ordained minister led the meeting; God did. And if the Divine Hand so moved a believer, she was compelled to speak his words through her voice.

Quakers believed that Christ was among them, and everyone—rich or poor, Black or white, male or female—could experience God in his or her conscience. Unburdened by a doctrine of original sin, Friends believed that Christ's seed might take root in a properly cultivated soul and, with God's Light, blossom into righteousness. God's Light was the same in each person, meaning there was fundamental spiritual equality. The only difference between individuals was in the amount of Light they experienced. Some basked in it, while others remained in relative darkness. Elders of the meeting encouraged the former and censured the latter, who did not follow God's will. No religious group in the colonies enacted their faith on a daily basis as much as the Quakers, which earned them both praise and ridicule.

The Religious Society of Friends had not always consisted of respectable sorts such as the Dickinsons. Quakerism arose during the chaos of the English Civil War, after Charles I was beheaded in 1649 by the Puritans, when the country was rife with religious and political experimentation. In their early years, Quakers were the lower sort of laboring people, seen as fanatics at the fringe of English society. In defiance of the world, they embraced the term of derision by which they became known—as they put it, "the people in scorn called Quakers." Their mission was to convince the world of the righteous path. Traveling in pairs, ministers, often women unaccompanied by a male chaperone, set out to publicize, dissent, educate, disrupt, provoke, and, ultimately, *convince* through an inward process—not *convert* through external force. They targeted those they deemed most at risk of damnation—the English Anglicans, the New England Puritans, the Ottoman sultan, the Chinese emperor, the Romish pope—and performed their faith in ways designed to elicit reaction. They stood outside churches and shouted down ministers. They smeared their bodies with ashes and strode into the services.

They ran naked through the streets to symbolize the spiritual nakedness of the unconvinced. Calling themselves "the first publishers of Truth," they sought to shock the consciences of imperiled souls.

In this, the Quakers were successful. Englishmen feared them even more than they feared the papists, who they believed were plotting to overthrow the government and doom them to eternal punishment. In a strange twist, they equated Quakers and Catholics—one religion stripped of all rituals and icons, the other centered on them. Where the Catholics had the pope, Englishmen reasoned, the Quakers had the Light within—or the "pope within," as they called it.[13] Both Quakers and Catholics recognized a higher authority than the king, which meant that their allegiance lay outside the nation and they did not consider themselves bound by the government or laws of England. No reasonable person, they believed, could ignore the similarities between the Quakers and the Anabaptists who had overrun the German city of Münster in 1532. Following their charismatic leader Jan van Leyden, the Anabaptists had ousted the civil authorities, executed nonbelievers, and proclaimed the End of Days to be nigh at hand. Then ensued scenes of depravity and debauchery as Europe had never before seen, with Leyden reigning as Christ come again. While he ate the best meat, wore robes of velvet, and took other men's wives, his followers starved and suffered. Eventually, in 1735, the authorities stormed the walled city. After executing Leyden's followers, they locked him in a cage, tortured him, and carted him around the countryside as an example to anyone else entertaining ideas of his own divinity.

With the restoration of Charles II in 1660 to the throne of England, religious as well as political order was restored. Parliament passed laws to force dissenters to pay tithes to the Church of England and specifically to prevent Quakers' public preaching or meetings. Yet Friends persisted in their usual manner, braving beatings, whippings, and tongues bored through with hot irons to bear their testimony for Christ. With brands on their foreheads and broken bodies languishing in jail, their spirits soared, producing some of their most compelling writings, including William Penn's 1669 *No Cross, No Crown*. Martyrdom was not only a sign of righteousness; it was the best publicity for their cause. Non-Quakers would know the seriousness of their conviction, and it would be contagious.

When they traveled to New England to convince the arrogant Puritans of their spiritual danger, amid the punishments Quakers endured, one mercy the Puritans bestowed, or so they thought, was banishment from the

Massachusetts Bay Colony. While some Quakers accepted that sentence, others took it rather as a kindly invitation to return at a future date. Mary Dyer, for one, a Puritan turned Quaker, defied banishment, returning to Boston and proclaiming Luther-like, "Here I stand; I can do no other." Thus as Charles II ascended the throne, Mary Dyer ascended the gallows. This was the stubbornly righteous stock from which John Dickinson hailed.

In those days of suffering, it became clear to many Quakers that the radical mode was no longer sustainable. Those engaging in the most extreme dissent put the entire movement in jeopardy. One charismatic figure in England, George Fox, sensed a new leading, a new direction, towards pacifism. Though Quakers had fought in Oliver Cromwell's army, God now revealed that his creations were sacred and must not be destroyed. This sanctity applied to individual men and also the unity men created together as a society—the constitution of the body politic. Unity was divinely ordained, as were the structures and processes governing it. So the weighty Quakers (those with the most Light)—George Fox, his wife Margaret Fell, Robert Barclay, William Penn, and others—believed that Friends needed to establish their own church government to create good order among men. They also needed to hold sacred the civil government, which ensured equal treatment for believers and for nonbelievers. Both were ordained by God for his ends.

Quakers' core principles did not change with this new order—they still aimed to save the world—but their methods did. After 1660, they would use only peaceful means, means that did not harm individuals or destroy the unity of the polity. They became a people of processes, recording their sufferings, breaking only unconstitutional laws, such as tithing, and then accepting the punishments with love in their hearts. In short, the Quakers became a people of laws, out-lawyering the lawyers and using the very system that oppressed them to gain their freedom. It was due in no small part to their persuasion that James II issued the 1687 Declaration of Indulgence, granting a measure of toleration to religious dissenters. Now, Quakers believed, salvation for the world no longer meant that everyone needed to become Quaker in name. They needed only to act like Quakers.

Indeed, the idea of what was or was not "Quakerly" was never unanimous among Friends. Since the 1690s, there had been a sense among some Quakers that holding their fellow men in bondage was un-Christian. As the trade in human chattel increased in the next century, one man in particular could be silent no more. Benjamin Lay was an odd individual. Standing only four feet tall, he had an intense and defiant gaze, his restless energy much more like that of the early Quakers. He had already made his testimony against slavery public by smashing his wife's tea service to protest the sugar produced with slave labor. In 1737, Lay published a tract directed at Quaker slave owners called *All Slave-Keepers Apostates*. The following year, he attended meeting dressed as a soldier—abhorrent to pacifist Friends. After preaching vigorously against slavery, he plunged a sword into his Bible, which had been hollowed out and filled with a bladder of red pokeberry juice, spilling forth the "blood" of slavery's innocent victims, splattering bystanders and shocking their sensibilities. Lay was swiftly disowned from the Society.[14] To Quakers, the means never justified the ends; rather, if the means were not appropriate, they might invalidate the ends.

Samuel and Mary Dickinson were not rigid Quakers, but Lay's radical behavior did not resonate with them. They held that as long as the enslaved people were treated humanely, the institution was compatible with Christianity. Through their example, they believed, those they enslaved could imbibe Quaker principles and be saved, and they entertained no thoughts of liberating them.

The Dickinsons' flexibility in their Quakerism was also evident in the education they desired for their children. Although some Friends wanted a "guarded" education, to stave off inevitable sin as long as possible, Samuel had always sought the best education for his children—hence he had sent his three sons by his first marriage to England, where they had died. With no schools in the region, the Dickinsons brought tutors into their home, preferring talented immigrants from Scotland or Ireland.

In April of 1739, Mary Dickinson gave birth to another son, whom they named Philemon. The family was expanding in other ways as well. Johney's half-sister, Elizabeth, called Betsey, now eighteen, had found a serious suitor. Charles Goldsborough was a thirty-two-year-old lawyer who lived on a large plantation on Horn's Point, directly across the Choptank River from Crosiadoré, in Dorchester County. His first wife had died, leaving him with a son, Robert, a year younger than Johney. Goldsborough was an Anglican, and the marriage took place in the Church of England. While the Dickinsons did not mind whom their daughter married, the Religious Society of Friends decreed that certain processes had to be followed for obtaining "clearness" for a marriage. No clearness could be given for a marriage with an Anglican. The elders of Third Haven Meeting thus wrung their hands over the "disorderly" marriage of Elizabeth Dickinson. Because Samuel was responsible for Betsey and he allowed the marriage, he had transgressed as much as she. The matter lingered unresolved in the community over the summer and into the autumn.

Following Quaker process, appointed members visited with Samuel to discuss his transgression and convince him to show contrition. Samuel held his ground. In October, Friend James Berry reported "that Samuel returns this answer that he did not reason himself a transgressor in the case of his daughter's marriage." Third Haven's dilemma was that Samuel was one of the wealthiest and most powerful members of the meeting, and they could not easily disown him. In November, the elders finally decided their course of action: they summoned Samuel to appear before them to give him "advice of our ancient Friends on such like occasions." They did not, as with some other transgressors, bear their testimony against him.[15]

Samuel Dickinson never discussed his official standing in the Society and whether he had been disowned within his sons' hearing, and Johney grew up unaware of what exactly had transpired.[16] Yet although he inherited his father's dislike of rigidity in religion, he was no less influenced by his mother's continued devotion to the Society of Friends.

In 1741, Samuel Dickinson moved his family north. For many years, he had conducted business in the Three Lower Counties on the Delaware River in Pennsylvania. These counties—from north to south, New Castle, Kent, and Sussex—contained excellent resources and were within reach of Philadelphia. Samuel's forebears had accumulated a significant amount of land near the St. Jones River in Kent County, which he inherited and enlarged. In Kent, he had both fertile farmland and access to water. He had already begun traveling between Crosia-doré and Kent, conducting business and making contacts with lawmakers and legislators. With such opportunities denied him in Maryland by the now-Anglican establishment—the Calverts had converted to the Church of England to retain the colony—he consented to be elected judge of the Court of Common Pleas in Kent County. Though not a trained jurist—few men were formally trained in the law in this place, at this time—what mattered most was that he was a propertied gentleman with learning and virtue, which, it was assumed, meant a commitment to disinterestedness.

In January, the Dickinsons left their Maryland homeland in the hands of son Henry and moved sixty miles northeast. They named their newly constructed house Poplar Hall.[17] Though modest by the standards of Philadelphia, the three-story house was one of the most elegant in the Lower Counties. Its size and pointed pediment, a nod to classical architecture, distinguished it from other brick houses of the region. Entering through the main door, visitors were received into an airy foyer with polished wide-plank floors and an ample staircase leading to the second floor. A large drawing room to the right, filled with natural light from four large windows, contained a marble fireplace with built-in shelving on either side. There were two small parlors, one for the gentlemen and one for the ladies, each with its own fireplace. Behind the two parlors was a more intimate family room with a wood stove, a large bank of cupboards, and stairs to the attic. Atop the main stairs were four bedrooms, one very large one and three smaller, all but one with a fireplace. A cellar with the kitchen ran the length of the house. Elegant English mahogany furniture was upholstered in silk.

After the move, Samuel expanded his landholdings, and the plantation developed into a thriving center of industry and amenity. The fertile land was ready for all manner of crops. There was ample pasture for grazing and marshland for reeds that could be made into baskets or bedding. Jones's Creek, located at the southern boundary of the property, provided good fishing and oystering, as well as a landing where crops could be dispatched to Philadelphia. Samuel later added a second house, four barns, two granaries, a dairy house, a tanning yard, and fifteen other outbuildings of various descriptions, including slave quarters. There were five apple orchards, a peach orchard, and a lush garden with cherry and other fruit trees.[18]

The lifeblood of the planation was a sizable community of enslaved Black men, women, and children, without whom all business would have ceased. Of the backbreaking labor, tobacco was perhaps the worst crop to work. The stench burned noses and throats, and the poisonous nicotine seeped through the skin. In addition to the field laborers, members of this Black community possessed the expertise that allowed the plantation to function like a self-contained town. There were tailors, cobblers, tanners, and carpenters. The planation lacked only a blacksmith. Without enslaved Black people, there would be no Poplar Hall, no Dickinson fortune.

Those enslaved by the Dickinsons were provided the basic physical necessities of life—coarse muslin for their clothing, ground meal and salt for their hoecakes, a morsel of salt pork. Their dwellings were typical of slave quarters and primitive by comparison with the main house. Each one-room cabin was constructed of rough-hewn logs sealed with mud and covered with a shake roof. The floors were dirt, and a single window was covered with cloth. A fireplace for cooking also heated the room—tolerably in the winter, unbearably in summer. The inhabitants slept on pallets or on the bare floor. The furniture—a table, a chair, perhaps a small chest—was coarse. Each dwelling was allotted a small garden plot where the inhabitants could cultivate a few vegetables.

The Dickinsons were fond of those they enslaved. But like most white people, they pretended the relationship was voluntary on the part of Black people, referring to them euphemistically as "our people," "servants," or even "family." They treated them well by the standards of the day. Unlike planters to the south, they provided those they enslaved with decent clothing and did not compel them to go about partially clad or naked. Mary kept careful track in her ledger of who received stockings, breeches, coats, and petticoats.[19] The Dickinsons also consulted the enslaved on matters that concerned them, including whether they should be sold. Because Quakers believed in the spiritual equality of the races, they also provided their people with education to enable them at least to read the Bible. But no earthy kindness can compensate for depriving another human of his or her liberty.

"Massa Johney," as the enslaved people called young John Dickinson, was kind, gentle, and good humored, a favorite among them.[20] From a young age, he took a genuine interest in them and their concerns. He was someone to whom they could turn if they needed help. To him, they were humans in a regrettable situation, one that he sought to ameliorate. Though there was talk of slaves being happy in their situation, Dickinson sensed that any notion that Black men and women were content as slaves was self-deceit.

Recent events had made this truth perfectly clear. The largest slave rebellion in the colonies erupted on September 9, 1739, when Johney Dickinson was seven, in South Carolina. A group of twenty newly arrived Kongolese slaves recruited around sixty others, killing whites along the Stono River on their way to their anticipated freedom in Spanish Florida. They did not make it. Intercepted by the militia, those who did not fight to the death were executed or sold to a more brutal life in the West Indies. With enslaved people constituting almost one-quarter of the population of the Lower Counties, Governor George Thomas advised slave owners to protect themselves. "Our slaves," he warned, "have given us too much reason to fear, that they will become troublesome to us in the like manner as Negroes have been in some of our neighbouring governments."[21]

Once old enough for serious instruction, Dickinson received tutors to ensure he would obtain the education necessary for him to claim his rightful place in colonial British society—that of a gentleman. His older siblings had been instructed by a serious young Presbyterian minister named Francis Alison, who had since gone on to establish a well-regarded Latin school in New London. The most significant of Dickinson's tutors was another young Presbyterian named William Killen, who had emigrated from Ireland in 1737 at the age of fifteen. When the Dickinsons moved to Poplar Hall, Killen moved in with the family. Only ten years older than Dickinson, Killen was erudite, upright, and honorable, the perfect mentor. The two young men became more than tutor and pupil, growing into friends and, later, colleagues in the law.

The foremost requirement for a gentleman—after possessing land and wealth, of course—was the leisure time these assets provided for a liberal education. He would use the time and resources he gained from the labor of those he enslaved to acquire broad learning in the arts and sciences. Dickinson's general education books provided an overview of what he should know. The French historian Charles Rollin's *The Method of Teaching and Studying the Belles Lettres, or an Introduction to Languages, Poetry, Rhetoric, History, Moral Philosophy, Physicks* and William Guthrie's *A New Geographical, Historical, and Commercial Grammar; and Present State of the Several Kingdoms of the World* gave him a foundation for the more advanced material he would cover as he came into adulthood. The Bible also figured prominently in his education for its instructive fables.

Despite the claims of their detractors, Quakers did indeed value the Bible, especially the New Testament. But they believed it came from the same source as God's Light. Just as humans could misunderstand God's will as it came through the Light, so might those humans who transcribed God's will in the Bible have made mistakes. Though God was infallible, men were not. The teachings of the Bible, therefore, were not to be viewed too narrowly or applied too strictly without consideration of other sources. Biblical parables could be very helpful, but they were not taken literally, and they needed to be tested against the Light within and subsequent revelations. In his commonplace book, young Dickinson copied the Latin phrase *temporis filia veritas*— truth is the daughter of time—and listed discoveries in the study of religion, philosophy, astronomy, and geology that disproved older beliefs. These were evidence that divine revelation was indeed progressive.

Dickinson's was an ecumenical and liberal course of study. He drew from a wide variety of sources to find wisdom that comported with his family's Quakerism. He seemed to discover it almost anywhere—even from the pagans, the papists, and the infidels; all had something to teach him. In his commonplace book, on the topic of prayer, along with a passage from Ecclesiastes, he jotted a line from Samuel Richardson's novel *History of Sir Charles Grandison*: "The Persians' prayer to the rising sun—Oh thou by whom thou art enlightened, illuminate my mind, that my actions may be agreeable to thy will." This Islamic prayer resonated with Dickinson's Quaker values. He likewise found much enlightenment in the ancient authors and read as much as he could of the Greeks—Aristotle, Plutarch, Homer, Plato, Lycurgus, Aesop's *Fables*—and the Romans—Cicero, Pliny, Sallust, Virgil, Ovid, Horace. Their insight into man, morals, and politics transcended time.[22]

To cut an acceptable figure in colonial American society, first and foremost, a gentleman should be conversant with history and political theory, which required extensive study. Dickinson found his masters. Niccolò Machiavelli offered trenchant observations on republican governance. Hugo Grotius, the Dutch jurist and theologian, wrote on natural law and law of nation, contributing to the understanding of rights of persons and how they are protected. Samuel von Pufendorf, the German philosopher, likewise expounded on the law of nature and nations. Frenchman Jean Bodin wrote on history, law, economics, and natural philosophy. Above all, the figure who was emerging as Dickinson's greatest intellectual hero was the English philosopher and statesman Francis Bacon, "whose Discoveries have entailed a debt on all the Human Race," as Dickinson later wrote to his mother.[23] He developed the scientific method of inductive reasoning—the method of observing nature and taking a skeptical approach to avoid being misled—something Dickinson himself aspired to practice.

His education was not merely in things long past. The colonial elite kept close watch on political developments in Great Britain and Europe. Indeed, the pages of the newspapers were largely foreign "advices," so Americans knew more about what was happening three thousand miles overseas than in neighboring colonies. Most compelling, of course, was news from "home," as colonists of English extraction considered Great Britain. Whether they had been there or not, London was the vantage point from which Britons in America viewed the world. As British subjects, most Americans gravitated towards a particular political perspective. Since the restoration of Charles II to the throne after the English Civil War, Englishmen had entrenched themselves into opposing political factions—the Tories versus the Whigs. Where

Tories were conservative supporters of the monarchy and the divine right of kings, Whigs were liberal proponents of the rule of law and the rights of the people. Americans tended to be Whigs.

Of paramount concern to Whigs in the early eighteenth century was the spread of "popery." Everywhere, it seemed to Englishmen, the minions of the pope were making inroads against the righteous Protestant empires— the Catholic French and Spanish against Great Britain and Holland. As Dickinson entered his adolescence, the War of the Austrian Succession raged in Europe. The conflict led to the naval War of Jenkins's Ear with Spain and then to King George's War in the British colonies in America, in which the French and Indians battled with forces marshaled by William Shirley, the governor of Massachusetts. But New York and New Hampshire seemed much farther away than Scotland, where a more nefarious plot was afoot. The Tory Jacobites—supporters of the dethroned King James II and the House of Stuart—still refused to accept the outcome of the Glorious Revolution of 1688 and rose up periodically in an attempt to reclaim the throne for James's descendants. These efforts stoked Whig fears of popery and arbitrary government, resulting in a flood of political treatises. In 1745, Charles I, son of James II and the so-called Young Pretender to the throne of England, fomented another Jacobite rebellion in Scotland.

Dickinson avidly read the letters Thomas Gordon and John Trenchard wrote under the pen name Cato denouncing the threat these Catholic sympathizers posed to the liberties Englishmen held dear—those of speech, the press, and rule of law. Though he did not subscribe to their virulent anti-Catholicism, he thrilled to their trumpeting of these fundamental rights. He also greatly admired the Whig perspective of Frenchman Paul de Rapin in his *History of England*, as well as Jacobite-turned-Whig theorist, the Viscount Bolingbroke, whose *A Dissertation upon Parties* taught him about English constitutionalism and the danger of political factions. Bolingbroke's distinction between factions, which he viewed as always destructive, and opposition parties, which could provide salutary resistance to arbitrary power, may have reminded Dickinson of his Quaker forebears.[24] The Irish satirist Jonathan Swift, whose *Drapier's Letters* alerted the Irish people about English plans to devalue their currency, taught him about English rule and methods of resistance.[25]

Whig ideals of the rights of Englishmen and constitutional protections of liberties resonated strongly for most in the American colonies. The farther a British subject was from the center of imperial power, the more vulnerable he tended to feel to arbitrary uses of authority. Thus, American Whigs gravitated towards the more extreme pronouncements of their ancient rights, liberties, and privileges embodied in the British constitution. They looked with reverence to the heroes of the Glorious Revolution—James Harrington, Algernon Sydney, and the monarchs William and Mary—who implemented the new revolutionary settlement, including the Bill of Rights, that secured the rights and safety of the people.

Although the Dickinsons were sympathetic to the Whig cause, they were not Whigs, exactly. They were Quakers first, and Samuel Dickinson's position as a jurist provided him with a different perspective from most colonists. Quakers were proponents of rights, but they were peaceful and cautious in their activism. Moreover, because of their belief that the Light of God might shine in all humans' consciences, they tended to consider that all men—and women—deserved to have their rights protected.

It was understood even before John Dickinson was born that he would study the law, as his father intended for all his sons. Samuel directed them to the law not because there was wealth to be had; indeed, colonial lawyers generally could not make a living in the profession, compelled as they were to spend their time chasing small debtors and interpreting wills. Rather, knowledge of the law was instrumental to other ends. Certainly, it was an asset in business, but for Quakers it was also a means of doing good in the world, of performing service to others, whether prosecuting a trespass, representing the wrongly accused, or serving in the legislature.

Knowledge of the law was the most important tool for advocating human rights and resisting oppression—whether by the government or other individuals. Even as early Quakers had confronted those who manipulated legal procedures to persecute them, they educated themselves in the law to challenge their persecutors on their own ground. Quaker Philadelphia had become home to the leading legal minds in the colonies, and Samuel believed his sons should be among them. It became apparent to him that Johney was his best hope. He had precisely the sharp mind, unflagging work ethic, scrupulous honesty, and devotion to justice necessary for excellence in the profession. Most of all, however, his motives were pure. Even at a young age, he evinced a sense of honor that forbade compromise to base motives. His emotions sometimes got the better of him, but Dickinson's parents suspected it was just youthful exuberance and that maturity would moderate his temper.

Like the rest of his education, John Dickinson's legal study began at home with his father serving as his example. Under the watchful eye of William

Killen, he acquired the skills he would need to master the knowledge. If he wanted eventually to practice law, he needed to know not only principles and maxims, the important cases, and the statutes of Parliament but also the languages of the law—Latin, French, and the amalgam of these with English in the specialized medieval legal language known as Law French, a legacy of the Norman conquest of England nearly seven centuries earlier. Though British jurisprudence had moved away from using Law French in case books and in the courtroom so that ordinary people were no longer completely excluded from the proceedings, many of the older case books and much of the legal vocabulary still used this language. Dickinson thus applied himself to learn it.

He came to revere the legal sages he studied. Foremost among them was Sir Edward Coke, who wrote the jurists' oracle *Institutes of the Laws of England*. Serving under three monarchs, from Elizabeth through James I and to Charles I, Coke was the chief justice of the Court of the King's Bench and framer of the 1628 Petition of Right to curb the tyrannical behavior of Charles I. Had Charles minded the petition, he might have kept his head upon his shoulders. Though many law students' efforts foundered on Coke's writings, which were dense and technical, Dickinson devoured his teachings, finding many occasions to quote "My Lord Coke." Many other jurists—Edmund Plowden, Malachy Postlethwayt, Thomas Siderfin, William Salkeld, Peyton Ventris—came to form a constellation of ideas and values at the foundation of Dickinson's legal study. Trained at the Inns of Court in London, these men wrote reports and commentaries on the cases they heard that became the basis of both the common law and legal education. They were scholars, often religious and political dissenters, sometimes agitators, and fiercely protective of English rights and liberties. Dickinson yearned to follow in their footsteps.

Yet he was also taught that a mind continually engaged in the same difficult employment would contract and stiffen. In polite society—and especially in conversation with the ladies at the tea table—a gentleman should also be familiar with literature and poetry. Mary especially, who was well acquainted with the best authors, ensured her son read widely.[26] He thus read Cervantes's *Don Quixote* and La Fontaine's fables, and he enjoyed Shakespeare, admiring both his wit and his political commentary. His favorite poet was Alexander Pope, whose works captured his imagination. Pope was relatable in other ways as well. Not only was he a Catholic, a religious dissenter like Dickinson himself; he also suffered from health problems, including tuberculosis of the spine. Although Dickinson was much more robust, his own periodic bouts of illness made him even more sympathetic to Pope's plight and ideas. But what endeared the poet to him most was Pope's devotion to his parents. "Of all the Good Qualities he possest," Dickinson exclaimed to his mother, "I esteem him for none so much, as the filial Piety which glows in his Works; and I am convincd, A man whose Soul contained so divine a Tenderness for his parents, must have been a complete good man."[27]

By his eighteenth year, Dickinson had learned much from his parents and tutors, and now it was time to extend his legal knowledge. This could not be done at home. In 1750, he departed quiet Poplar Hall, with its pleasant agrarian rhythms, for the burgeoning metropolis of Philadelphia. There he was to serve a three-year term as a legal apprentice. Through his family's connections, he had secured a premier clerkship with John Moland, the leading legal mind in Philadelphia, former king's attorney, head of the Pennsylvania bar, and member of the Provincial Council. Known for his erudition and devotion to his clients' interests, Moland was also a severe master, holding his clerks to the highest standards of performance.

Dickinson joined George Read, another young man from the Lower Counties, who had already been reading with Moland for a year. Like Dickinson, Read had bound himself to Moland for a term of years "to learn the science, business and mystery of an attorney at law," during which time the apprentice "truly shall serve, his master's secrets shall keep close, his commandments lawful and honest everywhere he shall gladly do." Their behavior would be strictly controlled so as to mitigate youthful indiscretions such as gambling and fornication. "From the service of his said master day nor night," the indenture stipulated, "he shall not absent or prolong himself." In return, in addition to teaching his young apprentices the law, Moland would "provide for his said apprentice meat, drink and lodging."[28]

Second Street, where Dickinson lived, was one of the better sections of town, inhabited by the leading merchants. Should he feel homesick, two sets of maternal aunts and uncles lived nearby. His Aunt Hannah and her husband, Samuel Morris, who was a successful merchant, and his six young cousins were close. And his uncle, the eminent physician Dr. Thomas Cadwalader, and his wife Hannah Lambert, lived across from Black Horse Alley with their two children, Lambert and John.[29] Uncle Cadwalader was a lapsed Quaker, but he agreed with Friends about vain and idle ceremonies in other sects that were "imposed upon ordinary people by wicked, politics, and designing priests." Dickinson was inclined to agree with him that these superstitious rituals had "contributed very much to corrupt the manners of men, turning their thoughts from true morality and virtue."[30] He was well connected and could introduce his nephew to the eminent personages in the city who could be of use to him in the future, such as the secretary of the province, William Peters.

One hundred miles from Dover, Philadelphia still possessed the feel of a country market town. The city, and indeed the province, was expanding quickly and was much changed from the days when the first settlers huddled in caves along the banks of the Delaware River. Now with fourteen thousand inhabitants in 1750—only about half the population of New York City—Philadelphia took an entire day to traverse on foot.[31] In some ways, Pennsylvania's founder, William Penn, who died in 1718, would have been pleased at what his colony had become; in other ways, he would not. A forerunner in what historians would, centuries later, refer to as "the Enlightenment," Penn had had a vision for his colony from the overarching ideals to the minutiae of urban planning. But Pennsylvania was the embodiment of the disjuncture of theory and practice, in many ways a casualty of its own success. As the political theorists knew, liberty could easily lead to license, or the abuse of liberty, as unintended consequences appeared.

Penn's primary aim was for the colony, founded in 1681, to be a haven for religious dissenters, a "holy experiment" reflecting the love for mankind—hence the name of his capital city—embodied in the ideals of his Quaker faith. The government, initially modeled on that of England, consisted of an executive (Penn and his deputies), an upper house of legislature (the Provincial Council), and a lower house of legislature (the Assembly). Penn originally planned to allow each branch an equal vote on legislation. But perhaps fearing the anarchic tendencies in early Quakerism, at the last minute, Penn had given himself a treble vote. His Quaker brethren, viewing this move as a betrayal of Quaker principles of equality, bridled at the power imbalance and resisted implementation of the plan of government.

Thus, despite Penn's lofty visions of a well-ordered and well-behaved society, Pennsylvania had developed a reputation on both sides of the Atlantic as an unruly and contentious colony. Though claiming to be a "peaceable people," the Quakers' political style bordered on riotous at times, leading many onlookers, including the British ministry, to consider them ungovernable. Over the first twenty years of the colony's existence, the Quaker-led Assembly had wrangled with Penn, his deputies, and his Provincial Council until, in 1701, its members implemented a new constitution—the

Charter of Privileges—that effectively nullified the power of the proprietors and Council, making Pennsylvania the only major colony with a unicameral legislature. That constitution provided the Quakers with unique liberties within the British Empire—the freedom to be Quakers and to "Quakerize" the colony, as one detractor put it. Thus Quakers dominated the government even as their numbers gradually declined in relation to the non-Quaker population.[32]

By the 1720s, the Quakers' power seemed to be dissipating until the arrival of William Penn's son Thomas in 1732, which had the effect of coalescing them into a faction against him. Whereas previous generations of Friends had contested William Penn's power, a rising generation revered the elder Penn as their founder and saw his son as greedily amassing his fortune at the expense of ordinary Pennsylvanians. Seeking to bring the Assembly to heel by starving it of funds, in 1751, Thomas Penn issued, from London, instructions disempowering the Assembly from passing bills that enabled them to print paper money unless they afforded him veto power over expenditures. The contest between Penn and the Quakers would only become more acrimonious.

Contrarian Quaker politics notwithstanding, religious liberty flourished. As the only major colony with liberty of conscience constitutionally protected—thanks to the Charter of Privileges—all professions of faith were welcome, and no one was harassed for his or her beliefs. So intriguing was this climate that visitors toured meeting houses, seeing them as far greater entertainment than anything else afforded by the Quaker city. At a Quaker meeting they might witness the spectacle of a woman preaching. As to whether that was stranger than a whole body of people sitting together in silence, visitors were often uncertain. Whatever brought them in, Friends cared not. Either way, they might convince these strangers of the Truth in God's Light.

Quaker civic-mindedness also led to more voluntary associations in Philadelphia than in any other American city. All were intended to improve the daily lives of the inhabitants through education, safety, and Christian charity. The Library Company, the only lending library in the colonies, was thriving in 1751, its nineteenth year. The city had three newspapers, two in English and one in German. It had two volunteer fire companies. In 1752, a new fire bell was installed on Fourth Street, where the entire city could hear it, and water pumps spaced every fifty feet or so facilitated rescue efforts. Insurance companies helped those who had experienced disasters to re-establish themselves. The Overseers of the Poor and the Quaker Almshouse cared for the indigent. Still, residents worried about the increasing numbers of sick people on the streets and complained that mentally ill individuals who wandered the city were "a Terror to their Neighbours" and in danger of being preyed upon by "ill-dispos'd Persons wickedly taking Advantage of their unhappy Condition."[33] But more than this, Philadelphians knew that the suffering of poor persons for want of food, shelter, and medical care must be alleviated. A movement by some residents was therefore afoot, led by a physician named Thomas Bond and Uncle Cadwalader, to build a hospital where these people could obtain care at a small cost. In fact, the Assembly had passed a bill to begin construction, which commenced the year after Dickinson's arrival. The legislation explained, "the relief of the sick poor is not only an act of humanity but a religious duty."[34]

Pennsylvania's reputation for enlightened policies had traveled across the Atlantic, where the French took notice. The *philosophe* Voltaire proclaimed that "WILLIAM PEN might glory in having brought down upon earth the so much boasted golden age, which in all probability never existed but in *Pennsylvania*."[35] Though there was some justification for this view, such acclaim bordered on the mythological, rooted as it was in the misconception that the Quaker rulers took a laissez-faire approach to religion.

Contrary to Penn's vision, many living within the province found the Quakers' version of religious liberty to be oppressive. Though there was no established church, the Quakers controlled the government more tightly than any Puritan regime. They passed laws peculiar to their society that all must follow, and taxes supported Quaker policies. Where their laws could not reach, Quakers dominated the culture of Pennsylvania. Not only did they stifle gaiety and diversions found in other colonies, but they also thought nothing of offering "close hints" to those not of their society about the spiritual risks of frivolities, such as curled hair or an embroidered waistcoat. One could hardly turn about without having one's conscience pricked by a Quaker admonishing them to prepare "for a time nigh at hand, when the Messenger of death is to be sent."[36]

Philadelphia's physical layout reflected the enlightened rationality of Penn's plan. Rather than allowing the city to expand organically, following the feet of men and animals as they beat paths through the wilderness, Penn had a novel design for the City of Brotherly Love. Wide streets were cut, forming a grid with spacious blocks of land for dwellings, shops, gardens, and orchards stretching between the Delaware and Schuylkill Rivers. Penn envisioned settlements evenly spaced between the two rivers, spread out to avoid the contagion of fire and disease.

But Philadelphia was a city of merchants and seamen who were loath to be far from the Atlantic port. So even as the population exploded, most clustered within a few blocks of the wharves on the Delaware River, which were the busiest in the New World and had made the Quaker merchants the wealthiest in the empire. The year Dickinson arrived, 317 ships glided into the harbor, carrying goods, passengers, and sometimes illnesses from around the colonies, the empire, and the globe.[37] The crowding in Philadelphia rivaled London, with more dwellings, shops, and warehouses wedged in with each passing year. Though some sections of the city contained crudely crafted buildings, many of the houses and other buildings were large, some as many as four stories, constructed of stone or brick. Some dwellings had balconies on which residents could find relief from the scorching summer heat. The estates outside of the city were modeled on those of the British aristocracy and almost as grand.

Goods were sold in shops and at a public market, the largest in British North America, which was held twice per week on High Street. Penn had designated this street to be exceptionally wide to accommodate the commerce. Stretching two blocks, the marketplace began at the courthouse and was covered with a gabled roof on brick columns and stone walkways. On Wednesdays and Saturdays, farmers and craftsmen rented stalls and came from the Pennsylvania countryside and New Jersey to sell produce, meats, livestock, and all manner of food, drink, and household goods. Visitors to the city found that the amount and quality of the goods for sale there rivaled European markets.[38]

The Quakers' openness to religious dissenters, their lenient penal code, and their benevolent institutions brought unexpected difficulties. Tolerant of even Roman Catholics, who were pariahs in most colonies and in England, Quakers did have some limits. A young upstart Anglican minister named George Whitefield was disrupting traditional religion in the colonies. Scandalously, after first priming listeners with religious pamphlets distributed before his arrival, he preached to them out of doors, whipping them into fits of religious enthusiasm. Every year of Dickinson's apprenticeship, the spectacle of the Reverend Whitefield's open-air evangelizing riled the city. The streets became clogged with thousands of curious seekers from the surrounding farmland and wilderness. Had he ventured close to Whitefield's platform on the steps of the courthouse, Dickinson would have seen the cross-eyed minister waving his arms above his head, exhorting his listeners to reject the worldly business of accumulating wealth—a distraction from the perilous state of their unconverted souls. In response, his listeners would cry out or faint in fits of enthusiasm. Whitefield's publicity campaign and popularity were such that he became the world's first celebrity, with a frenzy of admirers and a no-less-devoted cadre of detractors.[39]

To some, this was an alarming spectacle. Whitefield filled his listeners' heads with dangerous ideas, proving irresistible to the feeble-minded women and boys among them. He preached of spiritual equality and anti-intellectualism, thereby undermining the established hierarchy. Whitefield's "New Light" ministry borrowed heavily from an early incarnation of Quakerism, and Friends, who had since become more reserved, disapproved of his tactics. Nor did Whitefield's message resonate with Dickinson; his Quaker upbringing and rational turn of mind rendered him unsusceptible to the enthusiasm at the heart of the preacher's show. Despite Whitefield's rhetoric of piety, Dickinson had doubts about the morality of a man who seemed to exploit the hopes and fears of common people with little education.[40] Yet he may have taken note of Whitefield's innovative use of the press and his persuasive oratory.

Pennsylvanians might well have heeded calls for greater morality. The colony was frequently called "the best poor man's country,"[41] and, indeed, it drew more than its share of impoverished immigrants from the British Isles and Europe looking for new opportunities and better lives. The result was one of the most diverse colonies in peoples, languages, and religions. But although there was little overt religious strife, crime was a growing problem. In the decade before Dickinson arrived, there were seventeen homicides in the colony, and that number doubled during the next decade. Moral crimes such as gambling, swearing, and sexual misconduct, especially fornication and bastardy, were also rising sharply around 1750, whether despite or owing to Whitefield's ministry, no one was certain.

William Penn had desired a humane penal code for Pennsylvania, with justice for individuals and without the brutal physical punishments that prevailed in England and were applied disproportionately to the poor. For the first four decades of Pennsylvania's history, the death penalty existed only for murder and treason, and it was only applied twice. Some complained that Great Britain treated Pennsylvania as a penal colony, depositing its criminals on its shores. In 1751, the legislature passed an act to stem the tide.[42] The truth was, however, that America, and particularly Pennsylvania, cultivated its own criminals perfectly well. The orderly proceedings of the city during the day gave way to a different scene after nightfall: raucous gatherings of servants, enslaved people, vagrants, and those hawking illicit services. Their activities were frequently fueled by rum and accompanied by drumbeats on milk pails. In various neighborhoods, residents were plagued by the lighting of fireworks, which led to house fires. Beginning in 1751, perpetrators were forced to pay a fine unless they were servants, Black people, or Indians, in which case they received the lash and hard labor in the county workhouse. With few streetlights to ward away the dark, the nightly watch frequently had more trouble than they could manage.[43]

The Quaker government took various steps to remedy the problems, including passing legislation, such as that to regulate the nightly watch and streetlighting.[44] It had been forced to abandon the more lenient code to please the Crown, and punishment now looked more like that in other colonies, though Quaker judges were still reluctant to apply the harshest measures. Their religion dictated rehabilitation and reform rather than condemnation and death.[45] Nevertheless, it was not unusual to read in the papers about heinous crimes and ensuing executions.

One day, Dickinson would take very seriously his duty as a defense attorney, often for the poor and unfortunate. But for now, he was merely a clerk. The life of a legal apprentice was inglorious. Though not quite as lowly as a scrivener, the clerk toiled at much the same drudgery, copying letters, depositions, and contracts, while also making alphabetical lists of legal terms with definitions in a commonplace book, researching cases for his master, and learning how to argue by debating with his master and other clerks. A wonderful boon to the clerk was that his master's vast library was open to him—legal classics waiting to be plucked off the shelf and devoured. But they were a temptation in which Dickinson could not often indulge. Most of his time was spent at his desk, copying and commonplacing in the noisy office. But Dickinson had been raised to believe that there was intrinsic value in work, and he felt that once one had chosen to pursue law, knowing well its tedious nature, "to continue complaining & loitering is unmanly & foolish."[46] But the countless hours spent hunched over papers and books, frequently by candlelight, began to take their toll. He experienced an unaccountable pain in his breast that became increasingly distracting. It was difficult to know the cause or the cure, and the disruption to his work vexed him.

Attending court was a welcome break from the grind of copying. The State House, where the Assembly and the Supreme Court sat, opened in 1752 and was just a short walk from Moland's dwelling in Second Street (Fig. 4). Three justices sat at a high bench overlooking the chamber. Central in the room was the dock, a wrought-iron fenced platform where the accused stood. The jury box was to the right of the justices and the witness stand to the left. At the entrance was the bar, the railing behind which spectators stood. It was every law clerk's aspiration to pass the bar both literally and figuratively and join the court proceedings. In sessions, the apprentices listened intently, trying to follow the arguments.

At the end of the day, Moland and his apprentices might head across Chestnut Street to Clark's Inn for a bite and a draught or to the Indian King on Market Street, between Second and Third. There were nearly a hundred other establishments they could choose from. For his part, Dickinson patronized only these respectable establishments and avoided the tippling houses, which trafficked illegally in strong drink. His indenture with Moland specified "taverns he shall not frequent."[47] Philadelphia had, as yet, no proper public coffee house, though there was talk of one.[48]

Although most legal apprentices in the colonies received only practical instruction in copying, Dickinson was more fortunate. First through his parents and tutors, then through Moland, he was introduced to a theoretical understanding of the law. His broad and deep reading in literature provided him a humanistic foundation for the legal maxims he was learning. These maxims, coming from ancient and modern sources alike, were, he believed, "established on wisdom and experience of ages and proved by utility." Edward Coke's *Institutes* and Francis Bacon's *A Collection of Some Principall Rules and Maximes of the Common Lawes of England* became his scripture, the basis of his code of honor for serving his clients and country.[49] By fully understanding their meanings, putting them together, and committing them to heart, he was beginning to form his jurisprudence, his philosophy of the law.

One foundational maxim was Coke's "The People is unhappy when the Laws are unsettled."[50] It was said that "the People, whose law is incertain, endure the most miserable Slavery."[51] Therefore, their objective was "to settle Great Britain's Rights by public & positive Laws" and "clear & indubitable" rules."[52] Thomas Wood's *A New Institute of the Imperial or, Civil Law*, one of the standard law texts of the age, explained, "If any Case happen which is not provided for by any known or written Law, it shall be determin'd by the natural Principles of Equity, which is an universal Law, and extends to all possible Cases."[53] For jurists well knew that "want of right and want of remedy is the same thing."[54] Dickinson found that one of the simplest but most powerful maxims was "equality is equity."[55] This little phrase could be narrowly understood to mean that unless there are extenuating circumstances, all heirs to property should receive equal portions. But it could also be understood more generally to mean that every person deserved equality under the law. As Dickinson would learn, however, the simplest maxims could be the most difficult to realize.

During this period of study under Moland, Dickinson was also beginning to think more broadly about how to realize his ideas of justice. Whether the lawyer is interpreting a will or defending an individual charged with a crime, an abiding maxim was the "intent of the client is the pole star." This maxim could apply to a variety of circumstances, such as the lawyer's need to enter the mind of a semi-illiterate farmer who did not understand legal language when he wrote his will or so that he could put himself in the place of the man who had killed another in the dark of night and subsequently been charged with murder. Intent here was everything, as Dickinson knew. Was the act intentional, meaning it was murder? Or was it an accident, meaning manslaughter? The answer could mean the difference between life and death for his client. "An act," ran the maxim, "does not make the doer of it guilty, unless the mind be guilty." And if the person were charged, more maxims applied. "In criminal cases," said one, "the proofs ought to be clearer than the light." When no clarity was present, read another, "it is always safer to err in acquitting than in punishing, and on the side of mercy than of justice." For Quaker jurists who opposed the death sentence, this was an abiding principle.

There were also maxims Dickinson found relevant to his professional and personal conduct. One from ancient Roman law held that "the law assists those who are vigilant with their rights, and not those who sleep on their rights."[56] Others held that men possessed not only rights, but also responsibilities. "Everyone not only has a Right but *ought* to prevent every dangerous or Wicked act."[57] Whether the person preventing the wicked act were Dickinson himself or one of his future clients, he believed "no one should be damned for doing his duty."[58] He would always do his best for his clients and his country. Should he fall short of success, a maxim from the Roman senator Cassius Longinus provided solace: "In such attempts, 'tis glorious e'en to fail."[59] The deeper Dickinson became submerged in study, the clearer another of Bacon's maxims became: "Every man is a Debtor to his Profession, from which as he expects to find Profit & Emolument, So he ought to make Returns of Advantage to the World."[60]

In trying to apply and live this juridical wisdom, Dickinson married it to what he had already learned from his study of history, literature, poetry, and Scripture. He grounded his jurisprudence in a humane learning. Here Moland was a significant influence. Much like Samuel Dickinson, Moland exemplified personal dignity and liberality. He was a man not just of the law but of letters. He gradually accepted his new clerk not just into his practice but also into his home. Dickinson would, on occasion, journey the twenty-some miles north to Moland's estate in Bucks County, a fine stone house that also served as the county seat. There Dickinson became fond of Moland's lively family—his wife Catherine and their seven children.

The British legal calendar began to govern Dickinson's life. Since the Medieval era, there had been four terms, based on the Roman calendar: from January to April was Hilary Term; from April to May was Easter Term; from June to July was Trinity Term; and from October to December was Michaelmas Term. During terms, the clerks helped their master prepare for court. In between terms, they copied and commonplaced endlessly.

In September 1752, an extraordinary event disrupted Dickinson's work. On what should have been September 3, the *Pennsylvania Gazette* announced, "This day, being the fourteenth of September by the late Act of Parliament, begins the New Style." The British Empire was finally joining most of Europe and Scotland in adopting the New Style calendar implemented by the Roman Catholic Church in 1582. The old calendar, based on one proposed by Julius Caesar, was inaccurate, so Pope Gregory XIII had offered a more accurate version. But England, a Protestant country, was disinclined to adopt a papist calendar. There was a difference of eleven days between the two. When Parliament passed the Calendar Act of 1750, officially adopting the Gregorian calendar, the next year was shortened, lasting only 282 days, and for the first time, in 1752, the new year began on January 1 instead of March 21. But the English calendar was still misaligned with Europe's and Scotland's. To remedy the problem, in September of that year, the calendar was corrected by omitting eleven days. Time thus jumped overnight from Wednesday, September 2 to Thursday, September 14.

In an era when more people measured time by the almanac than by the clock and their lives were governed by the seasons and the accompanying festivals, this change took some adjustment. For Dickinson personally, the new calendar meant a new birthdate. Whereas he had been born on November 2 according to the Old Style, this year he would celebrate the advent of his twentieth year per the New Style, on November 13. For law clerks across the empire, the effect varied. Happily, Parliament had chosen September for the adjustment so as not to interfere with the court schedule. It also decreed that property rights would not be affected and were to run their allotted course in actual days, regardless of the calendar date. Nonetheless, when landlords demanded the usual rent, lawyers' offices around the empire received queries from tenants worried about losing eleven days of payment. These and other confusions were gradually resolved, either by practice or legislation.[61]

In the spring of 1753, Dickinson's second year of apprenticeship, the new State House bell, which later generations would call the "Liberty Bell," was ready for the tower. It was to be a great occasion, with food and drink provided in celebration. The bell-founders John Pass and John Stow set it up for a test ring. The sound it made was so discordant that Philadelphians laughed in derision, saying that it sounded like two coal scuttles being knocked together. The founders retreated hastily with their bell to make another try.[62] Finally, in June, the bell was in place. On June 7, the *Gazette* reported, "Last week was raised and fixed in the Statehouse steeple, the new great bell, cast by Pass and Stow, weighing 2080 lb. with the motto," chosen by Quaker Isaac Norris Jr., "Proclaim Liberty throughout the Land, unto all the Inhabitants thereof; Lev. xxv: x."

Dickinson passed the bar in Pennsylvania and his future became certain—his parents had decided to risk their son's life for a chance to give him the best legal education in the empire, at London's Inns of Court.[63] Having received permission to join the Middle Temple, where his legal heroes had studied, he sat with his parents and planned his course of study and finances in detail. His plan was to stay two years and return to America as a solicitor, without being called to the bar in London. Their calculations determined that it would cost him £100 per year to live in London.[64] It was a prodigious sum, but manageable for the Dickinsons. From his father's time in London decades earlier, Dickinson would have friends awaiting him, ready to help him get settled. The Hanburys and the Barclays, with whom Samuel apprenticed when he was in London, were part of the transatlantic Quaker network looking out for their own and advancing Quaker causes.

One month shy of his twenty-first birthday, Dickinson packed for his journey and prepared to take his leave of all he had known. "I am now preparing for my voyage to another world," he announced to his friends George Read, who himself had just been admitted to the Pennsylvania bar, and Samuel Wharton, an aspiring merchant. The Middle Temple seemed to him like Heaven, a place where he could immerse himself in law books in an environment suffused with the spirits of his intellectual heroes. "I believe few Christians expect their departure with more resolution and alacrity."[65]

On Sunday, October 15, the *Scipio* weighed anchor and eased out of the port. With a cargo of his father's tobacco in the hold beneath him and a future of promise ahead, John Dickinson was bound for London.

2

"The Noblest Aim of Human Abilities & Industry"

Legal Training in London, 1753–1757

Young John Dickinson, tall and willowy, stood on the deck of the *Scipio*, swaying with the rocking of the ship. He had only recently gained his sea legs, and the easterly wind, though chilling in December, was invigorating after five weeks confined to his cabin. Upon leaving the port at Oxford, Maryland, on October 15, 1753, high winds had kept them along the coast until the twenty-seventh, when they sailed into the vast Atlantic. Between the rough seas and illness, Dickinson spent his twenty-first birthday and most of the voyage miserably below deck. Captain Hill took a special interest in the young gentleman, whom he found engaging company despite his wretched state. He had an openness about him, an unostentatious manner, and a cheerful disposition, which made him a good conversationalist. The friendly feelings were mutual. "His behaviour to me, all the passage over," John wrote to his parents, "was not only civil & polite, but extremely tender & affectionate. . . . Indeed, he treated Me with all the Goodness of the nearest Relation."[1]

The *Scipio* dropped anchor at the port of Deal on the English coast on December 15. Dickinson's first impression of London, which he reached a few days later via a small boat, was that it looked much like the wharves on Front Street in Philadelphia—crowded with buildings and teeming with activity—except that it was seemingly never-ending in all directions. A thick layer of smoke lay over the city, obscuring his view. What he could discern was bigger than he could have imagined, with buildings of several stories and three-quarters of a million inhabitants.[2] Beyond the riverfront, the curved streets and haphazard edifices kept him from seeing much beyond the docks, except for church spires. Barely visible through the smoke was the heart of Anglicanism, St. Paul's Cathedral, whose massive white dome defied sectarian competition. In the foreground was London Bridge, spanning the Thames like a fortress to prevent tall ships from passing. Although the centuries-old bridge, completed in 1209, had in the past been the scene of gruesome displays of executed traitors to the Crown, it was now a mere spectacle of decayed elegance.

Upon disembarking, Captain Hill escorted Dickinson to John Hanbury's elegant residence on Great Tower Street. Hanbury was a Quaker, exceedingly wealthy, and very well connected politically. He was the leading tobacco merchant in the city and the London agent for many of Pennsylvania's Quaker merchants, including Dickinson's father. Knowing that his friend and kinsman Robert Goldsborough, son of his brother-in-law, was also studying at the Temple, Hanbury arranged to have Dickinson taken there.

A mile and a half upriver from Hanbury's establishment was the Honourable Society of the Middle Temple of the Inns of Court, the British Empire's legal center (Fig. 5). Here Dickinson planned to spend the next two years learning how to practice law from the greatest British jurists. His carriage approached along Fleet Street, which ended at Temple Bar, an imposing gateway between the City of London and the City of Westminster. In the Middle Ages, it could be shut to deter invaders, but it was now ceremonial. Beyond the bar was another bustling thoroughfare, the Strand. Entering the Temple through a gatehouse, Dickinson found a city within a city. In contrast to the London hubbub, it was relatively quiet, a little sanctuary of order and reason. He walked down Middle Temple Lane, which stretched the length of the community with some twenty shops, from bookstores and stationers to barbers and cobblers. Jurists strode the lanes, as did gardeners, watchmen, butlers, laundresses, and washerwomen. The lane ended at the Thames with the Temple's southward pediments, which were mere paces from the water and festooned with the loud obscenities of the dockworkers.[3]

Seeing an old acquaintance far from home was a cause for rejoicing; Americans were scarce at the Temple, with only 150 attending over the course of one hundred years.[4] Goldsborough immediately offered Dickinson part of his bed until he could procure chambers of his own. On December 21, Dickinson enrolled himself and arranged to rent a set of rooms at Middle Temple Lane, No. 2. The head of the society, Under-Treasurer Charles Hopkins, with whom Dickinson struck up an immediate friendship, promised to have the rooms fitted up in genteel fashion, which entailed having them newly painted and the floors whitewashed. Hopkins gave them to Dickinson for £12 per year instead of the usual £15. This was welcome news to Dickinson, who worried about money—although his family had enough. Whereas most Middle Templars lived on £200 or even £300 per annum,

Dickinson resolved to make do with £120. He still had to consider the cost of looking like a gentleman in the most expensive city in the world, which required silk stockings, properly cut wigs, and carriage hires, as well as dining at respectable establishments and attending the theater.

Dickinson's entry into London life was physically and mentally taxing. During a "seasoning" period, he immediately caught a cold that lasted a week. Despite this, he gladly accepted an invitation from another American to Christmas dinner. Mrs. Rebecca Covington Lloyd Anderson was, like Dickinson, originally from Maryland. Daughter of the former royal governor of the colony Edward Lloyd II, she had moved to London when she married William Anderson, a wealthy merchant. A patriotic spirit moved her to invite her countrymen to dinner each Christmas, an invitation Dickinson accepted every year he was in London. He was immediately taken with Mrs. Anderson, who, he reported to his mother, "has something most surprizingly like You in her manner, & in her person there is a Resemblance."[5] And when she spoke of Mary Dickinson as one of her dearest and most valuable friends, his heart swelled.

Dickinson had arrived between terms at the Temple, so rather than attending the courts of law at Westminster Hall, he settled into a domestic routine. He rose at five o'clock each morning to study. At seven o'clock, the laundress arrived with a breakfast of bread, butter, and milk. She would light the fire and put the teakettle on, and then leave. It was strange to Dickinson at first that he and Goldsborough had to serve themselves at breakfast, but he soon adjusted. The laundress returned later to make the bed and sweep the room.

The remainder of the day was generally spent at study. Dickinson would collapse his tall frame over a case book and try to untangle the arguments. It was labor he thoroughly enjoyed. "I have taken as much Pleasure in unravelling an intricate Point of Law," he wrote to his father, "as a Florist receives, When he sees some favourite flower, which he has long tended himself, at last unfold its glowing Colours, & breathe its sweet Perfumes."[6] At three or four o'clock in the afternoon, when dark descended on the city and reading became difficult, he would unfurl himself, and he and Goldsborough would adjourn to a chophouse for dinner. From there they would continue to a coffeehouse, where they could purchase and discuss the latest pamphlets until they retired at ten o'clock.

Templars were required to dine a certain number of times per term in the Middle Temple Hall (Fig. 6). A relic of Elizabethan architecture, its massive double hammerbeam ceiling hung imposingly overhead, and its walls were carved with the coats of arms of past Templars. At the far end of the room was the high table where the governors of the Temple, the Masters of the Bench, or Benchers, sat. The table itself, a gift from Queen Elizabeth, was constructed of four massive oak planks from Windsor Forest and so large that it had had to be transported via the river and installed before the structure was completed. The other distinctive feature of the hall was its mode of heating. Lawyers are a backward-looking lot, so rather than feature the latest heating technology, namely a cavernous fireplace at one end of the hall, they preferred the medieval style: a fire pit in the middle of the room with an opening in the ceiling for the smoke to escape. But Dickinson could not experience the grandeur of the hall just yet. He would have to wait until he was properly bonded to dine in Commons, meaning a gentleman in good repute must vouch for him. Then he would also participate in the legal exercises that took place there, such as the moot trials to practice argumentation and handling of evidence.[7]

As he became acquainted with London and the opportunities it afforded, Dickinson became acutely aware of the moral dangers to which youth could be exposed. Unlike his apprenticeship with John Moland, young men in London were left to their own devices. "Every person lives without Controul in his Chambers &, according to his Disposition, may either prosecute his Studies with the greatest Quiet, in them, or employ them to the worst Purposes," John explained to his parents. Inattention would be enough to ensnare one in a debauched life. "Virtuous Company," he reckoned, "is the strongest Guard to a person's Morals. He not only reaps a benefit from their Conversation, but by them he is preserved from falling into bad, & defended from Attacks on his Innocence."[8]

Though Dickinson knew only a few people, they were all sober, industrious, and perfect gentlemen. He counted on his bosom friend Goldsborough to help guide him, as well as on other Americans, including William Hicks from New York, Nicholas Hammond Jr. from Philadelphia, Edmund Jenings and Charles Carroll of Maryland, John Blair and Thomas Mason of Virginia, and William Drayton of South Carolina. Eventually, a set of eight or ten of them formed their own little society, meeting each week at one another's apartments to argue points of law raised in the previous week.[9]

Such virtuous men, some lamented, were becoming harder to find, even at the Temple. One of Dickinson's recent predecessors, a jurist named William Blackstone, was deeply concerned at the declining quality of lawyers in

England. He was currently on a lecture tour to explain the law as a logical system, and he was working on a multivolume project called *Commentaries on the Laws of England*, which he hoped would replace Edward Coke's *Institutes* for lawyers in the empire. "We must rarely expect to see a gentleman of distinction or learning at the bar," Blackstone lamented. The ideal lawyer, in his view, was a landed gentleman whose independence raised him above the fray of commoners and allowed him to serve the cause of justice disinterestedly. He should care about the principles of the law rather than the manipulation of it for particular parties. "What the consequences may be," he warned, "to have the interpretation and enforcement of the laws (which include the entirety of our properties, liberties, and lives) fall wholly into the hands of obscure or illiterate men, is a matter of very public concern."[10]

Blackstone need not have worried about young Dickinson, who, in most ways, was the very model of the aspiring lawyer he envisioned. He was well read, serious, and heir to significant property in land. Most importantly, his reasons for studying the law were altruistic. Reflecting on the good fortune that had brought him to the Temple and closer to realizing his professional goals, Dickinson wrote to his mother, "Next to the gratifying my Honourd Parents I find no Consideration of equal Weight with defending the Innocent & redressing the Injurd— That seems to me the Noblest Aim of Human Abilities & Industry."[11] On the other hand, as an American colonial, he could never quite embody the stature Blackstone expected. Some in the Old World doubted that those in the New World were capable of producing men of intellect. It was widely believed that climate and geography determined human nature. Although British Americans would never be inherently as savage as the natives of the howling wilderness where they were born, nor could they be considered on a par with men born and bred in the Isles.

Dickinson hoped to prove them wrong. He longed for recognition, for renown, and believed that the only way he could—or should—achieve it was to earn it through diligent application to his studies and virtuous actions. "Labour is the Path to Glory," he wrote his mother, "and by Divine Command, 'In the sweat of the brow' are the Goods of Life to be purchas'd."[12] He credited his parents with establishing him on firm ground. "You on your part have given Me all the Advantages necessary, and now by your Generosity I am placd, where all the Benefits to be acquired in my Profession, are to be reapd."[13]

Settling into life in London, Dickinson found himself in a "Social Wilderness, as much at a loss amongst Houses and Men as in the strangest

Forest."[14] He was disoriented by the cultural and structural landscape of the city. London was incredibly noisy. The clatter of carriages rattled in his ears, yelling and rushing men and women jostled him in the streets, and smoke choked his lungs. Criers hawking produce and wares—everything from parsnips to pots and pans to cast-off baubles from the wealthy—added to the din. Simply traversing the crooked and winding streets was a harrowing adventure. Narrow, dark alleys with innumerable dangers and temptations lurking in their shadows jutted to the sides. It would be all too easy for an imprudent young man or one lacking in moral fortitude to allow himself to be lured down one of these vicious paths to his demise.

Here, filth abounded and stench assaulted the senses. The city government directed inhabitants to sweep household refuse into neat piles each week to be collected by sanitation workers, but such refuse accumulated and frequently was not removed. Muck piles were festering, stinking heaps of not just human and animal dung but food scraps, building materials, animal carcasses, and even, sometimes, tiny human remains. The very year Dickinson arrived in London, one of his colleagues at the Middle Temple published a pamphlet called *Public Nusance Considered*, describing the problems, including bad roads, butchers infesting the streets with their foul remains, vagrants, the desperate poor, robberies, and murder.

As Dickinson arrived in London, poverty was rampant and crime was flourishing. But it was not merely the lower sorts who were to blame. A popular song evoked parallels between the filth in London streets and the corruption in the higher ranks. In "The Kennel Raker," the poor sweeper of the gutters sings:

> Tho' I sweep to and thro' old Iron to find,
> Brass Pins Rusty Nails they are all to my mind,
> Yet I wear a sound Heart true to George our King,
> Tho' Ragged and poor with clear Conscience can sing,
> Tho' I sweep to and thro' yet I'd have you to know,
> There are sweepers in high Life as well as in low

The raker implicates the upper sorts for sweeping in their offices—the statesman, the parson, the doctor, and the lawyer; they, too, all rake the gutters, taking anything valuable to themselves and pushing the rest out of the way. The lowly kennel raker, at least, has an honest heart, while the others laugh as they swindle their clients.[15] London provided examples of all sorts.

London homes of the gentry were a respite from the clamor of the streets. Happily, Dickinson had plenty of invitations to such homes, and he was charmed by the hospitality of his hosts, marveling, "I never was treated with more Tenderness & Kindness, by my nearest Friends, than I have been by perfect Strangers to Me."[16] The Hanburys and the Andersons were at the center of this world, and also the Barclays. David Barclay, a wealthy merchant and banker, was the son of theologian Robert Barclay, one of the founders of the Society of Friends, whose 1676 work, *An Apology for the True Christian Divinity*, provided guidance to those seeking an understanding of Quakerism. He lived in Cheapside, a street in the financial district that, despite its name, was lined with fine shops and expensive dwellings.

These respites notwithstanding, only one month into his stay, Dickinson found London more than he could bear. It was known that the senses were the guardians of one's innocence and morality and that repeated assaults on them by clamorous noises and noxious fumes could have a detrimental effect, especially on someone accustomed to the clean air and tranquility of Pennsylvania's Lower Counties. He resolved to quit the city at once for more wholesome environs. On January 23, the first day of Hilary Term, Dickinson and Goldsborough retreated to a charming country village called Clapham, remarkable for its pure air, about four miles south of the city.

Once settled in Clapham, the pair hired coaches to take them to London for court. Westminster Hall offered a veritable buffet for the curious student of the law. With most of the courts under one roof, one could wander as one pleased from Common Pleas to King's Bench to Chancery. The hall itself was cavernous, loud, and bitterly cold. The oldest building in the parliamentary estate, by the 1750s it was in dire need of repairs. Inside the hall was a hodgepodge of panels to divide the courts, timbers to support the medieval hammerbeam roof, and tarpaulins to keep out the rain. Periodically, the justices complained of the indignity that they—and by extension, the law—suffered in this venue.[17]

On his first day, Friday, January 25, 1754, Dickinson sat in the Court of King's Bench, located in the southeast corner of the hall. He learned that if he wanted a seat, he would have to save one by leaving a key or a glove on one of the benches.[18] The greatest of the common-law courts, the King's Bench heard a wide range of matters: civil, criminal, appeals, and anything concerning the king. It also controlled the lesser courts. Dickinson flipped open his new booklet and scribbled notes on seven cases being presented, writing more and faster with each case. By the end of the term in April, he had written thirty-eight pages in that book and had begun a second to absorb the overflow. These books would become references for his education and future practice.[19]

Dickinson also witnessed cases argued before the House of Lords. "This Noble Assembly has not the Awefulness I expected," he wrote his father. Much to his surprise, he found that "they meet in a Room much inferior to that appointed for the Representatives of Pensilvania. And as it was not any solemn Occasion, they were dressed in their common Cloaths, which were mostly plain, & some quite indifferent." Yet he witnessed the Lord Chancellor, Philip Yorke, issue his opinion on a ruling in one of the clearest, strongest speeches he ever heard.[20]

A place of special interest to an American colonial was the Cockpit at Whitehall Palace. Once the most extensive palace in England, and indeed Europe, after a number of devastating fires in the 1690s, Whitehall now consisted of a few buildings. One of them was a theater, called the Cockpit-in-Court, adjacent to St. James's Park. Once used for cockfighting or as a playhouse, it was now the seat of the Privy Council, the king's closest advisors. The Board of Trade also met here, and it was this body that most interested Dickinson. It reviewed legislation passed by the colonial assemblies and advised His Majesty on whether to approve it, nominated governors, and wrote their instructions. Once or twice a week, it also heard complaints, during which the best lawyers at the bar argued the cases.

"I now have an Opportunity of seeing and hearing the most learned Lawyers & the finest Speakers," Dickinson wrote excitedly to his father. He was enthralled with William Murray, "the Solicitor," and extolled his virtues at length. "He enjoys from Nature, all the Advantages an Orator can wish for," he began his homage. "His person is very good, and his Voice is Musick itself. His Language is not only easy & flowing, to captivate the Ear, but so refined as to delight the Mind, & his Arguments so nervous," that is, vigorous, "as to force the Assent of the Judgment." Dickinson believed that Murray "undoubtedly has attained the Height of Perfection: Every Motion speaks, Every Attitude has a Charm. His Action has nothing affected, nothing forcd in it, but seems a Confirmation of his Words. . . . The Eye & Ear, are absolutely his Captives."[21] He studiously memorized every inflection and gesture of the man.

In general, Dickinson marveled at the grandeur and solemnity of the courts of law. "The very Appearance of Justice is aweful," he wrote his father, "& the Dress of the Judges is calculated to inspire Respect."[22] Their scarlet silken robes billowed around them, and their wigs draped ponderously on their shoulders. Although by this time, elaborate wigs were falling out of fashion in London, the law was one profession that still required them, for both judges and barristers. Heavy, hot, and itchy, these wigs made from human or horsehair distinguished the wearer yet soon became greasy, misshapen, and clumped with old powder and dander. Come Trinity Term and summer heat, given the limited opportunity for bathing, they contributed to the stench of human sweat, grime, breath, urine, and feces. It was almost enough to make one long for the bone-snapping cold of Hilary Term. As imposing as the judges' and barristers' attire was, "how trifling, how despicable are these things," Dickinson observed, "Compard with their Wisdom & Knowledge."[23]

Each day in Clapham, Dickinson grew more robust. His appetite returned, and he soon felt renewed and revived. On February 23, he settled his accounts and returned to London, now able to bear its smoke and dirt as well as any tradesman of the city.

Dickinson's lot was not all work. London abounded with diversions, and he occasionally indulged. "You will not imagine," he told his mother, "I have been a Stranger at the Play Houses." But he was generally unimpressed. "Some Actors," he explained, "especially David Garrick and Mrs. Pritchard," who were famous even in the colonies, "are exact Pictures of Life, & easily perswade You they are the very persons they represent." A young lawyer might study these professionals for courtroom techniques.[24]

On March 2, Dickinson donned a new wig and went to the Theatre Royal to see Thomas Otway's *Venice Preserv'd; or, A Plot Discover'd*, a tragic tale of love, betrayal, and treasonous revenge. More noteworthy than the play was one fellow theatergoer—none other than His Majesty, George II himself. Dickinson knew his mother would relish details. "He is a small Man," John began, "but has a very grand walk. He has Nothing else that is remarkable, except that he had the most chearful face in the whole house. The Moment he came in, he clapped up his Glass, & took a Survey of all the Boxes, but did not bow to any, tho I observed, he did to some Noblemen that came into his box." His Majesty was spry at seventy-one years old. "At the End of every Act," said John, "he got up with all the Liveliness of a Man of Forty, & stood for eight or ten Minutes, till the next Act."[25] Dickinson's parents did not disapprove of the theater, though many Quakers would object, royal company notwithstanding.

He studiously did not mention where the theaters were located, in Covent Garden. A vast piazza surrounded by stately arcaded buildings, the Garden was once a produce market; now, however, it traded mostly in pleasure. Each night, numerous public houses disgorged their patrons into the square, street performers sang and danced for small change, a profusion of men with their "doxies" buzzed about the brothels, and mollies—homosexual prostitutes—cruised furtively behind cover of the arcades. The pleasure trade was now so brisk that the first edition of *Harris's List of Covent-Garden Ladies*, the annual directory of the district's prostitutes, would soon appear. It was a little more discreet than a previous guide, *A Catalogue of Jilts, Cracks & Prostitutes, Nightwalkers, Whores, She-Friends, Kind Women and Other of the Linnen-Lifting Tribe*. Although it was easy to side-step the night walkers in the square, more dangerous was the bawd, or the "procurer," as she modishly called herself. She solicited gentlemen on behalf of the higher-quality doxy. "Her chief place of rendezvous," warned a 1746 pamphlet, "is at the *play-house*, that's the [ex]change she never fails to be upon; and indeed is the most proper place for her to put off her damaged commodities."[26] Mollies sought their custom more discreetly, of course, since sodomy was a crime punishable by hanging. So infamous was the locale that the peculiar diseases one could acquire there were termed "the Covent Garden ague."

If Dickinson saw any bawds, procurers, doxies, or mollies, he thought better of confessing it to his mother. Rather, in the same letter, he offered something to allay her fears—and perhaps his own. "As to the Vicious Pleasures of London," he assured her, "I know not what they are; I never hear of them, & never think of them." His virtuous friends with their respectable motives would protect him. "We never go into the way of Vice," he insisted, "& therefore are never injured by her; for in contending with her, the greatest Cowardice is the Noblest Courage, and the most precipitate flight, the bravest Resistance." Then he quoted Alexander Pope, always his reliable guide:

> Vice is a Monster, of so frightful Mien,
> As to be hated, needs but to be seen;
> Yet seen too oft; familiar with her face,
> We first endure, then pity; then embrace.

It was no coincidence that here vice was feminine. He continued for some time in this vein, extolling the joys of virtue and the miseries of vice, finally concluding, "This is the Voice of Reason, which Religion confirms by pronouncing, the one Heaven, the other, Hell. May I be able to preserve these Sentiments, & give them Life by Practize."[27]

As one of the coldest winters in recent memory finally eased into spring, Dickinson continued to reside with Goldsborough while awaiting his chambers to become available. At the moment, it was vacation between Hilary and Easter Terms, so his main occupation was reading. Nothing else interested him. "I fly to Books," he wrote his father, "to Retirement, to Labour, & every Moment is an Age, till I am immersed in Study."[28]

Yet he had learned that it was unhealthy to spend all his time at the law books and thus turned to literature and poetry for entertainment. He also enjoyed horseback riding, "as it is a very fine Exercise." Now that the streets were drier and one could venture outside without becoming splattered with muck, Dickinson purchased a map of the city and began walking for exercise as well. He felt himself growing stronger every day and believed that the English climate would transform him for the better. "There are numberless Instances of it, in my Countrymen," he wrote his mother, "even within the Temple, Who have come here, in a much worse State than I did, & in two or three Years, have become different Persons."[29]

On his walks, if he turned left out of Middle Temple Lane onto the Strand, he would eventually come to Westminster Hall and then to St. James Park, a favorite haunt in the warm weather. The fields beyond the park were, he found, especially lovely. In January, the weather had been too cold to enjoy them, but a hard freeze allowed him an unexpected diversion—"Skeeting." Formerly exclusive to the aristocracy, ice skating became a favorite activity of all classes in London, and Dickinson joined in the crowds on Rosamond's Pond for the fun. Come spring, "in a fine Day," he wrote his mother, "those fields are filled with People in Coaches, on Horseback, and on foot, rambling about for an Airing. The Mall though, is the most frequented Walk, and is crowded with a gay Assembly, amongst whom, it is very agreeable to mix, & Saunter an hour, before Dinner."[30]

If he turned right out of the Temple onto Fleet Street, St. Paul's Cathedral was only fifteen minutes away. It was a "prodigious thing," but such grandeur seemed only what one should expect in so great a city. It did not spark his imagination or incite his admiration.[31] Just north of St. Paul's was Britain's other house of worship, the 'Change, the Royal Stock Exchange. He found it to be a fairly unpleasant place, teeming with "Noise, Dirt, and Business." The raucous men on the street were contemptuously called "Cit," as in "citizen of the town." These were tradesmen, not gentlemen. They were after money, not honor or glory from service to others. And when they got money, it did little to improve their manners. In addition to the trade in goods, there was another flourishing trade near St. Paul's and the 'Change. Along with Covent Garden, these areas were well known as molly cruising places. In truth, the pleasure trade flourished everywhere in London and catered to all tastes. Even on Middle Temple Lane strolled harlots hoping to lighten the students' purses.

Continuing north from the 'Change, Dickinson came to St. Bartholomew's Hospital, which had been expanding recently and where physicians were conducting path-breaking medical research. "Barts" increasingly bore less resemblance to its neighbor immediately to the north, Smithfield, the live-stock and butchers' market. The sounds and scents of cruelty reached the ears of passersby long before they saw the piles of meat and rivers of blood and fat. It was generally believed that beef would be of poor quality unless the animal were baited by dogs before slaughter. Panicked screams of cattle, hogs, and aged horses awaiting the knacker's knife wafted on the breeze along with the stench of their excrement as animals were butchered in the cellars under the market or inexpertly behind private shops and dwellings. Along with live-stock at Smithfield, a woman might be sold to the highest bidder by her dis-gruntled husband. Though illegal, it was a form of common-law divorce that struck few as untoward in an era when wives, like animals and children, were considered almost as property.[32]

Turning towards home, Dickinson would pass Newgate Prison and the Old Bailey, London's criminal court, which was even busier than usual during this crime wave. Whereas the victims of crimes had been allowed for some time to have solicitors help them prepare and prosecute their cases, it was not until the 1730s that any of the accused were allowed counsel to aid in their defense, excepting in cases of felony. Even then they could only consult with counsel on specific points of law, and they must prosecute their cases on their own. The accused often did not learn of the charges against them until the trial began, and they could not compel witnesses to testify on their behalf. Their innocence was judged on their natural and spontaneous responses to the evidence against them. Many jurists believed that defense counsel would only muddy the waters and make a guilty person appear innocent. Now, however, a defense lawyer could be seen on occasion working for a client. But the accused was still required to speak for him- or herself and with no presumption of innocence. Counsel was barred from speaking to the jury. This lack of advocacy in London stood in sharp contrast to Pennsylvania, where lawyers swarmed the courts, actively soliciting clients, and it was rare to see a defendant without counsel.[33]

Dickinson took note of the situation of ordinary people and their need of lawyers. "We see how the Courts of Justice are crowded," he wrote home, "by people who know nothing of the Law; how much more agreeable then must it be to Us, who understand every thing that is said."[34] More than his limited work in Philadelphia had, the London courts impressed him with a sense of the service that lawyers could provide to the lower sorts especially, who, without assistance, could be at the mercy of the harsh common law.

Gradually, Dickinson was acclimating to London and, thanks to his family's connections in Philadelphia, was finding his way into elite circles. His Uncle Thomas Cadwalader had sent him a letter of introduction from William Peters, the secretary of Pennsylvania, to the proprietor and governor of the colony, Thomas Penn, who lived in London. The letter, describing Dickinson as having "a sweet Disposition," eventually resulted in a friendship with William Penn's second son.

With an invitation in hand, on March 22, Dickinson hired a coach to take him to Governor Penn, who lived at a fine townhouse near Charing Cross. Although William Penn had been one of the leading lights of early Quakerism, Thomas had drifted away from the faith. When Dickinson met him, he hadn't worn the plain dress of Friends for a decade, nor did he use the plain speech. Now, with his new wife, an Anglican, he considered himself a member of the Church of England, though he still would not take the sacrament.[35]

Penn was eager to hear from Dickinson about the Penn family's province and the wealth it could bring him, and he listened attentively while Dickinson regaled him with accounts of the bountiful orchards, fields, and waters of the Lower Counties on Delaware. Penn took a personal interest in the earnest young law student, grew to enjoy his company, and became concerned for his well-being. "He behavd with a great Deal of Goodness and Kindness towards me," Dickinson told his mother, "and a Young Gentleman that lives with him, tells Me, he often asks him, if he has seen Me & how I do."[36] In young Dickinson, Penn surely believed he had an acolyte.

Dickinson, in turn, admired the governor's magnanimity and his professed political principles. Although talk in the province depicted Penn as a tyrant-in-waiting, intent on stripping the Quakers of their hard-won political power, in truth, he told Dickinson, he was a friend of liberty. Far from looking to deprive the people of their rights, he protested, he was interested in establishing balanced government, where the different branches would check the power of the others.[37] All the political theory and history Dickinson had read disposed him to agree with Penn—at least in principle.

In reality, he knew the situation in Pennsylvania was messy and that neither side was blameless. For his part, Penn disliked the "levelling republican system of government so much adopted by the Quakers," and because he knew control of the government was out of reach, he attempted to control the funds of the province, whence he believed their power flowed.[38] Penn thought the Assembly misspent funds they raised from taxation for frivolous civic improvements. "I think," said he, "their hospitals, steeple, bell, unnecessary library with several other things, are reasons why they should not have the appropriations to themselves."[39] Of course, it was precisely these attributes that made Philadelphia the cultural center of British North America. Thus, although Dickinson tended to agree with Penn about the imbalance in the Pennsylvania government and fractiousness of the Quakers, he could not agree with the proprietor's aims to accrue power in his own hands to the detriment of the people. "I cannot conceive," he wrote his mother, "how he got the Dislike of the Philadelphians so much, for I never conversd in all my Life, with a more agreeable, affable Gentleman."[40] Although Dickinson remained his own man, in a few years' time, he came to understand both sides' complaints.

London's politics were even more fraught than Pennsylvania's. The big event of the spring was the general election of the House of Commons, which occurred between April 18 and May 20. "It is astonishing to think," Dickinson reported to his father, "what Impudence & Villainy are practizd on this Occasion." Voters were pressured to elect particular candidates or kept drunk until the election had passed, and officials could not swear the oath against bribery with a straight face. "I think the Character of ancient Rome will equally suit this Nation, 'Easy to be bought, if there was but Purchaser.'"[41] It put him in mind of a stanza from "The Kennel Raker," which remained a touchstone:

> The Statesman he sweeps in his Coffers the blunt,
> That shou'd pay the poor Soldiers that Honours does hunt,
> The Action tho' dirty, he cares not a Straw,
> So he get's but the ready, the Rabble may jaw.

"Bribery is so common," he reported to his father, "that it is thot there is not a Borough in England where it is not practicd." It would be nearly impossible to root it out. "It is ridiculous and absurd," he proclaimed, "to pretend to curb the Effects of Luxury & Corruption in one instance or in one spot without a general Reformation of Manners"—by which he meant *morals*—"Which everyone sees is absolutely necessary for the Wellfare of this Kingdom. Yet Heaven knows how it can be effected. It is grown a Vice here to be Virtuous," he observed. So blatant and widespread was the corruption in the 1754 election that the painter and satirist William Hogarth produced a series entitled *Humours of an Election*. In four paintings, Britons schemed, connived, bribed, and threatened one another on their way to the voting place.

England was in desperate need of election laws to curb the corruption. But, Dickinson knew, "Laws in themselves, certainly do not make Men happy." Rather, "they derive all their force & Worth from a vigorous & just Execution of them—and where there is any Obstruction to this, from Ignorance, Villainy or Cowardice—People are just in the same Condition as if they had no Laws."[42] He also knew that even enforcing good laws would be insufficient. There must be more, something within the individual. "We have a Maxim in the Law that 'The People is unhappy when the Laws are unsettled,'" he wrote, quoting Coke. "But I think with much more Truth it may be said, 'when Religion is unsettled.'" Such, he found, was the case in England at the moment. "People are grown too polite to have an old fashiond Religion, and are too weak to find out a new, from whence follows the most unbounded Licentiousness & utter Disregard of Virtue which is the unfailing Cause of the Destruction of all Empires for it is as impossible for Publick Dignity & Security to exist without private Virtue & Honesty."[43]

On May 1, with the start of Easter Term, Dickinson's routine altered. Rather than spending the day hunched over books, he left his room and headed to Westminster Hall to be there by nine o'clock. If he was late and the walk was brisk, at least he would be warm for a time before the chill set in. He stayed there until two or three o'clock in the afternoon, often shivering.

Now almost six months into his stay, Dickinson was finally enjoying the full experience of the Temple. On May 3, he signed a bond to the Temple, agreeing to perform the required duties of membership, such as attending services in the Temple Church, and settle the required expenses, such as paying the cook in the dining hall. To ensure the fulfillment of these requirements, students recruited co-signers on their bonds. Dickinson enlisted a few respectable men to vouch for him, laid down his £20, a significant sum, and agreed to pay all fees and abide by the rules of the Temple, which, among other things, included not practicing law while still at study. He was now a full-fledged member. And he likewise signed a bond for his friend William Hicks, a New Yorker.[44]

Dickinson now entered into Commons, that is, dining in term with the barristers and students in Middle Temple Hall. Always among them were the Benchers—as the senior members of the Inn were called—and frequently some of the judges and greatest lawyers. Sitting at the fire pit in this grand hall, with the crackle of flames in the air, sparks floating to the heavens, and the firelight dancing in his eyes, Dickinson wondered to find himself at the epicenter of legal learning in the British Empire and pondered what his future might hold. "I dayly behold Objects which call me to my Duty," he wrote to his father. "Here may I be fir'd with Ambition at the Honours which are paid to deceased Merit: Here I view the Glory to which Industry exalts itself. I tread the Walks frequented by the Ancient Sages of the law; perhaps I Study in the Chambers, where A Coke or Plowden has meditated. I am struck with Veneration, & when I read their Works, by these familiarising Reflections, I almost seem to converse with them."

Dining in Commons made him feel exalted. "When I view the Hall, where the most important Questions have been debated," he mused, "where a Hampden, and a Holt have opposed encroaching Power, and supported declining Justice, in short upon whose Judgments, the Happiness of a Nation has depended, I am filled with Awe & Reverence." His heart swelled and he longed to emulate them. "When I see Men advanced by their own Application, to the highest Honours of their Country—My breast beats for Fame! Such are the Rewards of Diligence," he knew. In his heart, he also knew "the same means are in my Power."[45] He wrote in his commonplace book, under the heading "Fame," a quote from Tacitus: "To despise Fame is to despise the Virtues by which it is acquir'd."[46] And yet, one must be careful what one wishes for.

Dickinson was aware of the vagaries of fame and already leery of them. "Fame is so much more preposterous in Our Days than in Virgil's," he observed to his father, "'when She stood on the Ground; & hid her Head in the Skies.'" The ancient Greeks called her the goddess *Pheme*. He knew of many famous men who did not deserve her. Rather, Dickinson had another rule to live by. "I will endeavor to behave so that no man shall be able to say any ill of Me, and that is the most stable Foundation that can be laid for a lasting <u>Credit</u>." He reassured his mother, "I value Reputation above every other human Possession."[47]

By this point, others were taking note of Dickinson's eagerness and nascent talents. Under-Treasurer Hopkins saw the potential in the earnest young American and thought it would be a pity if he remained only a solicitor, doing legal work in an office, when he could well obtain the degree of barrister and represent clients in court. In truth, unlike in Britain, American lawyers typically assumed both roles, but Dickinson's argumentative skills were such that he should be recognized as a barrister in England as well. Hopkins suggested that he be called to the bar two years early. With this offer, Dickinson knew he must prevail on his father to allow him to stay an extra year in London. This was his last opportunity to polish himself before his first public appearance in Philadelphia.

After long hours working, and with the days warming and lengthening, Dickinson indulged in an occasional evening out. On May 14, with a group of friends that included Peyton Randolph, a fellow Templar and the attorney general of Virginia, he visited Vauxhall Spring Gardens, which, since opening in 1729, was the most fashionable entertainment venue in the empire.

They entered around six o'clock along an elegant walk, with an orchestra to the right playing a piece by George Frideric Handel, and found themselves in the middle of a grove. A little beyond was the Chinese temple, under which were placed seats for companies of visitors. The whole garden was laid out in meandering walks bounded by a William Hogarth painting to one side or a statue of a nymph on the other and punctuated with more seating. When it grew dark, a thousand lamps hanging from the tree branches lit up the garden, so many in fact that it seemed as though a new day were rising. At various times, the garden was the site of masquerades and fireworks— and also illicit liaisons. Vauxhall possessed at least as much vice as Covent Garden, though perhaps more perfumed and respectably clad.

Inspired by what he had experienced at Vauxhall, two days after this pleasant evening, on a whim Dickinson purchased a violin and an instruction book, which may have been *The Art of Playing on the Violin Containing All the Rules Necessary to Attain to a Perfection on That Instrument* by Francesco Geminiani. That the violin was never heard from again suggests that the notes emitted by Dickinson's hand were less perfect than his new book promised.

Trinity Term began on June 14, and as Dickinson returned to court, the London streets were nearly deserted. The nobility and gentry had fled the city for their country estates, escaping the heat and stench of the season. "It is surprising to see what a dead dull place London now is," he wrote his father. "Most of the Houses shut up, so few Coaches rattling thro the Streets or People walking, it seems as if there was some publick Calamity."[48] He did not mind the post-apocalyptic scene. It gave him more space to think as he hurried to court, strolled about town, or rode out on horseback.

When he roused himself from his books to wander the urban streets and the country lanes, Dickinson likewise allowed his mind to wander, "making Excursions backwards and forwards," ranging in all directions in an attempt to comprehend world and self.[49] His reveries took him first inward. "I love to trace my Soul thro all her Turns & Flights," he wrote.[50] He did so with the aim of improving himself, of disciplining his emotions and rooting out misconceptions. "When she is under the Influence of some Passion," he told his father, "I am pleasd to beat her out of the false Lights & Losses." Though this inward journey was not exactly the quiet Quaker waiting that happened in meeting for worship, it bore a resemblance. He frequently began with "a Hint from the book of Psalms," and then advanced through a confusion of poets, historians, philosophers to the ancients, Galen, and Hippocrates, who said, "art is long, life is short." He agreed with Plato, writing his words in his commonplace book: "For the soul to know itself, must contemplate the Divine Soul of wisdom, of which ours is but the image."[51]

By taking himself to task, critiquing his thoughts and thought processes, and interrogating his motives, Dickinson held himself to account. His industriousness was satisfying, but when he was inclined to be lazy, the reproaches he gave himself were stern. In the end, he believed, "a young fellow is like a Lame Person, who ought to use all the Crutches & Aids he can get, to keep him from falling—And tho it is a glorious, yet it is a difficult Victory for Youth to persuade itself, that Application is preferable to Pleasure."[52] He was thinking not only of himself, but also his brother Phil, about whom he worried. Even as he envied Phil his "Strawberry Time" in life, he knew their parents' expectations were all that could keep "the Giddiness of Youth from Shipwreck."[53]

Dickinson frequently contemplated the social hierarchy and its effect on manners, attitudes, relationships, behavior, and even language. The upper sorts in London were not what he expected. Raised with tales of the grandeur and sophistication of the British aristocracy, he was, truth be told, disappointed. "The Nobility in general," he wrote his father after visiting the House of Lords, "are the most ordinary Men, I ever saw. And if there is any Judging by the Heaviness, & Foppery of their looks & behaviour, Many of them are more indebted to Fortune, than their Worth, for a Seat in that August Place."[54] He especially disliked those who refused to show due condescension to social inferiors. "I shall always scorn that Brutal, Mean, false Pride of some people, who because they are Independent, think no Oblidgingness, no Honour, due to any Person."[55]

With the city relatively empty, the few remaining inhabitants were those creatures of business, the Cits, who circled, vulture-like, around the 'Change and were thoroughly despised by the upper sorts. The name "Cit," John explained to his mother, "bears the same Signification here, as Clown does with Us, or rather worse, for it means an awkward imitator of Gentility." Although he didn't share the locals' contempt for these people, Dickinson understood what provoked it. With more money than manners, they didn't know how to comport themselves and were "perfect Whales in company, so clumsy & so unweildy! and all their Mammon cannot support their Spirits under the visible disparity." Trying too hard to ape those above them, their affected speech sparked linguistic fads that Dickinson found absurd. To praise something, for example, they would say, "It is *the* thing," making that little word the most important in the Queen's English.[56]

Otherwise, Dickinson found a "universal Elegance reigning thro all Ranks of People." Outside of the city, he was especially charmed with the humble English cottages, each one neatly appointed with a little yard and gravel walkway, adorned with flowers and vines. "To see these little Hovels so genteely set off," he exclaimed, "gives Me more pleasure than a View of the most magnificent Palace."[57]

English society, in turn, caused him to reflect on home. The rigid hierarchy and predetermined, inflexible divisions between ranks of people here contrasted with the relative egalitarianism in Pennsylvania, where people could move up in society. An American could, with ingenuity and the right patrons, remake himself and rise from laborer to gentleman. The printer, turned scientist, turned deputy postmaster general Benjamin Franklin had refashioned himself thus.

But if America, without a landed gentry and titles of nobility, couldn't reproduce the same social stratification as in England, it was not for lack of trying. It was paradoxical that the more equality there was in America, the more the upper sorts strove to make distinctions between themselves and their inferiors, usually by rigidity of manners and ostentation—elegant clothing, furniture, carriages, and, perhaps most importantly, tea equipage, which allowed them to perform their superiority in elaborate rituals calcu-lated to delineate the well bred from the rabble. Whereas Dickinson could observe the striving of the Cits with some detachment, those in his native land who sought to deny fundamental human equality and lord their power over others riled him. "Equality," he believed, "instructs Us in Humanity & Wisdom."[58]

Yet there were many men in America, especially in his chosen profes-sion, who refused this "instruction." The aspirant "<u>Nobility</u> of Kent" in the Lower Counties were his fellow lawyers. "I declare," he wrote to his mother, "I don't know Whether to Laugh or be angry—at the ridiculous Folly of men who make themselves Slaves for the Priviledge of setting four foot above other People—or rather of shewing to all the World what Asses & Scoundrels they are."[59]

Worse than the lawyers were the gentlemen slaveholders and their sons. Their particular kind of education was at the root of the problem. It was the opposite of equality. "What a Nest of Vices shall we find in the Education of a Gentleman's Son in America!" he exclaimed. "The little mortal can no sooner talk than he is exercising his Commands over the black Children about him; no sooner walks, but he is beating them for executing his Orders, too slowly or wrong." This "education" created exactly the wrong kind of person, unfit for polite company or leadership. It stoked their passions, inflaming vices such as pride, selfishness, peevishness, violence, revenge, and cruelty. "By governing Slaves from his Infancy, he becomes a Slave himself. From amongst them, he is out of his Element. He dreads the Sight of an Equal; He is Cowardly & Sheepish before Persons of any Fashion; barb'rous & tyrannical amongst Inferiors." It was lamentable that "this in a great Measure is the Case in the Colonies: By conversing constantly with Slaves, they acquire a mean groveling way of thinking with the utmost Pride & Conceit."[60]

Sentiments such as these—that slavery was at least as bad for the enslavers as it was for the enslaved—were not unusual, even among slaveholders, and were at least as old as Aristotle. For planters such as his father, and especially those to the west in Virginia and to the south in the Carolinas and Georgia with vast tracts of land, slavery was considered an evil, but a necessary one. Most knew the moral hazard it created for the master. Few except for the most serious Quaker considered the effects on the person enslaved.

At this stage of his life, Dickinson followed his parents' example, the Quaker way, believing that because those whom they enslaved were treated well, no one was at risk. For those gentlemen's sons who were in danger, he had a solution. He believed that a solid liberal arts education, of the kind he had received from his parents and tutors, would inculcate a sense of equality and prevent the hubris that led young men to be tyrants to their social inferiors and sycophants to their superiors. He pitied children denied such an education and wondered if their ignorance was their happiness. Surely when they grew up and realized their disadvantages, they would be miserable. Moreover, it was obvious that "Ignorance is not only the Mother of all Errors, but of all Vices."[61]

Dickinson was distinctly aware of his privilege and the advantages it bestowed on him. "I had the Happiness of a more Liberal Education, than most of my Countrymen," he acknowledged. But like weeds in a flower bed, "yet I find a good many Mistakes, which I am dayly pulling up, and which I hope in time to have quite eradicated." For Quakers, perfection was attainable, though, without vigilance, it could be more easily lost than won. Ultimately, he concluded that "the Hearty & the Wealthy are, in a great measure, ignorant of the Blessings they enjoy, because they are unacquainted with the Miseries, which they avoid, & which the Sick & Poor are subject to."[62]

As he compared the Old World with the New, as enchanting and diverting as England was, Dickinson gained a sense of identity he had never quite possessed before and with it an appreciation for America. "There is something surprizing in it," he thought, "but nothing is more true, than that no place is Comparable to our Native Country." He was overwhelmed with a sense of patriotism and mused, "It is some strange Affection Nature has implanted in Us—for her wise Ends."[63] Traveling abroad had taught him like nothing else could that he was an American.[64]

Although he, along with other Americans, referred to England as "home," he confessed he didn't "seem to have any Connections with this Country; I think myself only a Traveller, & this the Inn: But when I think of America," he effused, "that Word produces a thousand pleasing Images; There Life is a Stream pure & unruffled—here an Ocean briny & tempestuous. There We enjoy Life, here We spend it."[65] He didn't think he would be happy until he returned to his true home. This new perspective on America would enable him to serve his countrymen much better than had he always remained among them.

Reflecting on his privilege and acutely aware he could not have come this far alone, Dickinson was deeply grateful for the "Divine Hand" guiding his life. His "Honour'd Parents" were the best gift. "As they have contributed so much to my Happiness, may I be enabled to make some Retribution to them."[66] It was a prayer he uttered often.

That summer of 1754, as Dickinson made short jaunts outside London, he found inspirations to reinforce his sense of humility and gratitude. In St. Michael's Church, a quiet country chapel twenty miles north in St. Albans, Hertfordshire, he was surprised to find the tomb of Sir Francis Bacon. The experience was deeply moving. It was not the statue of Bacon that elicited his awe and grief. Rather, it was his chosen final resting place. "To see the greatest Man that ever livd, whose Mind was reckoned a Counterpart to Nature, Whose Merit raised him to the highest Dignities of his Country, . . . laid in a little Parish Church, in a private Place, & amongst Ploughmen & Labourers, had Something in it inconceivably affecting."[67] The scene caused him again to ponder his own life's purpose, which brought to mind one of his favorite passages from Pope's *Essay on Man*:

> So Man, who here seems principal alone,
> Perhaps acts second to some sphere unknown,
> Touches some wheel, or verges to some goal;
> 'Tis but a part we see, and not a whole.[68]

This Quakerly idea that the individual might create change in the world captured Dickinson's imagination. "While Each pursues his particular Scheme," he marveled, "he unknowing and undesignedly serves as a Wheel to effect the general Good." Unlike Pope, however, Dickinson was not afraid of the change that an individual could make. Rather, he saw it as leading to "future Happiness" for humanity. He himself was filled with a sense of his duty to the greater good and his reasons for studying the law. To his mother he wrote, "There cannot be upon Earth, a nobler Employment than the Defense of Innocence, the Support of Justice, & the Preservation of Peace and Harmony amongst men."[69] He had high aspirations, but uncertainty moderated his expectations, and if he could not "shine amongst the Orators of Philadelphia," he told himself, "I may be a very useful Member of Community in Kent, by prosecuting small Debts."[70]

But though he was drawn to the "Noble Retirement of Kent," his choice was to "engage the busy Scenes in another Place," at least for a time. With youthful sanguinity and a touch of prophesy, he then imagined himself a farmer. After he had distinguished himself, he thought, "I am sure I shall turn Husbandman, & till the Bed, which in a short time will receive Me." There was a certain honor and dignity in farming the land and being connected to the soil. His Roman authors and his Quaker relatives had taught him that. Whatever his fate, he knew that with virtue on his side, he could chart his own course. "He that never climbs can never tumble," he wrote his father. On the other hand, it was also true that "He that never climbs can never rise."[71]

In the autumn, the nobility and gentry returned to London from their country homes. With them returned the noise, hurry, dirt, and confusion so that by the end of November, Dickinson anticipated, "London will be a perfect, or rather imperfect Chaos."[72] Many of them were no doubt eager to view the grand spectacle of the city, taking place on the ninth, which was to be Lord Mayor's Day, on which the lord mayor of London would be presented and sworn in at the Royal Courts of Justice.

The morning of the festivity, Dickinson received an invitation from the Barclays to come to their house and watch the parade. It seemed all of London had gathered for the pageantry. Throngs crowded the streets and ladies and gentlemen gathered on balconies and at windows to watch the spectacle. He was pleased to find Thomas Penn and his wife, who engaged him in conversation the entire afternoon. Penn asked him if he had ever been to the royal court. When Dickinson replied that he had not, Penn invited him to join him in attending the king's birthday party the following day. Dickinson eagerly accepted, though he was worried he would be underdressed in his suit of broadcloth, while others wore silk and velvet. Penn told him not to worry.

On November 10, the two men drove to St. James's Palace, George II's primary residence. The festivities began at one o'clock with the firing of the guns in the park and the tower. "Birthdays are always excessively fine," exclaimed Dickinson, "but this exceeds any that has been these many Years." Through avenues lined with guards and spectators, they entered into a large anteroom filled with noblemen and gentlemen. The ladies in resplendent finery, reminding Dickinson of the streamers from the Lord Mayor's Show, passed through to a separate room on the right, and to the left was the king's drawing room, where he received visitors. Dickinson and Penn stood for a half hour, the air thickening with the scent of sweat and ambergris, the musky gentleman's perfume extracted from the intestines of sperm whales, which never quite lost the scent of decay and digestion. The door to the king's drawing room was finally thrown open and the company ushered in. "I found Myself in the Presence of the Greatest & Best King upon Earth."

"Nobody spoke a word to the King unless addressed by him," Dickinson wrote his mother. "He stood with a Gold laced Hat under his Arm, with all the Modesty of a Woman, & every now & then he said a few words to somebody about him—which I could not hear—but by the Manner, I am sure were nothing but common Enquiries & Answers." The king's awkward demeanor made Dickinson uncomfortable. "Between his Speaking he constantly cast his Eyes on the Ground—in short," said he, "this seemd so painful a Tax upon his Majesty that I pitied him."

As Dickinson observed the courtly etiquette with avid interest, the great moment of the event occurred—the singing of what he described as a "wretched Birthday Ode," though it was "exquisitely performed by a Band of Instrumental & Vocal Musick."[73] Each year for the past twenty-two years, the poet laureate Colley Cibber had written an ode for the king's birthday. Cibber's efforts had few admirers. Dickinson now understood as never before Pope's mockery of him in The Dunciad, where the anti-Catholic Cibber is portrayed as the "Antichrist of wit."[74]

By three o'clock, Dickinson was thoroughly tired of the grandeur and feeling peaked with an empty stomach, there having been no refreshments served at the celebration. Penn had a prior engagement and departed with an invitation for Dickinson to visit him at his country seat at Maidenhead, located thirty miles east of London. Dickinson then walked back into the city and "satisfied in a little Chophouse—the Hunger which I had procurd in a Palace."[75]

Dining alone, Dickinson's mind raced with all he had experienced and, as he sorted through his emotions, he waxed philosophical. He did not welcome the ambition fired in him by moving in the highest circles of British aristocracy. He thought about the difficulty in rising to a higher station and the villainy such striving would encourage in some. "But what," he asked himself, "are the mighty blessings to be attained by the most happy ambition? What Rewards for all its Toils & Cares? What Recompense for all the Peace & Ease forfeited by its Pursuit?" Perhaps the aim would be to stand next to the king, to become a member of the exclusive Most Noble Order of the Garter and wear a blue sash.[76]

Dickinson preferred his own station in life. "To a Reasonable Man," he decided, "a good Broadcloth Coat should be much more valuable than a bit of

Ribbond." But he knew that most people did not share this view. "We see dayly & constantly Men sacrificing Virtue, Ease, and Reason to Vice, Disquiet, & Folly—to gain those things to which Mankind have falsely annexd, confused Ideas of what is really desirable." After they had spent their lives running after the perceived prize, they found it not worth the "vain & presumptuous Chace." He did not want to be driven by that kind of ambition.[77]

On November 13, Dickinson marked his twenty-second birthday, thankful that he was in his modest chambers with no wretched odes sung on his behalf. "For really," he proclaimed, "another Birthday woud make Me a Philosopher."

With his first year in London behind him, Dickinson felt satisfied with the work he had accomplished and the knowledge he had acquired. He was fortunate to be surrounded by dear friends. He lacked only his family, whom he missed very much, to make his happiness complete. His parents did not write as frequently as he wished, and sometimes many months passed with no word. Occasionally feeling sorry for himself, jealousy welled up in him towards little brother Phil, and he suspected that his mother was "so employd with her other Son, that She had no time to bestow on him that was absent."[78] Usually, however, he thought fondly of Phil, worrying about him incessantly. He knew from experience the difficulty of boys in devoting themselves to their studies. His Uncle Cadwalader had taken the "pretious fellow" in, which Dickinson hoped would do him good.[79] But the new year brought good news from home. Samuel Dickinson approved his son's request to remain in England to achieve the rank of barrister. His father's magnanimity made Dickinson feel like "a bankrupt in gratitude."[80]

After an entire winter of reading and taking notes, Dickinson exclaimed, "I find myself to be in the most profitable way of study I was ever in." He planned to present his notebooks to his father,[81] having copied speeches by some of the greatest men in Westminster Hall so his father could have "some idea of that Species of <u>Humour</u> which is usd there."[82] He also sent his parents Chancery books, that is, those pertaining to the Court of Equity, whose purpose it was to correct mistakes and ensure justice is done. His father had described how his mother had set herself the task of studying them. It charmed Dickinson more than he could say to think of his "Honourd Mother's designing to add to the Students of this Profession." He knew she was up to the task; he didn't even need to translate his Latin quotations for her. He wanted nothing more than to join them. "I wish I could possibly study with You," he said wistfully, imagining the three of them sitting together by a cheerful fire with their law books. "It woud be the most engaging Employment."[83]

In her way, Mary Dickinson was as much a role model for her son as his father the judge. They had an unusual relationship for the age. Not only did she read law with him, but they also debated one another like a couple of lawyers. When, for example, John worried about Mary taking on too many familial duties, he argued his case for her to hire a maid, saying, "at least my Honourd Mother will permit a Lawyer to altercate a little." He then proceeded, as though in a courtroom, making his points and answering his mother's objections. "If I am wrong," he concluded, "permit my Motive to plead my Excuse; for I cannot be indifferent to any thing that concerns your ease & Happiness."[84] If Mary did not relent, at least she would be entertained by John's loving argumentation.

As a consequence of Dickinson's intensive labors, before the end of Hilary Term, the old pain in his chest, with which he had been troubled during his apprenticeship in Philadelphia, returned. As time passed, he grew worse and developed a fever. Finally, Hanbury insisted that he seek out the best physicians in London for their opinion. They might have suspected what future physicians would recognize as pericarditis, an inflammation of the membrane containing the heart. Such a condition, which can recur for years, would be exacerbated by prolonged periods bent over books. The doctors prescribed the correct course of action when they ordered him to cease all study immediately, move to the country, and begin exercising.

Accordingly, Dickinson and Goldsborough secured lodgings a quarter mile outside of Kingston, a village ten miles to the southeast of London, across the Thames from Hampton Court Palace. He felt relief immediately. And it was not merely physical. "I am always most pleasd when in the Country," he confided to his mother, "because it bears some greater Resemblance to my Dear Home than this dirty, noisy City—the Din & Confusion of which banishes thought & Peace—& takes Me almost from Myself." Although spring was nearly upon them and Kingston had its distractions, he informed his parents that "We . . . are resolved to remember We are **Americans**—to live soberly & prosecute our Business."[85] Dickinson's nascent patriotism was becoming a badge of honor and distinction.

Dickinson may have been speaking more on his own behalf than on Goldsborough's, who had met a young lady and immediately fallen in love. Sarah Yerbury, called Sally, was beautiful and, at twenty years old, heiress to a small fortune since the death of her cloth-merchant father. Although the two had known each other only a short while, they were already inseparable and their courtship serious. Shortly before Goldsborough and Dickinson were settled in Kingston, the romance had heated to the point that Sally insisted they should be married. Goldsborough had wanted his father's permission and consulted Dickinson for his opinion on marrying without it. "It was not what I should chuse to do," his friend advised. "Parents had a right to be consulted—if not implicitly obeyd in that important Affair of Life." But, as the senior Goldsborough's proxy in London, Mr. Hanbury saw no need to wait. He consented to the match and agreed to write Goldsborough's father in favor of it. With the matter settled, Dickinson held his peace.[86]

After a hasty marriage, Sally moved in with Robert and John at Kingston. They were a congenial trio, though Dickinson tried to keep himself busy and out of their way. With the Thames not forty feet from their door, he went fishing every day and hired horses for daily rides. Dickinson's presence thus interfered little with wedded bliss, and Sally was soon expecting. He imagined that his mother would now worry that her son was on the verge of eloping with any number of women. But her worries were misplaced. "I am very glad I think so much like my Honourd Parents with respect to Marriage," he reassured her. "I never shall think I am at Liberty to dispose of myself, without their Consent who gave Me Being— And if I should ever be so mad as to do it, tho you shoud forgive Me, I shoud never forgive Myself."[87]

There were, in fact, rumors about Dickinson's intentions with several young ladies, but that is all they were. His mother's uneasiness, he insisted, was unwarranted. Though there were women he admired, "I solemnly declare I don't know a Woman upon Earth, for whom I have had a single thought as a Wife—but am as free from any Engagement of Affection that way, as the instant I was born."[88] Indeed, he worried that he might become some silly quixotic figure, chasing an imaginary princess. "I am very much afraid," he confessed to his mother, "I shall grow one of those foolish fellows—who have annexd so many fine Qualities to the Ladies that shall enslave them, that they never find any possest of one half & Loiter away life in expecting a Dulcinea that exists no Where but in their own Imagination."[89] Dickinson would also compare any future wife to his "Honourd Mother," with whom he could read law and have friendly arguments. How likely was he to find such a woman?

Because of Dickinson's condition, Easter Term came and went and Trinity began without his engaging in any serious work. "Nothing can equal the Uneasiness I feel from the Necessity of being idle," he lamented to his father.

"It is such an Interruption to a glorious Course of Study, I cannot bear to think on it."[90] He worried about not living up to his potential and dishonoring himself and his parents. "Life without Honour is the only Death I dread— To leave this world is the Lot of Human Nature, fixd by the Decree of our Creator, but to continue here ignobly, is the voluntary Choice of a mean Mind."

By the end of summer, he had resumed his reading. He could now walk four or five miles and ride twelve or fifteen without the least fatigue. With thanks to his "All-Gracious Maker and Preserver," he realized that "The Complaint in my Breast with the fever, have both entirely left Me." Writing to his father, he announced, "I am sure by the End of the Fall, to be as strong as ever I was."[91] Indeed, at the end of October, he felt it was time to return to the Temple and prepare for Michaelmas Term, which would begin shortly. So he packed his belongings, hired a coach, and left his happy abode with the young Goldsboroughs. Besides, Sally's lying-in time was nearly arrived, and studying with a baby in the house would likely be difficult.

The first day of term was Thursday, November 6, and he attended court faithfully, except in bad weather. To prevent a return of the pain in his chest, the doctors advised that he obtain a standing desk. He purchased one that, though appearing unusual, worked perfectly. The desk was a box with sloping sides that sat on a spindle through the center (Fig. 7). It could be raised or lowered by spinning it right or left. Books could be propped on the sides, or the sides could be opened and lowered for use as a writing surface. When he positioned the desk at the upper part of his breast, he stood perfectly erect while prosecuting his work. This posture "agrees with Me extremely well," he explained, "and tho it was a little troublesome at first, Yet I can now stand two Hours together without any Trouble." Joking to his mother, he wrote that he now may be called "a Peripatetick Lawyer." But he really did believe that nature intended people to be active and that the upper sorts did not exercise enough.[92]

He thus continued to exercise as well. Although he couldn't do as much as he had done in the country, he found other opportunities. He took up fencing, a common sport since it was decriminalized. An Italian fencing master by the name of Domenico Angelo had recently come to London and begun instructing young noblemen and gentlemen. He described fencing not in terms of war but as a means to gain health, graceful movements, and poise.[93] It suited Dickinson well. He might have compared the parries, thrusts, and dodges to future duels in court with opposing counsel. He had no intention of ever fighting an actual duel.

Another pastime was playing battledore and shuttlecock. A battledore was a small racquet, and a shuttlecock was a piece of cork trimmed with pigeon feathers. Played by two or more people, indoors or out, the object of the game was to keep the shuttlecock aloft as long as possible by hitting it upwards with the battledore.[94] Though some ridiculed it as a pastime for children and ladies, gentlemen commonly played as well. Dickinson played with his friends in the Middle Temple garden or St. James's Park, darting and lunging, his long limbs giving him a decided advantage.

Although Dickinson's life in London, with the rigor of study and the novelty of new pastimes, could make America seem very distant at times, in the new year, 1756, troubles in the colonies reverberated in London. When Dickinson had first arrived, there was news of ominous activities on the Pennsylvania frontier. For decades, the British and French had contested ownership of North American lands that had long been inhabited by Native peoples. At stake were not just settlement, the bounty it offered for trade, and navigation of the Mississippi River to transport the trade goods. It was also a contest for souls. Catholic France and Protestant Britain each eyed an opportunity to fulfill what they believed to be God's will to populate the land with believers. The French saw Protestants as heretics, and the British believed Catholics were in thrall to the pope, who was the Antichrist.

Tensions between the empires had increased since the French began encroaching on British settlements in the Ohio Country. When hostilities became open in 1754, the Pennsylvania Assembly and Thomas Penn were still at odds over expenditures in the province. Now their feud reignited. Frontier settlers petitioned the government, demanding it raise a militia to protect them. This, of course, would require funds. But Penn refused to allow the Assembly to raise taxes or to print paper money. The Assembly insisted that it should control the finances of the province, ignoring the reality that the executive branch controlled the purse strings in the British system.[95] On the other hand, the Assembly asserted, justifiably, that it had the right to tax the proprietor's lands equal with other inhabitants. Penn refused to submit. The impasse between the two branches left the people of Pennsylvania in the middle, unprotected from frontier violence. Some speculated, with good reason, that the Assembly may not have actually wanted to defend the frontier at all and was stalling merely to maintain complete control of the colony.[96]

Meanwhile, an incendiary pamphlet appeared in Philadelphia in April 1755 called *A Brief State of the Province of Pennsylvania*. Because criticizing the government was illegal, the pamphlet was published anonymously. But it was suspected that the author was one William Smith, an Anglican minister and inveterate enemy of the Quaker party. He vented his spleen in the pamphlet, levying insults at the Assembly that would undoubtedly leave him open to accusations of seditious libel if his authorship could be proved. He likewise went after the Quakers, whom he accused of concocting an unholy mixture of religion and politics to achieve their designs and dupe unsuspecting Germans into trusting them. Those poor people, he said, should beware "the arts of a Quaker preacher, more than of a lurking French priest." The shock waves the pamphlet caused in Pennsylvania did not subside for years. But Smith was not yet finished. In 1756, he published a screed called *A Brief View of the Conduct of Pennsylvania*, which suggested "ridding the Assembly of Quakers" by requiring an oath or "cutting their throats."

After news of British general Edward Braddock's defeat at the hands of the French and Native fighters in the Battle of the Monongahela, at Fort Duquesne, reached Philadelphia in the summer of 1755, the Assembly finally acted for the defense of the colony. Repeatedly, it passed bills to supply the militia by a land tax, and repeatedly the governor vetoed them. Among many protests, one prominent resident of Chester County, Justice of the Peace William Moore, submitted a petition signed by thirty-five inhabitants to the Assembly on November 5. It called Quakers to account for their lack of action "by Reason of their religious Scruples" and insisted that they no longer "neglect the Defense of the Province." The Assembly dismissed the petition summarily.

On November 24, two factors broke the impasse. First, Penn agreed to present a "gift" for the war effort in the sum of £5,000, which equaled roughly the amount of the taxes he would have owed. Second, a mob of several hundred angry German frontiersmen descended on Philadelphia with the intent of dispatching the assemblymen per Smith's suggestion. Accordingly, the Assembly passed a £60,000 supply bill. The next day, the Assembly did something unprecedented in Quaker Pennsylvania—it passed a militia law. Shortly thereafter, the members discovered that Penn's "gift" was actually nothing more than bad debts he had passed along to them for collection.[97]

Though the crisis of defense was averted for the moment, the political situation was volatile, with the Assembly enraged against the proprietor and angry petitions from both factions en route to the Board of Trade.[98] Now, as those petitions were to be heard on February 26, 1756, in the Cockpit at Whitehall Palace, Dickinson was ready with his notebook. He listened as the hearing began with a reading of a petition and then as it proceeded to arguments.

Counsel for the petitioners presented a portrait of Quakers so damning it could have come straight from the pen of Reverend Smith. The Quakers had grossly mismanaged the province, their "Zealous & bigoted"[99] pleas of conscience were just a ploy to remain in power, and their supply bills were nothing more than "Evasive, tricking, & Vain" machinations "for converting Proselytes to Quakerism." In conclusion, argued the plaintiffs, "they have brought the greatest Miseries on the Provinces, Miseries which must continue unless we have a Government with different Principles."[100]

Counsel for the Pennsylvania Assembly mounted a robust defense, attributing the flourishing of the colony to Quakers, who were "a People of the greatest Industry, Prudence, & Virtue." They spoke of the history of liberty of conscience in Pennsylvania and described the refusal of Penn to allow taxation of his lands. Warning of a civil war between factions should the Quakers be ejected, they maintained the Quakers were being scapegoated for problems having nothing to do with them.[101]

After listening to the entire argument, Dickinson returned to his chambers and set himself to the task of transcribing the hearing into longhand, filling in as many blanks in the account as he could remember. He then made a fair copy, which he sent to his Uncle Cadwalader. Ultimately, the Board did not grant Penn's request to remove the Quakers from power, and the dispute continued.

The need for action not just by Pennsylvania but by the British government was made plain in the next letters Dickinson received from home in March. The previous November, fifteen hundred French and Indians had burnt the town of Lancaster to the ground and were proceeding southward, terrorizing the inhabitants as they went. "I cannot imagine that Kent is in the least Danger," he assured his mother. "It is quite removed from the hostilities & defended by Nature from Incursions & the other Inner parts of the Province must be secure too, at least now, when something has been done by the Legislature." He reassured her with descriptions of the "Most vigorous Measures for Our Assistance & Protection" the government was taking.[102]

It was not until May 17, 1756, that the king finally issued his Declaration of War against France, beginning what became known as the Seven Years' War on the European continent and the French and Indian War in North America.

Dickinson witnessed the ceremony of the Declaration, which included sym-
bolically locking the Temple Bar, the gate to the City of Westminster, ostensibly against foreign invasion. But he did not feel as though a mere paper
declaration made much material difference; it was only acknowledging what
already existed. Nor did he approve of the policies adopted by Great Britain.
Most troublingly, there were now around eight thousand Hessians and four
thousand Hanoverians—German soldiers all—on the shores of Britain to
protect against foreign invasion. What were these mercenary troops themselves but a foreign invasion?

As Dickinson knew from reading history and political theory, to preserve
liberty, executive power should be held in check and the defense of the state
should be in the hands of the people. In ancient Rome, it was the brave and
patriotic citizen-soldier who defended his community. Only when the empire began to hire mercenary soldiers, foreign barbarians, who fought not
for country but for money, that the people's rights vanished and the empire
crumbled. Now Dickinson worried about Britain's fate. She had long been
in need of a revised militia bill to provide for her defense at home. One had
been in the works for some time and was finally up for consideration, but it
appeared to be doomed. On May 24, Dickinson sat in the House of Lords,
observing intently as the members debated and then rejected a bill, 59–23,
that the Commons had passed unanimously.

"This is a Piece of Policy," thought Dickinson, "that has disobligd the
Nation extremely, for instead of raising a Certain Natural & sufficient Power
by a Militia, a Whole People are to depend for Protection on the Precarious
External & Slender force of Foreign Troops." But that was the least of the
problems. "If they stay here," he continued in a letter to his mother, "it must
be very disagreeable to all men Who value their Liberties & Constitution, by
setting a Precedent, which in Cases of the Crown has ever been found an immutable Law, for the Increase of the Regal Powers: The Strides of which since
the Revolution of 1688 have been Gigantick."[103]

Every Briton, Dickinson believed, should be concerned about the power
of the executive encroaching on the rights and liberties of the people. "Can
one Single Reason be assigned why that important Trust of defense shoud
be committed to Slaves & Foreigners rather than to Freemen & Natives, but
that it pleases the King?" There could be no other reason except that "<u>it will
encrease his Power</u>. When Concessions are made to Princes, it is ridiculous
to think of Stopping" them. He warned, "There is no means in Nature for
altering his Course but Violence," which Dickinson and Quakers in general

abhorred. "I think a moderate Acquaintance with the English History, will teach one this Truth." It was also true, he observed, "that most of our Civil Wars have been Claims & Complaints, . . . which had either been given up singly or winkd at in Parliament." Yet he was astonished to hear some of the arguments used against the bill coming from the mouths of Englishmen. "Such is the Complacency these great Men have for the smiles of their Prince that they will gratify every desire of Ambition & Power, at the Expense of Truth, Reason & their Country."[104]

When the spring issues of the *Pennsylvania Gazette* began to arrive, he read them with dismay. Deputy Governor Robert Hunter Morris had declared war on the Indians—the first time the province had ever declared any war— and placed a bounty upon Indian scalps. This was certainly not what William Penn had in mind when he had reached out to Native peoples as friends and partners in his young colony. Quakers within the doors of the State House and without wrung their hands.

Then, on June 4, a number of Quakers made a dramatic motion of protest against the war. Six members of the Society of Friends resigned their seats in the Assembly rather than violate their consciences by waging war against the Indians.[105] It had become clear to many Friends that they could not be both good Quakers and good politicians. To preserve their consciences, they abdicated their seats and let others take over the responsibilities of protecting the colony. Shortly after the October election, four more Quakers followed suit. It was nothing short of a reformation of Pennsylvania Quakerism.[106]

But though this development changed the Assembly in some ways, depriving it of the strictest Quaker element, opponents of Quakerism lamented that it was not changed enough. Many Quakers remained, as did their allies who had been "Quakerized" by the culture of the province. Most notably, Isaac Norris Jr., a Friend in good standing, remained as speaker. Other influential men who had adopted some Quaker beliefs and behaviors, such as Benjamin Franklin, remained. But their partial Quakerism was more dangerous than the real thing. They pursued some aspects of the Quaker agenda—resistance to the proprietors and accruing power to the Assembly— without the check of Quaker principles to restrain them. They were not pacifists and cared not about peaceful processes. They were thus inclined to use any means to achieve their ends. In this instance, to maintain their power, members of the Quaker Party pled pacifism and refused to raise a militia to defend the frontier. But neither would they allow Thomas Penn to intervene, as they believed it would diminish their control of the province.

"I am extremely sorry to find such violent Animosities & heats as appear
in the Pennsylvania Papers," lamented Dickinson to his mother. "It is really melancholy to think of returning to one's Country groaning under the
double Miseries of War & Discord—Fire & Slaughter raging round, & Parties
& Dissensions weakening & distracting Us within. How soon do men lose
sight of Public Good, when under the Influence of Private Passion? or—"
he reflected on his conversations with Thomas Penn, "which Side shall an
honest Man espouse where both are in the wrong, as constantly is the Case
when such Passion is raisd?"[107]

Contemplating the partisanship in the Assembly reminded Dickinson of
his meetings with another Pennsylvanian recently arrived in London. Tench
Francis was a fellow Middle Templar and, until the previous year, the attorney general of Pennsylvania. Francis and Dickinson occasionally dined
at the home of their mutual friend Anthony Bacon, a London merchant
with whom Francis lodged. Francis was in the thrall of the Assembly, thoroughly identified with the Quaker interest, and no friend of the governor's
party. Dickinson suspected that the Quakers had sent him over to make their
case against raising a militia to the public, for there were several items in
the papers that seemed to be offspring of Francis's pen. His own good sense,
supported by his Uncle Cadwalader's advice, dictated that he hold his tongue
and utter not one word about Pennsylvania.

Dickinson could say that there were few people he disliked, but Francis
was one of them. Pretentious and affected, he was an example of what
Dickinson aspired not to be. When Francis spoke warmly about settling the
Ohio Country, Dickinson suspected that he had some scheme for profit.
Francis dropped hints half carelessly, half self-importantly, about Secretary
of War Henry Fox being interested in speaking to him about the territory.
But, he said, he declined the honor when it became clear he would be subject
to interrogation and not allowed "to harangue at Liberty."

When Francis extolled London as "the best Place in the World to teach a
Man the Knowledge of himself, & the Folly of Pride & Haughtiness," however, Dickinson agreed, though he thought this sounded something like a
confession. Francis seemed to him a man who had read too much but knew
too little. "His Notions are extremely confusd," Dickinson observed, and "he
has such an important way of hesitating and travelling round a thing, that
if he spoke less, he would speak better, but if he spoke better he would not
appear so wise to common People as he does." Francis stood in stark contrast to those jurists Dickinson admired. "He has, read the Roman History,"

he noted, "but does not understand anything of the Civil Law nor of their customs."

"I think, young man," declared Francis, "you will find that I have a valuable knowledge of the classic works."

Dickinson fought to keep his eyes studiously upon Francis instead of rolling them heavenward. "I have read Tacitus this Winter past," he replied, enjoying Francis's expression of surprise.

"Is that so! Why," he spluttered, "there are but three or four men in Philadelphia who can read it." Looking sidelong at Dickinson, Francis said artfully, "Ah, but surely you haven't read Sallust."

"Indeed, I am a great Admirer."

"I have just bought a volume! I will fetch it," at which Francis went up to his room and brought it down. The conversation then turned to Caesar's famous speech for the conspirators. But they soon differed in their paraphrase, and an argument ensued on the Roman laws, on which Dickinson exclaimed proudly to his mother that her son *omne tulit punctum*—"carried every point." He did not mind those who were ignorant but intensely disliked those who pretended to knowledge they did not possess.

It was not merely that Dickinson bested the braggart on his chosen ground that pleased him but that he did so as a gentleman should, affording his opponent a decent retreat. It was an entirely civil exchange. When Dickinson bade them farewell and the door closed behind him, Francis exclaimed to Bacon, "That young man is the most polite Scholar of his Years I have met with!"[108]

To ensure that he would never become like Francis, Dickinson immersed himself in learning the law and devising new study methods. He found that when he set down a single point of law, he was at a loss as to how to form an opinion about it. There were so many distinctions and exceptions, all dependent upon one another, and all scattered in different places, that it was difficult to see the very fine connections between them. He struggled until he hit on an idea. "I have endeavoured," he explained to his mother, "to throw the Law relating to each head together, & to marshall them in such a Manner, that Some Maxim or General Principle shall seem, as it were, the Trunk of the Tree, the Larger Divisions the Branches, & all the little Niceties & Minutenesses the Twigs & Leaves."[109]

Dickinson was not only an avid student; he was a natural teacher. He never enjoyed knowledge so much as when he could convey it to others. He described to his friends in some detail how his tree of knowledge would save labor and "keeps Our Learning like a Sword always bright & ready to be drawn." At last, he wrote, "I am convincd by Experience that a Person must be led into Endless Mistakes, Unless he has the Substance of his Knowledge arranged in a Regular Manner." He also described his practices to his mother, which he realized was unusual. "Perhaps if this Letter shoud fall into the hands of some People," he speculated, "they might think it a little odd to talk so much to You about the method of Studying Law." But John and Mary did not have a usual relationship. "They would excuse it," he elaborated, "if they knew the Tenderness with which You regard every thing that concerns Me, & how little Pleasure I take in any thing unless sweetened by a Consciousness of Your Knowledge & Approbation of it."[110]

During his final summer in London, Dickinson drove himself, relentlessly reading the Chancery reports. Saving these reports for last was also part of his method. He had endeavored to become acquainted enough with every branch of law so that when he practiced at home, he would be traveling along a familiar path. Chancery was the final touch. To his mind, the laws of England were like bones and muscle, but without the flesh. "The most fond Admirer of our Common Law must allow," he wrote his father, "that there are some Cases in which the Severity of its Rules, requires some little softening." The Chancery is what made English law beautiful.

Because Dickinson believed so strongly in the maxim of the Chancery that "equality is equity," it called to mind a problem in the court system in which he would soon be practicing. Although there was a Chancery Court in the Three Lower Counties, there was none in Pennsylvania. Thus, one might say, there was no need for him to study Chancery law to practice in Pennsylvania. "It woud be much properer to say," he thought, "every court there is a Court of Equity, for both Judges & Juries think it hard to deny a Man that Relief which he can obtain no where else." Considering every court as a court of equity was a noble aim, but with terrible consequences. The judges and juries ignored the problem "that Equity never intermeddles, but where Law denies all manner of Assistance." Because of this, "Every Judgment, Every Verdict is a confusd Mixture of private Passions & Popular Errors; & Every Court assumes the Power of Legislation." The result in Pennsylvania was insufficient separation of powers between the branches of government, which invariably corrupted justice.

"The Inconvenience of this extensive & arbitrary Authority is severely felt already," he wrote his father, "& will hardly decrease till the Source is stopd." But he resolved to resist the corruption in the system by resorting to his training and his virtue. "I shall continue my Application to my studies that

I may be able, when a wrongful Judgment is given against Me to produce Coke, Plowden, Ventris, Salkeld, etc. and show *victrix causa illis placuit, sed victa peritis*—'The victorious cause pleased them, but the vanquished cause pleased those who had perished.'" He resolved to meet wrongs with erudition and to stand for right against power, regardless of personal cost or outcome. "That tho they gave Judgment for the plaintiff, Yet all the Learned were of Opinion with the Defendant." Even a loss on the side of justice was a victory, and young John Dickinson would be a willing martyr.[111]

With his ideals clear, his resolve hardened, and having fulfilled his requirements at the Middle Temple, Dickinson received his call to the bar on February 8, making him a full-fledged English barrister. He relinquished his chambers the next day and soon sailed home to make his mark on the British American colonies.[112]

3

"Defending the Innocent & redressing the Injurd"

Practicing Law in Philadelphia, 1757–1759

Dickinson returned to America in the spring of 1757 a different man. Now twenty-four years old, he was worldly, he was robust, and he was a barrister. His homecoming was a joyous occasion. He traveled alone as far as Dover, and then his father sent the chaise to convey him to Poplar Hall. Meanwhile, his mother made her wishes known to the "family" of enslaved people. Amidst the other preparations for his return, she ordered, "Let the coloured children be dressed clean and come to see their young master."[1]

When the chaise approached the house, "we came like a flock of blackbirds," recalled Violet Brown, one of the enslaved children who was about six years old at the time. She and the other little ones crowded around Dickinson, all atwitter. They were eager not only to see him but also for the cakes promised them by their mistress. He looked down fondly upon them, pleased to see the "little bodies"—his special term of endearment—he had missed and who had grown so in his absence. The most venerable of the Dickinsons' enslaved people, Old Pompey, kissed Dickinson's hand, glad of the safe return of Massa Johney, the boy he had known since infancy.[2] Though his sentiments may have been genuine, what real choice did he have?

Dickinson remained at Poplar Hall for a few months, recovering from the voyage and reacquainting himself with his Kent County home and his dear family and friends. The quiet expanses of fields ready for planting, the fragrant fruit trees in bloom, and the soft lapping of the waters at their landing must have seemed a salve to his senses after so long in London's smoke, din, and grime. And now he was finally able to realize his fondest wish over the past three years—that of joining his beloved parents at their hearth and pouring out every detail of a journey that he could only inadequately express with his pen.

But in this time of war, the serenity at Poplar Hall belied the sense of anxiety pervading the province. The governor declared a day of fasting and humiliation in July to please the Divine Power, and clergymen lamented the "gloomy" situation since General Braddock's defeat, preaching about the "servility and servitude, popery and French tyranny" that threatened British liberty.[3] Although Dickinson didn't hold with such religious bigotry, news of battles and the prevailing martial sentiment stirred conflicting sentiments. On the one hand, he was keen to serve. "I wish I was amongst my Gallant Countrymen with a Musket on my Shoulder," he had written his mother the previous year. But his predominant desire was for peace. "I wish too, that the Operations of their Campaign may never be more dangerous than the Chusing their Officers."[4]

After a few restorative months at home, business called, and Dickinson returned to Philadelphia. Since his departure almost four years earlier, much had changed. The city had been greatly improved by the installation of pavement for carriages and pedestrians. The safety of the public was also ensured by streetlights and a nightly watch.[5] On the southwest corner of Front and High Streets, the London Coffee House had opened in 1754. William Bradford, a printer, was the proprietor.[6] It had become a favorite haunt of merchants and politicians, a place to conduct business, hear the latest news from around the empire, and debate provincial politics. Although it was a locale for the well-to-do, raucous auctions were also occasionally held there for goods, livestock, and land.

The Pennsylvania Hospital, which had only been in a temporary location on High Street when Dickinson had departed, was now housed in a splendid new building at Eighth and Pine Streets and had admitted its first patient in late 1755.[7] That same year, the College and Academy of Philadelphia opened, under a charter granted to Reverend William Smith, the inveterate enemy of the Quaker Assembly. The past spring, it had graduated its first class of seven men. Phil Dickinson had even enrolled and was to be a member of the third class in 1759, after which time he would clerk in his brother's law office.[8]

The Library Company, too, was flourishing. It had been established when the members of a discussion group called the Junto determined they needed to consult books during their deliberations. Because few men of the middling sort owned many books, they had decided to pool their resources to estab-lish a subscription library. For eleven years, the secretary had been one of its founders, Benjamin Franklin, who had recently sailed for London to serve as an agent for the province. He left the records in such disarray that it took his successors a great deal of work to bring order to them, and some gaps would never be filled. Still, the institution was growing and was now also a museum with some rare items, such as Roman coins and "Eskimo" parkas. Its entire collection was located in the State House, easily accessible to most Philadelphians.[9]

The most significant changes during Dickinson's absence, however, had occurred within the Society of Friends. The departure of eleven Quakers from the Assembly in 1756 was only part of a sweeping reformation taking place in the Society. Many Friends had come to believe that their success as merchants had led them into worldliness, luxury, and excess, making them forget their testimonies of simplicity and frugality and their duty to serve the less fortunate. Scandalously, some young Friends were heard using the formal "you" rather than the plain "thee" and "thou." During meeting for worship, certain vain members would rush outside to cover their saddles when it rained. And recently, some meeting house benches had been covered with soft cushions. Many feared that this attention to worldly concerns could only lead to spiritual destruction.

Another concern had arisen as well. In 1754, Friend John Woolman had published a tract entitled *Some Considerations on the Keeping of Negroes.* Woolman had witnessed Benjamin Lay's virulent protests against slavery in the 1730s and Lay's subsequent disownment by the Society and knew he had to approach matters differently. He bided his time, waiting for the weightiest slave owners to die before he brought his message forth. Where Lay had been accusatory and provocative, Woolman was gentle and sympathetic. Where Lay had sought to explode the institution of slavery, Woolman used persua-sion. It worked. Where Lay had been ejected from the Society, Woolman was heard and heeded. Friends believed that Divine Providence was speaking through this human oracle and that they must heed his new revelation. That September, Philadelphia Yearly Meeting published *An Epistle of Caution and Advice, Concerning the Buying and Keeping of Slaves* to help their members "to guard, as much as possible, against, being in any Respect, concerned in promoting the Bondage of such unhappy People." These were the small beginnings of something much larger—or so Friends hoped.

With £500 from his father to establish himself, Dickinson re-entered the Philadelphia legal world amidst this period of prosperity and turmoil.[10] No longer a green law clerk, he was now a full-fledged English barrister. He alone among men of his generation in this city had walked the halls trod by the likes of Edward Coke, attended court at Westminster, sat in the Cockpit, and been challenged by the learned Benchers in Middle Temple Hall. As he rejoined the other Philadelphia attorneys, his proud mentor and family welcomed him.

Others were not so well disposed, including one Joseph Galloway, the youngest lawyer in Pennsylvania history to argue cases before the Supreme Court. He was sharp and ambitious, but he lacked Dickinson's facility with language, both in writing and in oratory. He also felt keenly his lack of London training, for which he compensated with a haughty air. By all rights, Dickinson and Galloway should have been friends. Born only months apart, both hailed from Quaker families and had devoted themselves to the law. Having already established his legal career and begun serving in the Pennsylvania Assembly, Galloway might have shown Dickinson the ropes. Instead, Dickinson's advantages needled Galloway, who looked on him as a threat.

As Dickinson built up his practice, he made the acquaintance of other young gentlemen. One was Thomas McKean, also a lawyer, from New Castle County, who had been educated in the Latin academy founded in 1743 by Presbyterian minister Francis Alison, a former tutor in the Dickinson household. With characteristic openness, Dickinson took the initiative to write him a friendly letter of introduction. "As I flatter myself that We are to look upon Ourselves as friends to each other throughout Life," he began familiarly, "I hope You will not expect any declarations of my Esteem, but will be convinced by all my actions & the unaffected freedom of my Behaviour towards You, that it is very great." Believing it was important to signal where he stood on the political issues roiling Philadelphia, Dickinson said of the separate Assembly in New Castle that he hoped it would "treat the Governor with more respect than ours, & shew the world You have at least more good-manners if not more Christianity than We peaceable people."[11] His sarcasm at the expense of the Quakers was not lost on McKean.

Young, bright, and energetic, Dickinson, McKean, George Read, and another former Alison student, Irish-born Charles Thomson, soon formed a congenial quartet. Eager to make their marks on the world, each cared deeply about the welfare of his province and sought to bring his moral sense to bear upon it. Though Dickinson was the only one of the four to be raised Quaker rather than Presbyterian, and the only one not to have attended Alison's Latin School, the bonds they formed were lasting.

Initially, much of Dickinson's practice involved ordinary matters—property disputes, debt collection, and interpretation of wills. He embraced it all with alacrity, determined to apply his legal knowledge to helping the "Innocent & Injurd." As routine as these cases appeared, the problems and questions they raised in the colonies were at the heart of the British—and American—conception of rights. Under the British constitution, property ownership was one of the most fundamental rights. As John Locke stated this truism of British jurisprudence in his *Second Treatise*, "being all equal and independent, no one ought to harm another in his life, health, liberty, or possessions." Dickinson took this maxim to heart.

Yet matters were more complicated in America than in Britain. British immigrants had attempted to transplant their intricate systems of courts and laws into colonial governments. But these systems rarely took root easily, and the law adapted to the American environment. Of course, neither was the law static in England. "Circumstances of things have changed in England," Dickinson observed, "& the Law has changd with them."[12] An example he liked to cite was the unenlightened law preventing non-Christians from testifying in court. The law changed in 1744 with the opinion in *Barker v. Omychund*, which held, "It is a very narrow Notion, that no one but a Christian can be an honest Man; God has imprinted in the Minds of all Men true Notions of *Justice* and *Injustice*, *Virtue* and *Vice*."[13]

Similarly, Dickinson believed, the law must be adaptable to American circumstances. For example, the rules of evidence could not be set in stone. Common law could be very strict and reject certain kinds of evidence. For Dickinson, this represented "the strongest Reason why those Rules should not be severely observd" in the colonies. They were merely "**artificial Rules**," as he put it, "which are to be departed from to observe the Eternal & immutable Rule of Justice." Several circumstances unique to America should be considered, among them that when the rules originated, the colonies didn't exist. Similarly, the distance between the colonies and home was a factor, as were the "Infancy of the Country," the "Ignorance" of its inhabitants, and the "Irregularity" of proceedings. Moreover, "Records cant be expected here as perfect as in Westminster Hall," as he put it. Indeed, there was no equivalent to it in America. Therefore, he concluded, "Whatever Liberties have been allowed at home should be much more allowable here." How far this new maxim could extend, no one yet knew.[14]

Dickinson navigated this legal wilderness guided by his training, legal maxims and principles, his local knowledge of the people of Pennsylvania, and his sense of justice and humanity. Much of his work consisted in helping people settle their final affairs. Here he found "Greater Latitude . . . to be allowed in construing wills . . . than in England."[15] Most did not write wills, or they wrote them *inops concilii*—that is, without legal counsel. The problem is that "Country Men," he observed sympathetically, "are not Masters of Language."[16] Indeed, they were not versed in legal terms, "tho acquainted with those Points of Right & wrong." Also, wills were frequently written *in extremis*, or at the point of death, when the testator could not have been in full possession of his faculties.[17] Dickinson thus saw that "Things of one Nature will pass by Words meaning Things of another Nature."[18] Time and again, he saw the difficulties that occurred. "Many Estates are lost contrary to the Testator's Intent" by misinterpretation of the will.[19]

In aiding his clients, Dickinson held that interpreting wills meant finding their intent, which was the "Pole Starr" that guided them. That meant that the document could not be taken at face value. Rather, it must be treated as one piece of evidence to be examined and deciphered. When the testator did not know the legal meaning of the words he or she used, Dickinson conducted a forensic analysis. He frequently found that the testator's intention could "be spelt out by little Hints" throughout the document. "The Intent is not to be guest at," he warned. As his lawbooks made clear, "it must be drawn from the Words of the Will itself & must be agreeable to the Rules of Law—The Pole Starr."[20] More than this, even, the "Interests of the Testator are sacred."[21]

Disputes over wills often brought the parties to court. When that occurred, the educator in Dickinson emerged as he sought to teach his clients and the juries about the law. "Appeal to all the Jurymen," he noted to himself. "Do they know those points of Law? How can they suppose it known to a Farmer in this young Country in 1706?" He would invite the jury to consider what the testator actually meant. "Explain it to the Jury," he instructed himself. "What is a Fee simple? What is a Fee Tail?"[22] If he did his job well, he would make the jury see the pole star as clearly as he himself did.

One case in particular revealed how Dickinson sought intent. The children of William Paxton sought to recover land they believed had been held illegally by Henricus Van Dyke. In 1718, Paxton, struggling to provide for his young family, borrowed a small sum of money and mortgaged his farm as collateral. He died the next year, not having repaid the loan. Ten years later, his widow and the children moved to another county for better opportunities. Meanwhile, the mortgage transferred to Van Dyke, and now, thirty years later, Van Dyke continued in possession of the land, reaping profits from it well over the amount of the original loan. The children hoped Dickinson could help them reclaim their land in the Chancery Court in New Castle.

Opposing him would be his mentor, John Moland, and the attorney general of Pennsylvania, Benjamin Chew. Dickinson felt inexperienced and overmatched but took the case anyway, believing that "this Case is so clear that We evidently have the first Principles of Equity, Reason, Honesty, & Truth on our side." The unfortunate should be protected from exploitation in times of hardship. This concern was, in fact, a first principle of Quakerism, enunciated in 1676 by the Quaker theologian Robert Barclay, who had declared that the purpose of the law and civil government is "the Care of the Poor, of Widows and Orphans." Dickinson took this to heart and agreed with Barclay that "love and compassion are the great and the chiefest marks of Christianity."[23] This principle became a key element of his argument.

To remedy parties such as the Paxton children was precisely the purpose of the Chancery Court in New Castle. In his argument, Dickinson reminded the court that the Chancery is premised upon "The Laws of Humanity & Equity." Its three "grand Objects" were to prevent "**Frauds, Accidents,** and **Forfeitures**." To achieve this it needed to soften the "Rigour of the Common Law" so that its rule could be "Equality is Equity." In other words, no party should have an unfair advantage over the other.

Because his clients risked losing their property, he also explained the nature of forfeitures, which had "No Equity in them, no quid pro quo" and should be decided so that no party suffered, particularly the most vulnerable. The Chancery should "become the Parent of Orphans & the husband of Widows." It should protect the weak against the strong and, further, remove "the rough hand of Violence too often supported by Law and affords a healing Plaister to those poor wretches who have been torn by the thorns & Briars of the Law."[24]

He directed the court to the pole star—both parties' intent at the beginning of the affair—"notwithstanding all the endeavours of certain Gentlemen," meaning opposing counsel, "to muddy it—& give it an ugly complexion."[25] Their client now claimed that he purchased the land and that it had been in his possession so long and he had made so many improvements that he should keep it. Dickinson conceded that "much time had passed" since the original loan, but insisted that it was not "too late," as opposing counsel argued. At the time of the loan, argued Dickinson, "we were Infants & Feme Coverts"—a woman with no legal standing—and could thus take no action. He explained that there can be no purchase if the other party had no knowledge of it. "**Purchase without notice** is not good in Law or Equity."[26]

The circumstances of this case were straightforward: someone borrowed money and offered his land as security. "Is it not plain," Dickinson asked, "that on Repayment the Land shoud return to the first Owner?" As an illustration, he invoked Aesop's fable about the hound bitch and her companion. A pregnant dog asked her friend for the use of his kennel while she gave birth. He lent her his kennel, but after she whelped, she refused to leave. When the pups were grown, they were too big to evict. This case was the same, a simple equation. "We repay him the money; he has taken profits for many Years; We get our Land again . . . Who can be discontented" with such a judgment, he queried, "but the greedy Person who desires to swallow all & not leave a Morsel of their Parents' Inheritance to his poor Children?"[27]

Dickinson concluded by appealing to the judges' consciences, prodding them with Scripture. "I dont doubt but You will fulfill the words of good Job, 'That You will pluck the spoil out of the spoiler's mouth, & cause the Widow's heart to sing for Joy.'" Imploring the judges not to deny the plaintiffs their inheritance, he reminded them that "Poverty is an infirm old man that walks slowly— Wealth is lusty & often throws him down." He urged the judges to do the right thing.[28]

When the verdict came down several months later, Dickinson had prevailed over his former master and the attorney general, and his clients regained their land.[29] This victory proved that he could hold his own with the best legal minds in the city.

Apart from these routine cases, the war with the French and Indians shaped Dickinson's early practice in many ways. Even the small cases concerned the basic liberties of the people. A Quaker widow in New Castle County, for instance, feeling her religious liberty violated, hired him to recover her cow, confiscated by the government as compensation for her son's refusal to serve in the militia.[30] Such an injustice, however, attracted little notice from those besides Quakers.

Other cases riled thousands. Dickinson had been honing his skills on small cases for only a matter of months when he found himself at the center of a major political controversy, one involving defense of the frontier. The Pennsylvania Assembly, still dominated by Quakers and their supporters, turned on its critics, focusing its ire on the Anglican minister William Smith, who had published two scathing pamphlets against the Quakers, *A Brief State of the Province of Pennsylvania* in 1755 and *A Brief View of the Conduct of Pennsylvania* in 1756. Another target was Smith's ally William Moore, a Chester County judge on the Court of Common Pleas and a justice of the peace. In November 1755, Moore had sent a petition to the Assembly asking its members to cease neglecting the defense of the province because of their religious scruples, which the Assembly dismissed. In the 1756 election season, Moore and Smith had campaigned vigorously, though unsuccessfully, to defeat the Quakers.

In retaliation, the Assembly attempted to remove Moore from the bench. It published a blistering attack against him, accusing him of "divers Misdemeanors, fraudulent and extortionate Practices" and claiming that he "wickedly and corruptly, thro' an avaricious Disposition" did design "to oppress and distress the poor inhabitants."[31] Outraged in turn, Moore responded with an *Address* but had trouble getting it published.[32] When he approached David Hall, publisher of the *Pennsylvania Gazette* and official printer of the House of Assembly, Hall declined. He did not want to be accused of seditious libel by the Assembly. Moore demanded he print it out of fairness and on the principle of liberty of the press. Hall thus sought and received approval from two attorneys who were also members of the Assembly, Joseph Galloway and William Masters, as well as the venerable Quaker Isaac Norris, longtime speaker of the House. Moore's *Address* appeared in the brief window between the adjournment of the 1757 Assembly and the convening of the 1758 Assembly. Like Smith's pamphlets, it was an inflammatory piece, though in proportion to the Assembly's attacks on him.

As talk of the *Address* circulated, the German population of Pennsylvania was dismayed that no translation of it had appeared in the German-language newspaper. Smith took action. As a trustee for the Society for Promoting Religious Knowledge and the English Language among the German Emigrants in Pennsylvania, his responsibility was to ensure that the German papers covered the same news as those in English. He therefore arranged to have Moore's *Address* translated and published in *Die Philadelphische Zeitung*.

When the Assembly reconvened for its second term in early 1758, Moore and Smith were promptly arrested for libel on January 13, marched through the streets like criminals, and held without bail in the common jail. Since stopping Smith was the Assembly's main object, the members of the Assembly ignored Moore and scheduled a trial only for Smith. Accordingly, Smith requested Benjamin Chew as his attorney, but since Chew was the attorney general of the province, that request was denied. Smith then settled on John Ross, another senior Philadelphia attorney, along with his twenty-six-year-old colleague, John Dickinson. Smith would need a good team. So far, proper legal procedure had not been followed as Smith was denied bail, private meetings with counsel, and any official charge against him.

Unbeknownst to his lawyers, just before Smith's trial began, the Assembly had passed several resolutions that its members knew would be central to Smith's defense. They specified that to publish a libel on the Assembly's proceedings violated the members' rights, that Moore's *Address* was "a false, scandalous, virulent and seditious libel," and that the Assembly had jurisdiction over the matter and could examine complaints into the behavior of public officials, such as Moore, who "promoted and encouraged wicked Men in oppressing and distressing the Community."[33]

Meanwhile, Ross and Dickinson, unaware of the Assembly's resolves, planned three main arguments in Smith's defense. First, despite claiming the same rights, privileges, and powers as the House of Commons in England, the Assembly did not possess them. The Crown had proscribed certain powers from the Assembly, which did not have the right or power to erect itself into a court of justice. This was a matter for the common-law courts, and by holding Smith, the Assembly was denying him his liberty for an offense that was bailable in common law. In so doing, the Assembly not only deprived Smith of the sacred right of an Englishman to be tried by a jury of his peers, but it also put him at risk for double jeopardy; that is, he might be tried again in the regular court and punished twice for the same crime.

Second, Smith's lawyers planned to argue that the *Address* was no libel. Because it was written and published as self-defense, the law was clear: nothing contained in any proceeding in a regular course of justice would make the complaint amount to a libel, even if the matter should be false and scandalous.

Third, Ross and Dickinson would argue, Smith had no hand in writing or publishing the *Address*. It was Moore's alone. Moreover, he did not know it was a libel, since two lawyers, who were also members of the Assembly, had said it was not, and the item had already been published in two Pennsylvania papers.

As Dickinson hurriedly prepared for trial, he understood that this was the first meaningful test of his abilities as a lawyer. While a mere law clerk, he had longed to begin the *militia forensis*—the battle of court debate—but, if he were honest with himself, his courage had always been a little false, "like a Young Soldier's in his first Regimentals." He suspected he would tremble at the first sign of battle. He comforted himself, however, that "a little Cowardice has been the fault of the greatest Orators."[34] He was about to discover the stuff of which he was made.

When the proceedings opened on Tuesday, January 17, a large audience packed the gallery. All eyes watched the prisoner being brought in by the sergeant-at-arms. Then they turned to Thomas Leech, an Anglican merchant, who was serving as acting speaker in the place of Isaac Norris. Leech frequently filled in when Norris was indisposed, which often coincided with politically uncomfortable moments. Norris's indisposition did not, however, prohibit him from attending.

Leech ordered the clerk to read Moore's *Address*. He then turned to the prisoner. "Mr. Smith," he began, "this house has thought proper to make the following Resolves in your case & orders them to be read, that You & your Counsel may not Meddle with those points which they have already determind."[35]

Dickinson and Ross glanced at each other, unsure of Leech's meaning.

"Resolved!" cried the clerk. "First: That Mr. Smith or his Counsel shall not be allowd to speak or argue against the Authority or Power of this House to take Cognizance of the Charge against him. Second: That Mr. Smith or his Counsel shall not be allowd to speak or argue that the Addressed William Moor Esq. is not a Libel."[36]

Dickinson, Ross, and Smith sat stunned at this development. They had felt confident that they could get the charges against Smith dismissed, and these resolves had yanked their strategy from beneath them. Ross collected himself and rose to address the House.

He had, he said, "the greatest Reverence for Parliaments, & for the Constitution of this Government." Still, he added, the Assembly had taken away "the very points we intended to have insisted on." He then briefly enumerated the arguments he had planned to make. "But," he demurred, "as this Honorable House has been pleasd to make these Resolves, We are debarrd from speaking to any but the last." Smith looked on, dismayed, as

Ross continued at length, falling over himself to appease the Assembly and crossing the line from due deference to obsequiousness.

Seething at Ross's acquiescence to the House's restrictions, Smith rose and interrupted his own counsel. "Mr. Speaker!" he interjected. "I beg that I may be indulgd with a few words on this occasion as My Counsel has given up points that I never consented to." Before an objection could be made, he continued, "This House has been pleasd to make some Resolves in my Case, which have entirely deprivd Me of my Defence: It is impossible Mr. Speaker, for Me to consider these Resolves as Laws." He then requested that the House offer evidence to him and the audience that their conduct was in keeping with parliamentary precedent.[37]

Old Norris, unable to restrain himself, then interrupted: "I take it May it please the speaker, that this house has a Right to Prescribe the Modes of their own Trials; this every Court does." He asserted that the authority of the House shall not be disputed.

Although Dickinson had many objections to such an assertion, he remained quiet, deferring to his senior colleague.

Joseph Galloway then interjected with exactly the false comparison that Dickinson had anticipated. "It woud be easy," he proclaimed, "to shew Numberless Instances & Precedents upon Precedents where the House of Commons have proceeded in this Manner against Criminals." Indeed, Dickinson thought, but the Pennsylvania Assembly was not the House of Commons.

By now, Mr. Smith and his counsel were unsure of their next move. Smith turned from Ross towards Dickinson. "Is it possible," he asked Dickinson, "to bring the Points determind in the Resolves into the Consideration of the House again?" The mood of the House being clear, Dickinson sensed how dangerous the ground was on which they were treading. "It is impossible to attempt it," he replied, "without enraging the Members."[38]

Smith persisted with his request. Seeing that Ross would not act in the interest of their client, Dickinson assumed the role of lead attorney and turned to address the Assembly.

"Mr. Speaker," he said to Leech, but with an eye towards Norris and Galloway, "I appear before this Honourable House, as counsel to assist Mr. Smith in making his defense." He explained the dilemma he now faced. "We designd to have proceeded Sir, in the manner that has been mentiond by Mr. Ross; but as the House has disapprovd of that Order, We have been so much disconcerted, as scarcely to know what Method to pursue." He was caught between conflicting imperatives. On the one hand, he did not want to offend the honor of the House. But, from his earliest moments at the Middle Temple, he had vowed to himself that he would always do right by his clients. "On the other hand, Sir, I shoud think myself greatly blameable, if I shoud fail in my Duty to Mr. Smith by omitting any thing that may be urgd in his favour when perhaps his Reliance upon Me has prevented his engaging the Assistance of others in his Cause."[39]

Though Dickinson was torn between clashing duties, in some ways the matter was fairly simple. Although the Assembly was duly and legitimately elected, it was grossly overstepping its authority, violating the jurisdiction of the courts, and trampling on Smith's rights as an Englishman granted in the Magna Carta. Dickinson therefore knew what he must do. He was compelled by his conscience and his entire education to resist this arbitrary power and assert the rights of his client. The challenge was to do so without also incurring the wrath of the most powerful body in the province. He would have to proceed carefully, demonstrating deference at every turn, while also speaking the truth of the law to the power of the Assembly.

"I woud beg Leave to observe with great Respect, is that the Members of this House now sit as Judges in their own Cause; And tho I am perfectly satisfied how well their Integrity will guard against every Insinuation of Prejudice, Yet permit Me with submission to say; It will be more difficult to guard against the Reflections of the World."[40]

Dickinson hoped that if he appealed to the honor of the House of Assembly, their sense of justice, and their desire to preserve their reputation, they would take his meaning. In truth, the Assembly already had a reputation for being the most contentious in the colonies and one that served its own ends rather than those of its constituents. Its whole pursuit of this case against Smith was mystifying. Did the members not understand the law? Or was it that they understood it and, in their quest to quash a critic, simply didn't care? The matter went much beyond liberty of the press. It involved the freedom to meet with friends in private, to have free discussions, and freedom of thought. It was about due process and all that entailed—the right to self-defense, to bail and habeas corpus, to a trial by a jury of peers before a disinterested court. It was about separation of powers. The Assembly was usurping the power of the courts and threatening the rights of all Pennsylvanians.

"This is the Cause of every man in the Province," asserted Dickinson.[41] "This interesting Point is now to be determind," he added. "**Whether this House can try a man according to the Forms of the Courts of Law, &**

imprison him for an Offence that is cognizable in those Courts . . . & is bailable there; that is, can they restrain A Man of his Liberty, when by the **known** laws of his Country, & in the **usual** way of Proceeding he would enjoy it?"[42] He added that it was "a favourite maxim of Britain's Policy to settle her Rights by public & positive laws: So that no man coud be deprivd of his Reputation, his Liberty or his Life, but by Rules as clear & indubitable the acknowledgd Values & Beauty of those Blessings." This transparency in British law was due in no small part to early Quakers who demanded to see the laws they were accused of breaking and, in so doing, secured for dissenters religious toleration. "How far," Dickinson asked, "can this Proceeding be said to be governd by the 'Law of the Land'? . . . The Power of this Honourable House is undoubtedly extensive. But," he drew a line, "it cannot be unlimited. For an **unlimited** Power was never heard of under an English Constitution."[43]

Anger built visibly among the members as this newly minted barrister, standing tall before them, presumed to school them in the fundamentals of British law. But Dickinson was determined to say what he must. "For, Sir," he cautioned, "a small Acquaintance with History will convince Us, that Acts of power not very alarming in themselves, have afterwards provd Precedents for dangerous Demands & dreadful Determinations."[44]

Here Norris, Galloway, and several other members rose up one after another and asked the members of the Assembly to remember their resolves. Smith's counsel, they charged, had actually been speaking on those very points on which they determined the defense should not speak. The members were exposing themselves to ridicule by making resolutions they had not firmness enough to adhere to, and their lenity had extended too far already. It was unbecoming to their dignity.

After much deliberation, the House determined that Dickinson should not say anything more on the two first points but that the witnesses should be called and examined.

For the remainder of this day and the next, the witnesses paraded in and out: first Dr. Thomas Bond, at whose house Smith had allegedly edited the *Address*, and next his brother, Dr. Phineas Bond, who was also present. Then followed the printer William Bradford, who had also printed the *Address* and was thought to have the original manuscript; Robert Levers, the copyist for the printer; and then the two Germans, translator Friedrich Handschuh and printer Anton Armbrüster. The last was thrown in jail when he refused to answer questions. Not only did all of these witnesses seem "more Criminal" than Smith—who played the smallest part in the affair—but Dickinson noticed that the clerk of the Assembly did not always record their testimony faithfully.[45]

On Wednesday, January 18, the final and most significant witness was the printer David Hall, who had obtained permission in the first place from members of the Assembly to print Moore's *Address*. Dickinson asked, "Did you acquaint any body with the Contents & ask them if it might be safe in printing it?"

Hall replied, "I delivered the Contents as well as I coud & askd if I might print it."

"Who did You shew it to?"

Hall paused, uncertain how to continue. He began slowly, "I can't so well answer that question unless I enter into some Circumstances previous to it." The House allowed Hall to describe at length how Phineas Bond pressed him to print the *Address* and how he had sought approval from Norris, Galloway, and Masters. "I went to some Gentlemen of the Assembly," explained Hall, "& told them of the nature of the paper as well as I could from once reading it over—they told me if it was signd, I might print it—that the Liberty of the press might be open, which they desird." On this advice, Hall published the paper.

When the Assembly's lawyers began cross-examination, even their questions seemed to support Smith's claim to innocence: "Whether You would have printed this paper if these Gentlemen had not given you consent?"

"No," replied Hall.[46]

This next exchange in particular would remain in Dickinson's mind for years.

"May it please the Speaker," said Galloway, "the question may be askd Mr. Hall: whether did You directly or indirectly explain to those Gentlemen any one Paragraph or Assertion in that Address otherwise than by informing them, that it was a virulent & harsh Paper containing Gross Reflections against the late Assembly."

As Galloway spoke, Dickinson rose from his seat to object to the question. Yet only when Galloway finished did Dickinson move to speak. "Mr. Speaker—" he started. But before he could go further, Galloway cut him short.

"**Pray**, Mr. Speaker," he sneered, "let some Notice be taken of that **Young man**: Was ever such Audaciousness seen? I shoud be glad to know Whether he is to stop my mouth or I his. I claim the Protection of the house from his Insolence, or I must go off & quit my Seat. The **Young man** forgets the Difference between Us: though We may be something upon a footing in the Courts of Law," Galloway continued, "yet here I am his **Superior**, I am his **Judge**, & I pray Mr. Speaker, that he may be taught a proper Respect for the Dignity of the Members of this house. <u>Never</u> in my Days did I <u>ever</u> see such a **stork** brout into any publick place. I desire Mr. Speaker, that this **Young man** may be obligd to hold his Peace, & that the Witness may answer my Question."

As Dickinson burned with indignation, Speaker Leech, blustering with manufactured outrage, cried to him, "What no Decency, no Decency Young man; Do learn how to behave Yourself, or We must take some other Method!" He turned to Hall. "Mr. Hall, Answer the question that has been askd you."

Hall looked on, flumoxed by the startling scene unfolding before him. He could scarcely remember the question. After the clerk repeated it, Hall proclaimed, "I did not."

Leech turned to Dickinson. "Now, Young Gentleman, You have the Leave of the house to say what You want."

After expressing his gratitude for the opportunity, Dickinson began a response in defense of his honor. "The first part of the Charge indeed, 'that of being a **Young man**,' gives Me very little Uneasiness," he said, "tho something was certainly meant extremely reproachful by the frequent Repetition of those words, & the manner of pronouncing them." In fact, Dickinson was not even a year younger than Galloway. After noting that he did not think the Determinor of Providence should be blamed for bringing him into existence later than others, Dickinson added, "Every Moment Carries away part of <u>my Guilt</u> on its wings." In parting, he said, "I can only wish that while I advance in years, I may not partake the bitter Potion of <u>those</u> Who continue **ignorant**"—his eyes flicked meaningfully towards Galloway—[47]"with Opportunities of Instruction and **obstinately** persist in Errors, because they once **foolishly** adopted them."

Moving on before Galloway could muster an objection, Dickinson concluded his defense. For the moment, at least, he would ignore Galloway's mocking his appearance by calling him a "stork." But he would not forget it. He then proceeded to school the House on the fundamentals of examining witnesses. "The Member," he said, meaning Galloway, "was dictating a Question to the Clerk, to have it proposd to Mr. Hall. That question did not allude to certain facts, & desire the Witness to tell what they were." Rather,

Galloway told the story and merely asked Hall to affirm or deny it, which he explained, was a "leading question"—something forbidden in British courts of law.[48]

Galloway bristled at this and again attacked Dickinson for insubordiantion. But the House, without passing any censure on Dickinson, resumed questioning Hall. When the House adjourned for the day, Dickinson retired to prepare for the next.

In the morning, the House reconvened, summoned Smith's counsel, and ordered the sergeant-at-arms to bring Armbrüster before them. Chastened by his night in jail, Armbrüster begged pardon of the House for his misbehavior and proceeded to give direct answers to the questions. What became obvious was that all the other witnesses had been much more involved in the writing and printing of this so-called libel than Smith had been.

With the task of defending Smith complicated by the strictures laid on them by the House, Dickinson and Ross knew they could not be ready the next day to argue effectively for him. On Thursday afternoon, they requested a deferment of the trial until Saturday so they could "consider and sum up" the evidence. Their request granted, they withdrew to continue their work.[49]

But come Friday, Ross gave up entirely and turned the defense over to Dickinson, allowing him only a half day to prepare. He worked frantically all the night, sorting through the Assembly's many spurious claims and marshaling evidence to disprove them. By morning, Dickinson felt exhausted, unprepared, and ill; his old complaints from excessive work were recurring.

When Speaker Leech brought the House to order at 9:00 a.m. on the twenty-first and the trial resumed, Dickinson mustered himself to address the House. "Nursd in the arms of Liberty for the greatest part of my time spent in this Province, here I learnt the lessons of Freedom—that every man is entitled to the Laws—that no man should be looked on as guilty till he is condemned.

"This is a Cause of utmost importance as Præogative of the Crown, Authority of this house, & Liberty of Subject are concernd . . . because it is drawing into this Jurisdiction, an Offence that hitherto has been punished in the Courts of King at Common Law: The Authority of this House is concernd, because your determination will settle your Jurisdiction in causes of this nature & the Subject is interested because he is deprivd of his Liberty in an extraordinary manner."[50]

Dickinson felt acutely his deficiencies—his inexperience, unpreparedness, and poor health. And after the attacks he had endured from the members previously, he thought he might briefly explain his predicament. He began humbly, but the mood of the House was far from indulgent. "We <u>dont</u> want <u>none</u> of your Reasons nor your Excuses!" Speaker Leech shouted. "Go on with the Prisoner's defense!"

Dickinson had intended to speak to the fundamental injustice of the House sitting in judgment of an alleged crime committed against it. He wanted to warn members that Pennsylvanians would always have a stronger impression of the *authority* of the House than of its *justice*. But he thought better of it.

Instead, he continued, "Every man who is acquainted with Law books, knows that they are filld with Dictates, Whether particular facts amount to the Crimes of which the respective Persons are accusd." Had Smith been in a court of law, he would have been entitled to dispute two points: first, the fact itself, and second, the criminality of that fact. In deference to the House, he agreed to waive this right. He hoped, however, "that Humanity will incline the House to consider Arguments relating to the liberty of a Fellow-Subject."

He then described what they would have argued. First, the Assembly could not take notice of anything before it had convened. The House couldn't be offended because there was no House sitting at the time the pamphlet was published. Second, the Assembly had no jurisdiction over an offence punishable by law; that was for the courts. "That thus taking things out of the Common Course of Justice is an Infringement of the Magna Carta, that grand Confirmation of the Rights of Englishmen; A Suspension of the Habeas Corpus Act, the Bulwark of English Liberty; and an Introduction of the greatest Injustice, as a man might be punishd twice for the same Offence."[51] Finally, the Assembly could only punish contempt and breaches of privilege, which were not charged against Smith.

After enduring continuous interruptions and reprimands, Dickinson turned to reviewing the testimony of the witnesses. He noted what seemed to be a most fundamental point: that Smith's examination cannot be legal evidence, as it was not signed by him. Then he argued that every witness against Smith confessed to having been more involved in abetting and promoting the publishing of Moore's *Address* and therefore more criminal than the person accused. "What strange fate or unknown Wickedness it happens, that what is Criminal in him shoud prove blameless in others; and that the Nature of things shoud seem changd, when done by <u>him</u>, & when done by <u>those</u>

who give Evidence against him."[52] By "unknown Wickedness," Dickinson meant that Smith was suspected of being the author of *A Brief State* and *A Brief View*, which was the underlying cause of all the Assembly's resentment against him.

There was only one point of the testimony he wished to refute. Robert Levers, the transcriber, had said that he could not be sure of the handwriting on the manuscript but that it bore resemblance to Smith's. Should the House accept this testimony as evidence, it would be a dangerous thing. He reminded the House of the 1683 trial and execution of the Whig hero Algernon Sydney for allegedly fomenting the so-called Rye House Plot against James II. He was convicted of high treason on the basis of the similarity of handwriting—"a Judgment," Dickinson reminded them, "lookd upon with detestation by every Lawyer—& every honest man since."[53]

After a pause to let his argument settle among his listeners, he continued, explaining that Smith was a dutiful trustee for the Society for Promoting Religious Knowledge and the English Language among the German Emigrants in Pennsylvania. When Smith republished Moore's *Address*, it was simply at the request of German speakers, who complained they hadn't seen it. "As nothing is more disagreeable," explained Dickinson, "to those who pay for News-Papers than to hear of remarkable things in other Prints & not have them in such as they take." Smith gave only one encouragement to Friedrich Handschuh. "He told him it could not displease the Assembly to have the Address printed, when it had been publishd by Hall, their own Printer."[54]

Dickinson then embarked upon his third point, the evidence in Smith's favor. The defense had called only two witnesses, and only one of consequence—David Hall. Dickinson reminded the House that Hall had at first refused to print anything derogatory about the Assembly, as he was its official printer. "However," said Dickinson, "after much pressing, he thought fit to consult some of the Members. He applied himself to Mr. Isaac Norris the Speaker of the late Assembly, and of those present at the first Sessions, to Mr. William Masters and Mr. Joseph Galloway two other Members. With the Advice & Consent of these Gentlemen, Mr. Hall printed the Address."

Here Dickinson was interrupted by Norris and Galloway. "These are base, mean, scandalous, villainous Attempts to misrepresent the Evidence!" shouted Galloway. He accused Dickinson of attempting to smear the Assembly. "Whatever we have done," Galloway insisted, "was with a Design to preserve the Honour of the Assembly that we might not seem to restrain the

Liberty of the Press. If we errd, we humbly submit ourselves to the Censure of the House."[55] There was, however, nothing humble in Galloway's tone.

After being censured by the speaker, Dickinson proceeded, struggling to restrain his mounting frustration. "I was saying, Sir," Dickinson resumed, "that Mr. Hall's Apprehensions were removd by his Conversation with Mr. Norris, Mr. Masters & Mr. Galloway: & that with their **Advice & Consent** he publishd Mr. Moore's Address."[56]

Norris and Galloway again accused Dickinson of misrepresenting the evidence and spoke at length about the liberty of the press. Dickinson leapt at the opportunity to note agreement with his opponents. "I rejoice to find," he said, "the Members of this House, possest of such noble & just Sentiments of Liberty, Sentiments so becoming the honourable Station, to which their Country has calld them. We join in their Opinion!

"The Freedom of the Press is truly inestimable," he effused. "It is the Preserver of every other Freedom, & the Antidote to every kind of Slavery. By the Assistance of the Press, the Language of Liberty flies like Lightning thro the Land, and when the least attack is made upon her Rights, spreads the Alarm to all her Sons & raises and rouses a Whole people in her Cause." His conclusion was this: "Freedom of the Press is so opposite & dreadful to the Usurpers of unjust Power & the Enemies of Mankind, that **Liberty** however maimd & wounded **still** breathes & struggles, while that prevails."[57]

In closing, Dickinson challenged the Assembly to consider on what grounds Smith could possibly be denied these freedoms. All the witnesses in this trial are "more Criminal than Smith but my poor Client seems to be the Common Scape Goat to bear every bodys Offences."[58] Dickinson pointedly did not say what he really thought: "Liberty of the Press was only pretended" by the Assembly, "and by that have we been deceivd & entrapd into the situation We are now in."[59]

Norris and Galloway had been taking notes while Dickinson spoke, and now Norris interjected, again, that Dickinson had smeared the Assembly. He claimed that Dickinson had said "**that it was Mr. Smith's duty to print the Address.**" Norris expanded upon these words a long while to prove the indecency and disrespect with which Dickinson had treated the House with this argument, since they had resolved the *Address* to be a libel.[60]

Meanwhile, William Allen, chief justice of Pennsylvania, had grown increasingly agitated during the proceedings. When Norris finished speaking, Allen rose ponderously. "The Young Gentleman has usd the Words he was chargd with," he declared, but added that "there was nothing to blame in what had been mentiond." Allen expanded upon Dickinson's obvious respect for the House and the "great Earnestness" of his argumentation and chided the members for "sitting coolly to catch any unguarded Expression he should drop." In courts of justice, words could not be cherry-picked as evidence. After summarizing Dickinson's last point, he concluded, "I do not see anything in it liable to Censure."[61]

Dickinson was doubtless pleased to find an unexpected ally. But when he attempted to confirm his sense of respect for the House, Speaker Leech interrupted him, "We dont want none of your Apologies, for you only break our heads, & then give us Plaisters! Go on with the Prisoner's defence."[62]

In order to avoid bringing the wrath of the House down upon him again, Dickinson decided to read Hall's words from his examination, transcribed by the House's own clerk, highlighting again how Hall had secured the advice and consent of Norris and Galloway. But throwing their own witnesses back in their faces had a predictable effect. Norris once again denounced the brash young lawyer. Galloway railed against Dickinson and suggested that the sergeant-at-arms ought to be called to bring him to order. In some people's minds, there was little distinction between the guilt of the accused and the arguments of the lawyer on his behalf.[63]

"Mr. Dickinson sticks to this Point as though his Salvation & Redemption depend upon it!" bemoaned one assemblyman. Another leapt up and demanded he be stopped, warning the young lawyer that he would be guilty of treason if he continued. But Dickinson refused to be intimidated by such threats. Instead, he was determined to conduct himself as "an honest Man engagd in an honest Cause."[64]

Treading on dangerous ground, he then drew a comparison between the reign of the Roman ruler Tiberius, whom the historian Tacitus charged with implementing the "law of violated majesty," or treason, wherein "this Law was grown so extensive & uncertain, that while it was unknown to the People, what was within it, everything was construed by the Senate to be within it. Words became Capital Offences, and a cheerful Evening spent with one's friends, frequently producd an Order to dye in the Morning."[65] But Dickinson refrained from making any extensive comparison between them and very carefully confined his allusion to the point of evidence. Instead, he extolled the virtues of the government and constitution of Pennsylvania to warn of its demise. "If Crimes are to be sought for at our peaceful Firesides & social Tables, the next step must be to our Beds—and even Dreams will be criminal."[66] He was describing something for which his age did not yet have a word—a totalitarian state. God willing, it would never come to pass in a land of English liberties. "If the Sentence of this House shoud be unfavourable to Mr. Smith, he will be reducd to a more miserable situation than the most profligate & abandond Villain. For if this Assembly coud confine Mr. Smith for this fact which happend during the former Assembly, every following Assembly woud certainly have the same Right to commit him, that the present had."[67]

Here Dickinson was interrupted with excessive rage by several members objecting that he once again was disputing their authority. Dickinson was then allowed to go on. But each time he attempted to summarize a point, he was forced to stop as assemblymen broke in to censure him. Finally, he felt so fatigued and ill that he could no longer continue. He concluded perfunctorily. "Thanks for your Indulgence at this, my first Appearance before such honourable Judges," he said with a bow. "I hope that every moment of youthful indiscretion will add to my Knowledge so that the next time I have the honour to appear before you my performance will be much improved."[68] With this, Smith and his counsel withdrew to await the decision of the House.

When the Assembly resumed consideration of the Smith affair on Tuesday, January 24, only one part of Dickinson's argument seemed to have resonated with it. Agreeing with him that similitude of hands was insufficient evidence, they threw out Levers's testimony on that count. Then, after debating the evidence, the majority of the House found Smith "guilty of promoting & publishing the Libel."[69] Smith and his counsel must have been shocked but hardly surprised, given the farcical nature of the trial.

The following day, Smith was brought back to the House, and after his counsel was seated and the audience shuffled in, Speaker Leech announced that Smith was to be committed to jail until he made "satisfaction" with the House. He must ask for forgiveness for his crime. When he refused, he was also denied an appeal to the king or his council, nor was he allowed to post bail for his release.[70]

Red-faced with rage, Smith could no longer remain silent. He cried that he had been singled out "as the peculiar Object" of the Assembly's "Resentment," adding "I cannot in Conscience make any Acknowledgments or profess Sorrow and Contrition to the House for my Conduct." Then, striking his chest, he proclaimed, "I assure you, no Punishment you can inflict, would be half so terrible to me, as suffering my Tongue to give my Heart the Lie!"[71]

The courtroom erupted in a cacophony of hissing, stomping, and clapping from the spectators in favor of Smith. The speaker ordered the doors shut and anyone disrupting the proceedings arrested. Allies of the Assembly rushed to the front to give what information they could about the perpetrators of the disorder. After several men were seized and brought to the bar, they begged pardon and were ordered to attend the House in the morning. With the crowd contained and dismissed, the sergeant-at-arms carried Smith off and delivered him to the sheriff.[72] Smith immediately submitted a petition to Chief Justice William Allen for a writ of habeas corpus. But the House had voted to compel the sheriff to disobey any such writ. Allen, though sympathetic to Smith, felt bound to follow the rules.[73] Isaac Norris wrote gleefully to Benjamin Franklin, who was monitoring the situation from London. "Our old inveterate scribbler has at length wrote himself in a jail," he chortled.[74]

The conflict continued for more than a year. As public sentiment favored Smith, he prepared to go to the highest authority for justice, the King-in-Council. Enlisting the help of New York lawyers, he submitted a document that made use of Dickinson's arguments.[75] The House was compelled to release Smith during its summer recess, at which time Smith departed for England to plead his case. There he had the support of Thomas Penn, while the Assembly had Franklin. Smith and Franklin were determined to destroy one another's reputations. Franklin slandered Smith to booksellers to ruin his credit, and Smith attempted to convince the dons at Oxford University not to award Franklin an honorary degree.[76]

With Penn reproducing Dickinson's arguments before the Privy Council, the Council found for Smith on June 26. The decision was a devastating indictment of the Pennsylvania Assembly. It agreed with Dickinson's arguments, first, that the House could not try an offence against a previous Assembly that had since adjourned, and second, that even if the House of Commons in Britain had such a power, the Council and the attorney and solicitor general believed "that this extraordinary power ought never to be suffered in these inferior assemblies in America who must not be compared either in power or privileges to the Commons of Great Britain."

The final verdict indicted the Assembly's behavior at length, finding it "guilty of a high and unwarrantable Invasion, both of your majesty's Royal prerogative and the Liberties of the Subject." And it admonished the governor to represent the king's displeasure at "all such unwarrantable proceedings and Oppressions of the Subject" and to protect the king's "prerogative against all Usurpations and Encroachments whatsoever by the Assembly of that province."[77]

Such was Dickinson's introduction to the practice of law in Philadelphia and to the provincial Assembly. Smith was now a free man, but his—and Dickinson's—entanglements with the Assembly were far from over.

As Dickinson's reputation was burnished by his growing experience, demand for his services likewise increased. Although he had made enemies of some powerful men and his client had remained in jail, inhabitants of Pennsylvania now saw him as someone who would take the part of the people against the arbitrary powers of the government.

His case docket expanded beyond the routine work, and he began taking on wealthy clients, particularly in the Vice Admiralty Court. Over recent decades, several of these courts had been established throughout the colonies to handle maritime disputes without necessitating long trips back to England. Dickinson had an abiding respect for the institution. "The Admiralty," he believed, "is establishd on the generous Principles of Humanity & Publick Good."[78]

Admiralty cases could also be quite lucrative, dealing as they did with the transatlantic trade. Now many of the cases dealt with wartime prizes. Dickinson hadn't even needed to spend the entire £500 his father had given him as seed money for his practice; the money flowed in, and he was pleased with his success.[79] Still, he didn't have his eye on profit but on justice. He tended to represent the weaker party against the stronger one, as in the case of Danish sailors suing their captain for refusing to pay their wages at the end of the voyage after they had been called home by their king to join the militia. Although the ship was secured in port and the captain knew of their obligation to their king, he nevertheless withheld their wages. Dickinson cited several similar cases from the law books and ancient laws in favor of the sailors that detailed sailors' being called away due to other engagements yet still being paid. He then reminded the court of the eternal principle that "**Publick Rights** must always be preferred to **Private Contracts**."[80] These sorts of cases had long been tried in the Admiralty and usually went in favor of the sailors.

During the war between Britain and France, other cases became frequent. Prize cases, where privateers—government-sanctioned pirates—captured a ship and commandeered its cargo, were frequent. One client was Captain John Macpherson, a legend on the high seas for his exploits. The newspapers frequently reported how his ten-gun vessel, the *Britannia*, captured ship after ship laden with sugar, coffee, and other valuable wares. On February

23, 1758, French privateers had captured the snow—a large, fast two-mast vessel—called *Desire* on her journey from Rhode Island to Surinam. Three days later, the *Britannia* captured her, and, in short order, six other vessels as well. When the owners of the *Desire* refused to turn over their cargo to Macpherson, he brought a libel, or a claim, against them in the Admiralty Court, with Dickinson as his "proctor," or attorney. They prevailed, and Dickinson earned a handsome fee.[81]

Cases in the Admiralty could be quite controversial as Americans continued their trade during wartime. Many were honest sailors, merchants, or privateers trying to make a living, but others had nefarious designs and were intent on making a profit at the expense of their country. Dickinson would not represent parties that traded with the enemy in illicit goods. Other attorneys in Philadelphia had no such qualms about representing parties with traitorous intentions.

One such case was *John Campbell v. The Owners of the Spry*, in which Campbell, captain of the *Prussian Hero*, an eighteen-gun privateer, brought a libel in the Admiralty Court against the *Spry*, another privateer, for intercepting and seizing his vessel and cargo, claiming it was done illegally. He had engaged John Ross and Joseph Galloway as counsel; the owners of the *Spry* hired Dickinson to defend them. The *Spry's* claim was just, Dickinson believed, because Campbell was attempting to sell arms to the French, a clear act of treason. Campbell's court action was brazen, as he attempted to sue his captor for apprehending him in the commission of a crime. Dickinson could muster little respect for Campbell's counsel during this trial.

Though Campbell's intent to trade arms was apparent, his story was convoluted, which the defense attempted to exploit to cover his crime. His official commission was to sail to Jamaica with a cargo of dry goods, for which his crew signed articles of agreement. But instead, he deceived them, keeping his true mission to sell arms to the French a secret, and sailed to several neutral ports in the islands looking for buyers until they ended up in Monti Christi, also a neutral Spanish port. When he feared he might be discovered, witnesses saw him throwing the arms overboard in the dead of night.

Now his defense was likewise a tangled web of deceit. Ross and Galloway experimented with several options to put the captain's actions in an innocent light, including that the Admiralty Court didn't have jurisdiction, that the depositions of his sailors ought to be dismissed, and that Campbell might not even be British. Dickinson knocked down each attempt.

To begin, he brushed away the weak claim that the Admiralty did not have jurisdiction. Stating the obvious, he said, "There is no other Jurisdiction for trying Crimes at Sea." Next, he turned to the prosecution's motion to suppress the depositions from the crew. Of course, they did not want them admitted as evidence. The testimony was damning, revealing that Campbell "intended to go from Monti Christi to London, quite contrary to the Voyage agreed on with the Sailors and that he was loaded with Dry Goods, which was false and contradicted by Campbell's own Claim." But the sailors, who had endured "prodigious Cruelty, threats, and Hardships" under Campbell's command, should be heard, and it would be cruel, Dickinson argued, to deprive the defense of key evidence in the case.

The prosecution did its best to throw doubt on Campbell's nationality. "Ross says he was an Englishman," said Dickinson. "Galloway says he was an English Dutchman"—an absurd claim, Dickinson argued. Campbell sailed to different ports in hopes that doing so would somehow dissolve his allegiance to Britain and make him Dutch. But neither of these identities would absolve him of a crime. "It may be proper to take notice," Dickinson said, "of the great stress laid on Campbell's sailing from one neutral port to another. He has indeed tried every shape, but he must be an Englishman or a Dutchman," Dickinson argued. "Even granting this amphibious Gentleman to be a Dutchman," he quipped, "surely no Treaties allow them to furnish our Enemies with Arms. They expressly forbid it. See the Treaty of 1674."

Campbell's explanations for the large amount of arms on board were also revealing in their variety. One moment he claimed the arms were for privateers in Jamaica, the next moment they were for the Spaniards, and then later, the arms were allegedly for the use of the ship. But the several chests and great number of cannonballs, still in evidence after having been fished up from the harbor, were too many for one ship.

The prosecution's dissembling throughout made Dickinson think of a poem by Samuel Butler called *Hudibras*: "Fear does things so like a witch / We cannot tell which is which." But the law books were clear, and the prosecution was attempting to obscure treason with their distractions. "I have always thought the Paths of <u>Honesty</u> streight and plain," Dickinson told the court. "No Windings or Intricacies. One may perceive the Traveler at a distance but in the crooked Walks of <u>Cunning</u>, he is almost always hid, at most but a Glimpse and then lost again." Campbell dodged and weaved so frequently during testimony that even he couldn't keep his story straight anymore. "Men engaged in **unlawful designs**," Dickinson advised, "should have good Memories."

Ultimately, Dickinson argued that "this was worse than a Piratical Act; it was a treasonable Act." His client's capturing the *Prussian Hero* was "a kindness to Campbell, as he would have forfeited his Life & Fortune both if his Act had been accomplished." It certainly took a remarkable degree of hubris for a man guilty of treason to libel his rescuers and expose his own crime![82]

For all their twists and turns, cases such as Campbell's were relatively clear—selling arms to the enemy was a high crime. But the other, more ambiguous cases in the Admiralty captured Dickinson's interest on a deeper level. He focused on those that arose in the course of what was called the flag-of-truce trade.[83] The livelihood of many merchants in Pennsylvania depended on the valuable sugar trade with the French islands. In addition to sugar's being used in cooking and hot beverages, it was also used to make molasses; from molasses came rum; and rum was not just a drink but also currency laborers received as compensation. Before the war, Britain began scrutinizing trade between the colonies and the French islands more closely. When war erupted, Britain authorized the Navy to seize vessels trading goods such as sugar, which it deemed contraband.

Colonial governors, eager to protect the economies of their provinces, allowed merchants to trade by issuing passes called "flags of truce," which permitted the exchange of prisoners and the purchase of French goods. Under the protection of these passes, merchant vessels, also called "flags of truce," sailed to neutral ports belonging to Holland or Spain and traded goods. Pennsylvania became a center of this trade in 1759 when Deputy Governor William Denny, seeking to ingratiate himself with the Pennsylvanian merchants and line his own pockets, began selling many more flags of truce than other governors and, eventually, more cheaply. But the British government did not recognize the trade as legal, and invariably, many of these flag-of-truce vessels were seized by the Navy or privateers, their cargoes were forfeited, and the owners ended up in the Admiralty Court contesting the seizures and forfeitures.

As he worked these cases, Dickinson became convinced that the imperial mercantilist stance of the British government in disallowing the trade was untenable and unconstitutional. Although he did not deny that in general it was appropriate for Britain to regulate trade, he believed that it must be in keeping with British law and that free trade should reign when possible.

Goods used by civilians should not be considered contraband in the same category as arms and munitions or wartime provisions. He refused to sanction or defend those who used the flag-of-truce trade as a cover for these truly illicit activities that undeniably aided the enemy, but he was becoming increasingly adamant that free trade was a basic right and the government was unjustly infringing on Americans' rights.

Dickinson's was a risky stance. One's position on this trade was seen as an indication of one's patriotism, and he wagered his reputation by defending those potentially viewed as traitors to Crown and country. "Had it not been for this illicit and pernicious traffic," wrote one angry Briton, "the last French fleet could not have sailed to Europe, as the enemy is thereby furnished with those sinews of war, money and provisions."[84] Many Americans were also opposed. As the *Pennsylvania Gazette* reported, New Yorkers complained that it was "a most pernicious trade, by which means the French, our most inveterate enemies, have been enabled to purchase provisions from the neutral islands at a cheap rate, and by which means the country is drained of that very specie which his Majesty, out of his paternal goodness, has ordered to be lodged here for our support and defence."[85]

Dickinson disagreed, and he had strong arguments on his side. Of his flag-of-truce cases, one in particular commanded his interest and prompted him to consider action beyond the courtroom. In the matter of *Benjamin Spring v. The Ospray*, he represented the defendants. The *Ospray* was an English flag of truce out of Rhode Island that was seized illegally, Dickinson believed, by the *Spry* privateer, piloted by Captain Spring, whose owners Dickinson had represented against Campbell. The *Ospray* had French sugar on board as it made for Port-au-Prince in Hispaniola.

Dickinson made two overarching arguments: First, "that the Brig *Ospray* has done nothing unlawful." And second, that "if She has, the Commander & Officers of the *Spry* Privateer have no Authority or Right to seize upon or demand her as Prize."[86] There were, then, three reasons for the *Ospray*'s innocence: First, she strictly obeyed her commission and did not trade in contraband. Second, no injury was done to England by her trade. Third— a philosophical argument based in part on the work of French thinker Montesquieu, whose work Dickinson greatly admired—the English were by nature a commercial people whose laws were designed to facilitate their activities. Any unwarranted abridgement of their liberties in this regard would be dangerous. In addition, and most significantly, there was no law that made the *Ospray*'s actions illegal. Dickinson sought to prove not merely that the flag-of-truce trade was not treasonous but that it was "lawful, humane, and commendable."[87]

Dickinson opened by addressing the libellants' argument. "It is said," he began, "We supply them with Money, the Sinews of War."[88] But the very nature of the trade was that it was more beneficial to the British than the French. "We do not supply the Enemy with any warlike or naval Stores, or with Provisions," he explained. "This is universally acknowledgd to be unlawful."[89] He marshaled statistics on the trade to show the remarkable profits that American traders reaped, to the benefit of the British Empire and the detriment of the French.[90] In short, the British would conquer the French more completely through commerce than in battle.

Dickinson extended his arguments to a critique of the British Navy itself, arguing that rather than attacking the French, it expended its energies and resources attacking American traders. This argument led Dickinson to his second point, which was that the trade was not, in fact, illegal because there was no written law against it. The matter of written law was important and not one that all Englishmen recognized. "It has ever been thought a peculiar Happiness by Englishmen to have their Property as well as their Lives & Liberties secured by plain & public Laws." He cited the legal maxim "That the People, whose Law is uncertain, endure the most miserable Slavery."[91] Here, again, Dickinson's Quaker heritage was evident. His Quaker forebears, who were frequently charged with crimes under the unwritten common law, protested in court. "Show me what law I have broken," they would say to the judge. "I shall not believe thee now, except thou read the law to me."[92]

Likewise, Dickinson believed that Americans should not be punished except for breaking clearly defined laws that have been set down in writing for all to know. "Statutes," he explained, "may be called 'political revelations.' They contain <u>truth</u>, <u>certainty</u>, and <u>safety</u>." He supported his claim with Scripture, citing Saint Paul: "Where there is no law," that is, no revealed law, "there is no transgression." Not only had Americans broken no laws, but they believed themselves protected by precedent: no trade had been prohibited in the War of Jenkins's Ear. There was no statute prohibiting commerce during war. Moreover, a royal statute was continued that very year to protect the sugar trade.

The libellants objected, claiming that the king's Declaration of War prohibited trade with France. To this, Dickinson cited Coke, explaining that "the King's Proclamation is no part of the law, for he cannot make that unlawful, which was lawful before." Dickinson was always wary of the executive's accruing too much power. Surely, he asserted, British subjects did not want to return to the days "when too much Respect was paid to the royal Prerogative." Before the Glorious Revolution of 1688, the English had suffered under absolute monarchs who wielded their power arbitrarily. But now, he reminded the court, "every Englishman must behold with Pleasure the milder Methods of Government, that succeeded the Revolution" under their constitutional monarchy.[93]

Dickinson had always admired the Admiralty Court for its impartiality, but if the law were misapplied, the court could easily take a troubling turn from being the disinterested arbiter of maritime disputes between diverse peoples to one slanted in favor of certain segments of British society against others. "What can be more justly <u>alarming</u> to Englishmen," he queried, "than to see the Admiralty assuming to itself unbounded Power, over one of its most precious Possessions, its Commerce?" An unchecked judiciary could be as dangerous as an unchecked executive. One abuse of power in the judiciary could lead to others. Like the Chancery Court, which was instituted for equity, the Admiralty was a civil law court governed by the same rules. Forfeitures of private property, therefore, should have been "odious" to it. He called on the libelants and the judges to cite the statute that authorized such forfeitures. They could not, of course, because one did not exist.[94]

Rather than a legal course of action by the *Spry* in seizing the *Ospray*, Dickinson found a "surprizing Declaration of War made in his Majesty's name against his Majesty's Subjects."[95] And the Admiralty Court was legitimizing this war, creating what Dickinson referred to as a constructive offense—creating a crime where there was none. Moreover, the punishments for these fictive crimes were unduly harsh. "If the Child of a tender Mother shoud commit a Fault, which for the future She might prevent by her Commands, woud she chuse rather to disable him by a dreadful Beating, or by cutting off one of his Hands?"[96] Such behavior would be equally damaging and irrational as the flag-of-truce trade being punished with forfeiture.

So strongly did Dickinson believe that American rights were in jeopardy that he wanted to take his case to the public. Around 1759, he began composing an essay on this topic, called "Reflections on the Flag of Truce Trade in America." He wouldn't publish it under his own name, which could have been dangerous. As he well knew from William Smith's trial, any publication that was considered disrespectful of government could be termed "seditious libel," and he could join Smith in jail. So he gave himself a pseudonym. He needed one that would give him the most credibility with readers, something that implied both knowledge of the subject matter and disinterest, that is, impartiality. He decided on "An English Merchant." This gentleman would be a patriot and have concern for the rights of his countrymen in America. He prefaced the essay with an epigraph from Montesquieu. "Other Nations have made the Interests of Commerce yield to those of Politics," he explained. "The English on the contrary, have always made their political Interests give way to those of Commerce. They know better than other People upon Earth, how to value at the same Time these three great Advantages, Religion, Commerce, and Liberty."[97]

Dickinson knew that in order to convince the public, he could not alienate those with opposing views. Instead, he took the Quakerly approach: confronting people's false ideas while showing sympathy with their position and then working respectfully to win them over. He began with the very issue he confronted in the courtroom. "It is certain that Popular Opinions are often wrong," he explained, "and yet nothing is more difficult, & sometimes nothing more dangerous than to oppose them." What is worse, these mistaken opinions gain strength in numbers "till at last, like a Flood swelled with Rains, it breaks all Banks & bears down every Thing before it." During this unjust war, some turned on these American traders and accused them of assisting the enemy.[98] Now, however, he hoped that the public was calm enough to hear his argument.

He proceeded cautiously, demonstrating his thinking to be like theirs. "I must acknowledge," he added, "that this Charge seemd to proceed from such a Respect for the General Good, and was enforced with so much Zeal; that I was catchd by it, and greatly condemned this Trade." But after studying the matter, his mind had opened and changed. He had become "quite satisfied, that the Americans have been very much injured by the Representation made of their Behaviour."[99]

He laid out the same arguments as he would to a jury. He took care to define and describe the different kinds of law and the roles of the various courts. Rather than citing a multitude of law books and statutes as he did in his case notes, he kept his citations brief and accessible to the average person without legal training, and he translated his Latin quotes. Finally, he concluded with a startling observation: "American merchants alone," he charged, "have undergone, in this happy Period of Public Liberty, the uncommon Fate of being punishd, not by a <u>Law</u> made, but what is infinitely more to be abhorrd, by a Construction of some unknown Mystery calld Law, **ex post Facto**," that is, a law made after the fact.[100] It was a stark warning for Americans: their rights and liberties may no longer be protected by the Admiralty Court.

To negate any charges that this essay was somehow unpatriotic because it advocated trading with the enemy during wartime, Dickinson followed the logic of the epigraph by Montesquieu. Because the British—including Americans—were a commercial people, free trade would be all they would need to defeat their enemies. British merchants would buy French sugar at shockingly low prices and sell it at a profit around the empire. With such a weapon at their command, "Can they be any more our Slaves?"[101]

Dickinson crafted the essay over the next few years, writing, revising, rewriting, adding footnotes with statistics and citations, cutting, and writing some more. Sometimes he added extensions to pages by tacking extra leaves with sealing wax. He added a title page and a table of contents to his little booklet, which was fifty-two pages long. By this time, however, the war seemed to be drawing to a close and the flag-of-truce trade was no longer an issue. He had missed his moment. He realized that if he wanted to engage the public on current affairs, timing was everything. He didn't publish the manuscript, but it helped him hone his ideas about trade and foreign relations as well as his argumentative skills.

Dickinson now saw as never before how his work in the law would enable him to be of service to his countrymen in the halls of government. They badly wanted legislators who understood both their needs and how to write legislation to meet those needs. They required leaders who knew the proper role of government and would use it in service of the people, not against them. More than ever, Dickinson looked forward to the fall elections.

4

"Congratulate Me on my Salvation"

Election to Public Office, 1759–1763

As the son of a gentleman and a man of property, Dickinson had long anticipated serving in one of the legislatures, either of Pennsylvania proper or the Three Lower Counties on Delaware. With Pennsylvania being one of the largest colonies, a seat in that Assembly was the greater prize. It included thirty-six legislators from eight counties and the City of Philadelphia, representing 184,000 inhabitants. As the only major colony with a unicameral legislature and religious liberty protected in its constitution, the 1701 Charter of Privileges, the people had more freedom and more power than in other colonies—at least in theory.

The province had always been dominated by party politics. There were no formal parties as would develop in the next century, organized and with platforms. Rather, they were loose affiliations of like-minded men who supported certain religio-political ends or opposed others. For most of the history of Pennsylvania, the Assembly had been so thoroughly dominated by Philadelphia Yearly Meeting, the governing body of the Quakers, that the government was effectively a theocracy, creating enemies by imposing Quaker doctrine on non-Quakers. Even after the Quakers' "reformation" in 1756, during the French and Indian War, that had prompted eleven Friends to abdicate their seats, that Assembly was still controlled by the Quaker party, though now it consisted of men who were not Quakers. Other factions of Presbyterians, Anglicans, and supporters of the Penns contested against it for power while the Quaker party defended its position against encroachments by them as well as the Penn family and their deputy governors. It's no wonder that the colony—and particularly the Quakers—had a reputation on both sides of the Atlantic as being "ungovernable."

The Assembly of the Lower Counties had broken away from the Pennsylvania Assembly in 1701, when it became clear that its members' interests were separate from those of the Quaker party. It was only half the size of the Pennsylvania Assembly, with six legislators from each county, representing 33,000 inhabitants. Although New Castle, Kent, and Sussex counties were as religiously and ethnically diverse as the eight upper counties and also contained Quakers, their legislature was generally less contentious and worked with the Penns and their deputies rather than against them. It was a more forgiving environment in which to begin a career in politics.

In October 1759, Dickinson was elected to serve as a representative from Kent County. Of the candidates, he received the fifth-most votes, with 501 out of 5,000, surpassing more notable persons, including Attorney General Benjamin Chew and Judge John Vining, a wealthy planter. Election officials noted irregularities along with the returns. "It is well Known," they wrote, "that their is many Scattered votes taken no notice of by the clarks which would make a greater Diference if they had been kept." On the other hand, in this instance, "it is noted that there is a far Greater number of votes this year than Ever has been before ocasioned by the Inspectors taking a great many votes that had no Right by Law as appears by the Several Lists."[1] It seemed that, despite their best efforts, those without property were voting, and democracy was creeping into their system.

Although he now lived in Philadelphia, Dickinson was closer to the seat of government of the Lower Counties, which was in New Castle, than other representatives from Kent and Sussex counties. He traveled the thirty-six miles to the quiet little village for the eight-day session, which began on October 20. The journey, which he made frequently for court, was a pleasant one. After leaving Philadelphia and passing through a few miles of pleasing gardens and orchards, he took Gray's Ferry over the Schuylkill River. The Delaware River soon came into view and remained his companion for the better part of the trip. Ships low in the water with their burdens slipped to and fro while waterfowl fished and river otters frolicked on the banks. Before long, the landscape turned to some of the most beautifully cultivated farmland in the colonies, with fields of grain, flax, and clover ripe for harvesting. Dickinson passed through Chester, where he frequently attended court, and then crossed the border into the Lower Counties. Wilmington was the first village of any size he came to. It was a pretty little place, small but growing, and also laid out on a grid, like Philadelphia. New Castle was small even compared to Wilmington. There were only around a hundred dwellings and two houses of religion—a Quaker meeting house and a Presbyterian church. There was also a market house and a small courthouse.[2]

Although the courthouse had a modest room that could accommodate the eighteen assemblymen, the members frequently met in a private home. At this first session, after swearing in the members, the initial order of business was to elect a speaker. They chose Jacob Kollock, a long-serving Anglican from Sussex County. They then passed several bills, some of particular interest to Dickinson—for relief of the poor and regulation of roads in Kent County, and for easier recovery of small debts.[3] As usual, Deputy Governor Denny attended one day of their session.[4] Among the bills the Assembly presented him for approval was one appointing trustees vested with the power to protect New Castle Common, a thousand-acre tract of land designated by William Penn to be for the benefit of the public to graze livestock, collect firewood, and cultivate crops. Increasingly, conflicts had arisen over the land, so the Assembly sought impartial oversight of it.[5]

The Assembly adjourned at the end of the week. Dickinson had his clerk tally the pay and mileage of several representatives, himself included, for reimbursement by the government.[6] Like the others, Dickinson earned around £3 for his services, but he resolved always to donate his earnings from any type of public service. Widows, orphans, veterans, and the poor were generally the objects of his benevolence. He also had resolved never to seek offices of profit or emoluments for himself, directly or indirectly. In these ways, he believed, he could remain a disinterested servant of the public weal.[7]

The Assembly was not scheduled to reconvene until late spring 1760, but the urgency of the ongoing war with the French and Indians required Deputy Governor James Hamilton, who had replaced Denny, to request their action sooner. So back to New Castle Dickinson went in April. Hamilton explained that the colony must raise men and send them to a rendezvous point to be named, where the king would supply them with arms, supplies, and provisions. At least as many men as last time, or more, needed to be raised, and they would muster at Lancaster, York, and Carlisle to be led by General John Stanwix. Hamilton would protect their rights, but they must fulfill their duty. "I shall study," he assured them, "to protect you in the full enjoyment of all the Civil & Religious Liberties to which You are entitled by the Laws or Constitution of the Country."[8]

The Assembly responded with their congratulations to Hamilton on his appointment and their gratitude for his assurances that he would protect their liberties. They also understood that it was the prerogative of the Crown to requisition troops and that they should show their support for the war. But the Lower Counties were struggling economically and could no longer afford to give as freely as before. With Parliament promising compensation, however, they would do what they could.[9]

The next day, the Assembly presented two bills to the governor for his assent, both of which particularly interested Dickinson. One was to make his friend from his London days, David Barclay Jr., the agent for the Lower Counties. The agent acted as an advocate for their interests before the Board of Trade and with bankers and merchants. Of the assemblymen, Dickinson was one of the few who knew Barclay personally, and he could vouch for his integrity. The second bill was even more important. For many years, the Supreme Court of the Lower Counties had not been functioning effectively, and an earlier act to restore its ability to mete out justice to the inhabitants "had not answered all the good purposes intended."[10] This new bill repealed all sections of the law—nine total—pertaining to that court. As the only member of the Assembly with legal training at the Inns of Court, and now with some experience before the Supreme Courts of both Pennsylvania and her Lower Counties, Dickinson was in a prime position to contribute to the crafting of this bill. Governor Hamilton appreciated the import of these two bills and, recognizing their value as bargaining chips, told the Assembly that he wouldn't act on them until he had the funds they promised for the war. Accordingly, when they sent him the money bill, he approved those on the court and the agent.[11]

In one of the last points of business, Dickinson presented a report he had written on a committee with two other assemblymen, Evan Rice of New Castle County and Benjamin Burton of Sussex, to settle the campaign accounts from the previous year. The previous Assembly had voted £7,000 for the king's use, and their task was to describe exactly how much had been spent on everything, from clothing and provisions to pay for the officers and troops, as well as what remained in the hands of the Lower Counties. They found that a total of £6,880 had been spent. This exercise was a good example of the ordinary business of colonial governance, giving Dickinson experience in the management of soldiers and funds.[12]

But the very ordinariness of the Assembly business was itself extraordinary, considering the controversy similar exercises wrought in the Pennsylvania Assembly, which contorted itself to avoid funding a militia. For some members, their opposition originated from an earnest desire to protect the lives of their Indian allies. For others, it was a means to preserve political power in the face of proprietary encroachments. Dickinson felt strongly that a militia for self-defense was critical for the survival of a free people and should be funded accordingly.

Overall, Dickinson's performance in his first year as a legislator impressed his colleagues. Jacob Kollock had served on and off as speaker of the Assembly of the Lower Counties for the previous forty years, and some members thought this new, energetic young lawyer might well serve instead. For now, however, Dickinson turned to family matters. His mother had been overseeing Poplar Hall for several years as his father's health declined. Samuel Dickinson had long suffered from gout but in recent years had been in a great deal of pain. Yet he bore his lot with patience and resignation, and visitors found him to be in good spirits, always giving thanks to the Supreme Being for his worldly happiness.[13]

Earlier in the year, Samuel had had to turn over most duties to Mary. She now managed hundreds of acres, determining what crops were to be planted—tobacco, flax, wheat, corn, and barley—as well as their schedule for harvesting and sale. She kept the accounts, not just of crops sold but also of their tenant farmers in Kent and across the border in Maryland, as well as all work done at Poplar Hall by more than sixty enslaved people on the plantation and hireling workers abroad. Among the latter were smiths, weavers, knitters, tailors, cartwrights, and tanners. She had to ensure their "family" was as happy as possible, which meant feeding and clothing one and all.[14] It was a responsibility she felt keenly and did not enjoy.

Unfortunately, Mary's life would not get easier in the short term. Samuel Dickinson died on Sunday, July 6, 1760. Although his decline was long and his passing surprised no one, none of his sons was able to reach Poplar Hall in time to be by his side. Yet Mary reported that his end befitted a Christian who had lived a good life. At the last, he was cheerful, sanguine that he would be going to a better place.[15]

Dickinson felt the loss of his father acutely. Stern but loving, he had been a role model in many ways. That fall, Dickinson missed his counsel as he once again was elected to represent Kent County in the Assembly of the Lower Counties. After the members were sworn in on Monday, October 20, Dickinson was chosen speaker of the House. He was now in a position to realize his vision for the Lower Counties. Yet most of the legislation that was passed under his direction was routine, such as An Act to Encourage the Building of Good Mills. There was a supplement to the act the Assembly had passed the previous year on regulating the king's roads in Kent County, and it repealed an act empowering New Castle County to remove obstructions to fisheries.[16] Nothing passed was as consequential as last year's re-establishment of the Supreme Court, except for one act, designed to remedy a law passed twenty years earlier.

In 1740, the Assembly had passed An Act for the Better regulation of Servants and Slaves. It covered the usual issues—terms of indenture; punishments for runaways and rewards for their captors; the requirement that masters provide securities for setting enslaved persons free so they would not become burdens on society; and the assurance that children would be bound out, that is, placed as servants in another family, if parents couldn't care for them, and so forth. A supplement in 1752 added provisions for how disputes between masters and servants should be settled.

But Dickinson believed this law was defective in a significant regard. With laborers hard to come by, he had observed how free Black and "mulatto" people were being unlawfully held as slaves by those pretending to be their masters and mistresses. Moreover, these pretended masters had prevented their hostages from securing proof of their legal freedom. Dickinson believed that the law must provide a "mode for settling and determining, in a short and summary manner, the claim, or right, of any persons pretending to be entitled to their liberty."[17] Although there were common-law remedies for people of color, these were unreliable. Their liberties needed to be protected with a written statute, which, Dickinson explained, "contain Truth, Certainty, and Safety."[18]

Dickinson thus acted to protect the rights of free Black people and to ensure their access to fair court proceedings. The new law before the House provided that if an unlawfully detained person submitted a petition to a justice of the Court of Common Pleas, the justice must summon the pretended master or mistress before him to answer the charge. If the pretended master hid or refused to relinquish the hostage, the pretended master would be arrested. Because the attempted enslaver would likely have help and sympathy even from those empowered to enforce the laws, the bill provided further that if the sheriff refused to arrest the enslaver, he himself would be fined the monumental sum of £100, and that sum would be given to the victim. The victim could also seek further damages against the former enslaver by bringing an action of trespass or false imprisonment against him or her. If the victim was sold out of the colony, the pretended master must pay £100 and cover the court costs for these actions.[19]

When the bill passed, it became the only one of its kind in the colonies and one of the few pieces of legislation protecting the basic rights of people of color. Up to that point, not even Pennsylvania, with its growing contingent of Quaker abolitionists, had put such protections in place. Over the course of his tenure as speaker of the House, whether because of this or other legislative endeavors, Dickinson made enemies among his colleagues in the Assembly of the Lower Counties.[20] Acquiring enemies was, he believed, a small price to pay for following his conscience and a sign of his own righteousness. He didn't return to the Assembly of the Lower Counties, which allowed him to set his sights on a bigger prize—a seat in the Pennsylvania Assembly.

At the end of the year, in another substantial personal blow, Dickinson received word that his friend and legal mentor John Moland had died on December 30, in his sixtieth year. After Dickinson's parents, Moland had been the greatest influence in his life, the man who taught him how to be a rigorous and upright lawyer. They had served together as a team in court, but also on opposite sides. Just this year, they had done battle in the provincial court, sometimes with Moland winning the day, other times Dickinson. Yet their professional admiration for and trust in one another never allowed courtroom skirmishes to affect the friendship they had developed over the previous decade.

Moland had imparted his own traits to his young clerk. Dickinson reflected on these things as he wrote an obituary for the newspaper. In Dickinson's own "severe and steady Application to Study" and his "uniform and zealous Attachment to the Interest of his Client," he felt his mentor's influence. These traits in Moland were "joined to a clear Apprehension and tenacious Memory." During his life, Moland "was eminently and justly distinguished, for an easy Dignity in social Life—superior Abilities in his Profession," and "extensive Knowledge in polite Literature." Most importantly, however, he was revered "as a warm and faithful advocate."[21]

Moland's death was not a loss Dickinson bore lightly. His sorrow felt boundless as he thought how Moland had only recently retired from his law practice, intending to enjoy the flowers in his garden and the large oak tree leaning over the brook on his property. He could hardly imagine not conversing late into the night with his friend about the finer points of law and literature.

Dickinson's mentor was buried on his estate in Bucks County on January 2, 1761, with prominent Philadelphians, such as Elizabeth and Henry Drinker, in attendance.[22] Moland left behind a large family, who now turned to Dickinson for assistance. His widow, Catherine, had eight children to care for, ranging in age from three to twenty-two. She needed help managing finances and the behavior of some of the children, who had already troubled their parents. John Jr., the oldest, had been an aspiring apothecary at the Pennsylvania Hospital. When he had to resign because of ill health, Moland agreed to pay for the drugs he had invested in for his practice. But John had so displeased his father that in his will Moland revoked his oldest son's executorship and withdrew his bequest of his watch, sword, and cane.

His next oldest son, Thomas, was worse than a disappointment; he was an embarrassment. A year shy of his majority, he already languished in debtors' prison and was, in effect, banished from the family. Moland stipulated in his will that the condition of Catherine's keeping her inheritance was that she not converse with Thomas, to whom he left one single shilling.

The remaining children were still in good standing. Elizabeth, seventeen, and Hannah, sixteen, were the executors of their father's will. Their younger brothers, Billy, eleven, and Robert, fourteen, were to be put out as apprentices at the expense of the estate, and Joseph, seven, called Josey, wasn't mentioned, nor was little Grace, the youngest. Dickinson, already familiar with the details of the family's travails, knew that his role might not be easy. It would fall to him to manage the estate's funds and dispense moral advice, difficult duties that, while trying, he fulfilled for well over a decade.

Equally momentous in its way was the death of George II in October 1759. At that time, the Assembly of the Lower Counties was halfway through its legislative session. The death and accession of a monarch had significant implications for critical functions of the colonies, all the more so when it could not be known for months. At issue was what actions would be valid if they occurred during this interregnum. The questions included small matters, such as what name subjects should utter when taking an oath or affirmation of office, to larger issues, such as whether laws passed during this period were valid. Soon Dickinson joined his fellow jurists in Philadelphia in thinking about two specific problems, one real and one academic.[23]

The real problem was an ongoing controversy in Pennsylvania about judicial tenure, namely whether judges held their commissions for life during good behavior or whether they served at the pleasure of the king. Naturally, the Assembly considered that judges served for life, with their removal for malfeasance upon petition to the House; it had passed an act in 1759 to that effect, and several judges had been appointed by the governor. The Penns, however, believed that the Assembly was overstepping its bounds and petitioned the king for the repeal of the act, which was granted. When news of the king's demise reached Pennsylvania, the governor accordingly revoked the judges' commissions. But the judges refused to resign. Dickinson considered this matter to be one of utmost importance to the administration of justice in Pennsylvania. As a matter of common law, he believed that judges should serve for life on good behavior to allow for their independence from both the executive and legislative branches. It was a fundamental principle of government that the branches be separate and serve to check one another. The proprietors complained to British Attorney General Charles Pratt.

While Pennsylvanians awaited Pratt's response—which took several months—they made an evening's entertainment out of a similar question. A group of jurists gathered to debate whether court proceedings occurring in the six months after a monarch had died and before the colonists received notice were valid. Dickinson was assigned the negative position—that they were invalid—the opposite stance he took in the actual controversy with the Pennsylvania judges. He found it a challenging exercise to argue a position with which he did not agree, but he made a compelling case. Ultimately, Pratt's decision favored Dickinson's actual position—that they were valid—and to the proprietors' embarrassment, he proclaimed that the very question perplexed him since the judges were not the king's—they were the proprietors'—and the circumstances of English judges did not necessarily apply in the colonies.

In the fall of 1761, Dickinson thought that the people of Pennsylvania were familiar enough with him to put him in the Assembly, where he hoped he might do good, but though his name was put forward, he was not elected. Instead, he gained entry through a side door. The following spring, Thomas Leech, the member who had served as speaker during the infamous Smith trial, died, and on March 11, 1762, Dickinson was chosen to fill his seat.[24] Because he was attending court in the Lower Counties at the time, he did not take his seat until the September session.[25]

By now, Dickinson was under no illusions that the Pennsylvania Assembly was any sort of pantheon of disinterested legislators. After the House adjourned in May, disgruntled at the governor's refusal of their latest supply bill and having accomplished nothing effectual besides, Dickinson wrote to his dear friend John Hall of Annapolis, also a lawyer and legislator, comparing the members to a crowd of rowdy drunks. "I beg your Pardon for speaking so freely of these civil Heroes," he wrote sardonically. "Their Motives may be commendable— Tho I acknowledge their Conduct woud appear as laudable to Me, if they were quite idle—as when they are so busily employd—in doing nothing."[26]

Before he joined the fray in the Assembly, Dickinson still indulged in diversions of various kinds. He told Hall that he was not "too much of a Lawyer, Politician, or Philosopher" to avoid the horse races, and he enjoyed acting the sportsman, even picking up enough lingo so he could "almost hold a Dialogue in the Stile of the Turf." He teased his friend Hall about a recent defeat of a Maryland favorite by a Pennsylvania horse. But because the new term in the courts was about to begin, Dickinson would need to put frivolous pasttimes aside. Still, given his propensity to overwork, he reminded Hall, and himself, to "mix Pleasure with Business—& Innocence with Pleasure— Application & Fatigue may procure Reputation & Wealth—But destroy Health & Happiness."[27]

In the spirit of mixing business with pleasure, Dickinson accepted an invitation to travel with a delegation of Quakers to attend a meeting in Easton at the end of June with the Lenape tribe about the so-called Walking Purchase of 1737. The Lenape had agreed to sell the Penns as much land as a man could walk in thirty-six hours. But the Penns had hired runners to cover vastly more ground than the Lenape anticipated and thus swindled the tribe out of more than a million acres. Now the Quakers wanted to help them renegotiate. When they abdicated their Assembly seats, Quakers, having long striven for good relations with the Indians, formed a benevolent society called the Friendly Association for Regaining and Preserving Peace with the Indians by Pacific Measures. The organization was also a way for them to retain a degree of political influence. At this point in his life, Dickinson was not as yet much interested in Indian affairs. Rather, he told his mother, "I expect great Entertainment & Advantage from this Trip."[28]

This new opportunity would alter his plans to travel to the Jerseys with Thomas McKean, the young lawyer from New Castle County who, as Dickinson hoped, had become his close friend. They had both been working too hard, not just with their own cases, but frequently appearing in court for the other. He offered McKean the same advice he had given to Hall. "Moderation in every Thing is the Source of Happiness," he admonished. "This has been said a thousand Times—always believd—& practicd against—It is still true."[29] Now he cajoled McKean to join him in Easton, luring him with the prospect of seeing "a glorious Country" and "a thousand Indians." He added, "I think We may spend a Week there with great Pleasure, & after that You may transport Me to the Jerseys."[30]

The conference seemed to have a sobering effect on Dickinson, giving him a sharp lesson in the dynamics of power—proprietary and royal interests against Quaker and Indian interests. Not normally allies, Sir William Johnson, a British superintendent of Indian affairs, and the Penns discovered they could unite on the basis of their dislike of three things: the Quakers, especially Israel Pemberton, their most powerful leader; the Lenape tribe and its leader, Teedyuscung; and the Susquehanna Company of Connecticut, which was planning to plant settlers in Pennsylvania's Wyoming Valley.

Also present was another member of the quartet, Charles Thomson, the Irish Presbyterian. He was the head Latin instructor at the Friends' Public School in Philadelphia. As an active member of the city's intellectual community, he worked with Benjamin Franklin to found the Society for the Promotion of Useful Knowledge. His facility in taking notes was such that, at the request of Israel Pemberton, he had been the secretary for the meeting between the Delawares and the Penns the previous year. Thomson quickly became a champion of the Delawares' rights. They would later show their appreciation for him by adopting him into the tribe and naming him "The Man of Truth."[31]

The meeting did not go well for either the Quakers or the Lenape. Leveraging the threat of Connecticut settlers to the advantage of the British, Johnson humiliated Teedyuscung and Pemberton. He reprimanded Pemberton for meddling in government affairs concerning the Indians, effectively silencing him; and he shamed Teedyuscung, causing him to withdraw his complaint about the Walking Purchase. But a map kept secret by Penn and his agents displayed the depths of their deception. It showed clearly the scheme to miscommunicate to the Lenape how much land the proprietors would actually take. Though this map would not come to light for centuries, the transaction was so obviously duplicitous at the time that even friends of the proprietors could see it.[32] Dickinson referred to it as the "pretended purchase."[33] The meeting was a demoralizing defeat for the Quakers, a devastating loss for the Indians, and it opened the way for decades of bloody conflict between residents of Pennsylvania and Connecticut. Thomson's ire was such that the next year he published a pamphlet entitled *An Enquiry into the Causes of the Alienation of the Delaware and Shawanese Indians from the*

British Interest, which Dickinson surely read. He began to take relations with the Indians more seriously.

If Dickinson hoped to gain more business for his law practice by associating with prominent men on the Easton trip, it worked. As the summer ended and he anticipated the next Pennsylvania Assembly election, he was hired by Israel Pemberton for various work. Some of it related to Quakers' charity efforts with the Public School for educating poor children of both sexes and races, facilitating land transfers.[34]

Another case was tragic. Pemberton's stepson, a troubled young man named Joseph Jordan, had committed a terrible crime. On September 22, Josey, as he was called, came home drunk and abusive. Only his stepsister, Sally, was at home. She fled the house in fear and sought the help of other family members. Her uncle, and Josey's good friend, Thomas Kirkbride, rushed to the house to restrain him. Thomas entered the home and followed Josey upstairs, where he intended to lock him in a room. But Josey, enraged by drink and delusion, resisted and fought. As the men struggled, Josey stabbed Thomas in the stomach. Thomas died a painful death, and Joseph was immediately apprehended and put on trial for murder.

Those closest to Josey knew that he had not been in his right mind. Israel and Mary, Josey's mother, were bereft. Josey was Mary's only child from her first marriage, and his future had seemed so promising. He was very bright and loved learning. But as he grew, his family and friends noticed a change in him. His faculties decayed, and he transformed before their eyes from a bright young man full of potential to someone they no longer recognized. He turned to alcohol, which destroyed what understanding he had left. It seems likely that he suffered from schizophrenia.

Knowing their son would face execution if found guilty of murder, the Pembertons turned to Dickinson. Not only was he now recognized as the ablest lawyer in the province; he had also known Josey when they were boys. Dickinson was only two years older. Indeed, Dickinson himself had witnessed how "All the Traces of Learning are obliterated by the dreadful Disease that seizes him, from his Mind—like Marks on the Seashore Sand, by the Wave that washes them away."

Dickinson agreed to take the case, and he did so pro bono. "I confess," he said, "this has excited my Compassion in the highest Degree." Although it would be a difficult defense, he assured the Pembertons, "I have some Reason to hope" that when the jury is informed of all the circumstances, they "will in the most calm & sacred Manner enquire into the Truths & that their Lips will utter a Sentence dictated by feeling and unprejudicd Hearts." Josey's only hope of avoiding the hangman's noose was if Dickinson could convince the jury of his insanity. Dickinson promised, "I do not intend to misrepresent facts—or deceive by artful Arguments."

Taking such a case was not an easy decision for Dickinson. Although Pennsylvania considered that the accused had a right to counsel, there was as yet no firm presumption of innocence under the law, and some lawyers were reluctant to place themselves alongside one charged with so heinous a crime for fear the stain of guilt should transfer to them and ruin their reputations. In effect, Dickinson was putting his own reputation on trial with the accused. Some years later, he represented a man accused of murdering a night watchman, an officer of the law, in the line of duty. He began again by assuring the jury, "If I thought Death was intended by my client, no Consideration shoud tempt me to speak on this Occasion." In this case, the law and the evidence were clear. An officer of the law must announce himself properly before advancing to keep the peace. In this instance, the officer did not, and the killing was accidental.[35]

Now Dickinson addressed the jury, knowing he needed to allay their suspicions about him and his own motives. "Of all Causes," he began, "there is none in which I shoud so unwillingly engage, as in a Cause of this Nature." He needed to signal his agreement with their thinking about the usual penalties in such cases. Though Quakers opposed the death penalty, if there were non-Quakers on the jury, they would expect a punishment that would align more with the Old Testament than the New. "My Reason is—that no Maxim of Justice or Morality is more clearly establishd in my Mind than this—that wherever one Man maliciously destroys the Life of another by the most just Retaliation—the Aggressor shoud suffer in the same Degree." But there were caveats to this maxim, and "the utmost Caution should be usd in extenuating a doubtful Offence." He therefore prepared the jury for his argument against capital punishment in this case. After assuring them that he would receive no payment for representing an accused murderer in order to preserve "the approbation of my own Conscience & a Character unspotted with the sordid Love of Gain," he placed the onus on the jury to approach their verdict with compassion for the accused. "Listen to the Cries of Affliction," he implored them, "& to relieve Distresses owing more to Misfortune than to Guilt, becomes a worthy Man, & therefore cannot be displeasing to You."[36]

The trial ended quickly and as favorably as possible. Four days after the murder, on September 26, Joseph was declared a "lunatic" and committed to the Pennsylvania Hospital. For the next decade, he sat in a dark, damp cell, unheated year-round. Because most believed the insane did not feel the cold, those conditions were acceptable to his family. He and the other patients also endured the crowds of spectators who came to gawk at the curiosities. Shortly after Josey's arrival, to stem the tide of the curious, the managers of the hospital thought it only proper to charge admission. Lunatic patients routinely escaped their chains and slipped through the bars; some escaped only by taking their own lives. Josey died of natural causes at just thirty-six.[37]

Dickinson's defense of Jordan did not hurt him with the people of Pennsylvania. At the provincial election on October 1, he was finally chosen directly as a representative to the Pennsylvania Assembly from Philadelphia County. It was a moment he had imagined for many years, and he wrote ebulliently to George Read when the election returns came in. "You may Congratulate Me on my Salvation," he said with gleeful sarcasm, "for I am certainly among the Elect—& may enter into the Assembly of righteous Men—as I hope they all are."[38] Of course, he was keenly aware that election to the Assembly was quite unlike ascension to heaven. But he was elated at the honor and knew he would work as earnestly for his constituents as he did for his clients. He reported for duty punctually, but because a quorum wasn't achieved immediately, he was compelled to return to the court circuit and did not take his seat until the second session in January 1763.

The session began slowly, with little work until the war came to an end. "The last Advices in the newspaper make Peace to be quite doubtful," Dickinson dourly wrote to his mother. Many believed that only William Pitt, the British cabinet member who had successfully led the war effort, could secure it. He was a hero to Americans. But as much as he wanted an end to the war, Dickinson was apprehensive. "No Doubt we shall make an immensely advantageous or rather gainful Peace." But this was not necessarily for the good. "Our Commerce will be incredible. Our Riches exorbitant— Our Luxury unbounded— Our Corruption in Time universal—& our Ruin—certain." The student of history lamented "the inevitable fate of Empires."[39]

In the House, Dickinson was appointed to no fewer than seven legislative committees. His work was primarily on regulation of various activities. Tradesmen who transported or hauled goods, including wagoners, carters, draymen, and porters needed to register their vehicles or face fines. They would also be fined if they demanded more than the fixed rate for their services. The courts needed better regulation and to have continuances limited. Infrastructure and other public services also demanded Dickinson's attention. Thoroughfares needed to be pitched and paved, and the city needed a new public dock on the Delaware River; funds must be raised for these purposes. And relief for poor people in the province needed to be more efficient and effective.[40]

The legislative work was, of course, in addition to his law practice, which kept him on the circuit. While in Kent in early February attending the Court of Common Pleas, Dickinson received word from Charles Thomson, secretary of the Library Company of Philadelphia, that he had been unanimously elected a director of that institution.[41] He imagined telling his mother, thinking she would smile at the honor, perhaps because the institution was so closely associated with Dr. Franklin, on whom Mary knew her son's sentiments. "You'll be pleased, tho, when You know that the Choice is made by Men of Sense & Virtue," he informed her, "whose Approbation You have always taught Me to esteem a Blessing."[42] Uncle Cadwalader and the former Dickinson family tutor, Presbyterian minister Francis Alison, were also shareholders and directors.

Dickinson did his best to attend meetings of the directors, but he was not much inclined to join organizations, and his work schedule made attendance difficult. In 1759, he had been elected to the Junto, a club founded by Franklin years ago for debate and inquiry. It had recently been revived after languishing for many years. But he never attended.[43] He was a founding member of the Gloucester Fox Hunting Club in October 1766, undoubtedly hoping it would provide a diversion from work. They would have exhilarating rides accompanied by hounds with such names as Tipler, Singwell, Bumper, Slouch, and Sweetlips—all nods to the heavy drinking that occurred on such occasions. But his nonattendance at the first meeting did not bode well for his future participation.[44]

Towards the end of the Assembly's second session, most of Dickinson's legislation went smoothly through the process, was passed by the House, approved by the governor, and then sent to the Board of Trade for royal approval. There were a few snags, however. The committee to evaluate the colony's poor laws did not accomplish its task. And the bill for regulating the courts passed the House but was halted when the governor refused his assent on the grounds that it would be "subversive of justice" because he believed judges should make the rules in their own courts. The House debated it further but eventually dropped the matter in favor of more pressing business.

Dickinson was more concerned with the fate of a law he did not write, An Act for Preventing Abuses in the Indian Trade, which was brought before the governor in late February. Because it contained a provision for taxing the proprietors equally with other Pennsylvanians, the governor rejected it. But the bill's significance to the well-being of Native peoples was clear. Just before the House adjourned on March 4, it heard a petition from the Friendly Association, explaining that the Indians very much wanted to continue trading with "persons who treat them with justice and equity" and urging them to pass a bill. It was imperative that only "men of probity and conscience" trade with them, or "we cannot reasonably expect they will be easily convinced of the excellency of the Christian religion, nor continue alliance with us."[45] The Association requested that the House find some other way to raise money aside from taxation that would allow the governor to pass it.

Dickinson was in full agreement. Since his trip to Easton last spring, where he saw firsthand the exploitation of the Indians, his attitude about them had become more serious. "I think both Prudence & Good Faith require the Continuance of the present Act," he said, "which was calculated to preserve the Indians from the Impositions of the most infamous & extortionate Rascals who trade amongst them— And repeated Promises have been made to the Indians, that the Trade shall be carried on as it now is."[46] Dickinson believed that British subjects should honor their word to all people, especially the Indians, who were treated so poorly in general. With such urgency on this matter, the Assembly removed the offending taxation clause, and the governor passed the bill on April 2. Finally, as bad weather threatened and the members were eager to get home, the House adjourned until the autumn.[47]

The spring brought both sorrow and joy. A friend dear to the Dickinson family, Thomas Willson, whom they called Tommee, died after struggling with illness for some time. He left not only a grieving wife, Elizabeth, but also two children, John, twelve, and Sarah, thirteen. He had named Elizabeth executrix of his will and Dickinson executor. Tommee's death changed Dickinson's life considerably. His will stipulated that Dickinson be named guardian of John and Sarah. He would take the boy immediately into his care, feeding and clothing him with an inheritance of £300. As for his sister, it would not be proper for her to dwell with an unmarried man, so she was to be set up with a family in Philadelphia for one year, her expenses also paid from her inheritances, and she would be under Dickinson's "inspection and direction."[48] She also received two enslaved people, a boy called Bozman and a girl called Rachel, each valued at £18.[49]

Dickinson's life thus altered, seemingly overnight. He had some experience dealing with the Moland children and the family required much attention, but the younger children remained with their mother. Now Dickinson went from living freely as a bachelor to being a surrogate father. But it was a welcome burden. John Willson would be Dickinson's legal apprentice. Dickinson had long enjoyed mentoring the young people in his life—his brother, the children of friends, and his legal apprentices. He was a natural teacher. "I shall think Myself very happy," he would say to them, "if my little Experience can furnish you with any hints that may be of Service to You; & if You will permit Me to look on You as a Brother, I assure You I shall think & write with the same Affection & Freedom as if this was directed to Phil."[50]

On April 28, news arrived that a Treaty of Peace, ending the Seven Years' War—called the French and Indian War in America—had been signed in Paris.[51] The fighting was over. Or so it seemed. Before the celebrations of the peace had subsided, disturbing reports of Indian attacks made their way to Philadelphia from the frontier. By the end of June, it was clear that the government would need to address this renewed violence in their western lands. Governor Hamilton convened the Assembly in an emergency session on July 4 and addressed the House the next morning on the matter.[52] Though the Assembly agreed that the frontier must be protected, its members knew they did not have the funds to pay for such an effort. They also knew they would need a new law to regulate the troops protecting the frontier settlements. Dickinson was appointed to a committee with eight others to draft An Act for Regulating the Officers and Soldiers in the Pay of this Province, which mainly concerned their rights and punishments should they engage in misbehavior or mutiny. A funding bill would have to wait until the House reconvened in September.

Released from his legislative duties, Dickinson tended his law practice and enjoyed distraction from the seriousness of the ongoing hostilities. He was very well these days. In fact, he hadn't felt so robust for several years and was now entirely free from the pain in his breast and the headaches that frequently accompanied it. Money flowed in from his practice, and, as not every lawyer could make a decent living, he felt proud of himself; though it did put him in mind of the line of Scripture he had written in his commonplace book.[53] Proverbs 30:8 said, "Remove far from me vanity and lies: give me neither poverty nor riches; feed me with food convenient for me."[54] He felt as though he could take time to visit the Morris and Cadwalader clans in New Jersey. They were well, and the visit was pleasant, though he came down with a fever and had to stay in bed.

Once back in Philadelphia and fully recovered, only the ongoing violence on the frontier, continuing clashes between Native peoples and British Americans, intruded upon Dickinson's peace. News of Colonel Henry Bouquet's defeat at Bushy Run earlier that month had reached the city, and he could think of little else. It spilled into his letters to friends and family. "Great Numbers of our Frontier Inhabitants have felt the most dreadful Distresses." Now the British seemed to have driven the Indians to retreat for the moment, but, said Dickinson, "We expect them on our Frontiers again in the Fall."[55] He regaled his mother with more harrowing details of the war than she might have liked. His brother Philemon was currently with her in Kent, so Dickinson's mind was more at ease on her account.

Phil, however, was another matter. Dickinson and his mother both worried about "the fellow," as Dickinson affectionately called him, and his plans for the future. Although he had graduated from the College of Philadelphia in 1759 and then studied law with his older brother, he hadn't passed the bar, which they understood to be his design. They hoped his marriage might be imminent. "If he has a Mind to make You—Me—himself & another Person completely happy, he knows the Way," wrote Dickinson to Mary. He need only to propose to the young lady. Yet Dickinson expressed his concern that Phil might miss his chance. "There is that lucky Moment in most People's Lives, that opens Opportunities of Reputation & Dignity— The Prospect neglected & closd, the fantastic Idler languishes in toilsome Obscurity, & venerates for the Remainder of his Days, the Advantages when possest by some wiser Rival, which he himself might have securd." Dickinson hoped that he would have the opportunity of seeing his honored mother soon at one of the Friends' meetings in Philadelphia in October, when they could discuss Phil's prospects for matrimony.[56] They would have to wait four years before Phil wedded his first cousin, Mary Cadwalader.[57] Surely Mary also worried about her eldest's plans.

Dickinson's friends were falling into matrimony one by one. Thomas McKean had just married the lovely Mary Bordon, whom he had been traveling to New Jersey to court. George Read had married Gertrude Ross late last year. Now only Dickinson was unwed. He admitted he was "a little apprehensive" that Read's affections would "be drawn into so small a Circle that You will forget to love your Friends. If You do, I will revenge Myself upon you," he teased, "by taking a Wife, and ceasing to be, if my Heart will permit it, Mrs. Read's and your very affectionate" friend.[58] In truth, at thirty-one, like many men of his age, he longed to be married. But he still had no serious thoughts about anyone in particular. Occasionally, some young lady would capture his imagination, perhaps a piece of his heart and, for a time, he might even become hopelessly besotted. He would write doggerel, begging advice from "Ye shepherds, ye learned in love."[59] But these paroxysms usually passed.

When the September session of the Assembly drew near, Dickinson reflected on his duties and what would be expected of him. Thus far, he hadn't yet spoken at length in the House, but he knew he should be ready for the opportunity. One day, he stepped out to David Hall's shop on Market Street, where he purchased several books that promised to improve his abilities. He believed that "a lawyer should not only be learned, but should have an agreeable and elegant manner of communicating that learning to others."[60] He thus added to his library James Burgh's *The Art of Speaking*, along with Isaac Watts's *The Improvement of the Mind: or, a Supplement to the Art of Logick: Containing a Variety of Remarks and Rules for the Attainment and Communication of Useful Knowledge, in Religion, in the Sciences, and in Common Life*, and also John Ward's *A System of Oratory . . . to Which Is Prefixed an Inaugural Oration, Spoken in Latin*. Though he doubted he would have the opportunity to deliver or attend many lectures in Latin, the style and methodology, he thought, could prove useful. For good measure, he also purchased *Law Tracts* by Blackstone and a ream of paper.[61]

Dickinson was ready when the Assembly was to reconvene on Monday, September 14, though the anticipation of the moment was such that he developed a nagging pain in his jaw.[62] But any anxiety he felt was for naught. A quorum did not appear on that day. Nor did it the following day, nor the next, at which point the clerk was ordered to send the sergeant-at-arms with letters to the delinquent members, notifying them that their presence was required.[63]

Dickinson took the opportunity to respond to his mother's last letter. She planned a significant change in her own life. Tending to Poplar Hall had become exhausting without Samuel. Although she had been managing the plantation largely by herself before he died and for the three years since, she was now sixty-two, and it was too much. She wanted to sell the enslaved people and leave plantation life behind to be in the city with her son.

About selling "their people," her son was in accord. "I can only say," Dickinson told her, "that whatever is agreeable to you, will be perfectly so to me." In particular, he continued, "I believe our sentiments with respect to selling are the same. I would by no means approve of it, unless the People desire it. In such case," he assured her, "I would sell, taking care to get them good masters."

Then, having so thoughtfully considered the welfare of these human beings under his control, he continued, speculating on the market value for their flesh. "If we sell, I think it would be proper to advertise, as prodigious prices are given in New Castle County and in this province. I should expect seventy or eighty pounds at least for women and children on an average." As yet, he was not much troubled by the hypocrisy. The Dickinsons, after all, were kinder than most, though not yet united with Friends in the abolitionism that was quickly gaining momentum in the Society.

"I shall be quite happy when You are disencumberd from the Fatigues of such a Family," he confessed, "& settled in Peace & Ease among your Friends here." He was looking forward to his mother's coming to live with him. "I think You will be much pleasd with the Situation and Conveniences of this House. There is a fine open Passage for the Air backwards; a large pleasant Garden—& the Rooms very good. I am charmd with the Place—so is Aunt Cadwalader—& She says You will be so."[64] There was plenty of room, even with his ward, young John Willson, under his roof. And Mary might well be a help with John and his sister. Though Sarah was in a family, what did Dickinson know about the "inspection and direction" of a young lady?

The Assembly finally achieved a quorum on Friday, September 16 for its final session. Regular business resulted in Dickinson's being placed on several committees to draft legislation for such public necessities as funding a lighthouse on Cape Henlopen, placing buoys in the Delaware River, regulating the nightly watch, and lighting and paving the streets of Philadelphia. By September 30, the last day of the session, all of this legislation passed smoothly through the approval process.

The most important issue, however, held over from the emergency July meeting, remained unresolved: defense of the frontier. Dickinson had been appointed to a committee to draft legislation to fund a militia, which produced a bill to raise £25,000 for the king's use and to allow paper money to be used as legal tender in the colony. But, predictably, Governor Hamilton had vetoed it, claiming it was an injustice to the proprietors to expect that they would accept payment of rents in low-value paper money. They wanted sterling silver, something impossible for poorer inhabitants. Not wanting to give the Penns special treatment, the House refused to budge, and the legislative year ended at the usual impasse and with the frontier undefended.

5

"So long and so dangerous a voyage"

Towards Liberty in Pennsylvania, 1763–1764

October 1, 1763, was election day, and Dickinson was again chosen as a representative for Philadelphia County. Thus far, his mettle as a statesman had hardly been tested. He had proven himself adept at writing and debating legislation, but the last years had been relatively free of controversy, the war and subsequent conflicts with Indians notwithstanding. This was about to change.

The Assembly met on Friday the fourteenth to face the same intractable problem. When Governor Hamilton addressed the House, he described "Accounts of many barbarous and shocking Murders, and other Depredations, having been committed by *Indians* on the Inhabitants of *Northampton* County."[1] He implored the members to put the disagreement with him aside and pass a bill to fund the troops. Seeing the urgency of the matter, the House appointed a committee that included Dickinson and six other members to draft a bill for £24,000 for that purpose. The same committee was also instructed to prepare a bill to prohibit selling guns and other warlike stores to the Indians. A recent report from the governor's office revealed that Indians befriended and converted by the Moravians, a pacifist Christian sect, were trading with enemy Indians and may have been involved in recent murders in Bethlehem. The report recommended bringing the Moravian Indians closer to Philadelphia to monitor them. Proving that they could, indeed, act when they wanted to, members found a creative way to fund the troops by reallocating funds, both bills were passed on October 22, and the House adjourned until January 16.

Thomas Penn had long been dissatisfied with the course of events, which had just drawn a stern rebuke from British officials Sir Jeffery Amherst, commander in chief of the British Army, and Sir William Samuel Johnson, superintendent of Indian Affairs. In the recess, he replaced Governor Hamilton with his nephew, John Penn. Although the younger Penn had no political or executive experience, his appointment on October 31 was celebrated, and all parties looked to him as the solution to their problems.

The British government also signaled that it wanted conflicts with Indians to cease. On December 8, news of one of the most consequential decisions by George III reached Philadelphia. As part of the new settlement at the end of the war, he had issued a proclamation setting a new boundary line for American colonists for their westward settlements. Now, among other things, they were no longer permitted to settle west of the Appalachian Mountains. This meant that the much-coveted Ohio Territory would remain in Indian hands and out of reach of European settlers and land speculators.

To many colonial Americans, this was an infringement on both their livelihoods and the Divine Will. How many prayers, days of fasting, and days of thanksgiving had they offered up? How many personal sacrifices had they endured? To them, their victory over the French papists was a clear sign that God had favored the Protestant cause and wanted them to march forth to their promised destiny, to take the land and convert its heathen inhabitants. The Proclamation of 1763 could only be a sign that the administration did not share this religious imperative.

Though Quakers and those in their orbit, such as Dickinson, did not share this view of Divine Providence, most inhabitants on the frontier, who were mostly fiery Scotch-Irish Presbyterians, did. Tensions between the frontiersmen and the Indians whose land they coveted had never been higher in the seventy years since Pennsylvania had been founded. On December 14, it finally erupted in a shocking spate of violence, the likes of which the colony had never experienced.

Philadelphia remained ignorant of the calamity on the frontier for a week. In the meantime, Lieutenant Governor Penn had called the Assembly back into another emergency session to comply with a request from General Amherst to raise more troops to join those of other colonies in defending against the Delaware, Shawnee, and other tribes that had attacked Britons. Dickinson presented a spirited advocacy for it, along with John Hughes, Joseph Galloway, and Benjamin Franklin, who was returned from England. All of these men except for Franklin, as well as eight others, were designated a committee to bring in an answer to the governor's speech. Though predominantly a Quaker Assembly, even Friends were in favor of measures to, as assemblyman Samuel Foulke put it, "subdue the savages who infest our frontiers."[2] Even Quakers, it seemed, had learned to distinguish between their Indian friends and enemies. But their increasingly bifurcated Indian policy was breaking down.

As the House debated on the evening of the twenty-first, news of the calamity on the frontier known as the "Paxton Riots" finally made its way to the city. A group of militant Scotch-Irish Presbyterians called the Paxton Boys, angered by the inaction of the government, had taken matters into their own hands and slaughtered a group of six Indians at Conestoga Manor. Allegedly, their provocation was that an Indian named Renatus had murdered an innkeeper. But the Paxtons' victims were peaceful Christians. They had been butchered, and had others in their community not been away at the time, all would have been murdered.[3]

The Assembly, and indeed most of Philadelphia, was horrified. But before they could respond to that atrocity, news of another massacre, again by the Paxtons, reached them. On December 27, they had murdered and mutilated the remaining Conestoga Indians who had survived the first attack— fourteen men, women, and children—who had been placed in a workhouse in Lancaster for their protection.

As eyewitnesses came forward, the public learned the gruesome details. William Henry of Lancaster reported that a group of men had come "equipped for Murder." They had tomahawked men, women, and children. "Towards the middle of the gaol Yard, along the West side of the Wall, lay a stout Indian, whom I particularly noticed to have been Shot in the Breast, his Legs were chopped with the Tomohawk—his hands cut off; and finally a Rifle ball discharged in his Mouth so that his Head was blown to atoms; and the Brains were splashed against, and yet hanging to the Wall, for 3 or 4 feet around." All the victims had been "Shot—Scalped—hack'd—and cut to pieces."[4]

The governor decided to escort 140 Moravian Indians who were being held in protective custody in Philadelphia out of the province to safety in the colony of New York. But before they could cross the border, officials from that colony turned them away. The Indians were not the only ones in terror of their lives. As they made their way back to Philadelphia, the governor received a report that the Paxtons were mobilizing to march on the city and wreak havoc upon their enemies, the Quakers. Rumors flew that "fifteen hundred Men would come down in order to kill the said Indians, and that if Fifteen hundred were not enough, Five thousand were ready to join them."[5] As Philadelphians anticipated the Paxton Boys' arrival, Lieutenant Governor John Penn ordered troops to be at the ready and to shoot anyone approaching the barracks where the Indians were being held. First, however, he needed an updated riot act before he could deploy His Majesty's troops against subjects of the Crown. Speaker Norris was too ill to attend the Assembly in the State House, so, on February 3, 1764, the members met at his bedside in the home of his younger brother, Charles Norris, one block away at Chestnut and Fourth Streets.[6] They appointed two men, Dickinson and Galloway, to revise and extend an act passed under George I. The men returned that afternoon with a draft, which the House debated.[7]

Rather than adjourn for the day as usual, they reconvened after dinner, at which time they passed Dickinson and Galloway's revised Riot Act, authorizing Penn to deploy troops against subjects of the Crown. When they delivered the bill to the governor, they also informed him that the Paxton Boys were on the march. Penn quickly assented. The following day, Penn called all Philadelphians to meet at the State House. When some three thousand people had gathered in a cold, driving rain, the governor, accompanied by his Council, the Assembly, and the city magistrates, had the new Riot Act read aloud.[8]

A large group of men then formed an association for the defense of the Indians, and the governor issued an urgent message to the House that "the same Spirit and frantic Rage, which actuated those who lately put to Death the *Indians* in *Lancaster* Country, still prevails among them." He had good cause to believe that a murderous mob was heading their way. He believed that force would be necessary, because "they have already given abundant Proof, that neither Religion, Humanity, nor Laws, are Objects of their Consideration."[9]

A few days later, Philadelphia was in a frenzy of preparation, bells ringing and drums beating to summon inhabitants to action. The Quakers had particular reason to be afraid. Not only did their Society still control the Assembly in numbers disproportionate to the general population of the province, but Israel Pemberton's Friendly Association also continued to work closely with Indians. Pemberton and his brothers, James and John, worried rightfully that he was a special target of the Paxtons. Many Scotch-Irish believed that he had planted spies and agents among them and profited illicitly from the fur trade at their expense. He rushed to remove his family and himself from harm's way.[10]

Most shockingly, about two hundred young Quakers were now bearing arms to meet the Paxtons. One disgruntled observer wrote that "when their King and Country call them to Arms, they plead Conscience, and will tell thee, with a pious Air, and meek Countenance, 'they would rather perish by the Sword than use it against the Enemies of the State.'" Once threatened, however, Quakers were no different from the Paxtons, "eagerly desiring Combat, and thirsting for the Blood of those his Opponents."[11] It was a display of hypocrisy that the Scotch-Irish would not forget.

Dickinson now thought about how best to preserve human life. Though not opposed to the use of martial force when necessary, he was also not convinced that calling up arms against their fellow subjects should be a first resort. Instead, he thought about how to diffuse the anger and calm inflamed tempers. Whereas Penn believed that the Paxtons were godless and appealing to religion was useless, Dickinson disagreed. He knew that religion was likely at the very heart of things. The Paxtons were Presbyterians. Theirs was an angry Old Testament God who demanded an eye for an eye and decreed that his chosen people had not just a religious duty to God but a moral right to protect themselves by defending their covenant with him. When that covenant was threatened by Satan masquerading as savages, the faithful were obliged to destroy them. But there was more to the Bible than vengeance, as Dickinson hoped to remind them. Yet he also knew that religious arguments alone wouldn't work; they must be combined with an appeal to the Paxtons' self-interest.

Dickinson thus took up his pen and wrote "A Letter to the Inhabitants of the Frontiers," taking the same Quakerly approach he had used in his essay "Reflections on the Flag of Truce Trade." He would not alienate the Scotch-Irish, as most publications had, by condemning them for barbarism, although this was precisely his view. Instead, he would win their confidence by casting himself as a sympathizer with their grievances, an ally in their cause, and an admirer of their bravery. He chose his words carefully so as not to suggest any negative judgment or betray his true sentiments about their actions. They couldn't know that he had just written the Riot Act under which they would be punished or that he was assisting the lawyer defending Renatus, the Indian who had supposedly murdered the innkeeper, in his trial.[12] In this strategic move, Dickinson accepted that the virtue of honesty had to be sacrificed for the higher principle of saving human lives.

As with his flag-of-truce essay, he began by signaling his respect for the Paxtons and sympathy with their position. "My dear Countrymen," he wrote, "Permit a sincere Friend to offer his Sentiments to your cool Consideration." Appealing to them as brave men who appreciated candor, he explained that he trusted he could speak frankly to them about their plans to kill the Indians in government custody. "I am extremely sensible of Reasons You have for detesting the whole Indian Race," he continued. "My Heart weeps Blood, for the dear Relations You have lost by their Savage Barbarity."

He then appealed to the Paxtons from several angles, mixing his honest sentiments with untruths and feigned bigotry. Playing on their racial prejudices, he signaled solidarity with them, referring to Indians as a "sett of poor miserable despicable, yellow Wretches." Counting on their deeply held religious beliefs, he then pivoted to Scripture, comparing the Paxton Boys to Joshua, who spared the lives of the deceitful Gibeonites. "Many of these Indians," he reminded them, "have been instructed in the Doctrines of our most holy Religion . . . reclaiming them from their Savage Customs & changing them into civilizd People." He next appealed to their common sense, arguing that violence begets violence, and massacring the Indians would only invite retaliation. With every Indian they killed, he argued, they also killed a white person. Moreover, further bloodshed would invite a military occupation by the British government. "It is a well known Truth," he warned, evoking the general fear of a standing army, "that the People of England have been a long Time desirous of establishing a military Force in America, to be maintained at our Expence. They have waited hitherto for some Pretence or Excuse for this." The Paxtons' actions would be all they need to compel Americans to support troops among them.[13] Despite having written a riot act to punish them only days before, he also assured them that he was "no Government Man" and reminded them that God had placed them under the Pennsylvania government, which was actively working to protect them. Finally, and most importantly, he closed with a deeply held principle, one that justified all previous untruths—he urged unity. "The worst Enemies We have," he said, "are those who attempt to weaken the Strength of this Province at this Time of Public Danger, by dividing Us into Parties—& making wicked Distinctions of Countries & Religions— But my Brethren," he asked, "are We not all Christians & Pennsylvanians? Is not the Cause of each of Us the Cause of all?"[14]

When a delegation of religious leaders rode to meet the Paxtons on the outskirts of Philadelphia, they surely used some of Dickinson's logic to persuade the men to put down their arms and pick up their pens to write a declaration of their grievances. The Paxtons abandoned their violent plan and instead wrote two documents, a Declaration and *Remonstrance of the Distressed and Bleeding Frontier Inhabitants*, containing their grievances and demands, and sent them to the Assembly. Although the crisis of the moment was averted, tensions between the frontiersmen and the government continued to simmer beneath the surface for the next decade.

Meanwhile, the House was again required to pass legislation to fund frontier defense for the year 1764. And again, the proprietors adhered to their usual strictures against taxing their lands. Now they also prohibited rents to be paid in anything but sterling. In response, Franklin proposed legislation for issuing interest-bearing bills of credit to restore a measure of equality between the wealthy and the poor.

In the debates, Dickinson vigorously supported Franklin's bill, which would have denied the Penns significant income. Although he considered Thomas Penn a friend from his London days, he would not be swayed from his principles. He declared that "it is the interest of this province that the People should grant no further Prerogatives to the Honourable Proprietary Family, than what they now possess—& that such a precedent as is at present insisted on, will be of very dangerous Consequence." Believing, as the Chancery Court held, that "Equality is Equity," Dickinson argued passionately that "the same Justice is due to the meanest Person in the province" as was due the proprietor. To do otherwise was contrary to the "Sprit of Liberty."[15]

Dickinson's speech was, if anything, a little too convincing. Quaker Assemblyman Foulke was so moved that he proclaimed that to remove their necks from beneath the foot of the tyrant, he hoped it would "please Our Gracious Soveraign to interpose & take the Government out of ye Hands of the Proprietaries, which I believe is the wish of every one who retains a Just sense of Freedom."[16] But this took Dickinson's idea of resistance too far. Taxing the proprietors fairly was one thing; removing them—which also meant abolishing the Charter—was something else altogether. Indeed, it was the most dangerous suggestion anyone could make. This would not be the last time Dickinson's energy for a cause would be misconstrued by those with less forethought and lead to unintended consequences. The ship of state began to list to the left.

As the spring legislative session drew to a close, the Assembly continued wrangling with the governor over the supply bill. By now, a sizable faction of the House believed a conspiracy theory promulgated by Franklin and Galloway that Penn had been not just placating the Paxtons but also secretly encouraging them to terrorize the Assembly in order to force it to bow to the Penn family's legislative agenda.[17] Franklin and Galloway had drafted twenty-six resolves, each of which leveled sharp indictments of proprietary power in Pennsylvania and accused the Penns of everything from extortion to corruption of morals in the colony to undermining the prerogatives of the Crown. While Dickinson was confined to his bed with fever, each resolve passed unanimously.[18] The Assembly then adjourned for six weeks.

When Dickinson obtained a copy of the resolves, he saw that the most alarming one was the proposal to abolish the proprietary government and the 1701 Charter of Privileges and make Pennsylvania a royal colony. His alarm was not for love of the Penns; rather, the constitutional implications concerned him. Should the Charter be abolished, all the distinctive rights and privileges that Quakers enjoyed would cease. Someone like Franklin, who did not share the Quakers' faith and only allied himself with them for political purposes, could not be expected to concern himself with such matters. Dickinson found Galloway's approval of the plan more mysterious, considering Galloway's Quaker heritage. But given his affinity for power and prestige, which Dickinson had long witnessed, perhaps it was not so mysterious after all.

During the recess, Dickinson engaged in other duties, including preparing for court, aiding the Moland family with their problems, and attending meetings of the Library Company. Primarily, however, he pondered how to respond to the resolves and began drafting a speech against the abolition of the 1701 Charter of Privileges.

As he wrote, Dickinson was spurred to new urgency by news from England. With funds running low, Parliament had determined that it could tax the colonies despite Americans' lack of representation in that body. The members of Parliament cited the depressed state of the nation, with Britain overloaded with taxes and debt from the late war, a good amount of which was incurred by defending the American colonies. Accordingly, they passed the Revenue Act, also called the Sugar Act, which updated a duty on molasses, a staple not just in American cooking but also in making rum.

More ominous than the duties in the Sugar Act was a line stipulating that violations of the act could be tried in *any* court of record. Previously all such cases had been tried in the Vice Admiralty Court in the region where the vessel was seized, keeping the accused at home before sympathetic judges. But just before the passage of the Sugar Act, a new Vice Admiralty Court had been established in Halifax, Nova Scotia, that would preside over all the others. Thus, the accused would be removed from his local environment and tried at a distance, costing him time and money and denying him friendly judges and witnesses who could testify on his behalf. Such an affront to justice, thought Dickinson, made the British government's interference in the flag-of-truce trade appear mild by comparison. The papers also reported that Parliament was pondering a worse plan still—imposing a stamp tax to raise a revenue on the colonies.[19]

That Franklin and Galloway were at this moment proposing to abolish the current government and place the colony in royal hands struck Dickinson as extremely dangerous to the people of Pennsylvania. The Crown had long disapproved of how Quakers governed Pennsylvania, and now, with Parliament's new, ominous stance towards the colonies, throwing aside the charter that protected them would mean the end of William Penn's "holy experiment" and many of their civil liberties.

When the House reconvened in mid-May, a fissure in the Quaker party that had been forming for some time deepened. Over the first fifty years of Quaker rule, Friends had come to care less about members of the Assembly "bearing the cross"—as they put it—of being true Quakers, as long as they adopted the outward forms of Quakerism—using the plain speech, dressing plainly, and supporting the Quaker agenda. When Quakers reformed their Society in 1756 and the most devout Quakers abruptly abdicated their seats in Assembly, they left it to those who took their testimonies less seriously. Now these members were led by a man many devout Quakers believed was dangerous. Though Franklin could play the part of a Quaker when it served his purposes, he didn't really share Quakers' faith and practice. Now he was leading a set of "young hotspurs," as Isaac Norris thought of them, with Joseph Galloway, a Quaker turned Anglican, first among them.[20]

The issue of religious liberty was personal for Dickinson, and not merely because his dearest relations were Quakers. Though one of the youngest members of the House, Dickinson felt a kinship with the older members, who were like his parents. These were men who took their faith seriously but also knew how to fulfill their duties to their constituents, understanding that doctrinal rigidity would help no one. But Dickinson was not an actual Quaker and would never become one. He was a dissenter among dissenters. Although he was what Quakers would later call a "birthright" Friend, born to Quaker parents in good standing with their meeting, he had no desire to formalize his membership. Doing so would entail applying to Philadelphia Monthly Meeting and enduring a months-long scrutiny of his beliefs.[21] And although he agreed with Friends on most major theological tenets—spiritual equality, universality of salvation, and the ability of all people to preach the Gospel—since the Quakers' reformation during the late war, he knew that his conviction about the necessity of militias for self-defense would put him at odds with the leadership. He thus preferred to remain independent from any faction in order to adhere to his deepest convictions. Pennsylvania's 1701 constitution protected the consciences of all people, and to lose sight of this fact was reckless.

On May 18, two petitions to the king appeared before the House, one from the freeholders of Pennsylvania and the other from members of the Society of Friends praying that his Majesty "would be graciously pleased to take the Government of this Province into His immediate Care and Direction."[22] Dickinson could only imagine what methods Franklin and Galloway had used during the adjournment to induce thirty-five hundred inhabitants to sign petitions for the change. Men who were poor and unable to read or write were easily led by their unscrupulous "betters." But these were only a small fraction of the 300,000 souls who lived in Pennsylvania.[23] Dickinson knew that if the rest could be made aware of the dangers, they would choose more wisely.

At this most inopportune moment, Dickinson's fever returned. On May 23, he awoke feeling unwell, and for the first time this session, he was compelled to remain in bed. Although still very ill the following day, he forced himself to attend the Assembly. He was astonished at what had transpired during his one-day absence. Norris had tried to prevent any business of substance from being conducted until more members were present, but Franklin and Galloway began debate on the change of government and had a committee appointed to draft a petition. Later the same day, the committee presented the petition. It was as though they had waited precisely for the moment when Dickinson was not present to object. When the petition was read for the second time on the afternoon of the twenty-fourth, Dickinson took his first opportunity to speak against it.

Galloway and his allies complained that Dickinson's dissent was premature, that he should have waited for the petition to be transcribed or even signed. But since the twenty-six resolves had passed so easily, Dickinson felt he couldn't wait and gathered his notes quickly. Although assemblymen always spoke extemporaneously, he believed it was his duty to be well prepared. When Franklin had noticed him preparing notes on an earlier occasion, he had praised his young colleague for introducing the method.[24]

At this moment, Dickinson assumed a role that would define not merely this moment but the remainder of his life: that of the trimmer. The nautical metaphor of the trimmer was an old one in politics, and it had two opposite meanings. A trimmer might be the person who trims the sails of the ship to catch the prevailing wind, that is, a political opportunist. He is a contempt-ible figure because he is reliable only in his pursuit of his self-interest. By contrast, the other meaning of trimmer is the person who shifts the ballast, or cargo, to prevent the ship of state from capsizing and to keep it on course. This principled trimmer, while appearing to shift his position in relation to the opposing sides—starboard or port, right or left—is actually allowing the ship to steer a straight and true course to the final destination: liberty. In the late-seventeenth century, English statesman George Savile, Lord Halifax, explained in his pamphlet *The Character of a Trimmer* that "Our *Trimmer* owneth a Passion for liberty. . . . [H]e thinketh it hard for a Soul that doth not love Liberty, ever to raise it self to another World, he taketh it to be the foun-dation of all vertue, and the only seasoning that giveth a relish to life."[25]

Acting the trimmer and throwing his weight to counter the radical measures, Dickinson began by asserting that to protect the people of Pennsylvania, cooler heads should prevail, and they should ponder their next steps carefully. As was his wont, he reached first for common ground with his opponents, agreeing that the proprietary instructions that prohibited taxing the Penns' land were unjust.[26] Indeed, he had spoken against them repeatedly. But, he continued, the House would be acting rashly if it abolished its sacred charter. The remedy should be in proportion to the disease and undertaken only after due consideration. "It seems to me," he explained, "that a people who intend an innovation of their government, ought to choose the most proper *time*, and the most proper *method* for accomplishing their purposes; and ought seriously to weigh all the probable and possible *consequences* of such a measure."[27] He then considered examples from history, both modern and ancient, in the governments of England, Denmark, Holland, and Rome, before he addressed each of the conditions in turn.

First, the *timing* of their petition was especially poor. Drawing on his per-sonal experience in London when he witnessed the debate over the behavior of the Assembly before the Board of Trade, Dickinson assured the House that the king and his ministers did not look favorably on the Assembly. If His Majesty's Council was against them then, he queried, "What reasonable hope can we entertain of a more favourable determination *now*?"[28]

Second, the *method* of requesting the change was objectionable. They were enraged and seeking change not out of reverence for the king but ha-tred for the proprietors. Moreover, "At the same time we mean to preserve our privileges: But how are these two points to be reconciled?" he asked.

"Certainly it will be thought an unprecedented Stile of petitioning the crown, that humbly asks a favour, and boldly prescribes the terms, on which it must be granted."[29] He described the possible scenarios of requesting a change while insisting their privileges remain intact. None was viable. Their choice was either to "renounce the laws and liberties framed and delivered down to us by our careful ancestors: or we may tell his Majesty with a surly discontent, 'that we will not submit to his *implored protection*, but on such conditions, as we please to impose on him.'"[30]

Finally, the consequence of a change would be disastrous. "At this period," he warned, "when the administration is regulating new colonies, and designing, as we are told the *strictest reformations* in the old, it is not likely that they will grant an invidious distinction in our favour." He reminded them of the Sugar Act, passed on April 5, and ominous tidings of Parliament contemplating a stamp duty.

Lest the House forget the unique privileges its members enjoyed, Dickinson enumerated them. First, "we here enjoy that best and greatest of all rights, *a perfect religious freedom*." He went on to describe the participation of religious dissenters in all facets of the government when "posts of honour and profit are unfettered with *oaths* or *tests*." These were particularly Quaker liberties, and they were in danger of being lost.[31] In Pennsylvania, Quakers were allowed to affirm their loyalty to the government rather than swear, which enabled them to serve in the legislature, on juries, on the bench, and as witnesses.

The matter of religious liberty was not merely academic to Dickinson; he himself was a religious dissenter—in some ways even more than the Quakers themselves. Although raised as a Quaker and deeply religious in Quakerly ways, he disliked organized religion. He rejected some aspects of Quakerism, such as endogamy, that is, marrying only within the meeting, which is what had alienated Samuel Dickinson from Quakerism when John's sister married an Anglican. He found that church or meeting structures could lead believers to become too rigid, valuing the superficial shows of virtue and piety while ignoring deeper faith and motives. Just because someone dressed plainly or used "thee" and "thou" did not, alone, make him a good Quaker, obedient to God's will. This was precisely why the Pennsylvania Assembly was now dominated by men such as Benjamin Franklin, who deftly adopted political Quakerism—the virulent dissent against the authorities—while ignoring religious Quakerism, especially pacifism broadly construed to mean doing to others as they would be done by and preserving unity in the province. In the name of resisting the proprietors, these men might well destroy Pennsylvania by abolishing the Charter of Privileges. Dickinson thus valued a civil constitution that allowed him to remain "unchurched" while following the dictates of God in his conscience.

Dickinson also celebrated the democratic nature of the Pennsylvania government, with a powerful unicameral legislature that suffered "no checks, from a council instituted, in fancied imitation of the House of Lords," sat upon its own adjournments, and was re-elected each year. Although Britons generally believed "democracy" was a derogatory term akin to "anarchy," in Pennsylvania, the people had more say in the laws and government than elsewhere in the empire.

"Let any impartial person reflect how contradictory some of these privileges are to the most antient principles of the English constitution, and how directly opposite other of them are to the settled prerogatives of the crown." He challenged his colleagues to consider "what probability we have of retaining them on a *requested* change."[32] Any request for greater liberties than what Englishmen enjoyed in Britain would be considered not liberty but license, a critical difference in English political theory. Liberty was the proper and just exercise of rights; license was overstepping those proper bounds and grasping for what they shouldn't have. License invariably led to anarchy.

Yet another threat Dickinson foresaw was the imposition of Anglicanism. Through much of early Pennsylvania history, Quakers contended with Anglicans' attempts to oppress them and worried about a possible establishment of the Church in Pennsylvania and the installation of an American bishop in the colonies. Either of these developments could reduce Quakers to being "Dissenters in their own Country."[33] In the past they had suffered brutal persecution at the hands of the Church of England, and they should not wish for a return of that condition. Dickinson warned that Anglicans "will be extremely desirous to have *that* church as well secured, and as much distinguished as possible in the American colonies: especially in those colonies, where it is overborne, as it were, by dissenters."[34] It was not only the "ungovernable" Quakers who would have to worry, Dickinson advised; the Crown knew that the Presbyterians, another dissenting sect, were responsible for the Paxton Riots. "Thus the blame of everything disreputable to this province, is cast on one or the other of these dissenting sects—circumstances that I imagine will neither be forgot nor neglected by his Majesty's Council."

Dickinson challenged his colleagues to remember their duty to the people of Pennsylvania. They had been chosen by the people of the province in free and fair elections under the present constitution. "The measure now proposed," he explained, "has a direct tendency to endanger this constitution; and therefore in my opinion, we have *no right* to engage in it, without the *almost universal consent of the people*, expressed in the plainest manner." The constitution of Pennsylvania was not simply a piece of paper with their rights and liberties written upon it; it was the body of the people themselves, whose will the Assembly must follow. "Our *Trimmer*," said Lord Halifax, "admireth our blessed Constitutions, in which Dominion and Liberty are reconcil'd."[35]

As Dickinson acted the trimmer, shifting the ballast with an eye towards religious liberty as Pennsylvania's destination, he described the province as a ship of state heading into uncharted waters. "Let not *us* then, in expectation of *smooth seas*, and an *undisturbed course*, too rashly venture our *little vessel* that hath safely sailed round *our own well-known* shores, upon the *midst* of the *untried deep*, without being first fully convinced, that her *make* is strong enough to bear the *weather* she may meet with, and that she is well *provided* for so long and so dangerous a voyage." The trimmer serves a noble purpose, but his is dangerous and thankless work. He literally holds sway, and both sides want his weight with them. When he refuses, he becomes the target of both extremes. If one prevails, it could doom the vessel and crush him in the process.

With this danger in mind, Dickinson concluded by echoing the resolution he had made to himself as he finished his training at the Middle Temple: to stand for right regardless of personal cost. "To have concealed my real sentiments, or to have counterfeited such as I do not entertain, in a deliberation of *so much consequence* as the present, would have been the *basest hypocrisy*," though it "would have been the most *politic* part for me to have acted." He would not play politics with the happiness of the people. "I *detest* and *despise* all its *arts*, and all its *advantages*." By standing strongly against certain powerful men, he knew he would incur the wrath of some. "A good man," he insisted, "*ought* to serve his country, even tho' she *resents* his services." It was his duty to obey "the *unbiassed dictates* of my *reason* and *conscience*."[36]

When Dickinson finished, Galloway rose and spoke for about four minutes but Isaac Norris appeared so ill that the House thought it proper to adjourn. Several members, including Norris, approached Dickinson and declared he had fully spoken their sentiments. John Ross affirmed that he had clarified the issues, and he was glad to have it more thoroughly considered. Dickinson was requested to leave his notes on the table, but he demurred, as the notes were imperfect. He would prepare them as soon as he could.[37]

A few days later, Isaac Norris resigned as speaker again, citing his health. Despite his encouraging words to Dickinson, he requested that the House elect Franklin as speaker, which meant the petition would advance over Dickinson's objections. In addition to readying his speech, Dickinson also summarized the main points into a succinct protest for inclusion in the official minutes of the House. But when he made the motion to include it, seconded by two members, only three out of the twenty-seven members voted in favor. Outmaneuvered and feeling betrayed, the three resolved amongst themselves to publish the protest in the papers. It appeared in July, angering Franklin and Galloway.[38]

One day after an exhausting and tense session, as the members filed out of the State House, perhaps Galloway, who thought nothing of publicly mocking another man, made a snide remark on Dickinson's defeat, knowing Dickinson would overhear it. Whatever the provocation, suddenly, the two men were facing off on the steps of the State House.[39] The anger Dickinson had suppressed towards Galloway for the past six years finally erupted. Since the Smith trial when Galloway had publicly humiliated him, Dickinson had managed to tolerate his colleague's arrogance and rigidity sufficiently to serve as Galloway's co-counsel in court and to draft legislation together. But he had reached his limit. Fisticuffs ensued. Someone might have seen Galloway make a grab for Dickinson's prominent nose.

As the men were pulled apart, Dickinson, losing all composure and forgetting his Quaker principles, did something he had never imagined he would do—he lost all composure and challenged Galloway to a duel.[40] Galloway, perhaps sensing that he had pushed things too far, declined to respond. Dickinson was enraged by this and likely relieved as well.

Though the petition was now on its way to Richard Jackson, the Assembly's agent in Great Britain, some of Dickinson's warnings had gotten through to the members. The Committee of Correspondence was ordered to "proceed with the utmost Caution." If Jackson felt there was any "Danger of our losing those inestimable Privileges," he was "to suspend the presenting of the said Petition."[41]

Dickinson was glad to put the matter behind him once the Assembly adjourned. When Isaac Norris pressed him to publish his speech, he resisted. But when some gentlemen in the city, his constituents, requested a copy, believing it his duty to comply, he sent it to them. He then left for a vacation in the Jerseys to regain his health. While he was away, the gentlemen in possession of his speech decided to publish it without consulting him. And they also added a preface by the one person who was calculated to enrage Franklin and Galloway more than anyone: none other than William Smith.[42] Smith had recently stepped off a ship from England, just in time to be informed of the controversy and lend a hand.[43] There remained abundant raw feelings between Smith and the Galloway-Franklin alliance, which had done its best to ensure Smith languished in prison after his farcical trial by the Assembly.

The endorsement of his speech by Smith, a solid supporter of the proprietary, was problematic for Dickinson, linking him to a faction that he did not represent and, in fact, disagreed with frequently and vehemently. On June 29, before he returned from the Jerseys, the *Speech* was available for purchase, and in short order it went into a second edition and one in German. It took several months before Dickinson learned who had authored the preface.

Responses to the *Speech* appeared swiftly with both praise and ridicule. The first, an anonymous pamphlet probably by Galloway, was called *The Maybe*. It was a derisive, mocking piece, designed to draw attention to the uncertainty of the dangers Dickinson highlighted and, predictably, cast him as a supporter of proprietary power. "On the first view of his performance," sneered the author, "I was surprised at the wonderful depth of his *logic*, and the prodigious labour he was at in collecting so great a number of *ifs* and *maybe's* to support the cause of liberty." To this author, fear of losing basic liberties was nothing more than visions of "Raw Head and Bloody Bones," the bogeymen children imagine in the dark.[44] In fact, Dickinson had proven himself as a staunch opponent of preferential treatment for the proprietors and an advocate only of the charter privileges of the people of Pennsylvania. Moreover, the alarms he raised were solidly in the Whig tradition of due vigilance at the encroachment of power against the people.

The most consequential effect of the *Speech* and Dickinson's work against the move for royal government was the transformation of old factions in the Assembly and the formation of new ones. He masterfully built a new coalition for his cause, demonstrating his inherent understanding of what was important to the people of Pennsylvania, his keen observation of factional politics, and his considerable powers of persuasion. The Presbyterians had become convinced that the Quaker party was pursuing royal government with the aim of subduing and oppressing them. They began mobilizing to resist the change, with leading lights such as evangelist minister Gilbert

Tennent preaching sermons against it. When Tennent died unexpectedly, Presbyterians looked for a new leader and set their sights on Dickinson. But as a principled trimmer, he was no more a tool of the Presbyterians than he was of the proprietors. Their motives differed significantly: the Presbyterians opposed the change because they distrusted the political Quakers; Dickinson opposed it because he wanted to protect religious liberty. He thus became the de facto leader of a growing segment of the Quaker party, consisting of older members such as Norris, that rejected Franklin-Galloway politics. Instead, they hewed to an older model of Quaker politics that valued the Charter, understood how to navigate their commitments to their faith that did not compromise their civil obligations as legislators, and would work with the proprietors and the Crown on matters such as defense.

Among the converts to Dickinson's cause were George Bryan and Charles Thomson. Both were merchants and "Old Side Presbyterians," meaning that they disapproved of the revivalism of Gilbert Tennant; they were also fervent patriots.[45] Both became Dickinson's friends, and Thomson and Dickinson formed a bond that would last a lifetime. For all their similarities, they could have been brothers. They were equally articulate and even looked alike, both tall and thin with prominent noses. And now that Dickinson's *Speech* had pried Thomson away from Franklin, who was untroubled by a possible stamp tax, he and Dickinson along with Thomas McKean and George Read, began keeping a close watch on British measures.

Over the hot summer of 1764, most Pennsylvanians were so consumed with their partisan battles that Parliament's new taxation acts went into effect with little notice. New Englanders, however, were paying attention. Massachusetts lawyer James Otis published a pamphlet that caused a great commotion throughout the colonies. *The Rights of the British Colonies Asserted and Proved*, challenging the legality of the new taxes, was reprinted widely in the colonies and London. But it got mixed reviews. Though many, including Dickinson, praised it for supporting American rights, others found that it conceded the rights of the colonists in favor of parliamentary power.

The pamphlet was also unclear, treating complicated legal issues that Otis failed to explain in ways that his readers, even well-informed ones, could understand. Otis's shortcomings inspired Dickinson to believe that he could do it better. He suspected Otis was wrong when he argued for no distinction between internal and external taxes. But he would have to ponder the matter further. For now, he was inclined to agree with Otis's central claim: that Parliament should be obeyed. Dickinson decided to bide his time and await further developments. One thing of which he was certain, however, was that this was not the moment to abandon the Pennsylvania constitution.

On August 11, as Dickinson prepared to leave for court in the Lower Counties, a pamphlet appeared called *The Speech of Joseph Galloway*, which Galloway claimed to have given in the House the same day that Dickinson gave his speech.[46] Dickinson was incredulous that it had been published, for Galloway had spoken not one sentence of it in the House. Galloway's "pretended speech," as Dickinson thought of it, attempted to undermine Dickinson's arguments, inflate the threat from the Penn family, and express confidence that the king and ministry would protect the rights and liberties of Pennsylvanians, all the while casting aspersions on Dickinson.

Galloway was aided in his effort by Franklin. Annoyed by the personal abuse he had experienced at the hands of the proprietary party and feeling he had restrained himself long enough, Franklin retaliated against Dickinson as well, though his junior colleague had never uttered a word against him. Pretending to offer Dickinson avuncular counsel, he wrote a preface to Galloway's speech. In sarcastic tones, he explained that Dickinson, "tho' long hated by some"—undoubtedly Galloway—had become a leader of the proprietary faction. To the supporters of the Penns he was "a *Sage* in the Law, and an *Oracle* in Matters relating to our Constitution." Franklin continued, "I would only advise him carefully to preserve the Panegyrics with which they have adorn'd him: In time they may serve to console him, by balancing the Calumny they shall load him with, when he does not go *through* with them in all their Measures."

After the preface came a nasty little "Advertisement" that served as a prelude to the speech, wherein Galloway and Franklin accused Dickinson of neglecting his duty to his constituents, saying he "seldom attended" the House due to his "Indolence." But these charges were fabricated. Dickinson had a clear record of opposing the proprietors; his motives for preserving the Charter were rather about protecting religious liberty; and he had attended the House diligently all spring, excepting two unavoidable absences due to fever. Perhaps feeling twinges of regret, Franklin later confided to Richard Jackson about his preface. "To cooler People," he confessed, "it may possibly seem too severe."[47]

Dickinson set off for court in the Lower Counties with his anger refreshed. He was also mystified by Galloway's behavior. He should not have been surprised that a man who would make up a speech he never gave would also attack the character of others. But why? "Why should he engage in this *preposterous* project? *Why* should he so industriously endeavour to exhibit me as a villain to my country, for speaking my sentiments in that place where my country had commanded me to speak them?"[48] As someone who was confident in his place in the world and attempted to conduct himself with scrupulous honesty, Dickinson was at a loss to understand the motives of an opponent without such scruples. His youthful idealism collided with political realities.

Over the next weeks, Dickinson traveled from New Castle to Dover and back up again, his time almost wholly consumed by the schedule of the courts. In small intervals, he stole moments to write a reply to Galloway's pretended speech, struggling to keep his anger in check. "To act honestly and to be traduced," he knew, "has been the fate of many men. To bear slanders with temper, and to entertain a proper pity or contempt for their weak or wicked authors has been the lot of few. I hope I shall be able so far to suppress the resentment naturally arising from a sense of unprovoked injuries." As he began his reply, his resolve to maintain his temper quickly failed; he could not resist swiping at his opponent for not responding to his demand for a duel. So he took his shot against a man who "wields the weapons of wordy war—*the only weapons he dares to wield*."[49]

Dickinson then dismantled Galloway's pretended speech piece by piece. He explained circumstances that Galloway presented as contradictions in his thought or actions. He dispelled misguided notions Galloway offered as reasons why their privileges would be safe. He corrected Galloway's misunderstandings of history. Above all, Dickinson wished his readers to understand his own reasons for opposing this effort to become a royal colony in this particular moment. "Of one thing we are *sure*," he emphasized: "that we are in the *utmost discredit* with the king and his ministers." It would make no sense, and, indeed, be the height of folly to seek a change now, yet "Mr. *Galloway* is willing to risque the *perpetuating* those demands of unequitable taxation, which have been constantly made by the proprietors—at a *time*, when *we are certain* that the crown and its ministers look on these demands as highly just and reasonable."[50]

The contempt Dickinson felt for Galloway suffused his response. So absurd were some of his constructions that Dickinson could not resist addressing them. Galloway represented all Dickinson despised. "Weakness and ignorance when attended by modesty, are naturally entitled to pardon and to pity," he thought. Galloway only pretended to possess wisdom and knowledge; he sought power he didn't know how to use and honors he didn't deserve. He used his good fortune in life to harm his country, abusing those who attempted to stop him. And he demanded respect he had not earned. Dickinson's feelings towards Galloway were "*contempt* and *ridicule*, if not of *hatred*." He had no more patience. Unable to restrain himself, Dickinson stooped to Galloway's level. In retaliation for Galloway's having called him a "stork" during the Smith trial in 1758, he asked whether Galloway could be a "long supporter" of the rights of the people because he is a "short man."[51]

It wouldn't seem proper to address these character flaws in the body of his reply, so he vented his spleen in an appendix. There he stated that he didn't intend to note Galloway's "continual breaches of the rules of grammar; his utter ignorance of the English language; the *pompous obscurity* and *sputtering prolixity*"; or his "innumerable and feeble tautologies." But that is precisely what Dickinson undertook, eviscerating Galloway's pretended speech with abandon, heaping scorn at each possible turn, dissecting his opponent's malformed prose and mixed metaphors.[52]

As he wrote, an image took shape in his mind of Galloway and Franklin preparing the pretended speech. Galloway was an empty vessel and Franklin, the scientist, was following a recipe for a potion. As soon as he finished his *Reply*, he jotted it down. Franklin would take the dried leaves of the law, a pinch of history, and pulverize them together. Add two handfuls of words such as "liberty," "property," "proprietary," "power," "injustice," "slavery," "thraldom," and "magic charms" to "midnight gloom" and "fatal death"—two of Galloway's most ridiculous terms. *What kind of death is not fatal?* Dickinson wondered. Franklin would then strengthen the concoction with "Impudence, Malice, Envy, Hatred, Ill-Manners, and all Kind of Uncharitableness" and moisten it with two bottles of old Madeira wine. Pour it all into an empty head and stir with an electrified rod. Cover the head with a large and well-powdered wig and let it ferment for eight weeks until it grows very violent. When it is at its height and the mixture is turbid and thick, pour it on the highest quality British-made paper. A good dose of this mixture will exhilarate schoolboys and, when opened in a room full of company, will set them all laughing. Dickinson could muster a sharp sense of humor when provoked.

When he returned from the circuit in early September, Dickinson looked over his *Reply* once more and then sent it to the printer. It was impossible for him to prepare his pamphlet for the public in the manner he wished.

He hoped his readers would be kind enough to excuse the inaccuracies he should have corrected if his business had not prevented him. He might have hoped that they would also excuse his vindictive tirade in the appendix, however amusing it might be.

So pleased was he with his clever recipe idea that he could not refrain from putting it on paper. Calling it *A Receipt to Make a Speech. By J——- G———, Esquire*, he sent it to the printer as well. His authorship would be obvious, but he no longer cared. When he received the broadsides a few days later, he flipped one over and jotted a song he remembered from his London days. It was "The Kennel Raker." The stanza on the corrupt lawyer encapsulated Galloway perfectly:

> The lawyer with quibble and subtle pretence—
> Still keeps in doubt till he pockets your pence
> Till he's swept all your cash he assures you tis law
> And till you're a bankrupt ne'er finds out the flaw[53]

With the upcoming election, tensions among the factions were higher than ever when the House reconvened later in September 1764. In addition to routine business, members were reminded of their unfinished work regarding defense of the western counties when they read the petitions before them. One from freemen in Berks County complained of poor representation in the House and another about the insufficient number of troops raised for their protection.[54]

Equally unsettling, and surprising to many members, was a letter from the House of Representatives of the Massachusetts Bay Colony. The previous spring, while the Pennsylvania House was locked in bitter partisan fighting, the Massachusetts House had been considering the Sugar Act and the threat it posed to the rights of the colonists. "Those measures," they wrote, "have a tendency to deprive the colonies of some of their most essential rights as British subjects, and as men; particularly the right of assessing their own taxes, and being free from any impositions, but such as they consent to by themselves or representatives." They also explained that they had instructed their agent in London to remonstrate against the measures, to endeavor to repeal the said act, and, if possible, to prevent further such duties and taxes on the colonies.[55]

Dickinson was heartened to hear of these efforts, and though he was troubled by the new ministerial measures, he felt vindicated that he had accurately gauged the temperature of the political climate in London. Whatever his feelings about the Penns, moving the colony under the direct purview of the Crown would be disastrous for colonial liberties.

At the end of September 1764, the Philadelphia Yearly Meeting of the Religious Society of Friends and its subordinate body, the Meeting for Sufferings, took place. These meetings were among the most influential gatherings affecting provincial elections. The former was the overarching governing body for Quakers in this region; the latter was to document and resist persecution. In theory, neither was a political body, but in Pennsylvania, they obviously were. Throughout much of the history of the province, candidates for political office were chosen within Philadelphia Yearly Meeting, and an endorsement meant certain election. While Friends had retreated somewhat from such active politicking, the body was still a powerful force. The newspaper reported that the Meeting for Sufferings had informed Quakers in England of their disapproval of the royal government scheme.[56] Dickinson's message in his May 24 *Speech* had resonated as he hoped. This development enraged the royalist faction, which knew re-election would be made difficult when the Quakers came out against it.

On election day, the complex and shifting alliances of the Pennsylvania population mobilized—rural and urban Quakers, New Side and Old Side Presbyterians, pro- and anti-royal government people, pro- and anti-proprietary people, frontier farmers and urban laborers, and German, English, and Scotch-Irish voters. The result was Dickinson's re-election and the ouster of Franklin and Galloway. The margins were narrow, but, ultimately, William Smith's efforts with the Germans seem to have made the difference, proving that the 1758 Assembly was right to fear his work with them. In private, Franklin exclaimed, "They carried (would you think it!) over 1000 Dutch from me," while publicly he brayed about voting fraud, "double tickets, and whole boxes of forged votes" that he claimed had cost him the election. Galloway, meanwhile, fumed as he began to plot his comeback.[57]

The members of the new Assembly met on October 15 and unanimously chose Isaac Norris as their speaker. Then they immediately considered a letter from the Rhode Island Assembly about the new taxes laid on the colonies with the Sugar Act, the likelihood of a stamp tax, and the associated "fatal consequences" for English liberties. Finally, Pennsylvania would neglect this matter no longer. The House formed a committee to draw up instructions to Richard Jackson about the dangers, which were finalized and sent on October 20.

The same day, the House revisited the petitions for a change of government to discuss what to do about them. Dickinson had been successful in convincing most members that a change was undesirable. They also agreed with him that the proprietors ought not to receive preferential treatment in taxation. But rather than take Dickinson's cautious approach of abandoning the petition for change altogether, the majority had another plan, and events took a turn Dickinson did not foresee. Members now sought to use the Franklin-Galloway scheme as a bluff to extract concessions from the Penns.

As was frequently the way when things became messy, Norris pleaded indisposition and requested another speaker be chosen. Dickinson was quite disillusioned with Norris. There was no doubt the elderly man was ailing, but it was equally clear his ailments worked to his advantage. Dickinson felt as though he had done Norris's bidding in taking the lead against the change of government, only to be abandoned when he needed reinforcements. The situation worsened when the House voted to appoint Franklin as another agent in London, along with Richard Jackson, and have him present the petition for the change.[58]

On the morning of October 26, a number of Philadelphians petitioned the Assembly, expressing concern about losing their privileges and liberties under a royal government and objecting to Franklin as agent. Known as Franklin was for fomenting the movement for change in the first place, they believed "he may be justly supposed to have a fond Partiality for his own Schemes." Moreover, because Franklin and his son held offices of profit and honor under the Crown, they didn't believe that "a Gentleman of his moderate Fortune will sacrifice his Interest for the Sake of the Province." The House appointed Franklin anyway, over the dissent of twelve members. It then adjourned until January 7.[59]

It was clear that those who appointed Franklin were not in favor of royal government but rather only looking to use him for their own purposes. It was rumored that Penn ally Chief Justice William Allen had let slip that Penn had acquiesced to taxes on his unimproved lands. The anti-change faction hoped to threaten Governor Penn with the most offensive tool they had—Franklin—in hopes they could extract more concessions from him.

It was a dangerous thing, indeed, to play political games so carelessly with a people's basic rights. Those who should have been Dickinson's allies in stopping the petitions now toyed with their own destruction. Dickinson thus was not done with his protest. Since the House had refused to allow the dissenters to enter their protest in the minutes, he decided to go public. The protest detailed the many detriments of Franklin's appointment: his partiality as the author of the change; his bias against the proprietors; how, because he was disliked by royal ministers, his appointment could be seen as disrespectful to the king; that he was disliked by many reputable inhabitants of the province; the undue haste of the House in making his appointment; and that Franklin cost the province too much money. Finally, instead of appointing Franklin, the dissenters suggested naming Dr. John Fothergill, a widely respected English Quaker, to assist Jackson.[60]

With the unethical behavior of the assemblymen—first the falsehoods published about his attendance record by Galloway and now this risky effort to extract concessions from the proprietors—Dickinson regretted the failure of a motion he had made near the beginning of the year. In early March, a petition had arrived in the House from a number of inhabitants of Philadelphia who had serious concerns about what their elected representatives were doing behind the closed doors of the assembly room. They thought they should be "admitted to hear the Debates in the House, and thereby be informed of the true State of such Matters under the Deliberation of the Representatives of the People." They therefore requested that a standing order be issued to allow them access. Dickinson motioned that such an order be given, on the grounds that the assemblymen were the servants of their constiutents and should keep no secrets from them. A committee that included Franklin was then formed to investigate the practices of the House of Commons and the legislatures of other colonies. After they reported—incorrectly—that the House of Commons disallowed "strangers" to witness the deliberations and they found the other colonial assemblies to be mixed on the practice, the matter was dropped without a decision.[61]

When Franklin responded at length to Dickinson's protest, he again chose not to attack Dickinson, whom he knew to be the leader and author, and instead turned his ire on William Allen, treating him as the author instead. Noting how Franklin closed his remarks—"I am now to take leave (perhaps a last leave) of the country I love"—Dickinson surely hoped that he had seen the last of Franklin.[62] Dickinson and Franklin's other critics found the fanfare orchestrated at his departure absurd. They marveled at, as Dickinson put it, the "*vainglorious triumph* puffed off at his Embarkation, for which silly pageantry, ship Guns were borrowed in Philadelphia, and sent down to Chester—the use there made of them, with other vain Exultations."[63]

Because Dickinson had led in the controversy to this point and had put his name on public documents, a few members now pressed him to write an answer to Franklin. But Franklin's diatribe was aimed mainly at William Allen, although he did quote Dickinson's words to show Dickinson's alleged partiality towards the proprietors.[64] He drafted a long response, but since Franklin had since departed, he thought better of publishing it. A number of people, including Assembly colleague Joseph Richardson and Uncle Cadwalader, reminded Dickinson that since he was unaffiliated with any faction, he would be particularly vulnerable if he went after Franklin.[65] He therefore thought it most prudent to place his draft response in his desk drawer and allow Smith to issue his vitriolic response.

Over the 1764 legislative year, Dickinson had grown exasperated with his colleagues and the political machinations of both sides. Even those with whom he agreed and who had supported him in his endeavor to preserve the charter had disappointed. As the Assembly went into recess and 1764 drew to a close, he resolved this would be his final term in the Assembly.[66]

There was one bright spot during this unpleasant time. As Dickinson's relationship with Speaker Norris evolved over the years from adversary to ally, he also accepted Norris as a client. Now Dickinson had frequent occasion to meet with him on various matters. Because Norris was often ill, Dickinson called at Fairhill, Norris's grand estate three miles north of Philadelphia in an area called the Northern Liberties (Fig. 8). Norris, long a widower, his wife having died in childbirth with their second daughter, lived with his maiden sister, Elizabeth; his two daughters, Mary and Sarah, called Polly and Sally; his nieces, Hannah and Mary Griffitts; and his elderly cousin, Mary Lloyd, called Molly.[67] Although Dickinson had been acquainted with most of them for years, he now began to know them better.

Fairhill, named for the nearby Quaker meeting called Fair Hill, was an idyllic place. The grand brick manor house sat on a hill with sweeping vistas of Philadelphia and the Delaware River. With his significant wealth from trade, the senior Isaac Norris had constructed the estate in 1712 as an expression of Quaker ideals of virtue, simplicity, and retreat from the world to country living. Built on the plan of Dolobran Hall in Montgomeryshire, Wales, the seat of the Quaker Lloyd family, the work had been undertaken by paid contractors and at least two men Norris enslaved, William and Addoo. The entire estate was designed for the edification of mind and spirit.

Numerous outbuildings, including the meeting house and schoolhouse, and extensive vegetable and flower gardens made the estate like a small, self-contained town. The structure that most embodied Quaker ideals was the greenhouse with attached library. Gardening was a spiritual activity for Quakers, who believed it brought them closer to God through tending his creation. They cultivated the land as they cultivated their souls for the planting of Christ's seed. And the library, perhaps the most extensive in the colonies, enhanced the mind with the best literature, poetry, history, and political treatises in English and Latin. Fittingly, it was attached to a green-house so minds could be tended with as much care as the rare and beautiful plants they grew.[68]

This congenial group of relatives, with the sisters at the center, formed a little society they called the Rural Circle, or Band of Friendship.[69] It was an imaginary village populated by nymphs and the occasional swain, who spent their days writing poetry for one another and other elevated pursuits. Aunt Betty achieved notoriety for studying astronomy using her own telescope and was the envy of men lacking their own scientific equipment.[70] They all had pen names to protect their identities should their lines be discovered. Polly was Felicia or Celia; Sally was Sophia; Hannah Griffitts was Fidelia; Aunt Betty was Eusebia; and Cousin Molly was Myrna. Even old Norris was honored with the name Aristobulas. They wrote to one another of their woes and joys and bore witness both to Divine Goodness and injustices in the world they inhabited.

The Rural Circle had a strict code of behavior for the few who were admitted. In the first place, they must withdraw from the world. Those who were "not so fond of Retirement" and "cannot reconcile themselves to forsake ye gaieties of life" were not suitable for membership. They must also com-municate with one another openly and engagingly. They admonished one another to write with "Charming, frankness & Vivacity. Remember, my dear Girl," said Sophia to Fidelia, "this is ye call of Friendship."[71]

Most importantly, they must be sincere. It would be unimaginable that a member would "think one Thing, & say Another on ye Same Subject." They "banish'd that Tyrant Ceremony" and demanded "an Entire Freedom" to "Visit, Talk, and write, just as it suits our Disposition." They deliberated at length before admitting another cousin, Hannah Harrison, to their group. They worried she was overly fond of society and would not be willing to "turn Hermit" with them.[72] When they finally admitted her, she was called "Sophronia."

For the Rural Circle, it was a blessed relief to abandon superficial niceties. They had severe language for those who conformed to polite decorum. They were "Time-killers," "Diverters Of a Dull Hour," "Triflers," and "Weaklings." Going into society meant risking contact. "If any such Weaklings should come in my way," Sophronia wrote with a sigh, "I would sometimes undergo the tedious Penance of an Hour or two's Conversation with them." These women were thus immune "to all ye Gaieties & Compliments of ye Town, or even to ye Gentlemen's notice, which you know is not of that Importance to me," confessed Fidelia, "as to Some others." More than that, they detested the rituals of flattering the opposite sex and the machinations that invariably ensued when people had "design[s] of entrapping one another" in matrimony.[73]

Indeed, the nymphs of the Rural Circle reserved their choicest words—and acute wariness—for the swains who sought their company. They spoke sardonically of men as their "Glorious Leaders," "Lords of Creation," the "Sex-superior," and "the Saucy Sex."[74] Independent-minded women were right to harbor suspicion; those of independent fortune even more so. A woman could be independent only if she remained single. To marry was, by default, to give up everything to a man.

By law, upon entering into marriage, a woman's entire identity was subsumed under her husband's and she became like a child or a lunatic—dependent, unaccounted, and unaccountable. It was called *coverture* and the woman a *feme covert*. She was covered, hidden, or obscured by her husband. She was a nonentity. Her entire property became his, excepting only her clothes. Her children were his. Her contracts and actions were not legally binding. She had few rights under the law and no responsibilities. Additional strictures were usually demanded of a wife by the husband and society. The woman should comport herself with deference to her husband. She should not attempt to converse on subjects falling under the male purview, such as politics. She should not speak publicly. She should be quiet, demure, and obedient. All a woman's efforts should thus be for the honor and ease of her husband and his children. Any education she received was only so she could please him in agreeable conversation.

A woman was dressed for the part. Beginning at around three months old, all infants were laced into stays, or corsets—ridged, conical undergarments stiffened with whalebone. Parents of the upper sort did not want their children crouched and crawling on the ground like beasts. Stays would ensure they grew upright, physically and morally. At age five or thereabouts, little boys graduated out of their stays and were trained up to be virtuous. Females, the weaker sex, changeable as the moon, remained in stays their entire lives. Because they inherently lacked virtue, which was a masculine trait, their stays would provide the structure and restraint denied them by nature.[75] The more fashionable the lady, the tighter the stays. The waist was cinched, and the natural bust was decreased by five inches. Deprived of the ability to expand her lungs for her entire life, she would faint at the slightest exertion. Quiet, demureness, and obedience would be assured. There would be no reason a lady would know that she, in fact, had the physical ability to speak forcefully or publicly, which requires the capacity to fill the lungs and project the voice. A poem published in the *Gazette*, entitled "Advice to a Young Lady lately Married," could have been written by one of the Rural Circle, summarizing their objections. It began, "Small is the province of a wife, / And narrow is her sphere in life."[76]

Quaker women could avoid all of these restrictions by rejecting marriage, social conventions, and vain and worldly fashions. Their stays might remain loose, and if they chose to marry, the could reject coverture to a degree by retaining their own property. They could devote themselves to education. They could preach the Gospel with the support of the entire meeting.

The Rural Circle saw men and their masculine systems of oppression as the cause of their misery. Daily occurrences confirmed it. Once, when Sophia (Sally) was riding out with her father, they came upon an instance of "Cruelty in Power." It was a man "showing his Superiority over a Woman" by beating her. The unbelievable brutality prompted Aristobulas to ask the man how he could "so Inhumanely Treat her." He responded in his Scottish dialect that "she is my Wife & pretends she cannot walk." They persuaded the man to stop for the moment, but they knew it would not be for long. Sophia considered him to be "the disgrace of our Country."[77]

Though men were, in general, not to be trusted, the Rural Circle was not opposed to marriage or to men entirely. Should a woman consent to wed, however, she should absolutely not "give her hand without her heart."[78] Another aunt, Mary Parker Norris, wife of Uncle Charles Norris, was an excellent model. As he was Theophilus, she was Theophilia. They lived a half block from the State House, and when Isaac was indisposed for Assembly business, he sometimes lodged with his brother, where Dickinson and the other legislators attended him. Theophilia and Theophilus had a beautiful young family. Little Isaac, named for his uncle and grandfather, was now four. Dickinson was especially fond of Debby, who was but three. He had noted her birth in his pocket almanac. "Born on this day of October 1761, Debbie Norris."[79] He took a special interest in the children.

Though the Rural Circle controlled its membership closely, Dickinson met the requirements for virtue, character, and conversation. As he joined them at the tea table, he found they brought fresh life to the sentiments set down long ago on dry pages surrounding them. He loved the directness and candor with which the sisters addressed him, the liberty with which they expressed their views, and the liberality of their views. The poetry of their little society was suffused with religious sentiments that revealed the depths of their faith. In their forthright erudition, the sisters reminded him of his mother, though their Quakerism was more pronounced than hers. There is such an inexpressible somewhat in their persons and behavior, noted a mutual friend, that as soon as they enter the room, reserve vanishes, and they converse with an intimate freedom. This was precisely the sort of relationship Dickinson prized above all others. He looked for it constantly but found it only rarely. Where sprightly Sally won his affection as a sister, the more sober Polly gradually won his heart.

6

"Created in us by the decrees of Providence"

Defining and Defending American Rights, 1765–1766

In early 1765, the repercussions of the royal government controversy reverberated on both sides of the Atlantic. Reviews of Dickinson's and Galloway's pamphlets appeared in London lamenting the strife, while proxies for the principals in Philadelphia continued firing. Some commentators attacked both sides, such as the author of the pamphlet *Nosum Nosorum: Or, a New Treatise on Large Noses* (Fig. 9). Relying on common knowledge of Dickinson's prominent nose, the author reflected on its "Magnitude, Power, and Potency," comparing it to the pyramids of Egypt. The author explained, "for the singularity, wonderful magnitude, apparent visibility, superiority and stupendocity of his Nose, he has been unanimously elected President of *The Society of Noses*, and will continue in that honorable Post 'til another may be found that has a more magnificent Nose than he." It cast Dickinson as the leader of the Worshipful Society of Noses, a parody of the Religious Society of Friends, in opposition to the "bull-dog noses," led by Franklin. Both were caricatured on the cover. Within was an absurd song about large noses, complete with vulgar language and barely veiled comparisons of a large nose to a certain other appendage pleasing to the ladies. It was indeed difficult to tell who got the worst of it—Dickinson with his flaccid hook nose or Franklin with his stubby little member.[1]

Dickinson was too busy to worry about such things. His schedule was replete with legislative work, and his case docket was full. In the Assembly, he wrote bills: one to release two insolvent debtors languishing in jail; one to erect a poorhouse in Philadelphia; one to protect poor German immigrants who were being exploited by ship masters and merchants; and one for a supply bill for the king's use. And he was on a committee to combine the poor laws into one act.[2] His court docket included a variety of cases. There was one of assault and battery by a master against a servant wherein Dickinson represented the master; another one in which he represented a "crippled apprentice" suing his deceased master's estate for support; and various trespasses, debts, and replevins.[3]

A type of case he took frequently was one municipality suing another over the support of a poor resident. In Pennsylvania, as in England, poor people had a legal right to receive a "settlement"—meaning legal residency and relief from their basic wants—from the parish or township where they lived. But the townships frequently attempted to skirt their responsibilities. Dickinson found this especially problematic where women were concerned. They were frequently left alone when a husband died or abandoned them. When young children were involved, their situation was urgent. One argument the townships used was that married women were *femes covert*—women with no legal identities apart from their husbands. When a woman married, her property became her husband's, and it was her husband's job to support her. On the surface, it seemed a reasonable argument. But Dickinson rejected this notion as it made women entirely vulnerable to the whims of their husbands. Neither should they be at the mercy of the whims of the government. "A Woman does not lose her Settlement by marrying a Man who had none," he argued.[4] This was not a surprising position considering his Quaker upbringing. Quaker women frequently refused coverture by keeping their property in their own names.

Another common case that likewise demonstrated Dickinson's thinking on the rights of women and other vulnerable individuals' rights to property concerned ejectments—removal of an individual from another's land. In one ejectment case, in order for his client to remain on a piece of property, he had to prove it was owned not by the plaintiff but by a woman named Abigail Alricks, who was generally believed to be "an idiot"—or *non compos mentis*, not of sound mind. Dickinson proved that she only suffered from a speech impediment and that it was simple prejudice that caused people to think ill of her. In the process of deposing the witnesses, he established not just Alricks's sound mind but also her human dignity. It was actually her refusal to marry that convinced one witness that she was competent. When told a man might court her, Alricks replied that "if he did, it must be for her Money—& then perhaps having got that, he might use her ill—but while She remained single, & kept her Estate in her own Hands, She would be usd well by somebody." The witness was surprised at her answer because she expected a foolish one.

Instead, she came away from the encounter believing "I am sure I could not have given so sensible an Answer."[5]

Not all of Dickinson's cases involved the lower sorts in Pennsylvania. His reputation was now such that he received business from around the colonies. Merchants in South Carolina, Virginia, and New York sought his services to defend their interests. He was hired by the elite and even nobility, performing work for the Penns, the London Land Company, and Frederick Calvert, Lord Baltimore, the proprietor of Maryland. The latter engaged him multiple times, once to secure payment for a debt owed him by John Vining, a wealthy judge in Kent County and a friend of Dickinson's.[6]

Never far from Dickinson's mind, however, was the increasingly tense imperial situation. Pennsylvanians had been too embroiled in the drama over royal government to pay Parliament's new plans for taxation much heed or join in the growing chorus of protests. Besides, the Franklin-Galloway faction did not want to give the king or his ministers any reason for a negative impression of Pennsylvania as they planned on presenting the petition to unseat the Penns as soon as possible.

Now the spring of 1765 brought ominous news. The April 18 *Gazette* published an extensive account of the new Stamp Act, written by Prime Minister Lord George Grenville and just passed by the House of Commons, complete with each resolve voted upon. It was clear that the effect on the colonies would be devastating if it received royal assent. This would mark the first time Great Britain had passed a direct tax upon the colonies for the purpose of raising a revenue. The colonial assemblies frequently raised revenue for the king by taxing the colonists, whom they represented. And Americans understood that Britain must regulate the trade of her colonies, which was the essence of the mercantile system under which they lived. But a tax by Parliament directly on the colonists to raise revenue was an entirely different matter. For that, the colonists must give consent. And for them to consent, they must have representation in the House of Commons, which they did not.

The Sugar Act was dangerous enough, but the Stamp Act's wide reach made it much worse. Unlike the Sugar Act, which mainly affected merchants, the Stamp Act affected everyone. It required that all vellum, parchment, and paper receive an embossed royal stamp costing a specified amount; otherwise, use of these materials would be deemed illegal and any business conducted with them null and void. The law applied to everything, from provincial legislation, to newspapers, to playing cards. Dickinson would be forced to charge clients more not just for the stamp itself, but also for the time it took to navigate the complexities of the law.[7]

He thought about those in the colonies who would be most affected, the laboring people who needed contracts drawn up for work. "How will our *merchants* and the *lower ranks of people*, on whom the force of these regulations will fall first, and with the greatest violence, bear this additional load?" he wondered. "I apprehend that this Act will be extremely heavy on those who are least able to bear it; and if our merchants and people of little substance languish under it, all others must be affected."[8]

On principle and in practice, Dickinson objected to this new tax. Aside from the obvious problem that Parliament had no right to tax the colonies, the tax itself was unjust. Taxation in America had always been assessed "by making as exact an estimate as could be formed of each man's estate" so that the taxes are "proportioned to the abilities of those who were to pay them." He believed that this "is the mode of taxation, which will be found to be least oppressive and destructive, and certainly the most equal." But he believed the Stamp Act would favor the rich, allowing them to escape paying their fair share of taxes while placing most of the burden on poorer people, "who most of all require relief and encouragement."[9] Americans were ill-prepared to shoulder such a financial burden. Though they might appear affluent to members of Parliament, buying manufactured goods from England at a prodigious rate, Dickinson saw this as less a sign of wealth than greed. When the Seven Years' War had ended, he worried that Americans would ruin themselves seeking after luxuries they could ill afford at the expense of their virtue.[10] By 1765, his prognostication seemed accurate. Americans were in over £2 million of debt to British creditors.[11] Finally, that those who disobeyed the act would be tried in the new Vice Admiralty Court in Nova Scotia meant that justice was out of Americans' reach.

Yet Pennsylvanians remained on the whole unconcerned. Other colonies, such as Massachusetts, raised the alarm. Statesmen in that colony, as well as in Maryland and Virginia, wrote pamphlets against the new taxation, launching the rallying cry "no taxation without representation." The Assembly of Massachusetts had also sent a letter to the Pennsylvania Assembly suggesting that there be a meeting in New York of representatives from all the colonies to deal with the situation. A new group calling itself the "Sons of Liberty" began organizing in Rhode Island and elsewhere with the aim of protecting their rights.[12] But with the Assembly currently in recess, nothing would be done until the fall session.

That summer, Dickinson took the opportunity to escape the sweltering heat of the city to tour Pennsylvania's upper counties for business and pleasure. He traveled first to Bethlehem, which hadn't seen rain for six or seven weeks, nearly destroying the crops of oats, flax, and hay. Then he was joined for part of his journey by his twenty-three-year-old cousin, Lambert Cadwalader. Whereas their father had been a physician, young Lambert and his brother John were already partnered as successful merchants. Dickinson was proud of his kin, who were keenly interested in current affairs and ready to resist the Stamp Act.

Dickinson's travels took him through Carlisle and then southward through boggy and humid York and Lancaster. Before he returned to Philadelphia, however, he made one more stop, at Wright's Ferry on the Susquehanna River, to visit his friend Susanna Wright, or, as he called her, "the Susquehanna Muse."[13] In her sixty-eighth year, small in stature, and plainly attired, Susee Wright was one of the most colorful people he knew, and one of the most remarkable. Her intellectual accomplishments made even Dickinson's achievements pale by comparison, proof on her own that women were as fit for any profession as men. She was proficient in Latin, Italian, and French and possessed of a library containing the works of Milton, Swift, and Dickinson's beloved Alexander Pope.

Like the Norris sisters, Dickinson's other female friends, Wright's Quakerism suffused everything she undertook, from her intellectual pursuits, to the spare yet tasteful decor of her house, to her refusal to marry. This last principle was dearest to her. Believing that even relatively egalitarian Quaker unions risked oppressing women, she chose to steer her own life entirely. She had even written a stirring poem to Polly Norris's Aunt Betty, celebrating her decision to remain unmarried and blaming men's misinterpretation of the Bible for making them somehow believe that they should govern women. Though men would try to seduce a woman into marriage, she should "shake off the yoke" and "sure his equal be."[14]

Wright and Dickinson had much in common and could talk for hours about mutual interests and shared political views. She was a vivacious conversationalist, and theirs was a friendship rather than a professional relationship. If they spoke of the law, it was in abstraction, not as lawyer and client.

Wright was an inspiration to Dickinson, and he was her "Very Good and Obliging Friend."[15]

Still, it was perhaps daunting for a man who might one day have marriage in mind to converse with Susee Wright. All the more so should that young man be inclined towards a young lady tutored by her. Early in Polly Norris's life, Wright undertook to mentor her from afar, sending her books in French. Six-year-old Polly gleefully promised to learn the language and wondered that "anybody can be so open handed to her without ever having seen her."[16] Wright was an honorary member of their Rural Circle.

When the Assembly convened in September for its final legislative session before the October election, it immediately dealt with the letter from Massachusetts proposing a congress in New York. During the recess, violent protests had erupted in Boston, threatening the lives and property of the stamp officers. Dickinson drafted resolves of the House, but some found his language extreme. He wanted the term "natural rights" to appear, and that seemed too radical for those who were used to thinking in terms of the "rights of Englishmen." The former came from God; the latter came from the British constitution and their status as subjects of the Crown. The more cautious members didn't want to give the impression that they were threatening the prerogative of the Crown or setting themselves above accountability to the British constitution. The controversial language was omitted in revisions, but ultimately Dickinson's view prevailed, and it was reinstated in the final version. The Assembly appointed him to the delegation to attend the Congress, along with George Bryan of Philadelphia and John Morton from Chester County.[17]

The delegation to the Stamp Act Congress took two days to reach New York and arrived the evening of September 29. Dickinson lodged with a relative on Wall Street, in the very center of town. Also on hand were his cousins John and Thomas Jones, both well-regarded physicians.[18] John, who apprenticed with Dickinson's Uncle Cadwalader, would later found a medical school at King's College and serve as physician to Benjamin Franklin and George Washington.[19] The Congress was to meet on October 1, but all the delegates did not arrive until October 7, which gave the cousins time to enjoy one another's company and exercise their "risible muscles," as Cousin John put it.[20] With the delegation from the Lower Counties including Dickinson's friends George Read and Thomas McKean, the gatherings were lively.

While awaiting the other delegates' arrival, news came from Philadelphia of the results of the provincial elections. In August, Dickinson had run advertisements in the Pennsylvania papers announcing his intention not to serve another term. He had become tired of the factionalism and endless battles. Working as the principled trimmer, he had been attacked viciously by one party and betrayed by the other. Now he preferred to focus on his burgeoning law practice. The Presbyterians had done everything in their power to get him re-elected, including running him instead of their favorite, George Bryan. Dickinson was grateful for their "generous Behavior" to him, but he was glad not to have been returned.[21]

When the delegates met in City Hall, they chose the conservative Timothy Ruggles from Massachusetts as their chairman over the brilliant but erratic James Otis, also of Massachusetts. But, in some ways, Dickinson was the de facto leader. Ruggles was not inclined to support any resistance to Great Britain, and Dickinson had come prepared with a draft of twelve resolves, which became the basis for the delegates' deliberations. Each one had to re-affirm the relationship between the colonies and Parliament, balancing the rights of the former and the power of the latter. And all this must be done while demonstrating their utmost deference to the king. But those assembled were not of one mind. They disagreed strenuously on how much power should be conceded to Parliament and the language asserting their rights.

The situation was seemingly intractable. Englishmen living in Great Britain generally assumed that ever since the revolutionary settlement of 1689, which created a constitutional monarchy, Parliament was sovereign over British territories. Thus, its statutes ought to be obeyed. But many colonists had not adopted this view. The inability of the colonies to be represented in Parliament logically prohibited that body from determining policy within the colonies or taxing them. This insoluble dilemma was captured in the maxim *imperium in imperio*, or state within a state—such a thing was impossible, a monstrosity, a beast with two heads. There must be a single superintending sovereignty. With Parliament now testing its strength with new taxation, Americans were compelled to decide where the ultimate authority lay: with the Parliament, the king, or somewhere else.

With those on either side wanting more extreme statements, there needed to be much compromise and adjustments in language as they moved from one topic to the next. Dickinson redrafted the resolves multiple times, with other members also editing his drafts. As they deliberated, they learned that the violent protests had spread southward to Philadelphia, and there were now riots, destruction of property, and intimidation of officials there.[22]

By October 19, the Declaration of the Stamp Act Congress was composed and approved, and the body turned to work on petitions to the king, the House of Commons, and a memorial laying out the facts to the House of Lords. Although Dickinson was not a member of these committees, he nevertheless drafted the Petition to the King. Before the work of the Congress was finished, he was called home on important business. On October 25, as the Stamp Act Congress adjourned, only six delegations were empowered to sign the documents; Connecticut and South Carolina were restricted by their instructions from signing anything; and the New York delegates believed they had no such mandate, not having been appointed by their Assembly.[23]

Though he had left early, Dickinson could be satisfied with the central part he took in the proceedings. It was not just that he had given the Congress a foundation on which to build; it was that he carefully listened to all members, even those with whom he disagreed, and tried to build consensus that was reflected in his revisions. Overall, the impression he made on his fellow delegates was quite favorable, solidifying friendships that would last decades. Most crucially, this work had given him a sense like nothing before that this was a struggle that transcended any one colony. Americans in every colony would have to work together to prevail.

While in New York, he had been thinking of what he might say to his countrymen about the crisis. Although other pamphlets from the likes of James Otis of Massachusetts, Richard Bland of Virginia, and Daniel Dulany of Maryland gave compelling theoretical arguments, which Dickinson wanted eventually to pursue, on why the Stamp Act was unconstitutional, of more immediate need from his perspective was practical advice to Americans on what they should actually do in response to the Stamp Act. Compliance was out of the question. Doing so would set a precedent that would affirm the legality of the act and open the door for similar legislation in the future. Riots were clearly not the answer, but neither was evading the act by not using stamped paper or otherwise skirting the law.

Dickinson offered something else. In a broadside addressed to "Friends and Countrymen," he gave his readers an alternative: the Quaker practice of civil disobedience, formulated in response to religious persecution. Civil disobedience is the public, nonviolent breaking of unconstitutional laws with the intent of raising public awareness about the injustice. Crucially, no harm can be done to persons or property, and those engaging in it must accept their punishment. Of course, such punishment would only draw further public disapproval and strengthen their cause. Faced with a virtual repeal of the law through mass noncompliance, the government would then be compelled to repeal the law officially. Dickinson's broadside recommending that colonists simply ignore the Stamp Act and "proceed in all Business as usual" marked the first instance of anyone offering guidance to the colonists for how to resist Britain effectively and the first instance when this quintessentially Quaker practice was recommended to non-Quakers. It would be two hundred years, however, before it would be widely used again.[24]

At almost the same moment—November 7—Charles Thomson, the leader of the Sons of Liberty in Philadelphia, held a meeting of merchants to organize a boycott of British goods until the Stamp Act was repealed. From this point onward, Dickinson and Thomson acted in tandem to defend American rights.

As his broadside circulated in several colonies, Dickinson also published a long treatise on political economy, entitled *The Late Regulations Respecting the British Colonies on the Continent of America*. Whereas "Friends and Countrymen" was directed to Americans of every rank, *Late Regulations* was aimed at the elite who would be conversant with the complex concepts and sources he used.[25] It possessed the qualities that were becoming hallmarks of Dickinson's public writings, particularly when directed towards audiences with whom he had profound disagreements—it was rational, it appealed to the readers' self-interest to motivate right behavior, and it utilized powerful rhetoric to command his readers' attention and sway them to his position. Here, much of the argument was laid out in elaborate footnotes, another hallmark of Dickinson's writing.

Throughout the treatise he discoursed expertly on paper money and monetary policy, markets and trade patterns, and taxation and regulation policy. Knowing that what mattered to the ministry more than anything was the accumulation of treasure, the sum of his argument was this: if Great Britain wanted the colonies to continue paying for British products, regulation of trade must be loosened and taxes not imposed. Otherwise, the results would be disastrous. Further, he highlighted the disadvantages under which the North American colonists labored. The favoritism of the ministry towards the sugar islands was foremost among them. "Should the interest of one colony be preferred to that of another?" he asked. "Should the welfare of millions be sacrificed to the magnificence of a few?" Ultimately, he argued, the welfare of the public in general ought to be preferred over individuals.[26]

With these two public writings printed and distributed, Dickinson had one more item to compose. He sat down and took up his pen to write to former member of Parliament William Pitt directly. Though Pitt was not currently in the government, Dickinson knew of no other person who might have both sympathy with the plight of the colonies and the influence to change policy. Known as "the Great Commoner" because he refused to accept a title of nobility, Pitt was revered in the colonies as the man who had orchestrated Britain's victory in the French and Indian War and as a friend to American interests.

Dickinson addressed him with the deference due his station and pled the cause of America. The lengthy letter was a brief primer on how to prevent American independence. Laid out in clear terms, the formula was simple. The colonies, explained Dickinson, won't seek independence unless Great Britain drives them to it. "They will not engage in such a Scheme unless they unite in it," he wrote, "and they will not unite, unless it be in a Common Cause that points all their Passions at one Object."[27] If America tried for independence, Dickinson assured Pitt, they would succeed. But not only would America's success be bad for Britain, depriving her of much wealth, it would ultimately mean the end of America, "Crimes and Calamities," and "Centuries of mutual Jealousies, Hatreds, Wars and Devastations; till at last the exhausted Provinces shall sink into Slavery under the Yoke of some fortunate Conqueror."[28] He sent the letter and hoped for a good reception.

Soon into the new year, 1766, the *Pennsylvania Journal* reported glorious news: the petition for royal government had been presented and resoundingly rejected by the king and council. "Thus we hope we have got rid of this unhappy bone of contention, and now peace, good will and brotherly love will take place," read the news.[29] But Dickinson didn't believe it. The petition can't have been presented. The Assembly's instructions to the agents made clear that they were to take the utmost care only to present the petition in circumstances most favorable to Pennsylvanians. With the protests against the Stamp Act, circumstances could hardly have been worse. Nor had there been any report from the agents that they had acted. No agent, thought Dickinson, could be so stupid as to think a proposal for change at this time would gain ministerial favor. He was certain "that no Rashness, no Views, no Passions of their own, will tempt the agents to hazard the Liberties of Pennsylvania amidst such mighty Dangers."[30]

But that is exactly what had transpired. More news from London confirmed it. Against the advice of his fellow agent and in utter disregard of his
instructions and Pennsylvanians' liberties, Benjamin Franklin had, in fact,
enthusiastically presented the petition to the Privy Council as soon as he
arrived in London the previous November. It was a misjudgment that cost
him his cause. Franklin's loss, however, was Pennsylvania's gain. Whether he
had proceeded so recklessly from mistake or malice, Dickinson could not
tell. But now, although Dickinson had given him the benefit of the doubt,
he now knew with certainty that Franklin was not to be trusted. At least the
matter of the change of government was now favorably concluded.[31]

As the Stamp Act crisis continued to roil the colonies, Americans could
not know that measures were already underway for its repeal, some by Pitt,
who hadn't yet received Dickinson's letter. The Sons of Liberty in the Lower
Counties proclaimed they were "exasperated, by the implicit Obedience paid
to the Act in the Cessation of Public Business." They had hitherto taken no
action against the act, but, roused by their compatriots in colonies to the
north and the south, they decided to mobilize.

They, too, had read "Friends and Countrymen," and, finding it an expression of their sentiments, wrote to the *Pennsylvania Gazette* to request the
identity of the author. Upon learning it was Dickinson, they assembled at the
Court House in Lewes-Town, the seat of Sussex County, on March 15 and
demanded the keys to the main public buildings. They then proceeded to
take possession of the courthouse, the county magazine, and the flag. As they
drank toasts to the king and liberty, and to the confusion of the Stamp Act
and its supporters, they fired a cannon and cheered. Gradually, the protesters
adjourned to the courthouse, where they read "Friends and Countrymen"
aloud. The Sons of Liberty then called before them, as though they were a
tribunal, the officials of the town, most of whom pledged upon their honor
to go about their "business as usual," as though the Stamp Act had not been
passed.[32]

Although Dickinson believed he had addressed the Stamp Act sufficiently
with "Friends and Countrymen," he soon found this was not the case. News
arrived on May 1 that the Committee of Correspondence in Barbados had
written to that colony's agent in London pleading for repeal of the Stamp
Act.[33] In doing so, the committee had adopted a submissive tone and

sought to distance Barbados from the mainland colonies, calling them "rebellious." Angered, Dickinson again took up his pen to refute their claims and explain the principles of peaceful resistance. Calling his pamphlet *An Address to the Committee of Correspondence in Barbados*, he signed it, "A North-American."[34]

Central to Dickinson's argument was a distinction between three different responses to tyranny. First was the Whig response, what the Barbados Committee accused the American colonists of—violent mobs disrespecting government and fomenting rebellion. Though indeed it was true that mobs had rioted in Boston, New York, and even Philadelphia, these mobs were, Dickinson asserted, "composed of the lower ranks of people in some *few* of the colonies." Abhorrent as these displays of violence were, they did not rise to the level of rebellion. They were, Dickinson explained, merely the acts of subjects driven to desperation by oppressive measures. As regrettable as such actions were, they were common forms of popular discontent, even by loyal subjects of the Crown.

On the other extreme were the Tories, those who believed the government was infallible. This seemed to be the position of the Barbados Committee. It reminded Dickinson of Tories in the years before the Glorious Revolution of 1688. In fear of revolution, they had published a tract advocating the divine right of kings and denying the lawfulness of any response to tyranny except praying and petitioning for redress.[35] If those measures failed, the subject's only recourse was to submit and obey. "Had you lived in those days of ignorance," Dickinson exclaimed, "with what lucky assistance might you have propp'd up the tottering tyrant, by maxims of law to prove, *that kings can do no wrong*; and texts of scripture to shew, *that submission is due to the powers that be!*"[36] Now it appeared to Dickinson that the men in Barbados were extending this theory to Parliament. Such a position would deny the revolutionary settlement of 1689 that established a limited constitutional government in England and her realms.

These Barbados men clearly did not understand the distinction between "the disgust of government and the administration of it." Government, Dickinson believed, was a necessary good, but sometimes the administration of it fell to bad men. Those who sanctioned rebellious mobs that threatened to overthrow the government conflated poor administration with government itself. Similarly, those who submitted timidly to tyrannical ministers showed only fear, not respect. Such behavior was "subversive of those sacred rights which God himself from the infinity of his benevolence has bestowed upon mankind." Dickinson proclaimed that submitting humbly to tyranny "is deserting and betraying as much as you can, that principle, on which the constitution of *Great-Britain* is established."[37]

The Quakerly measures Dickinson had advocated in "Friends and Countrymen," the third perspective he discussed in the *Address*, contrasted with both the Whig and Tory positions. Peaceful protest against unjust, unconstitutional laws showed respect for the government by returning the constitution to its first principles. Most fundamental of those principles is a recognition of the origins of those rights. "We claim our rights from a higher source," explained Dickinson, "from the King of kings, and Lord of all the earth. They are not annexed to us by parchments and seals. They are created in us by the decrees of Providence, which establish the laws of our nature. They are born with us; exist with us; and cannot be taken from us by any human power, without taking our lives. In short, they are founded on the immutable maxims of reason and justice." The purpose of government is to protect those God-given rights. When it does not, it must be reminded in an appropriate manner. Though some in the colonies engaged in violence, other protests manifested "not in *action*, but negatively, in a *refusal to act*, in a manner destructive to them." He meant noncompliance with the unjust law to use stamped paper. "Perhaps you think," he suggested, "they were guilty in forming and persisting in their universal determination not to use stamped papers, as they were commanded to do."[38] But they would have done more injury to themselves had they obeyed the unjust command. He dismissed the idea that such an injustice might have been remedied by a well-penned petition. They had tried that in the Stamp Act Congress to no avail.

Delays meant that by the time Dickinson's pamphlet appeared, news of the repeal of the Stamp Act had reached the colonies, and "A North-American" was accused of simply trying to prolong the controversy. Dickinson's intended audience in Barbados had seen only radical principles in the pamphlet. Several objected to Dickinson's inflammatory use of "natural rights," claiming that "by propagating his Principles of natural Freedom," Dickinson has "made himself accessary to the Robberies, Plunderings, Demolition of Houses, and other Excesses" in the colonies.[39] Another compared him to a religious zealot, saying, "His Zeal for natural Rights . . . was carried to an intemperate Excess."[40] British pamphleteer William Knox decried the absurdity of the doctrine of the natural rights of mankind that Dickinson included in Pennsylvania's resolutions on the Stamp Act. Knox scoffed that this doctrine "will render the blessings which British subjects enjoy under their excellent constitution universal to all people." Such a thing was unthinkable. Knox was sure it was "a doctrine unknown to all civilians, except the assembly of Pennsylvania."[41]

Though Americans were warming to the idea of natural rights, most believed that rights were conferred by particular governments and, in the case of the British, only applied to white, Protestant men of property. But Dickinson had a Quaker understanding of rights, one that most Britons, including Americans, did not generally accept. It was more expansive. When rights come from God, they inhere in everyone. Quakers believed that God's Light in mankind meant that all humans, regardless of sex, race, material standing in this world, and even whether they had heard of Christianity, could find God in their consciences and thus were possessed of inviolable rights.

Dickinson was prepared for negative reactions. Enduring them was part of the sacred process of public deliberation. As the conflict with Britain escalated, he laid down the Quakerly principles to which he was determined to adhere. First, "on all Occasions where I am call'd upon as a Trustee for my Countrymen," he thought, "to deliberate on Questions important to their Happiness, disdaining all personal Advantages to be deriv'd from a Suppression of my real Sentiments, and defying all Dangers to be risqued by a Declaration of them, openly to avow them."

"Secondly," he continued, "after thus discharging this Duty, whenever the public Resolutions are taken, to regard them tho opposite to my Opinion as sacred because they lead to public Measures in which the Common Weal must be interested, and to join in supporting them as earnestly as if my Voice had been given for them."

A third and final step was perhaps the most challenging. Dickinson knew there could be serious consequences for his inflexibility. But these consequences must be accepted with love. "While I believe in my Conscience that I am faithfully serving my Country," he continued, "I shall deplore but not dread her Resentment if I happen to offend her. She is my Parent. As a dutiful Son, I shall kiss her correcting Rod. Let her strike—but let her also hear Me." He knew that he might be wrong or his motives misunderstood. "But sufficient it will be for my Vindication, if it be decided, that my Conduct is influenc'd by what I think right, for then it must be influenc'd by Honesty and Affection." He had faith in Americans. If his contemporaries could not judge him fairly, posterity would.[42]

This was the Quakerly code of conduct Dickinson resolved to follow regardless of personal cost. And he explained and modeled it for his countrymen repeatedly in hopes they would behave in the same manner.

News of the repeal of the Stamp Act arrived in May 1766, to the delight of the colonists, who celebrated the moment for years to come. For Dickinson, however, his joy at the repeal was quickly tempered. By the middle of June, it became known that immediately before Parliament had repealed the Stamp Act on March 18, it had passed a piece of legislation called the Declaratory Act. This law declared that Parliament had the right to legislate for the colonies "in all cases whatsoever." It was a most alarming decree. Though few Americans allowed it to dampen their celebrations, constitutional lawyers such as Dickinson took it as a shot across the bow and awaited Parliament's next move with trepidation.

All was not well in Pennsylvania either. Although the campaign for royal government had ceased, another threat to Pennsylvanians' religious liberty loomed. This one came from Dickinson's former client and political ally William Smith. He and other Anglicans had long wanted a bishop installed in the colonies to extend the reach of the Church of England and make it easier for American clergy to be ordained. Dickinson and other religious dissenters saw this as no less dangerous to their civil liberties than the threat from the royal government campaign. After all, escaping the dictates and corruption of the Church of England was a major reason why many dissenters had come to the colonies in the first place.

This new effort gathered momentum as one of Pennsylvania's greatest champions of religious liberty passed from their midst, signaling the end of an era. On July 13, 1766, the venerable Quaker Isaac Norris died at age 65. As his time drew near, Norris, reflecting on his long life of public service, exclaimed, "No man shall ever stamp his foot on my grave and say 'Here he lies, who basely betrayed the liberties of his country!'"[43] With perhaps the exception of the Smith trial, Dickinson could agree. His legacy was literally forged into the State House bell by the Scripture he chose: "PROCLAIM LIBERTY THROUGHOUT ALL THE LAND UNTO ALL THE INHABITANTS THEREOF, LEV. XXV:X."

Polly and Sally felt the loss of their beloved papa acutely. In the best of times, Polly's verse was never blithe. Now her lines reflected her present disposition, dark and sorrowful. Unfortunately for his bereft daughters, Norris died intestate, leaving them to navigate the complexities of the legal system themselves while managing Fairhill. "I feel the loss of his guardian arm every moment," confessed Polly.[44] Norris had indicated that Fairhill, worth thousands of pounds, should eventually belong to Polly's young cousin, six-year-old Isaac Norris, son of Mary and Charles.[45] Little Isaac, Debby, and babies Josey and Charlie had themselves lost their father earlier that year, when he was only fifty-four.

Dickinson, too, mourned his colleague, but when he called on the sisters, they did not seek his help with the estate. Instead, Polly stepped ably into her father's role to manage the vast estate with its many tenant properties, though the grand house slipped into a state of disrepair. Occasionally she sent a polite missive regarding business to Cousin James Pemberton in the guise of seeking advice, both knowing it was rather an announcement of intention.[46]

Now that Aristobulas was no more, Fairhill transformed. No longer a locus of political power as the home of the speaker of the Assembly, now it was exclusively a Quaker poets' sorority. Members of the Rural Circle wandered the gardens, read in the library, and worshipped in the meeting house. Free from male entanglements and oversight of fathers and husbands, they blossomed fully into their *noms de plume*, taking inspiration from the glories of nature and finding consolation amid their sorrows in dedicating verse to one another.[47]

Another female literary light on the periphery of the Circle was Elizabeth Graeme. Many in Philadelphia had read her travel journal, which circulated after her two-year trip to England from 1762 to 1764. Now Graeme and her widower father hosted what they called "attic evenings" at their estate, Graeme Park, twenty miles north of Philadelphia. Many traveled the considerable distance for conversation, debate, poetry readings, and music. Though only loosely connected to the Rural Circle—she was an Anglican and delighted in the gaieties of society—Graeme and its members shared poetry and other literary endeavors.[48] Although Dickinson moved fluidly in both high society and the reclusive Rural Circle, he preferred the latter.

At this moment, Dickinson's life was brimming with possibilities and potential. His law practice was gaining renown and making him wealthy. Amid the tense relations with Great Britain, he had proven to himself and others that he could contribute to the American response with confidence and wisdom. And in the Rural Circle, he had found a society in which he might like to apply for membership. He seemed to be poised for great things.

7

"By *uniting* We stand, by *dividing* We fall"

Creating American Identity and Unity, 1767–1768

As 1766 gave way to 1767, Dickinson's flourishing practice was now a veritable school for talented young apprentices. Among them were Peter Z. Lloyd;[1] James Sayre; James Wilson, a brilliant Scotsman; Johney Willson, Dickinson's ward; and the relatives of a couple of friends: Jacob Rush, younger brother of Benjamin Rush, and John Macpherson Jr., son of the eccentric Captain Macpherson, the privateer made famous for his spectacular captures with his ship *Britannia* and whom Dickinson had represented several times in the Admiralty Court. Dickinson put these clerks through the same paces he had been put through by Moland. He also believed an aspiring lawyer's mind ought to be shaped with literature, which he believed "would insensibly refine & polish his Taste in Composition" and "give a Grace to every thing a man does." And, he told them, it would serve as "Relaxation from your severer Studies." He especially recommended Alexander Pope.[2]

Dickinson modeled how a liberal-minded jurist should practice, accepting cases most lawyers wouldn't take. One such case was *Dominus Rex v. Rachel Francisco*. Francisco was a servant girl, employed by Elizabeth Cremaine of Kent County, who was charged with infanticide and concealment—murdering her illegitimate child and concealing the body. Most lawyers wouldn't touch such a case; making things more complicated, Francisco was a "mulatto."[3] These factors meant the odds were against an acquittal. But Dickinson, believing everyone had rights deserving of protection and that Francisco was innocent, accepted the case and worked diligently on her behalf. Perhaps the sentiments of the Rural Circle echoed in his mind, making him more sympathetic to women's causes.

Infanticide and concealment were among the most serious crimes a woman could commit, and the punishment was death. The law assumed that the child had been born alive and had been murdered unless the woman could prove it was stillborn. In effect, the woman was assumed guilty unless she could prove her innocence. Convictions for this crime were not unknown. In 1759, a Berks County woman named Elizabeth Crowl was executed for the murder of her illegitimate child.[4]

When the trial began, Dickinson addressed the court with two aims: to gain their sympathy for the defendant and to gain their trust in him. "Women have suffered, no doubt, for the Concealment of a dead Child," he began. One could only imagine, he said, the horror a woman must feel first to experience such a grave loss at the very moment when there should be the joy of new life; but then to be assumed guilty would naturally prompt secrecy. It is a "Harsh Statute" under which they must suffer, he argued. He begged the court to depend on his own "Sense of Honour," which would not allow him to defend a murderer.

He first argued that her actions were not those of a guilty woman. Though he granted the incident might appear to be murder, there was proof it was not. There were no marks of violence found on the child and no blood where the child lay. The fact that Francisco had borne an illegitimate child before was crucial. The murder of a first child would seem more likely, and the murder of a second, when the first one had not been killed, would be highly unusual. As to the matter of concealment, Francisco's secrecy was not from guilt but from shame, and she buried the body out of a sense of decency, not malice. She had voluntarily confessed that she had borne a child. She also possessed old clothing from her former child, which indicated a good character.

One of Dickinson's central aims was to challenge the prosecution's expert witness, Dr. Nicholas Ridgely. The doctor claimed Francisco was guilty because the infant's lungs floated when submerged in water, which supposedly indicated it had drawn breath. Dickinson sowed doubt in this conclusion. "Various Operations of physic and nature have been known only recently," he suggested. "The Circulation of Blood is a modern Discovery. Till then, a contrary notion prevailed. The Motion of the earth" is likewise a "new Discovery." He intended to convey that the conventional wisdom such as Ridgely's was obsolete and that more recent scientific experiments would disprove the theory.

He raised other doubts about established medical wisdom as well. When the prosecution argued that the umbilical cord being cut too short signaled malice and murder, Dickinson responded by asking if Francisco had had such "a malicious Intent, how much more strongly might She have exprest it? The Child bore no Marks of Violence. She is very ignorant and woud not have known how to cut the String, which is evident in that she was surprized by the Child being dropt from her in the Kitchen." In his conclusion, Dickinson made his key point, "If there is the least Doubt, there is great Misfortune in Condemning an innocent Woman to Death." He hoped the jury would err on the side of life.

Despite Dickinson's efforts, Rachel Francisco was found guilty of the charge of infanticide and concealment. Yet all was not lost. Her counsel was making applications for her reprieve. Though the jury was not swayed and Justice Vining had convicted her, even he said, "I wish they may succeed." He did not seem to harbor a grudge against Dickinson for commencing a lawsuit against him for the debt he owed Lord Baltimore. Indeed, all the judges in the case believed that there were several favorable circumstances in her trial and strongly recommended her as "an object truly worthy of compassion and mercy." Indeed, Francisco was given a twelve-month reprieve, which lapsed into permanence when the governor neglected to issue a warrant for her execution.[5]

The year since the repeal of the Stamp Act had been quiet, but it was an ominous quiet with the Declaratory Act hanging over Americans' heads like the sword of Damocles. Then in late spring and early summer of 1767, the British ministry, led by Charles Townshend, Chancellor of the Exchequer, followed through on its threat with a new wave of invasive and oppressive acts designed to bring Americans to heel. Called the Townshend Acts for their creator, these were five new laws passed in June and early July. The first, the New York Restraining Act, passed on June 5, prevented that colony from passing new bills until it complied with the 1765 Quartering Act, which allowed the British Army to house soldiers in outbuildings on colonists' property. The Revenue Act, passed on June 26, not only taxed glass, paper, lead, and paint, but it also gave customs officials the power to use writs of assistance to search private property for smuggled goods. Next was the Indemnity Act on June 29, which protected the East India Company from competition from smuggled tea by reducing taxes on the tea. And last, the Commissioners of Customs Act, passed on June 29, created a new customs board based in Boston to enforce the new acts.

Dickinson was alarmed but not surprised. It was only a matter of time before Parliament tested its power again. As he awaited public outcry, he again picked up his pen. When autumn came and no one had objected, it was becoming clear that Americans had been lulled into a sense of complacency by the repeal of the Stamp Act, and now, in Dickinson's view, the Declaratory

Act alarmed them insufficiently. Seeing no sign that the colonists would protest this new, unprecedented attack on their rights and liberties, he realized
that he must act. For some time, he had had in mind an address he wanted to
deliver to his countrymen. Over the next weeks, he began its execution. His
objective was to explain the new laws to all Americans, the elite and laborer
alike, describing in the clearest terms the danger to their rights and liberties,
and convince them to act.

One significant problem, however, was that Americans did not see themselves as Americans. Rather, they thought of themselves as Britons, connected
by their common loyalty to the Crown of Great Britain. Dickinson knew that
must change if they were to resist this encroachment on their liberties, and he
had a plan to reach as many people as possible.

He imagined this address as a series of letters he would publish in the
Pennsylvania newspapers, similar to Jonathan Swift's *Drapier's Letters*,
published in 1725 to alert the Irish of a ministerial scheme to depreciate
their currency. Dickinson would assume a pseudonym, but he did not do so
simply to protect his identity. Rather, he imagined a persona, a figure who
would embody the ideal qualities of a British North *American*. He would be
someone who could be trusted and admired by all ranks, someone whom
Dickinson himself aspired to be. This gentleman would be independent, well
educated, civic-minded, and disinterested. In short, he would be the very
model of virtue. He would be tied to the land and far from the bustle and
distraction of the city. Like Dickinson's own father, or John Moland, or Isaac
Norris, he imagined this character owning a tract of land on the banks of the
Delaware River in Pennsylvania. But he did not want to use the term "planter,"
which had connotations of not just vast wealth and luxury but also the injustice and inequity of slavery. Instead, he sought to evoke something more intimate with the land and accessible to all Americans. He settled on "Farmer,"
someone close to the land but not a yeoman, with sweat on his brow and dirt
beneath his fingernails. The farmer persona harkened back to a Roman ideal
of the free citizen, living independently on his land. But it was more than
that. It was also a Quaker ideal, and one that Dickinson shared—to remove
himself from the corrupting influences of the city and the State House and
retreat inward, to his books and fields, to converse with the sages of old and
commune with the Divine Author. These sources would then compel him to
turn outward to the community and aid those in need.[6]

Dickinson published the first letter in the *Pennsylvania Chronicle* and
the *Pennsylvania Gazette* on December 3, 1767, introducing Americans

to the "Pennsylvania Farmer," who would explain to them their rights and responsibilities and inform them about the legislation threatening their liberties.[7] He spoke particularly to those "whose employments in life may have prevented your attending to the consideration" of public affairs. They, too, had an obligation to engage. "As a charitable, but poor Person does not withhold his *Mite*, because he cannot relieve *all* the Distresses of the Miserable," he counseled, "so Let not any honest Man suppress his Sentiments concerning Freedom, however small their Influence is likely to be. Perhaps he 'may touch some Wheel,'" he added, citing a favorite line from Alexander Pope, "that will have an Effect greater than he expects."[8] Whereas many pamphleteers gestured towards the common people, these writers saw politics, such as horse racing, as a gentleman's sport. The lower sorts, they believed, had no other role than to defer to their betters. Even the quotation he used from Pope was from a poem urging men to accept their place in the hierarchy and not to strive above their stations. By contrast, Dickinson wanted all Americans to engage in these important political deliberations regardless of their status in society. He wanted to raise them up.

While explaining the Townshend Acts, he reiterated the importance of immediate action against unjust law to avoid setting a precedent with their acquiescence that would lead to more oppression. In doing so, he again clarified that violence was not an appropriate response. "Sorry I am to learn," he wrote, "that there are some few persons, who shake their heads with solemn motion, and pretend to wonder, what can be the meaning of these letters." They believed that the established powers were so strongly set against them that they could do nothing to defend their rights. Such men thought they had either to remain silent or take up arms. "To talk of 'defending' our rights, as if they could be no otherwise 'defended' than by arms," he explained, "is as much out of the way, as if a man having a choice of several roads to reach his journey's end, should prefer the worst, for no other reason, but because it *is* the worst."[9]

He had imagined that some readers would question his purpose with these letters. "The meaning of them is," he explained, "to convince the people of these colonies, that they are at this moment exposed to the most imminent dangers; and to persuade them immediately, vigorously, and unanimously, to exert themselves, in the most firm, but most peaceable manner, for obtaining relief." He continued as clearly as possible: "The cause of liberty," he asserted, "is a cause of too much dignity, to be sullied by turbulence and tumult." He knew that the Quaker ways of peace he would recommend were seen by most as ineffectual at best, cowardly at worst. But the greater risk was those looking to stoke the fires of rage that could lead to war and perhaps independence, which was unthinkable. "I hope, my dear countrymen," he therefore said, "that you will, in every colony, be upon your guard against those, who may at any time endeavor to stir you up, under pretences of patriotism, to any measures, disrespectful to our Sovereign and our mother country."[10] Instead his "dear countrymen" should continue the various methods of peaceful protest they had used against the Stamp Act, namely civil disobedience and other nonviolent means, including boycotts, another Quaker method of resistance. They should appeal to the mother country as a child who had been wrongly struck—respectfully and dutifully. And they must give their measures opportunity to work. "Our *Trimmer* believes," explained Lord Halifax, "there can be hardly any such Disease come upon us, but that the King may have time enough to consult with Physitians in Parliament."[11] Likewise, the Farmer said, "*Venienti occurrite morbo*. Oppose a disease at its beginning."[12]

Foremost in the Farmer's plan was encouraging Americans to understand themselves as Americans and to unite with one another. Although he asserted that they were and must remain British, they were naturally also *Americans* whose interests and fates were intertwined. When Parliament attacked one colony, it attacked all. "Let us consider ourselves . . . *separated from the rest of the world*, and *firmly bound together* by the *same rights, interests* and *dangers*." Dickinson's promoting civil disobedience during the Stamp Act had been novel. So too was this call for unity. It germinated something that had never existed before: a sense of an American identity, distinct from being British. In 1755 at the Middle Temple, Dickinson came to understand himself and his fellow colonists clearly for the first time. They were Americans, which to Dickinson meant that they were capable of defying vice and embracing virtue and could "live soberly & prosecute our business."[13] An "*American's* character," he now explained, "is most distinguishable, for his loyalty to his Sovereign, his duty to his mother country; his love of freedom," and "his affection for his native soil."[14] Unity with his countrymen would be his salvation.

The Farmer cultivated Americans' view of their relationship with Britain, training it in a new direction. With independence not a viable option—they were, after all, British as well as American—to some, parliamentary sovereignty seemed an all-or-nothing proposition. Dickinson thus sought to shift the debate away from the unproductive terms of the location of taxation to the intent of the taxation. Until now, most commentators had said that parliamentary taxation external to the colonies—that is, on goods before they landed on American shores—was acceptable, while internal taxation—on goods once they were in America—was not. Instead, Dickinson argued that taxation for the purpose of regulating trade was acceptable but that for raising a revenue was not. Whether in construing wills, defending a murderer, or writing legislation, what mattered was the pole star, the intent.

Dickinson imagined two distinct but overlapping spheres of government—imperial and colonial—each with its own jurisdiction: one for the regulation of trade; the other for raising revenue. This new articulation suggested something most Britons believed impossible: *imperium in imperio*, a state within a state. Indeed, the practice already existed; it just needed to be defined. Dickinson made a start, but Britons were convinced that a body politic with more than one head would be a monstrosity. Dickinson's experience with the various tiers of the Quaker ecclesiastical structure had taught him otherwise. Within the overarching Philadelphia Yearly Meeting were progressively smaller meetings, from the quarterly meetings at the county level to monthly meetings at the municipal level. Although all were subject to the general rule of the yearly meeting, the quarterly and monthly meetings regulated local matters. Something similar could work for civil government.[15]

Concluding on February 18, 1768, and quickly appearing in pamphlet form, the *Farmer's Letters* captured the spirit of the moment and Americans' imaginations like nothing before, selling more copies than any other pamphlet to date. The response was immediate and resounding, going far beyond anything Dickinson could have anticipated. Even before all the letters appeared, he began receiving notice. At the end of January, he was elected into the American Society for Promoting Useful Knowledge and the American Philosophical Society. These honors, however, were coincidental, as his identity as the Farmer was not yet known. In any case, he was uninterested in attending meetings of either.[16] On the other hand, members of the Massachusetts legislature responded precisely as Dickinson had hoped. Following the Farmer's advice, Samuel Adams wrote a circular letter to all the colonial legislatures, imploring them to join together in a nonimportation agreement.[17] This letter led to the first intercolonial boycott of British goods by most of the colonies.

"I would propose," said Adams shortly thereafter, "that this Town, at their next Meeting should take into Consideration, and adopt some proper Method to evince their Regard to a Gentleman who has so gloriously labored for the common Good."[18] The people of Boston accordingly thanked the Farmer and published their gratitude in the newspapers. "'Tis to YOU, worthy Sir! that America is obliged, for a most seasonable, sensible, loyal and vigorous Vindication of her invaded Rights and Liberties," the article effused. "You seasonably brought your Aid, opposed impending Ruin, awakened the most indolent and inactive to a Sense of Danger." After continuing at length in this vein, they described the town meeting. "To such eminent Worth and Virtue," they said, they "express their earliest Gratitude." And they assured the Farmer that they would continue to follow his advice. "Actuated themselves by the same generous Principles, which appear with so much Lustre in your useful Labors," said the people of Boston, "they will not fail warmly to recommend, and industriously to promote that Union among the several Colonies, which is so indispensably necessary for the Security of the Whole."[19] When reprinting the article, one Pennsylvania newspaper remarked, "This is the *First* honour of the kind that ever was conferred by a city on any person in America."[20]

There were more "firsts" to come. The Massachusetts response was only the beginning of a wave of adulation for the Farmer. Many Americans had the same experience as John Devotion in Connecticut. "The *Farmer's* Letters," he said, "have alarmed or opend my Eyes that Fears are now quite as high with me as on Account Of Stamp Act."[21] Letters of gratitude thus poured in from other towns and groups. Poems, pamphlets, and soon books were dedicated to him. Newspaper articles appeared, singing his praises and echoing his sentiments. Even members of the Rural Circle took up the Farmer's challenge to act. The following year, after the Farmer's identity was known, Cousin Hannah Griffitts demonstrated that "female Patriots" could contribute their might to the cause better than their inert Quaker brethren, even without their civil rights. She began,

> Since the Men from a Party, or fear of a Frown,
> Are kept by a Sugar-Plumb, quietly down.
> Supinely asleep, & depriv'd of their Sight
> Are strip'd of their Freedom, & rob'd of their Right.
> If the Sons (so degenerate) the Blessing despise,
> Let the Daughters of Liberty, nobly arise,
> And tho' we've no Voice, but a negative here.
> The use of the Taxables, let us forebear . . .[22]

With praise rolling in from every corner, the Farmer had clearly struck some chord in Americans, causing them for the first time to think of themselves as a distinct people, a people with inherent rights and liberties they had a duty to protect. It was a political awakening, and it made the friends of the ministry and Crown nervous. In the first instance, they feared the Farmer's popularity among the lower sorts. They recognized that he wrote so as to be understood by as many people as possible. William Franklin, Benjamin Franklin's son and royal governor of New Jersey, lamented that the *Farmer's Letters* "being wrote in a smooth, easy flowing stile they pass off very well with great Numbers of the common people in America."[23] Accusing the Farmer of demagoguery, another warned that his readers "are led into such gross idolatry, as to worship liberty without knowing what it is."[24]

A few critics focused on the Farmer's attempt to overcome the problem of *imperium in imperio*, with predictable results. William Hicks, Dickinson's companion from his Middle Temple years, sought to shatter the budding theory of divided sovereignty, which he considered naive, and convince Americans that Parliament was entirely corrupt, bent on oppressing the colonists.[25] This angered Dickinson, who believed this line of argumentation was dangerous, shutting the door to reconciliation and opening it for conflict, wherever that might lead.[26] On the opposite extreme, some argued that Parliament's power was supreme throughout all the king's dominions. About the Farmer's suggestion, they asked "What a political jumble would this create?"[27]

Benjamin Franklin's reaction was emblematic of the limited thinking on this topic. Still in London angling for a position in Parliament, he had no answer to the problem of *imperium in imperio*. "The more I have thought and read on the subject," he confessed, "the more I find myself confirmed in opinion, that no middle doctrine can be well maintained, I mean not clearly with intelligible arguments. Something might be made of either of the extremes; that Parliament has a power to make *all laws* for us, or that it has a power to make *no laws* for us."[28] As imaginative as Franklin was as a scientist, he was far less so when it came to political philosophy.

For months people speculated as to the Farmer's identity. Governor Bernard of Massachusetts suspected someone in New York, perhaps that upstart Alexander McDougall. Some suspected Marylander Daniel Dulany. Lord Hillsborough suspected Franklin. Franklin guessed Oliver Delancey of New York. Franklin was savvy enough to recognize that resisting the wave of the Farmer's popularity would be futile and dangerous. So instead, he took cautious steps to promote the *Farmer's Letters* in England but with an added disclaimer in a preface: "How far [the Farmer's] sentiments are right or wrong, I do not pretend at present to judge." Still Dickinson was very pleased with it. An edition appeared in Ireland around the same time.[29]

In early May, Dickinson knew his secret was out when he received a visit from the representatives of the Society of Fort St. Davids, a gentlemen's fishing and hunting club. They delivered a speech and presented him with a wooden box, carved from heart of oak—a symbol of British patriotism—with an inscription "to the author of the *Farmer's Letters*" that read "in grateful testimony of the very eminent services thereby rendered to this country." Dickinson was, in fact, deeply pained when the tribute, along with his response, was published around the colonies and as far away as Quebec, feeling that it "exceeded all Bounds of propriety" and that not even the "Fervor of the Time" could excuse it. He sincerely wished it had not been published.[30]

In Pennsylvania, only one major group disapproved of Dickinson's efforts: the Quakers. Although they had embraced resistance to the Stamp Act, now they reconsidered their position. They found the fervor stirred up by the *Farmer's Letters* alarming. Worried that a spark might easily be fanned into a conflagration, they thought the *Letters* "imprudent." Thus began a rift within the Society of Friends over whether and how to resist Britain. On the one extreme, those who controlled the Society gradually adopted neutrality as their official stance, abandoning their tradition of civil disobedience; on the other, a faction eventually formed into a separate meeting of "Free Quakers" who were willing to abandon the peace testimony and take up arms. Many were in the middle. Regardless of their stances, all were united in their desire to protect their religious liberties codified in the 1701 Charter of Privileges.

As maddening as the Quakers could be to those in favor of resistance, they were not wrong to be afraid. Threats to their religious liberty were everywhere. In the spring of 1768, Dickinson turned to another ongoing concern. The previous year, a pamphlet had appeared, entitled *An Appeal to the Public, in Behalf of the Church of England in America*, written by Anglican minister Thomas Bradbury Chandler of New Jersey. Building on momentum begun by William Smith and other Anglicans in 1766, it was a plea to Parliament to install a bishop in America. The call for yet more parliamentary interference in the colonies was troubling, especially to religious dissenters, many of whom had fled to the colonies to evade oppression by the Church of England. Protecting religious liberty was, of course, one of Dickinson's primary concerns as well, as he had proven throughout the course of the royal government controversy. Now he joined former family tutor and friend Francis

Alison, the Old Side Presbyterian minister, along with a few other committed religious dissenters, in a response. Following the Farmer, they likewise decided to publish a series of letters in the papers, called "The Centinel."

The first number appeared on March 24, and the authors planned on issuing them regularly at least until the summer. On April 28 and in the beginning of May, Dickinson's contributions appeared, the sixth, seventh, and eighth, and possibly the sixteenth numbers of "The Centinel."[31] His arguments about constitutional rights and the preservation of religious liberty allowed readers to identify him quickly as the author. Two of his principal arguments were, first, that establishing or regulating religious institutions in the colonies was a matter of their internal police, in which Parliament had no business meddling; second, there ought to be separation of church and state. "Religion and government are certainly very different things," he explained, "instituted for different ends; the design of the one being to promote our temporal happiness; the design of the other to procure the favor of God, and thereby the salvation of our souls." Improperly mixing them had "deluged the world in blood."[32]

Pennsylvania, he noted, was the best example of this separation, which allowed even the despised Catholics to participate in the political and civic life of the colony. He did not mention that despite the separation of the institutions of church and state in Pennsylvania, the Quakers there had established the only real theocracy in America. For decades, the leading members of the meeting were also the leaders of the Assembly. The imposition of their religion on members of other sects caused deep resentment towards them and the colonial government. The Quakers' policy of pacifism, for example, was often blamed as the root cause of the Paxton Riots in 1763. The truth was that Quakers had enemies on both sides. Whether Presbyterians threatened from below or Anglicans from above, the Quakers' religious liberty was protected only by their unique constitution.

As the last of Dickinson's Centinel contributions appeared, he welcomed a new friend to town. Arthur Lee of Virginia had decided to pass through Philadelphia to meet the Farmer on his way to London for medical training. The two men felt an immediate kinship, which soon extended to Lee's brother, Richard Henry, who sought a correspondence with the Farmer. Dickinson agreed, beginning a warm friendship based on their similar political views.

Meanwhile, Arthur Lee and Dickinson began work to convince the Quakers in and out of doors to join the resistance. Dickinson wrote two pamphlets, one of them bristling with sarcasm and ridiculing the Quakers hiding behind their pacifism and the other accusing Quakers of prostituting their patriotism to their self-interest when they refused to join the nonimportation agreement. Writing as "Pacificus," he mocked them: "With a happy foresight therefore our assembly perceived, that any steps taken by them towards a 'harmony' or union with the other colonies, for obtaining a repeal of the late acts, must bring upon them such reproaches from his Majesty's *ministers* and our *other friends* at home, as might tend to *disturb the* PUBLIC TRANQUILLITY."[33] If his tone were too subtle, he then wrote in the guise of a "Gentleman in Virginia" to a Quaker merchant in Philadelphia. Because Charles Townshend "saw clearly to the Bottom of your Hearts," he knew that Quaker merchants would approve of his tax scheme for the colonies. "Thus have the People of your Province been deceived into a Pacific Compliance," he charged. "You did not esteem it your Duty, as Merchants nor as American Freemen, to oppose it; BECAUSE IT DID NOT DIRECTLY AFFECT YOUR PRIVATE INTERESTS."[34]

He wished Americans could see Quakers as they used to be—unafraid to speak truth to power. As William Penn put it in 1682, "Where it is Lawful, to be sure, it is best to be *Neutral*." "But," he added, "where *Right* or *Religion* gives a *Call*, a Neuter must be a *Coward* or a *Hypocrite*."[35] Far from being hypocrites, the Quakers in the early years of Pennsylvania enacted their faith publicly. "There was a certain turbulent Spirit in our Forefathers," Dickinson explained, "which never would suffer them to sit down in Silence and Submission under any Attack upon their Priviledges or Liberties." He couldn't think of any people who were quicker to defend their rights than the Quakers. To be perfectly clear that he was not advocating violence but rather civil disobedience, he continued, "Their Turbulence was of such a kind, that no other turbulence can be compard with it. It was the Turbulence of Sense, Spirit, Virtue, Meekness, Piety, employed . . . in Defense of publick Happiness. It was cautious: it was firm: it was noble: it was gentle: it was devout. In short, their Policy was like the Religion they profest."[36] He wished that Quakers would again set an example for their countrymen.

Having vented his spleen, Dickinson had another idea for how to rouse Americans. Although he had long since given up writing poetry, he "ventured to invoke the deserted muses," as he said to James Otis, and wrote a patriotic song, to which Arthur Lee contributed a few lines.[37] Set to the tune "Heart of Oak," which all Americas knew as the song of the British Navy, it caught on immediately and was sung in taverns throughout the colonies.

> COME, join Hand in Hand, brave AMERICANS all,
> And rouse your bold Hearts at fair LIBERTY's Call;
> No *tyrannous Acts* shall suppress your *just Claim*,
> Or stain with *Dishonour* AMERICA's Name.

He sent the song to James Otis for him to give to the newspapers in Massachusetts. Inhabitants of Boston were especially enthusiastic about it. A lawyer named John Adams found that it "is cultivating the sensations of freedom."[38] Yet Dickinson's efforts were misappropriated in some instances to commemorate behavior he didn't condone. The newspapers described large crowds gathering on the anniversary of the destruction of Governor Thomas Hutchinson's house during the Stamp Act protests. Before or after they toasted the Farmer, they sang the "universally admired *American* Song of Liberty," which was "fraught with a noble Ardor in the cause of Freedom."[39] The end of the song was punctuated with cannon fire and cheers from the crowd. This first-ever American patriotic song popularized the line "By *uniting* We stand, by *dividing* We fall." Dickinson had coined America's first national motto.

In advance of the provincial elections, Dickinson and his allies knew they must apply more pressure to the Quakers if Pennsylvania was to unite with the other colonies in nonimportation. Dickinson had been chosen to address a meeting of merchants in April to persuade them, but there was little response.[40] Now he drafted instructions to the representatives of the City and County of Philadelphia in the Assembly for how they should respond to the Massachusetts circular letter and the Townshend Acts.

On July 30, the State House bell rang to summon inhabitants to the yard. Organized with the help of Chief Justice William Allen, the meeting was presided over by Dickinson and Thomson, the two most eloquent orators in the city. Their first purpose was to convince the Quaker merchants to join in nonimportation with the other colonies. Their second was to induce the Assembly to act. They collaborated on a long and fiery speech, making the same plea they had made for months in meetings and publications. Dickinson and Thomson made quite a pair. Both tall and thin, with prominent noses, both masters of persuasion and fervent about the cause of resistance, they appeared as brothers before the crowd. It didn't matter that one was Presbyterian and the other leaned towards Quakerism. They spoke of "the iron rod of power" that hung over the colonies. After reiterating the major points about taxation and representation, resistance to the Stamp

Act, and the reduction of American freemen to "slaves" to Britain, Thomson concluded by quoting at length from the Farmer, the sum of which was "our vigilance, and our union, are success and safety; our negligence and disunion, are distress and death." The instructions to the representatives, which were read after the speech, noted that their sister colonies were being deprived of their power to govern themselves for refusal to comply with ministerial measures and directed the representatives "to exert yourselves as soon as the House meets, that a Petition to his Majesty, a memorial to the House of Lords, and a remonstrance to the House of Commons, be immediately drawn up and transmitted home." When the speech ran in the newspaper, it ended with the new American motto.[41]

Joseph Galloway, meanwhile, would not let Dickinson's efforts go unchallenged. Disarmed at first by the sudden popularity of the Farmer, he now orchestrated a concerted attack. He and his supporters mocked Dickinson from behind such pen names as "Country Farmer," "Thomas Peaceable," "Ironicus Bombasticus," and his counterpart, "Satiricus Sarcasticus." "Little John" parodied in doggerel Dickinson's letters of thanks to those in other colonies who had written to the Farmer. Calling him "John-a Nokes, or Dick-a-Stiles," they accused Dickinson of ambition, pride, pandering to the ignorant, and hypocrisy. The Farmer was a "snake in the grass" inflaming dangerous democratic tumults; he sought to "stir up the people to violence, outrage and bloodshed" with his writings and shamelessly "blazon them forth with *Italics*, SMALL CAPITALS, and CAPITALS without number, that they might make the greater impression on his readers."[42] It was true that Dickinson used every available typographical technique to reach the general public. If Dickinson was bad, his critics believed, his admirers were worse. They ridiculed them for worshipping him like a deity, naming those who echoed his calls for resistance "Fools" and "Parrots."[43]

But these attacks gained no traction. A supporter of the Farmer summarized the weakness of the efforts: "Sensible of the force of the FARMER's reasoning, they oppose it, with a very few arguments of importance, and a torrent of calumny."[44]

Dickinson was philosophical about the attacks; he expected them. When the Anglican minister Thomas Barton presented him with an ornamental perpetual fountain in gratitude for his efforts, he responded that he wished a perpetual fountain "may water the tree of American liberty." He added, "I am extremely sensible of my own frailties, and yet I think I have so much charity, that I reflect with pleasure, that perhaps these very people who abuse me, may derive some little advantage from those very actions of mine for which they abuse me." Content that he had done his duty conscientiously, he summarized, "It is all the revenge I desire to take of them; and this I think, is a Christian revenge."[45]

From the end of July, through August, and into September, almost every issue of every paper in Pennsylvania consisted largely of writings by Dickinson, to him, or about him. Galloway's smear campaign notwithstanding, most of it was favorable from around the continent. The papers reported that the Farmer was toasted not once but twice by the Sons of Liberty in Boston at a celebration commemorating their resistance to the Stamp Act, and again when they dedicated a tree to the goddess Liberty. During the ceremony, they sang Dickinson's "Song of Liberty," which was becoming an anthem of British-American patriotism and resistance. Americans throughout the colonies praised his writings, his character, and his patriotism. No one had ever captured their imagination like Dickinson's Farmer. In addition to the paper tributes, vessels began to appear on the registers at the Port of Philadelphia with names such as *Pennsylvania Farmer*, *Farmer*, *Farmer's Delight*, and *Dickinson*. Other writers on issues of national importance called themselves "Farmer": a "Chester County Farmer" (Galloway), a "Connecticut Farmer," a "Winchester Farmer" (Samuel Seabury), a "Continental Farmer," an "American Farmer" (Crèvecoeur), a "Federal Farmer" (Richard Henry Lee), "A Westchester Farmer" (Alexander Hamilton), "A Maryland Farmer," "A Farmer" (David Cooper, George Logan, John Francis Mercer), and others.

Dickinson's friend Elizabeth Graeme was likewise inspired by the Farmer. Deeply moved by his eloquence, she wrote a new poem called "The Dream, A Poem, The Philosophical Farmer."[46] Graeme imagined the Farmer in a divinely scripted scene. The narrator falls asleep on the banks of the Delaware River and in a dream is transported across the waves to see Albion, the personification of England, chastising Pennsylvania for disobeying her. "Dare they reject my commerce and my power, / And spurn my influence in a fatal hour?" Albion demands. "Retract your claims / And learn to tremble at a Briton's name."

As Albion's indignation causes the sea to roil, the narrator witnesses "A form celestial, venerable, good" descending from the heavens. It is Pennsylvania's founder, William Penn, come to remind Albion that her power is limited by God and reason and that the land had been settled by those devoted to religious liberty. But now, Penn sees that his sons are tyrannizing the inhabitants. Liberty's fire still burns in the breasts of many, but it is difficult to know who truly believes in liberty and who only mouths the word. Then Penn unfurls a sacred scroll, which he gives to the narrator to transmit to the people of Pennsylvania. Among the multitudes she sees that "One youth conspicious tower'd above the rest / His country's freedom had inspir'd his breast." This youth is John Dickinson. To him she relinquishes the scroll so he can deliver Penn's message to the people. He bows gracefully and then conveys the message to the crowd.

As Graeme painted a portrait of the Farmer in verse, an actual portrait of him was advertised in the Philadelphia papers. The printer Robert Bell was selling a copperplate engraving by James Smithers. It depicted the Farmer standing before books, one of them Coke's *Institutes*, leaning on the Magna Carta, and holding a copy of his *Letters* (Fig. 10). Before the end of the year, it was for sale in many colonies.

Dickinson had become the nascent country's first celebrity. The Atlantic World had known only one previously, the English-born Reverend George Whitefield, who preached from the 1730s through the 1750s. But Dickinson was now the first American to reach that status. Two other Americans were known, and even famous. George Washington's journal from the French and Indian War, published in 1754, had introduced him to the literate in England and the colonies. And Benjamin Franklin had become famous for his scientific experiments. But neither of these men had anything like Dickinson's status; he was celebrated by swooning admirers and imitators and possessed unmatched influence over public opinion. Unlike those who were merely famous, he reached a sort of mythical or quasi-divine status as people around the colonies invoked his name to demonstrate their patriotism. On the other hand, as Dickinson would soon learn, celebrity also evokes the opposing sentiment in some people, stirring their resentment instead of their admiration. They, too, would have their say. For better or worse, this was most certainly more "bustle" than Dickinson had anticipated he would make when he first entered politics.

The aims of Dickinson and Thomson in their July speech were achieved after the election, when the House appointed a committee to draw up petitions to the king and Parliament for the repeal of the Townshend Acts.[47] A further indication of the success of the *Farmer's Letters* and the popular pressure they created was that the most stubborn of factions, the Quaker merchants, was finally moved to consider real resistance, albeit tentatively.

They met on November 1 and drew up a memorial to their counterparts in London, laying out the facts and pledging to adopt a nonimportation agreement in the spring if Parliament failed to address the complaints in the Assembly's petitions.[48]

For the time being, Dickinson returned his attention to ordinary matters. He had been so consumed by the hurry of business and the furor following the publication of the *Farmer's Letters* that he had let his personal relationships lapse. This included paying his respects to Polly Norris and her family. He felt it time to pay a call, for he had an important matter to discuss with her. He rode to Fairhill to ask for her hand in marriage.

He may have been nervous, rehearsing his case to himself along the way. Perhaps he requested a private audience. Surely he presented her with an impassioned and yet reasoned case. He certainly had the blessing of his honored mother, without which he would not have proceeded.

Polly did not favor him with an answer immediately, nor when he called again several days later. In the course of conversation—and perhaps as a test of his heart—Polly informed him that Fairhill did not belong to her and Sally. Rather, they intended to deed it to their young cousin Isaac Norris, as was their father's wish. Dickinson believed this would diminish the sisters' inheritance by about one-half. He also learned that the sisters intended to lend all the money they had in England to their Aunt Mary Norris for the benefit of their cousins. Considering that the children were too young to pay even the interest, Dickinson regarded it as a gift by another name, a gesture of how deeply they loved their cousins. Other Norris women had impoverished themselves by such generosity, and Dickinson did not wish to see this with Polly, especially if she refused his hand.[49]

Polly's wealth—or lack of it—made no difference in Dickinson's pursuit of her. He neither needed nor wanted her money. Nor did he need her social status. He had already secured more fame than he could ever have imagined, and he had a vast inheritance from his own father, a thriving and lucrative law practice of his own making, and considerable wealth from tenant properties that increased each year. Though Polly's fortune would be reduced to a very modest one, Dickinson's sentiments and behavior towards her remained the same. "How much soever Miss Norris might lessen her Estate," he thought, "she cannot lessen my Passion for her." He wrote her letters professing his love. But he worried that someone had planted the idea in the sisters' minds that he was primarily interested in Polly's fortune, and he despaired that Polly would reject his suit. Knowing her great regard for her sister's opinion,

Dickinson took up his pen in hopes he could enlist Sally in his cause, insisting, "I was not influenced by the Change in her circumstances."[50]

He scribbled and edited and scribbled some more. But the more he wrote, the more he sensed defeat, as though Polly had already made up her mind against him. He professed to Sally that he "loved Miss Norris with too faithful a Tenderness; she was the Blessing, the Treasure I wished to gain. Every Thing sunk in my View below the least regard, when compared with her inestimable Worth. I do not pretend to practice Piety or Virtue as perfectly as I ought," he confessed. He wanted only to devote his life and fortune to making her happy.

Knowing Polly was not the type of woman to trifle with a man's affections, he resolved not to be the quixotic fool chasing his Dulcinea and to conclude his correspondence with the sisters once and for all with his dignity intact. "I do not, dear Madam, mention these Things to you, in Order to engage your Favor on an Affair, which never more can be renewed," he said. "But I most sincerely wish, that my Conduct may have your Approbation."[51]

It seemed an eternity before he received a reply, but Polly finally accepted his hand. He was overwhelmed with joy. "What an enchanting Prospect of Blessings to me is now fixed on a Union with a Woman, possest of my Soul— whose Virtues promise Me temporal & eternal Happiness." Dickinson was all the more elated because he also had the approbation "of a most beloved & excellent aged Parent, who forms no wish for any greater Joy in this World" than seeing her eldest son wed.[52]

Only a few days after their engagement, however, a disagreement arose between John and Polly about how they should be married. Polly's Quakerism was a powerful force in her life, and she declared that she would be married under the care of Friends. Quakers' corporate exclusivity required that members in the Society of Friends have "orderly marriages" conducted according to the discipline. This meant that they should marry only members of their own Society and do so under the guidance of the meeting. To flout this stricture would be a significant transgression and could lead to her being disowned from the meeting. Polly's faith clashed with John's suspicion of organized religion. He thought a civil ceremony should suffice. He also recalled the difficulties his father had faced when John's elder sister Betsey married an Anglican against the advice and consent of Friends. Though he did not know exactly what transpired, even as a young boy, he had been aware of the tensions the rift created. This was a matter of principle for Dickinson, and where principle was concerned, he could be maddeningly stubborn. He thus dug in his heels and attempted to dissuade Polly from her devout path. When she was equally stalwart in her position, Dickinson again despaired and again turned to Sally, whom he now considered his "dear, amiable sister."[53]

He could not contain his emotions as he wrote to her. "I stand at this moment on the Brink of a Precipice and your kind Hand may save Me from falling & being dashed to Death— If Miss Norris resolves never to marry but before the Meeting, she resolves to make Me the most unhappy Man upon the Face of the Earth; and to this hard Fate shall I be subjected, by the Mistake of a Woman dearer to me than my Life."

Thoroughly unaware of the thin ice on which he trod, he continued. "Your charming Sister has been brought up, I fear, with such a Veneration for the Society of Friends, as teaches one to revere all Quaker rules as equally inviolable: But surely an unbiassd Judgment would make Distinctions between such as may be departed from, without any Immorality or Illegality." As was the way in the Dickinson family, he deployed his lawyerly argumentation. "If an Act is not contrary to the Laws of Virtue or of our Country, can any Rule of a particular Society, however positive it may be, make that Act improper or dishonorable? Unquestionably it cannot." Query asked and answered.

Despite Polly being a mature woman of twenty-eight years and as well read as any on the continent, Dickinson took a paternalistic approach, treating her as he might one of his law clerks. "The Force of Opinions impressed on the Mind by Education," he lectured, "is amazing even to the Persons themselves who have held them, when Experience, further information, mature Reflexion, & a freer Conversation, have enabled them to judge more justly."

He wanted Polly's thinking to be unfettered, as his was, by the arbitrary rules of Quakerism. "By always conversing with People who think & speak in one Way," he admonished, "our Minds are never excited to make Enquiries. We rest quiet in finding the same Sentiments perpetually repeated to Us, & therefore believe them to be universally right: But when a better Opportunity of acquiring Knowledge is presented, our Minds become more active, our Enquiries more frequent, and our Sentiments more just & liberal." These were the principles of liberal arts education that Dickinson held dear. "Let her only determine to consider the Reason of any Opinions inculcated by Education," he begged Sally, "and she will distinguish between those essential to Virtue & Piety, and those merely arbitrary & derived only from Rules of a certain Sett of private Men."[54]

He was right, Polly knew, about all of it. She also valued liberal education. But he asked too much. He assumed too much—or perhaps too little.

She would not be swayed from her faith and commitment to the practices of Friends. Her answer was a firm "no."

To Dickinson, this was an "inexpressible Misfortune" that "utterly destroyed all my Happiness on this Earth."[55] He gained a measure of sympathy from other members of the Rural Circle. Hannah Harrison and her mother were particularly kind. But none of them could prevail on Polly to give up her principles. He lamented not just the lost union with Polly but also the extended family he would have gained.

For her part, Polly had hoped to persuade John to her views on religion. In him, she saw an earnest and noble patriot, one whose liberal education had taught him to care for the unfortunate but also one whose laudable purposes would be thwarted by worldly concerns if he did not embrace religion more fully. Particularly dangerous, she believed, was the great fame he was acquiring, now stretching across the Atlantic World. It would bring him low if he were not cautious. So, as with all things meaningful to her, she put her sentiments in verse.

> For once a moment to advice attend
> and mark the prudent council of a friend
> the love of Pennsylvania fires my breast
> to wish the merits of her sons confest
> justly admired by all the wise and good
> and for their bright resplendent worth belovd
> first fire Religions Empire in your soul
> put ev'ry passion under her control
> and when religion laid the perfect plan
> join education to compleat the man
> let strict Politeness make the diamond glow
> And brave Humanity that melts at woe
> teach you to aid the poor man's friendless cause
> defend your Country's liberty and laws
> that so your virtues may like stars arise
> Shine in your life and fit for ye skies
> And to posterity transmit your fame
> the shining Honours of a virtuous name
> And Oh, beware of Pride & self-conceit
> for if you've these you'll n'ere be good or great

Here it was Polly who tutored John in the great lessons of life and admonished him in turn. Below, Polly drew a line across the page and added a further thought: "Simple thou art and simple thou must be / for I despair of ever teaching thee / Oh had I but a head like thine / and thou a little heart like mine."[56] These hard-headed people would complement one another perfectly, were they not both so stubborn. Now all Dickinson could do was mourn the love lost and what might have been.

8

"Pursue moderate measures with vigour"

Leader of the Resistance, 1769–1773

In early 1769, as Americans awaited the results of their appeals to Britain about the Townshend Acts, Dickinson spent time responding to correspondence he had received during the tumult of the previous year. A long letter from Richard Henry Lee remarked on the maddening lethargy of the Pennsylvania Assembly and the progress of resistance in Virginia.[1] Though some planters were hesitant, others had taken the Farmer's warnings to heart. Lee was most concerned as to whether the Virginia Assembly would stand against the Declaratory Act.

Dickinson shared his friend's sentiments. He had been informed that William Pitt believed that the Declaratory Act made taxing Americans constitutional and that the Administration would "pursue vigorous measures with moderation." Dickinson wanted to reverse the maxim: "We shall pursue moderate measures with vigour." He praised Virginia's spirit of resistance and was pleased to report that Pennsylvania had finally sent petitions home. But there were new causes for concern on two fronts. In Pennsylvania, the Quaker leadership had become more serious about opposing efforts to resist Britain. Leading Friends had recommended to their members that they resign from resistance committees. But they were also increasingly divided on the matter, and it was unclear which way things would go.[2]

Affairs in London were worrisome. "We perceive with grief," Dickinson wrote to Lee, "but not with despondence, that the conduct of his Majesty's most dutiful subjects, had been grossly misrepresented to our excellent sovereign."[3] Recently, the transcript of a speech George III gave to Parliament the previous November had arrived in Philadelphia, and it emphasized the dire necessity of using *only* peaceful means of protest.

"I have seen that spirit of faction," said the king, "which I had hoped was well nigh extinguished, breaking out afresh in some of my colonies in North America." He singled out Boston as being in a "state of disobedience to all law and government," revealing "a disposition to throw off their dependance on Great Britain."[4]

His Majesty was not wrong that Boston and other New England cities had engaged in violence. Their Calvinist religion taught them that militant defense of rights was both a duty to God and their sacred right. It could easily be taken too far. They were not necessarily aiming at independence, but the actions of some rash people allowed the enemies of America to represent them all as rebels. Now the king would be less inclined to come to their defense against his corrupt ministry. A gentleman in London found fault with both sides of the American controversy. "While the advocates for the right of Parliament would reason the Americans into absolute slavery," he observed, "the Americans, on the other hand, run into the contrary extreme, and are very near proving too much; for their arguments, if allowed their full scope, would establish an entire independency." But there was an exception that gave him hope. "In some letters I have lately seen subscribed A FARMER, and written with a spirit and decency that does America honor, the author appears fearful of this extreme, and fairly acknowledges the dependency of the colonies to be necessary for their own sake."[5]

In the meantime, Philadelphians finally began acting on Dickinson's advice. The effort was led by a committee of twenty-one politically active merchants, including Charles Thomson, with Quaker John Reynell as the chairman. Having received no reply to the memorial they had sent to their counterparts in London last fall, the merchants realized they must act now to honor their word. They met on February 6, canceled spring orders of British goods—paper, fabric, china, glassware, paint, and all manner of things not made in America or hard to come by—and pledged no new orders before March 10, by which time they expected a response to the memorial. When they did receive a response, however, it was disappointing. Although the London merchants were sympathetic to the Americans' plight, they had been advised by members of Parliament, such as Tory Edmund Burke, not to lobby on the Americans' behalf. Thus, on March 10, Philadelphia merchants entered into a solemn agreement not to import goods shipped after April 1.

Other Pennsylvanians joined in. Several companies of firefighters vowed to cease eating mutton. Instead, the sheep would be used to boost the budding manufacture of woolens in the colonies. Other citizens pledged to wear leather coats rather than those made from imported cloth. The idea was that Americans could soon produce their own fabric, grown and spun at home, and the colonists could achieve at least sartorial independence from Great

Britain. At first, they would have only coarse, rustic fabrics. But ingenious individuals, such as Dickinson's friend Susee Wright, were already producing their own silk. The following year, the American Philosophical Society established the Society for the Cultivation of Silk, which presented Wright with a prize for the largest number of cocoons raised by one person.[6]

Dickinson's celebrity continued to grow. Years later, Charles Thomson would recall that "during all this time, Mr. D. was considered as the first champion for American liberty."[7] By March 1769, the Pennsylvania papers reported that "Mr. Dickinson's Farmer's Letters, have carried his name and reputation all over the British dominions."[8] Indeed, the *Farmer's Letters* had already been published in at least twenty-seven editions, extending Dickinson's fame beyond British territories. From Spanish Florida to French Quebec, people spoke his name and admired his work. The Farmer was toasted in Savannah, Georgia, and thanks were given and poems were published for him in Portsmouth, New Hampshire.[9] Patriots around the colonies celebrated the repeal of the Stamp Act and raised their glasses not just to the "ingenious Farmer" but now also to John Dickinson himself. In England, the radical journalist John Wilkes had enquired after Mr. Dickinson: his *Farmer's Letters*, said he, "are superior to anything of the kind that was ever published in any age or country."[10] The College of New Jersey at Princeton conferred upon him an honorary Doctorship of Laws.[11]

The *Farmer's Letters* also became known in Europe. Shepherded to France by Benjamin Franklin, they were translated into French. The French were keenly interested in things American, and especially the Quakers in Pennsylvania. To the *philosophes*, Quaker Pennsylvania had brought about a golden age of reform and freedom.[12] They imagined Quaker Pennsylvania to be a state based wholly on rationalism and free from religion. Though it was a myth, it was at least true that Pennsylvania had no established church. As the Quakers' enemies knew, however, that sect still exerted firm control over the colony. Benjamin Rush told Dickinson that the *Farmer's Letters* were well known in France and "added to the Seeds of liberty planted in that Country by Montesquieu, Ruisseau, & Voltaire."[13] The French interest in them was different from that of English-speaking peoples. To them, the *Letters* exemplified the theories of natural philosopher François Quesnay, whose ideas had gained popularity throughout France. Quesnay believed that Americans, and especially Quakers, were healthier, wealthier, and more fertile than Europeans because of their simplicity and frugality and the fact that they lived according to natural law, evidenced by their farming. Pennsylvania Quakers had, in fact, gained their wealth as merchants, but this pamphlet from a Farmer in Pennsylvania seemed sufficient evidence to confirm their favorable biases.

Pierre Samuel du Pont, a protégé of Quesnay, also took a keen interest in the Farmer and eventually established his own residence on the banks of the Delaware River. During this time, most Europeans believed that human characteristics depended on the land in which they lived. While it was assumed that the wilds of America would produce "savages," Dickinson was evidence that the New World could produce men with the civility and intellect to rival any in Europe.[14] Du Pont imagined that his own name might well take root in such fertile soil.

Eventually, the Farmer had made his way to Vienna, where excerpts from *Brief eines Prachters* were published in the *Wienerisches Diarium*.[15] Count Zinzendorf, a prominent German Protestant, himself read the Farmer enthusiastically, which was one piece of radical Americana that was not banned by the oppressive Habsburg monarchy.[16] Poland, too, knew the Farmer, with his *Letters* residing in the libraries of the king and other statesmen.[17]

It was not all applause; the Farmer's celebrity abroad endangered Dickinson's life. There were reports of anti-American speeches in the House of Lords. Lord Grenville, the former prime minister, called the *Farmer's Letters* "an impudent, seditious, and infamous libel."[18] Lord North, Chancellor of the Exchequer, went further, calling for the execution of men responsible for "inflaming the minds of the people." This, he thought, would serve as an effective deterrent to others seeking to stir up trouble. Threats notwithstanding, by May Americans were following the Farmer's advice. The three major ports, Philadelphia, Boston, and New York, were now unified in nonimportation. As the effects of the action were felt, manufacturing in Pennsylvania accelerated, which was cause for rejoicing for the laboring men of the city.[19]

Dickinson was uncomfortable with his newfound status. Although when he was young, his "breast beat for fame," he could not have anticipated this. He found the constant attention and adulation burdensome. Taking Polly's advice, he turned to his work "to aid the poor man's friendless cause." One satisfying case this spring was *Dominus Rex v. John Holland*. The Crown was prosecuting Holland, a butcher by trade, for the murder of William McIlherring, a tanner. To Dickinson, it was a clear case not of murder but of manslaughter. The two men had been sharing a drink and a meal when McIlherring instigated a quarrel by demanding that Holland demonstrate his commitment to Freemasonry by singing a song with him. After Holland declined, McIlherring, indignant, hurled insults, at which point, Holland attempted to leave. When McIlherring followed him out of the house, Holland turned to him, holding out his sheathed sword. But Holland was unaware that the scabbard was missing the last eight inches. McIlherring ran into the blade, effectively stabbing himself. Holland was beside himself, running to fetch the barber-surgeon and tearfully offering any amount of money to save McIlherring's life. He then turned himself in to the night watch. At this point, McIlherring's mistress, Elizabeth Moore, who had witnessed the whole scene, swore she would see Holland hang.

Dickinson took the case, confident in Holland's innocence. His actions after the stabbing were not those of a guilty man. And Moore's testimony was rife with inconsistencies. Dickinson also easily found character witnesses who would attest to Holland's sober, civil, and obliging behavior and Moore's poor character. Indeed, she had recently been banished from the township for disorderly behavior. Upon receiving word of his acquittal, Holland was overcome with relief and gratitude. From his cell, he wrote Dickinson that his "extreme goodness in condescending to plead my cause, has conferred an obligation on me too strong to be conveyed in the common language of mankind." He enclosed a promissory note for £20, but Dickinson always took murder cases pro bono.[20]

Between his work for his clients and monitoring the progress of the resistance, Dickinson had again let personal matters languish. One day in June 1769, he recalled a promise he had made to Sally Norris the previous summer, one that the devastation of Polly's rejection had caused him to forget. He was to show her a bust of Cleopatra in death. It was a fine piece, and he knew Sally would appreciate the work. But just as he was about to write her, word came from Fairhill that Sally was gravely ill with smallpox. The cause was a mystery. There was no contagion rampant in Philadelphia, due in part to the new practice of variolation, the ingesting of pulverized scabs from smallpox victims to achieve inoculation. Though the practice was becoming more common, it was still not widely adopted.[21]

In early June, Sally had complained of a fever, followed by an upset stomach. At first it appeared to be a common flu and her vomiting a favorable sign. But when sores appeared in her mouth and the telltale blisters erupted on her skin, a sense of dread settled over the household. Yet they were not without hope. Many people survived smallpox, even if they were scarred or blinded. The Rural Circle's faith in Divine Providence was strong.

Though Polly sat by Sally's side with broth at the ready, swallowing was much too painful for Sally, with the sores covering her throat. As the blisters afflicted her entire body, they ruptured, producing a stench like rotting flesh. Noxious though it was, the doctors hoped that the release of fluid from the pustules would lead to Sally's recovery, so they encouraged the process by applying plasters to her skin and letting blood to release the corruption from her body.[22] The days crawled by, and Sally's condition only deteriorated. The ruptured pustules multiplied, and she slipped in and out of delirium. Polly bemoaned the "cruel disease" as she viewed Sally's fair form lying "all spotted" before her. She must "seal her lips lest she offend her God with all the anguish of a sister's heart." Sharing in Sally's pain, she whispered, "I feel for thee with every rising breath."[23] Sally smiled at her sister "to sooth her Grief & make her Suffering less."[24]

On Saturday, June 24, at age twenty-three, Sally died, taking a part of Polly with her. "Snatched from my arms," she lamented, "a victim for the grave."[25]

Though distracted by grief himself, Dickinson had business to attend to. He wrote to clients about their cases and to his friends about the resistance to importation. He told Arthur Lee that he had faith that Americans would persist in their support of nonimportation, though the British were equally sanguine that Americans' vanity and carelessness would break their resolve. But this was not Dickinson's main concern. He felt that unscrupulous politicians were manipulating American public opinion, driving them towards independence from Britain. "If we may consider the connection between Great Britain and this continent, as a marriage—a condition, in which the parties are always happiest, when they never dispute about their rights, then these flattering statesmen, may justly be called political adulterers, who utterly poison the peace of families." He looked forward to hearing from Lee that public affairs were placed in the hands of men possessed of virtue and good sense.[26]

As he wrote to Lee, Dickinson received a visit from one Captain William Duddingston. The captain had become known to the colonists since the previous September, when he had taken over command of His Majesty's

schooner *Gaspée* to enforce the Townshend Acts. He had already seized
several prizes off the coast of Massachusetts. Now Duddingston visited
Dickinson on behalf of David Hay, an artillery captain in the British Army
and husband of Hannah Moland, John Moland's daughter. He conveyed a
letter from Hay, written aboard the *Gaspée*, where he apparently remained,
and mentioned to Dickinson that there had been a scuffle between Hay and
a man named Davis Bevan, a Chester County tavernkeeper. Hay wrote that
he feared the man might take out a summons against him. "I rely on your
friendship," wrote Hay, "to make the best of a bad market for me, & I enclose
a fee for no other reason, than that you may with a safe consience declare you
are engaged."[27]

Dickinson accepted the fee and awaited further news, which arrived almost immediately from none other than Bevan himself. Obviously battered,
Bevan informed him of several circumstances Duddingston had omitted.
He was fishing when he saw the *Gaspée* and hailed her, wishing to speak to
the pilot. His boat was seized, and "and in a piratical manner" Bevan was
dragged on board, where he was "accosted with the most abusive language."
Soon Hay arrived and joined the verbal abuse. Duddingston, Hay, and the
other crew members then proceeded to beat Bevan "in a most cruel manner."
After chaining Bevan in the hold of the ship, they eventually returned him,
bruised and bloodied, to his own boat. Once on shore, Bevan followed both
men to Philadelphia, where they attempted to bribe him to not file a lawsuit.
So now Dickinson also knew that Hay was in town, not on the ship, and had
chosen not to approach Dickinson on his own behalf.[28]

Dickinson believed that Bevan's case was the cause of every freeman who
might unfortunately fall within the power of those who seem to think that
their office entitled them to abuse their fellow subjects. He was so uneasy
about this new information that he felt it would be impossible for him to
represent Hay. Writing to him immediately, Dickinson said, "I beg You will
excuse my returning the Fee. If I can serve You as a Friend in accommo-
dating this Affair," he added, "it will give Me Pleasure to express the Esteem
I feel for You."[29] But he thought, "Whenever I am engagd in a Cause by being
misinformed, & find it in Truth too unjust for Me to prosecute, no offers
however extravagant shall tempt Me to undertake the sordid Employment of
acquiring Gain by violating my Conscience."[30]

Signaling his awareness of the lie Duddingston told him about Hay's location, Dickinson sent his response to Hay's home rather than to the *Gaspée*. It
was Hannah who replied. Chagrined by her husband's behavior, she said he

now acknowledged that he had carried things too far. "I am convinced that any thing you do to settle matters, will be agreeable to him," she wrote. "I shall esteem myself much obliged to you if you will do all you can to soften matters and bring this affair to an end without much expense."[31]

Over the next weeks, the incident became a hot topic of conversation in Philadelphia, with Bevan's account published in all the papers. As it happened, however, Dickinson's intervention was unnecessary. After Bevan complained to the civil magistrate, Hay was taken into custody by the sheriff. But before justice could be done, Duddingston took the writ from the sheriff and took Hay off in his ship.[32] The impunity with which British officers could flout American laws was galling.

On Thursday, June 29, Dickinson set aside his work and joined a small crowd at Arch Street Friends burial ground. With many in the Quaker community in attendance, Sally was to be interred near her parents.[33] Though it was customary at the funeral of a young, unmarried woman for the female mourners to wear white, the Rural Circle did not follow such vain fashions. Nor did the funeral display the usual grandeur and ostentation, with an elaborate coffin and lavish gifts for the mourners. Cousin Hannah G. wrote a last tribute as Fidelia to her Sophia, "the dear lamented Maid."[34]

Weeks later, when Polly finally brought herself to sort through her sister's possessions, she found a letter Sally had written her, in the event she should die first. "If it be thy lot to Survive me, I charge thee not to mourn. It will be Inconsistent with that love which had ever subsisted between us."[35] But she could not accede to her sister's wishes. Instead, she responded in verse:

> With woes Opprest admist this awful gloom
> When evry fainting power submits to grief
> How shall I weave a laurel for thy tomb
>   What words can reach—or yield my soul relief.[36]

Later that summer, Dickinson still mourned dear Sally while the bust of Cleopatra remained on his desk. He regarded it as belonging to Sally, so he settled on presenting it to one of the Rural Circle. But he did not want Polly to see it in her vulnerable state. "I am afraid," he thought, "so strong an expression of departing life may affect her too sensibly." Instead, he addressed a letter to her cousin, Hannah Harrison. "I shall receive a particular pleasure, if you will accept it, as a small mark of my perfect affection." Thinking of his broken engagement with Polly, he added, "I once hoped, it would have been in my power, to have given farther proofs of that affection." He now despaired of any union with Polly.

Before he closed the letter, he added a last request. "I am told, Madam, that you have a Profile in Paper of your late dear Cousin— If I may be allowed to take the Liberty of making such a request, I beg to be favored with a Copy of it, which will extremely oblige Me."[37] Because Sally had never sat for her portrait, a silhouette of her profile was the only image he could have by which to remember her (Fig. 11).

With Sally gone, Polly now lacked the "partner of my soul."[38] Feeling Polly's palpable grief, Dickinson could not leave her to mourn alone. He resolved to give her whatever comfort she would accept and resumed his visits to Fairhill. Ever attentive to her needs and promising to shoulder her worldly burdens, he slowly became her "dear Johney Dickinson," and Polly found herself reconsidering his offer of marriage. On reflection, perhaps she could understand his position regarding the marriage ceremony. It was true—she had allowed herself to be cloistered in the Rural Circle, and they didn't often interact with those of dissimilar views. It could well be that her standing on the rules of Quakerism in this instance was unnecessarily rigid. And Dickinson, whom she did indeed love, clearly felt so strongly against it that she might be willing to acquiesce. While she awaited guidance from the Almighty Being, she wrote,

> The swain whose lot to gain my stubborn heart
> Must think no toil to great my love to share
> His words must flow with ease and void of art
> Him to reward shall be my constant care.[39]

At the end of March 1770, Polly finally agreed that it was time they declared their intentions to marry. They did so on the twenty-fifth and set a date of July 19 for a civil ceremony at Aunt Norris's house, with justice of the peace George Bryan to preside.[40]

As Dickinson was minding his business and attending to Polly, he was encouraged that the nonimportation agreement seemed to be holding. But tensions suddenly escalated. News arrived from Boston that on March 5,

British soldiers had shot and killed several inhabitants. There had been "some trifling provocation of a soldier," and then inhabitants gathered, though "without any appearance of arms, or weapons of any sort." But "the officer present ordered the soldiers to fire on the people, which they fatally did, and killed four people outright, and wounded a number more." The soldiers who had fired were committed to jail to await trial.[41] Eventually, the matter was revealed to be more complicated than initial reports had suggested. Actually, a large, club-wielding crowd had surrounded the soldiers and thrown rocks. Why firing began, no one knew; the officer had not given the command. For now, however, it appeared to the colonists to be a "massacre" of Americans by the British.

A few weeks later, the *Gazette* reported another disturbing turn of events. After the New York Assembly had refused to enforce the Quartering Act, Parliament dissolved that Assembly and installed a compliant one. In response, a young merchant named Captain Alexander McDougall had published an anonymous pamphlet accusing the newly installed Assembly and the dominant faction—led by the prominent De Lancey family—of betraying their constituents by voting to enforce the act.[42] The result was explosive. The New York Assembly arrested McDougall, charging him with libel, and then a skirmish erupted between British troops and the Sons of Liberty in New York on Golden Hill. Though one death was rumored, it seemed there were only a few injuries. Nevertheless, both clashes, in Boston and New York, suggested that His Majesty's soldiers would indeed turn on their own countrymen.

The letter in the *Gazette* described Captain McDougall in sympathetic terms—he was an honorable and industrious Scotsman, educated and well spoken, though fiery at times, as his people were known to be. Now he languished in jail. "His Friends, however," said the letter, "hope, that in a cause of such expectation and consequence, the virtuous sons of the law will distinguish themselves by their readiness to assist him; and that the eloquence OF YOUR FARMER will come and defend the principles his pen has inculcated, and which may perhaps have excited the very zeal, so painful to our old patrons of the Stamp-Act, and their present adherents." This case could only remind Dickinson of William Smith's libel trial with the Pennsylvania Assembly. Although blood had now been shed, Dickinson retained hope that Americans would take the righteous path. "Homespun Cloaths are all the Armor—Spades & Plow Shares the Weapons We shall use in this Holy War."[43]

By early May, not long after Americans had finished toasting the Farmer and other patriots in celebration of the repeal of the Stamp Act, they learned the glorious news that all of the Townshend Acts were repealed except for the Tea Act.[44] The Philadelphia merchants now divided into two groups: those who believed the resistance should continue until the Tea Act was repealed and those who thought it should end. As merchants relaxed their boycott and again allowed British goods to be unloaded, the industry that had emerged during the boycott was threatened with annihilation. The craftsmen of the city were therefore in favor of making nonimportation permanent. There were good reasons why resistance should continue everywhere. The merchants of Boston made their position clear. "We recommend," they announced, "that sententious line in the Song of Liberty, composed by our celebrated Farmer: *By uniting we stand, by dividing we fall.*"[45]

The happiest of days, July 19, fell on a Thursday. Because of Dickinson's celebrity, John and Polly tried to keep their nuptials quiet, inviting only family and a few close friends to the little ceremony at Aunt Norris's Chestnut Street home. Despite it being a civil ceremony, presided over by Presbyterian justice of the peace George Bryan, John and Polly had a Quaker-style marriage certificate, with all fifteen guests signing as witnesses. In addition to his mother and Phil's family, on Dickinson's side were the Cadwaladers. On Polly's side were the Norrises; Cousin Sarah Logan; members of the Rural Circle, Hannah Harrison and Molly Lloyd; and Peter Z. Lloyd, who was both Polly's relation and John's clerk. Despite their best efforts, news of the Farmer's wedding could not be contained; bells pealed from Christ Church, and they received enthusiastic well-wishes from groups such as the German community and the workmen in William Bradford's print shop who had set the type for the *Farmer's Letters*. Overbrimming with patriotic enthusiasm, the printers congratulated the Farmer on his "Happy Nuptiuals with Miss Norriss" and assured him that "This Letter is wrote on American Manufactur'd Paper."[46]

The Dickinsons immediately left Philadelphia to spend a few weeks with Phil's family in Belville, New Jersey. After that, they took a little honeymoon in Pennsylvania, accompanied by Cousin Hannah H., first to Norristown, then to Yellow Springs, where they took the waters, and then on to Reading. The mountains overlooking the town tempted the trio to clamber up and take the view. They wished only for Cousin Hannah G. to capture the moment in verse. John was pleased to find that Polly was "a most excellent Traveller." Her presence made everything more agreeable. And he proudly reported to Aunt Norris that "Yesterday completed <u>two</u> months of Marriage, without <u>one</u> Quarrel."[47]

Next it was on to Carlisle, where Dickinson attended to some business.[48] While there, he received a second letter from Alexander McDougall, requesting his legal assistance in his trial for libel against the Assembly in his province.[49] But after his experience with William Smith, Dickinson may have believed that McDougall's case would be handled best by the able lawyers in New York, who knew the characters they would confront.

When the couple returned home, in what was undoubtedly the most unconventional living arrangement of any leading gentleman in the colonies, Dickinson simply moved into the Quaker poets' sorority at Fairhill and lived among them. At Polly's behest, her husband began steps to transfer her financial assets into his name. Although many Quaker women chose not to be *femes covert*, after Sally's death, Polly no longer wanted the burden of managing Fairhill and its tenant properties. Dickinson therefore took it off her hands and enlisted Cousin Hannah G.'s help in managing the tenants.[50] He himself undertook renovations of the grounds and outbuildings, which had been neglected since Isaac Norris's death. Polly was surely also relieved that her transgression of marrying a non-Quaker in a civil ceremony earned her only a reprimand from her meeting and not disownment.

Returning to work after his honeymoon, Dickinson confronted two developments. First, the nonimportation agreement in Philadelphia had collapsed. The Quaker dry goods merchants had long been dragging down resistance efforts. Dickinson had faith that the majority of Pennsylvanians were disinterested enough to still want a boycott. He wrote to his friends Arthur Lee and the famous British historian Catharine Macaulay, both in London, expressing his confidence in Americans. He admired Macaulay greatly, expressing that her works would be instrumental in "rendering Justice" and would undoubtedly "facilitate the Endeavours of future Patriots throughout the British Dominion in every Age."[51]

Second, without his approval, Dickinson had been re-elected to the Pennsylvania Assembly (Fig. 12). He did not want to serve, but his friends had gone to great lengths to get him elected. This would be his first service since 1765, when he felt he had been pushed out by the rank partisanship in that body.[52] Now, at least, he could try to motivate the Assembly, still dominated by Quakers and their supporters, to act against British measures.

When the House convened in October, Dickinson must have felt somewhat vindicated by a pamphlet written and published by printer William Goddard called *The Partnership*, which detailed his troubled professional relationship with Joseph Galloway. Goddard painted a picture of Galloway as a petty, jealous, and tyrannical man taking advantage of a young printer just beginning his career. Goddard confessed that he had allowed Galloway to bully him into publishing many of the anonymous articles that appeared against the Farmer in the summer of 1768, which he since regretted.[53] Nevertheless, Galloway was elected speaker of the Assembly, which meant Dickinson's ability to accomplish his priorities would be limited.

To increase his chances of success, no sooner had the committee assignments been made than Dickinson revived a subject from the 1764 Assembly. He motioned again that the doors to the assembly room be left open so that the property owners and other respectable inhabitants could hear the debates. Knowing the motion would meet with resistance, this time he had a speech prepared. "We are servants of the people," he began, "sent here solely for their Good, not for our own Benefit. They have a right to know what We are doing & know it as soon as possible. We have no Secrets to keep from our Constituents." He painted a picture of unscrupulous politicians with "their own dirty self Purposes" who might "misrepresent out of Doors every Step taken here by those who have Honor & Courage enough to oppose them." He compared Pennsylvania with the House of Commons and the legislatures of other colonies, which granted public access. Pennsylvania had "one of the best Constitutions" that was "favorable to Freedom" and accountable to the people. "Why should We be distinguished from almost every British Government in this particular?" In conclusion, he also motioned that the minutes of the House be printed at the end of each day rather than at the end of the legislative year. This time, he was partially successful. The House voted to allow constituents to witness their deliberations.[54] With this important victory, Dickinson faced the serious problems before them.

Over the previous year, a war had erupted between inhabitants of Connecticut and Pennsylvania over control of the fertile Wyoming Valley, which straddled the border of the two colonies at the head of the Susquehanna River. It was a problem for the Assembly to deal with and evidence of how hard it would be to unite Americans against the British. Pennsylvania land speculators and Connecticut settlers both claimed the land, a feud that had been brewing since 1762 when the Penns had used the settlers as a threat against the Indians at the meeting in Easton. Not only had the Penns failed to secure their land, but the conflict had escalated into what would be called the First Pennamite–Yankee War in 1769. In December 1770, the war continued and an old Quaker enemy resurfaced. Lazarus Stewart, one of the Paxton Boys who had committed the atrocities against the Indians in 1763, was the leader of a band of men who had joined the Connecticut side of the skirmish. He had been arrested in the fall but had escaped. Now he had reassembled the Paxton Boys and ambushed Fort Durkee. The Paxtons' hatred for the Pennsylvania government put them on the side of the Yankees, as the Connecticut settlers were called.[55]

Early in 1771, Dickinson was placed on the committee in the House to respond to Governor Penn's request for aid in bringing the miscreants to justice. In the response Dickinson drafted, they suggested first a proclamation offering a reward for Stewart's arrest. But in the fighting, Stewart slipped away into Connecticut.[56] Dickinson could not know that this controversy would still be demanding his attention more than twenty years hence. But it was immediately clear that it could affect America's response to Britain if not resolved.

The beginning of the second legislative session was filled with routine business, including various bills for regulating fishing, improving waterways, and aiding the poor. Dickinson did his own part by donating to the Overseers of the Poor for "assisting such poor persons in this City whose Modesty may prevent their asking Relief."[57] He was also charged with inspecting the Pennsylvania Hospital, another cause to which he donated, to ensure it was serving patients effectively.[58] Along with his first cousin John Cadwalader, Dickinson was a founder of the Friendly Sons of St. Patrick, a benevolent society for aiding Irish immigrants. Although only an honorary member, he regularly attended dinners.[59] Dickinson's benevolence was becoming widely known, enough so that the following year the Sons of Tammany invited him to join them to "form such useful charitable Plans, for the Relief of all in Distress."[60]

Dickinson also hoped to advance the cause of resistance. He motioned that there should be an address to the king from the House requesting repeal of the Tea Act, the only Townshend Act still in effect. The motion passed, and he was placed on the drafting committee, which, as usual, meant that he was the primary draftsman. Dickinson wrote a spirited petition to the king, but he feared that ministerial influence had reached even to their own State House and that it might be difficult to pass the petition he had in mind.[61]

His concern prompted him to introduce two bills he had long thought necessary and were now, he believed, critical. One would prevent members from holding posts of profit, either from the Crown or Parliament; the other would prevent the Assembly from conferring such posts on members. Perhaps with former members such as Benjamin Franklin in mind—Franklin was known to seek emoluments—he gave a long speech on the topic.[62] "Liberty is founded on Constitutional Independence," he began. "The Tide of Corruption . . . is rising fast upon Us, and threatens to overwhelm us down beneath its Weight." He used copious classical references, which would resonate with his colleagues, who knew the main cause of the fall of the Roman Republic was the rampant corruption of public officials. Fully aware he might alienate himself from some of his colleagues, he said defiantly, "I will do my Duty—I will speak what I think for the public Good—if I fail, it is in a just Cause." The cause was against corruption, and those whose votes were bought and sold.

Frequent elections were "no sufficient Security against persons being returnd, who have accepted Offices that [compromise] their Conduct in this Room." He described how someone with the right family or connections but a mean spirit could advance. "It is astonishing what a contemptible Creature, by such Arts can crawl into Office," he said. Dickinson had faith in the Assembly as a body, but some members were "silly Scoundrels" and "abject Wretches" representing "men of sense and virtue." Quoting Scripture, he insisted, "No Man can serve two Masters." The only master an assemblyman should have is his constituents. "Let our Security be made to depend on the Force of Laws—Let them say, who are not fit to be employed in making Laws."[63]

Dickinson's words had no discernible effect. Neither of the bills advanced, and the petition to the king was muted. Certain members, not wishing to offend their ministerial masters, pruned it down. Now, rather than a bold statement of rights, it became something acceptable to Galloway, only timorously reminding His Majesty that the remaining tax on tea meant that they were still taxed without their consent.[64]

Because of this and other thwarted efforts in the Assembly, Dickinson believed he could work more effectively for the public in a private capacity. Although he knew he could win re-election, and perhaps gain more power as Galloway's power faded, when the provincial elections approached, he made clear his intentions not to be re-elected. The electors respected his wishes, but not gladly. "Permit me to say," his kinsman Quaker James Pemberton told him, "I am sorry the public is deprived of thy services in the Assembly; but as things are there circumstanced, I cannot blame thee for withdrawing."[65]

Dickinson was now happily returned full time to his practice and his family. The timing was fortunate. Not only was he exhausted by the continued political controversies, but his family was about to expand. Polly's lying-in period was almost here, and the entire household at Fairhill was busy with anticipation and preparations. Much to Dickinson's delight, his mother moved to Fairhill to assist Polly with her new duties.[66] He also busied himself with plans for a new house in town. He purchased two adjoining lots on the north side of Chestnut Street between Sixth and Seventh, near Aunt Norris's house and caddy-corner from the State House. He would build an impressive structure in front of an old house, and Polly's cousin David Evans would do the work.[67] He hoped to live in town at least while the Assembly was sitting.

Come December, with more joy and pride than he thought possible, Dickinson informed his former clerk James Wilson of the happiest news. "On the fourth of this month," he said, "Mrs. Dickinson presented me with a little girl, as hearty as if she had been born in the Highlands of Scotland." He could think of no better description for the ear-piercing wails emitted by this tiny little creature, which brought to mind the screech of bagpipes meant to call the clans across hill and dale. Wilson, himself a Scot, would surely appreciate his meaning. "I hope, in a few Months," said Dickinson in reference to Wilson's newlywedded state, "You will know, how much more Truth there is than You ever thought in the Expression."[68] They named her Sarah Norris, after her deceased aunt, and likewise called her Sally (Fig. 13).

As the Dickinsons adjusted to having a "young Stranger" in the house, as the Reverend Francis Alison put it in his congratulations, their extended family grew as well.[69] Dickinson had long been something of a surrogate father to an increasing number of young people. He had many apprentices of all ages in his office, from twelve to their early twenties, and he received letters from parents around the colonies hoping to place their sons with him. Other children came under his care when friends died and designated him guardian or he otherwise felt obligated to assist. He continued to advise the Moland children, and family friend Thomas Willson died in 1763, leaving the care of his son and daughter to Dickinson.[70] Johnny Willson had been his clerk. Now, in 1772, Dickinson's dear friend from the Middle Temple, William Hicks, died after a long illness, leaving five orphans in Dickinson's care. Although most were bound out to other families until their majority, at least one infant came into the Dickinson household.[71] Thus, before he had even one child of his own, Dickinson was *in loco parentis.* He enjoyed mentoring young people as he had his own brother. Some of these relationships lasted decades as he ushered them into productive adulthood. Dickinson was a born educator. It was a role he gladly took on for the young people in his life, his clients and juries, colleagues when necessary, and the American public.

As happy as Dickinson was in his wedded state, he did not immediately notice that not all of his acquaintances wished him well. Some of his Presbyterian friends considered it a betrayal that the man they believed the champion of their political causes and enemy of the Quaker party would marry a lady educated so strictly in that Society—and the daughter of the party's leader, no less. As he conversed more with Friends, attended meeting more frequently, and removed to his new country seat amid the Rural Circle, their mistrust deepened the less they saw of him. He began to sense a certain coldness and understood that they might not continue to support him against his enemies, especially if his public conduct should vary from their judgment. They would suppose that he was influenced by "too strong an addiction to the Society of Friends."[72] For the moment, however, being with Polly in his ignorance was bliss.

Early in 1772, Dickinson heard from his former clerk, Jacob Rush, who had enrolled at the Middle Temple. The previous fall, Dickinson had sent him advice about his studies, practices he himself had employed, such as reading the reports of the Chancery Court and attending that court diligently. Rush informed his mentor that he was gaining much from attending the Court of the King's Bench. Lord Mansfield, the Lord Chief Justice, whom Dickinson had also witnessed during his time in London, had a reputation for his efficient handling of cases. His courtroom presented a great opportunity for acquiring knowledge.[73]

Indeed, that very year, Mansfield issued one of his most consequential rulings, in the case of *Somerset v. Stewart.* James Somerset was an enslaved African whom Charles Stewart, a British customs officer, had purchased in Boston and transported to England in 1769. After Somerset escaped and was captured, Stewart planned to send him to Jamaica for hard labor. But Somerset had been baptized into the Anglican Church, and his godparents stepped forward to prevent his re-enslavement and deportation. He soon acquired substantial support from a team of five attorneys, the abolitionist Granville Sharp, and widespread public outcry against slavery.

Somerset's attorneys argued that regardless of American laws permitting slavery, neither the English common law nor statute law allowed enslavement;

further, contract law forbade one to enslave oneself. Later that spring, Lord Mansfield issued his judgment. "The state of slavery," he found, "is so odious that nothing can be suffered to support it, but positive law. Whatever inconveniences, therefore, may follow from the decision, I cannot say this case is allowed or approved by the law of England; and therefore the black must be discharged." With that, Somerset was liberated. But it was unclear what precedent this ruling set or the extent of it. While Mansfield himself denied that the ruling had far-reaching implications for the institution of slavery, and it certainly had no application in the colonies, others found it a precedent with which they could chip away at the institution.[74]

Although the ruling would not be known in the colonies for a couple of months yet, the injustice of slavery was already on Dickinson's mind. He could not ignore the obvious problem with claiming rhetorically, as he and many others did, that Americans were "enslaved" by Britain's taxation policies, while Americans themselves—Dickinson *himself*—held their fellow creatures in bondage. For Dickinson, Sharp's words resonated powerfully: "Why is it that the poor sooty African meets with so different a measure of justice in England and America, as to be *adjudged* free in the one, and in the other held in the most *abject Slavery*?"[75] Why, indeed.

In fact, Dickinson's conscience troubled him increasingly. By now, the Quakers had almost eradicated slavery among their members, and they further considered how they might publish their testimony and bring abolition to the wider society. It was impossible to live in a household with Quaker women and not have slavery a frequent topic of conversation. Dickinson was not yet prepared to free those he enslaved. He was surely worried about the financial loss and the long-term welfare of the Black people themselves. He thus continued to delude himself with the notion that he could make their enslavement comfortable for them.

In the midst of these musings, an enslaved woman named Dinah came to him. She had long been owned by the Dickinson family, first by Samuel and then Philemon. Now Philemon had sold her to a man who intended to sell her and her little girl, Nancy, three or four years of age. But Dinah did not want to be sold away from her home and family, so she turned to Dickinson for help. Dickinson explained, "At her Request I bought her & her Child, to prevent their being sold against her Inclination to a person in Maryland." He paid the tidy sum of £75, though her master wanted £100, and placed mother and child with William Thompson, who lived in Kent County.[76] Soon another enslaved woman, Nanny, requested Dickinson purchase her and her four children to prevent them from being "sold to disagreeable Masters," which he also did.[77] But this tactic was an insufficient resolution to a growing concern, because, although it alleviated the immediate distress of individuals, it perpetuated the institution of slavery.

During the early 1770s, when Americans anxiously awaited the outcome of peaceful protests and the next move by the king's ministers, the Farmer was at the height of his celebrity. So great was his reputation and influence that the colonists would hardly make a move against Britain without consulting him or his writings. If they acted without consulting him or heeding his counsel, they soon regretted it. In the trials following the Boston "massacre," the attorneys for the soldiers were two native sons, young lawyers named John Adams and Josiah Quincy Jr. The latter opened the defense by invoking the peaceful methods of resistance advocated by the Farmer. "Lest my opinion should not have any weight," proclaimed, Quincy, "let me remind you of an author, whom, I trust, and wish in the hands of all of you. One whom I trust you will credit. I am sure you ought to love and revere him. I wish his sentiments were ingraven in indelible characters on your hearts." He then preceded to quote liberally from the Farmer's third letter, extolling the virtues of his position. "Finally," Quincy concluded, "to finish with the justly celebrated Farmer, '*Hot, rash, disorderly* proceedings, *injure* the reputation of a people as to *wisdom, valour,* and *virtue,* without procuring the *least benefit*.'" Quincy asked whether the same was true of this trial. "Who then," Quincy asked, "would sacrifice his judgment and his integrity, to vindicate *such* proceedings?"[78] No reasonable jury would side against the Farmer, he rightly surmised. The defense was largely victorious. Of the eight soldiers on trial for murder, six were acquitted and two were convicted of the lesser charge of manslaughter.

Another ill-considered act by the colonists in 1772 prompted further tensions with British administration and more need for Dickinson's counsel. On June 9, the British schooner *Gaspée*, still commanded by Captain Duddingston, was lying in wait for smugglers off the Rhode Island coast. While chasing an American sloop, the *Gaspée* ran aground. The *Gazette* reported that "a great number of people in boats boarded the schooner, bound the crew, and sent them ashore, after which they set fire to the vessel, and destroyed her."[79] The newly appointed secretary of state for the colonies, Lord Dartmouth, sent a letter to Rhode Island governor Joseph Wanton calling the plundering and burning of the *Gaspée* "an act of high treason, that is, levying war against the king." The letter stated that the offender "should be brought to England to be Tried."[80]

Panicked, the Rhode Island Assembly wrote to Dickinson. Noting "how fatal such a precedent once established in this little colony will be to all the other colonies, in America," they wanted Dickinson to "give us your opinion in what manner this colony had best behave in this critical situation."[81] Others were also eager for Dickinson's thoughts on the *Gaspée* affair. The incident had captured the attention of colonists from New England to Virginia, with the latter colony now calling for inter-colonial committees of correspondence to promote unity and coordinate resistance to Dartmouth's commission. Richard Henry Lee also sought Dickinson's opinion on the matter.[82] He replied that the actions of the British ministry "undoubtedly are the most insulting violation of the rights of Americans that could be devised."[83]

Various groups sought his legal services on local matters unrelated to the controversy with Britain. New York attorney Abraham Yates wrote on behalf of the city of Albany, which was contending with wealthy New York families over rights to land. The controversy had been ongoing for decades, and now the families looked to Dickinson to press their claims. Yates explained, "From your former studies and observations (your *Farmer's Letters*, for which every good man in North America thinks he stands beholden to you) I think you will be the most apt and capable to direct us the steps the most proper to be taken."[84] He provided Dickinson with their petition to the governor and council and begged a speedy reply. Certainly, property rights was one of Dickinson's areas of expertise, but, like the McDougall case, this New York matter seemed too remote for him to become involved.

This summer another request arrived from closer to home. Prompted by pamphleteer and politician Daniel Dulany, several gentlemen in Maryland had contacted Dickinson for his opinion on 1702 legislation in their province allowing the Anglican Church to tax inhabitants for every forty pounds of tobacco.[85] Dickinson had confronted a similar situation more than a decade earlier in Pennsylvania, after the death of George II caused the legal and political establishments to question the validity of laws and court proceedings. Only here was a law passed after the death of William III and the succession of Queen Anne. Members of the conservative Anglican clergy, not just in Maryland but also in Pennsylvania, were keenly interested in legal arguments that would bolster their perceived right to levy taxes to support the Church, while non-Anglicans believed the law had been invalidated and this was a case of taxation without representation. In May 1773, the presiding judge, Samuel Chase, had ruled that the law was valid.[86]

As a religious dissenter himself, Dickinson's sympathies lay with the country party; he dreaded an Anglican establishment in the colonies. But the legal question was, if not clear, then at least answerable to a degree of certainty. "I am of opinion," he wrote, "that the clergy of Maryland are entitled to the forty pounds tobacco per head granted by the contested acts."[87] If the liberal faction wished to oppose this law, it must do so through the legislative process.

As the elite in the colonies honored Dickinson in their way, ordinary Americans were expressing their idolization of Dickinson as well. Ships and taverns were named for him, as was a stud horse called "Pennsylvania Farmer."[88] Dickinson's likeness appeared on canvas, in miniatures, etched in copper, molded in gold, and carved in wood. Sisters Rachel Wells and Patience Wright were daughters of the Quaker John Lovell of Long Island. When both women were widowed, to sustain themselves and their children, they began carving figures from wax. In 1771, they opened a waxworks house in New York City, which was destroyed by fire. They managed to save a few pieces and started touring the colonies with statues of the two most notable men in the British Empire: the celebrated Mr. George Whitefield and the beloved Farmer of Philadelphia. "Gentlemen acquainted with those admired personages," reported the *Massachusetts Spy* when they arrived in Boston, "confess their obligations to the skill and industry of these ladies for . . . presenting his numberless friends in Boston, with the living image of John Dickinson, Esq."[89]

Mrs. Wright, though more flamboyant than most of Dickinson's female Quaker circle, was typical in her outspokenness. Her manner and behavior were controversial, and she offended people in the usual ways they were offended by Quaker women, behaving in ways considered unladylike. Abigail Adams would one day refer to her as the "Queen of sluts."[90] But no one loved flattery as much as the social elite, and flattered they were when she produced from the warmth of her skirts, as though giving birth, their exact likenesses reproduced in wax.[91]

A weaving competition in Pennsylvania announced Dickinson's image as a prize. The medal for first place for best homespun wool cloth "contained an ounce of gold neatly finished—On one side the bust of the Pennsylvania

Farmer, with this motto: *Take away the wicked from before the King, and his throne shall be established in righteousness.* The reverse, a woman spinning on the big wheel, the motto: *Frugality and industry make mankind rich, free, and happy.*"[92] The Farmer had eloquently extolled the virtue of frugality and American industry, and this prize would inspire the best products from patriots of all denominations. Another clothier marketed his American-made velvet by advertising that the Farmer himself wore a suit of it.[93]

American-made fabrics were improving in quality. Dickinson purchased a length of American silk made by Grace Fisher, a Quaker minister, as a present for Catharine Macaulay.[94] It was both a token of his esteem for her and a mark of American ingenuity. Her response delighted him. "It was with some difficulty," she confessed, "that I could prevent my heart the being somewhat elated with vanity on the reception of a present from, a man of the most dignified character on the other side the Atlantic nor can I ever wear the example of American quality and ingenuity without feeling a very sensible pleasure." When she added that she hoped Americans would "always be satisfied with "the produce of their plentiful country" and imitate the "virtuous periods of the Greek and Roman States" rather than the ruinous decadent periods, she spoke Dickinson's mind exactly.[95] As much as he loved his countrymen, he saw the potential for them to become fatally distracted by the pursuit of luxuries.

This very concern animated other residents of Philadelphia. Francis Alison was monitoring the cloth market in the city and finding reason for alarm. "Such an immense quantity of English goods as are now on hand has almost drained the whole patriotic fund among our merchants," he wrote to Dickinson. This was a problem for the fledging American manufacturers of cloth, who needed the support of the merchants. In particular, Alison was thinking of an Irishman named James Popham in Newark, New Jersey, who produced coarse fabrics for the lower sorts of people. He was "overloaded with patriotism," but without the merchants, explained Alison, "he must depend on the farmers, as he is most likely to promote their interest." Alison turned to Dickinson as *the* Farmer to advocate for him.[96] Believing that American manufactures were critical to the country's survival, Dickinson would do what he could to help.

Cloth production was not the only industry Dickinson supported. When Polly asked him to put her finances into this name, that included a one-third ownership in Elizabeth Furnace, an iron forge in Lancaster County. Henry William Stiegel, its flamboyant German proprietor, had also begun producing fine glass—not only tableware, but items for scientific experiments, such as glass tubes. "We have been prohibited," said the Farmer, "from manufacturing for ourselves." Because Britain demanded that Americans purchase necessities from her and also taxed these necessities, "We are therefore exactly in the situation of a city besieged," he said.[97] Further, between the bills "artfully framed" by devious ministers and the "extraordinary inattention" of members of Parliament when legislating for the colonies, laws passed such as the 1764 Sugar Act, which disallowed American iron to be sold to any buyer but Great Britain.[98] Dickinson's solution was civil disobedience on a grand scale. Even before he acquired Polly's share of the Furnace, he began actively supporting Stiegel in his endeavors as friend, advisor, patron, and attorney.

Although Stiegel was undoubtedly a talented artist, he proved to be a poor businessman, living beyond his means and indulging in extravagances. He traveled with an entourage that included a pack of hounds, and he entertained with lavish banquets featuring a multi-piece orchestra and multiple cannons fired at the arrival of guests. By the early 1770s, he had fallen into debt, and Dickinson's funds stopped flowing, replaced with hints that a lottery might be Stiegel's financial salvation. It was not, and in 1774, Stiegel ended up in debtors' prison, awaiting the mercy of the Pennsylvania Assembly to relieve him with legislation. Although Stiegel continued to lobby Dickinson for support to regain the business after his release, eventually Elizabeth Furnace passed into the hands of the capable ironmaster Robert Coleman, who employed the unfortunate Stiegel on the property he had once owned and became the wealthiest man in Pennsylvania.[99]

As Dickinson was learning from the throngs who approached him for funds, for legal aid, or simply to be in the presence of the Farmer, celebrity had its drawbacks. He had lost much of his privacy. His every move was scrutinized by friend and foe. But Dickinson could not have anticipated the degree to which his fame would make him a target to more than just his political enemies.

One of the strangest episodes in Dickinson's life was occasioned by his friend and former client Captain John Macpherson, the renowned privateer during the French and Indian War, losing his senses. Macpherson had recently published a poem in honor of the Farmer. His fifteen-year-old son, John Jr., was also one of Dickinson's law clerks. The captain was known for his eccentricity, but what had been mere quirkiness took a dark turn to erratic behavior. Doctors were summoned, Macpherson was declared insane, and he was imprisoned in an outbuilding on his estate, called Mount Pleasant, for one hundred days, beginning in May 1769. During his confinement and upon his release, he sought vengeance, and his sights settled on Dickinson.

Where Macpherson had once seen a friend and patriot hero, he now saw an enemy who had conspired with Mrs. Macpherson to imprison him and turned John Jr. against him. Dickinson's motive, Macpherson claimed, was that Macpherson knew that Dickinson was not the sole, or even the primary, author of the *Farmer's Letters* and he didn't write the "Song of Liberty." Macpherson's ravings were demonstrably false. His own son had grown weary copying the *Farmer's Letters* so that Dickinson's handwriting wouldn't be recognized by the printers.[100] Macpherson implied that he had authored some of the works that Dickinson had taken credit for and described him as his "bitter enemy," "the most ungrateful and basest of wretches God ever created," and an "ungrateful monster." He claimed that Dickinson feared Macpherson would reveal his secret, so Dickinson had had him declared insane and imprisoned. Macpherson now ranted against Dickinson in several long, erratic, and positively delusional pamphlets, called him names such as "Oliver Cromwell, Jr.," and levied threats against him, as well as against Mrs. Macpherson and John Jr.

Dickinson could see for himself the pressure John Jr. was under because of his father's mental illness. "You must leave the base ungrateful *John Dickinson*," Macpherson railed to his son. "If you love me better than *John Dickinson*, you will obey me; if you love *John Dickinson* better than me, obey him; he or I shall fall in fame." It was no surprise, then, that John Jr. now approached Dickinson and requested a release from his indenture on the grounds that his father would disinherit him if he remained.

Dickinson agreed to release him. "I shall always be ready to do you a real service," he said, "but as the fiercest threats against my person and reputation, have not prevailed on me, so I hope you will excuse me, if vain threats against you cannot prevail on me, to act in a manner, that, in my opinion, would injure my character." He then encouraged the boy to do what he thought best and would not blame him.[101]

Dickinson's unease with his celebrity manifested itself in his adhering even more tightly to his sense of virtue and honor. These were not abstractions to him. Rather, they were strict guides for his personal and professional conduct to which he attempted to adhere. Dickinson's friends and family knew well that his principles could make him maddeningly stubborn. They must bend or lose him.

His friend Elizabeth Graeme learned this when she invited the Dickinsons to her clandestine wedding to Henry Fergusson in April 1772. Fearing her gravely ill father would not approve, Betsey wished to keep it from him. Eleven years Betsey's junior, Henry Fergusson, though accomplished and handsome, was also unpropertied and without immediate prospects. One could see how Dr. Graeme might object to such a match. If they married, Graeme Park would immediately become Fergusson's when Dr. Graeme died. Though Dickinson was fond of Betsey and wished her well, he could not sanction a clandestine marriage that could very well defy Dr. Graeme's will. He had always believed that parents should be at least consulted, if not obeyed, when a child married. This meant young men as well as young women. He no more approved of Betsey's decision than he had of Robert's at the Middle Temple. He was later confirmed in his decision as the occasion became the subject of gossip around Philadelphia.

"Believe me," Betsey later wrote, "I never resented your declining to be present at the ceremony, though it was by my desire you were solicited." She hoped that Dickinson would give her legal advice concerning her recently deceased father's debts and her inability to pay them now that her husband owned the property. He refused to be her attorney, but he called on her to affirm that he would remain her friend. She expressed her gratitude by sending him a copy of her epic poem based on the Farmer.[102]

Some friends were not as tolerant of Dickinson's strict code. His old friend and former tutor William Killen knew him well and was less inclined to accept his rigidity. As the 1772 elections neared, the contest for sheriff in Kent County concerned Killen greatly. Two men sought the post: Philip Barrett, a liberal-minded friend of Killen's, and John Cook, a conservative Anglican. Killen feared that Cook would be a tool of the conservative party and, rather than protecting the welfare of the people, would allow them to be taxed unjustly. Killen sought Dickinson's influence on Barrett's behalf, "to request your good offices with the governor," he explained, "to procure for him the sheriff's office of Kent County, in case he should apply to you for that purpose."

But he knew Dickinson might refuse him. Killen thus took the liberty Betsey Graeme could not and chided him preemptively. "You will therefore permit me to entreat you for once," he wrote, "to lay aside that obstinate dignity, that has hitherto prevented you from asking favors for yourself or others, and befriend an oppressed people with your credit and that of your friends." Knowing that Dickinson cared deeply about "redressing the injured," Killen suggested there was more dignity in that than in adhering to some maxim about never being indebted to government.[103] Killen was blunt in his friendship, knowing Dickinson's strengths and his failings—which could be one in the same—as well as anyone. Dickinson would always act and speak freely when he believed it right and was equally adamant that he would never compromise his integrity. Sometimes, his friends believed, his inflexibility was detrimental to both others and himself.

If Dickinson relaxed his stance and obliged his friend, his efforts were for naught. The conservatives prevailed and Cook was elected sheriff. But his wishes for his own election were fulfilled. In late summer, he published an announcement of his desire not to sit in the Assembly during the next year, and he was not returned.[104]

At the anniversary of the Boston "massacre" in March 1773, Samuel Adams sent Dickinson an oration on the occasion and apprised him of proceedings in the Massachusetts Assembly. The governor had demanded the members' sentiments on the supremacy of Parliament, but they were uncomfortable expressing an opinion until they heard from Dickinson. Considering Dickinson the "ablest advocate" of the public interest, he wrote, "Could your health or leisure admit of it, a publication of your sentiments on this and other matters of the more interesting importance would be of substantial advantage to your country. Your candor will excuse the freedom I take in this repeated request."[105]

Dickinson was grateful for the oration and heartened by the actions of the Massachusetts Assembly. "Time shall ripen the period for asserting more successfully the liberties of these colonies," he replied, assuring Adams of his love for his countrymen, for liberty, and for peace. "But, sir," he demurred, "tho these are my Sentiments, I must beg you will please to excuse Me from enlarging on them in any Publication," adding, "I never took up my Pen as a Volunteer; but always as a Man prest into the Service of my Country, by a Sense of my Duty to her—and tho for a little while I may have endeavourd to maintain a Post, yet it has only been, till a better Soldier could come more completely armed to defend to it."[106]

Adams also desired that Dickinson might meet a young Massachusetts lawyer who would be traveling home from South Carolina. He would only give his initials, "J.Q." Dickinson soon learned the gentleman's name was

Josiah Quincy, the same who had defended the soldiers in the so-called massacre using the Farmer's words. They met a few days later at a turtle dinner with the Supreme Court justices and the entire bar of Philadelphia. The next morning Dickinson called on him at his lodging, where they spoke for another hour, and Dickinson invited him to dinner at Fairhill the following Monday.[107]

Quincy was taken with Dickinson and could not understand the distinct impression that he was unappreciated by a number of gentlemen in Philadelphia. "Compared with the honors paid the Farmer in *all the other provinces*," he thought, "one may justly say 'A prophet is not without, *save in his own country*.'" While on a three-hour ride with another Philadelphia lawyer, Joseph Reed, Quincy plied his host for information about "the Farmer's manners, disposition, and character."[108]

On the evening of May 3, John and Polly held a lavish dinner party at Fairhill, where the guests, including Quincy, were elegantly entertained.[109] Dickinson served turtle, the best claret and Burgundy in the empire, and Berkeley cheese from Gloucester.[110] The conversation turned to politics, and Quincy learned much, confiding to his journal, "I this day had confirmed to me, what I ever believed—that a certain North American Dr. Franklin is a very trimmer—a very courtier."[111] Quincy used "trimmer" in the sense of one who trims the sails of the ship to go with the prevailing winds—an opportunist. As a political analogy, this was the opposite work of the trimmer shifting the ballast to maintain course. Opportunistic trimmers were rightly suspected of self-interest in politics.

Quincy was clearly intrigued by Dickinson. "This worthy arch-politician, (for such he is though his views and disposition lead him to refuse the latter appellation) here enjoys *otium cum dignitate*—leisure with dignity—as much as any man." Quincy went on to describe his house, paintings, antiques, gardens, bath-house, study, fish pond, fields, and vistas, including the Delaware River in the distance, as proof that Dickinson must be the "happiest of mortals." "I verily believe he enjoys much true felicity," mused Quincy. And yet, so perfect was no man's life. On further consideration, Quincy added, "Did you ever see a man of his station without a *but*? I am mistaken, if this engaging, and strictly speaking charming man, has not his."[112]

Through the summer and into the fall of 1773, Dickinson bided his time, waiting for the right moment to resume his activism in the American cause. As he had predicted, Parliament offered another provocation. In May, it had passed a new Tea Act, which was to go into effect in the fall. Pennsylvanians seemed little exercised over the new measure until it was revealed that four Quaker merchant firms had been given exclusive rights to sell East-India tea in Philadelphia. Radical leaders then called a public meeting, the first American protest of the Tea Act, and a committee of twelve met with the Quaker merchants and halted their plans to sell the tea.[113] Thomas Mifflin, a merchant and warm supporter of the resistance, and Charles Thomson, along with Benjamin Rush, then began publishing a torrent of articles and broadsides against the act.[114]

Dickinson believed that the time was now right for him to take up his pen again. For the moment, however, he strategically withheld his identity from the public. He had two approaches in mind, each for a different audience. First, in early November, he published an essay in Bradford's *Journal* under the guise of "an extract of a letter to a gentleman in this city." It was a cool and rational explanation of the offending act, a brief lesson in economics.[115] Thus Dickinson targeted the elites. Second, later that month, he published a broadside under the penname "Rusticus." Here he let his emotions show. Incensed that this act was passed "with a View not only to *enforce* the *Revenue Act*, but to *establish* a *Monopoly* for the *East-India Company*," he again sought to explain the offending legislation. It was a scheme by the government intended solely to prop up this failing company by subsidizing it with taxpayers' funds so it was cheaper than smuggled tea. He demanded to know "whether WE, our WIVES and CHILDREN, together with the HARD EARNED FRUITS OF OUR LABOUR, are not *made over* to *this* almost *bankrupt Company*, to augment their Stock, and to *repair* their *ruined Fortune?*" If Americans purchased the tea, they would be implicitly accepting the taxes Parliament laid on it in the Townshend Acts of 1767.

Rusticus gave a rousing call to patriotic action by Americans of all ranks to "disappoint [Parliament's] Malice." He urged Americans to unite "and publish to the World your Resolutions" not to receive the tea, not even to let the vessels moor at their wharves, not to unload or store it." He that does "shall ever after be deemed an Enemy to his Country, and never be employed by his Fellow Citizens." Even the dock laborers were with him, for, he asserted, "there is a Spirit of Liberty and a Love of their Country among every Class of Men among us, which Experience will evince, and which shew them worthy of the Character of free-born *Americans*."[116] The Sons of Liberty in New York, recognizing the work of the Pennsylvania Farmer, reprinted the broadside on December 4, explaining that it described "the Measures that should be adopted to Baffle the present Design of the *Ministry*, and the *India Company*, to enslave *America*."[117] Philadelphians, however, did not suspect the Farmer.

In view of the threat from the latest Tea Act, two new factions had clearly emerged to replace those of the previous decade. No longer was the controversy about making Pennsylvania a royal colony; now it was entirely about how to respond to British oppression and whether one took a conservative approach, as did most Quaker merchants, or a radical Whig one, as did Dickinson and his friends.[118] But "conservative" and "radical" are necessarily relative. What was radical in Philadelphia looked tepid to those in Boston. By the end of December, Philadelphians learned about the startling event that occurred in Boston on the sixteenth of that month. "The people immediately, as with one voice, called for a dissolution" of the tea, and "they repaired to Griffin's wharf, where the tea vessels lay, proceeded to fix tackles, and hoisted the tea upon deck, cut the chests to pieces, and threw it over the side." When the vandals noticed one man "filling his pockets" with the tea, "they treated [him] very roughly, by tearing his coat off his back, and driving him up the wharf, through thousands of people, who cussed and kicked him as he passed." Another protester turned looter was "paid a visit" by "a company of natives, dressed in the Indian manner, armed with hatches, axes, etc." Fortunately for the looter, he was quarantined after receiving inoculation from smallpox, so "they deferred proceeding to extremities."[119] In the end, ninety-two thousand pounds of tea, worth £9,659, was destroyed.

Like the so-called Boston Massacre and the destruction of the *Gaspée*, the so-called Tea Party was not, to Dickinson's mind, an honorable act. As understandable as Bostonians' anger was, the destruction of property and terrorizing of individuals did not follow the Farmer's directives for peaceful protest. Neither did clandestine acts perpetrated by those disguised and cloaked in the dark of night. Such tactics were not civil disobedience but civil violence. There would certainly be swift and terrible repercussions to follow such immoderation. Accordingly, as the radical leaders in Philadelphia whipped up support for the Tea Party, the Trimmer shifted his ballast slightly to the starboard side.

9

"Freedom or an honorable Death"

The Continental Congresses, 1774–1775

The spring of 1774 was a time of joy and trepidation for the Dickinson family. On May 7, Polly presented John with their second child, whom they called Mary, after her grandmother. She was hearty and immediately brightened their lives. But at the same time, public affairs were grim—and predictable. News reached Philadelphia that Parliament had begun passing punitive measures in response to the unrest in Boston, which the British called the Coercive Acts. The first was the Boston Port Bill, which closed the port and required payment for the destroyed tea. Samuel Adams, Josiah Quincy, and Arthur Lee implored Dickinson's help to instruct Americans on their course of action. Knowing that this new punishment was because of how Bostonians had "imprudently acted our Past," Adams sought his advice.[1] Quincy and Lee both expressed a desire for a "general Congress" to determine how to resist, and they knew "your Colony must take the lead in this Matter."[2] Dickinson had already begun writing a second series of letters to his countrymen.

On May 18, Paul Revere, a Boston silversmith, arrived with a letter from the Committee of Correspondence in that town appealing to all colonies to suspend their trade with Great Britain.[3] They were following the same path the Pennsylvania Farmer had taught them in 1768. And, again, Pennsylvania's participation as the most central of the colonies, culturally, economically, and geographically, was critical.

In response, a triumvirate of Whig leaders of the resistance in Philadelphia—Joseph Reed the lawyer; merchant Thomas Mifflin; and Dickinson's old friend, Charles Thomson—planned a meeting for Friday, May 20, at City Tavern to determine a course of action. They knew that Pennsylvania must present a unified front with Boston but also that the Quakers would be out in force to resist anything they devised. Both sides— Quaker and Whig—hoped the Trimmer would throw his weight their way. This balancing act of unity and resistance was Dickinson's specialty. It was precisely why he had written anonymously on the Tea Act last fall, in order to maximize his influence when the time was right. This was it.

Although generally the Whigs knew that Dickinson was in favor of resistance, they were unsure of what he would actually condone at this moment. They also knew that their success depended on his attendance at the meeting and approval of their plan. "At this time Mr. Dickinson was in the highest Point of Reputation & possessed a vast influence not only over the public at large but among the Quakers in particular, in consequence of his marriage into that sect," Reed later recalled. "No person in Pennsylvania ever approached as a rival in personal influence."[4] It was not just Pennsylvania; the eyes of all the colonies were upon him.

Dickinson confided his sentiments only to Thomson, and together they devised a plan for a public performance that was calculated to bring as many Philadelphians as possible of all persuasions along with them.[5] At the meeting, Thomson would come out strongly and rashly in favor of Boston, enlisting the other Whigs, including Mifflin and Reed, in support. Then, when tempers at the meeting reached a fevered pitch, Dickinson would propose moderate measures. These would appear so mild by contrast with the Whig proposal that Quakers could not but acquiesce.

Come Friday morning, the triumvirate rode to Fairhill. Reed and Mifflin believed they were there to convince Dickinson to attend the meeting that evening. The Farmer put on a show of reluctance. He was distant and cautious, offering excuses for staying away, including alleged fears for his reputation and fortune. There was, of course, more than a grain of truth in his position. He had made no secret that because he loved the people of Boston "with the Tenderness of a Brother," he implored them "by every Thing dear & sacred to Men of Sense & Virtue, to avoid Blood or Tumults." It was not that he was afraid of violence per se. Nor had he ever worried about losing his fame and fortune. Rather, if Americans were to be successful, they had to remain peaceful and unified. "Give the other Provinces Opportunity, to think and resolve," he instructed. "The Cause is the same to all—but the rash Spirits, that would by their Impetuosity, involve Us in unsurmountable Difficulties, will best left to perish by themselves, despised by their Enemies, & almost detested by their Friends." He meant Philadelphians as well as Bostonians. "Nothing can ruin Us but our Violence."[6]

Reed, for one, was taken in by Dickinson's performance, fully believing that Dickinson's "nerves were weak." Angered and frustrated, he asserted to Dickinson, "It was owing to his farmers letters, and his conduct, that there was a present disposition to oppose the tyranny of Parliament that his reputation was high." It was therefore incumbent upon Dickinson to live up to that reputation. Failure to do so would mean "he would be branded as an Apostate from the cause of liberty, & accounted too timid a person to be depended upon in time of danger." Everything, he insisted, depended on Dickinson.

The meeting at City Tavern transpired more or less as Dickinson and Thomson had planned. Mifflin and Reed arrived first, so as not to give the appearance of coordination with the other two. The Long Room of the tavern was packed with two or three hundred men of all ranks and political persuasions: Quakers for and against resistance, Presbyterian Whigs, and Anglican supporters of the proprietary. Reed attempted to begin the meeting but found that he couldn't get far without Dickinson there to lend legitimacy to the proceedings. Now even Mifflin seemed to be having second thoughts about the extreme measures they planned to propose.

When Dickinson and Thomson finally arrived, the crowd murmured approval of Dickinson's presence, and the show began. Reed opened the meeting, the letter from Boston was read, and then Reed, in moderate terms, proposed support for Boston. Mifflin now stepped forward and spoke on the same topic with more warmth. Then it was Thomson's turn. He launched into a fiery speech advocating a declaration in favor of Boston. He spoke with such vigor in the hot and crowded room that he fainted and had to be carried away to recover. Though not part of their plan—Thomson was functioning on very little sleep—his incapacity served their purposes well. Dickinson now rose and, according to Paul Revere, "spoke longer and with more Life and Energy than ever he had done on any former Occasion."[7] He proposed writing a petition to the governor that would call for the Assembly to be brought back into session. The purpose would be to plan for a congress that would coordinate resistance among all the colonies and work for reconciliation with Britain. With the "Spirits of the People raised to an high Degree," as Revere observed, Dickinson departed.[8]

Although the turmoil and confusion continued for some time, those in the meeting were greatly relieved. "Mr. Dickinson's great weight," recalled Reed, "precipitated the company into an adoption of [his proposal]; which being so gentle in its appearance, was a great relief against the violence of the first." Although the Quakers were not in favor of it, they felt compelled to agree with it as a compromise. Ultimately, the meeting agreed to form a committee of correspondence consisting of Dickinson and eighteen other members.

Confidence in Dickinson was so high that he topped both the radicals' and the conservatives' lists. This Committee of Nineteen would take several steps: write a letter of support to Boston with copies going to New York and the Southern colonies; request that the governor call the Assembly into session; and call another meeting of inhabitants of the province when necessary. On the twenty-first, the letter was given to Paul Revere, who left for Boston.

By early the next week, on June 1, Dickinson's new letters to the inhabitants—four in all—began appearing in the papers, repeating his calls for resistance and arguing as strongly as ever that their methods should be firm but peaceable.[9] Reminding Americans of his call for civil disobedience during the Stamp Act and ignoring the riots and other violence, he said, "You behaved as you ought. . . . You proceeded in your usual business without any regard to the Stamp Act. . . . The act was thus revoked by you" before it was formally repealed by Parliament.[10] They should do the same against the new measures. He ended with a call for the collection of the sentiments of all the North American British colonies. For this purpose, he joined the New England colonies in calling for a congress. The letters were reprinted in Boston with an introduction from the editors of the newspaper, Benjamin Edes and John Gill. "The *illustrious Farmer* is once more exerting his *Genius—for his oppressed Countrymen*," they wrote. They were clearly "the Work of that great and good Man, *John Dickinson* of Philadelphia;—whose Name will be revered and loved, while Knowledge, Sentiment and Spirit invigorate this Northern World."[11]

Over the next weeks, the remainder of the Coercive Acts became known. In addition to the Boston Port Act were the Massachusetts Government Act, which abolished that colony's charter and placed Massachusetts under royal control; the Administration of Justice Act, which allowed the royal governor to send individuals out of the colony for trial; the Quartering Act, which stipulated British soldiers could be quartered in any colony; and the Quebec Act, which expanded the Quebec territory and gave Catholics freedom of religion. Each threatened American liberties in different ways.

The petition to Governor John Penn to call the Assembly met with unsurprising failure on June 7, when it was laid before the Provincial Council, and Penn summarily rejected it. Yet it was an important procedural step to preserve the appearance of legality in the actions of the radicals, who could now mobilize with greater dispatch. The Nineteen held a meeting on the tenth to, among other things, debate how delegates to the Congress should be chosen and what measures they should take. Dickinson offered a novel proposal, one that would have far-reaching consequences he neither intended nor anticipated: that all Pennsylvania counties elect committees that would select delegates in a special convention and provide them with instructions. With Galloway as the speaker of the Assembly, it suited Dickinson fine that Penn refused to convene it. Dickinson was foremost among those who distrusted the Assembly, especially with Galloway at the helm—and with good reason. From the beginning of his career with the Smith libel trial, he had watched that body and that man disregard principles of justice and sound procedure to achieve ill-conceived or corrupt ends. Over the years, he had tried numerous times to introduce reforms that would make it truly accountable to the people, but very little had worked. Aside from distrusting the Assembly, he had other reasons for wanting this "committee-convention" plan of choosing congressional delegates, namely that an assembly called into an unofficial special session would lack the constitutional authority to deliberate on behalf of the people and would essentially be a form of virtual representation.[12] But with many opponents advocating choosing delegates through the Assembly, the deliberations continued through the next day. Finally, the Committee of Nineteen adjourned until the eighteenth, which would also allow voters in far-flung areas to attend and weigh in.

The meeting on June 18, co-chaired by Dickinson and moderate merchant Thomas Willing, comprised several thousand voters who gave a ringing endorsement to Dickinson's committee-convention plan. It was a significant victory for the radicals. A new Committee of Forty-Three was formed, representing all ranks above unskilled laborers and all political persuasions. It was more democratic than anything Pennsylvania had ever seen, which was critical to ensure all parties remained invested in the cause. As a concession to moderate members, the Forty-Three then agreed to request that Galloway call the Assembly so they could attempt to work in conjunction with that body. Some colonies would choose their congressional delegates with conventions, and others would use their assemblies; Pennsylvania was the only colony attempting to use both. The idea was that the convention would provide the delegates and instruct the Assembly, and the Assembly would instruct the delegates to Congress. This way, the delegates would be legitimized from the bottom up and the top down. Meanwhile, during the last week of June, Dickinson, Thomson, and Mifflin left to tour the counties to garner support for raising committees. They needn't have bothered; the process was already well underway.

While they were gone, the Forty-Three made progress on several fronts. A circular letter went out to the other colonies setting the date for the meeting of the Continental Congress on September 1. Another circular letter went to the counties calling a meeting of the new convention on July 15. It secured a promise from Galloway to call the Assembly, which turned out to be unnecessary, as Governor Penn was compelled to call it for July 18 to deal with Indian unrest on the frontier.

Although the various factions in Philadelphia—and, indeed, the colonies themselves—were more unified than anyone could have imagined even a few months before, this unity was not perfect. Just as Dickinson worried about Massachusetts adopting extreme measures ahead of the other colonies, there were elements of Pennsylvania society that also concerned him. The militant Scotch-Irish Presbyterians on the frontier could be problematic, as could urban tradesmen. The latter now felt betrayed by compromises made by the radical leaders, compromises they felt gave too much voice to the moderate and conservative elements. In particular, they wanted a ban on importations immediately, exactly the sort of hasty move Dickinson wanted to avoid and which, in any event, would never occur without cooperation from the Quaker merchants. In a long and scathing letter, they unleashed their fury on Dickinson, their leader. The letter alternated between deference to and reverence for Dickinson on the one hand and insults and threats on the other. "The People begin to assemble in companies to consult what they ought to do," the tradesmen warned, "if any Attempt should be made to have any of those who are obnoxious to the People appointed Members of the Congress, it will certainly produce a Riot, and perhaps endanger their Safety." "You we revere & you we depend upon," they told Dickinson. "Your Love to the Cause will readily pardon our Freedom & Fears."[13] This extraordinary letter left little doubt in Dickinson's mind of the danger he would be in if he were perceived as going against their interests. That men of the lower sort would speak to their better in such a manner was a sign of deep currents of unrest that, if stirred up, could overturn the social order. The Forty-Three ignored these and other grumblings of the laborers.

Mid-July brought a flurry of activity for both the convention and the Assembly. The convention met on the fifteenth in Carpenters' Hall, down Chestnut Street from the State House, and began deliberating on the course they wanted the resistance to follow. A subcommittee of eleven men was charged with drafting instructions to the delegates to Congress. Dickinson had already been working on them since July 4, along with a lengthy treatise he would title *An Essay on the Constitutional Power of Great Britain over the Colonies in America.* In it, he labored diligently to distinguish between "rights of the mother country and those of the colonies" and "when resistance becomes lawful." "By the laws of God," he asserted, "and by the laws of the constitution, a line there must be, beyond which her authority cannot extend."[14] In scholarly fashion, he supported his argument with copious footnotes, which themselves had footnotes. He did himself no favors, working almost to the point of collapse. "Whenever Health permits write," he jotted in a note to himself. "Tho an afflicted Heart pours forth its Sensations without Art, while an aching Head is incapable of the Labor of Correction."[15] He might have been heartened to know that Americans would be finding inspiration in this work three decades hence.[16]

Dickinson's instructions, however, were too extreme even for some radical members of the convention. They demanded that Parliament renounce all internal legislative power over the colonies, all taxation, including "external" duties on trade, all quartering acts, and the extension of the Admiralty Courts and other offensive trade regulations.[17] Joseph Reed, for one, resisted, complaining that England would never agree to such terms, and pressed for a plan with a list of minimum demands. It was the same as Dickinson's list, except it left in place current trade duties. If Reed's cold feet on resistance seemed strange in light of his criticism of Dickinson's alleged weak nerves only a few weeks before, Arthur Lee, writing from London, provided a possible explanation: "this Gentleman maintains a constant correspondence with Lord Dartmouth," secretary of state for the colonies and one of "the bitterest enemies America has in this Kingdom."[18]

Meanwhile, the Assembly had convened on July 18 to deal with Indian unrest on the frontier and the matter of the Congress. It voted to allow its deliberations to be open to the convention only; although Dickinson had convinced the House to allow the public to view its deliberations in 1771, it had since reverted to secrecy.

On the morning of July 21, members of the convention walked up Chestnut Street to the State House to present to the Assembly their work and their delegates—Dickinson, his former law clerk James Wilson, and Thomas Willing. The Assembly ignored them. That evening Galloway published a pseudonymous attack on the convention as illegitimate. He called Dickinson a "new *Cassius*," in reference to the vain and ambitious Roman politician who was active in the plot to assassinate Julius Caesar.[19] The next day, the House reversed its decision to allow the convention to witness its proceedings.

Behind closed doors, Galloway appointed a slate of delegates to Congress drawn from the House membership, including himself and other ultra-conservative members.

Although the convention did not prevail in the selection of delegates, meaning Dickinson was excluded from their number, Dickinson's impressive talents as a political leader had been on full display over the spring and summer months. Although he did not work alone and depended on a few key allies, no one could have done what Dickinson accomplished in uniting historically hostile factions of Pennsylvania society and, with the committee-convention system, bringing them into stride with one another to present a more or less united resistance to Britain just as delegates from the other colonies arrived in Philadelphia. This remarkable achievement meant that Dickinson's influence would be felt—it would be sought after—whether he was a delegate or not. No man in America wielded more power than did Dickinson at this moment.

As for the complaints of Galloway and his followers, although the committee-convention system was indeed extra-legal, it was not, if the sentiments of most Pennsylvanians mattered, illegal. It had the full endorsement of a broad spectrum of the people. Although Dickinson proposed it initially as a way to do the work the Assembly could not or would not do for the Congress, it remained in place, a permanent fixture on the Pennsylvania political landscape, functioning almost as a shadow government alongside the Assembly. What this would mean for the future was too early to tell.

In late August, as delegates from the colonies began to arrive in Philadelphia for the Continental Congress, Dickinson was the main attraction for many of them. George Washington and Patrick Henry sought out the Farmer, bringing with them a letter of introduction from Dickinson's friend from the Middle Temple, Thomas Mason. "They ardently wish to love Mr. Dickinson's Person as much as they admire the Farmer's Abilities, and Character," Mason explained.[20] The delegates watched him closely, noticing not only his opinions on the issues that concerned them but also his manners and appearance. To them he was the epitome of gentility, with a gracious air, an impressive estate, and liberal views. In his conversation they found him to be genuine and easy, learned but not pedantic. His expressions were polished but without ostentation. Listeners attended "with unmixed delight," hoping that when he stopped "another sentence would be added."[21]

John Adams of Massachusetts, a newcomer to the resistance, was often at the table with Dickinson during these weeks. As star-struck as anyone, he eagerly consigned to his diary every detail of his interactions with the Farmer. He was especially honored to be invited to Fairhill. "Mr. Dickinson has a fine Seat," he wrote, "a beautiful Prospect, of the City, the River and the Country— fine Gardens, and a very grand Library." He added, "Mr. Dickinson is a very modest Man, and very ingenious, as well as agreeable. He has an excellent Heart, and the Cause of his Country lies near it." About another encounter, he wrote, "A most delightfull Afternoon we had. Sweet Communion indeed we had—Mr. Dickinson gave us his Thoughts and his Correspondence very freely."[22]

The adulation Dickinson received from his colleagues caused him unease, which manifested itself in a dream. While lodging at Aunt Norris's house on Chestnut Street, he dreamt he was walking down a street in Philadelphia with Benjamin Franklin—who in reality was in London at this time—conversing about public affairs. Distracted by the conversation, Dickinson suddenly noticed that they were on a long, narrow street with tall buildings. "How we came into this gloomy place I know not." Before he knew it, they were stumbling through a vast heap of ashes. Franklin then disappeared, leaving Dickinson struggling to get clear of the ashes, "frequently falling, almost smothered and scarcely hoping to escape with life." When he finally emerged, he had a sprained right ankle. As he limped along, "all at once I heard the gayest music, and saw the way before me splendidly illuminated." The melodies and light came from magnificent apartments along each side of the street. "In these apartments," said Dickinson, "were very lovely women. They offered me a variety of liquors and refreshments, that were recommended by a fragrance I had never known before, and invited me with every temptation to enter their glittering chambers." Perhaps this was the abode of the ancient goddess Pheme, whom Dickinson knew from reading Virgil. She was a relentless gossip who, on a whim, could raise a man up to renown or destroy him with scandal. She was also a close acquaintance of Dr. Franklin, who frequently did her bidding.

As Dickinson fought the desire to accept the invitation, a beautiful little black-and-white-spotted dog approached him. Although the dog first seemed friendly, he bit Dickinson's wounded ankle. As he kicked the dog away, it occurred to him that it represented vice. Before long, an unattractive little black dog approached. Dickinson was wary, expecting another attack. But when he gazed into the dog's eyes, he saw his good nature. Dickinson patted the dog, who then took Dickinson's wounded ankle into his mouth and healed it. He knew then that the dog was the embodiment of virtue and allowed himself to be led along by his new "friendly companion," who would periodically glance back to ensure he was being followed. As they proceeded, Dickinson was torn between the "powerful fascination" of the ladies' chambers and "the protecting energy of truth" leading him forward. His mind was "convulsed with agony," and he felt a "tempest of conflicting agitations." Like his Quaker ancestors, his "whole frame trembl[ed] at the eternity of guilt by a violation" of virtue. Eventually, at a great distance, he noticed a light resembling a star. "The more eagerly I pressed towards the starlike light," the weaker the temptations became. "At last," he concluded, "without any expectation of such a deliverance, to my inexpressible joy, I found on my right hand a flight of steps, that led me directly up into the light of day."[23] When flattery flowed so freely, Dickinson felt challenged to adhere to the path of virtue and follow his pole star.

The First Continental Congress met on September 5 in Carpenters' Hall, rejecting Joseph Galloway's proposal that they meet on his territory, in the State House. On the first day, Charles Thomson was just alighting from his horse to pay a visit to Mary Norris, the aunt of his new bride, Hannah Harrison (Sophronia), when the messenger of Congress "accosted" him with a request that he come to Carpenters' Hall. Upon entering, he saw "an august Assembly. And deep thought and solemn anxiety were observable on their countenances."[24] Although Dickinson was not among them, his presence loomed large. It was his vision of the twin goals of peaceful resistance and reconciliation that dominated the proceedings. In pursuit of these aims, Congress was unified with virtually no dissent. And it was not just Dickinson's vision that prevailed; despite his absence from the Congress, he drafted the documents that would guide America in its early days.

On September 17, Congress was presented with as thorough a statement of the Pennsylvania Farmer's vision as he could have wished. Paul Revere brought a copy of the Suffolk Resolves, passed in Massachusetts a few days before. The points contained precisely what Dickinson had urged—peaceful protests through economic measures and disobedience of Britain's unconstitutional laws—and no suggestion of violence other than preparations for self-defense by colonial militias. Congress endorsed them unanimously.[25]

Come election day on October 1, the talk of Philadelphia was whether Dickinson would be chosen so he could take his rightful place in Congress. So eager was the public that larger than normal crowds, including many of the delegates, gathered to watch the returns. When he was elected as a representative from Philadelphia County, celebrations ensued. He took his seat on

October 17, contributing to the ongoing debate on the Articles of Association, which would leverage America's economic power against Great Britain, and continuing his work on the other documents. Thomson later recalled that Dickinson "was the most eloquent Speaker in the first congress," adding that "the eloquence of Patrick Henry was much overrated." Ultimately, wrote Thomson, "some of the most admired productions of the First Congress were from his pen."[26] Of the six documents it issued, Dickinson was the primary draftsman of three of them—the Petition to the King, "To the Inhabitants of the Colonies," and *Letter to the Inhabitants of the Province of Quebec*—and likely the lead on the Bill of Rights and List of Grievances.[27]

Perhaps the only document on which the delegates and Dickinson did not see eye to eye concerned Quebec. Whereas most delegates were virulently anti-Catholic and saw the presence of a Catholic territory on their northern border as a serious threat to their liberties, Dickinson, with his Quakerly ecumenicism, saw the Quebecois as friends and potential allies. As William Penn had been willing to work with Catholic James II on the matter of religious toleration, Dickinson likewise could work with Catholic Canadians. He wrote to encourage them to unite with Americans to resist the British on the same grounds as the Americans—the protection of their civil and religious liberties.[28] All people of every religion deserved that. Dickinson's authority in Congress was such that his draft prevailed.

But though most in Congress generally agreed with Dickinson's positions, with so many strong personalities in the room, tensions inevitably arose. At least one member was rankled by Dickinson's leadership in authoring the documents. Thomson observed that "squabbles" ensued when some members, eager to make their mark, wanted their entire speeches and all their motions recorded, even those that failed. "There was a jealousy entertained of Mr. Dickinson's talents by the Lee's of Virginia and some others," explained Thomson, "but in eloquence none exceeded him."[29] One of the "others" was John Adams. After working hard on the Bill of Rights and List of Grievances, as well as the Petition to the King, Adams became peevish when his versions were dissected by Congress. The Petition in particular Dickinson found to be "written in Language of such asperity, as little accorded with the conciliatory disposition of Congress."[30] Both documents were replaced with Dickinson's versions. When Adams realized he would not be credited as a celebrated author, his enthusiasm for the work in Congress turned to tedium and his admiration for Dickinson soured into vindictiveness. Now his colleagues were "nibbling and quibbling as usual," and Dickinson was no longer "agreeable" and "ingenious." Instead, he was "delicate" and "timid"—feminine attributes.[31] He began plotting Dickinson's downfall.

One unusual thing in Dickinson's personal life excited Adams's notice as something he could use against him—the outspokenness of his mother and wife. Most men of the time were unaccustomed to women taking part in political discussions. Despite being married to an outspoken and politically astute woman himself, Adams confessed "a Terrour of learned Ladies."[32] He projected his discomfort onto Dickinson and misunderstood Dickinson's insistence on peaceful resistance as pressure from Mary and Polly. Recalling the time decades later after his ardor for Dickinson had cooled, Adams painted Dickinson as a pitiable, browbeaten husband. "Dickinson had a wife and a mother who were both Quakers," said Adams, "and they tormented him exceedingly, telling him that he was ruining himself and his country by the course he was pursuing. If I had such a wife, and such a mother, I believe I should have shot myself."[33] Elaborating, he said, "If my Mother and my Wife had expressed such Sentiments to me, I was certain, that if they did not wholly unman me and make me an Apostate, they would make me the most miserable Man alive."[34] But this view entirely misrepresented Dickinson and his relationship with his female family members. He valued women's opinions on political matters but made up his own mind and would not budge, even for his beloved Polly, if he did not think it right. Moreover, he had been urging peaceful resistance long before he married.

If interference by Dickinson's female relatives irked Adams, that they were also Quakers compounded the matter. During the First Congress, Adams likewise became firmly set against the "Broadbrims," a derogatory term for Quakers, based on their style of hat. As he later recalled, "The Laws of New England and particularly of Massachusetts, were inconsistent with liberty of conscience, for they not only compelled Men to pay to the Building of Churches and Support of Ministers but to go to some known Religious Assembly on first days, &c." When the Quakers learned about these laws, Israel Pemberton, Polly's cousin, and other leading Friends, summoned Adams and the other Massachusetts delegates to a meeting at Carpenters' Hall where Pemberton and other leading Quakers admonished them on behalf of religious dissenters. Adams was miffed to be lectured to by these haughty sectarians, and his resentment took root.[35]

After Congress adjourned, in November the radical faction in Philadelphia, heartened by the recent election and Congress's measures, sought to formalize a new alliance that excluded any conservative or moderate members.

Calling themselves the "Committee of Observance and Inspection," the members ultimately numbered sixty-six, with Dickinson one of their key leaders, along with others such as Charles Thomson and Thomas Mifflin. Similarly, the Pennsylvania Assembly finished its business for the year by endorsing the *Journal of Congress*, to which the conservative members, led by Joseph Galloway, objected strenuously.[36]

These days, Dickinson was increasingly impatient with the unending factionalism, which was especially trying as he labored under "a great deal of Sickness."[37] "I have found it almost impossible," he thought, "to act with Integrity, without displeasing a powerful Faction—among the weak of whom, their Views are Despicable, & among the artful, selfish."[38] But the public demanded he serve. His reputation had never been higher. "The present Distraction of public Affairs induces Me to serve this year, but I am resolv'd to decline, as soon as I think, my Duty will permit Me."[39] He would have to wait some time.

Meanwhile, struggles continued in Pennsylvania between the contending factions, with a new ultra-radical wing gaining strength in the Committee of Sixty-Six, as it was now being called. Seeking to follow their counterparts in neighboring colonies, some members called a convention, hoping to establish a militia for armed resistance. Dickinson and the other leaders of the Sixty-Six knew that such a premature move would strengthen the resolve of the conservative faction and undo all their gains in the Congress. At the convention on January 23, 1775, the ultra-radical element was restrained, but all the same, the next day, Quakers issued a "testimony" condemning Congress and all radical activity.[40] Though claiming to be apolitical, their highly political stance had the opposite effect, splintering and weakening the conservatives in the colony. News of disunity in Pennsylvania fired up the presses in New York, a growing bastion of Toryism, which falsely claimed that the Pennsylvania Farmer had abandoned the radical cause.[41] They undoubtedly hoped he would.

As radical and conservative factions in the North American colonies became more contentious, Dickinson's influence was convincing other provinces to join the resistance. Although his 1774 attempt to bring Quebec along had failed, an excerpt of a letter from Jamaica, reprinted in the *Pennsylvania Journal*, reported that "Mr. Dickinson is in high reputation here; his writings are pronounced superior to every thing of the kind that has appeared." These writings had been passed along to the government, which inspired the members of the legislature to write their own Humble Petition and Memorial of the Assembly of Jamaica to the king, issued on December 28, 1774, protesting laws imposed on them without their consent.[42]

While the colonists waited apprehensively for the British response to their latest missives, they received only discouraging signals. Among other intelligence, Dickinson had begun receiving letters from Patience Wright, one of the sisters who had sculpted his likeness out of wax a few years prior. She was now in London, a warm partisan determined to aid her countrymen with useful information. Dickinson was eager to receive it. In turn, he informed her that the outlook from the colonies was grim. Only calamities befalling Americans could reconcile them "to the thoughts of bearing Arms, against the powers of our Sovereign & parent State." He himself had come to terms with the idea of a civil war pitting British-Americans in one or more of the colonies against the British government, but not with the idea of a war for separation of the colonies from Great Britain. "Where our struggles will end," he mused, "what strange Revolutions will take place, no human Creature can guess, if once the Sword is dipt in blood, for drawn it already is. For my part," he reflected, "I can only say, there are two points on either of which I shall esteem it my duty, when called upon, to lay down my Life. First, to defend the Liberties of my Country, against their meditated Destruction. Secondly, To preserve the Dependance of those Colonies on their Mother Country."[43]

Then the tension ruptured. The king declared Massachusetts to be in a state of rebellion, and it was rumored he had also designated a number of men, including Dickinson, "actual rebels," directing that they should be tried and executed.[44] At the end of April 1775, British regulars attacked the militia at Lexington and Concord. "The rescript to our Petition," Dickinson wrote to Arthur Lee, meant that "the impious War of Tyranny against Innocence has commenc'd."[45] The king's decree would define the main purpose of the Second Continental Congress, which was scheduled to meet on May 10. The previous December, in anticipation of the next meeting of Congress, the Assembly had added Benjamin Franklin, Thomas Willing, and James Wilson to the delegation. Joseph Galloway, whose Plan of Union had been spurned by the last Congress, was hardly a presence and ceased to be an obstacle for Dickinson or the resistance. He would eventually flee to New York for sanctuary with the British, leaving his wife, Grace, in Philadelphia to fend for herself as the spouse of a Loyalist.

As Dickinson sorted through the latest reports from Britain, he crafted a long letter to Arthur Lee, apprising him of the situation and formulating the American response. "All the ministerial Intelligence concerning Us is false," he said. With defiant optimism, he then conveyed a vision of America. "We are a united, resolved People—are or quickly shall be well arm'd & disciplined— Our Smiths & Powder Mills are at work Day & Night.— Our supplies from foreign Ports continually arriving. Good Officers, that is, <u>well experienc'd</u> ones, We shall soon have— And the Navy of Britain cannot stop our whole Trade." Americans, he knew, were willing to sacrifice for the cause. "Our Towns are but Brick and Stone & Mortar & Wood. They perhaps may be destroyed. They are only the Hairs of our Heads. If shav'd ever so close, they will grow again. We compare them not with our Rights & Liberties." In politics as in religion, there was a clear and direct channel to the sacred and divine. "We worship as our Fathers worship'd," he proclaimed, "not Idols which our Hands have made."[46]

At this fraught moment, all was not well in the Dickinson household. Little Mary was ill, and after a week or two, it became clear she had contracted smallpox, the same disease that had taken her three uncles so long ago, as well as her Aunt Sally. Her parents watched with excruciating helplessness as their little girl suffered from blisters and fever, and on May 5, two days before her first birthday, their bonnie little girl succumbed. The next day, her parents requested of Philadelphia Monthly Meeting that she be buried as a Quaker.[47] The grief they and her older sister felt was overwhelming. A poem of condolence arrived from Cousin Hannah G., who bore witness in verse to the many deaths of their age. Mary, "a Spotless sacrifice to God," was "releist from all the Painful scenes." She now dwelled with "kindred cherubs" in the "full beams of Love-Divine."[48]

Susanna Wright likewise wrote from Lancaster County to express "how deeply we have felt for you." She and her family were mourning a loss of their own—her youngest brother James, Dickinson's former colleague and ally in the Assembly—and she now turned to Dickinson, "my truly Honored & Humane Friend," for assistance with James's seven children. As she reasoned, "Thy kind Regard" for her brother must "be transmitted to his Orphan Children." She had written in April for his advice about whether she should secure a new patent for the children to preserve their ownership of Wright's Ferry across the Susquehanna River. Receiving no answer and having reflected further, she was now writing to ask another favor, "that thou would Kindly allow thy name to be joynd to ours as a

Guardian to these Orphan Children." She promised him that she would do all she could to ensure that it would not "subject thee to any degree of Inconvenience or trouble." Wright was fully aware of the demands of public affairs on Dickinson's time and attention and knew she would have to wait for his affirmative response.[49]

Indeed, he hardly had time to mourn his own loss. Days after burying Mary, Dickinson returned to his work for the Second Continental Congress, although other delegates noted that "he was, and indeed still is, much affected with the loss of his youngest child."[50] Whereas the goals of the First Congress had been resistance and reconciliation, the primary purpose of the Second was to prepare for "this most unnatural and inexplicably cruel War," as Dickinson described it.[51] A letter from colonial agents in London explained that, although the American cause had some support in Parliament, considerable British troops had been ordered to America.[52] Beyond that, Congress needed to deliberate on its course of action. The body was restless amid the drastic turn of events. With hostilities now open and civil war upon them, a martial spirit was rising, though few members knew what should happen next.

Dickinson shared the martial spirit. "Freedom or an honorable Death," he said to Lee, "are the only objects on which Americans' Souls are at present employed."[53] But although he believed ardently in "the lawfulness of defensive war," he saw it as an unfortunate necessity, not a first resort.[54] "Preparations for war," he said, "must go pari passu"—hand-in-hand— "with Measures of Reconciliation."[55] He thus planned to propose a course of action to Congress. Most members, he knew, would be receptive to his proposal; he was willing to risk the disapproval of the few who would not.

Dickinson laid out his plan. James Duane and John Jay of New York and Samuel Chase and Thomas Stone of Maryland joined him. They agreed that there should be a second petition to the king. On May 15, Jay made the motion, and Dickinson seconded it.[56] The next day, Richard Henry Lee of Virginia and John Rutledge of South Carolina wanted to know whether their aim was independence or reconciliation with a restoration of rights. John Adams responded in his "lengthy, and Argumentative" way that "independence on Parliament is absolutely to be averred in the Americans, but a dependance on the Crown is what we own."[57] In other words, Americans would remain loyal to the king.

In this spirit, Dickinson offered various approaches to the situation, explaining the advantages and disadvantages of each as well as the probable course of events. "We may act in any of these three Ways," he said. "First, We may prepare with the utmost Diligence for War, without petitioning, or sending Agents to England, to treat of an Accommodation. Second, We may prepare as mentioned and also petition, but without sending Agents, &c. Third, We may prepare, petition, and send Agents, &c."[58] This last option included joining a second petition to the king with a treaty.

He favored the third option and argued over the next days as forcefully as he ever had, though some members, who were beginning to consider the possibility of separation, disliked his message. Whereas previously the same people had considered his words to be prudent and reasoned, now they found them to be "timid." Some criticized Dickinson. A few members—Silas Deane among them—even felt "disgust" at his proposal for further reconciliation efforts.[59]

The frustration was mutual. Dickinson grew impatient with a small number of his colleagues who seemed determined to miss his point. "The Gentlemen have confided themselves singly to this Question: Whether petitioning and negotiating would procure Us Redress of our Grievances." But, he again clarified, "That is not the Ground on which I offered it to Consideration." He then repeated seven advantages it would reap, including the strategic ones of "Encreasing our Friends in Europe," "preventing Reinforcement coming over" (namely mercenaries), and "enabling Us to be better prepared" both militarily and commercially. He stated the obvious: "Delays should be courted in Defensive Wars." To those who believed that his plan was "timid," he said, "We may treat in such a Manner as to shew our Courage—& that We are influenc'd not by Timidity or Despondence, but by such Sentiments as ought to animate Men, Freemen, Christians— I go further— I say, We may treat in such a Manner as to shew our Magnanimity and yet most exactly to regulate our Demands with Precision, according to the Dictates of Reason & Policy, by the Exigencies of Affairs, whatever they may be, and to calculate the Concessions We will make, in every Event favorable or unfavorable, that can possibly occur."[60]

Ultimately, the vast majority of delegates found his arguments convincing and supported his proposals. On May 26, they adopted four resolutions. First, they unanimously placed the blame squarely on Parliament for the present situation of the colonies; second, they unanimously resolved to defend themselves against hostilities by the British; and third, they unanimously resolved to send another petition to the king. The fourth resolution, that they should conduct formal negotiations with the British, passed, though not unanimously.[61] Samuel Adams declared himself to be greatly satisfied with their resolutions, believing "matters are finally well decided."[62]

During these debates and into early June, John Adams's favorable opinion of Dickinson seemed restored. At the end of May, he wrote home to family and friends that "the martial Spirit" in Pennsylvania was "astonishing" and "amazing" and "the Farmer is a Colonel."[63] The militant members of Congress knew that Dickinson was right and that the public would support only reconciliation efforts and self-defense, no more. Adams echoed Dickinson's language, asserting that they should "proceed with Warlike Measures, and conciliatory Measures Pari Passu."[64] Moreover, even the opponents of sending agents, such as Adams, recognized the advantages such a course would give them. Although Adams believed negotiations would detract from preparations, he also saw that Dickinson's point in pressing for diplomacy was precisely that it would give them more time to prepare and to become more united. Adams admitted the need for prudence, unity, and uniformity of pace. He explained to Abigail his agreement with Dickinson about how Congress must proceed. "America is a great, unwieldy Body," he said. "Its Progress must be slow. It is like a large Fleet sailing under Convoy. The fleetest Sailors must wait for the dullest and slowest. Like a Coach and six—the swiftest Horses must be slackened and the slowest quickened, that all may keep an even Pace."[65]

In June, preparations for defense began in earnest. Inhabitants of Pennsylvania had already begun petitioning the Assembly to move beyond parades, which were nothing more than "useless Shew," and put the colony on a proper footing for defense.[66] On June 14, Congress directed that Pennsylvania raise six companies of riflemen. Dickinson, with fresh military intelligence in hand from Patience Wright, immediately drafted instructions for their enlistment.[67] Among the criteria upon which prospective riflemen would be chosen, in addition to their physical abilities and attachment to America, would be their sobriety and "moral Character." Two other key points spoke to the control the government would maintain over the men and the arms: each man would be provided with a rifle, and each must swear an oath that included the line "I will lay down my Arms whenever I shall be ordered so to do by the present or any Assembly of this Colony."[68]

The next day, June 15, George Washington was unanimously voted the commander of the Continental Army. Although his days as a colonel in the Virginia militia had been almost twenty years earlier, that he had any military experience at all made him an attractive choice. No American army actually existed yet; he would form it from militia units in Massachusetts and New York. Units from Pennsylvania, Maryland, and Virginia would join them. A few days later, Congress resolved that Pennsylvania should raise two additional units, which would compose a battalion with the other six. Dickinson was placed on the Assembly committee to "consider of and report to the House, such measures as may be expedient for putting this City and Province into a State of Defence" and also on the new Committee of Safety.[69]

The First Philadelphia Battalion of Associators, approved by the House on June 30, was Dickinson's to command as colonel. He later reflected, "I had the command of the whole militia of *Pennsylvania* from its establishment— though, indeed, with the title only of first Colonel."[70] In anticipation of this duty, he had subscribed to purchase a copy of *The Prussian Evolutions in Actual Engagements*, a military manual. It would come with *Prussian Manual Exercise* and *The Theory of the Art of Gunnery*.[71] He would be as ready to lead his men into battle as possible. As his battalion began to drill, it attracted notice—or rather, its commanding officer himself did. Tall and trim, Colonel Dickinson cut a dashing figure in his uniform. When a young apprentice physician, Nathaniel Luff, was encouraged to seek the position of assistant surgeon in Dickinson's battalion, he jumped at the chance. Dickinson was a neighbor of his father in Kent County. Luff knew him to be the most celebrated character in the Atlantic World and admired him greatly. Seeing the Farmer in his uniform inspired imitation. Dickinson sported a white paper crown around his cocked hat, which was inverted in military form. His soldier's coat was short and colored brown with buff trim. When Luff enlisted, donned his own military attire, and marched with the unit, he would have been hard pressed to say whether he was more proud to be an American or to look like John Dickinson.[72] John Adams could regale James Warren with the impressive preparations for war in Philadelphia, assuring him, "The Spirit of the People is such as you would wish."[73]

With military preparedness underway, Congress turned its attention to executing other aspects of Dickinson's plan. The first element became known as the Olive Branch Petition. John Jay attempted a draft, but it was deemed inadequate, so Dickinson drafted it instead. In the humblest of terms, it prayed for redress from the king, begging him to intercede with Parliament on behalf of the American colonists. It made no demands, articulated no rights, and only expressed their love and loyalty to the king. As Congress worked, the Battle of Bunker Hill took place on June 17. Even so, the petition passed on July 5 with no member commenting on the debates and all members signing.

Charles Thomson later said that the petition "ought to have redounded to Dickinson's credit as a politician."[74]

Although Adams was mildly annoyed at both the petition and the prospect of future negotiations, he also recognized their necessity. "We must have a Petition to the King, and a delicate Proposal of Negociation &c.," he explained to James Warren the day after he signed the petition. "This Negociation I dread like Death. But it must be proposed. We cant avoid it. Discord and total Disunion would be the certain Effect of a resolute Refusal to petition and negotiate." Moreover, Adams also was convinced by Dickinson's argument that if America did proceed to negotiations, these could work to the Americans' advantage. "We may possibly gain Time and Powder and Arms," he observed.[75] Although there were a few "lukewarm" men in Philadelphia—Thomas Willing, William Smith, and Israel Pemberton—they were "obliged to lie low" for the moment.[76]

While Dickinson drafted the Olive Branch Petition, the second part of his plan for peace was in the works: A Declaration on the Causes and Necessities of Taking Up Arms. His colleagues didn't quite understand his aim. John Adams described it as "a Strange Oscillation between . . . Preparations for War, and Negociations for Peace."[77] The drafting committee had submitted an unsuitable version written by John Rutledge, which led to two new members being added, Dickinson and a delegate from Virginia, Thomas Jefferson. Jefferson took the lead and likely presented his draft to Dickinson in private. Dickinson then made a few minor edits, which Jefferson, disliking any changes to his prose, ignored. But his draft was also unsatisfactory to Congress—meek, uninspiring, flaccid. Dickinson registered his objection in the committee, which then charged him with writing yet another version.

Although Dickinson used Jefferson's draft as the basis for his own and retained several paragraphs, he changed the structure and tone of it entirely, as well as many particulars.[78] Reproducing the same ideas he had expressed in April to Arthur Lee, he added forceful and militant language that was lacking in Jefferson's version. "Our cause is just. Our union is perfect. Our internal resources are great, and if necessary, foreign assistance is undoubtedly attainable." He was, of course, bluffing. "With hearts fortified with these animating reflections," he wrote, "we most solemnly, before GOD and the World declare, that, exerting the utmost energy of those powers, which our beneficent Creator hath graciously bestowed upon us, the arms we have been compelled by our enemies to assume, we will, in defiance of every hazard, with unabating firmness and perseverance, employ for the preservation of our liberties, being with one mind resolved, to die Freemen rather than to live Slaves."[79]

The Declaration passed Congress on July 6, and a copy accompanied General Washington to Boston, where he would assume command of the troops. It was read to the men by the president of Harvard College, occasioning, according to one newspaper, "huzzas by the army, and a pertinent prayer to which the army shouted a loud Amen."[80] By October, it had been translated and republished as far away as Austria.[81]

Issuing these two documents, the Second Petition to the King (known as the Olive Branch Petition) and the Declaration, one humble and beseeching, the other assertive and belligerent, was the move of a chess master controlling the board. Together, they served the same purpose: to achieve reconciliation. Independently, they also served critical functions. Dickinson had no illusions that the petition would itself produce results. It was mainly a legal and political document intended to serve several purposes. First, it would show their friends in Great Britain and elsewhere that they had exerted every effort to reconcile, perhaps even embarrassing the ministry by highlighting its tyrannical behavior. It would do for America what martyrdom did for Quakers—it would show Americans' innocence and convince the British public of their cause. The public would then pressure the government to change. Second, it would give the colonists time to prepare for the coming civil war by building their army and winning France to their side. Third, it would give the colonists legal cover for their defense by force of arms. Should independence occur, the petition would show they had done all they could to avoid it. It would also unite Americans and bring those hesitant Pennsylvanians along towards resistance.

The purpose of the Declaration was simpler: to inspire patriotism and unity in Americans and produce such "apprehensions" in the British that they would think twice about waging war against the colonists and Americans might "procure Relief of all our Grievances."[82] So satisfied was John Adams that he exclaimed, "It has Some Mercury in it, and is pretty frank, plain, and clear. If Lord North dont compliment . . . us, with a Bill of Attainder, in Exchange for it, I shall think it owing to Fear."[83]

With the last element of Dickinson's plan—negotiations—on hold while Congress awaited response to the first two elements, other business ensued. On July 21, Benjamin Franklin produced a draft document called the Articles of Confederation and requested that it be laid before Congress for a vote. But having reached consensus to continue reconciliation measures, few wanted the disruption that would be caused by discussing a document that assumed separation from Great Britain.[84] Too many members were still loyal to the king and convinced that reconciliation was possible.

During this time, John Adams grew increasingly disgruntled with his colleagues. His grievances, it seems, pertained to how military officers were appointed.[85] Unable to control himself, he repeatedly violated congressional secrecy to complain to friends in Massachusetts. On July 23, he blamed his colleagues in general and the Massachusetts delegation in particular. "Many Things may be wrong," he wrote to James Warren, "but no small Proportion of these are to be attributed to the Want of Concert, and Union among the Mass. Delegates."[86] The same day, writing to Abigail about Pennsylvania's preparations for war, he changed his tune and abruptly turned on Dickinson—despite Dickinson's being among those most responsible for Pennsylvania's preparing at all. After calling him an "overgrown Fortune," Adams described his military activities, which he had so recently praised, as only "pretending to be very valiant."[87] The next day, he wrote a fateful letter to Warren. "A certain great Fortune and piddling Genius," he said of Dickinson, "whose Fame has been trumpeted so loudly, has given a silly Cast to all our Doings."[88] The reason for Congress's secrecy became apparent when the British intercepted the letter and published it in the *Massachusetts Gazette* on August 17.

Adams's recollection of how this insult originated, written thirty years after the events and without use of available sources, would fuel mythology for centuries. Having forgotten that he voted in favor of the Olive Branch Petition and signed it, Adams first imagined that he gave a speech against the petition that "terrified" Dickinson and made him "tremble for his Cause." His tale then became more incredible. Adams claimed that he stepped out of the chamber and into the State House yard on other business, only to have Dickinson follow him and, "in as violent a passion as he was capable of feeling," berate Adams as a master would a schoolboy. In a "rude," "rough," and "haughty" manner, Dickinson allegedly yelled that he and other members of Congress would break from New England and conduct the resistance in their own way if Adams did not conform to his "pacific system." Although Dickinson could indeed be pedantic when he believed someone was in the wrong, given that his primary objective since the beginning of the contest with Britain was to unify the colonies, Adams's claim that Dickinson threatened to cause disunity himself strains credulity. Adams's narrative continues with his responding to Dickinson in a calm, measured, and jovial manner.[89] Those acquainted with both men might rather have reversed the descriptions.

Some months after the publication of the letter, when Charles Lee, a British officer who had adopted the American cause, confronted Adams about the insult, Adams retreated. "I took the liberty," said Lee to Dickinson, "to ask him what Devil could incur him with a low opinion of your parts? He honestly confes'd that He had wrote in a pet just after a warm squabble He had with you, and just in such a moment a Man was apt to own into gross misrepresentations, that He really thought He had incurr'd the guilt, for that you were indisputably a Man of genius and integrity."[90]

Adams never apologized to Dickinson. Instead, the next time they passed each other on the street in mid-September, Adams doffed his hat and carefully observed Dickinson's response.[91] Although the comment rankled Dickinson, having learned a lesson from his bitter engagement with Joseph Galloway, he chose to ignore Adams, who by now had a reputation in Congress as a malcontent. Besides, Adams earned his own punishment for his albeit-unintentional public venting of his spleen. In solidarity with Dickinson, members of Congress shunned Adams for weeks thereafter.[92] Dickinson was confident in his position and actions; he needed nothing from Adams. Adams, meanwhile, found other friends who shared his views. Had Dickinson known that a day later, Captain Macpherson, Dickinson's former friend and admirer and now his sworn enemy, invited Adams to dinner, he could have imagined what these two would have to say about him.[93] Adams doubtless expressed his belief that Dickinson was "warped by the Quaker interest."[94]

In the summer and through the autumn of 1775, Dickinson was as busy as ever. He hardly had time for family. Polly, still mourning their daughter, was "dark & comfortless." Although she attended meeting almost daily and could frequently be found in prayer, it was "a time of Spiritual desertion." She was "surrounded by outward blessings," namely Aunt Betty, Mary Dickinson, and James Pemberton, but it was a time of sickness and death. Mary Harrison, sister of Hannah, was very ill, so Polly paid a visit to her at Somerville. Nancy Piet, Little Mary's nurse, died in early September of the flux, after which Polly felt "very low & tired at meeting." Then a few days later, Cousin Molly Lloyd, a member of the Rural Circle who had lived with Polly for more than twenty years, also died after a short, painful illness. On this occasion, however, Polly did feel "the inexpressible Consolation of God Almighty's power & love."[95]

Most of Dickinson's duties during the fall involved military matters, working in the Assembly and on the Committee of Safety and as colonel of the First Battalion of Associators, putting the colonies onto a footing for war. Among his assigned duties were drawing up a memorial to the Assembly requesting funds for "Drums, Colors and other Necessaries," as well as to employ adjutants, sergeants, drummers, and others for the Association and to recommend the construction of armories.[96]

Other matters revealed the deep internal opposition threatening to undermine the American cause. Colonel Dickinson was charged by the Committee of Safety with presenting to Congress the case of two traitors. In August, Dr. John Kearsley and Isaac Hunt, the latter an enemy of Dickinson's since the controversy over royal government in 1764, had been threatened by a mob with receiving "an *American* coat of tar and feathers" and then being expelled from the province for being "violent enemies to the cause." But when the committee determined that the men's physical safety was in danger, the plans were aborted in favor of vandalizing Hunt's house.[97] Kearsley, along with James Brooks and a Quaker named Leonard Snowden, had written letters to England casting aspersions on America and requesting that five thousand Redcoats be sent to Philadelphia. He was now under guard at his house, and the letters had been retrieved before the ship carrying them had sailed too far.[98] Dickinson informed the committee that because Congress had already passed a resolution for arresting and detaining such traitorous persons, they now would only agree that they should be "closely confined."[99]

The Committee of Safety also took several steps for the defense of the province on the waterways. Dickinson was charged first with inquiring whether Associators possessing provincial muskets would be willing to serve on boats the committee was planning on building to defend the province and, later, to discover who possessed those arms so they could be requisitioned.[100] The first boats were christened the *Ranger*, the *Congress*, and the *Dickinson*.[101] Civilians out on the Delaware Bay or the Delaware River were liable to be captured and impressed by British men-of-war, so the committee passed several resolutions for their protection. The committee also resolved that anyone helping the British navigate the bay or river would be "deemed an enemy to *American* liberty, a traitor to his Country, and as such published and held forth to the publick."[102] Committee members hoped that navigation of those waters could be made more difficult. The committee resolved that a defensive weapon devised by Polish engineer Tadeusz Kościuszko called *chevaux de frize*, or "Frisian horses"—portable frames with iron-tipped spikes protruding from them—should be sunk in the Delaware River to deter enemy ships attempting to enter the Port of Philadelphia.[103]

In October, despite attempts to discredit him by ultra-radical members of the Sixty-Six, Dickinson, with his "pacific system," was resoundingly endorsed by the voters and returned to his seat in the Assembly.[104] He was also immediately reappointed to the Committees of Safety and of Correspondence.[105] Shortly thereafter, it became clear that Congress's efforts at reconciliation and negotiations during the summer had been for naught. On October 31, the colonists learned that the king had declared them to be in rebellion on August 23. Days later, when the Olive Branch Petition arrived in England, he had refused to entertain it. This disappointing though unsurprising news did not deter Dickinson or his supporters in their conviction that reconciliation remained the correct path. Events unfolding in Pennsylvania dictated it. Congress, however, inched closer towards preparing for separation from Britain by discussing how to implement republican governments in the colonies. In this, John Adams took the lead.[106]

Myriad problems presented themselves at the beginning of the Assembly's first session in late October, all of them directly affecting how well the Pennsylvanians would respond to British aggression. The House was pelted with competing memorials. The Committee of Safety reminded the Assembly that "the Sum of Money, granted by the House" was depleted "and that a considerable Sum is still necessary" for procuring arms and other accoutrements of war.[107] But Pennsylvanians were polarized on the idea of war. On the one side, the officers of the Military Association for the City and Liberties of Philadelphia submitted a memorial presenting their "great Concern that fatal Mischiefs will arise to the Associate from the Lenity shewn towards Persons professing to be conscientiously scrupulous against bearing Arms," namely the Quakers. They believed that very few people actually avoided military service for reasons of conscience and that most simply were afraid to risk their lives and fortunes for the cause. They wanted the Committee of Safety to take action against them.[108]

On the other side, the Quakers submitted their own lengthy memorial on October 31 protesting any forced participation in warlike measures as violating "that most essential of all Privileges, *Liberty of Conscience.*" They reminded the House of the language in the Charter of Privileges. "No Person or Persons," it read, "who shall confess and acknowledge one almighty God . . . and profess him or themselves obliged to live peaceably under the Civil Government, shall be in any Case molested or prejudiced in his or their Person or Estate, because of his or their *Persuasion or* Practice."[109] They concluded, "We fervently desire the most conciliatory Measures for removing the impending Calamities, and for restoring Peace to the Colonies in general, may be pursued."[110] Several petitions responding to the Quaker memorial complained that, among other things, it "bears an Aspect unfriendly to the Liberties of *America*, and maintains Principles destructive of all Society and Government," in part because, they believed, it unjustly released certain people from military service but also because it disparaged "the glorious Revolution which placed the present Royal Family upon the British throne."[111] Americans, it seemed, still harbored some loyalty to the Crown.

The Assembly responded to the situation with an unprecedented move. It passed a militia bill that, for the first time in the colony's history, required all able-bodied men of military age to serve or be fined. Dickinson served on the committee in the Assembly to draft *Rules and Regulations for the Better Government of the Military Association in Pennsylvania*. But although this seemed like a victory for the resistance, in reality, the fines were so low that they didn't actually pay for the pacifists' absence; the Associators still sacrificed more by outfitting and equipping themselves and leaving their occupations.[112] Long a cause of contention in Pennsylvania, now the rift between those who would bear arms and those who would not was the central contest over control of the province.

The tensions between Quakers and militants was not the only threat to Pennsylvania's unity. On the northern border in the Wyoming Valley, violence had flared again in the ongoing dispute between Pennsylvanian and Yankee settlers from Connecticut. Competing memorials were read, and Dickinson was placed on a committee to respond. It remained to be seen whether the Continental Congress could step in and decide the dispute. Another memorial from the Committee of Chester County represented "the present weak and defenceless Situation" of Pennsylvania.[113]

Such was the unsettled situation in Pennsylvania on November 4 when Dickinson was reappointed as a delegate to Congress and charged with writing new instructions for the next session. With the will of his constituents in mind, he took this opportunity to respond to John Adams's efforts in Congress to establish new republican governments in the colonies. "Though the oppressive measures of the British Parliament and administration have compelled us to resist their violence by force of arms," he wrote, "yet we strictly enjoin you, that you, in behalf of this colony, dissent from, and utterly reject, any propositions, should such be made, that may cause, or lead to, a separation from our Mother Country, or a change of the form of this government."[114] Passing in the House on November 9, these instructions would prove pivotal as events developed over the coming months.[115] Most immediately was a consequence Dickinson surely didn't intend. Rather than excluding the possibility of independence, the instructions invited public discussion of it. Various pseudonymous authors weighed in. While some favored the instructions and others did not, one styling himself after Dickinson as "A Continental Farmer" observed that all options should be considered.[116] The Pennsylvania Farmer's hold was now being tested on his home turf.

Even as the debate over independence began tentatively in Pennsylvania, a neighboring colony was risking resistance for the entire continent. Congress hurriedly dispatched a committee consisting of Dickinson, John Jay, and George Wythe of Virginia to meet with the New Jersey Assembly. It planned to send an address to the king proposing some accommodations or concessions to ministerial demands. Just as Dickinson didn't want any one colony to advance to extreme measures before the others, neither did he want any to cave to Britain's pressure. He spoke to the legislature for more than half an hour, reminding them of the recent history of the controversy with Britain and the very reasonable measures Congress had recently taken to attempt reconciliation, namely the Olive Branch Petition. "But," he pointed out, "it was necessary to convince Britain that we would fight, and were not a Rope of Sand." "The Eyes of all Europe are upon us. Until this controversy, the strength and importance of this Country were not known." According to one witness, Dickinson then "bragged of our success and courage." When he finished, Jay spoke for twelve minutes and Wythe for eight. Governor William Franklin, son of Benjamin Franklin and a Loyalist, ultimately concluded that the address of the House "would probably have passed" had the congressional committee not "harangued" them into dropping it.[117]

Although this episode in the New Jersey Assembly demonstrated what men such as Dickinson and Jay knew—that many Americans were still eager to reconcile with Britain, even at the expense of their liberties—they also knew that some members of Congress had turned towards independence. As the year ended, voices from within Pennsylvania as well began to call unambiguously for independence.[118] America thus balanced precariously at a tipping point between reconciliation and revolution. Whichever way things broke, preserving unity would be both essential and impossible.

10

"As the rock among the waves"

Supporting America against Americans, 1776–1777

Pennsylvanians were indecisive about how to respond to their monarch declaring them to be in rebellion. Clarity dawned for some in mid-January 1776, when word arrived of George III's October address to Parliament denouncing Americans. At the same time on January 9, a pamphlet appeared, entitled *Common Sense*. Addressed to "the Inhabitants of America," it was actually directed primarily to the people of Pennsylvania. The reputed author, Thomas Paine, had just sworn allegiance to Pennsylvania and been instructed by Benjamin Franklin and Benjamin Rush to focus his work on his adopted colony. Because Pennsylvania was the geographic, economic, and political center of America and one of the largest and wealthiest colonies, no move for independence would succeed without it. But while the Quakers controlled the government and Dickinson's instructions to the delegates remained in place, nothing would happen. Franklin, Paine's "political father," and others knew that there could be movement, if only certain segments of the population were properly motivated.[1] The pamphlet argued passionately for independence but also ridiculed the king, the monarchy as an institution, and the idea that vast America could be governed by England, a small island. Without expressly naming Dickinson or the Quakers—there was no need—it denounced him as being part of "a certain set of moderate men who think better of the European world than it deserves," a group that "by an ill-judged deliberation" would be "the cause of more calamities to this Continent" than even its enemies.[2] The pamphlet sold as well as the *Farmer's Letters* had, and for the first time, independence from Great Britain was open to public debate.

Dickinson, along with a shrinking cadre of delegates who had once been the radical members of Congress and were now holding the middle ground, still pressed for reconciliation. Nothing material had changed in the previous six months, so neither had Dickinson's resolve to oppose independence. "My

Principles were formed very early in the Course of this unhappy Controversy," he said. "I have not yet found Cause to change a single Iota of my political Creed."[3] Many Americans still desired a connection with Britain, and they were still grossly unprepared for independence. "Torn from the body, to which we are united by religion, liberty, laws, affections, relation, language and commerce," warned the Farmer, "we must bleed at every vein."[4] Even as he and James Wilson sought a way to secure military aid from France, they continued to draft procedures for the third phase of the plan Dickinson had outlined in May 1775 for negotiations with Britain, including a peace commission that would travel to England. They also awaited a delegation that was supposedly coming from Great Britain. Dickinson argued that Congress had no right to establish an independent government and that its only business should be defense. "Celebrated Writers," he reminded his colleagues, "deny a Power to change a Government without a full & free Consent of the People plainly exprest. The Sense of America as exprest is for Reconciliation."[5] Should reconciliation fail, he continued to prepare Pennsylvania militarily and otherwise, at least with the appearance of unity with the other colonies, for the moment of separation from Britain.[6]

But their work became increasingly futile as the debate over independence intensified. There were voices both for and against separation, but the tide was clearly turning in favor of what Dickinson saw as a drastic and dangerous move. Among other developments, the Quakers handed Paine and supporters of independence a gift by responding to *Common Sense* with a "testimony" they hoped would be calming but instead had the opposite effect. It chided Americans for their disrespect to the king and suggested that their greedy and sinful behavior, particularly that of enslaving their fellow men, had brought on divine punishments in the form of Britain's policies. They also asserted that Quakers themselves never meddled in politics, a patently false claim they would soon come to regret.[7] The testimony was signed by Polly's cousin James Pemberton as clerk of Philadelphia Yearly Meeting.

Paine could not let the Quakers' blatant hypocrisy stand. Having been raised a Quaker himself, he knew exactly how to attack them with their own writings, which he did to devastating effect in an appendix to the third edition of *Common Sense*. "O ye partial ministers of your own acknowledged principles," he exclaimed, before quoting Quakers' only theologian, Robert Barclay, in support of his charge. If Quakers truly believed their testimony, they would stay out of the debate over independence. "The very publishing it proves," he said, "that either, ye do not believe what ye profess, or have not virtue enough to practice what ye believe." He added ominously, "Say not that ye are persecuted, neither endeavor to make us the authors of that reproach, which ye are bringing upon yourselves."[8]

As the pamphlet war in Pennsylvania escalated, so did the civil war with Britain. It was rumored that General Henry Clinton, the British commander in chief in North America, was sailing south to lay siege to New York. At the behest of Major General Charles Lee, Congress resolved on February 12 to send detachments of the four Philadelphia Battalions of Associators. Dickinson, who had already been in extensive contact with Lee, "cheerfully offered" to march, though members of the Pennsylvania Committee of Safety begged him not to go, as they wanted him for pressing business in the Assembly.[9] But Dickinson held to his offer.[10] When word arrived that the Redcoats had departed New York without landing, Dickinson was ordered to stand down. His and other officers' eagerness to defend the country were good for morale in Pennsylvania. Noting Dickinson's readiness in particular, the *Pennsylvania Packet* reported, "The competition and spirit which appeared among the officers and privates, upon this occasion, indicated that the citizens of Philadelphia are upon a footing with the foremost of the colonies, in resolving to die freemen rather than to live slaves."[11] Dickinson told Charles Thomson that as long as Britain "only sends her own troops to fights us, I shall consider the contest only as a family quarrel." However, he added, the moment that "foreign incendiaries" were hired "to cut our throats," he would join "in preparing for a Declaration of Independence."[12] He vowed to "adhere with Roman firmness" to his plan.[13]

The debate over independence raged in print. Dickinson was distracted, however, by a personal blow. His mother, at seventy-six, had been ailing for some time. While with Philemon in New Jersey, she died on March 23, 1776.[14] It was a profound loss. Dickinson had been close with both parents; he had considered his father a friend. But he had a special bond with his "Honored Mother." She, perhaps even more than his father, had been a role model for the virtue Dickinson aspired to attain in his life. He could confide in her, talk about any topic that interested him, and seek her advice in matters personal and public. From Mary he learned to respect women's opinions, abilities, and particular struggles in a male-dominated society. With hearts heavy, John and Polly sent Sally off with her Cousin Debby to Aunt Norris's house on Chestnut Street while they traveled to Trenton. With them they brought items Phil had requested for the funeral, including black cloth with which to drape the coffin.[15]

Dickinson returned to Philadelphia in April to find Congress inching towards independence in various ways. It was attempting to forge alliances with the Indians. The Lenape had already been working with Quakers for some years. Now Captain White Eyes, chief sachem of the Lenape, was interested in Americanizing his people and requested that whites—especially Quakers—reside among them to instruct them in Christianity, the liberal arts, and handcrafts.[16] Congress saw in this an opportunity to secure the Lenape people's allegiance before the British could. On April 10, it passed a series of resolutions to meet White Eyes's requests. The Friendly Association for Preserving Peace with the Indians wanted to support Congress in this effort, and James Pemberton requested that Dickinson facilitate the efforts. "I have made the Motion in Favor of Captain White Eyes," Dickinson reported. The captain would receive $300, two horses, two saddles, and two bridles, and his interpreter would be given $50. But Dickinson was apprehensive. "I am afraid, they will lose the Money or waste it," he fretted, "and wish that some Friends would not lose a moment in getting the Money & laying it out for them."[17] This attitude was in keeping with Quakers' paternalistic relationship with the Indians. That Congress and the Quakers aided one another was no more than a case of mutual convenience; the Quakers were as set against American measures as ever.

Meanwhile, John Adams was pressing for the colonies to establish republican governments in preparation for separation from Britain. To that end, he published a little pamphlet called *Thoughts on Government*, which he had been formulating since spring of 1775 when he published his first contribution to the controversy with Britain, *The Letters of Novanglus*. It was essentially a blueprint for the structures of self-government. His ideas were influential in Virginia, North Carolina, and, later, his home of Massachusetts.[18]

By the end of April, the radicals in Pennsylvania, whipped up by Paine's fiery language, were restless. They and their counterparts in Congress hoped that a by-election in Pennsylvania on May 1 would remove the stolid Quakers from their seats and install revolutionaries in their place. But their hopes were disappointed when nothing changed. The election only proved that Pennsylvanians were evenly divided on the question of separation from Britain.

Events then conspired to assist the radicals. First, on May 6, Philadelphians learned that the British had hired mercenaries—Hessian soldiers—to fight them, despite opposition by several members of the House of Lords.[19] Then, on the eighth, the HMS *Roebuck* attacked Pennsylvania's gunboats on the

Delaware River. At the same time, Paine struck again at the Quakers. Writing as "The Forester," he published another attack against them and their government, equating them with Tories and maligning their seventy-five-year-old constitution that protected their unique religious liberty. He reminded Pennsylvanians—or, rather, certain Pennsylvanians—of their anger that had prompted the Paxton Riots. "We can trace the iniquity in this province to the fountain head," he wrote, "and see by what delusions it has imposed on others. The guilt centers in a few, and flows from the same source, that a few years ago avariciously suffered the frontiers of this province to be deluged in blood." Paine then leveled a threat: "And though the vengeance of Heaven hath slept since, it may awake too soon for [the Quakers'] repose."[20] He later called them "a fallen, cringing, priest-and-Pemberton-ridden people," referring to Polly's cousins, John, James, and Israel, the most powerful Quakers in America.[21] It was an old insult to equate Quakers with Catholics, the other religious group Englishmen suspected of seeking to undermine their liberties.

On May 10, Congress finally acted, instigating a final struggle between John Adams and John Dickinson. Adams motioned that all provincial governments that were either royal or otherwise not "sufficient to the exigencies of their affairs" should be replaced.[22] He had Pennsylvania particularly in mind. "It was a measure which I had invariably pursued for a whole year," he confessed. "These [Quaker] cloggs are falling off."[23] The resolution passed, opening a path for the radicals to advance. But Dickinson did not see the resolution in this light. His response was that the Pennsylvania Assembly was neither royal nor insufficient for the needs of Pennsylvanians. Adams thus responded on May 15 with a preamble to the May 10 resolution recommending that any government requiring an oath or affirmation to the Crown be replaced. This did include Pennsylvania. Aware of the implications this move could have for Quakers, when Congress recommended a day of fasting for May 17 to bolster the American cause, the Committee of Philadelphia issued an order that inhabitants "forbear from any kind of insult to Quakers, or any others who may, from conscientious scruples, or from a regard to their religious professions, refuse to keep the said Fast."[24] But such protections would not long remain.

In mid-May, business took Dickinson down to Dover, and in town, he encountered Thomas Rodney, brother of his longtime friend and neighbor in Kent, Caesar. Rodney had just heard about the resolution to change the governments and observed to Dickinson the "many advantages that would follow our framing Governments." Dickinson agreed, adding "that it would not prevent but perhaps promote a more speedy reconciliation, because the longer they let Governments exist before they offer Terms the more firm that Government would be, & therefore the more difficult to effect a reconciliation." Rodney also wished for peace and reconciliation but also "never to mix our Governments with Britains." He warned his brother Caesar, however, that Kent was rife with Loyalists.[25]

On May 20, the Pennsylvania radicals took advantage of the opening made for them by Congress. After holding a public meeting in which they essentially announced the end of the legally constituted and elected Assembly, they then sent a petition to that body affirming their agreement with the May 15 preamble to Adams's May 10 resolution. Unwilling to acquiesce to the coup of a legally elected body, Dickinson drafted and the House passed a resolution on May 24 rendering oaths and affirmations unnecessary.[26]

But the Assembly was in its death throes, and this act was a last gasp. Dickinson was forced to confront the reality that the movement for independence was advancing rapidly, regardless of the wishes of half the population of Pennsylvania. With Hessian mercenaries on their way, Charles Thomson, long Dickinson's partner in the resistance, reminded him, "You are pledged to us." Dickinson responded, "It is so."[27] Although the Quaker-led Assembly still limped along, Congress mobilized for the next big steps. June would be busy, with several critical documents that needed to be crafted, all in preparation for what Dickinson dreaded: declaring independence from Great Britain. As much as he did not want this for America, Dickinson had been the central figure in facilitating it. No other leader had done as much, bringing his colony along, keeping the others in line, and facilitating preparations. There were other leaders, such as Samuel Adams, critical to their particular colonies. They all looked to Dickinson for guidance.

First, before they could proceed, he would need to remove the single most significant obstacle: the November 1775 instructions to the Pennsylvania delegates that prohibited them from voting in favor of independence. On June 5, the Assembly appointed Dickinson to a committee for this purpose. As he was drafting the instructions, he attended a meeting of officers of the militia, the Pennsylvania Associators, on June 6. They were enraged that the Assembly had taken it upon itself to appoint brigadier generals to command the Associators. The officers believed that it was their prerogative to choose their leaders.[28] One officer censured the Assembly harshly and reviewed its rash conduct as evidence for why this body should not be trusted with the appointments. In so doing, he targeted Dickinson's November instructions. "The authors & abettors of these instructions woud find they had lost the Confidence & affections of the people!" the officer proclaimed. Dickinson now moved to the fore to defend the Assembly's actions—and his own—noting the contradictions of the men's demands. The printer of the *Pennsylvania Journal*, Major William Bradford, witnessed his speech.

"We are blamed," Dickinson began, "for appointing men who had not the confidence of the people and we are also blamed because we gave not these suspected men unlimited power. You say the Assembly has no right to alter the constitution without the consent of the people, & you condemn the Assembly because they gave not their delegates power to alter it."

He then turned to the heart of the men's grievances: the central role he had played in delaying separation from Great Britain. This moment was not merely about explaining what he believed to be best for America, the land he loved. It was about his honor. And he was not speaking merely to the men in front of him at this moment but to all Americans, present and future. "It is true," he owned. "I am the author of the instructions. I appeal to my Maker for my integrity in this matter." The audience stood transfixed by Dickinson's words. Bradford described him as moving fluidly among the men, his voice the fountain of his heart. "The loss of life," he continued, "or of what is dearer than life itself, the affection of my countrymen shall not deter me from actions as an honest man. These threats then that we just now heard might have been spared. I defy them. I regard them not—I stand as unmovd by them. As the rock among the waves that dash against it—I can defy the world, Sir, but—I defy not heaven; nor will I ever barter my conscience for the esteem of mankind! So let my country treat me as she pleases, still I will act as my conscience dericts."

Dickinson was sincere and persuasive. "His graceful actions, the emotions of his countenance & a plaintive yet manly voice strangely improved upon my judgment. He was clearly wrong," Bradford said, "yet I believed him right: Such were the effects of his oration."[29]

Dickinson's moving speech notwithstanding, something had shifted profoundly. As the officers proceeded to protest the Assembly formally, he saw that his work as the principled trimmer was effectively at an end. America's course had changed, even if its destination hadn't. And the attacks began. By the end of the month, Dickinson was accused in the *Gazette* of "steering an indefinite course, sometimes agreeing with one side, sometimes with the other;

seeming upon the whole to have no other fixed object in view than HIMSELF." This mischaracterization of Dickinson as the opportunistic trimmer was calculated to minimize his influence.[30] Even at this point, Dickinson recognized that his adversaries "were indefatigable and successful."[31]

The month of June was the most consequential of the era, and Dickinson's busiest. On June 7, Richard Henry Lee motioned in Congress that the colonies should be independent. The motion passed in the affirmative. The next day, Dickinson's new instructions allowing the colony's delegates to concur with Congress on independence were approved by the Pennsylvania House. Congress then appointed a committee to draft a declaration of independence. Had Dickinson been in favor of one, there is little doubt he would have been the lead draftsman, as he had been for most other congressional documents. Instead, on June 11, Congress appointed him to a committee, along with Franklin, John Adams, and others, "to prepare a plan of treaties to be proposed to foreign powers."[32] Focusing on commercial activity, this Plan of Treaties would be a blueprint for the new nation's diplomatic relations. Dickinson had, of course, been thinking about American foreign trade since he began work in the Court of Admiralty in the late 1750s. He had refined his views in his unpublished essay, "Reflections of the Flag of Truce Trade," in which he argued that war was unnecessary when opponents could be dominated with economic might. With reference books on treaties and maritime law close at hand, Dickinson scrawled thirteen draft articles of the Plan of Treaties, adapting their provisions strictly for maritime commerce. Later, John Adams prepared the final draft version, making a clean copy of the first thirteen articles and copying the remaining seventeen from various law books and treaties. The joint efforts of these two political adversaries would create the basis for America's foreign policy that lasted far beyond what either man could see. Adams never acknowledged Dickinson's work.[33]

While still in the midst of the treaty, the following day, June 12, Dickinson was appointed chairman of a thirteen-man drafting committee to write America's constitution.[34] This was where Dickinson spent most of his time. "An agreement upon the terms of our confederation," he believed, "ought to precede the assumption of our station among Sovereigns." America would not receive foreign recognition or support if its government was not properly constituted. He therefore took the lead writing the Articles of Confederation.[35] When time permitted, he also worked on a draft essay on a new government for Pennsylvania and notes for a speech he anticipated giving in Congress on the topic of independence.

Although Dickinson had Benjamin Franklin's 1775 draft of the Articles before him, and he retained some provisions, such as one for forming an alliance with Indians and securing their land to them, he added a number of revisions and new provisions, making the document his own. What he produced was remarkable for its forward vision. He knew that any new American constitution had to be a suitable replacement for the British constitution, by which the colonies were currently connected. Therefore, his first clause called for the creation of a strong central government, with the states subordinate to the larger Union, providing that colonies would retain sovereignty "in all Matters that shall not interfere with the Articles of this Confederation." He also included a provision that would allow Congress to raise troops in a state without the cooperation of that state. Dickinson had been saying it for over a decade: without unity, America would not survive.

If Dickinson's first priority was stabilizing the new nation, his second was truly revolutionary, more so, even, than the Declaration of Independence currently being drafted: a lengthy clause protecting religious dissenters. Even as he wrote, he was witnessing the slow demise of Pennsylvania's 1701 Charter of Privileges, and he therefore copied its language almost verbatim into America's new constitution. The clause would freeze the laws in each colony so none could pass new laws infringing on the rights of conscience. For some, such as Massachusetts, that would mean dissenters would have only religious toleration. But Dickinson's main concern, as always, was Pennsylvania, where the Quakers' sworn enemies were wresting control of the government and poised to turn the tables on their perceived persecutors. He sought first to secure the religious liberty Quakers had always enjoyed.

What he did next with the language of the 1701 Charter went well beyond that. As he drafted the clause, he began copying from the Charter: "No person or persons, shall be molested or prejudiced in his or their religious persuasion or practice. . . ." Then he stopped and considered his language carefully. As worded, the clause was insufficient. It did not, as Abigail Adams had implored her husband to do that spring, "remember the Ladies" when defending American rights.[36] Abigail's husband merely laughed at her for being "saucy" and compared her to a disobedient child and an "insolent Negro."[37] Dickinson, by contrast, had Polly in mind, and all female Friends. He thus crossed out "his or their" and replaced it with "his or her" (Fig. 14). Nothing like this—explicit protection for the fundamental rights of women— had ever been written into an Anglo-American constitution. And those who understood Quakerism knew that it meant more than just religious liberty.

When he used the word "Practice" to refer to religion, Dickinson considered that for Quaker women, to *practice* their religion meant to preach publicly. This clause was thus a protection for women's public speech, a right most women did not even consider they possessed—indeed, it was a right that women with fashionably tight stays would be physically unable to exercise.[38]

Another concern that Dickinson alone expressed repeatedly was on the matter of slavery. He initially queried whether Congress ought to define and regulate the practice. In a subsequent draft of the Articles, he asked, "Should there not be an Article to prevent those who are hereafter brought into these Colonies, from being held in Slavery within the Colonies?" But his colleagues were no more ready to regulate or end slavery than they were to protect women's religious liberty and speech.

Other aspects of Dickinson's Articles of Confederation were also noteworthy. There was a provision prohibiting public officers from accepting foreign emoluments, one prohibiting standing armies but requiring militias, one allowing free trade between states and foreign nations, except when that trade interfered with the Union, and several more. He did not give Congress the power to tax, because the people were not represented in or by that body, only the states with one vote each.

Even as Dickinson prepared America constitutionally for separation from Britain, word arrived in Philadelphia of Loyalists in Sussex County, the southernmost of the Lower Counties on Delaware, preparing to resist any such move. "There is Reason to apprehend," wrote John Hancock, president of Congress, "those deluded People are supplied with Arms and Ammunition from the Men of War of our Enemies." Congress ordered the Assembly to send a battalion from Chester County to assist the government in Sussex.[39] This news made very clear that Americans were far from united on the course Congress was charting.

On June 13, Pennsylvania's Quaker-led Assembly met for the last time with a quorum under the Charter of Privileges. The following day, Dickinson's new instructions were nevertheless signed by the speaker and conveyed to Pennsylvania's delegates to Congress. They did not direct the delegates to vote for independence. Indeed, the instructions did not mention "independence" at all. "We therefore hereby authorize you," Dickinson wrote, "to concur with the other Delegates in Congress" in adopting "measures as shall be judged necessary for promoting the liberty, safety and interests of America." The instructions merely removed the restrictions so the delegates could vote their consciences. And they added something else Dickinson thought critical.

The delegates should take care to "reserve to the people of this colony the sole and exclusive right of regulating the internal government and police of the same."[40] With his religious liberty clause in the Articles of Confederation and this line about internal policing, Dickinson expressed his concern over the rights of religious dissenters in Pennsylvania and attempted to protect them. Without such protections, he knew well, Quakers could again be persecuted.

After Dickinson finished drafting the Articles on June 17, the congressional committee bickered and disputed each clause. Some committee members, including Dickinson, lost hope of ever agreeing on an American constitution. Others, such as Edward Rutledge of South Carolina, grew impatient with Dickinson, accusing him of possessing "the Vice of Refining too much"—as though a constitution could be too refined.[41] Ultimately, the two most important articles—for a strong central government and for religious liberty, with its gender-inclusive language—were excised. Thus the Articles of Confederation as Dickinson wrote them did not even make it out of the drafting committee intact. They were altered by his colleagues immediately before they were passed along and then further altered in 1777. The final version, not ratified until 1781, bore little resemblance to his vision and was ill-crafted for the realities facing the nation. In the meantime, America had no constitution.

No sooner had Dickinson finished his attempt to protect Americans' religious rights than others were working to deny them. With the Quaker Assembly now defunct, on June 18, the radicals called a convention to govern the state and write a new constitution to replace the 1701 Charter. In their way, they were merely following the logical course Dickinson had laid out in the spring of 1774 when he had established the committee-convention plan to elect delegates to Congress by skirting the uncooperative Assembly. Thomas McKean was elected president. Their next steps were also foreseeable. Among their first orders of business was to impose a test act requiring an oath. In pointed disregard of the 1701 Charter, this test was intended specifically to exclude Quakers, who refused to take God's name in vain, from voting and holding office.[42] At the same time, they abolished property requirements for voting, thus transferring power to those who felt most aggrieved by Quaker rule. Dickinson's fears about persecution of dissenters were already justified.

On Monday morning, July 1, Congress met to debate the question of independence. After other business was dispatched—reports read from generals in the field, funds allocated to Virginia for stores and provisions, and

Maryland's instructions to its delegates read—the body resolved itself into a committee of the whole.[43] Dickinson came prepared with notes outlining the concerns he had expressed since separation seemed likely. He had attempted to write them out in full, but the demands of him in the last weeks had been extraordinary, and the notes devolved from heavily edited full sentences that progressed fluidly to cryptic and disorganized abbreviations.[44]

The task before him was daunting. He knew this would be the most important speech of his life, and he was candid about what it would mean for him and his country. "My Conduct, this Day," he began, "I expect will give the finishing blow to my once too great, and my integrity considered, now too diminished popularity." He did not care about fame. He was willing to "sacrifice my private Emolument to general Interests." Reiterating the principle he had stated throughout his career, he said, "I might indeed, practise an artful, an advantageous Reserve upon this Occasion"—if, that is, he only cared about his own fortunes. "But thinking as I do on the Subject of Debate," he clarified, "Silence would be guilt. I despise its Arts. I detest its Advantages. I must speak, though I should lose my Life, though I should lose the Affections of my Countrymen." He knew that if he were to say nothing against independence and simply fall in with the majority, he would remain the most celebrated and most powerful man in America. If the revolution were successful, he could have his choice of posts and be immortalized as the leading founder of the greatest nation on earth.

He offered a prayer, imploring "Almighty God, with whom dwells Wisdom itself, so to enlighten the Members of this House, that their Decision may be such as will best promote the Liberty Safety and Prosperity of these Colonies." He also prayed for his own ability "to speak the Precepts of sound Policy."

He then proceeded to reiterate the many reasons why now was not the time for independence. "Our Interest is to keep Great Britain in Opinion that We mean Reconciliation as long as possible," he began. He painted a picture of the devastating war executed by a British ministry provoked and the nation united against it by a declaration of independence. "The War will be carried on with more Severity, Burning Towns Letting Loose Indians on our Frontiers." If victorious, Britain would impose Anglicanism on them. If America prevailed, the cost would be too dear. "We shall weep at our Victories, Overwhelm'd with Debt," which he calculated would be six million in Pennsylvania currency.

When confronted with the calamities of a long war, he observed, the people will justly "complain about our Rashness & ask why We did not first apply to foreign Powers; why We did not settle all Differences among Ourselves; Take Care to secure unsettled Lands for easing their Burthens; Why not wait till better prepar'd and We had made an Experiment of our Strength?" Ultimately, the Congress was answerable to the people, so its members, their servants, ought to think carefully about where they were leading them. Echoing the same nautical metaphor he had used to preserve the Pennsylvania constitution in 1764, he said, to embark on the journey before they were prepared was to "brave the Storm in a Skiff made of Paper."

In the contest, Americans currently held the moral high ground. Their peaceful resistance using civil disobedience was slow, but it was working. The Stamp Act had been repealed. All the Townshend Acts but one had been repealed. Dickinson cited an address from the City of London to the king supporting the Olive Branch Petition. It expressed "abhorrence of the tyrannical measures pursued against our fellow subjects in America, as well as of the men, who secretly advise, and of the ministers, who execute these measures" and urged the king to grant the colonies relief.[45] This deliberative process of changing laws by changing minds was the foundation of a free society, and it took time. If they proceeded as he had recommended in 1775 in "the most desperate Prosecution of the War & the most pacific Negotiations at the same Time, We shall be Heroes in the Field and Philosophers & Christians in the Cabinet. It would Stamp the Character of our Country for every brave Quality & every good one so that We may take our Rank among the Nations of the Earth for undaunted Assertors of our Liberty & the most passionate Lovers of Peace."[46]

Turning next to the strongest arguments he had heard for declaring independence, Dickinson raised and dismissed them one by one. First, supporters of a declaration claimed that foreign governments wouldn't assist Americans until they declared independence. This was incorrect, and Dickinson named several historical examples, such as France assisting Parliament before Charles I was executed in 1649.

Second, they said that Americans would be overjoyed at declaring independence, and it would motivate them to fight. But this, said Dickinson, would mean they were motivated too much by resentment. "I fear the Virtue of Americans," he confessed. "Resentment of the Injuries offered to their Country, may irritate them to Counsels & to Actions that may be detrimental to the Cause, they would dye to advance." He discoursed at some length on the history of wars, ancient and modern, and the extremes men were drawn into—massacres and the destruction of innocents, women and children. "If

Convenient & Advantageous," these will be called "just actions. Shall We proclaim this to be our Creed to the World?"

Third, supporters of the declaration claimed it would accelerate the establishment of new governments. But, countered Dickinson, the "people are going on as fast as they can." Fourth, they said it would hasten the suppression of Toryism. Dickinson replied that the establishment of new governments would suppress Toryism.

Fifth, the people expected it, they said. Dickinson replied that the people could be told "it is only deferred till a Confederation or a Treaty with foreign Powers is concluded." These two issues were critical. The delegates seemed to understand that America needed allies. If they could get favorable terms from France, "let Us declare Independence. If We cannot, let Us at least withhold that Declaration, till We obtain Terms that are tolerable." It was a concern that "We have many Points of the utmost Moment to settle with France." On the other hand, after all this time, Dickinson was less certain his colleagues understood how important internal American unity was, or how precarious. "Not only Treaties with foreign powers but among Ourselves should precede this Declaration," he insisted. "We should know on what Grounds We are to stand with Regard to one another." His experience drafting the Articles of Confederation had been revealing. "The Committee on Confederation dispute almost every Article," he explained. "Some of Us totally despair of any reasonable Terms of Confederation."

Sixth, members of the army had their hearts set upon it and it would encourage them. Catering to a standing army is a "Terrible Enforcement of an Argument," said Dickinson flatly. Besides, the Continental Army would have its day without a declaration. "Great Britain after one or more unsuccessful Campaigns may be induc'd to offer Us such a Share of Commerce as would satisfy Us—to appoint Councillors during good Behavior, to withdraw her Armies, to Protect our Commerce, Establish our Militias—in Short, to redress all the Grievances complain'd of in our first Petition."

He stated the obvious: "I am alarm'd at this Declaration being so vehemently prest." He was also disappointed in his colleagues, whom he discovered had not been speaking plainly. He had learned "that people in this House have had different Views for more than a 12 month." He found it "Amazing, after what they have so repeatedly declared in this House & private Conversations—that they meant only Reconciliation." He couldn't resist a tinge of sarcasm, adding, "But since they can conceal their Views so dexterously, I should be glad to read a little more in the Doomsday Book of America."

In conclusion, he reminded his colleagues that the fate of their new nation was in God's hands. Invoking Enrico Caterino Davila, the sixteenth-century Italian historian of the religious wars in France, he again used a nautical metaphor: "The Skilfulness of the Pilot avails but little, if the Gale of Divine Favor, which governs human Affairs with eternal Providence, does not help to bring our Actions to their desired Port."

Dickinson's notes to himself expressed his deepest motivations for this stance against independence that would, long after his death, define his entire life. At this moment, he disregarded himself, his self-interest. "The self," he wrote, "falls like a drop in the Ocean." He was admittedly afraid of what was to come—for his country and for himself. But he was determined to act with virtue. "A Man's Virtue may cost him his Reputation & even his Life." In case his meaning of the term wasn't clear, he added, "By Virtue, I mean an inflexible & undaunted Adherence in public Affairs to his Sentiments concerning the Interests of his Country." He then summarized the dilemma of the principled trimmer: "In one Country he would be a Rebel, in another a Traytor—& for what? for pursuing the Medium that leads to the Interests of both, which are inseparably united." Lord Halifax likewise explained that virtue itself is a trimmer, "dwelling in the middle between the two Extreams; That even God Almighty is divided between his two great Attributes, his Mercy and his Justice. In such Company, our *Trimmer* is not asham'd of his Name."[47]

When Dickinson finished, the room remained silent for some time. Then, finally, John Adams rose to respond to Dickinson's objections. It was the last scene in a lengthy two-man drama that had been unfolding since the fall of 1775. With most in Congress already in favor of independence, Adams's argument, which likewise recounted his position of the last months, carried the day. It was clear that in the vote to be taken the following day, Congress would declare independence.

With the decision made, Dickinson believed that it was imperative that it appear unanimous. It would be the only hope of convincing Britain and the world, especially potential allies, that they were united. Because his conscience would not allow him to vote for a measure he believed in his heart to be a grave mistake, Dickinson had only one other option: follow the Quaker process of dissent. In the Quaker tradition, after a member of the meeting has spoken his mind but the body has resolved to go in a different direction, for the sake of unity, the dissenting member must step aside to allow the body to move ahead. On July 2, Dickinson thus abstained from the vote on independence, not even attending Congress on that day.[48] Crucially, removing one's objection is a tacit endorsement of the action to be taken. The member must therefore wholeheartedly support the meeting in its endeavors. He would then be obliged by his sense of right and honor to do everything in his power to support his country.[49]

As Dickinson explained it, "Though I spoke my sentiments freely, as an honest man ought to do, yet, when a determination was reached upon the question against my opinion, I received that determination as the sacred voice of my country, as a voice that proclaimed her destiny, in which, by every impulse of my soul, I was resolved to share, and to stand or fall with her in that plan of freedom which she had chosen."[50] If patriotism means placing country before self, Dickinson suppressed every sentiment of foreboding in his heart and threw himself entirely behind the American cause.

Pennsylvania thus voted in favor of independence, with Benjamin Franklin, John Morton, and James Wilson voting aye; Charles Humphreys and Thomas Willing voting nay; and Dickinson and Robert Morris abstaining.[51] The day the Declaration was adopted, on July 4, Charles Thomson recalled that "the measure frightened and appalled even its well wishers. The Citizens vastly kept aloof, the Crowd that assembled at the State House was not great; and those among them who joined in the acclamation were not of the highest-order, or the most sober and reflecting."[52] It was an inauspicious advent of a new era.

Although Dickinson neither wrote, approved, nor voted on the Declaration, more than any single person, he was responsible for its coming into being. Through force of personality, deft maneuvers, and strategic use of his weight, he had led Americans in their resistance for almost a decade. He had educated Americans on their rights and the protection of those rights. He had, with help from friends and allies such as Charles Thomson, Thomas McKean, and Thomas Mifflin, wrested Pennsylvania, the most fractious and reluctant colony, into tenuous and imperfect internal unity. Without Pennsylvania, neither resistance nor revolution could occur. One of the largest colonies, and also the cultural, political, economic, and geographical center of America, it was riven by strict Quakers on the one side and ultra-radical Presbyterians on the other. With the help of local leaders in other colonies looking to him for guidance—the Lees of Virginia and James Otis, Samuel Adams, and Josiah Quincy in Boston—Dickinson had molded the colonies into a semblance of a union. Then, as American unity seemed to propel the country ever faster towards independence, knowing his countrymen were not yet prepared for it and always with his eye on liberty as the final destination, he heaved his weight to the other side. For eight months, his 1775 instructions to the Pennsylvania delegates to reject independence were the bulwark against separation. If America was to prevail, this crucial delay would be the reason why. Immediately after the Declaration passed, John Adams admitted that Dickinson had been right and that "the delay of the Declaration has many great advantages attending it." Among other things, he said, "This delay will cement the Union, and avoid those Heats and perhaps Convulsions which might have been occasioned, by such a Declaration Six Months ago."[53] In this assessment, however, he was quite mistaken.

Thus, while at the moment of independence, it appears that Dickinson was compelled to shift his allegiance from Britain to America—from the ancient British constitution to the imperfect American one—that is not precisely what happened. Living in London as a young man had revealed clearly to Dickinson that he was, first and foremost, an American, and America was always his priority. His British identity was secondary, and Britain was not his home. However, keeping America under the protection of the British constitution—especially because it would allow the preservation of the Pennsylvania 1701 Charter of Privileges—seemed to Dickinson the best way to preserve American liberties. The destination was always American liberties.

Despite his making the Declaration of Independence possible through education, unity, and delay, Dickinson had been consistent from the earliest days of the contest with Britain about not wanting independence. Many of his admirers, however, willfully disregarded his repeated assertion of this fact. Some in Pennsylvania imagined that he had taken them to the brink of independence only to abandon them. In other places, it took years to set the record straight. More than a decade later, in 1787, a French newspaper claimed that "a single voice, a single man, pronounced the independence of the United States. It was John Dickinson. America owes him eternal recognition; it was Dickinson who set her free." In Paris at the time, Thomas Jefferson hastened to correct them.[54] In 1776, only the most zealous Pennsylvanians felt—or claimed to feel—betrayed at his refusal to take them the last step. Out of this sense of betrayal grew the convulsions that Adams thought were avoided by delay.

On July 4, immediately after the Declaration was adopted, intelligence arrived from General Washington that New York had been invaded by the enemy and militias were required. Dickinson, who was then meeting with committees and officers about defense, was ready when Congress adopted a resolution to send his battalion to support Washington.[55] Unbeknownst to Dickinson, however, at the same time at a meeting in Lancaster, privates and officers of the Philadelphia Associators were voting to install two brigadier generals over him. He "felt the stroke" against him, as leadership of the Associators was a post he valued highly, not for military honors but for allowing him to do his duty. As they prepared to depart, Dickinson addressed his battalion, expressing his disappointment but also saying, "As we are soon to go into service, my affection for you, and my attachment to the common cause, should prevail over other sentiments, and I will perform with you the expected tour of duty."[56] Then, when most members of Congress did not take up arms, Dickinson marched with his men into New Jersey to meet the British at New York. This was no longer a civil war; now it was a revolution.

Colonel John Dickinson, accompanied by his second in command Colonel Jacob Morgan Jr. and his brother Brigadier General Philemon Dickinson of the New Jersey militia (Fig. 15), marched with his men as far as Trenton, but then, exhausted and unwell, he dismounted and continued by carriage to Elizabethtown, where he arrived on July 10.[57] Deployed directly across the harbor, less than half a mile from British forces in New York City, Dickinson's unit was part of a "flying camp," a highly mobile force that could meet the enemy anywhere it chose to attack along the Hudson River.

Polly wrote letter after letter to "my dear Johney Dickinson, for whose sake I suffer more than I am well able to bear," but he had been unable to reply aside from sending her a few lines from Trenton. She worried about him in the heat and the elements, not knowing whether he even had a tent to sleep in. Charles Thomson, Peter Lloyd, and other friends looked in on her and delivered what news they had, and Polly kept John apprised of developments at home with business and family. "Thy Baby is well and daily asks for Papa's kisses," she told him. But now all she could do was pray he came home to them. "May Gracious Heaven protect thee in the midst of danger and never suffer thy heart to fail as mine does."[58]

Dickinson worked hard to hold his unit together, obtain crucial equipment and provisions, and strategize with other officers, even as he ruminated about the reaction to his stance on the Declaration of Independence. Friends attempted to persuade him that he had been wrong. "I cannot agree with You," Dickinson explained to his friend, Major General Charles Lee, "that a

Declaration of Independence <u>at this Time</u>, will promote the Happiness of my Country. I have tried, I have toil'd to thrust the Belief of the Proposition into my Mind." Although he valued the opinions of Lee and other trusted friends who worried that he was sacrificing his reputation, or at least his popularity, for a political "Herecy," there was too much Quakerism in him to disobey his conscience. "I have so much of the Spirit of Martyrdom in Me," he continued, "that I have been conscientiously compell'd, to endure in my political Capacity the Fires & Faggots of Persecution, rather than resign my impious Persuasion." Of course it occurred to him that he was wrong and "suffering for a most absolute Falsity," but that "Falsity" was, nonetheless, "sacred to Me." Seeing his virtue as a protective cloak, he said, "I dread nothing more than offering Violence to my Integrity."[59]

In truth, Dickinson was deeply relieved to have rejoined the ranks of mortals, finding both the constant adoration and critical eye of his countrymen exhausting. To Charles Thomson he exclaimed, "no youthful Lover ever stript off his Cloaths to step into Bed to his beautiful Bride with more Delight than I have cast off my Popularity." His relinquishing his celebrity was not merely "voluntary," as Thomson described it; it was "ardent." "Whether I shall ever put on the cumbersome Robes" of popularity, he added, "I know not & care not." He left Thomson with a quotation from Homer: "The man who is tenacious of purpose in a rightful cause is not shaken from his firm resolve by the frenzy of his fellow citizens clamoring for what is wrong, or by the tyrant's threatening countenance."[60]

While Dickinson was within sight of the enemy, prepared to give his life for his country, the radicals who overthrew the Pennsylvania government, and who were distant from the fighting, wrote a new constitution and appointed new delegates to Congress. Although Dickinson still had three months left in his term, he was now out of the Pennsylvania government.[61] Having anticipated this drastic change, he had quickly written thoughts on a new Pennsylvania constitution and gotten them to a printer. *An Essay on a Frame of Government for Pennsylvania* was ready for sale on July 27.[62] He laid out a government with a bicameral legislature and an executive council, led by a governor, with power to approve or disapprove legislation. After describing the powers of each branch, he stipulated that "to preserve the sacred rights of Conscience inviolate," all persons would possess the same rights as under the 1701 Charter. And he used the same gender-inclusive language as he had in his draft of the Articles of Confederation. After listing other provisions, he stated that amendments could be made with approval of two-thirds of the legislature and two-thirds of the counties. Finally, he suggested laws that might afterwards be passed on various topics, including his priorities of "Education of youth, and promotion of piety and virtue," prohibiting enslavement of those brought into or born in Pennsylvania, ensuring trial by jury, and preventing corruption of officials. The radicals ignored the essay.

As news of political developments in Philadelphia reached him in Elizabethtown, Dickinson grew angry in spite of himself. After all he had done and continued to do, he felt betrayed. Moreover, as news of the new Pennsylvania constitution emerged, Dickinson's friends and even his enemies wished he were in office to guide their efforts. The radicals drafting the new constitution were unequal to the task. The leaders were Robert Whitehill, a backcountry farmer; Benjamin Franklin, a printer and scientist; James Cannon, a mathematician; Timothy Matlack, a brewer; George Bryan, a merchant; and Thomas Paine, a propagandist. Even John Adams saw the merit of Dickinson's presence as a moderating force and wished that he "may be restored to office, at a fresh election."[63] His legal talents, political skills and experience, and even temperament were desperately needed in a convention of men who possessed few of these qualities.

Thomson chided Dickinson for his decision on independence that got him tossed out of office. "I know the rectitude of your heart & the honesty & uprightness of your intentions," he said, "but still I cannot help regretting, that by a perseverance which you were fully convinced was fruitless, you have thrown the affairs of this state into the hands of men totally unequal to them." He described the Pennsylvania radicals as fervent patriots eager to serve their country. "But sure I am when their fervor is abated," he said, "they will do justice to your merit. And I hope soon to see you restored to the confidence & honors of your country."[64] But Thomson's optimism was misplaced. "The poor *Trimmer* hath all the Powder spent upon him alone," observed Lord Halifax. "There is no danger now to the State (if some Men be believ'd) but from the Beast called a *Trimmer*."[65]

Dickinson's time at the front was brief. His unit, like most other state militias, was no match for the most powerful professional army in the world. They were minimally trained and unprepared, both materially and mentally, to meet the challenges of war. Patriotism was an inadequate substitute for these necessities, and even that seemed in short supply. Despite the best efforts of Colonel Dickinson and his superior officers, the enlisted men deserted in significant numbers, some returning home to tend to their crops, others even attempting to defect to the British.[66] Dickinson duly informed his superiors and the Pennsylvania government of the crisis.[67] His appreciation for the remaining men, many of whom were "in low circumstances," was such that he directed that his pay be distributed to their wives and children.[68] Dickinson's performance as colonel was singled out for praise by his commanding officer, General William Livingston, who wrote to George Washington that his "Behavior does honor to his Province in particular and America in general."[69] Those back in Philadelphia were pleased to learn, "by all who come from the Camp," that Dickinson was "regaining that Influence, which your Superior Wisdom & Abilities must sooner or later give him."[70]

Nevertheless, in some quarters, Dickinson's reputation continued to suffer. On August 18, a friend paid Dickinson a visit at his quarters in Elizabethtown to warn him of a campaign being mounted against him. He informed Dickinson in detail of a great number of malicious falsehoods about him circulating in Philadelphia concerning the Presbyterians and their clergy. His enemies claimed that Dickinson abhorred the Presbyterians' aims and ridiculed "the Manners and Pretenses of their Ministers." Dickinson was astonished. Upon reflection, however, he admitted that he had noticed "a certain Coldness in my Presbyterian Friends," which he attributed to his closer relationship with Quakers since his marriage. He had some misgivings about two men—Joseph Reed and Benjamin Rush. He found that while "I religiously performed a friend's Duty" to them, they "totally estranged themselves from Me, and did not act kindly with Regard respect to my Reputation." Dickinson made it clear to his visitor that he could share these complaints with both Reed and Rush.

He then specified the maxims he strove to live by. The first was "Never to solicit or seek directly or indirectly any Post of Profit or Honor," and the second was "In public Affairs to pursue solely the Good of my Country, and then to defy the World." "In other Words," he clarified, "to fill the Place assign'd Me, according to my apparent Duty, with an Inflexibility immoveable by Fear, Sollicitation or Temptation, but never myself to try to enlarge the Sphere of my Duty or Activity." He then recounted several occasions on which he had refused power and profit to prove he was "govern'd by the Dictates of his Conscience."

Although he knew his friend didn't doubt his integrity, he also understood that others did, so he pivoted to logic. "What can be more evident," he queried, "than that I have acted on Principle? Was there a Man in Pennsylvania, that possest a larger Share of the public Confidence, some Months ago, than did I? Or that had a more certain Prospect of personal Advantage from

Independency, or a smaller Chance of Advantages from Reconciliation? Can it be supposed, that I was so stupid, as not to consider and understand these Things?" Even his worst enemy knew that had Dickinson tossed aside all his misgivings and voted for independence, he could have held virtually any post he desired in the new government. "Any man not more than half an Ideot might perceive the situation and the immediate Consequences of such a Behavior," he added with disgust. "I know most assuredly, & publicly declared in Congress, that I should lose a very great Part of my Popularity— and all the Benefits an artful, or what some would call a prudent Man, might coin it into—I despise them, when to be purchased only by Violations of my Conscience—I should have been a Villain, if I had spoken and voted differently from what I did."

"Whom was I trying to please?" he demanded. "The Proprietary People are known to have uniformly been my deadly Foes throughout my Life. Was it to please the People call'd Quakers? Allow it— What was I to obtain by pleasing them? All things were verging to a Revolution in which they would have little Power. Besides, I as much disquieted them by other Measures I took as I did others by opposing the Declaration of Independence. Thus I displeased both Sides—one by going too far; the other by not going far enough." Such is the fate of principled trimmers, "who with singleness of Soul consult the public Wellfare, without basely attaching themselves from selfish Motives to either of contenting Parties." [71] Knowing this truth did not make it easier to accept.

By September 1, 1776, Dickinson's unit had been sent home, narrowly missing the disastrous Battle of Manhattan that took the lives of militiamen from Delaware and Maryland. He believed his conduct as colonel was universally approved.[72] That he was immediately appointed as a justice of the peace by Pennsylvania's revolutionary convention suggested the members' confidence in him.[73] At the behest of his men, he retained his colonelcy so that he could again lead them when the time came. But the convention went beyond its mandate and confirmed two new brigadier generals to lead Dickinson's battalion. He accordingly resigned his commission in protest, resolving never to be accountable to those he considered merely "lately inspired patriots" who might well use an error or a misfortune against him.[74] At that moment, Dickinson planned a move unheard of by a gentleman of his wealth and stature: at the next call for enlistments in the Pennsylvania militia, he would join as a private. The grim work of war was performed by enlisted men, and a few women, of the lower sorts. Gentlemen were officers who traveled, dined, and slept in relative comfort, rarely risking life or limb. He would rather be with those who ran those risks.

In the meantime, Dickinson turned to the alarming political situation in the state.[75] A new, faulty constitution was being imposed on the people of Pennsylvania as a fait accompli on September 28; there was no vote to approve the system that would govern the people. When Dickinson saw the declaration of rights that was included, he eviscerated it with his pen, rewriting clauses and including missing protections for dissenters' rights.[76] His primary goal became to amend the flawed constitution. The root of the problem was that the radicals, contrary to all sound theory of the day, were democrats who had taken the extreme step of abolishing property requirements for voting, which allowed all men who paid taxes to cast a ballot. It was a dangerous act to give such power to men without education or principles who were dependent on others for their livelihoods and ideas. Like most leaders of the day, Dickinson believed that "the People are not proper for Sovereigns—because that requires as much Attention to foreign Affairs as to domestic—& Experience is absolutely necessary." But he did believe that "common sense & the general Ideas of Justice are sufficient to determine whether the laws are rightly administered & whether they are happy or not. Therefore, the People are good Judges whether the Government is well administered but not fit to govern."[77] These Pennsylvania men were sworn enemies of the Quakers, which might even have compromised their ability to judge the efficacy of the government.

Pennsylvania radicals' snub of Dickinson was made even more glaring by the leaders in Maryland, who were attempting to draft their own constitution and bill of rights. Although their statesmen were experienced, they nevertheless sent their work to Dickinson for comment and begged him to come to Annapolis to advise them. Thomas Stone and Samuel Chase both expressed that he "could render very great and essential Service to our State." Dickinson could not oblige the latter request, but he did return his comments on their work.[78]

Ahead of the November 5 election to seat a new post-Quaker Assembly, Dickinson, along with Thomas McKean—Dickinson's longtime friend and now president of the convention that formed after the fall of the Quaker Assembly—led a public meeting to voice their concerns about the new constitution. Now that the Quakers were out, the Assembly was divided into two new political factions: the Constitutionalists, who supported the radical constitution, and the Republicans, who objected to violations of the rule of law they found in the proceedings of the convention and the provisions of its hopelessly flawed constitution. Among the thirty-one points they outlined in the meeting were that the convention had gone beyond the powers entrusted to it, that it did not show due respect for religion, and that it created irregular and improper power and judiciary structures in defiance of Congress and sound theories of government. "The said Constitution is confused, inconsistent, and dangerous." It was, moreover, not presented to the people for their consideration, disapproved of by a majority, and ought to be amended immediately.[79] The dangers were apparent even to outsiders. "The people of Pennsylvania," John Adams noted in a letter to Benjamin Rush, "will be glad to petition the crown of Britain for reconciliation in order to be delivered from the tyranny of their Constitution."[80]

At the election, Dickinson was returned to office in Pennsylvania as a member of the new Assembly and also in Delaware to serve as delegate to Congress.[81] He promptly wrote to the Delaware Assembly to decline to serve. He was honored by their confidence in him. But, "for several weighty Reasons," he begged to be excused from accepting the post.[82] There was simply too much to do in Pennsylvania, and it would separate him from Polly.

But even with the volume of work, bitter factionalism within the Pennsylvania Assembly caused his tenure there to be short-lived. On November 27, he put forth a proposal to amend the constitution, but the motion was rejected.[83] The government would hold to the provision that the constitution could only be amended every seven years, and then only by a body called the Council of Censors. Guided by instructions from his constituents, Dickinson and his faction protested vigorously, causing an opponent to speculate that he was seeking a position of power for himself. Dickinson responded that he would never again hold office, regardless of how the government was regulated.[84] But it did no good. "The behavior of some persons on that day," he later explained, "and the disagreeable circumstance of entering into contests scarcely to be avoided with Gentlemen I had for a long time esteemed, added to what had passed before, induced me to decline any further opposition to the Constitution."[85] After his proposal to amend the constitution was rejected, he resigned his seat in the Assembly, taking his allies with him.[86] Achieving a quorum now would be nearly impossible.

Benjamin Rush, with whom Dickinson had reconciled upon his return from the front, tried to convince him to reverse course, assuring him that, "in Spite of all their cunning & malice," the radicals would soon reform the

Pennsylvania government. "The eyes of the whole city are fixed upon you." As General Howe bore down on Philadelphia, the sound of drums echoed in the streets, and merchants shut up their shops.[87] Rush hoped the Pennsylvania militia would deter Howe. "We expect—we are sure you will head your battalion," said Rush. "The whole State of Pennsylvania will be influenced by the City of Philadelphia—and the city waits only to see what part you will take," he said to Dickinson.[88] With the Assembly floundering, Congress declared martial law and announced that it would take over the government if necessary. The radicals, humiliated, turned their full ire on Dickinson, whom they now considered a traitor.

On December 10, the British were in Trenton, poised to take Philadelphia, and Congress was preparing to flee to Baltimore. Terrifying rumors circulated about shocking "Outrages of a Soldiery intoxicated with Success," as Dickinson put it. He asked James Pemberton to take his family to his farm in Kent.[89] Pennsylvania papers soon reported on atrocities committed by the British Army in New Jersey. Soldiers had held several women and girls hostage, raping them repeatedly over three days. Their victims included thirteen-year-old Abigail Palmer, her two friends, and a woman five months pregnant.[90] Dickinson knew that he and his family would be targeted "more especially as the part I had taken from the very Beginning of the present controversy, and my having born Arms." He feared this "might have drawn peculiar Insults and Injuries on those who were connected with me. I believe," he thought, "there was not one Man at that Time in Philadelphia, who had acted as publicly in the Common Cause as I had done."[91]

Dickinson's plans were foiled when Polly refused to leave without her husband. So they packed their belongings and together climbed into their four-horse carriage, along with Sally and one of the Hicks orphans. Two servants attended a baggage carriage. They traveled slowly—no more than twenty miles per day—along main public roads and lodged in public houses in Chester and New Castle Counties. Along the way they met many acquaintances, including John Hancock, president of Congress, and his family, who were also fleeing.[92]

Upon arriving at Poplar Hall on December 16, the Dickinsons' tenant was kind enough to let the family have two rooms in the house.[93] Polly was not pleased to be displaced from her Philadelphia home. "I am now seperated from my Brethren and fathers house, a stranger in a strange land," she lamented to her friend Sally Fisher. She thought about Fairhill, the poetry she had written about it, and the time she had spent with her father, sister, and the Rural Circle, "when I had no more thoughts of moving, than of going to Rome."[94]

Dickinson soon learned that the Pennsylvania Council of Safety, now the executive power in the state, had begun actions against him. They were encouraged by Dickinson's erstwhile admirers such as Samuel Adams, who once considered him a "True Bostonian" but now accused Dickinson of having "poisoned the minds of the People" since September 1774.[95] Claiming they had received a complaint that Dickinson had refused to accept Continental currency, and pretending no knowledge of his whereabouts, Council members intercepted and read a note from him to Phil and imprisoned the enslaved man who was carrying it. No sooner was Dickinson out of town than they appropriated his new and recently renovated Chestnut Street house, converting it to a hospital. They also leveled "charges" against him: that he had opposed the Declaration of Independence; that he had deserted his battalion when it returned to the field in December; that he opposed the American cause; that he had abrogated his duties to the State of Delaware; and that he had told his brother not to accept Continental currency.[96] Dickinson was now effectively an enemy of the state. Rumors flew about Philadelphia that he had been arrested, and his enemies published libels in the papers.[97]

Dickinson refused to be intimidated by these false charges and immediately began drafting a defense of his actions. "Every Artifice has been incessantly practised to hack down my Reputation," he began. He saw the Council's smear campaign as an extension of John Adams's efforts to impeach his character, which had begun in the summer of 1775. "Even when my Heart has escap'd Censure," he continued, "the Mediocrity of my Genius & the Greatness of my Fortune have been thought proper Subjects of Animadversion. I admit the Justice of the Charges, and can truly say," he parried, "I envy not the Men of exalted Genius & small Fortune their present Triumphs."[98]

As soon as his family was comfortably situated, Dickinson returned to Philadelphia to confront his accusers and demand a public hearing to vindicate his reputation. But after a meeting with the Council on Tuesday, January 14, 1777, it stonewalled him, refusing to meet again or accede to any of his demands. Dickinson had only asked that Council members issue a statement clearing him "from all Suspicions of Intentions unfriendly to the Cause of America" and that they repeat publicly what they had told him about why they had opened his letter to Phil, jailed the enslaved man, and turned his house into a hospital.[99] But before he got a response, news from Kent of his house almost burning and Polly's distress necessitated his departure. His hurry and a violent cold also prevented him from lingering in New Castle to decline his appointment to Congress in person before the Assembly.[100] Instead, he asked George Read to convey his regrets. Once back in Kent on January 21, he continued writing his defense, which took him until the end of February to finish.[101]

The matter of the Continental currency and the intercepted letter concerned Dickinson the most. On the way to Kent, he had indeed written hastily to Phil, who was currently commanding his New Jersey regiment on the front, cautioning him against accepting Continental currency from his tenants or other debtors while in the field. The danger of being mere miles from the enemy and of Americans regularly stealing from one another was too great. To stain Dickinson's reputation, the Council leaked only portions of the note without context. Dickinson would have rather it published the entire thing so the public could see that he had said Phil should not accept Continental currency "while he continued with so much hazard in Camp."[102] The Council also claimed, preposterously, that Dickinson had urged Phil to resign his commission.[103] As for his own alleged refusal to accept Continental currency, just as he was leaving Philadelphia, Dickinson had accepted payment of two substantial debts in it. He had signed affidavits to prove it.[104]

Despite knowing the full context of the letter and also the falseness of the complaint against Dickinson, the Council nevertheless sent a copy of the letter to George Washington.[105] Dickinson was misinformed that Washington "never took any notice of it in his Correspondence with the Council." Actually, Washington had indeed responded, saying, "Nothing ever amazed me more than the Note said to be wrote by Jno. Dickinson Esqr. to his Brother the General."[106]

The damage was not only to his reputation; it was material. Dickinson estimated that the Council's seizure of his house had cost him well over £10,000, but he did not demand reparation. Moreover, if Council members had only asked, he would gladly have given it to them. His love for the wounded soldiers was such that he would have "opened my best House and the best Rooms in it." He would have "cut down my best Woods for the Relief of such unhappy people."[107]

Fully confident of the disinterestedness of his conduct, he refused to bend, defending his honor in the strongest terms. "I have acted in Conformity to what I Judged to be right," he announced.[108] "Would I but have consented only to become a Villain, and to regulate my public Conduct by my private

Interest, I should at this Hour be called a patriot by those, who now persecute me."[109] Moreover, "the Council of Safety knows, I might have reigned with them, if I had been so false to my Countrymen, as to abuse the Trust they reposd in me, only by concealing my real sentiments for fear of displeasing them."[110] But such contemptuous behavior was never Dickinson's way. "Little do they know me," he proclaimed, "if they suppose, their artifice will induce me to swerve one tittle from the truth."[111] He wanted to be perfectly clear. He did not address them now because he was afraid of them. "I defy your Power," he asserted, "and if any of You bear Me Malice; I would have You assuredly to know, I equally defy <u>that</u>."[112]

Dickinson's Uncle Cadwalader, who served the American cause as the medical director of the army hospitals, was incensed at the treatment of his nephew by the "scandalous wretches" in the Council. "My Heart glowed with Indignation, at the Insult," he said. When Phil told him how thoroughly innocent John was of the charges, Cadwalader was pleased and proud. He praised Dickinson's address for its "cool candid & short manner." Still, he thought Dickinson's honor demanded more. "Tell them to their faces, that you looked upon their Cruel treatment of you, owing to the malice of some of their members." He also warned, "If you do not treat them in this manner, you will invite Insults of this kind, during your whole life."[113]

Dickinson knew that his uncle was right, but he could only do so much from Kent. He continued gathering evidence of his innocence by securing affidavits from tenants that he did, in fact, use Continental currency. He published articles in the Pennsylvania papers, in defiance of a seditious libel law, that criticized the government and called for amendment of the constitution.[114] And he planned other more dramatic displays of his patriotism.[115]

In the spring of 1777, for the first time since the Declaration of Independence had been issued, Dickinson had time to spend with his family, to read his books, and to walk his fields. His repose was marred only by six-year-old Sally's breaking her arm after falling from a porch.[116] As he reconvened with these beloved things and conferred with Polly about all he had endured in recent years—not only the loss of his infant daughter and honored mother, but also vicious attacks on his honor by a new breed of political enemy—he was able for the first time in years to meditate on the things most important in life. In so doing, he found that he had come to share Polly's Quaker priorities more than he had realized. He felt a surge of patriotism, faith in the Author of All Goodness, and love of his fellow men. Like a good Quaker, these moved him to action, but not back to Pennsylvania. "No Temptation, except serving my Country, America," he wrote Benjamin Rush, "could engage Me ever again to take any share in Pennsylvanian Affairs."[117]

Instead, Dickinson did two things unheard of for a gentleman in his elevated position. The first related to a matter that nagged at his conscience. His participation in the institution of slavery had long made him uncomfortable. Quaker slaveholders had told themselves for decades that their ownership of other human beings was acceptable in God's eyes because they were kindly masters who tended to the well-being of their "property" and led them to the Christian faith. But beginning in the 1750s, this attitude had begun to change. Now Quakers had instituted a new "antislavery testimony," meaning that they eradicated slavery from their Society. In 1775, they had turned outwards to do the same in America, forming the Pennsylvania Society for Promoting the Abolition of Slavery.

Dickinson had always disliked the institution for the danger it posed to the morals of white people. He was not alone in this sentiment. In this early phase of the Quaker abolitionist movement, even the most ardent advocates proclaimed that they were more concerned for the welfare of whites.[118] Exerting total power over another person corrupted the thinking of the enslaver, leading to abhorrent behavior. For most abolitionists, concern for the enslaved person was secondary.

This disregard for the lives of Black people led to hypocrisy among American leaders. Before independence, Dickinson was among those who spoke passionately about Americans' potential "enslavement" to Britain. It was a rhetorical trope he and others employed in many of their writings. In 1771, however, Dickinson articulated in more detail the stark difference leaders of his age actually recognized, but refused to acknowledge, between freedom and bondage. "Slaves," he wrote, "who have nothing but a miserable Life to lose and whose Minds must be infected by their Condition, are influenced only by their feelings." By contrast, he observed, "Freemen, possest of the Blessing, that gives a Value to Life, ever attentive to its Preservation, believe they have a Right to consider their Situation, & the Dangers that threaten them."[119] This was an assessment that was more nuanced, untinged

with the romanticism of the battle cry "liberty or death": without bodily autonomy, life had no value, and the individual's degraded position did not even
allow him to think. He could only suffer. Still, American leaders insisted that
Britain would make them "slaves" if they did not resist. By their definition,
taxation without representation reduced white men of property to slaves.

Dickinson found more opportunity for commentary, not just on white
Americans' potential "enslavement" to Britain but also on Americans' actual
enslavement of Africans. The 1772 case *Somerset v. Stewart*, whereby chattel
slavery was ruled to be incompatible with the British common law, caught
his attention. In a 1774 pamphlet published to promote the efforts of the First
Continental Congress, he hinted not just of his approval of the British ruling
but also of his condemnation of the legality of white Americans' enslavement
of Black people—and not Black *Africans*, but Black *Americans*: "Even those
unhappy persons," he wrote, "who have had the misfortune of being born
under the yoke of bondage, imposed by the cruel laws, if they may be called
laws, of the land, where they received their birth, no sooner breathe the air
of *England*, though they touch her shore only by accident"—here he cited the
Somerset case—"than they instantly become freemen." It was, he observed, a
"Strange contradiction" that "the *same* kingdom at the *same* time, [was both]
the *asylum* and the *bane* of liberty."[120]

Dickinson was inclined to favor the *Somerset* verdict not only because
it followed Quaker principles but also because it adhered to British law as
Dickinson understood it. With *Somerset*, the British constitution at home
was simply codifying what was already apparent in the Admiralty Court.
He believed that "the Admiralty is establishd on the generous Principles
of Humanity & Publick Good. It looks on the whole World as one great
society. Its rules are those of Civil Law & of Nature—that is of Reason &
Virtue— It makes no Distinction between Nations." And because of this, the
court regarded "the barbarous Inhabitants of Africka & the polite people of
Europe—with an Equal Eye."[121]

As was the norm in mid-eighteenth-century Quaker families, the
Dickinsons had subscribed to the fiction of the benign Christian slave-
holder and the happy slave. At one time, his family was one of the largest
slave owners in the Delaware Valley, holding more than 130 men, women,
and children in bondage. Most of them Dickinson then inherited from his
father. He had long expressed concern at the very least for the good treatment of his "bondspeople." In a 1764 advertisement for the lease of Poplar

Hall, he specified that because the slaves to be let with the plantation "are remarkably honest and well behaved, Care will be taken, that they are not put under the Command of any one, but a good natured humane Man."[122] Likewise, in his business dealings, if his slaves were part of a lease of a tenant property, Dickinson stipulated in the contract that they "shall be treated with Tenderness and Care, both in Sickness and Health, well fed and warmly and properly cloathed."[123]

For some time, he resisted acknowledging what he knew he must do, telling himself he could "render a State of Slavery easy to them." But Dickinson came to see that the benign master and happy slave was a convenient fiction whites used to justify a "horrid infatuation." The absurdity of comparing white Americans' position under the Tea Act and other British measures with that of chattel slavery gradually resonated for Dickinson, and his own words made the most obvious impression upon him—that Americans could not in good faith bemoan their own potential and rhetorical slavery while physically holding men and women in bondage. Now, as Dickinson generally adhered more closely to Quakerism, he came to realize that humane treatment of the enslaved was not enough. He "found his mind disturbed on their account."[124]

In 1776, the year after Philadelphia Quakers established their abolition society, Dickinson began to make his sentiments against slavery known more publicly. His queries while drafting the Articles of Confederation put his colleagues on notice that he felt that slavery was unacceptable. With the *Somerset* case no doubt in mind, Southerners such as Edward Routledge hated his draft because it would create a powerful central government that threatened their property by protecting the rights of "inhabitants" moving among the colonies.[125] Indeed, given Dickinson's own views on *Somerset* and its adherence to British jurisprudence, he opposed independence, at least in part, because he found better hope for protection of the rights of "all men" under the British constitution than as yet undecided American law.

Now, as he communed with the "Benevolent Author" and the words of the Declaration rang in his ears, he began the process of freeing those he enslaved. On May 12, 1777, he drew up a deed for manumission of the thirty-seven men, women, and children. But he was not yet prepared to release them unconditionally. The deed specified that they would remain in bondage for another twenty-one years. Any children born during that time would be free, unless Dickinson educated and maintained them, in which case they would

remain enslaved as long as their mothers remained so. Although surely not
what the Black people themselves hoped for, it was a start. Dickinson's sense
of duty on this matter was so strong that he believed Divine Judgment would
come down against him had he neglected it.[126]

His second patriotic act was to execute his plan to join the militia as a private. If some in Pennsylvania or elsewhere would impugn his patriotism,
he would demonstrate it so that it could not be denied. He thus joined
Captain Stephen Lewis's Delaware regiment, "and in that capacity served
with my musket upon my shoulder." He also followed orders to scour the
countryside, requisitioning arms and ammunition. When the British took
Wilmington in late August, despite the *chevaux de frize* he had directed to be
placed in the Delaware River, he was one of one thousand Delaware troops
sent to Christiana Bridge to deter the British invasion. When intelligence
arrived of much-needed ammunition left in the ferry house, he offered to
lead fifty men to acquire it.[127] His duties continued the entire summer, as the
Americans failed to prevent the British from landing at Head of Elk in their
attempt to take control of the Delaware River. After Washington's dramatic
defeat just outside Philadelphia at the Battle of Brandywine in September,
Thomas McKean, now president of Delaware, likely recognized that America
should not lose one of its best legal and political minds on the battlefield,
so he commissioned Dickinson as a brigadier general on September 26.[128]
Although he never acted on the commission and resigned in December
"on account of some objections relating to the militia and the militia laws,"
Dickinson at least was removed from harm's way.[129]

Other threats loomed, not just for Dickinson but also for his immediate
and extended family. They were precisely what he had anticipated when he
drafted the religious liberty clause in the Articles of Confederation. Working
in tandem and following suggestions by Thomas Paine in his writings,
radicals in Congress and the Pennsylvania government concocted a scheme
against the leading Quakers of Philadelphia. Paine's scathing attacks on
Friends beginning in 1776 had only escalated after independence was
declared and the war went badly for the Americans. The truth was that most
Pennsylvanians had never been very interested in overthrowing the British,
let alone fighting them. Their main goal had always been overthrowing the
Quaker government. With that accomplished, their patriotism flagged.
Paine knew this and sought to stoke the *rage militaire* by equating Quaker
pacifism with Tory loyalism, blaming Quakers for the fact that the war was
going poorly, and even suggesting that they be arrested. Quakers, many of

whom were actually on the American side, now endured harassment on the streets and broken windows in their shops and homes when they refused, on religious grounds, to observe the patriotic rituals demanded by the government.[130]

One congressional delegate in particular listened attentively to Paine. John Adams, along with a few other delegates, fabricated a story that the Quakers of the fictitious "Spanktown Yearly Meeting" in New Jersey had been informing the British about American movements. Accordingly, Congress ordered the Pennsylvania government to arrest the leading Quakers in Philadelphia and imprison them. Among them were Polly's relatives, Israel, John, and James Pemberton, as well as several of the Dickinsons' friends. Without a warrant, officials stormed into James Pemberton's home, ostensibly looking for guns. Recalling that it was Quakers' pacifism that had angered them and that finding guns was therefore unlikely, they searched his desk, confiscated papers, and demanded he accompany them. Pemberton, in the Quaker way of resistance, refused to rise from his chair, so the officials carried him seated in it from his home. He and more than twenty other men, mostly Quakers, were then held without charge in the Mason's lodge.[131]

The prisoners immediately petitioned the Pennsylvania Assembly for their right of habeas corpus, an ancient English right against unlawful and indefinite imprisonment. Chief Justice of the Pennsylvania Supreme Court Thomas McKean had issued them a writ, along with a letter to John Adams schooling him on the right, a copy of which McKean also sent to Dickinson.[132] But the Assembly passed an *ex post facto* law—a law after the fact—to deny it. When the prisoners petitioned Congress, that body claimed it had no jurisdiction and they must petition Pennsylvania, which was holding them. This charade continued as Friends were exiled to Winchester, Virginia, where some of them died, while others, whose families were left husband- and fatherless, saw their businesses fail and livelihoods destroyed.[133] Adams, who just a few months prior had declared Quakers to be no threat at all, now proclaimed, "We have been obliged to attempt to humble the Pride of some Jesuits who call themselves Quakers, but who love Money and Land better than Liberty or Religion. The Hypocrites are endeavoring to raise the Cry of Persecution, and to give this Matter a religious Turn, but they can't succeed. The World knows them and their Communications."[134]

Dickinson's worst fears about bigoted radicals leading Pennsylvania and no national constitution protecting dissenters' rights were now fully realized. The "Virginia Exiles" would be detained and deprived of their liberty without charge for nine months, before they were finally released unceremoniously, without explanation or restitution.

By the autumn of 1777, Polly and the children had returned to Fairhill, and the threat to Dickinson's immediate family took a dire turn. After Brandywine fell and Washington retreated, the British resumed their march to claim the American capital. At the end of October, while Dickinson was at Poplar Hall, he received word that they were nearing Germantown. Their next stop would be the Northern Liberties and Fairhill. Dickinson wrote hastily to Polly. She should, without delay, gather their little girl and his day book and find safe places for valuables. A friend would retrieve her and bring her to Poplar Hall.[135] He was sick with worry about Polly and their "precious one"; it didn't occur to him that he would never see their lovely house at Fairhill again.

Within days of Polly's safe arrival in Kent, the British descended upon the Northern Liberties. Having learned that Fairhill was the seat of the Pennsylvania Farmer, "that damned rebel," Colonel Thomas Twisleton took special delight in rendering the elegant mansion to ashes.[136] After all, as John Adams complained, the British considered Dickinson to be "the ruler of America."[137] Present at the burning was Loyalist Joseph Galloway, who, surprisingly, tried to do Dickinson a good turn. Rather than encourage the destruction, he told the soldiers that the true owner of the estate was Polly Dickinson's cousin, Isaac Norris. They proceeded anyway. Now Dickinson could truly assert, "For some time past I have been incessantly attacked on every side."[138] Although the manor house was lost, the spectacular library was spared.[139] Standing atop her mother's house on Chestnut Street, Debby Norris counted seventeen fires in the vicinity.[140]

Perhaps knowing the kindness done him by an enemy, in July of the following year, when Grace Galloway, the Loyalist's wife, was alone and struggling to retain her property, Dickinson "came & in the most friendly way offer'd his service & advice. He behaves so well," she reported, "that I am quite taken with him." Naturally, Dickinson worked for her pro bono.[141]

At the end of this bitter and terrifying time, Dickinson was exhausted. He resigned his commission in the Delaware militia and retreated inward to the solace of his family.

11

"From the Mist of Doubts to the Sunshine of Belief"

Quaker Politics in Congress and the Delaware Presidency, 1778–1782

After John and Polly had resettled into their domestic rhythms, Polly became restless in Kent, hinting to Susee Wright that she would prefer to be back in Philadelphia, especially when mosquito season came. The women in her circle could not imagine why her husband insisted on staying at Poplar Hall, where the air was so unhealthy. His physician uncle fretted that Dickinson wouldn't survive there much longer. But there were advantages to being far removed from civilization. Even as Susee commiserated with Polly, she warned of dire circumstances confronting Quakers in Philadelphia, who were now "suffering deeply" in the British-occupied city. "I fear those miscreants," she said of the British, "will never leave it without plundering, if they do without Burning."[1]

Life was little better in Philadelphia under American control. Benjamin Rush informed Dickinson that even the Executive Council of Pennsylvania had complained about the constitution and wanted it changed. "The ignorance of the Assembly, the tyranny of the courts of law, and of magistrates— & the total insufficiency of both laws and magistrates to defend the state from the insults & rapine of the Quarter Master Commissaries & military Officers," as Rush explained, meant that the people felt undefended, unsecured, and ready to take matters into their own hands.[2]

Wright and Rush did not exaggerate. Soon the British would evacuate Philadelphia, which would leave political and religious dissenters at the mercy of the Americans. In March 1778, the Assembly passed an Act of Attainder, which nullified the civil rights of Loyalists in absentia and pronounced a death sentence upon them. Almost four hundred individuals were attainted. Of the 130 who surrendered at the end of June, two were Quakers.

Eventually all were pardoned, except for the two Quakers, who were executed by the order of Executive Council President Joseph Reed, a Presbyterian and erstwhile Dickinson ally.[3] Friends had pled with the Assembly to restore the Charter of Privileges, and James Wilson had represented the two men. But Samuel Adams expressed the sentiments of many of the Revolution's leaders. "These Quakers," he said, "are in general a sly artful People." Their unity and insularity was cause for suspicion. "They carefully educate their Children in their own contracted Opinions and Manners," he complained, "and I dare say they have in their Heads as perfect a System of Uniformity of Worship in their Way, and are busily employd about spiritual Domination as ever Laud himself was."[4] The comparison of Quakers with Archbishop of Canterbury William Laud was as damning as equating their doctrine of the Light within to the Catholic pope.

In this grim climate were some glimmers of hope in the war. After several bruising defeats, a significant American victory at the Battle of Saratoga had a number of good effects. It naturally boosted the morale of the troops. It had also finally tipped the scales enough in the Americans' favor to convince the French to support their cause. A treaty of alliance was signed on February 6, 1778, the foundation for which Dickinson had laid with his work on the Plan of Treaties in June 1776. The pending departure of the British in mid-June was generally cause for celebration. And, just as Dickinson had predicted in his speech against independence, now that the British had experienced only mixed success in their military campaigns, they were ready "to redress all the Grievances we complain'd of in our first Petition to the king."[5]

To this end, on June 4, a three-member peace commission from Britain arrived in Philadelphia, led by the young Earl of Carlisle. Prepared to inform Congress of their "most earnest desire to re-establish, on the basis of equal freedom and mutual safety, the tranquility of this once happy empire," they wanted to lay old controversies to rest. Now they would offer Americans everywhere they could possibly have desired as colonists, and more, including free trade, no military forces on American soil, assumption of American debts, allowing paper currency and underwriting its value, and either American representation in Parliament or British representation in the legislatures of the American states. In short, they offered to support Americans and their institutions so that Americans "may have the irrevocable enjoyment of every privilege that is short of a total separation of interest, or consistent with that union of force, on which the safety of our common religion and liberty depends."[6] They would offer them everything, that is, but independence.

Congress, now sitting in York, Pennsylvania, received the so-called Carlisle Commission's letter on June 13 with disdain. So offended were they by the slights it contained against the French king—their new favorite now that a treaty was being finalized—that they refused to hear it through on first reading. On June 17, they responded that they would be willing to consider a peace treaty "when the king of Great Britain shall demonstrate a sincere disposition for that purpose." To them, this meant "an explicit acknowledgment of the independence of these states" or the withdrawal of the king's troops.[7]

The coming of the Carlisle Commission was known long in advance. Currently in Philadelphia, Dickinson was struck by a very Quakerly impulse. As early Quakers used to travel great distances to convince heads of state of the Truth of Quakerism, he now formed a plan to approach the commissioners with the goal of convincing them to acknowledge America's independence. Anything was worth a try for peace, and no one, he reasoned, was better qualified than he to explain why the improbable had become actual. He jotted notes for a speech. "Credit should be given to my Sentiments," he would explain, "because nothing less than the absolute necessity of accepting American independance could have reconcil'd Me to this Measure." He listed several pieces of evidence that proved how opposed he had been to independence, including his conduct as a member of the Assembly and Congress (they could check the published proceedings of the Assembly if they liked); John Adams's intercepted letter with the "piddling genius" comment; that he was turned out of both the new Pennsylvania government and Congress; his displacement from his command of the Pennsylvania militia; and, finally, common knowledge. Moreover, he assured them "I act wholly as a private person." He was not appearing before them at the behest of Congress or any other body. "I declare in the <u>most solemn</u> Manner," he insisted, "<u>upon my Honor</u>, that no such Body or Person has assented to my Conduct on this Occasion or even has Knowledge of it."

Next he cited three "incontrovertible Facts" to prove America was now, actually, independent. First was "the Unanimity of America in Support of Independence." The only people still unhappy about the Declaration of Independence, he explained, were Quakers and Tories, but they were a small minority. Second was "the Zeal of America in Support of Independence." This zeal was so powerful that if the British conquered the entire eastern coast, Americans would continue to fight them from beyond the Allegheny Mountains. A third reason was "her Strength—such an Army as We never had before." The American population was quickly replacing soldiers killed in battle, and American boys were raised up to be citizen soldiers; now they played at war with toy muskets. Finally, America could now produce the goods it used to get from Britain, such as salt and clothing.[8] All of these facts proved that America was already independent. Dickinson was confident that the new nation would prevail.

But regardless of how convincing Dickinson could be, the commission was not authorized to recognize America's independence. With the British evacuation of Philadelphia underway and America allied with Britain's greatest enemy, the commissioners knew they hadn't a chance of securing peace honorably. Thus they turned to bribery and threats, proving to Americans that their decision to separate from that corrupt regime was the right one.[9]

Once the British Army had evacuated Philadelphia, in the summer of 1778, the Dickinsons returned to stay with Aunt Norris on Chestnut Street. Polly welcomed the chance to be with her family since she was again with child. Dickinson, however, frequently returned to Kent. He had left around the first of August, and Polly fretted not hearing from him for three weeks, her imagination conjuring pictures of him on his sickbed. She herself complained of a disorder of the bowels that kept Dr. Redman and Nurse Wilson in attendance. A letter from Dickinson finally arrived on the eighteenth, expressing his concern for Polly's and seven-year-old Sally's health. "My Happiness, under Heaven, depends on You," he said, and instructed Polly to give Sally a dose of powdered bark each Monday. Polly should also remind her to be "extremely kind and gentle to every body—speaking kindly to all, rich and poor, young and old." He told of much-needed food for the extended family arriving by shallop at the Dickinsons' dock and reported that he was hearty, and although there were myriad demands on his time, "I go through them in my easy Way, so as to be a mere Philosopher the greater part of the afternoon." In closing, he sent "a multitude of kisses" for "our Precious baby," Sally. Polly replied that "Her eyes sparkle with Joy upon hearing of her papa's remembrance."[10]

Aunt Norris reported that on August 19, Polly had "an exceeding good Labor" in spite of the extreme heat and humidity, delivering their third child, a son whom they named John.[11] Aunt Norris did not write immediately, however. Although the birth was easy, Polly's disorder returned. Now Cousin John Jones also treated her, and he recommended Aunt Norris delay writing

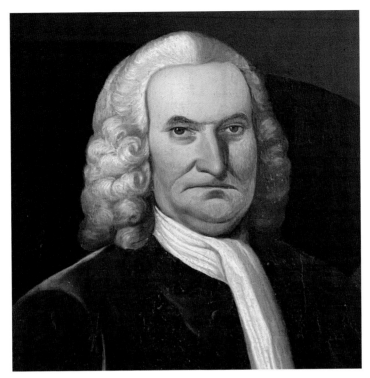

Figure 1. Samuel Dickinson, [n.d]. The John Dickinson Plantation, Dover, Del. .

Figure 2. Mary Dickinson, [n.d]. The John Dickinson Plantation, Dover, Del.

Figure 3. Charles Willson Peale, *A Portrait of Dr. Thomas Cadwalader*, 1770. Philadelphia Museum of Art, Philadelphia, Pa.

Figure 4. Nicholas Skull, et al. "A Map of Philadelphia and Parts Adjacent: With a Perspective View of the State-House," (1752). Library of Congress, Washington, D.C.

Figure 5. Joseph Nickolls, *A View of the Fountain in the Temple*, 1738. The Middle Temple, London.

Figure 6. Middle Temple Hall. *Penny Magazine* (May 31–June 30, 1835).

Figure 7. John Dickinson's standing desk. The Library Company of Philadelphia, Philadelphia, Pa.

Figure 8. *Isaac Norris, his House at Fairhill*, [n.d.]. Stenton, Philadelphia, Pa.

Figure 9. Frontispiece. *Nosum Nosorum: Or, a New Treatise on Large Noses* (1765). The Historical Society of Pennsylvania, Philadelphia, Pa.

Figure 10. James Smither, *The Patriotic American Farmer*, 1768. The Library Company of Philadelphia, Philadelphia, Pa.

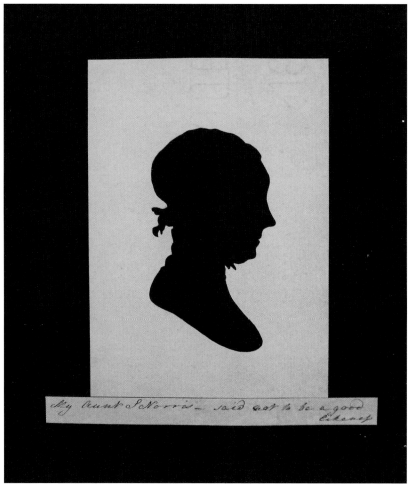

Figure 11. Sally Norris, [n.d.]. The Historical Society of Pennsylvania, Philadelphia, Pa.

Figure 12. Charles Willson Peale, *John Dickinson*, 1770. The Historical Society of Pennsylvania, Philadelphia, Pa.

Figure 13. Charles Willson Peale, *Mary Dickinson and Daughter, Sally Norris Dickinson*, 1773. The Historical Society of Pennsylvania Collection, Philadelphia History Museum, Philadelphia, Pa.

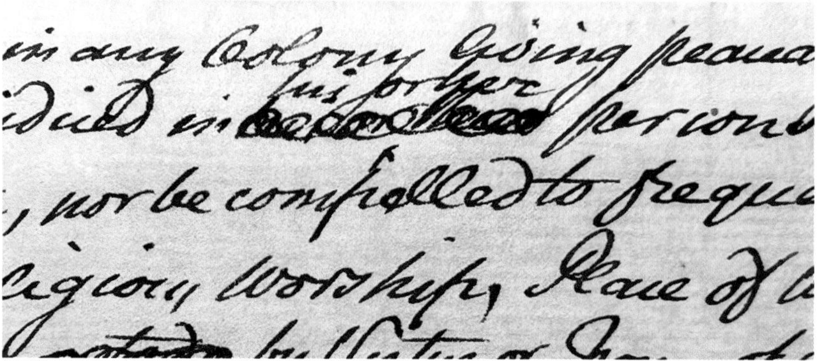

Figure 14. John Dickinson, Notes for the Articles of Confederation, [1776]. The Historical Society of Pennsylvania.

BRIG-GEN. PHILEMON DICKINSON.
Member of the Continental Congress.

Figure 15. Albert Rosenthal, *Brig.-Gen. Philemon Dickinson*, 1820. New York Public Library, New York, N.Y.

Figure 16. Pierre Eugène du Simitière. *J. Dickinson, Esqr.*, 1781. The Historical Society of Pennsylvania, Philadelphia, Pa.

Figure 17. Charles Willson Peale, *John Dickinson*, [c. 1782–83]. Independence National Historical Park, Philadelphia, Pa.

Figure 18. Lester Hoadley Sellers, *Peale's Arch of Triumph*, [c. 1969]. American Philosophical Society, Philadelphia, Pa.

Figure 19. Gilbert Stuart, *George Logan*, [c. 1804]. Atwater Kent Museum, Philadelphia, Pa.

Figure 20. Charles Willson Peale, *Deborah Norris Logan*, 1816. Stenton, Philadelphia, Pa.

Figure 21. John Dickinson's Market Street house, Wilmington, [n.d.]. The Delaware Historical Society, Wilmington, Del.

Figure 22. John Dickinson, [n.d.]. The Library Company of Philadelphia, Philadelphia, Pa.

Figure 23. John Dickinson ship's figurehead, American, [c. 1820-1840]. White pine, paint. Courtesy of David A. Schorsch and Eileen M. Smiles, photo by Mike Meyers.

to Dickinson about their new son until Polly's health improved—just in case. By the morning of August 21, she was much better. And although her baby seemed to be doing well days after his birth, he died on September 2, devastating his parents.[12]

By Christmas, the Dickinsons had returned to Poplar Hall, taking Cousin Debby Norris, now seventeen, with them as company for Sally. It was a charming domestic scene that John and Polly could paint for Aunt Norris. The family enjoyed the snow knowing they had "plenty of wood, a tight House, good flour, buckwheat, oates in plenty, butter, honey, partridges, turkeys, fowls, rabbits, beef, pork—and many blessings." They wanted only for a sleigh. The extreme cold kept them mostly indoors, and the children in the house "make such a racket," said Polly, "I know not what I write." Tending to their needs was Violet, who was born enslaved to the Dickinsons. Her room was next to the girls' so they could call upon her easily. Polly bore the winter well thanks to the fires Violet kindled in John and Polly's bedchamber fireplace each morning and evening.[13] Per Dickinson's manumission deed, she still had eighteen and a half years left to serve before she would be a free woman.

In this period of withdrawal from public life, Dickinson continued with his law practice and devoted attention to agriculture. The only sign that he was thinking about a future in public office is that he took an affirmation of loyalty to the State of Delaware in 1778.[14] This seemingly trivial act was actually a remarkably significant gesture. Choosing to affirm rather than swear revealed the profound shift in Dickinson's relationship with Quakerism since he had left office. War puts one's priorities in perspective like nothing else, and, in a sense, Dickinson had been at war not just with the British but with his own countrymen, especially those intent on using him as their political whipping boy. Rather than downplay his Quaker leanings, he signaled his alliance with Quakers publicly.

Dickinson could not avoid public service for long. He had narrowly dodged an appointment to a committee by the Delaware Council for giving an account of state expenditures despite not even being a member of that body. But before the members had a chance to inquire as to his willingness to serve, they concluded, "as that gentleman complains much of his want of health, we are induced to think he will decline the appointment, or that his indisposition will delay the immediate going on with this business."[15] Dickinson did not feel poorly all the time, but when he accepted an office of trust from his fellow citizens, he devoted himself to the work so entirely that exhaustion would inevitably take its toll. He was obliged to choose his assignments carefully.

Delaware finally prevailed on him in early 1779, appointing him delegate to the Continental Congress on February 1. This time, he felt he must accept. Polly wasn't pleased. "I am utterly sick of Politics," she complained. She didn't believe they would ever see the tranquility they had known before the Revolution.[16] The Dickinsons were now in Wilmington, which at least was closer to Philadelphia than Poplar Hall. But "it is very Lonesome when thee is absent," Polly wrote. "I should soon be tired of Wilmington, pleasant as it is."[17] Dickinson felt the same. "I am selfish, as almost to wish, the Time may be as tedious to You, as to Me," he would confess, "tho, I am afraid, to wish that, would be too cruel. However, if the pleasure of meeting is proportion'd to the Anxiety of Separation, perhaps it would not be very unkind."[18] Their anxiety was heightened by the fact that Polly was again with child.

Perhaps as a nudge to encourage Dickinson to take his seat, in March, the president of Congress, John Jay—another who refused to sign the Declaration of Independence—was eager to welcome him back to his rightful place at the head of national affairs. Philemon, who happened to be in Philadelphia and had spoken to Jay, followed up, clarifying that "the President of Congress desires me to inform you, that your presence is very necessary at this time, & beg you will not delay a single moment, as matters of the utmost Consequence are now under consideration."[19] Others also rejoiced at Dickinson's return. "Never was there a period when she wanted the aid of her virtuous Sons so much as in the present hour," said John Jones. To Jones's thinking, those currently in Congress were "unequal to the mighty task of American Empire."[20] American military and diplomatic successes notwithstanding, Dickinson reentered Congress at possibly the worst moment. The country was in crisis on several fronts, and the particular mixture of personalities and factional interests created a toxic environment.[21] Jay welcomed Dickinson's presence as a moderating force. But Dickinson was hardly an uncontroversial figure, determined as he was to stand on principle, self-interest be damned. As members attacked one another, he was as vulnerable as any of them.

He took his seat on April 23, and his first significant act was on May 5, along with Nicholas Vandyke, to ratify on behalf of the State of Delaware the Articles of Confederation that Congress had adopted on November 15, 1777.[22] The other Delaware delegate, Thomas McKean, had signed on February 22.[23] But as Dickinson did so, he also declared his objection to the fact that this version was drastically different from the draft he had written in

1776. Two of the most important articles were missing: that for a strong central government and that for the protection of religious liberty that included women's freedom of speech. He and the Delaware delegation expected that the document would be revised and altered at a later date.[24] The most important thing at the moment was to obtain ratification by all the states. Until then, the country would be without a constitution, and an inadequate one was better than none. There was much work to be done, and success would be limited under such adverse conditions.

Three complicated tasks demanded Dickinson's attention over the coming months, each potentially an existential threat to the infant republic: the dire financial situation, a confusion in marine affairs, and stagnant peace negotiations. All were, of course, linked to the war and were made more difficult by the unwillingness of members of Congress to put aside personal, factional, and sectional interests and work for the good of the Union. Other problems resulted from the lack of time and the inadequate expertise of the delegates. Dickinson began work on these three matters simultaneously.

First, on a committee with William Henry Drayton and James Duane, he drafted a lengthy broadside to the American public on the grim financial situation facing the country—the depreciation of the paper currency, the inability of America to fund the war, and the corruption of low-ranking public officials. It was a mixture of education, reprimand, and patriotic encouragement. The country was exactly where Dickinson feared it would be when he made his speech against independence on July 1. "*America*, without arms, ammunition, discipline, revenue, government, or ally, almost totally stript of commerce, and in the weakness of youth" is like David facing Goliath. He implored citizens to consider their own interests in light of what was best for the common good, to pay their taxes and resist corruption, monopolies, and price gouging.[25] "In vain will it be for your delegates," he admonished them, "to form plans of œconomy; to strive to stop a continuation of emissions by taxation or loan, if you do not zealously co-operate with them in promoting their designs, and use your utmost industry to prevent the waste of money in the expenditure." He ended with rousing sentiments designed to reinvigorate Americans' sense of patriotism. He encouraged them to "finish the great work you have so nobly carried on for several years past." They had already overcome so many disadvantages and achieved more than anyone believed possible. "Consider how much you have done, and how comparatively little remains to be done to crown you with success. Persevere; and you ensure Peace, Freedom, Safety, Glory, Sovereignty, and Felicity to Yourselves, your Children, and your Children's Children." As a practical measure, sound policy must work in concert with public spirit. So considering that much of the problem concerned paper currency, which was worthless, he drafted a plan to halt emission of bills of credit.[26]

A related concern was the management of the Quarter Master General and Commissary General Department (QMG&CG), which was paying prices so exorbitant for necessities, such as forage and provisions, that many feared it would ruin the American cause. President Caesar Rodney of Delaware had pressed Dickinson to look into this matter particularly.[27] Assuring Rodney that he shared his concern, Dickinson worked on two committees, one to investigate the finances of boards and departments and the other to explore ways of restructuring expenditures.[28] Both focused on QMG&CG. He sent out surveys to the commanding officers and drafted resolves for how the department might be managed better.[29] It became clear that deputy quartermasters and commissaries in the various states were involved in corruption and self-dealing to reap profits at the expense of the United States. Ultimately, Congress decided that there must be more oversight of the individuals by the executive branches of the various states to reform this department.[30]

Marine affairs—the navy, maritime trade, and maritime law—were in a disastrous state, due in part to the "useless" congressional Marine Committee, as President Jay described it. The committee consisted of one delegate from each state. But as Jay complained to General Washington, "Very few of the Members understand even the State of our naval Affairs or have Time or Inclination to attend to them."[31] As one of the few delegates who had extensive experience with maritime law in the Admiralty Court, Dickinson was the logical person to take on the matter. He was appointed to a committee to devise a plan for conducting the country's marine business and define the duties and powers of the commissioners.[32] He drafted a "Plan for a Commission of Marine," which was intended as a blueprint for the new Board of Admiralty that superseded the Marine Committee in December.[33]

One of the most contentious matters facing the Continental Congress concerned whether to negotiate for peace. It turned not merely on initiating talks with the British, which was difficult enough, considering they had not yet acknowledged America's independence, but on the relationship with foreign allies and sectional differences at home. Although the United States had secured the alliance with France, simmering tensions among the American ministers there—Silas Deane, Benjamin Franklin, and Arthur Lee—exploded. Deane, already recalled home, and Lee accused each other of intrigue and malfeasance in the Pennsylvania newspapers. Congress looked on, at first mildly amused, and then joined in the attacks. By 1779, it was clear that the dispute had serious policy consequences, and members of Congress lined up behind one man or the other.

The matter was effectively settled when Conrad Alexandre Gérard de Rayneval, France's foreign minister, asked Congress to appoint a minister plenipotentiary to engage in negotiations with Britain and to send instructions regarding the new republic's policy towards Spain, which was proposing to act as a mediator between Britain and America or, if Britain refused, to join the French. Gérard made it clear that he no longer wanted to work with Lee. Although Lee was Dickinson's old friend from the early years of the conflict with Britain, Dickinson was compelled by circumstances to vote against his continuing in France. His reasons, he explained, were not Lee's patriotism but rather the French refusal to deal further with him. Moreover, Lee's differences with Franklin precluded a harmonious relationship between the men. Taken together, these factors meant he simply could not be an effective minister to France.[34]

Lee was bitter about his perceived betrayal by Dickinson, saying, "I am unhappy to see your name among those in Congress, who were for passing a more than unmerited censure upon me without my being heard."[35] Lee's brother, William, attempted to comfort him by reminding him that Dickinson had been against independence and now "may have designs of oversetting independence."[36] But he surely knew this accusation was unfounded. It boded ill for Dickinson's reputation and legacy that less than three years after independence was declared, some were already twisting facts about him to suit their purposes.

As the battle over relations with America's principal ally raged, on June 17, Dickinson was assigned to the committee to draft the commission for the future minister plenipotentiary to France.[37] Like his other committee assignments, this, too, entailed significant difficulties. A conflict arose over the matter of fishing off the coast of Newfoundland. Securing rights to the fisheries, some of the richest in the world, was a paramount demand for New Englanders, but Southerners did not want this issue to obstruct peace negotiations, as the war was hurting their economy, dependent as it was on commerce with Britain.

Although Dickinson agreed with his New England colleagues about the importance of the fisheries, he would not consent to making America's access to them a condition of the peace for a few reasons. First, France, America's only real ally, did not want it to be a condition. And Spain, which had joined the conflict in support of France, concurred. Since the war was being fought largely at France's expense, Congress was bound to respect its wishes. Second, the sooner peace with Britain was achieved, the fewer lives would be lost. And Dickinson was not thinking only of the lives of American soldiers. On July 19, a motion was made as to whether the Marine Committee should be "directed to take the most effectual means to carry into execution . . . the burning and destroying of towns belonging to the enemy in Great Britain and the West Indies." Dickinson voted against the wanton destruction of civilian property, but the motion passed.[38] Finally, Dickinson had to think of Delaware, whose economy was dependent more on commerce than on fishing. As he told President Rodney, "It is my Duty to prefer the particular Interests of the State that honours Me with her Confidence & Merits Me with a share of her power, to the particular Interests of any other State on this Continent."[39]

Congress proved so inept in the deliberations on the matter of the peace treaty and the debate became so heated that Dickinson finally felt compelled to address President Jay with a solution. After reviewing past treaties and memorials from ministers and considering how little progress Congress had made and how dangerous the delays would be to American interests, he wrote "to propose another Mode of proceeding thereon for facilitating and accelerating those Deliberations." Since the middle of June, the committee to draft a commission to the ministers in France had been flailing, so now Dickinson suggested "throwing our Resolutions into the Form of a sett of Instructions" instead. He had sketched out his initial ideas of "the Turns that may take place in the Course of the Negotiation" and believed that Congress "can easily supply its Deficiencies." Dickinson knew it would be clear from what he laid out "that I would give my Vote for a Pacification" and that some members would object very strenuously to the terms he was proposing, namely that securing of the fisheries should not be a condition of peace.

Dickinson was not naive about what the reaction to his proposal would be, writing, "I am perfectly aware of the Reproaches I shall incur, and of the Hazards I shall run, by committing Myself in a Manner so contradictory as I now do to the Sense of great Numbers of my Countrymen more ardent tho not more zealous than Myself in our righteous Cause." Although attacks on him had already begun, he was there with the honorable motive of serving his constituents. He reiterated the two rules he had laid down for himself since the beginning of the contest with Britain: first, that he would always speak his mind freely on questions of the public happiness, and second, that if after doing so, the country decided to go another direction, he would support the decision as though it were his own. These were his actions at the moment of independence, and he would always continue so regardless of the personal consequences. Knowing also that his intentions and actions might be misrepresented in the future, he sought an insurance policy that placed his faith entirely in the hands of future historians. "Whatever may be the Merit or Demerit of my Behaviour on this great Occasion," he said, "I beg, that these papers signed by Me, may be receiv'd by Congress, and kept among their Records, that I may not be injured by Misapprehensions, nor have it in my power to elude a Charge, but, may stand or fall by Evidence under my own Hand voluntarily delivered by Me at the Time of the Transaction."[40]

In the end, this matter went better than he had hoped; enough members agreed with Dickinson that his plan went forward. On August 4, he was appointed to another committee to draft instructions to the future minister, who was to be John Adams. Dickinson made clear that American independence should be recognized and the peace treaty should be accomplished before any treaty involving commerce was negotiated. He should request of the French king that he secure fishing rights to Americans, but if the British refused, they should move on. Adams, a New Englander who prioritized the fisheries, was predictably displeased and resolved to strain the limits of the instructions.[41] Had he known the Pennsylvania Farmer had tied his hands, he surely would have gone further.

On some matters, Congress found unanimity. Dickinson felt honored to draft the resolutions awarding Major Light-Horse Harry Lee the medal of honor for his actions leading to the victory in the Battle of Paulus Hook in August.[42] And he was pleased, along with his colleagues, to bestow an unusual honor. They resolved to grant a partial pension and a suit of clothing to Margaret Corbin, who in November 1776 had taken the place of her fallen husband in the Battle of Fort Washington, valiantly manning his cannon. She still suffered from wounds she had received and had earned her reward as much as any man who fought.[43]

The unrecognized suffering of women was something with which Dickinson was familiar. It pained him to cause his beloved Polly anguish by his absence. He wrote her frequently, but letters were a poor substitute. On July 6, Polly's beloved Aunt Betty died, after "a great deal of pain in both body and mind."[44] Then, on the twenty-sixth, their second son was stillborn.[45] Polly wrote to her husband, "I never suffer'd so much in my life as I now do." She turned to "that Gracious Being" for strength, and she entreated her "Ever Dear Johny Dickinson" to do the same. "Thee has been led thro Scenes of great difficulty," she acknowledged. To one another they would be "an Assistant in Virtues rugged path."[46]

In the midst of his Congressional work, Dickinson received a letter from Elizabeth Graeme Fergusson. They hadn't seen each other since December 1776, but Fergusson told him that she was reminded sorrowfully of the Dickinsons each time she passed the burnt ruins of "poor Fair Hill!" Now she sought Dickinson's help regaining her family estate, Graeme Park, which had been confiscated after her Loyalist husband fled the country. She hoped Dickinson could use his influence with the Assembly.[47] He replied that the matter was, alas, "entirely beyond the extent of my Influence." Considering the terms with which he had quit the Assembly and the fact that since he had effectively been pursued as an enemy of the state, he informed her, "You hardly could have ask'd the Interposition of a person less likely to succeed."[48]

On November 18, Dickinson requested and received a leave of absence from Congress. By the time he left, he had served on twenty-four committees, including those most critical to the establishment and survival of the new nation, and written the reports and conclusions for many of them, demonstrating once again his value and his commitment to the American cause. But the workload combined with the poisonous atmosphere in Congress convinced him that the only way to preserve his honor and health was to return to private life. He worked dutifully throughout his tenure, but when he was again nominated for the seat in 1780, he declined the position.[49]

Apart from exhaustion and disgust with the partisan Congress, another reason for Dickinson's leave was because of the death on the fourteenth of his beloved uncle, Thomas Cadwalader.[50] Dickinson felt the loss deeply. His uncle, the reigning patriarch of the Cadwalader clan, had always been his champion and reliable counselor. Even before the death of Samuel Dickinson, Cadwalader had been like a father to John and Philemon both. His loss was lamented not just by his family. Dr. Cadwalader had been a leading figure in Pennsylvania and New Jersey for decades, and his public service and benevolence were well known. A renowned physician and one of the founders of the Pennsylvania hospital, he wrote the first medical textbook in America and was one of the first to inoculate people against smallpox. He served more than twenty years on the Provincial Council, was a founder and director of the Library Company of Philadelphia, and was a member of the American Philosophical Society. His generous philanthropy included £500 to found the

Library Company in Trenton. Although he was not a Quaker, he was buried in the Trenton Friends Burying Ground, near his sister.[51]

Dickinson's time was his own again for most of 1780. As well as enjoying his family and the "luxuriant Prospect of Plenty" at Poplar Hall, he also spent time on spiritual matters.[52] Over the last years he had progressed, as he put it in a letter to a friend, "from the Mist of Doubts to the Sunshine of Belief." "Yet," he added, "I must acknowledge, that tho my Faith is clear & strong"— he had always believed in the Divine Author—"my practise is still confused & fluctuating."[53] He was as ever inclined towards Quakerism but not so convinced that he had adopted all of their "peculiar" testimonies. Although he was taking the affirmation instead of the oath, he still did not use the plain speech. He continued to address Polly with the formal plural "you" rather than "thou" and "thee." Harmonizing "faith and practice" was an ongoing challenge for many Quakers. Even good ones struggled with adopting all the testimonies, whose purpose was to separate the believer from nonbelievers, making them conspicuous to the world and opening them up to ridicule. Since Quakerism was a faith that recognized human fallibility, members understood that though they might falter at times, there was always the possibility for redemption and perfection.

To now-nine-year-old Sally, "Pa's Precious," Dickinson was perfectly clear about his priorities for her, even while using the un-Quakerly plural. "At present," he explained, "I have such an Opinion of You, that I would not take Millions of Millions of Worlds all Gold and Jewells for You. But my Love is not worth mentioning in Comparison of the Love that your most gracious Creator will have for You, if You please him—" If she pleased God, she would please her father. "I do not pray, that You may be beautiful, or rich, or longlived; but only this, that You may be good— Happiness is joined to Goodness."[54] The Dickinsons, like all moderate Quaker parents, were less concerned that Sally formally became a Quaker than that her behavior was pleasing to God.

Dickinson did not have long for reflection. In a special election in November 1780, he was chosen overwhelmingly by the citizens of New Castle County as a member of the Delaware legislature, which would convene next on January 4, 1781.[55] The state needed him, and friends pressed him to accept the office. George Read even pledged on his friend's behalf that Dickinson would accept the office. "Your private Interest is deeply interested therein," Read reminded him, "for I am clearly of Opinion that two or three Years more of such Management as the last woud have left no little Property to be mindful of and this proceeded more from ignorance & Inattention than design." Though he himself hadn't anticipated serving either, Read said, "we are equally bound to exercise the different Talents given us for the good of the Society." Of utmost concern were the issues of paper currency and reforming the dysfunctional Delaware militia.[56]

Thomas McKean likewise wrote to Dickinson about their shared concerns for Delaware and the Union. He sent Dickinson copies of laws on currency and promised to send more. And he also hoped that Dickinson, once in office, would turn his attention to the Delaware militia. "Put them on as respectable a footing as the troops of Pennsylvania," he entreated Dickinson. "On our army, next under God, the success of our cause depends." He wanted the militia to be better regulated, which meant higher taxes for the people of Delaware. Prisoners of war were also a pressing matter. A number of officers had languished years with the enemy, and McKean hoped they could make exchanges. His overarching concern, however, was the entire state government. "It appears to me to have been too much neglected in Delaware," he said. "Unless the principal Magistrate, and Officers concerned in the administration of Justice, are supported in an honorable manner, the state will be governed by a parcel of ignorant & extortionate men." Few men of talent would devote themselves wholly to the public interest. Rather, they sought offices only "for their own emoluments."[57] He knew that Dickinson would prioritize the public welfare over his private interests.

The most significant problem facing the new republic, one that affected everything, especially in wartime, was finances. Dickinson and Charles Thomson had recently begun a conversation on the matter. "British hopes of subjugating us," said Thomson, "if they still retain any, must rest wholly on the derangement of our finances." If these could be managed properly, America would prevail over the enemy. "The arrangement and right management of our finances is therefore," he emphasized, "an object of the greatest importance."[58]

Dickinson agreed entirely. The core issue was raising funds, which must happen through taxation. But just as it was a central cause of the current revolution, so did it continue a problem in the new nation. There were two methods of taxation. One was the monarchical and aristocratic way. Under this model, merchants simply passed on their costs to the customers; the people never knew how much they were being taxed, and merchants could enrich themselves under cover of this policy. The republican way was to tax openly and directly so that everyone knew how much he paid and could be, Thomson said, "more attentive to abuses and misapplication in the expenditure and will of consequence be more watchful to prevent their rulers from bribing the people." He added optimistically, "The people of America are in general sensible and intelligent. Convince them that taxes are necessary and they will cheerfully pay them."[59] Dickinson also hoped this was the case, though experience suggested otherwise.

His friends' pleas notwithstanding, Dickinson was still not ready to return to public service, so he declined the position. Instead, he spent the first half of 1781 in Dover with Polly and Sally. He worked at his law practice, training young attorneys, such as the son of his friend Dr. Charles Ridgely,[60] and traveling between Kent and Philadelphia. Disaster struck in August, when the family was in the city. Poplar Hall was plundered by Loyalists. "As none of the neighbouring houses were plundered or molested, it is supposed," reported the *Pennsylvania Journal*, that "New York Loyalists had given particular directions for the robbery, in order to be revenged upon that worthy patriot and honest man, for the foundation he laid for the present revolution by his valuable writings."[61] Early in the morning, a group of men descended on the farm and demanded that Violet tell them whether Dickinson was at home. Taking keys to chests containing his valuables and ransacking the house, they stole silverware, clothes, food, and liquors estimated to be worth £2,000 as well as a trunkful of priceless personal papers, among which were likely the drafts of his *Farmer's Letters*. Rumor had it that these were scattered through the streets of New York City. The marauders also invited any enslaved people to join them, although the miscreants declared that they preferred their master. Only one man, Isaac, accepted the offer. Another, Nicholas, rushed to Dover for help. Around forty members of the Delaware militia arrived too late to do anything.[62] None of Dickinson's colleagues at the state or national level endured such violation of having one home burnt, another confiscated, and a third plundered.

Losing Isaac in this way was a catalyst for Dickinson's next act. Despite providing for the eventual manumission of his slaves, he had been uneasy for some time about continuing to enslave others. On September 27, he wrote another manumission deed for a small group of enslaved people unconditionally, including Violet. When he executed it on the twenty-ninth before Chief Justice William Killen, Violet, now about thirty, began her life as a free woman.[63] A few of those he freed—Violet; Joseph Martin, a mixed-race man in his forties; and two children (with the consent of their parents), Pompey, a fourteen-year-old boy, and Nancy, a twelve-year-old girl—indentured themselves to himself as servants for a term of years to ensure they would have livelihoods. In return for their service, they would receive the same compensation as white servants—"Meat, Drink, Cloathing, Lodging and Washing" along with "customary Dues," which could be goods or money—at the termination of the contract. He also struck out the overly restrictive language on the standard indenture forms that prohibited such things as marrying without the master's permission. Each individual signed with his or her mark at the bottom.[64] Dickinson still enslaved several other Black people, but their eventual freedom seemed more assured.

Business detained him longer than expected in Kent. He wrote Polly diligently. "I affectionately thank thee for writing so often," she replied, "it is ye greatest relief any distress'd heart can have which on thy Account has not rest." She had heard "it is very Sickly in Kent," so she urged him to "take the bark" for his health.[65] In October, on the verge of returning to Philadelphia, he awaited the results of the Pennsylvania elections on the ninth. Despite vowing never to serve that state again, he began to reconsider, thinking perhaps he could do some good. So he allowed himself to be put forward as a candidate for Philadelphia County. Before the Pennsylvania results were in, however, he was elected to the Delaware Council for New Castle County. He accepted and again affirmed rather than swore his loyalty.[66]

Shortly after the Assembly convened, the glorious news arrived that General Cornwallis had surrendered to General Washington after the Battle of Yorktown in Virginia. Both Polly and Dickinson's former clerk Peter Lloyd wrote him on October 22. This would likely mean the beginning of peace negotiations in earnest and the eventual end of the war. But Lloyd provided disappointing news as well. The Pennsylvania radicals, who still dominated state politics, had prevented his election in that state. The electors in Philadelphia County complained of "glaring and monstrous" partiality that had led to his defeat.[67]

Disappointed, Dickinson focused on the Delaware Council and, together with George Read, brought more energy and focus to the government than had been seen in many years. Their goal was to remedy the feeble government under Caesar Rodney. During the legislative session, Dickinson worked on several bills, all involving finances, including one for an operating budget in hard currency for the following year, one vesting Congress with the power to levy duties on imports to Delaware and prizes in its Admiralty Court, and a supplement to an act calling out of circulation old bills of credit issued by Congress and emitting and funding new bills.[68]

Dickinson had a clear vision for the state and the experience and expertise to realize it. His colleagues recognized this, and hence what came next was not surprising. On November 6, 1781, he was elected president of Delaware for one term of three years. This was, from his perspective, a most unwelcome development. From Dover, he complained bitterly to Polly. The vote was unanimous despite his declaring that he could not accept the office. "It is absolutely forced upon Me with one Voice not only of the Legislature," he clarified, "but of the People. How to avoid I know not." So determined had he been to leave Delaware that, just the day before, he had sent his goods and servants to Christiana Bridge to be loaded onto ships for Philadelphia. He could hardly express "how unexpected & distressing this Event is to Me, & how opprest I am with the Difficulty of evading an Appointment made in so remarkable a Manner."[69]

Dickinson had several reasons for his disappointment. In addition to his preference for being in Philadelphia, where he and Polly had more friends and relatives, the State of Delaware was in dire straits. With most of its structures and institutions on the point of collapse, it would take a mammoth effort to reform them. With his health uncertain, he may not have felt up to the challenge. Nevertheless, Dickinson put aside his personal desires and prepared to serve his state once again. He gave his acceptance speech and took the affirmation of loyalty on November 13, his forty-ninth birthday (Fig. 16).[70] Then, with the Assembly going into recess, he got to work.

Delaware was quite literally a failing state. Rife with Loyalists, such as those who plundered Poplar Hall, and plagued with incompetence and corruption, nothing was functioning properly. The courts did not meet, the crops rotted in the fields, and the militia had ceased mustering.[71] It would take ingenuity, strenuous work, and force of personality to turn the state around. In his acceptance speech, Dickinson thus informed the Assembly that there was "one *apprehension* I cannot dismiss, that I shall not be able to fill the station to which I am appointed, so advantageously as I wish, or as you may perhaps expect." He assured them, however, that he would try his best to compensate for his deficiencies, including in his health, and serve the state to his best abilities.[72]

Crises confronted him at every turn, and he attempted to ameliorate them as much as possible without the Assembly's help before it reconvened in January. As congratulations arrived from various regions and constituencies, one of Dickinson's first moves was to address the moral ills of the state.[73] Nothing, he believed, could be accomplished until the people were whole in their virtue. He therefore published a proclamation against vice and immorality. This was not merely about restoring republican virtue. Reflective of Dickinson's own deepening faith, the proclamation was very much a religious document. "AS it is undoubtedly pleasing in the Sight of ALMIGHTY GOD, that his rational Creatures should yield a chearful Submission to his Holy Laws," Dickinson began, "it appears to me my first and indispensible Duty, to call the Attention of the People of this State to a serious and due Consideration of these important Truths"—meaning obedience to the Divine Will and reason, as well as the awful "Threats and Punishments of irresistible Power against Offenders." To ensure that Delawareans recognized their own "Unworthiness" as well as their "Transgressions" and remained grateful for God's mercies, he explained, "I have thought fit to issue this Proclamation." His directives to the people of the state included not just that they should "earnestly endeavour to discourage and suppress all Vice, Profaneness and Immorality," but also to do so by worshiping "on every *Lord*'s Day, at a Service acceptable to him." He also expected that "all well-disposed Persons, and especially all Persons in Place of Authority, will by their own exemplary Conduct encourage and promote Piety and Virtue, guide the young, the weak, and the unexperienced into laudable Courses." He hoped that these exemplary citizens would cause the "dissolute and debauched" to "feel the Shame and Contempt into which they are fallen, may be prevailed on to reform their evil Practices." In effect, Dickinson was trying to effect a "Reformation" of society, taking on "Blasphemy, Profane Swearing or Cursing, Drunkenness, Lewdness, or other dissolute or immoral Practice." This included suppressing "public Gaming," "disorderly Houses," drunkenness, and not keeping the "*Lord*'s Day, commonly called *Sunday*." Finally, he encouraged lawmakers to enact bills to allow magistrates to punish offenders.[74] Later in his term, to bolster the proclamation, he directed that funds from marriage licenses that would normally go to him should be directed to clergy in Delaware, who "are not provided for in proportion to their Merit."[75]

Dickinson was in effect looking back to the earliest days of the founding of Pennsylvania, when Quakers were first establishing what William Penn called their "holy experiment." Although they set up no state church, the pressure they exerted over their constituents to conform to Quakerism effectively created the only theocracy in the colonies. But where Pennsylvania Quakers had met with resistance, Dickinson's proclamation was welcomed in Delaware, as well as in Pennsylvania, which struggled with similar problems.[76] Dickinson had no interest in establishing a theocracy with church leaders also serving as political leaders; he merely hoped to encourage civic virtue. To focus the minds of Delawareans, he also issued a proclamation for a day of public thanksgiving and prayer on December 13.[77] "How far it is possible to reclaim People from Folly, Madness, & Vice, I know not," he thought. But he was "unalterably resolved" to try.[78]

At the same time, several urgent matters pertaining to the war—though it was technically over—pressed upon him. He immediately appointed six new officers to take charge of various matters related to the defense of the state, including naval duties, supplies, and recruitment.[79] British prisoners of war in Virginia were escaping over the border into New Castle County on the way to New York, aided by Delawareans. The Tory infestation was so bad and the Delaware coast so poorly defended that, in December, British privateers were emboldened to plunder the town of Lewes in Sussex County. Dickinson thus issued a proclamation "strictly forbidding, under the severest Penalties of the Law, all Persons to harbor or employ any Prisoners of War, or in any Manner whatsoever to facilitate their going into the Quarters of the Enemy," under the severest penalty of the law.[80]

General Washington wrote to inform President Dickinson that a military hospital was desperately needed in Wilmington to treat soldiers wounded in Virginia. "Your Excellency must be sensible," Washington wrote, that "its execution can admit of no delay without endangering the loss of many brave and good Men."[81] Dickinson sprang into action, conferring with John Cochran, director general of the military hospitals of the Continental Army, and physicians to establish the facilities.[82] He was able to procure the use of a building at the College of Wilmington, but there were no public funds for anything else. Dickinson therefore used his personal funds to purchase wood and straw for warmth and bedding.[83]

In January 1782, he was distracted from work with worry about Sally, who had whooping cough, and Polly, with a severe cough of her own, which Dr. Jones had warned could end in a consumption.[84] "I intreat You to take all possible Care of Yourself & of our Darling," he wrote home. "I love You both as well as ever Man loved a Wife or Daughter. Get better & make Me happy."[85] But the legislative session demanded his attention. He immediately mobilized the legislature to act on the most urgent issues, the military and the economy, which were always tightly intertwined. The twin problem was that the British, British sympathizers, or perhaps only opportunists, had brought trade on the waterways to a standstill. Delaware's lifeblood was "interrupted and impeded by armed Boats and Cruisers of the Enemy."[86] Without trade, there could be no taxes. Without taxes, there would be no state.

Dickinson thus took two steps. The first was to encourage passage of An Act for the Protection of Trade of Delaware Bay and River. This law would allow Colonel Charles Pope, a former Continental officer and now captain and commander of the state schooner, aptly named *Vigilant*, to execute the instructions Dickinson had given him the previous November. He would cruise the waterways and, with his usual "Vivacity" and "Patriotism," seek out the enemy where they lurked. When the waterways were cleared, he would publicize the fact.[87] Ideally, not only would trade resume, but raids undertaken from the water would also decrease.

To this same end, the state's militia also needed reform. Dickinson believed that "a well regulated Militia is the proper and natural Defense of a free State."[88] But this one was in extreme disorder despite recent legislation. "The putting the Militia of this State upon a respectable Footing," Dickinson wrote to the brigadier generals of each county, "is so essential to its Honor Safety and Wellfare, that I esteem it my indispensable Duty to make every Exertion, in my Power for carrying this Design . . . into full Execution."[89] He would have to take a hands-on approach not just to ensure its survival but to realize his vision for what the militia should be in a republic, a vision that was more extensive than anyone's. Dickinson brought his prior military experience—both in policy and practice, as an officer and a private—to bear. His role as commander in chief was one he accepted with utmost seriousness.

Three of the seven bills the Assembly passed during this session were designed to re-establish the militia. In an unusual move for an executive, Dickinson himself took the lead on drafting the bills he wanted. It made sense, as he had both more legislative experience than anyone in the Assembly and a vision of what he wanted Delaware to be. His idea was to establish the militia for the use of not merely the state but also the nation and to remedy the depreciation of pay in the army. Rather than thinking of each state as an entity unto itself, each defending itself with its own army, Dickinson imagined that state militias would be something more. When required, they might be called up by the central government, as Dickinson envisioned in his draft of the Articles of Confederation, and work in concert to guard the entire nation from both internal and external threats. It was a novel concept for the age—a compromise between a standing army, which most Americans considered a stepping stone to tyranny, and uncoordinated state militias, which could hardly defend their own borders.[90]

The law stipulated that every freeman—that is, white man who possessed the minimum property requirements—between eighteen and fifty shall, at his own expense, provide himself with "a Musket or Firelock with a Bayonet, a Cartouch-Box to contain twenty-three Cartridges, a Priming-Wire, a Brush and six Flints, all in good Order." There were exemptions for ministers of the Gospel (which included all Quakers, since anyone might preach), judges, and teachers. But although individuals would own the arms, they were not free to use them as they chose. Far from it. These individuals were to be parts of a *well-regulated* militia, with the state providing the regulation. Individuals were required to muster at the behest of the state only, and only at the command of a commissioned officer, each month (except July, January, and February) and train—or face stiff fines. The state would use the revenue from these fines to purchase a store of public arms, which were to be returned after use. The regulation of the militia also meant that ammunition was controlled by the state and distributed to the troops as needed, with records diligently kept. Under this tight supervision, militiamen would train until they could fire their muskets three to four rounds per minute. The purpose of the militia was for the commander in chief of the state to prevent "Invasion, Rebellion or Insurrection within this State."[91]

Dickinson also began work on a new manual for the effective regulation of the troops. Taking the drill manual that Baron von Steuben had presented to George Washington for the Continental Army in 1779, Dickinson adapted it for the purposes of a state. In addition to drills to maintain order and discipline, he added his own preface describing the importance of the citizen militia to freedom in a republic. "You now form the Body of a free, sovereign Republic," he wrote. He explained what it meant to be self-governed. "Your Laws, your Manners, your Conduct, your Prosperity, all in a great Degree, depend on yourselves." Militiamen must be perfectly prepared "on the shortest Notice, and in the best Manner, to exert the whole Force of the State." At the same time, he was not unaware of the dangers that could come from within the state itself. "I hope," he added, "the martial Spirit of Americans will never be inflamed by the wild and wicked Suggestions of Ambition or Avarice, but I wish that noble Temper of Freedom always to prevail among them, that meaning no Harm to others, vigilantly guards against Injustice." At his own expense, he printed five hundred copies for distribution among the troops.[92]

He then began to put these principles into practice, overseeing the reforms personally. "I propose to do Myself the Honor," he informed the Council and the House, "in the Course of the Year of visiting & reviewing every Battalion in the State; and it will afford Me a very great Pleasure when I am inform'd, that the Battalions of a County are properly formed & disciplined."[93] And he wrote a similar letter to the officers of the battalions he would visit with more specifics and requests for information.[94] In October, after the officers had had a chance to implement his regulations, he reviewed Colonel Patterson's troops in New Castle, Colonel Dagworthy's troops in Lewes, and Colonel Collins's troops at Poplar Hall in Kent. They were now prepared to defend the state and the nation. His officers were pleased with Dickinson's having become "the Guardian of the militia." Patterson exclaimed that "a spirit pervades now . . . such as I have not seen for some time." It was remarkable how improved the militia was. "Where was more Roman Virtue Shewn in History?" he asked. "Never."[95] Dickinson's deepening Quakerism never overshadowed his conviction that a citizen militia was the foundation of a free people.

With Delaware's defense on the path to reform, Dickinson turned to civil matters. As someone who had spent decades in the courts of the Lower Counties, he was aware of the problems they faced. His old friend and former tutor William Killen, now chief justice of Delaware, warned that the courts were "very defective, to the great Delay of the due Execution of the Laws and Administration of Justice." Killen proposed several remedies, but his pessimism was such that he was "inclin'd to think, he may no longer preside in the abovementioned Courts, or serve his Country in any other Public Character."[96] David Finny, an attorney in Wilmington, also urged action. "Let not the Justices of your Supreme Court," he wrote Dickinson, "complain any longer of being neglected by the Assembly."[97] In response, Dickinson passed An Act for Increasing the Powers of the Justices of the Supreme Court. The justices would now be able to hold court when needed, levy fines to compel jury attendance, and have higher pay, among other improvements to the system.[98]

Dickinson got much of what he wanted from the internally focused legislation, but he did not get everything. The virtue of the people mattered little if their representatives were driven purely by self-interest. To curb corruption in the government, he had in mind to pass a law "to Exclude the Members of the General Assembly from Places of Profit." But he had no more luck in Delaware than he'd had in Pennsylvania a decade earlier. Although he produced a draft on February 1, it did not pass that session or that year.[99]

Dickinson also looked outward, beyond the borders of Delaware, and thought about the health of the entire union. From his year in Congress, he knew firsthand that the weakness of the central government under the

Articles of Confederation, which had finally been ratified the previous year, in 1781, needed to be addressed. He also knew that part of the problem was Delaware itself. Late in 1781, the newly elected president of Congress, John Hanson, had written to Dickinson to inform him of "a deficiency of a Representation from your State" in Congress and express his "hope that your Excellency's influence will be exerted to prevail upon your State to send forward and keep up a full Representation in future."[100] With only seven states currently represented, Congress could do even less work than usual. Robert Morris, superintendent of finance of the United States, wrote to urge Delaware's compliance with new acts for requisitions, explaining that "compliance therefore must be very punctual, for delays are equally dangerous and expensive; and if they should happen, the People must be burthened with new Taxes unnecessarily."[101]

Dickinson thus engineered the passage of An Act for Aiding and More Effectually Carrying into Execution Certain Acts of Congress. He spoke repeatedly to the legislature, asserting that "compliance of the several Legislatures with the determinations of that National Council, is absolutely necessary for establishing a system of regularity and efficacy in the affairs, and for maintaining the Honor of the United States."[102] Specifically, he urged the legislature to help make Delaware pay its taxes to Congress—"a measure essential," he asserted, "to the support of public credit"—and he guided the selection of four new delegates to Congress.[103] They were men he knew well and trusted implicitly: Caesar Rodney, Thomas McKean, Samuel Wharton, and Dickinson's own brother, Philemon. Dickinson then wrote their instructions himself.[104] Though none of these men currently resided in Delaware, which caused some objection, they would represent the state well in Philadelphia while he worked in Dover to ensure acts of Congress were carried into execution effectively.[105] He persuaded the Assembly to pass laws to facilitate this end.

In the spring of 1782, various issues vied for Dickinson's attention. On April 2, the war encroached on New Castle County when a band of raiders captured several ships and terrorized the town of New Castle. In May, there was an outbreak of smallpox in Kent, and anxiety ran high. Although some were inoculated against it, many were not.[106] Because of the pestilence, the House refused to convene, and the meeting was postponed until June.[107] Dickinson was anxious for it to meet sooner, but he did not want to overstep his authority in calling the House to meet in a different location.[108] That month he also addressed an urgent matter with General Washington. After an American officer had been murdered by British soldiers, Washington intended to execute publicly a British officer in retaliation, though that officer had nothing to do with the murder. Dickinson crafted a deferential letter—Washington was notoriously short-tempered and sensitive to perceived slights—suggesting that such an execution would be unjust and outlining six reasons why it would be "irregular." He ended by assuring Washington that his honor would be preserved: "I have not intimated to any person," wrote Dickinson, "that I should write on this Affair, nor have exprest my Doubt in Conversation."[109] In what became known as the Asgill Affair, Dickinson's was only one of many voices of protest, and eventually Congress ordered the officer's release.[110]

During his tenure, there were joyous occasions as well. In a message to the Delaware Assembly on June 12, he informed the members that the queen of France had produced a dauphin—a male heir to the Crown. France had supported the American cause since 1778, and Dickinson's former suspicion of the French had transformed into an abiding affection. He therefore orchestrated an elaborate public celebration, something he believed would incline Delawareans to patriotism and boost public morale. Because he was interested in "preventing those gross irregularities at places of public diversion, now become so frequent," including the usual, such as excessive drinking and the lighting of fireworks, he would plan the festivities himself.[111] He designed a triumphal arch in the Roman style and had it erected in the middle of the town square in Dover. It was decorated with pictures symbolizing liberty, justice, and humanity with Latin mottos accompanying each. To represent the Union, he imagined a solar system, a sun surrounded by thirteen stars and an eagle flying towards it. The motto read *Patrus Virtutibus*, with paternal virtues. The alliance between the United States and France was demonstrated by their respective flags flying on either side of the arch, which would be flanked by troops of the militia under the direction of the officers. The celebration and the dinner on June 22 were both festive and orderly and concluded with toasts, chosen by Dickinson, to many of the esteemed personages of both countries.[112]

Afterward, Dickinson personally extended his congratulations to the French minister, the Chevalier de la Luzerne, who at the same moment was extending an invitation to Dickinson to attend festivities he was planning in Philadelphia for July 15.[113] Dickinson was pleased to attend the more extravagant celebration—a concert, fireworks, and dancing—in the city, replete with a "brilliant Company of Citizens." One account stated that it "surpassed in Magnificence, every Thing of the Kind yet exhibited in this Country."[114] The celebration was centered at Dickinson's own house on Chestnut Street, which had been converted back from a military hospital and was currently leased to the French minister.[115]

The spring legislative session had been quiet compared to the flurry of activity in the winter. Only two bills were passed. Dickinson nonetheless saw the need for his action on a number of issues. The state schooner needed financing and the crew required better wages than the Assembly had proposed. In a message, he urged the Assembly to act on both matters. Ultimately, because the state coffers were empty, Dickinson provided the funds himself. He took another personal loan from Robert Morris in the amount of £1,000.[116]

He then issued two proclamations about ongoing problems identified by Congress. One concerned mail stolen in Maryland. Such theft happened frequently enough that Congress wanted the mid-Atlantic states to offer a substantial reward for the capture of the thieves. Also, despite Delaware's laws to the contrary, trade with the enemy continued. Congress believed that since force alone had not defeated America, her enemies sought to dispirit her citizens and weaken the public credit. Dickinson therefore enjoined Delawareans to report anyone trading with the enemy to the authorities. Finally, he wrote to officials on the safety of public records. In 1778, records of the state had been stolen, and, embarrassingly, now some had been recovered and returned by a British officer.[117] Dickinson was anxious that this should not happen again.

On November 7, 1782, in one of his final messages of his first term to the Delaware Assembly, Dickinson raised a subject that had been increasingly pressing upon him: the welfare of enslaved Black people. After freeing most of his own slaves, his attention was now on the state. A ban on the importation of slaves to Delaware had been debated since the late 1760s and finally made law in the new 1776 state constitution. But it was not enforced.[118] He urged the Assembly to follow the lead of Pennsylvania by "passing laws for alleviating the afflictions of this helpless, and too often abused part of their fellow creature." He also implored that Black families not be "cruelly separated from one another, and the remainder of their lives extremely embittered."[119] As he wrote those lines, he himself was in the process of purchasing Abigail, the pregnant wife of Nathan, one of his enslaved men, and her four children, to keep them from being sold away to Maryland.[120] His plea had no effect. Delawareans were as addicted to slavery as any other planters below the Mason-Dixon Line. He knew it would take much more for them to recognize human rights over their economic self-interest. The next day, he proclaimed another day of thanksgiving and prayer for November 28.[121]

During election season in the fall, Dickinson's political fortunes took a sudden turn. As his second term as president of Delaware was about to begin, unbeknownst to him, on October 12, he was elected to the Supreme Executive Council of Pennsylvania.[122] Learning this news during a trip to Philadelphia in early November, he immediately decided to remain, placing the leadership of Delaware in the hands of the speaker of the Assembly, John Cook.[123] A few days later, Benjamin Rush put him forward for the office of president of the Supreme Executive Council of Pennsylvania. Rush believed that Dickinson was the best and only viable candidate. And thus, on November 7, Dickinson was elected to the presidency, a post that also made him a judge in the High Court of Errors and Appeals, the highest court in the state.[124]

So unexpected was this development that he and Polly had been on the verge of moving into their new house in Wilmington, which they had prepared at great expense.[125] However, this was a post Dickinson very much wanted. About to turn fifty, he might have imagined that his life would be slowing down. Instead, he was the only public figure of the era to hold the executive offices of two states simultaneously, as he did for the next three months. On his way out of Delaware office, there were a few final points of business to resolve. He issued commissions to various individuals to serve as sheriffs and coroners in each county, and he granted permissions for various people to travel to or from the state. Finally, he recommended "exemplary Punishment"—harsh punishment to serve as a deterrent for others—for a jailer who released ten British prisoners of war in Dover.[126]

By the end of his first term, Dickinson had almost single-handedly reversed the course of Delaware from a failing state to a model for the rest of the country. Now he would attempt to do something similar for Pennsylvania. He did not formally resign his presidency of Delaware until early January 1783. Knowing that his leaving this post would cause rancor among some in the state, his farewell speech expressed the ambivalence he felt at that moment. Although he was resigning his office, he assured members of the Council and Assembly that his "Affection and Gratitude to the State I never will resign, but with my Life." He reminded them he had not wanted to accept the presidency, and now he had served to the best of his abilities for a year. He also added that he "could not avoid" accepting the Pennsylvania presidency without "involving Myself in Circumstances exceedingly disagreable."[127]

At the beginning of his term as head of Delaware's government, Dickinson had thought, "Happy I shall think Myself, if it can be said of my Administration at its Conclusion—that it made the People better."[128] Now at the end, he reviewed his accomplishments. "*The Delaware State* was the *first* of the Union," he said, "that introduced order into that chaos of politics and morals, in which strength and weakness, safety and ruin, virtue and iniquity, strangely met together, and wrought in wild conjunction—by stopping the rage of tender laws, and instituting equitable modes of adjusting, in all cases, the confusions that had been occasioned."[129] Even as he departed the state, Delawareans proclaimed, "We most earnestly wish you *to continue* your benevolent exertions for advancing a reformation of manners."[130] Dickinson's parting speech was perhaps too candid to placate all his listeners, and his resignation gave additional ammunition to the enemies he was about to face in Pennsylvania.

12

"Through a Wilderness of Difficulties"

President of Pennsylvania, 1782–1785

As president of Pennsylvania's Executive Council, Dickinson faced an endless slate of problems and crises. Not only was the commonwealth struggling under the same difficulties from the weak central government that plagued Delaware, but it also faced threats and controversies unknown in that much smaller state. Even as Dickinson spent time on Pennsylvania's economy, defense, crime, and factional controversies, he was continually distracted by all manner of emergencies: violent clashes with Indians on the frontier, an attempted secession, a boundary dispute that led to armed conflict, a significant diplomatic crisis, and a mutiny. Moreover, because as president of the state he was also the head of the judiciary of Pennsylvania, which served a dual function as the United States' court system, he oversaw several important cases that shaped national policy. He had to manage these matters without the help of a central government—sometimes even in opposition to it—and effectively with one hand tied behind his back: as the president of an executive council rather than a single executive, constitutionally he did not have the power to implement the necessary policies unilaterally with only the concurrence of the legislature. But this arrangement was more than acceptable to him; it was preferable in that it differed so strongly from monarchy. He liked that his powers were limited and that, on the Council, as he put it, he "sits with colleagues of real abilities and independent spirits."[1]

When Dickinson's election was announced, there was a parade and, the papers reported, "an unusual concourse of the most respectable citizens of Philadelphia, who expressed their happiness upon this occasion, by repeated acclamations of joy."[2] Dickinson's ascension in Pennsylvania, this most radical state, signaled something of an awakening among its citizens. They had experienced what leaders would soon recognize as "democratic despotism" or "tyranny of the majority" in the form of the denial of civil rights and persecution of religious and political dissenters. And this administration by the so-called Constitutionalists was hardly better than Delaware's struggle against Toryism. Returning Dickinson to office after having driven him off six years earlier and placing him at the highest level suggested that Pennsylvanians sought a return to reason and justice. Indeed, officers of the Pennsylvania troops in the Continental Army wrote their congratulations to Dickinson: "We consider your appointment as the returning dawn of that temper and good sense." They respected him for the "distinguished part" he had played in "bringing about the present Revolution."[3]

In Dickinson's acceptance speech to the Assembly, still filled with the radicals who had driven him out in 1776, he said the honor for him was not in holding the office but in the proof of Pennsylvanians' esteem. He would do his best and apologized in advance for the mistakes he would undoubt-edly make. Remembering the democratic despotism of the past, he also gave members of the Assembly a lesson in the principles of public service and citizenship, explaining that "he is an enemy to the state, who, in a public post, treats a *fellow-citizen* as an enemy to himself." Each man should "be as anxious and active for their combined happiness and honor, as for his own." Finally, reminding them who he was, he said, "My past Life has proved in several memorable Instances, that I dare offend my Fellow-Citizens, but, I cannot bear to injure them. I have experienced great Satisfaction from this honest Policy, and mean to persevere in it, regardless of Consequences."[4]

His first proclamation was the same as for Delaware—on suppressing vice and immorality. He lengthened and expanded it, with the most notable dif-ference being the addition of a paragraph on the education of youth, which was becoming one of his main priorities along with religion. The two matters were, in fact, closely related. More than simply writing about these things, he also donated land, funds, and books to new and existing schools in the area, including £100 to the college in Princeton, New Jersey.[5]

But Pennsylvania's problems were so deeply entrenched that even Dickinson's supporters were skeptical of how far he would get. In John Jay's congratulatory note, he was optimistic, writing that Dickinson's election was "an Event from which the Common Wealth will I am persuaded derive very essential advantages."[6] Privately, however, he confessed that although "Mr. Dickinson has talents and good intentions," and "it will not be his fault if Pennsylvania does not derive advantages from his administration."[7] The fac-tional conflicts in the state were extreme.

Those radicals who had ousted him in 1776 seem to have known that he would be back and had been preparing for that day. The attacks started even before his election. The first was on October 2, 1782, by "A Plain Common Freeman." Without naming Dickinson but describing him clearly enough, the Freeman called him a "sunshine patriot," a "summer soldier," and accused him of, among other things, deserting the public cause in 1776 and attempting to "seduce a near relation, and meritorious soldier from his duty to his country," meaning Philemon, "and to cover his brother with that dishonour which himself had embraced." Now "this delinquent," they said of Dickinson, "has the effrontery to offer himself a candidate for your suffrages at the ensuing election. He aspires to the patronage of those citizens whose command he ingloriously deserted in 1776, and indulges the extravagant delusion that he is shortly to preside over that very state which he but 'tother day abandoned to its enemies."[8] This was just the beginning.

The very day Dickinson assumed the presidency, one calling himself "Valerius" began a sustained and vigorous attack, the likes of which Dickinson had never before experienced. Valerius revived all the old charges by the radicals from 1776 and elaborated on them in twelve lengthy letters published in the *Freeman's Journal*. Although Valerius's identity was a mystery, Dickinson's relatives speculated it may have been John Armstrong Jr., one of Dickinson's former law clerks and someone known for underhanded dealings.[9] The charges, all of which Dickinson had already answered in one way or another, were that he had opposed the Declaration of Independence; that he had deserted his battalion and now opposed the American cause; that he had abrogated his duties to the State of Delaware; and that he had told his brother not to accept Continental currency. Dickinson was hardly the only politician among the so-called Republicans whom the radicals attacked; he was just the most visible and the most influential.[10]

Before his election, Dickinson wrote to each printer in Philadelphia, requesting that they publish nothing in his defense so that he could, as the printers explained, preserve "a noble disinterestedness with respect to the first office in the state."[11] But after the election, he could not remain silent. In an age where honor and reputation were everything and men died defending them, it was unthinkable that Valerius should go unanswered. Since his scuffle with Joseph Galloway twenty years ago, however, Dickinson had dueled exclusively with his pen. Reviving the defense he had drafted in 1777, he wrote four letters, one devoted to each charge. Allies likewise took up their pens. Under the name "Eugenius" came a scathing attack against Valerius. "Defamatory productions," he said, "appear to be only the malignant effusions of rancorous malice, or of disappointed ambition." Eugenius considered Dickinson's election to the presidency "as the *sun-rise* of public happiness."[12]

A salve to Dickinson's wounds were the letters of congratulation that appeared from all quarters—the officers of the troops of Pennsylvania in the Continental Army, the German Lutherans, the Baptists, the Seventh and Eighth Battalions of the Lancaster militia, and others.[13] He was especially pleased to hear from the religious and military groups, feeling as strongly as he did about both causes.

Missing, however, was anything from the Ninth Battalion of Lancaster. The commanding officer of that regiment, Colonel John Rodgers, led his men in questioning Dickinson's fitness for leadership. He sent out a circular letter to the other Lancaster battalions and to the *Pennsylvania Gazette* expressing their sense that their rights were in danger. He therefore proposed a meeting in which they would "mutually contrive such measures, as may tend most effectually to preserve our good constitution, and our dear independence and liberty."[14] Nothing could be more clear than that it was an invitation to mutiny.

On January 15, colonels of the Second, Fourth, Seventh, Eighth, Ninth, and Tenth Battalions of Lancaster met and duly elected Colonel Rodgers as their chair. Rodgers reported that "he was credibly informed that the President of the State of Pennsylvania was against the independence of America (at the time it was declared) and the constitution of this State, and that therefore our liberties are in danger." The question was then put: "Is it the opinion of the members present, that they approve of the appointment of John Dickinson, Esquire, as President of the State of Pennsylvania, or not?" To Rodgers's un-doubted consternation, each battalion affirmed that "a better choice of a President could not be made." The body then resolved "That we approve of Col. *Rodger*'s calling this meeting, in as much as it has conduced to remove doubts and unjust charges, that were circulating to the disadvantage of his Excellency the President of this State." Rodgers had to swallow his indigna-tion when they resolved "that such meetings may hereafter tend to suppress false and malicious reports, that thereby virtue may meet with its just reward, and vice be shewn its own deformity."[15]

By now, Dickinson was deep into the management of Pennsylvania (Fig. 17). Over the course of his first year, the state's difficulties included matters that were routine among the new states, such as financing the war, or ones that had long plagued Pennsylvania, including crime. Pennsylvania's fiscal situation was likewise grim. As in other states, funding the war had been a significant problem when taxes could not be collected. Dickinson thus began 1783 by advancing £1,000 of his own money to the state to cover recruiting expenses for the state militia.[16] Crime and finance issues intersected, as when tax money was stolen or counterfeited.

There was also conflict over Pennsylvania's borders. Since the founding of the province in 1681, the Penn and Calvert families had fought over the Pennsylvania–Maryland border, a dispute that resulted in the drawing of the Mason-Dixon line. For decades, there had also been a conflict over the northern border. In 1754, Connecticut's delegates to the Albany Congress had secretly purchased a tract of borderland from the Iroquois. Pennsylvanians, meanwhile, maintained that the land was part of their original charter. Dickinson gained firsthand knowledge of the problem when he attended the 1762 meeting in Easton about the Walking Purchase. The contest pitted Pennsylvania land speculators against Connecticut settlers in the Wyoming Valley, and periodically the tensions erupted in open hostilities, as they had in 1769 and 1774, known as the Pennamite-Yankee Wars. In 1771 and 1775, Dickinson had served on Assembly committees that had attempted to manage the problem. Now, although the Revolutionary War was technically over, the wartime chaos was not, and the border dispute reignited.

In January, Dickinson proclaimed that the Wyoming Controversy had gone to the Court of Commissioners, which, on December 31, 1782, had ruled in the so-called Trenton Decree that the land belonged to Pennsylvania. However, he had always sympathized with the Connecticut settlers, mainly struggling farmers who had invested significant labor in the land. His proclamation thus also forbade Pennsylvanians from confronting the settlers and instead mandated that the laws and the courts be allowed to work. Law enforcement officers were also to do their jobs in protecting the innocent.[17]

On April 16, Dickinson issued what was surely the most joyous proclamation of his executive service: the announcement of a peace treaty with Britain and cessation of all hostilities by Pennsylvania's land and sea forces. The provisional articles between Great Britain and America had been signed on November 13 of the previous year—as fine a birthday gift as there ever was—and those between Great Britain and France and Great Britain and Spain on November 20. After all the preliminaries were signed and ratified, ultimately Congress declared on April 11 that all hostilities should cease. Dickinson wanted a major celebration of the peace at the proper season. For now, there was other work to be done. As daunting as waging the war had been, it was already clear that transitioning to peace would have its own challenges.

Foremost among these was the situation on the southern border and western frontier. In March, Dickinson had issued a proclamation announcing the settlement of the southern border with Virginia, but, as in the north, the situation was still in crisis.[18] The problem was old and familiar, namely anti-government sentiment on the frontier. And the root cause was also the same: clashes between frontiersmen and Indians, which continued even worse than before the Revolution. The Indians who had sided with the British now needed to be informed of the peace treaty, which stipulated that Britain would cede western lands to the United States. Congress intended to use this land as payment to Continental soldiers. But, of course, everyone knew that the Native peoples would not simply hand over the land of their ancestors. Dickinson was therefore eager for Congress to execute a treaty with the Indian nations as well.[19]

April brought news that forty Pennsylvanians had been "killed and taken" by the Indians. Now the frontiersmen were planning the opposite of what the Paxton Boys had done. Rather than marching on Philadelphia, they attempted to secede from Pennsylvania to form their own independent state. Calling it "Westsylvania," it was the region in the southwest corner of the state, along the Ohio River. Between the fatalities, the threat of secession, and an Assembly controlled by radicals, Dickinson felt he had to take decisive action. It was, after all, the Pennsylvania government's refusal to defend the frontiersmen against Indian attacks that had propelled the radicals into overthrowing the Quakers and taking power. Now, as a Quaker fellow traveler, Dickinson himself was of two minds. On the one hand, like Quakers in general, he had sympathy for the Indians and what they had endured at the hands of whites. On the other, murder was intolerable, whether by whites or Indians, and he knew it was the government's job to defend its people. He thus issued a letter to Pennsylvania's delegates in Congress, making explicitly clear that the United States wanted to treat Indians "not only justly, but friendly," but that unless they ceased their outrages, America would "extirpate them from the Land where they were born and now live."[20] Congress immediately issued a resolve to this effect.[21] Until the treaty could be effected, Dickinson sent Reverend James Finley, an Irish-born Presbyterian minister, as agent to would-be Westsylvania "to bring over our deluded fellow Citizens to a proper sense of their Duty."[22]

Another crisis brewing concerned the soldiers in the Continental Army, who were now out of work. Some of them still suffered from wounds, and all of them were poor and hungry. To the north in Newburgh, New York, these men were increasingly disgruntled about the prospect of not receiving any pay or pensions when they were discharged. Events reached a boiling point when a letter circulated, apparently written by John Armstrong Jr., encouraging the men to give Congress an ultimatum. It had the making of a coup d'état. Fortunately, on March 11, General Washington placated the men, at least for the time being, with a moving speech.[23]

The very same day in Philadelphia, a petition arrived on President Dickinson's desk from a group of soldiers. "The Poor Petteion'd [Petitioned] Soldiers," as they describe themselves, "do beg for god seak to the honourable Governor; hoping that his Honourr will teak into Consideration and help the Poor Destressed Soul's that is now hear in this town." They were all in debt and could not leave town to look for work. They had applied to the Orphans' Court for assistance but had been told that there was no law to help them. "In the mean time," they pleaded, "the Petteioners is wating they are Starving to death; there is no kind of Work a Stirring that they Could help their selves to a bit of bread."[24]

Few things moved Dickinson as powerfully as his duty to ensure that soldiers who had sacrificed for their country were provided for. In February, the retiring officers of the Pennsylvania militia had also petitioned him about being "reduced to the most disagreeable situation."[25] Dickinson immediately addressed the Assembly on the matter. "After bravely and patiently encountering every danger and difficulty in the cause of their country," he said, "their former methods of life totally deranged, their fortunes injured or exhausted, their constitutions in many instances impaired, to be thrown, unpaid and unprovided for, upon experiments for the subsistance of themselves and their families, must be deeply distressing to persons, who feel any sentiments of gratitude and benevolence." He also informed them that a ship he had sent to New York with provisions and other articles to relieve American prisoners of war had been received.[26]

The next day, the Assembly passed An Act to Raise a Sum of Money for the Payment of the Officers and Soldiers of the Line of Pennsylvania. Though a start, Dickinson believed it required revisions. The instructions should be easier to follow and written so that "even the weak & uninformed may be guarded as much as possible against Distresses and Injuries." Further, he had researched into what other states paid their soldiers and found that several of them had offered "greater Compensations." Fair pay was crucial "not only for rewarding, but, also for encouraging Public Virtue."[27] When the legislators couldn't draft something acceptable, Dickinson stepped in to do it for them.[28]

Although due to Dickinson's leadership the soldiers and officers of the Pennsylvania militia were managed well, the Continental soldiers under Congress's purview were not. The Pennsylvania Line had the same complaints as the soldiers in Newburgh had with Washington. Rather than receiving their pay and pensions, they were furloughed. What happened next made Newburgh look tame. On June 19, a large group of armed soldiers came to Philadelphia from Lancaster County to join troops already there.

Congress appointed a committee, led by twenty-seven-year-old Alexander Hamilton, to deal with the matter. The committee demanded that Dickinson call up the Pennsylvania militia and put down the Continentals by force. Hamilton's temperament and inexperience stood in stark contrast to Dickinson's level-headedness and his long history with military matters. He knew that calling up the militia was not only dangerous but unrealistic. The militia could not be ready at a moment's notice. Nor was it at all clear that the general public—of whom the militia was composed—would support a decision to bear arms against their fellow Pennsylvanians wronged by Congress. Dickinson reasoned that the militia was just as likely to side with the Continentals. Moreover, such a directive might well run counter to the Militia Law, which only authorized using the militia to put down *insurrections* by citizens; this was a *mutiny* of soldiers. And, at the very least, if the militia did not join the Continentals, its very presence would undoubtedly provoke more violence. Moreover, it was the soldiers, not the militia, who currently controlled the magazine where the ammunition was stored. Dickinson considered the matter, deliberated with the Council, and together they determined that negotiations were their only option. Considering that the Council had exclusive jurisdiction over matters within state boundaries, Congress had to leave matters to Dickinson. Hamilton was furious.

On Saturday, June 21, armed soldiers marched to the State House, the meeting place of both the Pennsylvania government and the United States Congress. Their business was not with Congress, which did not meet on Saturdays, but rather to demand permission from Dickinson to form a committee to negotiate their settlements. The implication was that Pennsylvania was in a stronger position than the United States' government to redress their grievances. Although the soldiers did not instigate any overt violence, their actions were threatening. About fifty armed men stood outside the State House and demanded the Council respond to their demands within twenty minutes or "we shall instantly let in those injured soldiers upon you, and abide by the consequences."[29] sentries stationed at the door, this was a thinly veiled death threat. Meanwhile, as 350 additional soldiers arrived, so did members of Congress for an emergency meeting called by Hamilton. Congress's presence at the State House was unexpected; the soldiers had come to deal with the Executive Council of Pennsylvania. In calling Congress into session, Hamilton placed Congress in harm's way.

The actual threat turned out to be minimal. The soldiers and a gathering crowd of civilians mingled outside the State House, passing around the bottle. As Congressman James Madison reported, he and his colleagues feared "no danger from premeditated violence."[30] The president of Congress, Elias Boudinot, was confronted by some drunken soldiers as he left the building, but their commanding officer interceded, reprimanded them, and apologized to Boudinot. Notwithstanding the absence of a true threat, Boudinot pressed Congress to command Washington to march troops on Philadelphia. Hamilton, angered at the perceived insult to Congress and its authority by the rogue soldiers, recommended the body flee Philadelphia. He intended to use depriving Pennsylvania of the privilege of hosting Congress as leverage as he continued to press Dickinson to call the militia.

Although Dickinson was one of the leading proponents of a strong central government and had a clear record of pressing the state legislatures to support Congress, he also knew precisely when its power was legitimate and when it overreached. For Hamilton to demand that Pennsylvania deal with a committee of Congress rather than the actual body was inappropriate, and Dickinson refused to comply. Hamilton complained bitterly about the "weak and disgusting position" Pennsylvania assumed, though it was, in fact, Congress's impotence that enraged him.[31] Dickinson held the position of strength. Indeed, as the president of one of the largest states that also was the seat of the Confederation government, he was arguably the most powerful man in the country, similar to his position in 1775, when he controlled both Congress and the Pennsylvania militia. And he used this power in the same way: to keep the peace rather than succumb to pressure by either Congress or the soldiers for rash action. Dickinson was completely aware of the potential danger of the situation. But he and the Council consulted with militia officers, who approved the policy they had adopted, which was to wait until the negotiations failed or violence erupted before exerting force. Congress did actually leave Philadelphia, never to return permanently, but its reasons for leaving had little to do with the events that June. Those were only a convenient pretext.[32]

Even after he received news of Congress's departure from the city on Tuesday, June 24, Dickinson remained vigilant. With soldiers still at large and rumors of violence circulating, word came of a planned attack on the Bank of the United States on Chestnut Street. The soldiers intended to take their pay by force. Dickinson, along with General William Irvine, went to the bank and stayed up all night to protect it. The next day, the soldiers denied that there had been any plan to attack the bank and expressed eagerness to continue negotiations. But the Council wouldn't hear them until they apologized and submitted to Congress. The captains protested that the soldiers' intention had only been to apply to the Council for relief and any poor behavior was owing to a visit from three congressmen to their barracks the evening before. One congressman in particular, they said, had especially inflamed the men, otherwise they would not have gone to the State House at all. Although they declined to name him, it was clear that the congressman was Alexander Hamilton.[33] Nevertheless, Dickinson insisted that they should lay down their arms and come to his house in a show of submission.

That evening, the soldiers paraded before Dickinson's house. He emerged, climbed upon a table set outside, and, by candlelight, upbraided them for their "unprecedented and heinous fault" and "insisted on their giving a further evidence of their good disposition, and of their duty to the *offended Majesty* of the United States." Dickinson's speech, derived from the wording of the law, suggested the soldiers had come close to committing treason. He ordered the men "to repair to the Barracks under the command of their officers, then present, and behave themselves as soldiers ought to do," assuring them that he would attempt to secure pardons for them. After giving Dickinson three cheers, the soldiers "instantly obeyed."[34] An apparent concealing of information by Boudinot protected members of Congress, particularly Hamilton, from any charges of treason.[35]

Over the summer and into the fall, the mutiny was dissected and discussed in the State House as well as in the public houses.[36] Opinions were divided on Dickinson's handling of the situation. Predictably, some were angry. Charles Thomson reported that "Hamilton's resentment was wholly bent against the president of the state and nothing but Dickinson's ruin would satisfy him." But Thomson found that this was a "private resentment" and urged Hamilton "to consider the interest of the Union." Thomson himself was almost as irked with Dickinson, whose refusal to bend to Congress's will seemed to him to be mere pride rather than principle.[37] The friends differed in this regard. Neither had Thomson understood Dickinson's principled stance on independence. On the other hand, Benjamin Rush reported that "Mr. Dickinson's conduct in the close of business has met with universal approbation."[38] Into the autumn, Dickinson persisted in pleading the soldiers' cause to the Assembly and encouraging the members to honor the men who sacrificed for their country.[39]

Dickinson's handling of the so-called Mutiny of 1783 and his ongoing concern for soldiers in distress attracted the notice of a group of officers in town. On October 15, the Pennsylvania chapter of the newly established Society of the Cincinnati met at the City Tavern. The Society had formed in May to honor men who had served at least three years as officers in the Continental Army. But the Society agreed that a select few honorary members also be admitted for distinguished service in the militia or to the public. Dickinson's name was put forward and approved for membership.[40]

Despite continuing attacks from the radical faction in the state, there were signs that Dickinson's reputation was holding up. One of his greatest admirers, Benjamin Rush, founded a college in the frontier town of Carlisle and, in honor of the most important partnership of Dickinson's life, called it "John and Mary's College." Later the name was changed to "Dickinson College" to avoid any appearance of monarchy by association with the College of William & Mary in Virginia. Rush had a particular vision for this institution, which he'd been planning for years, and a reason for choosing the Dickinsons as its namesake. The frontier had long been characterized by bigotry, darkness, and violence. The Scotch-Irish Presbyterians, who had displaced the Indians, frequently by murdering them, and led the way in persecuting Quakers, were in desperate need of reform and enlightenment that a liberal education would provide. Rush also hoped it would keep Presbyterians from leaving Pennsylvania. A Presbyterian himself, he therefore had in mind an ecumenical institution of learning that would instill a love of religious liberty and other virtues necessary to a republican citizenry. To this end, he named it for two Quakers. Although Polly Dickinson was a Friend, many people, including Rush, didn't know that John Dickinson was not actually a Quaker. To emphasize religious diversity, Rush also appointed Dickinson as the president of the board. John and Polly helped the cause by donating land for the campus worth £600, along with five hundred books for the library from her late father's collection.[41] The college was chartered on September 9.

On November 6, Dickinson won re-election to a second one-year term as president. "The day was observed," reported the *Gazette*, with "the display of the State flag on Market-street wharff, the firing the United States salute by a company of the militia train of artillery, an elegant entertainment, the ringing of bells, &c. &c." For the Dickinsons, the festivities served a dual purpose. Also on the sixth, Polly, at the age of forty-four, gave birth to their fifth and last child. They named her Maria, and she was as robust as could be.[42] As Dickinson's own fifty-first birthday approached, he delivered his acceptance speech. There was much to be done, and to those who would undertake it "is delegated the sacred trust, of realizing the blessings of freedom, for which so many brave men have suffered—fought—or died—and of improving to the best advantage the signal favors, which Providence hath condescended to bestow upon the inhabitants of this land." Dickinson closed on a personal note. "I wish for no greater happiness in this world, than to be useful to my fellow-citizens, and for no higher honour, than to be esteemed by them."[43]

At the end of November, Dickinson began overseeing plans for a celebration of the peace to take place early next year. He had proclaimed October 18 a day of public thanksgiving, but all agreed that more should be done. A committee was formed to plan the "public Demonstrations of Joy," with acclaimed painter and consummate showman Charles Willson Peale at the head. The state had allocated the significant sum of £600 for the purpose, and because it was directing and funding the event, for safety's sake, no one would be required, or even allowed, to celebrate separately. Dickinson must have hoped that this event would match or exceed the previous year's celebration of the birth of the dauphin.

The focal point was to be a huge triumphal arch situated at the top of Market Street between Sixth and Seventh Streets (Fig. 18). It bore some resemblance to the arch Dickinson had designed for the birth of the dauphin, but on a much larger scale. Illuminated with some twelve hundred lamps, and with all other lighting in the city forbidden, the arch would be a spectacular sight. Constructed in the style of Roman architecture, the structure would be over fifty feet wide and thirty-five feet high, with a balustrade atop nearly four feet high. The opening of the main arch was to be fourteen feet, with smaller arches to the sides of nine feet each. The pillars supporting the arch, "adorned with spiral festoons of flowers," would be in the Ionic style.

Covering the edifice would be thirteen tableaus, one for each state in the Union, with images and inscriptions in Latin and English for the people to view and consider. Each was designed to guide the sentiments of the viewer towards feelings of gratitude and patriotism. As the public approached to pass through the arch, they would first see the Temple of Janus, the Roman god of boundaries, with the temple doors shut, as they were in times of peace. The inscription would read, "*By the Divine Favor / A great and new Order of Ages commences.*"[44]

Anticipation for the festivities increased in early December as General Washington arrived in Philadelphia. On December 8, Dickinson rode to Frankford outside the city, along with Robert Morris, Generals Arthur St. Clair and Edward Hand, the Philadelphia Troop of Horse, and several prominent citizens, to welcome Washington. After having bidden farewell to his officers in New York City, Washington was on his way to Annapolis, where Congress would sign the Treaty of Paris on December 23. He would also resign his commission as commander of the Continental Army. The *Pennsylvania Packet* reported, "His arrival was announced by a discharge of cannon, the bells were rang, and the people testified their satisfaction, at once more seeing their illustrious chief, by repeated acclamations."[45]

Washington stayed for several days, during which time he received and answered messages from officials and the citizens. President Dickinson, speaking on behalf of the Executive Council, congratulated him on the victorious peace and wished him "every happiness of this life." Washington responded with his gratitude. On the fifteenth, he departed and was accompanied a ways by the city troop of horse and "a number of gentlemen of the first distinction," including Dickinson.[46]

After the excitement of Washington's visit, in the new year, citizens of Philadelphia were primed for the public demonstration that was set for January 22. As the date approached, Peale and his workers constructed the triumphal arch and hung the paintings and the hundreds of lights that would illuminate it. Towards evening, a crowd of thousands had assembled to watch the illumination, which was to happen with a representation of peace personified, descending via pulleys and ropes from a nearby building. Then, at the right moment, seven hundred fireworks would discharge. "It is expected," wrote one Rhode Island newspaper, "that this exhibition will be the most magnificent that hath been made in America."[47]

Indeed, the event was spectacular, but not in the way they'd planned. Roughly an hour before the paintings were to be illuminated, "an unfortunate incident" occurred, reported the *Packet*. A New York paper described how the oil paintings caught fire and burned up almost immediately, and the fire set off many of the fireworks. A rocket entered the head of one Sergeant Stewart, of the artillery, killing him instantly, and several others were wounded.[48] The Pennsylvania paper concluded that it was remarkable how few injuries there were, "Considering the great number of people that were collected in so small a space."[49] The American poet Philip Freneau composed a poem "Occasioned by rejoicings in Philadelphia on the acknowledgment of the National Independence," which was a description of the arch, tactfully omitting the conflagration and fatality.[50] Poor Mr. Peale was also a victim of his own creation, having fallen onto the stage, broken several ribs, and sustained burns from which he suffered weeks in recovery.[51] Adding insult to injury, when it was all over, the event was over budget.[52] One could only hope the ill-fated arch was not a harbinger for the future of the new United States.

After this inauspicious beginning to his second term, Dickinson turned to other business. A priority was banking. The Bank of North America had been established by Robert Morris in 1781 to fund the war. But there was significant hostility to an institution perceived by some as an aristocratical threat to the nascent republic. Thus, in 1783, a rival Bank of Pennsylvania was planned for the sake of competition. Although the Bank of Pennsylvania garnered significant subscriptions, the Bank of North America quickly reduced the price of its shares and seemed likely to maintain its monopoly. Dickinson's main concern was "what Method of Banking will be attended with the greatest Utility to the Public," as he said to the directors of the Bank of Pennsylvania. Any profit to stockholders was secondary.

Dickinson, though no expert in banking, engaged the subscribers of the state bank to consider two questions. The first was whether the public good would benefit most from having one bank or two. If only one, the second question was whether the state and national banks would be consolidated and, if so, on what terms.[53] Although he shared many Pennsylvanians' desire for an agrarian state, he did not share their suspicion of banks. Rather, he believed that banks were necessary to encourage commerce, even in an agrarian economy, and to stabilize the economy by eliminating dependence on paper currency. Dickinson himself was inclined to believe that one bank would be best and suggested consolidating the two banks. In any case, the radical Assembly proposed to make the questions moot by revoking the bank's charter the following year. One writer, possibly Dickinson, attempted to convince other farmers of the need for a bank. As the Pennsylvania Farmer had done before the Revolution, now "A Philadelphia County Farmer" offered an explanation of a complicated matter in simple terms. He described himself as one of them, as someone who had once been opposed to the bank but had come to see its advantages. If Dickinson was not the author, his style had been carefully copied.[54] But it did no good. The Assembly revoked the bank's charter, and it wasn't restored until 1787. Until then, for better or worse, the people of Pennsylvania would have to rely on the Bank of North America for their needs.[55]

Turning to a subject on which he felt very qualified to treat, on April 8, Dickinson delivered an address to the newly appointed trustees of Dickinson College. He valued the opportunity not just to express his gratitude for the endeavor but also to expound on his principles of education, something of critical importance for the new nation. He laid out the ideas that should guide them: gratitude to God for the victory over Britain; a focus on promoting peace by advancing religion, virtue, freedom, and literature; and paying special attention to Pennsylvania's western frontier. "To do Good, is our Duty," he proclaimed, "and with what probability can so much be done, as by teaching the rising Generations, how to do Good?" He believed that it was "betraying Posterity, to leave them Wealth, without teaching them how to use it; & all the Cares & Toils of a Parents Life Prove to be utterly thrown away by a Negligence of Instruction." In conclusion, he assured them that their efforts "will be directed to prevent these & the innumerable Mischiefs public as well as private, that spring from defective Education."[56] In this spirit, Dickinson chose the Latin motto, the latter part of which was included on the official seal of the college: *Sine Vi, dabit precæpta Doctrina & Pietate tuta Libertas*— Without force, freedom is protected through piety and learning.[57]

When he returned from Carlisle, Dickinson launched an overdue project left over from the war. In 1775, he had been on the Committee of Safety that sank numerous *chevaux de frize* in the Delaware River and Delaware Bay. They did not work as well as hoped, however. After the British took Philadelphia, they managed to navigate around them and were able to bombard Fort Mifflin. Now the sharp iron-tipped spikes were proving a hindrance to peace-time navigation. Two contractors submitted a proposal on April 20 for the removal of the blockades. They charged £3,000 up front and another £1,500 upon completion of the job. Dickinson studied the proposal carefully to ensure the interests of the state were protected and then signed off. It would take six months to complete.[58]

In early May, Dickinson attended the general meeting of the Society of the Cincinnati as the representative of Pennsylvania, a position to which he had been elected the previous month.[59] As with most groups he joined, his fellow members soon pressed his pen into service to address a controversy about eldest sons inheriting titles and honors. Many people, some in very prominent positions, were troubled that it seemed positively unrepublican and, indeed, aristocratic. In a pamphlet published the previous year, entitled *Considerations on the Society or Order of the Cincinnati*, South Carolinian Aedanus Burke had raised the issue.[60]

Along with Richard Henry Lee and David Humphries, Dickinson co-authored a circular letter that went out to the members along with a revised constitution for the Society. They sought "to remove every cause of inquietude, to annihilate every source of jealousy." They then discussed several changes in the Society, including "that the hereditary succession should be abolished, that all interference with political subjects should be done away." They also suggested that its funds be supervised by state legislatures. The Society, they announced, was based "on these two great original pillars, FRIENDSHIP and CHARITY." Their purpose was "to diffuse comfort and support to any of our unfortunate companions, who have seen better days and merited a milder fate—to wipe the tear from the eye of the widow, who must have been consigned, with her helpless infants, to indigence and wretchedness, but for this charitable institution,—to succour the fatherless,—to rescue the female orphan from destruction, to enable the son to emulate the virtues of his father."[61] These assurances, bearing the signature of the new president general, George Washington, and accompanied by a new charter eventually put most of the criticism to rest.

Dickinson's efforts for the Society of the Cincinnati were light work compared to what followed in the remainder of his second term as president of Pennsylvania. The rest of 1784 was defined by two major occurrences: a civil war and an international diplomatic incident. From the spring through the autumn, these two crises unfolded simultaneously, with one resolving well, the other not at all.

The civil war gave lie to the notion of American unity and exemplified the weakness of the national government. After a lull in the fighting between Connecticut settlers and Pennsylvanians to combat the British, the American victory at Yorktown in the fall of 1781 allowed the conflict to resume. With the Trenton Decree affirming that the land belonged to Pennsylvania, Dickinson hoped that peace would prevail while the courts worked out how to decide competing claims. Tensions remained through 1783 and into the spring of 1784, when some Pennsylvania officials took it upon themselves to dispossess the Yankees of the land and burn their homes. During the summer, matters deteriorated, with skirmishes between the armed camps and Pennsylvanians attempts to destroy the Yankees' crops. Throughout the contest, and now more than ever, Dickinson was sympathetic to the Yankees, who were family farmers, rather than to the Pennsylvanians, who were land speculators. As news of atrocities committed by Pennsylvania officials traveled south, the Pennsylvania militias ordered to assist them also began siding with the Yankees. This was just as well, as Dickinson did not want militias called out for civil disturbances; those should be handled by civil magistrates and *posse comitatus*. Eventually, with no armed force at their disposal, the unscrupulous Pennsylvania officials retreated, and the Yankees stayed on the land. Though the fighting was over, the conflict continued well after Dickinson left office, even after the land claims of the Yankees were settled by the Assembly in 1787. It wasn't until 1799, when the Wyoming Valley was fully absorbed into Pennsylvania and the Yankees given full rights as citizens, that the half-century of conflict finally ended.[62]

As the conflict in the Wyoming Valley was escalating in May, another incident pitted Pennsylvania against the confederation government of the United States, and now also involved a foreign power. It turned on the rights and privileges of foreign diplomats and which court had jurisdiction if those were violated. A French cavalry officer, Charles-Julian de Longchamps, was charged with twice assaulting the French consul François Barbé-Marbois, though a witness claimed he saw Marbois land the first blow. Dickinson attempted to mediate the dispute, but the men refused conciliation, and the matter went to court. The question arose of which authority should try Longchamps: Pennsylvania or France. At present, Congress did not even have a minister of foreign affairs in place to advise on such matters, let alone a court in which to try an offender, since the Pennsylvania courts were still functioning as the national judiciary. Nor had the relations between the two nations normalized as they transitioned from wartime parties to a peacetime consular agreement. Eager to expand trade with France, Congress did not want to offend its ally, but since it was not positioned to deal with the situation, Pennsylvania had to take the lead. Although Dickinson attempted to have the Assembly pass a bill to protect foreign diplomats, he didn't succeed.[63]

All parties could agree that the law of nations should be upheld by whatever jurisdiction ultimately tried and punished Longchamps. They just needed to know where he would be held accountable, and Dickinson was caught in the middle. With France demanding the offender, and knowing that a state court was not the ideal venue but that Congress was less able, Dickinson sent queries to Chief Justice McKean about whether Longchamps could be legally delivered to the French, and, if not, whether his offenses in violation of the law of nations meant he could be imprisoned at the pleasure of the king of France, and whether the Executive Council could facilitate this imprisonment.[64]

McKean answered Dickinson's queries in the negative and then proceeded with the case of *Republica v. De Longchamps*, which began on June 24 in the Pennsylvania Court of Oyer and Terminer. Dickinson asked his former law clerk James Wilson to assist Attorney General William Bradford with the prosecution. Another of Dickinson's former clerks, Jacob Rush, was on the bench. In July, the court found that Longchamps was guilty of "an atrocious violation of the law of nations." His sentencing took place in October. He was fined, sentenced to twenty-one months at hard labor, and given seven years' probation. Dickinson could then write to the French diplomats that "it is with much Pleasure we observe the Respect therein manifested for the Law of Nations."[65] But it was clear that such cases would more properly be handled not by state courts but rather by a court of the United States.[66]

As Dickinson ended his second term, another ongoing matter resolved favorably. The Executive Council received a certificate from the warden's office that the contractors hired to remove and destroy forty-nine *chevaux de frize* had also "removed all the frames that were obstructions, and that the navigation, in both the eastern and western channel, is rendered perfectly safe."[67] Finally the Port of Philadelphia was fully open for business.

In the October 12 election, voters returned Dickinson for a third and final term, but they also made his job more difficult. The Republicans lost the majority in the Assembly, meaning he would have even less cooperation than usual. But voters did elect an ally named George Logan, a Pennsylvanian and cousin of Polly's on her mother's side. Logan had spent most of his life in England, returning only recently, after medical school. In 1781, he had married Debby Norris, one of Dickinson's favorite people (Figs. 19 and 20). Inspired by the Pennsylvania Farmer, Logan had been one of the founders of the Philadelphia Society for Promoting Agriculture in March, and Dickinson joined shortly thereafter.[68] And now he was elected to his first political office. Their relationship blossomed after Dickinson left office in 1785.

There was one final controversy of Dickinson's presidency. It began with a petition. Aaron Doan, a member of a Tory outlaw gang who had been sentenced to death, appealed to Dickinson for his life.[69] Doan and his brothers had been raised in a Quaker family that was Loyalist during the war. Rather than enlisting in the Bucks County militia as the law required, the men of the family had either fled or joined the British to avoid enduring forced service in the Patriot cause. Over the course of the war, the Doans had harassed state officials and those in favor of American independence, and by the end were marauding across several counties with a significant number of Indians and Black people among them.

In 1782, the state had proclaimed the Doans and their associates "outlaws," an ancient English legal remedy that placed the offender beyond the purview of the law and required every man to hunt him down and destroy his property. Never before had "outlawry" been used in Pennsylvania, so it was surprising when Chief Justice McKean had pronounced it on the Doans. Aaron Doan had been apprehended in August, brought before the Supreme Court in September, and given the death sentence in October. Now he complained that he had not received a fair trial. This was something Dickinson could not ignore, especially in a capital case in which he would be responsible for issuing the warrant of execution. He was concerned not just with the legality of the proceedings but with the effects such an action would have on the people of Pennsylvania.[70] He may have been recalling the appalling breach of justice in 1778 when two Quakers were singled out and summarily executed under an act of attainder. The man ultimately responsible was then-president Joseph Reed, a Presbyterian.

Supported by most of the Council, Dickinson wrote to the judges explaining that the Council had "perused and attentively considered" the proceedings, and considering that it was "a Case of a novel and extraordinary nature, which being once established as a precedent, may greatly affect the lives Liberties and Fortunes of the Freemen of this Commonwealth," they could not issue a warrant for execution "until the doubts and difficulties" were removed. "To take away the Life of a Man, without a fair and open Trial, upon an Implication of Guilt" was "so dangerous" that "Judges have allways exerted their Ingenuity & Humanity in reversing Outlawries upon slight Objections."[71] He thus submitted nine questions he wanted judges Thomas McKean and George Bryan to answer. He also noted a number of technical violations that should have led the warrant of outlawry to be set aside.

Dickinson and McKean, though lifelong friends and always very similar in their politics and jurisprudence, were now the nominative heads of Pennsylvania's opposing political factions, Dickinson of the Republicans and McKean of the Constitutionalists.[72] Despite their many commonalities, in some cases they disagreed on the finer points of law. Here Dickinson perceived his friend as disregarding the right of trial by jury; McKean thought his friend was trampling on the principle of an independent judiciary. McKean thus took his time answering the questions and then did so abruptly, making clear he believed Dickinson was overstepping his bounds as executive.

The matter dragged into the spring, with both men entrenched in their positions. The court refused to reverse the ruling, and Dickinson refused to issue the death warrant. In an attempt to broaden support for his position, Dickinson decided to send the matter to the Assembly, which declined to interfere. Although he and the Council could have pardoned Doan, it is possible they didn't because they wanted to emphasize the importance of trial by jury, an institution that Dickinson prized most highly his entire legal career, though he always sought lenity in capital cases whenever there was the least doubt about guilt or process. Ultimately, Doan remained in jail and continued to petition the Council after Dickinson left office. Eventually, the next Assembly president, Benjamin Franklin, pardoned him on the condition he would leave the country, which he eventually did.[73]

Aside from the Doan controversy, the remainder of Dickinson's final term was free from life-and-death questions regarding individuals but did concern questions about the health of both the United States and the Commonwealth of Pennsylvania. He opened 1785 with a lengthy message to the General Assembly about the problem of public credit. The question had arisen whether Pennsylvania should assume the debts of its citizens to the United States and establish a fund for paying the 6 percent interest rate that was being imposed upon those debts. This was yet another area in which the roles of the central and state governments were unclear, and Dickinson believed that Pennsylvania shouldn't be forced to take a position that properly belonged to the central government. He believed that Congress's powers "comprehend the whole management of the national debt" and that "their hands ought rather to be strengthened than weakened."[74] If Pennsylvania were to assume this debt, it must only be under two conditions: first, that only the original holders of the certificates that had been used to finance the war would be the ones paid, rather than those from dealers who had purchased them from distressed persons; and second, that paying these debts would not impoverish Pennsylvania and prevent it from paying taxes to the central government. Both of these conditions admitted difficulties, including how the first purchasers could be distinguished from the dealers; how paying the dealers would make the government of the United States appear to foreign allies, who themselves awaited repayment; and that the state could become overextended financially.

Moreover, still more accounting was required to determine how much Pennsylvania would owe, particularly when collecting taxes remained an uncertain and inefficient process. There was no guarantee that Pennsylvanians would be able to bear the burden required. Congress believed that simply printing more bills of credit would be the answer, but Dickinson thought that would only create more problems, including rampant inflation and the inequity to those who paid their taxes in specie, or coins. It would also create more speculators and invariably harm the most vulnerable. "We ardently wish," he clarified, "to save widows, orphans, officers, soldiers, and other worthy citizens who contributed their property by placing it in the Loan Office, or otherwise, to the use of their country, or have served her, and still hold their certificates from such unequal contests" arising from paper money.[75]

Dickinson believed that establishing a new system of revenue was the most important issue facing the state and, indeed, the nation. He envisioned a system "founded on just, and therefore salutary principles" that would be easy to understand, with clear laws and an efficient collection process.[76] He proposed bringing the various collectors of taxes and county treasurers under the purview of the comptroller general so that each individual and all the taxes could be assessed. This would allow funds to be easily traced and deficiencies, frauds, or neglects discovered. "Thus," he concluded, "every freeman will have the satisfaction of knowing that what he contributed has been applied to the general welfare, in which his own is involved." Abuses would be detected and punished, which would "be an encouragement to him to pay his taxes cheerfully."[77]

Before Dickinson left office, two other aspects of the commonwealth required improvement: certain laws and the regulation of prisons. Among the laws he wanted improved were those concerning immigration and determining the worthiness of foreigners to be naturalized; those for electing justices of the peace and sheriffs and determining voting districts; those concerning marriage so that divorce and alimony would be provided for; and, finally, the very first law he called for, the one to suppress vice and immorality, which allowed too much gambling. All needed to be amended and enhanced in one way or another.

Next he turned to a subject that was becoming an area of special interest for him: prison reform. "The regulation of prisons," he explained to the

General Assembly, "seems to be a care peculiarly becoming a free people. The slightest portion of affliction needlessly added to that which results from restraint of liberty, is an offence committed by the State." The plight of the incarcerated was dire. They lived in squalid conditions, and, because they were forced to pay for their own way, many of them were starving to death, depending on handouts from Good Samaritans to survive.[78] To alleviate suffering and promote reform of the individual, Dickinson presented the Assembly with a long list of categories covering most aspects of prison life, from general security, to the daily necessities of prisoners, to religious instruction and morals.[79] Soon after, he ordered the city commissioners of Philadelphia to raze the old jail and workhouse and purchase a lot for new ones.[80] It was at least a start towards more humane conditions; he would continue his reform efforts as a private citizen.

Although a good number of issues from Dickinson's previous terms remained unresolved, at least some had concluded well—or seemingly so. Towards the end of 1784, the Council had received word of the conclusion of a treaty with the Six Nations Indians, or the Iroquois Confederacy, whereby all their lands within Pennsylvania had been purchased, which, in turn, would allow soldiers of the Pennsylvania Line to receive payment in land.[81] To Dickinson, it was not just that this matter was concluded but also how. "The Indians," he wrote with evident satisfaction in his message to the General Assembly, "acknowledge themselves 'kindly' and 'generously' dealt with—declaring that Pennsylvania has never deceived or wronged them." The transaction was not just good for Pennsylvania. He believed that because the old friendship between Pennsylvania and the Indians was restored, the relationship could be further improved to the advantage of both parties.[82]

There is little doubt Dickinson believed this to be true. Over the years since he had attended that 1762 meeting in Easton, his affection for Native peoples had grown into admiration and a desire to ensure they were treated justly. Some years earlier, after he had begun courting Polly, he had an idea for a story he would write called "Indian Letters." In this romantic tale, the protagonist is captured in infancy and "adopted by an Indian Man & his Wife who had lost a Son in a former War." He feels "their Tenderness for him." He is ignorant of his English heritage until he takes his own captive, who taught him to read and write. The young man travels to Philadelphia, where he is appalled by the ways of whites. He then undertakes a "Comparison of English & Indian Life." The complexity of so-called civilization is "contrasted with Simplicity of Indian" ways. "The English labor for those Things which when obtaind they are not more contented than We are." The "Dress of Men & Women inconvenient & absurd." Also absurd are their laws, which "bewilder & elude Justice." Their priorities are inverted. "Criminals for capital Crimes are tried in a Day," but "a Dispute for a String of Wampum may last 7 Years." The whites have "Absurd Notions of carrying on Wars" and afterward, "None but their great Men are talkd of among them." There were "Miserable Dissensions between different Sects," and he has an "Abhorrence of them for this Reason." But in the midst of war, he takes "a lovely Prisoner" who "instructs him in Religion." He is compelled by the Supreme Being to love her. "Glory & Power are nothing in Comparison with her Virtues & Goodness." He is "More pleasd with Quakers than any others." Having been raised as an Indian, the protagonist gravitated to the religion most familiar to him. "Quakers say," he learns, "the Great Being condescends with their Souls."[83]

Although Dickinson never wrote more than sketchy notes for this novel, the Indians captured his imagination as they had captured his protagonist, romanticized notion though it was. Quakers had always attempted to deal fairly with Indians, purchasing their lands at fair prices and protecting them from their rapacious countrymen. Therefore, in acquiring Native lands, it was imperative to Dickinson that the Indians be treated fairly. Before the talks with the Iroquois Confederacy got underway in October 1783, he strove to set the tone for the negotiations with Pennsylvania's delegates in Congress. The Indians' opinion of Americans was consequential, he argued. "We think our Character and future relation to them must greatly depend upon the Conduct We hold towards them in the present Circumstances." There were two possible outcomes, depending on the commissioners' actions. "We may now convince them beyond Controversy or Suspicion, that We are an honest manly and generous, or a cunning unjust and selfish Nation." Not only was it in America's interest to deal fairly with the Indians; it was the country's duty.

He counseled the delegates to imagine themselves in the Indians' place. "Nature planted them in this Land," and if we could "intimately be acquainted with their Modes of thinking" we would understand that "they have endeavoured to consult the political Welfare of their country in the best manner" and learn "to revere the Principles of those Efforts, that have been so injurious to us, and so useless to them." He believed that the law of nations entitled Americans to some of the land, but not to the point that Indians would feel "a Resentment of hard Treatment." He wanted a combination of cession and purchase of lands that would "impress forcible on the Minds of the Indians, that We are a firm and worthy People, who are not to be provoked with impunity, and who may be trusted in our Transactions." Finally, he discovered an inequity in the language that must be remedied before any treaty could be accomplished. On the one hand, it stipulated that the United States would merely "endeavour" to restrain its citizens from encroaching on Native lands but that Indians "shall not" encroach on American land. "The expressions should be mutual," he insisted.[84]

The following year, 1784, he likewise instructed the commissioners. "In negociating with the Indians," he said, "you will regulate your conduct by the principles of Justice as well as the most exact Economy." In addition to obtaining the lands, he hoped they might also revive a trade relationship. The key was to use "utmost endeavors to conciliate their affections and gain their confidence rather than irritate their tempers or provoke their resentments."[85]

Dickinson's optimism concerning what was called the "Last Purchase" was ill-placed. Also known as the Treaty of Fort Stanwix, this first of several treaties with Indians after the conclusion of the Revolution was actually a crippling blow to the Iroquois Confederacy, which ceded claims to the entire Ohio Territory and land west of the mouth of Buffalo Creek, as well as some land along the Niagara River. Dickinson bore some responsibility for their plight. Rather than heeding his more recent instructions, the commissioners followed the first set he had issued in April 1783 and treated the Indians as a conquered people, precisely the treatment Americans had feared from Britain. The commissioners refused to acknowledge Iroquois sovereignty or control over the land and instead asserted the dominance of the United States. Although some tribes were satisfied with the treaty, the consequences were not yet clear to them. The negotiations nullified the power of the Iroquois Confederacy to participate in any future treaties and defined the western boundary of its lands, which would enable the United States, including land speculators such as George Washington, to move aggressively into its territory.[86]

The spring brought an event that Dickinson had surely imagined but perhaps never thought possible. In mid-April of 1785, a letter arrived from Samuel Adams introducing Catharine Macaulay and her husband, Dr. Graham. In truth, she needed no introduction. Dickinson had exchanged letters and gifts with her before the Revolution and admired her magisterial history of England as well as applauding her support for the American cause. "They wish to shew every Mark of Respect to Patriots & Heroes in our foederal Republic," Adams explained, "on the Success of their late Exertions in Support of the Independence Dignity & Happiness of Man."[87] The couple was traveling from the north to the south on their pilgrimage, arriving in Philadelphia on April 27. The *Packet* announced Macaulay's visit, describing her as "not more admired for her celebrated writings, than for those dignified virtues which adorn every true friend of America."[88] Dining with one of his favorite authors, and indeed one of the greatest of patriots of the age, must have been one of the highlights of Dickinson's life.

Where patriotism was concerned, Americans enjoyed expressing theirs. On the Fourth of July, Philadelphians celebrated by ringing bells, decorating ships in the harbor, and other festivities. The Society of the Cincinnati did so by waiting on Dickinson and Thomas McKean to congratulate them on the anniversary before they partook in an elegant dinner at the City Tavern.[89]

The anniversary also occasioned a renewed request to Dickinson from the artist Robert Edge Pine, who was painting a canvas depicting July 4, 1776, in Congress. For the second time, he wrote to Dickinson requesting permission to include him in the painting. "The Truth is," Dickinson repeated, "that I opposed the making the Declaration of Independence at the Time when it was made. I cannot be guilty of so false an Ambition, as to seek for any Share in the Fame of that Council. Enough it will be for Me," he explained, "that my Name be remembered by Posterity, if it is acknowledged, that I chearfully staked every thing dear to Me upon their Fate of my Country, & that no Measure however contrary to my Sentiments, no Treatment however unmerited, could, even in the deepest Gloom of our Affairs, change that Determination." He had done all he could to "promote their Happiness." He concluded, "I continued inflexibly attached to their Cause."[90] Patriotism was not something merely performed when it suited, whether by lighting fireworks or appearing in a painting.

Although Americans celebrated Independence Day with gusto, it was questionable how much farther beyond these demonstrations their patriotism extended. The ideal of republican self-sacrifice for the common good, while excellent in theory, had never seemed very robust in practice, especially where taxes were concerned. Dickinson believed that Americans needed structures to guide them. In this respect, he had never thought that the Articles of Confederation, as ratified, would be equal to the needs of the Union. In an August 1783 message to the Assembly, he had asked that they be "strengthened and improved."[91]

But nothing effectual had been accomplished in the ensuing two years. Now there seemed to be some stir about strengthening the powers of Congress. In New York, a meeting of merchants and other citizens considered "the embarrassed and critical situation to which the trade of America is reduced" because there was no national authority to regulate it.[92] They decided to form committees of correspondence in the various states to devise some way to empower Congress. To Dickinson, this seemed an excellent opportunity to act.

In considering the most necessary changes and how they could be accomplished, he sent two letters to Charles Thomson with queries and suggestions. One of them included a draft of a message he planned to deliver to the Assembly. Thomson, then in New York with Congress, which had settled there after the Mutiny of 1783, was perhaps the single most qualified person to advise about the changes needed in the central government and how to obtain them. As secretary of Congress, the main contact between the states and Congress, as well as its "executive manager," he was arguably the most powerful man in the least powerful body in the United States.[93] However, even Thomson was stumped by Dickinson's questions. He agreed that the central government was "weak and ineffective," but what to do about it was anything but clear. He agreed with Dickinson, however, that they should be cautious in overturning what they already had. And he was inclined to be significantly more conservative than his friend in both his optimism about and his ambition for change.

Naturally, Dickinson's queries stemmed from difficulties in Pennsylvania. Since the Longchamps-Marbois affair, he had wondered whether there should be a power in the central government "of punishing the officers of the confederated republic in some prescribed manner of proceeding." He felt strongly that there should be "due observance of the law of Nations." Thomson agreed, but he doubted whether that power should reside with the central government, as it would infringe too much on the sovereignty of the states. Dickinson disagreed.

On the matter of taxation, Dickinson posed two questions. First, he asked whether it would be wise for Congress to have the power "of adjusting the quotas of all charges & expenses by an equitable & certain mode." Thomson believed it would "be useless" and responded, "If the States will not furnish either returns of property or of inhabitants how would it be possible for congress to exercise the power of adjusting the quotas?" Second, Dickinson suggested a power in Congress "of imposing and collecting certain defined internal duties to be applied only as a sinking fund," that is, a reserve fund. Again, Thomson thought it would be ineffectual and might lead "designing Men" to discourage the people from what they were willing to grant, namely "the power of regulating commerce and of imposing duties at least on importations for the purpose of raising a revenue." He therefore wished Dickinson would "turn his whole attention" to that matter.[94]

With this exchange in mind, in August 1785, Dickinson issued the final substantive message of his presidency to the Pennsylvania General Assembly. Reminding the members that he had previously remarked on the deficiencies of the Articles of Confederation, he began by referencing the recent activities in New York. "We are pleased to find," he said, "an opinion generally prevailing at this time, that some amendment of the confederation is necessary." But "instead of stopping at *partial* provisions," he hoped that "it may lead to as *perfect* an establishment of the union as can be devised." Then, rather than taking Thomson's advice to limit his recommendations to raising tax revenue, he deferred to his friend by mentioning Thomson's priority first, but then added several of his own, including imposing and collecting postage in the same way as taxes; regularizing punishments of government officials; and maintaining the law of nations. In a further nod to Thomson and the New York merchants, he said, "Many persons are now very earnest to have the first of these powers lodged in Congress without limitation."[95] As yet, it was still unclear how or when these changes could be implemented, but Dickinson stood at the ready to do so if called.

Dickinson ended his presidency of Pennsylvania as he had begun it, with an appeal to the public on their duties as citizens. This time, it came in the form of an open letter to the judges of the state. As they rode the circuit to administer justice and punish "Evildoers," he wanted them to keep in mind "how vain are Laws without Manners. These cannot be expected, unless the strictest Attention be paid to the Education of Youth, and the Inculcation of a true Love and Fear of The Supreme Being." These things were most necessary in republics. "Where the People themselves are to govern," he explained, "their Virtue is essential to their Prosperity." He then reiterated the essence of his first proclamation on the suppression of vice and immorality in order to help the state's citizens to "ensure their own Felicity and the Honor of their Country" with "a just Regard for Industry, Frugality, Temperance, Morality, and Piety." This was what he hoped for in Pennsylvania. He also wished "that You would be pleased strongly to recommend in the several Counties, the

Establishment of Schools, Attendance at places of Public Worship, Provision for Ministers of the Gospel, and Observance of the Sabbath."[96] He was, in effect, suggesting that Americans behave more like the Indians of his captivity narrative.

By the end of his time in office, Dickinson had handled a potential mutiny, a civil war, and an international diplomatic incident, and he had set the wheels in motion for meaningful improvements in many of Pennsylvania's laws, policies, and institutions. On his watch, the final boundaries of the state had been settled, a secessionist movement had been quelled, and he had at least prepared Pennsylvania to advocate for a stronger national union. He had also been part of founding one of the first new colleges in the United States, which was named for him, and he had become an honorary member of a prestigious military society. Of course, he had not resolved everything in Pennsylvania to everyone's satisfaction, including his own, with the Indians the most significant casualty. Still, he had worked diligently to the best of his ability. Thomas Hartley, a lawyer and former Continental Army officer, admired what Dickinson had accomplished, writing, "Those who reviled and persecuted you have been obliged to join in Silencing the Tongues of Envy and Detraction and to declare you worthy of the highest Honour and Trust which the Common Wealth could bestow."[97] Hoping this was indeed the case, Dickinson was greatly relieved to return to his family in Wilmington in hopes of a lengthy retirement.

13

"A labour of public love"

Reconstituting the American People, 1786–1791

Dickinson again stepped down from public office, he hoped for the last time, and eased into retirement in Wilmington, finally reunited with Polly on a permanent basis. He would have preferred to live in Philadelphia, but, as he told Benjamin Rush, "the shattered Situation of my Affairs after the War compelled me to retire" to Wilmington.[1] Their mansion, which Dickinson had had built, was in the heart of the small city, on the corner of Kent and Market Streets, with the house facing Kent Street (Fig. 21). A garden surrounded by a high brick wall extended to Shipley Street to the east. "The situation is elevated," noted an observer, "commanding extensive views of the surrounding country, and for health and convenience, is excelled by few." One entered the house by a large and elegant hall adorned with architectural flourishes. On the first floor were four rooms, including a large dining room and kitchen with running water nearby, a bathing room, a smoke house, and other necessities. The second floor consisted of eight spacious rooms, all well lighted, some with large closets, and a lavatory. There were three rooms on the third floor besides the garrets. The house was "well-calculated to accommodate a large family in the best style." All agreed that the buildings were "finished throughout with taste and elegance."[2] The Dickinsons also owned a vegetable garden three blocks north on Market, across the street from the Presbyterian church.[3]

The whole family missed their friends and relatives in Philadelphia.[4] At fifteen, Sally especially pined for her circle of friends at the Norris house on Chestnut Street and the Logans at Stenton, feeling her isolation more acutely when the streets were too muddy to go out.[5] But they did receive some visitors, call on the neighbors, and attend meeting several times a week. The meeting house was nearby on Fifth Street, which was convenient. Usually the family traveled together in the carriage, but occasionally each would find his or her own way—Polly riding in a wagon with friends, Sally on horseback, and John walking.[6] Sometimes, the entire family would join Dickinson on his trips out of town, all piling into the carriage and enjoying the scenery on the way to Chester County or wherever his business took him.[7]

For Dickinson, spending time with his girls was a joy, if not always peaceful. Sally was "a Beloved Child," mature beyond her years. Polly remarked to Cousin Hannah G. that she "has been my Constant Companion thro Scene of great <u>distress</u>." Maria, on the other hand, now three, could be "a perfect Vixen" one moment, "yet Gentle as a dove the next Minute." When Polly felt she had to discipline her with two or three slaps, Maria bit, spat, and attempted to strike Polly in return, then lay on the floor kicking and "roaring." When her tantrum passed, she was again "Ma's Baby, good Baby, put her dear little Arms round my Neck and Kissed me." Polly could never remain angry with her for long and admitted being partial to her.[8] John seemed to feel the same way.[9] Maria reminded them of Polly's sister Sally at that age. Tantrums notwithstanding, Maria was a "Remarkable Sensible Child." Cousin Molly Lloyd had called Sally Norris "an Old Child."[10]

Dickinson finally had leisure to take stock of his life's ambitions. He had always been aware of his privilege and thankful to the Divine Author for it. In turn, he had done what he could to advance benevolent causes, such as giving to the Pennsylvania Hospital or donating his pay to the widows and orphans of religious ministers or military veterans. His cousin Debby Norris would later reflect that he was "remarkably kind & attentive to his poorest neighbors & acquaintance. This seemd something peculiar to his Character, for he excelled in it . . . He used to assist widows & unfortunate Persons with his advice respecting the settlement of their affairs, and would take a great deal of trouble to do them service."[11] Now he looked to the Society of Friends as the best means for enacting his charitable designs on a larger scale. "My Mind for a considerable Time past," he wrote to his kinsman James Pemberton in the spring of 1786, "has been much engaged by a Desire, to contribute to the promotion of an effectual sense of the Blessings of Virtue & Piety, especially among People of the poorer Class."[12]

Quakers believed that individuals could not find God in their consciences and reform their ways if burdened by physical hardships and the lack of basic needs. One could hardly consider one's soul if distracted by gnawing hunger, or oppressed by ignorance, or beaten down by a master's rod. For Dickinson, doing his Christian duty of relieving oppression was not merely about the individual's soul; it was about the survival of the republic. Social ills such as poverty, crime, and slavery would bring down the country as surely as a faulty government. So he turned his attention to the problems of reconstituting the

nation on firmer moral foundations, from both the top down, by restructuring the government, and the bottom up, by using his wealth to benefit
the poor.

Polly was his partner in these benevolent endeavors. They generally wished
to remain anonymous, and Dickinson was pained when their identities
were revealed. "Acts of this sort," he wrote to Pemberton in December 1786,
"ought to be done 'in Secret.'" He remained convinced that their gifts would
be better handled "under the Management of Friends" rather than personally. Still, there was a silver lining to their identities being known. "Perhaps,"
he mused, "Establishment being begun may stir up others, to contribute to its
Promotion."[13] Indeed, this was another Quakerly trait—setting an example
in the world for others to follow.

He had already begun some important measures. In 1785, Dickinson
attempted to abolish slavery in Delaware through legislation. "I took
some Pains in directing the Draft bill," he later explained to Pemberton,
"to make all the proper provisions, adverting to precedents in other
places."[14] There was already a law in Pennsylvania, which Dickinson had
no part in writing, and he used it as a model. Cognizant of a less receptive audience in Delaware, he first prescribed "a new Preamble—short—
& free from every Expression that can possibly be construed to reflect
on persons of different sentiments."[15] His approach was exactly like that
of Quaker abolitionist John Woolman, who gently persuaded Quakers
to give up their slaves in 1754.[16] Dickinson then proceeded to correct
the wording of the law, explaining that "for want of these Words great
Contests have arisen in Pennsylvania."[17] He went as far as to write new
sections and provisos, noting of the sixth section on the financial liability
for freed slaves, "much Confusion having arisen in Pennsylvania, from
the odd Manner of its being worded."[18] In January 1786, the bill was then
"taken to Dover when the Assembly was sitting" and put forward by Allen
McLane.[19]

While awaiting results on the bill, Dickinson worked for abolition in
other ways. After the death of renowned abolitionist Anthony Benezet,
Pemberton wrote to Dickinson proposing that some of Benezet's pamphlets
to be published posthumously. Because "it gives me Satisfaction to perceive
thy mind turned to promote his laudable views," explained Pemberton, he
would send a number of pamphlets for Dickinson "to distribute in such way,
as thou may judge most conducive to the pious intention of our endeared deceased friend."[20] Next, on May 11, Dickinson manumitted unconditionally

the remaining Black people he enslaved. This final deed would effectively nullify several earlier wills he had written that freed his slaves upon his death and provided them with funds to be divided among them to get them settled in their new lives of freedom.[21] Instead, many of them remained on Dickinson land, renting it for nominal sums and farming, and he assisted them as they needed, with special attention to the widows. Now he was as unencumbered by that evil institution as much as any Quaker, and they praised him for it, not even minding that he still would not accept the name "Quaker."[22] He estimated his financial loss to be between £8,000 and £10,000, but he gained "a peacefull easy mind."[23] He later wrote to his kinsman John Lloyd, the British abolitionist, explaining that he and Polly had "liberated all those, who by the erring Law of our Country, were called our Slaves. It was an Emancipation of our own Minds."[24]

With his conscience cleared, Dickinson acted like a Quaker and looked outward to reform the world. First, he added a codicil to his will regarding two plantations totaling five hundred acres. They would be given to the State of Delaware, and rents would be given to Quakers in Kent County for establishing inexpensive schools "for the instruction of Blacks and other poor persons in reading, writing and the principles of Christianity, and in prudently distributing books well calculated to promote habits of industry, frugality, morality and piety."[25] The following year he stipulated, "Let the old Blacks, Mary, Flora, Priscilla, Augustus, Jenny, and Pompey, live where I have settled them, and be comfortably provided for with Cloathing and other Things proper."[26] He continued his duty to them until his death, even after some of the women married and were legally the responsibility of their husbands.[27]

Unfortunately, by the end of May 1786, the abolition bill was dead. It had been considered and debated by the Delaware Assembly in February, but the pro-slavery faction had the upper hand, and, ultimately, the bill was deferred "for future consideration."[28] The most that Delawareans were willing to pass were laws prohibiting selling slaves out of the state.[29] Dickinson tried again at a later date to "bring the Affair forward," but "the Legislature were in such a temper, that it would be in vain then to renew the Attempt." He decided to keep the bill and wait for a better time.[30]

Although Dickinson's effort failed, Warner Mifflin, the most aggressive Quaker abolitionist, had some success the following year. The Delaware leg-islature passed a new law benefiting Black people in several ways, including reviving some of the provisions of the law Dickinson had passed as speaker of the Assembly in 1759, such as prohibiting the enslavement and sale of free Black people and levying penalties against the kidnappers. Additionally, although the bill denied them the vote, officeholding and the right to testify against white people in court, it did allow them the right to own property and seek legal remedy in court.[31] As poor white people knew, property ownership was a key stepping stone to the franchise.

The Dickinsons' greatest cause was education. Dickinson had long valued liberal arts education. Now that it seemed clear that white men of all ranks would eventually have the vote, he and Polly considered it central to the survival of the republic. It was the antidote to ignorance and slavery, both literal and figurative, two closely related ailments. "I look upon the protection of education by government," he wrote to Benjamin Rush, "as indispensably necessary for . . . advancing the happiness of our fellow citizens as individuals and for securing the continuance of equal liberty to them in society."[32] Dickinson had always supported education by donating funds to schools, by teaching a number of boys and young men in his law office, and of course, as one of the founders of Dickinson College. The Dickinsons now made a more concerted effort to create informed citizens.

"Lessening the Expence of Schooling & distributing suitably instructive Books, appeared to Me," he said, "very likely to render eminent services to those for whom I was concerned."[33] Their concern was for both boys and girls, and both Black and white children. They had a subscription to the Nottingham School, founded by a Quaker named George Churchman, and Dickinson directed that the remainder of it be paid. But the school was struggling and not exactly what they envisioned it to be.[34] They had also been involved with the founding of the Wilmington Academy to instruct poor children in the liberal arts, religion, and morality. Without regard for their origins, these children would be held to the highest standard of learning, expected to master mathematics, several branches of science, and Latin and Greek to read the ancient classics. Dickinson now served on an oversight committee.[35]

Dickinson had also spoken with a printer about adapting *The New England Primer*, the standard textbook of the day, into a new work he called *The American Primer*.[36] His idea came at the same time that New Englander Noah Webster sought his endorsement for his new textbook, *A Grammatical Institute of the English Language*, whose sales were flagging. Its third volume, *Rules for Speaking and Reading*, contained Dickinson's 1774 *Letter to the Inhabitants of the Province of Quebec*, published by the First Continental Congress. Dickinson praised this edition for its explanation of the pronunciation of American English, but he wished its reading samples would include "a clear yet concise Account of the Christian Religion," as well as poetry and literature "best calculated for improving the Understanding, purifying the Heart, and regulating the Conduct."[37] Webster obliged, but not until decades later, and with a Calvinist bent Dickinson would have rejected. In the spring of 1786, Webster embarked on a new marketing campaign for the *Institute* with endorsements from leading men around the country. The only two he mentioned by name were John Dickinson and Benjamin Franklin.[38] His edition became the standard textbook for the next forty years. Yet the Dickinsons had in mind something bigger than a textbook and began discussing ideas with Churchman, who considered Dickinson "a Partner in our Care for Poor Children."[39]

Meanwhile, the constitutional crisis in America was deepening under the dysfunctional Articles of Confederation, and public events made clear the necessity of civic education to national stability. In the summer and fall of 1786, residents of Massachusetts rose up against the state government in what became known as Shays's Rebellion. The state's response of calling out the militia to suppress it had the opposite effect when the militia refused to muster and then joined the rebellion; the state then had to call in a private force. This episode vindicated Dickinson's decision not to call the militia to deal with the soldiers in the near mutiny of 1783. Both incidents also confirmed Dickinson's concern about the viability of the Union under the current constitution. Enough other leaders were also concerned about the "imbecility," as Dickinson put it, of the Articles to organize a convention in Annapolis to remedy the problems. Having been retired from public office for less than a year, Dickinson traveled with George Read to attend from September 11 to 14 as delegates from Delaware.[40]

In their first order of business, the Annapolis delegates unanimously elected Dickinson as chairman. It made the most sense. He was the elder statesman among youngsters such as James Madison, Tench Coxe, and Alexander Hamilton. Of course, he had also written the first draft of the Articles of Confederation, which contained provisions that had been excised from the ratified version and now appeared necessary after all. And as a member of Congress and president of two states, he had had a prime vantage point for witnessing the failure of the Articles to unify the country. Unfortunately, little could be accomplished by this body. Only five states sent delegates, who were authorized only to consider the trade and commerce of the United states and, at most, frame an act that would unify the various systems of the different states. It quickly became clear that something more was necessary. To this end, the convention drafted a report that was read before Congress on February 21, 1787. It stated that commissioners agreed that all the states should send delegates to "meet at Philadelphia on the second Monday in May next to take into Consideration the situation of the united States, to devise such further provisions as shall appear to them necessary to render the Constitution of the Fœderal Government adequate to the Exigencies of the Union."[41] Dickinson accepted an appointment to attend the Federal Convention.

As the Annapolis Convention met, the Confederation Congress in New York made plans that included Dickinson. A long-running boundary dispute between South Carolina and Georgia had come before it, and, according to Article 9 of the Articles of Confederation, it would appoint a federal court for a hearing. Both Dickinson brothers' names were drawn as two of the thirteen judges, and they were required to be present in New York on June 18 of the next year. A letter from Secretary Charles Thomson informed John of this fact. He responded, saying he could not attend. He didn't give a reason, but there were many, including his poor health and that he hoped the Federal Convention would be meeting then.[42]

But Thomson refused to accept this response. Since Congress was not sitting, he wrote to Dickinson as a friend before he informed Congress, chiding him for neglecting his duties under the present constitution. "Government has claim upon individuals for services," he explained, "as well as individuals upon government for protection and these of so binding a nature as to be indispensable and so essential that a non compliance is a violation of the social compact." Though the Articles were indeed defective, this provision allowing appointment of courts was wise, Thomson argued. Moreover, he said, while president of Pennsylvania, Dickinson had benefited from the same court to settle the Wyoming Controversy. He didn't believe that Dickinson had a "invincible necessity" compelling him to decline.[43] Fortunately, their friendship was not tested by this difference, as the dispute between the states was settled out of court in April 1787.[44]

Early in 1787, John and Polly had gained clarity about their benevolent designs for education. Writing to Pemberton in December, they explained that they wanted "some Establishment in the Country, similar to that at Glaucha near Hall in Saxony, or to that at Ackworth in England."[45] The former was an orphanage in Germany, the latter, a Quaker boarding school founded in 1779. They hoped that everything would be laid out clearly so that "every needless Expence may be avoided." They initially planned to donate a lot in Philadelphia on the east side of Seventh Street between Market and Arch Streets for the school itself and two plantations in Kent County, totaling five hundred acres, for income. They hoped their plans might be "carried into Efficacy, as soon as may be."[46]

Another concern the Dickinsons shared with Quakers was prison reform. Having seen the inside of too many horrific prisons during their early years, Quakers had long tried to make them places of reform rather than punishment. But they had yet to reach beyond their Society to help non-Quaker prisoners or organize for that purpose. Dickinson had begun his efforts for prison reform as president of Pennsylvania. "My Mind has been very frequently & deeply concerned, in observing, how very negligent I have been 'in doing Good.'" He explained to Pemberton, "My Intention is, to make a permanent Provision towards the Relief of those Poor who may be 'Sick, and in Prison,' under the Direction of Friends in Philadelphia." Pemberton inquired whether he wished to help only Quakers. "The Persons intended," Dickinson replied, "were those confined on Account of the Conscience or for Debt, without any Distinction as to Religious Profession." He wanted these prisoners to receive medical treatment, tolerable accommodations, and debt relief. John and Polly intended to donate the ground rent of several lots in the Northern Liberties and Nice Town, which would provide an annual income of £14 for a benevolent society.[47] The Quakers began mobilizing.[48]

A new organization established in February fortuitously aligned with the Dickinsons' current priorities. Called the Society for Political Inquiries, it began meeting at Benjamin Franklin's house and included Thomas Paine, Robert Morris, and James Wilson. In one of its first meetings, Benjamin Rush, also a member, delivered a paper on an increasingly unpopular law passed the previous year. Called the "wheelbarrow law," it replaced capital punishment for low-level crimes with work repairing the public streets. Although fewer executions was a salutary development that Rush applauded, this law was far from benign. By also dressing the convicts in a "peculiar style," the purpose of the law was public humiliation. Rush argued that the law was counterproductive because it destroyed the prisoners' dignity and made them less susceptible to rehabilitation. Published as a pamphlet in April, Rush's argument brought timely attention to the cause of prison reform.[49]

The groundswell for action was significant. With their seed funds, the Quakers' organization efforts, and Rush's publicity, the Dickinsons' vision for prison reform was actualized in the establishment of the Philadelphia Society for Alleviating the Miseries of Public Prisons, the world's first prison reform society, in early May.[50] At the same time, the Society for Political Inquiries requested that Dickinson allow them to make him an honorary member. "They fondly hope," George Fox wrote, "that you will not be opposed, to assisting them, in their endeavours, mutually to improve themselves in the Science of Government."[51]

When Rush sent Dickinson a copy of his pamphlet, he also conveyed good news about Dickinson College, which was "in a very flourishing Condition." Students came from not just Pennsylvania but Maryland, Virginia, and North Carolina. This college, Rush hoped, "will issue rays of knowledge which shall finally reform our Constitution & laws, and humanize even the half civilized inhabitants of the western Counties of Pennsylvania."[52] Despite Dickinson's inability to attend meetings of the trustees, Rush refused to entertain his request to choose another president of the college.[53]

Dickinson, as he always had, continued his efforts to do good in small ways. He still cared for at least one of the orphans of his friend William Hicks. Richard Penn Hicks was now about seventeen. His father had bequeathed him an estate in New York, but the state was attempting to claim it. With the help of James Duane, Charles Thomson, and Dickinson's cousin John Jones, young Hicks received most of the estate. Duane thought it best the boy continue his studies in the law with Dickinson, writing, "I know that you will continue to him your truly paternal Care!"[54] Dickinson also wrote to the Delaware Assembly to present an inventor named John Fitch, who was attempting to introduce the steam engine. New Jersey had already passed a law to give him a fourteen-year monopoly for steam traffic on the waterways, and a similar bill was pending in Pennsylvania. Dickinson hoped Delaware would follow suit, as this invention seemed calculated "to promote the public Good."[55]

Since the beginning of the year, national affairs had also demanded Dickinson's attention. He and George Read discussed the Federal Convention, its potential outcomes, and how to protect Delaware's interests. They were alarmed that Virginia "hath again taken the lead in the proposed Convention" by already appointing delegates.[56] They agreed that Delaware ought to appoint delegates and enjoin them against departing from the fifth Article of Confederation, which gave each state one vote. In April 1787, the

Delaware Assembly appointed Dickinson, Read, Richard Bassett, Gunning Bedford Jr., and Jacob Broom as delegates.[57] Dickinson and Read also worried about what adding territory to the United States could mean for Delaware, and Dickinson did not want to close the door on future alterations in the constitution that might be "pleasing and beneficial" to it.[58]

The long-awaited Federal Convention, with delegates selected by the state legislators, met in Philadelphia on May 14. Dickinson couldn't attend immediately, but he wanted to prepare the American people for what was at stake. On May 12 he published a short essay entitled *Fragments on the Confederation of the American States* that, in four short chapters, sketched a few major ideas to improve the Union. He was very worried that, at this precarious moment, the United States could just as easily devolve into anarchy as reform itself. Aware of the public's adulation of George Washington, he dedicated the essay to him. "It is every good man's wish," he wrote, "that you may be as successful in preventing a revolution as you have been fortunate in bringing one about."[59] The chapters addressed the rights of Congress, the defects of the Confederation, amendments to the Articles of Confederation, and an "equalizing court" that would mediate disputes between the states.

The Delaware delegation was anxious for Dickinson to arrive, with George Read writing on May 21, "I wish you were here." Read knew their colleagues' ideas for the new government, and they troubled him. "I suspect it to be of importance to the small States," he said, "that their deputies should keep a strict watch upon the movements and propositions from the larger States, who will probably combine to swallow up the smaller ones." He urged, "if you have any wish to assist in guarding against such attempts, you will be speedy in your attendance."[60]

It was not easy for Dickinson to leave his family. Polly, her infirmities increasing with age, tolerated her husband's absences less well each time, and Maria, now four, was a handful. Sally was a great help, but Maria was precocious and into everything. Dickinson wrote a letter to Maria, who could already read. After admonishing "Pa's Precious" to love God, say her prayers, and not to go places in the house where she could get hurt, he said, "I have found many poor Children here, who can't read, and have no Books— You must send all your Books down to them." Seeking to impress upon her a sense of duty that comes with privilege, he told her about a boy named George whose father had died and left him and his mother destitute. "The poor little Fellow has never been one Hour at School in his whole Lifetime," Dickinson wrote, "and yet his Mamma & Grandmamma have taught him to spell very well and to read a little— And so Papa for You gave him a quarter of a silver Dollar, because he was so good a Boy." He instructed Maria to send him and his sister some books.[61] Dickinson loved Maria "as affectionately as ever a Father loved a Child," but he did not coddle her.[62] He had high expectations for the kind of women his daughters would become.

On the morning of May 29, Dickinson stepped out of the morning fog into the familiar surroundings of the Pennsylvania State House.[63] It had been twenty-five years since he had first been elected to the provincial Assembly. With him he brought his extensive experience in political, military, and legal offices—perhaps deeper than that of any other member. He was also the only delegate to have these experiences in one of the country's largest states as well as one of its smallest states. His practical experience was matched by his long study of history, the law, and political theory. Equal in importance was Dickinson's religion. Although some delegates were deists, many more adhered to traditional religions, such as Congregationalism or Anglicanism. No other, however, was so profoundly shaped by Quakerism, which would inform Dickinson's contributions to the deliberations.

Over the course of the three and a half months the Convention met, as the mild spring weather turned into summer heat, these contributions were significant. Sitting in the stifling atmosphere of the State House with windows closed against curious ears, his performance was hampered by health issues, including severe headaches. He was unable to speak with his usual charisma. Those who knew him only by reputation were unimpressed.[64] Yet though his powers of persuasion were blunted, he was still able to offer ideas on a wide range of topics from the largest that confronted the Convention to many minor ones as he served on the Committee of Assumption of State Debt, the Committee of Slave Trade, the Committee of Postponed Parts, and the Committee of Economy, Frugality and Manufactures.

On his first day, the Convention adopted a rule for the secrecy of its proceedings that would allow delegates the freedom to speak, disagree, and change their minds without fearing outside pressure. It also referred plans of government from Virginia and South Carolina to the Committee of the Whole. At the end of the day, Dickinson wrote optimistically to Polly, "My Hopes of something good for our Country are Strong— Virtue & Wisdom must be employed— May Heaven bless our Endeavour."[65] Likewise, although he couldn't reveal much, to a friend he wrote that not only was the

Convention "of excellent Temper"; "for Abilities" it "exceeds any Assembly that ever met upon this Continent, except the first Congress."[66]

Although he was in favor of amending the Articles rather than abandoning them and starting over, it soon became clear that the Convention intended to draft an entirely new constitution. Immediately, his and George Read's apprehensions about bigger states dominating smaller ones were validated when the Virginia plan proposed abolishing one vote for each state in the new legislature in favor of two houses with representation based on proportion of inhabitants.

It was clear to Dickinson and others that a bicameral legislature, which was the British model, was the only viable option. But how Americans should be represented in each house was unclear. Dickinson's most significant contribution to the proceedings concerned this difficult question. On May 30, he wrote notes for his plan. "Members of the first Branch ought to be chosen as they now are by the existing Confederation, that is, by the Legislatures of the several States, each State having an equal Vote." And then, "Members of the second Branch ought to be elected by the People of the several States."[67] In conveying his vision to the body, he repeated a sentiment from his first *Farmer's Letter*, namely that the business before them was so important "that no man ought to be silent or reserved."[68] He discoursed at length about the necessity of a bicameral legislature and the "accidental lucky division of this country into distinct States," which must be preserved.[69] Because he knew that the large states would never give up on proportional representation, "he hoped that each State would retain an equal voice at least in one branch of the National Legislature."[70] Proportional representation alone would seriously disadvantage Delaware, whose population was a fraction of Virginia's and Pennsylvania's.

In Dickinson's plan, the states would be subordinated to the federal government, but much of their autonomy would also be preserved. His plan was neither for a *national* government, which obliterated the individual states, nor for a *federal* government that held the separate republics together only loosely. It was a "national-federal" solution.[71] It is not likely a coincidence that this solution resembled the structure of the Quaker meeting, with its tiered levels of regional and local meeting, a structure that Dickinson had experienced his entire life.

On June 7, he offered a metaphor he had been using for at least five years to help his colleagues understand his idea. The national-federal system would be like the solar system, "in which the States were the planets, and ought to be left to move freely in their proper orbits." He elaborated: "The concentrated Energy of the Union may be compared to The Sun, full of Light and Life, and the several States to Planets of different Sizes revolving around it, and receiving its beneficial Influences. The peculiar Power of each State may be called its projectile force, and its constantly operating Tendency towards the central Sun, with the regular Observance by all The States of due Distances from one another, may, if the Use of Astronomical Language is here in a figurative Sense allowable, be ascribed to the force of Attraction."[72] When Dickinson had created the arch in Delaware to celebrate the birth of the dauphin, he had included a depiction of thirteen stars orbiting the sun. Dickinson's proposal was ignored, at least at first.

Four days later, on June 11, Connecticut delegate Roger Sherman reintroduced Dickinson's idea of proportional representation in one branch of the legislature and equal representation in the other.[73] The delegates still were not ready to accept the idea and referred it to a committee on July 2.[74] Meanwhile, on Friday, June 15, New Jersey delegates produced a plan for a system that looked much like the Confederation government, with a unicameral legislature and equal representation of each state. Virginia pressed for proportional representation there too. It was an unacceptable prospect, and Dickinson's patience for both plans wore thin. He said privately to James Madison, who was the architect of the large-state plan, "You see the consequences of pushing things too far." Those smaller states that wanted two branches would "sooner submit to a foreign power" than "submit to being deprived of an equality of suffrage, in both branches of the legislature, and thereby be thrown under the combination of the large States."[75]

Dickinson worked over the weekend, planning a long speech on Monday, June 18, to explain his idea of representation in detail. But when the time came, he felt too unwell to muster his usual performance. Whereas usually audiences sat rapt before him, with words such as "fire," "spirit," "elegant," "correct," "beautiful," "chaste," and "luminous" coming to mind, now his efforts seemed "irregular," "incorrect," and "like expiring flames."[76] Always alert to an opportunity, Alexander Hamilton, who had remained silent thus far, interrupted him and discoursed the entire day on a plan of his own design. Later called the "British plan" for its resemblance to the government America had so recently overthrown, his ideas—including an executive and senators who would serve for life, like a king and a House of Lords, and a legislature that could, like Parliament, pass "all laws whatsoever" for the states— were so out of step with the republican sentiments of the Convention that the body responded with silence. Rain pelted the State House windows.[77] Hamilton henceforth attended the Convention only sporadically. The next day, Dickinson suggested that comparing the Virginia and New Jersey plans and taking the best parts of each might work. Again he was unable to break through to his colleagues.[78]

The delegates thus wrangled over what representation should be based on, population or wealth. Some, including Dickinson, thought it should be based on each state's tax revenue, but the suggestion was ultimately rejected. Instead, the debate turned to slavery. Southerners wanted slaves counted, but should they be counted as persons and therefore part of the population? Or should they be counted as property and therefore part of wealth? Counting them as persons would give the slave states a substantial advantage over the others. When James Wilson put forth the motion that enslaved persons should be counted as three-fifths of a person, the Delaware delegation voted "no."[79] Dickinson was appalled. He made clear his belief that slavery was incompatible with republicanism for two main reasons. First, it denied their fellow creatures their basic rights to "life, liberty, and the pursuit of happiness." Second, it created a class of people, the enslavers, who themselves could not comprehend the principle of equality and were unfit to exercise their rights. As he had put it when he was a young man, the enslaver "is Cowardly & Sheepish before Persons of any Fashion; barb'rous & tyrannical amongst Inferiors."[80] Further, because Dickinson believed that in a healthy republic, citizens should be close to the land, America should be a nation of farmers. This could not happen if enslaved people performed all the labor. America's very survival and its international reputation were at stake. Believing that the Convention was "Acting before the World," he asked his colleagues, "What will be said of this new Government, of founding a Right to govern Freemen on a power derived from Slaves, . . . themselves incapable of governing—yet giving to others what they have not?"[81] In the end, with no better compromise in sight, on July 12 nine states voted in favor of the three-fifths provision, none voted against, and Delaware was divided.[82]

On July 16, the committee tasked with formulating a plan for representation in the two houses of the legislature produced its report. It contained both Dickinson's idea of proportional representation in one branch of the legislature and equal representation in the other and Wilson's three-fifths clause. It passed narrowly—five states in favor, including Delaware; four against; and one, Massachusetts, divided.[83] Despite Dickinson's having first proposed a key component, this solution came to be known as the "Connecticut

Compromise." Later, Dickinson explained the concept. "It has been said that the varied representation of sovereignties and people in the legislature, was a mere 'compromise.' This is a great and dangerous mistake." Assuming that proportional representation was the prevailing preference of the Convention, his proposal of "equal representation of each state in one branch of the legislature" had been "an original substantive proposition." Though not a new idea in itself—the Confederation had equal representation of the states—it was novel in conjunction with proportional representation in the other branch of the legislature. Dickinson reasoned that because America was such an extensive territory, it could only be governed "by a combination of republics, each retaining all the rights of supreme sovereignty, excepting such as ought to be contributed to the union." It was safest to have them represented equally in one branch of the legislature because if both branches had proportional representation based on population, as the Virginia Plan proposed, the states would "be annihilated."[84]

Dickinson's proposal thus solved the old problem of *imperium in imperio*—the once-unthinkable proposition of a state within a state—that had brought about the Revolution. When he had proposed in the *Farmer's Letters* almost twenty years earlier that such a thing might be possible, critics had scoffed. One of these was Benjamin Franklin, who now sat on the committee tasked with finding a solution to the representation problem. Despite Dickinson's clear description and rationale, Franklin still could not understand how such a bifurcated system could work. In his droll style, and violating the secrecy rule of the Convention, he regaled guests with an account of the proceedings, comparing America to a two-headed snake recently given to him. "If it was traveling among bushes," Franklin said, "and one head should choose to go on one side of the stem of a bush and the other head should prefer the other side, and that neither of the heads would consent to come back or give way."[85]

For his part, although Dickinson believed that "the preservation of the States in a certain degree of agency is indispensable," he worried more that the states would injure the Union than that the federal government would injure the states. He therefore proposed limits on the states, such as that the federal government should have some control over the state militias because "there might be a rebellion against the United States." He was also in favor of Congress's having the power to negate state laws. On the other hand, he argued that "no such power ought to exist" in the judicial branch. In other words, he disapproved of judicial review. "Judges were expositors of the Constitution" and should not "have authority to declare a law void." Neither should two or more states be able to combine into a new one without consent of the state and national legislatures.[86] Nonetheless, slavery remained on his mind. He believed that the biggest threat to the Union came from slavery, which, because of the three-fifths clause, was now bound up with representation. Dickinson feared that the Southern states would be encouraged to import more enslaved people and "Every Importation of Slaves will encrease the power of the State over others. This principle I wish to avoid."[87] Madison reported that "Mr. Dickenson considered it as inadmissible on every principle of honor & safety that the importation of slaves should be authorized to the States by the Constitution." Dickinson indeed believed that certain states could not be counted on to consider the best interest of the Union. He continued, "The true question was whether the national happiness would be promoted or impeded by the importation, and this question ought to be left to the National Govt. not to the States particularly interested." In response to Charles Cotesworth Pinckney of South Carolina, who defended slavery by citing examples in the ancient world and England's and France's approval of it, Dickinson said, "If England & France permit slavery, slaves are at the same time excluded from both those Kingdoms," which was a reference to the 1772 *Somerset* verdict declaring slavery incompatible with the common law. He added, "Greece and Rome were made unhappy by their slaves."[88]

Dickinson was appointed to the Committee of Slave Trade to consider the importation of enslaved people.[89] Although he wished to ban the trade immediately, some Southern states threatened to leave the Union if that happened. The committee therefore proposed giving the federal government the power to prohibit the trade after 1800.[90] Pinckney moved to change the date to 1808, and this motion passed.[91] Some Southern states, such as Virginia and North Carolina, had already banned importation, but hardly for altruistic reasons. Fewer imports would keep the prices of currently enslaved people high.

Dickinson wished that the word "slave" be included in the clause banning their importation rather than the vague mention of "such persons."[92] His reasoning was that otherwise, Americans' hypocrisy would be clear when the Constitution was published. "The omitting the <u>Word</u> will be regarded as an Endeavour to conceal a principle of which We are ashamed." His colleagues did not accept his change. Article 1, Section 9 of the Constitution omitted the word.[93]

Because transmission of information in the Early Republic was unreliable, Dickinson's actions with regard to slavery during the Convention received mixed reviews in the press. "A Countryman," probably Hugh Hughes, launched a full-throated condemnation of him for allegedly not living up to the Farmer's rhetoric. In two letters in the *New-York Journal* in November, he maintained that not only had Dickinson not worked against slavery, but he'd actually been instrumental in "opening a Trade which is a Disgrace to Humanity!"[94] Quoting the Farmer's first letter, in which Dickinson asserts that "Benevolence towards Mankind excites Wishes for their Welfare, and such Wishes endear the Means of fulfilling them," Hughes hit him hard: "What gracious Sentiments and how sweetly expressed!" "But what are Sentiments, or the tenderest Expressions, when not accompanied by corresponding Actions? They certainly render the Author a greater Object of our Pity, if not of Contempt." Then Hughes attacked Dickinson for his biggest antislavery achievement in the Convention: the prohibition of the slave trade, which Hughes considered a failure. "How is it possible, to reconcile the first Clause of the 9th Section, in the first Article of the new Constitution, with such universal Benevolence to all Mankind?" Hughes effectively charged Dickinson with virulent racism. "Will this Gentleman say," he queried, "that the Africans do not come within the Description of 'Mankind?' If he should, will he be believed?" He went on to malign Dickinson's character, claiming, "he was early instituted in Virtue, which, now, in advanced Life, he seems either to have forgotten or stifled."[95]

Although Hughes was mistaken about Dickinson's role in the Convention and his attitude towards Black people, that he would attack Dickinson specifically makes sense. As the Farmer, Dickinson had become an icon for liberty, and Americans continued to look to him to advance the cause for "all men." It is unclear why he assumed Dickinson was in favor of slavery or did not work against it. In addition to opposing it in America, Dickinson wrote to John Lloyd some years later, "When will the Cause of Humanity be adopted by Britain? How long will She dare, by national Acts to defy the Sovereign of the Universe? How much longer will they be the Inventor of Ranks, the Manufacturers of Miseries for their Brethren of Mankind?"[96] Britain obliged in 1807, convinced in part by Lloyd's publication *The Case for Our Fellow-Creatures, the Oppressed Africans.*

Other commentary on Dickinson was closer to the truth. After the Convention, the news that Dickinson had manumitted all his slaves—the only leading figure of the era to do so—made the newspapers. In "An Anecdote," a friend of Dickinson's asked, incredulous, whether the rumor was true. "Yes," replied Dickinson, "it is; and I *now* feel myself qualified to deliberate upon a form of government, for the preservation of liberty. For no man's understanding (added he) is *perfectly erect* on the subjects of liberty or govornment [*sic*], while he keeps a single slave." To this his friend replied, "May the same conduct be adopted by, and the same spirit pervaded all those citizens who should be called to share in the power and offices of the United States!"[97]

Dickinson made contributions to countless other matters in the Convention. Among them, he opposed qualifications for officeholding but advocated term limits for representatives; he offered that representatives and senators should receive equal pay but that they should not be paid by the states; he thought felonies were sufficiently defined by the common law and that ex post facto laws only applied to criminal cases; he thought money bills should be kept in the hands of the representatives of the people.[98] In an indirect contribution made years earlier, the case of *Respublica v. De Longchamps* (1784) in the Pennsylvania court—over which Dickinson had presided as president of the state—led the Convention to add a clause specifying that Congress, not the states, would define and punish offenses against the law of nations.[99]

The summer was not all work for the delegates. They enjoyed lively times at City Tavern, the Indian Queen, and other public houses. Some attended concerts and other public events. And they attended dinners and parties hosted by the elite of Philadelphia. One day, they left the heat of the State House to witness a novel sight. On August 22, the remaining members—several had already returned home—congregated on the banks of the Delaware River to see a demonstration of John Fitch's steamboat *Perseverance*, propelled by mechanical oars on either side. Although steam engines had been in commercial use for almost a century, this was the first American trial. The spectacle surely reinforced the delegates' sense that they were on the cusp of a *novus ordo seclorum*, a new order of the ages.

But, like Fitch, Americans would also require perseverance, for neither his contraption nor the Constitution was "a machine that would go of itself," as the poet James Russell Lowell later put it.[100] Rather, republics required concerted effort on the part of citizens to persist and flourish. Whether Americans would put in the effort and the patriotic self-sacrifice remained to be seen. Dickinson explained the fundamental principle of the American system. "*Each* individual must contribute such a share of his rights, as is necessary for attaining that security that is essential to freedom," he would later say, "and he is bound to make this contribution by the law of his nature; that is, by the command of his creator; therefore, *he must submit his will, in what concerns all, to the will of the whole society*." He must sacrifice for the common good. In return, he would gain freedom from fear, the protection and assistance of others, and tranquility of mind. The result would be that "*perfect liberty* better described in the Holy Scriptures, than any where else, in these expressions—'When *every* man shall *sit* under his vine, and under his fig-tree, and none shall make him afraid.'"[101]

On the one hand, a republic required virtuous citizens, with virtue defined as disinterestedness—the willingness to put aside self-interest to promote the common good. Virtuous citizens created a virtuous government. The "tranquility and prosperity" of republics, Dickinson explained, "have commonly been promoted, in proportion to the strength of their government for protecting *the worthy* against *the licentious.*" The Constitution was designed for this purpose. "The objects of government," he clarified, are "the safety and repose of the governed" and "the advancement of their happiness." It would mitigate against "errors, feuds, and frauds," as well as "wars, tumults, and uneasiness."

The Federal Convention itself exemplified how republicanism could function. Elected by the state legislatures, themselves elected by the freeholders, the delegates worked both for the interests of their respective constituents and the welfare of the Union. The Convention was "a labour of public love," and the Constitution was "a work formed with so much deliberation, so respectful and affectionate an attention to the interests, feelings, and sentiments of all United *America.*"[102] No delegate got everything he wanted. Everyone had to listen, compromise, and adjust his expectations. For example, two features of the new government that Dickinson sought concerned the executive. To avoid the dangers of monarchy or dictatorship, he proposed a plural executive, as there was in Pennsylvania. Those who wanted a single executive won the debate. He also wanted the executive to be elected directly by the people, "which he regarded as the best and purest source."[103] Instead, he had to settle for the Electoral College. In another provision early in the deliberations, he moved that the executive be subject to impeachment, a motion that failed—spectacularly, with only Delaware voting in the affirmative—on June 2. It wasn't until July 20 that the Convention returned to the subject and delegates agreed that this was a necessary provision in a similarly lopsided vote.[104] "The president will be no dictator," Dickinson observed with satisfaction. "He is removable and punishable for misbehaviour."[105]

During that arduous summer, tempers frayed, frustrations mounted, and doubts abounded. The delegates complained to friends and family at home about the slow process, the unpleasant conditions, and each other. Nonetheless, they were acutely aware of two things: first, that they were creating something that would serve posterity for decades, even centuries to come, and second, that their work was not perfect. They were fallible mortals whose efforts were inherently flawed. They "laboured to form the best plan they could," Dickinson knew. But given their shortcomings, none of them imagined their work was finished or etched in stone. "If all the wise men of antient and modern Times," he thought, "could be collected together for deliberation on the Subject, they could not form a Constitution or System of Government, that would not require future Improvements."[106] Therefore, framers of this system "provided for making at any time amendments on the authority of the people, without shaking the stability of the government."[107] The people could, he reiterated, "*amend* it, wherever it is *defective*."[108]

Here, whether they knew it or not, the delegates were following Quakers. In their early years, Friends had originated the practice of civil disobedience to amend the unwritten British constitution. At their first opportunity for creating their own government in 1681, not only did they write their constitution, but William Penn included a novel provision: an amendment clause. This way, as revelations came to the people of Pennsylvania, their legislators could introduce every salutary change to their laws as necessary. Now all Americans possessed the same power, one that would ensure peace, stability, and longevity of the Union. "Thus, by a gradual process," said Dickinson, "we may from time to time *introduce every improvement in our constitution*, that shall be suitable to our situation."[109] He believed that the United States would eventually be a "perfect body" that "corresponds with the gracious intentions of our maker towards us his creations."[110] Its purpose was to "advance" and "extend" public and individual happiness, which were "sacred concerns."[111]

Dickinson himself wanted several amendments to the Constitution, particularly concerning the election of the president. Since that office would not be chosen directly by the people, as he preferred, he proposed that "the Electors shall allways be chosen by the People—not by Legislatures." Also on this matter, he wanted "Frauds to be prevented." He sought another amendment that would make "the Power of deciding in disputed Elections of President & Vice President to be more clearly established." If it wasn't clear who the votes were for, "this Uncertainty may hereafter cause Convulsions in these States."[112] Time would tell whether these amendments would be necessary.

In both the Convention and future deliberations, Dickinson believed that "Experience must be our only guide; Reason may mislead us." Reason had not created "the singular & admirable mechanism of the English Constitution" nor "the absurd mode of trial by Jury." Instead, "Accidents probably produced these discoveries, and experience has given sanction to them."[113] This sentiment captured the imaginations first of Dickinson's colleagues and then posterity, who continue to quote him. To Dickinson, "experience" and "accidents" had meanings beyond the mundane. For him, they were imbued with religious significance. "Experience" included the experience of God's Light in the conscience, or revelation. And elsewhere he described trial by jury as a "Heaven-taught institution," suggesting that human "accidents" were actually part of the Divine plan for mankind.

None of the delegates, not even Dickinson, explicitly introduced religion into the proceedings or the Constitution. Experience had taught them how divisive it could be. The only provision they would agree on is that no religious test would be required in any oath or affirmation for office in the United States.[114] Citizens were free to practice any religion or none.

Learning from experience was why Dickinson believed Americans should be conversant with history. "History is entertaining and instructive; but," he cautioned, it was not simply a collection of facts or amusing stories. Americans must learn from the past. "One nation may become prudent and happy, by the errors and misfortunes of another."[115] Posterity might well learn from mistakes of the framers in this very Convention.

This process of amendment through experience unfolded with one of Dickinson's own contributions at the Convention. To ensure that the Constitution would serve as a promotor and protector of "the *worthy* against the *licentious*," he moved that state legislators should elect senators to the Congress. His rationale was that the people in general would elect the most virtuous among them to serve in the state governments. In keeping with what James Madison called "the filtration of talent" and Thomas Jefferson called the "natural aristocracy"—that the best people would rise up to positions of power—these virtuous men would then elect their betters to the Senate. The Convention adopted the idea and wrote it into the Constitution. Had Dickinson lived to see his provision in action, he would have been alarmed at how badly it failed, advancing the most corrupt men into the Senate. However, he might have rejoiced that Americans utilized the amendment clause in the Constitution to pass the Seventeenth Amendment in 1912, allowing senators to be elected directly by the people.

Over the months, both John and Polly suffered considerably from their separation as well as their respective ailments. Dickinson was absent from the deliberations for several days, sometimes for illness and other times to return briefly to Wilmington for business or family. It was not in Polly's nature to hide her true feelings. "I was not born," she wrote in a poem, "to carry smiles & sunshine in my face when discontent sits heavy at my heart."[116] But it was as hard on her husband to read her woeful letters. "You grieve Me with Complaints of my Absence, & more with Accounts of your Indisposition," he replied. Seeking to bolster her resolve for both their sakes, he continued, "It is one of the best Joys of my Soul to be loved by You, and I love You with the tenderest Affection— Let Us be content— Take Care of your Health— Be easy for a little While— and let Us trust in that Gracious Being from whom We receive so many unmerited Blessings Let Us strive to be happy here."[117] Dickinson believed it was their duty to God to be happy, and happiness was attained by serving others.[118]

Towards the end of the Convention, Dickinson's headaches were so severe that he was forced to depart on September 15, two days before it adjourned. But on the fourteenth he offered one last revision. Reviewing a clause to allow the capture and return of fugitive slaves, he objected to the language proposed by Madison and Wilson that stated, "no person legally held to service or labour in one state escaping into another." This clause effectively reversed the 1772 decision in *Somerset v. Stewart*, in which a British judge had ruled that a man enslaved in Massachusetts and transported to England could not be returned to slavery. In a futile attempt to resist the damage of this clause, Dickinson wanted "legally" struck because he thought it suggested that slavery "was legal in a moral view." He proposed instead that the words "under the laws thereof" be inserted after "state."[119] Dickinson had been expressing his belief that slavery should be illegal for more than a decade. In 1774, the comment "if they may be called laws," in his *Essay on the Constitutional Power of Great Britain*, explicitly questioned the validity of slavery laws in the colonies.[120] And in 1786 he wrote to John Lloyd about "the erring Law of our Country" that allowed enslavement.[121]

This small but significant change in the fugitive slave clause did nothing to prevent Americans from hunting down men and women fleeing to freedom and passing more laws to do so. George Washington himself spent the last years of his life relentlessly pursuing an enslaved woman who escaped his grasp into New Hampshire.[122] The seed the Farmer planted did take root, however, and it almost blossomed at a crucial moment. In 1856, as the issue of slavery was tearing the United States asunder, an enslaved man named Dred Scott sued his enslaver in the Supreme Court, claiming the man had carried him into free territory, which should, by law, make him free. When the court ruled against him, Justice Benjamin R. Curtis used Dickinson's language as one of the pillars of his dissent.[123]

With that final contribution, Dickinson departed Philadelphia, leaving his old friend George Read as proxy to sign his name to the document on September 17. With Dickinson advocating ratification, it is no coincidence that the State of Delaware became the first to do so on November 26, 1787. Others now repeated his solar system metaphor to advocate ratification in their states.[124]

At the end of this service for Delaware, Dickinson did something unusual. "It has been my intention," he explained to the state auditor, Eleazar McComb, "never to charge the State for any services." But times were difficult, and Dickinson believed the state had unfairly assessed his taxes. He was thus obliged to request payment for serving in Congress in 1779, as president in 1782, at the Annapolis Convention in 1786, and seventy-four days at the Constitutional Convention. McComb responded with a payment of £559, which Dickinson then donated to his charitable causes.[125]

Early in the new year, 1788, at home in Wilmington, Dickinson worked at his practice, managed his properties, and thought about philanthropic projects. By now the debate over ratification of the Constitution was in full swing, but it was not progressing as well as friends of the Constitution had hoped. The New Hampshire convention had adjourned without ratifying it, which put the entire movement in jeopardy. In the spring, Philadelphia merchant and keen promoter of republicanism John Vaughan traveled to Wilmington to prevail on Dickinson to again take up his pen for the American cause. Dickinson agreed, but on the condition that his identity would not be revealed. Dickinson later explained to Tench Coxe, a Pennsylvania politician, that he "did not wish to obtrude my Name in such momentous Business."[126] He thus began another series of letters, which he initially titled "Delaware Letters." He eventually adopted the penname "Fabius," under which these essays would be published.[127] Like his *Farmer's Letters* twenty years prior, these were directed to ordinary Americans, encouraging them to join in the debate. "What concerns all, should be considered by all," he now said more explicitly, "and individuals may injure a whole society, by not declaring their sentiments. It is therefore not only their *right*, but their *duty*, to declare them." He continued, "Let every one freely speak, what he really thinks, but with so sincere a reverence for the cause he ventures to discuss as to use the utmost caution, lest he should lead into errors, upon a point of such sacred concern as *the public happiness*."[128]

The letters explain the basic functions of the Constitution, along with the principles behind those functions, in terms that "unpolished but honest-hearted" Americans would understand. He also addressed the qualities American citizens should possess and fears the opponents of the Constitution harbored. His arguments were bolstered with lessons from history ancient and modern, as well as his religious principles. Overall, he sought to impress upon his countrymen that they must "cling to Union as the political Rock of our Salvation."[129]

This union would produce remarkable changes for Americans. Before independence, Dickinson did not believe that the people were "proper for sovereigns." His fears were justified during the Revolution, when pure democracy was suddenly unleashed on Pennsylvania and democratic despotism ensued, victimizing dissenters with violations of their basic civil rights. He still had grave reservations about whether certain of his countrymen could wield their liberties responsibly. But now that America was a "democratical republic," Dickinson embraced and promoted the idea. The United States Constitution would effect the "emancipation of one class of her citizens from the yoke of their superiors—A relief of other classes from the injuries and insults of the great." There would be "people of every rank, in a more flourishing condition . . . than they ever were" and more than anyone "thought it possible for them to attain."[130] He then clarified his understanding of the first principle written in the Declaration of Independence. "The very establishment of this freedom involves Equality; and this equal freedom is like Light. It is pure; it is gentle; it comes from Heaven; it gives to Earth its Value; and everyone enjoys the whole of it."[131]

Under the new Constitution, Dickinson hoped America would become a beacon of enlightened policy and practice and a force for good in the world. "Delightful are the prospects that will open to the view of United *America*," Fabius wrote effusively. "Her sons well prepared to defend their own happiness, and ready to relieve the misery of others—her fleets formidable, but only to the unjust—her revenue sufficient, yet unoppressive—her commerce affluent, without debasing—peace and plenty within her borders—and the glory that arises from a proper use of power, encircling them."[132] What system anywhere in the world could rival it? The Constitution would diffuse "the blessings of *equal liberty and common prosperity* over myriads of the human race."[133]

To allay fears that it would contain the "oppression of a monarchy or aristocracy," he repeatedly returned to the centerpiece of the new American government—"*the power of the people*." Even the Senate, that quasi-aristocratic body that Dickinson intended to resemble the House of Lords, would be "controulable by the people" and "THE WILL OF THE PEOPLE" would have "a decisive influence over the whole." Bad administrators would fall before "the *supreme sovereignty* of the people," he reiterated. "The wit of man never invented such an antidote against monarchical and aristocratial [*sic*] projects, as a *strong combination* of truly *democratical* republics."

But with great power comes great responsibility, which Fabius also sought to impress upon his readers: "IT IS THEIR DUTY TO WATCH, AND THEIR RIGHT TO TAKE CARE, THAT THE CONSTITUTION BE PRESERVED." Americans, as individuals and as a unified people, must possess certain traits. The *Fabius Letters* were effectively a lengthy definition of what it meant to be an American. His instruction about the Constitution was laced with hints and examples, both ancient and modern, for how they should behave. Americans would obviously be patriotic. In case his meaning were unclear, he specified that an American should have vigor and union of reason and passion to engage in robust deliberations about the nation's welfare. These deliberations would be informed by the citizen's enlightened spirit, experienced intelligence, and impartiality. An American should conduct him or herself in relation to others with benevolence, humility, soundness of sense, honesty of heart, and simplicity of manners. As a people, Americans should have "wisdom & virtue enough, to manage their affairs, with as much prudence and affection of one for another, as the antients did."[134]

These were the desirable traits. Fabius made clear that there were also undesirable traits that could lead to the downfall of the union. He was compelled to acknowledge them because, he said, "flattery is treason; and error, destruction." These traits included thirst of empire, folly, and wickedness. Dickinson worried especially about how Americans would manage their wealth. The pitfalls were many: luxury, ambitiousness, and avarice. "The abuse of prosperity," he said, "is rebellion against Heaven."[135] Injustice in wealth could return them to the British system they had just thrown off. And, he added, "If ever monarchy or aristocracy appear in this country, it must be in the hideous forms of despotism." But tyranny could come from democracy as well. "By this animating, presiding will of the people," he therefore clarified, "is meant a reasonable, not a distracted will. When frensy seizes the mass, it would be madness to think of their happiness, that is, of their freedom." One faction was liable to tyrannize another, as he had witnessed in Pennsylvania. He thus encouraged Americans in the right direction, planting a seed that, though far from true in 1787, he hoped his readers would make reality in the future: "Where was there ever a confederacy," he asked, "in which, the people were so drawn together by religion, blood, language, manners and customs, undisturbed by former feuds or prejudices?"[136]

For Dickinson, more than any other leading figure, nation-building was a profoundly moral endeavor. Although his generation agreed on this point, none engaged the public as intensely as he did. To forge Americans into one virtuous people, Fabius advocated something he had long thought necessary: a "reformation of manners," or *morals*. As president of Delaware and then Pennsylvania, he had issued proclamations on suppressing vice and immorality in hopes of instigating such a reformation. Liberal reformers in Great Britain were presently engaged in a similar endeavor. In June of that year, the king had issued his own proclamation on vice and immorality, which was proposed by the abolitionist William Wilberforce. Now Fabius insisted, "History sacred and prophane tells us, that, CORRUPTION OF MANNERS IS THE VERY BASIS OF SLAVERY."[137]

Dickinson wanted greater adherence to religion, but not just any religion. What he had in mind was not the intolerant Anglican or Congregational sort that preached salvation of the few and damnation of the many and forced dissenters to conform to their ways. It was not the irrational enthusiasm and anti-intellectualism of the evangelical churches. Neither was it the militantly violent and bigoted Presbyterian kind, such as the Paxton Boys practiced, that condoned persecution of other faiths and the slaughter of innocents in God's name. Rather, what Fabius imagined was an enlightened faith that acknowledged the potential for the Divine Light in all humans regardless of physical or social characteristics or place of birth; a faith that welcomed the light of learning through literature and science as a complement to the Divine Light; and a faith that was enacted in benevolence to one's fellow creatures and, above all else, admonished believers to do unto others as they would be done by. These characteristics could be present in any religion but were most often associated with Quakerism.

Yet Dickinson would not press even that religion on his fellow Americans. As salutary as Quakerism often was, he had never agreed with all of its tenets, and he remained unaffiliated with any church. Americans must choose their faiths for themselves under a government that did not privilege any one over the others. Like his forebears, Dickinson did not want Americans to become

Quakers, only to act like Quakers. Unlike in Quaker Pennsylvania, religiously based laws would not be forced upon them. The Constitution and the government it created were secular.

Although Dickinson continued to believe that church and state ought to be kept "distinct and apart," he did believe that "there is a Relation between the Principles of Religion and the Principles of Civil Society." He thus urged following the Bible, but not all of it, and not literally. Used correctly, "the Bible is the most republican Book that was ever written."[138] Its stories were useful "fables," and he urged daily readings in the New Testament.[139] "*Humility* and *benevolence* must take place of *pride* and *overweening selfishness*," he instructed. "Reason, then rising above these mists, will discover to us, that we cannot be true to ourselves, without being true to others—that to be solitary, is to be wretched—that to love our neighbours as ourselves, is to love ourselves in the best manner—that to give, is to gain—and, that we never consult our own happiness more effectually, than when we most endeavour to correspond with the Divine designs, by communicating happiness, as much as we can, to our fellow-creatures."[140] Although throughout his life Dickinson himself had found inspiration in a broad range of sources, including secular poetry and literature, the ancient pagan authors, and non-Christian religion, he knew that many Americans possessed only one book: the Bible.

Fabius also anticipated a significant objection to ratification that many Americans would have, namely that there was no "bill of rights" accompanying the Constitution. Enumerating selected rights on paper, however, would actually put other rights in jeopardy. Some ignorant or malevolent person might be encouraged to claim that these enumerated rights were the only ones individuals possessed. Dickinson's arguments on this head echoed his 1766 *Address to the Committee of Correspondence in Barbados*. There he said that rights "are not annexed to us by parchments and seals. They are created in us by the decrees of Providence, which establish the laws of our nature. They are born with us; exist with us; and cannot be taken from us by any human power, without taking our lives. In short, they are founded on the immutable maxims of reason and justice."[141] Now he argued that human rights would not be obtained by a written bill of rights. "They and all other rights must be preserved, by soundness of sense and honesty of heart. Compared with *these*, what are a bill of rights, or any characters drawn upon paper or parchment, those frail remembrancers?"[142]

Dickinson sent the letters one at a time to his friend Vaughan in Philadelphia, who rushed them into print.[143] In Philadelphia, the first number appeared on April 12 and the last of the nine on May 1. Many other publications appeared, both for and against the new Constitution. Perhaps the most sophisticated was a set of eighty-five *Federalist Papers* that appeared in the New York papers. Though they gave the most thorough and erudite explanations of virtually every aspect of the Constitution, they didn't reach much beyond the elite of New York. By contrast, the *Fabius Letters* appeared in the newspapers of at least seven states from South Carolina to New Hampshire, including three separate times in Philadelphia, once with the *Farmer's Letters*.[144] Vaughan was very happy with their reception, reporting that they "are admired by all who wish to be *injoind to do right* & Strongly approved of by men of weight & reflection."[145] Among these men were soon-to-be President Washington, who exclaimed to Vaughan, "The Writer of the pieces signed Fabius, whoever he is, appears to be master of His Subject; he treats it with Dignity, & at the Same Time expresses himself in such a manner as to render it intelligible to every Capacity." He hoped the *Letters* would get a wide circulation.[146] Caesar A. Rodney, nephew of Dickinson's late friend and later the attorney general of the United States, presented the *Letters* to British Whig jurist Thomas Erskine, writing that Dickinson "cannot be suspected of any other than the purest motives for the Good of his Country."[147]

Despite Vaughan's plea to Dickinson to divulge his authorship, his identity as Fabius was unknown until he republished the letters under his name in 1797.[148] Dickinson was eager to avoid reviving the celebrity he had once experienced. The following year, he was much discomfited when Philadelphia editor Matthew Carey took the liberty of reprinting in his magazine *American Museum* the 1768 tribute paid the Farmer by the Society of Fort St. Davids along with Dickinson's answer. He had been mortified in 1768; it was no better now. "There was an Indelicacy in its Appearance that wounded my Mind," Dickinson explained to Carey, "& for which the Regret of a whole Life cannot sufficiently atone." He requested that Carey refrain from publishing anything further about him in the *Museum*.[149] He couldn't escape all of it. In 1788, Philip Freneau, later known as the "poet of the American Revolution," dedicated a poem to the Farmer, writing, "Thou DICKINSON! the patriot and the sage, / How much we owed to your convincing page."[150]

By June 1788, the Constitution had been ratified by enough states to go into effect. It had not been in place long before a significant development threatened to undermine the new frame of government—the permanent establishment of a new capital city. After Alexander Hamilton had attempted to instigate a mutiny of Continental soldiers so that Congress would have an excuse to leave Philadelphia, it had spent several nomadic years in various other cities—Princeton, Annapolis, Trenton, New York City, and then back to Philadelphia in 1790. At the Federal Convention in Philadelphia, delegates recalled the near mutiny of 1783 and largely agreed that the seat of government should not be in a particular state but rather in a district unto itself, which was therefore written into the Constitution. In the first Federal Congress, Southerners, including Thomas Jefferson and James Madison, wanted the capital to be in the South, but they didn't have the votes. Hamilton's main goal was that the federal government would assume the debts of the states, which many thought would give it too much power. Neither did he have the votes. The men struck a deal, called the Compromise of 1790. Congress then passed the Residence Act in July 1790, which placed the seat of government in a district carved out of Maryland and Virginia. It would be called "Washington in the District of Columbia."

Dickinson was glad for the assumption of debt by the federal government, but he opposed locating the United States capital in the South. In a range of concerns, near the top of his list of ten queries on the subject was "Should the seat of Government for a free people, be fixed in a Part of their Territory, where the number of Slaves exceeds that of Freemen?" It would make the national hypocrisy that much more glaring. And believing as he did that slavery corrupted masters and turned them into tyrants, he was convinced that a Southern capital seemed an impossible atmosphere for disinterested and democratic leaders. Dickinson had other concerns as well, including that the remote location would "have a tendency to estrange them from the just Regards for the sense of their Country" and that a city with greater commerce would be preferable. Also, Dickinson had grave concerns that "the prodigious Magnificence that is to be displayed in the fœderal City, will have a baneful Influence upon many Persons, by indisposing their Minds to Republican Principles and Manners." How could Americans live the simple and frugal lives that Fabius recommended when surrounded by grandeur?[151] Only time would tell.

The final chapter in the American Revolution was the ratification in 1791 of the Bill of Rights. To secure ratification by the states, twelve amendments were made to the Constitution, with the first ten amendments naming certain fundamental individual rights. But this bill differed from documents traditionally given that name. It was not something separate from the

Constitution, like the English Bill of Rights or those in the various states, but rather amendments to that document. Moreover, the Tenth Amendment went directly to Dickinson's concerns in the *Fabius Letters*. It specified that the enumeration of some rights did not preclude the existence of others, and these were reserved to the states and individuals.

Now, the *novus ordo seclorum* truly began. The Old World hierarchy that was the Great Chain of Being was dealt a deathblow that reverberated around the world. The idea that all *men* were created equal and possessed inherent rights was the beginning of the end of the exclusive rule of white, propertied, Protestant men. Now, in theory, there was the possibility that other sorts of men might gain control over their own lives and fortunes. But for now, it was still only an idea. And still, those white, propertied, Protestant men retained their grip on the levers of power, finding reasons to deny protections and control to those unlike them—those who were poor, non-Christian, dark complected, or female were still subordinated. White men no longer thought in terms of the *rights of Englishmen*, but most still thought in terms of the *rights of man*. Only a few contemplated *human rights*.

But now that the ideas of rights and equality were stated for all to know, the contagion of liberty would spread. Some Americans rejoiced at this, while others would do everything in their power to conserve the old order. As America grew older and political factions hardened into formal parties, their very platforms would represent this divide. Like all of the Founders, Dickinson's feelings about the contagion were mixed. Among the leading figures, however, he stood out in that he generally facilitated the spread of liberty to those unlike him—although as the republic suffered growing pains, his limits were tested. In all cases, he tried to follow his conscience for what was best for America.

14

"I love Mankind"

A Citizen Activist, 1791–1799

After the Federal Convention, Dickinson aimed to retire from public life, once and for all. Although he was continually pressed to accept various offices, he was usually able to decline. In July 1788, Tench Coxe of Pennsylvania urged him to stand for the Senate immediately.[1] But he was much engaged with other work. In June, he had become the leading charter member of the Library Company of Wilmington, which he hoped would do as much good as the Library Company of Philadelphia had for the inhabitants of that city.[2] And he and Polly had many other projects afoot.

As he resumed his focus on faith and good works, Dickinson became a Quaker in almost everything but name. In later years, he would reminisce that it was his daughter Sally who inspired him. As he recalled, when she was around twelve, he asked her whether she would like dancing lessons, something all fashionable young ladies desired. He offered to bring in a dancing master to instruct her. When she hesitated, he suggested she think about it and let him know. Later she returned and proclaimed, "if Father pleases, I had much rather be a Friend." Dickinson was "mortified" to realize that his young daughter was more sober-minded than he. Her denial of herself this pleasure and other virtuous conduct "powerfully struck his mind."[3] In truth, however, his turn towards Quakerism began much earlier, under Polly's influence. By the mid-1780s, he was actively adopting Quaker priorities for benevolence and justice, putting his professional expertise and vast wealth to work for those less fortunate. By the mid-1790s, he was outwardly indistinguishable from the Quakers. He wore plain clothes, used the plain speech, and attended meeting several times per week. John may have won the battle to have a civil marriage ceremony, but Polly won the war for his soul.

As Dickinson's connection to Quakerism became more apparent to outsiders, Quakers increasingly looked to him to help realize their goals of social justice and welfare. They urged him to join them formally to become a Quaker in name as well as in deed.[4] Dr. Nathaniel Luff, who as a young medical student had been inspired by Dickinson to join the militia in 1775, was now his friend and said, "I could most earnestly wish my dear friend (Dickinson) would claim his privilidge amongst the People called Quakers: for he is growing Old, & I sincerely pray, he may end his days in peace."[5] But even as he resembled Quakers more outwardly, there were other signs that Dickinson's faith was still not perfectly in step with Quakerism, confirming in his mind that he would never be fully united with them.

He believed in a core theological tenet of Quakerism: "that any Body of Christians may form themselves into a Church; and that the Ministers by them approved and admitted, if really pious then are true Ministers of the Gospel."[6] He had also fully absorbed the doctrine of the universality of God's Light within and the measure of spiritual equality that this universality bestowed upon believers. Now, after the passage of almost sixty years, Dickinson finally sought information about his father's status within the Society of Friends. Despite Samuel's falling out with the meeting over his daughter's "disorderly marriage" to an Anglican, he had not been disowned.[7] For Samuel's son, the most obvious and profound area of difference with Friends was in their pacifism. Although Dickinson had always and still believed that peace was paramount and war should be a last resort, he was more of a pragmatic pacifist than a principled one. He believed ardently in the necessity of citizen militias.

Moreover, Dickinson found Quakers too rigid doctrinally, as when they adhered to certain testimonies too fixedly, losing sight of the meaning behind them. He agreed with Quakers that although "Christianity is an active, affectionate, and social Religion," in order to fulfill our "Duties to our fellow Creatures, it requires separation from them, though enjoining 'that we be not conformable to the World.'" He would cite Romans 12:2 on that point. But "in following the testimonies, the utmost Attention is needed, least distinction from others by plainness of Manners & Customs assume the place of Virtues, and become snares." He also objected when Quakers privileged the Light over reason.[8]

These theological differences could potentially interfere with the Dickinsons' desire to work with Friends on their benevolent projects. They continued pressing their plan, expressed to James Pemberton, for founding a Quaker boarding school. When results were not forthcoming by 1788, Dickinson wrote to another kinsman, Samuel Pleasants, "I find, that no Measure has been yet taken by Friends, with respect to the institution concerning which we have so frequently conferred."[9] It gradually became clear that the Dickinsons and the Quakers had different expectations of the curriculum. The Quakers were inclined to shun the liberal arts in favor of a "guarded education" for their youth. Unlike many Protestants, Quakers did not believe in original sin, but they did believe in inevitable sin. Their aim was to protect children from sinful influences for as long as possible. To them, this meant restricting education to a curriculum that excluded subjects and branches of learning they deemed unnecessary and detrimental to morals. As his kinswoman Debby Norris Logan later explained, Dickinson "was the enlightened and persistent advocate of public education at a time when . . . the Quakers hesitated for a long time to accept the Dickinsons munificent gift." The Quakers worried that "lest while knowledge might come, religion would linger."[10]

Some Quakers imagined that Dickinson was simply not humble enough before Christ to understand the purpose of education. Because God, Anne Emlen schooled Dickinson, "doth not distribute his Talents amongst Mankind, but according as they are capable of improving them," they should not "bestow an abundance of manure, on a barren Soil, that can never repay the Cultivator for this labor & expence." Emlen also wanted Dickinson to join the Religious Society of Friends, but, she thought, "Perhaps human Wisdom is not yet sufficiently reduced in Subjection to the 'Simplicity that is in Christ' to make thee as yet willing to stoop to the foolishness of the Cross, sometimes appearing in the Quaker."[11]

Dickinson objected to this line of reasoning. He had more faith in the children than did Emlen. "Some worthy persons," he chided, "slight learning too much, because wonderful Acts have been performed by illiterate Men"—which he then crossed out and replaced with the gender-neutral "Persons." "It should be allways recollected," he reminded Samuel Pleasants, "that these Persons were particularly called and qualified for particular Purposes." He believed that "Learning & Religion will be found perfectly to agree together." More specifically, he added, "Hypotheses or counterfeits substituted in the place of truths, have done unspeakable injury; and by these vanities the world is still deluded." He wanted them to avoid "'Foolish Questions,' 'Fables and endless genealogies,' 'Prophane and vain babblings, oppositions of science falsely so called'—and 'Winds of doctrine,' the apostle Paul has justly condemned; and these, to be sure, should be consigned to perpetual oblivion."[12]

Dickinson disagreed with the Quaker approach to education for theological reasons. He believed that children should study the "natural, moral, and revealed Truths" in order to "'do good' to their Fellow Creatures." If a proper approach were not taken, they could be misled, either by the skeptical philosophers of Europe or proponents of Quaker pedagogy. On the one hand, "Scepticism or Pride in rejecting what should be admitted, and," on the other, "Enthusiasm or Confusion in admitting what should be rejected, are perhaps equally adverse to the Acquisition of sound Knowledge." The Quakers' assumption that one truth is "injurious to another," he believed, was "adverse to the Acquisition of sound Knowledge."[13] "'The bringing Life and Immortality to Light,'[14] was never designed to supersede preceding universal Obligations: and the Principles of our Religion, admirable as they are, were never intended to degrade Reason. There is no such Incongruity in the divine Dispensations."[15] He cited the works of early Quakers William Penn and Robert Barclay in his attempts to convince Friends of his position. "If this subject be fully considered," he concluded, "it would be evident, that such a system of education may be adopted as will produce a more extensive diffusion of blessing public & private, than could at first view be apprehended."[16]

The following year, 1789, there finally seemed to be movement on the school. Owen Biddle, a Quaker carpenter and master builder, sent him an essay for his review,[17] which he published the next year, called *A Plan for a School On an Establishment Similar to that at Ackworth in Yorkshire, Great-Britain.* According to Dickinson's direction, it contained lengthy passages from a Friends' account of that school, along with one of the orphanage in Germany, followed by the plan for an American version.[18] Dickinson exclaimed, "I will confess that my Heart is set upon its Establishment." But, perhaps because there was still disagreement about the curriculum, he added, "There seems to be a strange Lukewarmness & Indifference [among Friends] where hardly to be expected."[19] As an inducement to them to continue, the Dickinsons deeded the Yearly Meeting a valuable lot on Seventh Street near Market in Philadelphia.[20] They intended the gift to be much larger, but Friends' delays caused them to worry it would never happen, so they put their resources to other uses.[21]

While Dickinson waited for Friends to act, he instructed his own children in Quaker principles. "Guard against Levity, vulgar Pleasures, Rudeness or Frivolity in Look, Word, or Action to any human Being," he admonished ten-year-old Maria, who required a stricter hand than her sister. "Lessen not the Happiness of thy fellow Creatures: but strive to encrease it."[22] He also stipulated that should he die, Phil should become their guardian, and

Dickinson "earnestly desired they may be educated in the Principles of Friends, but not with any other Restrictions respecting Conversation & Dress than those which Modesty & Moderation require."[23] In other words, they would not be required to use the plain speech or plain dress, testimonies that Dickinson believed verged on dogma if taken too far.

Having found what he believed to be the key to his earthly and eternal happiness, Dickinson returned to an idea he had held since he studied law at the Middle Temple. Seeing the corruption around him during the elections in London, he wished for a reformation of manners by a return to "an old fashioned Religion." Now, to advance the "Prospects of public Felicity," he wrote to Benjamin Rush that "It is my ardent Wish, that the People of The United States may make as great a Reformation in Manners and Customs, as they have made in Government." He rejected the notion that the old ways of Europe, of luxury and inequality, should govern Americans. He believed that observing and following Truth "is the Duty of a Nation professing Liberty of Action." Simplicity in all things was paramount. "Let us not Weakly, and meanly, and treacherously, and impiously neglect the Opportunity given to Us by God, of shewing by our Example to our Fellowcitizens of the World, how Freemen ought to live."[24] Rush was so taken with Dickinson's exhortation that he submitted the letter for publication to the *Universal Asylum, and Columbian Magazine* so many more Americans would see it.

The following year, 1791, a distressing episode occurred that surely vindicated Dickinson's sense that an American reformation was necessary. It also demonstrated that he could be even stricter than Friends were about adhering to principles of their faith. He sold a plot of land in Philadelphia to a man name William Geisse on Geisse's assurance that he would not use it for performing plays. But no sooner had the deed been transferred than actors were on site. Although Dickinson had enjoyed attending the theater as a young man, he had grown to share strict Quakers' objection to the pastime. Theater productions tended to encourage the very vice and immorality he had tried to prevent as president of Delaware and then Pennsylvania. He was thus horrified when he discovered Geisse had deceived him.

With the support of staunch Quakers in Philadelphia, he filed a suit against Geisse. But as it became clear that Dickinson would not prevail in court, he began to relent. The Quakers, however, had no intention of backing down. Their plan was for Dickinson to use his considerable wealth to win the case by drawing it out indefinitely and eventually compelling Geisse to accept defeat. Dickinson refused. "I cannot seek for a victory from the subterfuge of

Procrastination," he protested.[25] If he could not win the case on the merits, he would not "distress his Opponents, by the Weight of my Purse. I have never acted, and will never act in this Manner."[26] In making their pleas, the Quakers ran up against the immovable wall of Dickinson's principles.[27] Much to the Quakers' disappointment, Dickinson conceded defeat. Yet in this he was exercising a core belief of Quakerism—one that Quakers themselves seemed to be neglecting—namely that process was as important as the outcome, and the ends do not justify the means.

The year 1791 brought hardships to the Dickinson family in the form of ill health and death. Phil's wife Mary died in August, causing Dickinson to wish "We could have spent more Time together."[28] Phil soon remarried— Rebecca Cadwalader, Mary's sister.[29] The state of Polly's health was also worrisome. She hadn't been well since she returned home from visiting family in Philadelphia in October 1787. Later Sally would mark that moment as "the commencement of that lingering state of ill health which was assigned her." She suffered much but did so with "Christian resignation."[30]

For his part, Dickinson had not been successful in staying out of public office since the Federal Convention and had relented to serve as judge on the Delaware Court of Errors and Appeals, which was arduous work. He had to write notes as detailed as those he wrote as a barrister. Finally, however, headaches and back aches caused him to resign towards the end of 1791.[31] In addition to these physical ailments, Dickinson suffered from bouts of depression, which would only be exasperated by an inability to work and a dispute with an unscrupulous thespian. Birthdays could prompt melancholy, as they were a time to take stock of his life's achievements. On November 11, 1791, he wrote to Polly, "Next Day after Tomorrow I enter my Sixtieth Year. How long I have lived, and how uselessly. Inattention is the Destruction of Opportunities."[32] Should he desire them, there were more opportunities for usefulness forthcoming.

By this time, Delawareans had come to realize that their state constitution, written in 1776 by Thomas McKean, was not sufficient for their needs. As the citizens of many states did during these years, they decided they must have a new one. Among the problems legislators found were that "the general departments thereof are so blended together, and improperly arranged, as to prevent an impartial, beneficial, and energetic cooperation."[33] On September 8, the Delaware legislature had thus motioned that there should be a new constitutional convention, which would begin on November 29, either to amend the old constitution or to adopt an entirely new one.[34]

Dickinson attempted to avoid service by preemptively declining nomination.[35] The voters in New Castle County elected him anyway, and he duly joined the convention at Dover. Its first order of business was to elect a president. Rejecting secret ballots, it elected Dickinson by a voice vote on December 1, after which it elected other officers and established rules for conducting business. Next, the members sought to determine whether the 1776 constitution needed only amendments or to be replaced entirely. To that end, they appointed a special committee. But when those members disagreed, the entire convention decided to deliberate and refer only general propositions to the committee for their instructions. Beginning on December 6 and over the next ten days as the convention debated each point of a new constitution, Dickinson would vacate the president's chair and be replaced temporarily so he could participate actively in the deliberations. Despite feeling poorly, he became the most active member, making or seconding more motions than any other.[36] On the seventeenth, the special committee brought in an entirely new draft constitution, and the convention then worked through each article and section.[37]

In the first session, which lasted until December 31, the members took only one break from the proceedings, to hear a memorial from the Religious Society of Friends. Quaker Warner Mifflin entered the chamber on December 22. A few years earlier, he had praised Dickinson for liberating those he enslaved and had no doubt been one of the Friends who prevailed upon him to bring a bill for the gradual abolition of slavery to the Delaware House. Now he read a petition to the convention with two concerns. First, he believed that conscientious objectors should be exempted both from military service and the fines levied against those who could not, from religious scruples, serve. Second, he spoke at length on "the natural Rights of Man" and "the present debased state of the Blacks," who are subjected to "grievous, inhuman, and unchristian suffering of being torn from nearest connections as brute beasts, and in chains sent to more barbarous climes." He called it "savage cruelty." He then quoted the Declaration of Independence to his fellow members, hoping to prick their consciences. If they neglected to outlaw slavery, "it will be a disgrace to the state in the eyes of the nations upon earth; and that it will be a Rottenness in the Constitution." God's wrath might even overthrow the government.[38] At some point, likely after Mifflin's memorial, someone motioned to declare all persons born after the passage of the constitution free, leaving it to the legislature to determine the regulation of the care and education of Black people.[39] This was Dickinson's preference, but the motion went nowhere, and the convention adjourned until May 29 to allow the public time to consider the draft constitution.

In the spring session, Warner Mifflin attended almost every day.[40] On the morning of May 30, he was again allowed to address the convention on the same topics on behalf of the Quaker meeting with a memorial signed by James Pemberton. After again quoting to them the key line from the Declaration of Independence—"We hold these truths to be self-evident, that all men are created equal, that they are endowed by their Creator with certain unalienable rights, that among these are Life, Liberty and the Pursuit of happiness"—he suggested that they redress the grievances of Black people. That would give the world "a laudable proof on your part, that the declarations which have been extensively circulated in favour of civil liberty, and the natural rights of men, are not a mere empty sound of expressions, calculated for partial temporary purposes only."[41]

By now, Dickinson had been thinking about Black rights for many years. Even before he had freed all the Black people he enslaved, he was thinking much more expansively. During his Pennsylvania presidency, as he considered "Strengthening & improving our Union," he also pondered the "propriety of making Blacks freeholders & giving them Votes."[42] Currently, vague language in the new 1790 Pennsylvania constitution meant some Black people, those who were bold enough, were now exercising the franchise.[43] Perhaps this "accident" was, like trial by jury, an experience that Americans could use as a guide. As a Quaker fellow traveler, Dickinson believed there was "that of God" in the consciences of all humans, which made them spiritually equal. Civil equality should follow. His intent in providing education for Black children was that one day Black people could possess enough virtue to become full citizens. He planned to write an essay on the topic. In a note to himself he jotted: "Slavery to be gradually abolished—treat this fully!"[44]

Dickinson had a strategy for securing the abolition of slavery in the constitution. It involved first allaying white fears about potential Black power, and it was a characteristically Dickinsonian move—extend an olive branch to one's opponents and sacrifice lesser principles for greater ones. On June 6, the only day Mifflin wasn't present, Dickinson motioned that "none but white persons shall hereafter be capable of becoming freeholders within this state."[45] If this provision passed, it would reverse the single most important right that Black people were allowed to exercise in Delaware and that was protected by the 1787 law for which Warner Mifflin had worked so hard.[46] Although sacrificing property ownership would undoubtedly be a blow to Black welfare, it would also remove the single biggest obstacle to a provision for abolition in the constitution: the white fear of Black people wielding political power. This choice may not have been hard for Dickinson. After all, under this new constitution, property requirements for white people to vote had been abolished.

Subsequent deliberations did not go as Dickinson hoped. Some members wished to postpone the discussion of Black property ownership and instead rush into debating abolition. Richard Bassett, a Methodist from Kent County who had ushered through the 1787 law, and Robert Haughey, a Presbyterian from New Castle County, who was also one of the wealthiest men in Delaware and enslaved fifty-seven people, motioned that no one could be enslaved in Delaware or transported from the state as a slave except with permission from a court. Also, after a certain year to be determined later, no one could be born into slavery in the state. Thinking that the discussion of abolition was premature if Black property ownership weren't first restricted, Dickinson voted against having the discussion.[47]

When members of the convention returned from their midday break, they again took up Dickinson's motion to prevent Black people from owning property. But first he moved for a change to his initial proposal. He qualified it so that only white people should be allowed to purchase property in Delaware and that Black people could hold property if they had inherited it, if it had been given to them, or if they had owned it before the present constitution was written. The motion didn't pass.[48] Thus Black people retained the right to purchase and own property, and the topic of abolition was dropped.

That same day, James Pemberton wrote to Dickinson, eager to know the results of their deliberations in regard to the Quakers' petition. He was "hoping the subject matter will obtain the most Serious deliberation" and reiterated the Quakers' concerns about conscientious objection and slavery. He had reason for hope. He enclosed some papers showing "the alarm, which has taken place in Britain on this Subject, which presages the downfall of the horrid traffic."[49] Friends throughout the Delaware Valley were awaiting good news.

The result of the convention was a new constitution, one that remained in place for more than one hundred years. It now looked much like other state constitutions and the Federal Constitution. Although some similarities remained from the 1776 constitution, new provisions were added and old ones omitted. Now there was no religious test for officeholding and no right to bear arms, but there was a right to assemble. It also strengthened the executive branch and created more separation between the branches. There was a significant overhaul of the judicial system. The 1792 version also retained a key institution from the colonial era: a Chancery Court. Dickinson's old tutor and friend William Killen became Delaware's first chancellor. Rights of conscience and of Black men were not, however, fully protected.

On the last day of the convention, Mifflin, furious at Dickinson, handed him a letter. "Thou art as great an enemy to the cause of righteousness as is in that body," it said. He believed that if some random Presbyterian—Presbyterians were frequently the Quakers' enemies—had been in Dickinson's seat, "something would have been done in both cases." Dickinson was "in the way" of progress. "Those who come nearest to the truth and are not in it, and profess it, are its greatest enemies," said Mifflin.[50]

After the convention, Dickinson wrote to Pemberton to give an account of himself and the proceedings. Although, he began, "It is and has been for some Time past my earnest Concern, that Slavery may be gradually and totally abolished," he said he found his colleagues intractable on the issue. He explained how the debate had unfolded in the convention, first with abolition's being proposed in the first session to a poor reception, and then the Friends' memorial against slavery with the same result. At that juncture, the constitutional dilemma became clear: "Some of Us thought," explained Dickinson, "that any Prunings of this Tree of bitter fruits, would only strengthen it and make it last the longer. Alleviations of Slavery by the Convention, would have been constitutional Sanctions of it." The discussion then turned to enforcing the existing laws that prohibited the importation of slaves.[51]

The problem, as Dickinson saw it, was that the citizens of Delaware were not fully conscious of the problem or prepared to take measures to end it. "Information concerning the Injustice and Impolicy of Slavery is wanting," he explained. But there was reason for optimism. The signs of its inhumanity "are growing more and more obvious, and, I believe, will be in a few Years very generally acknowledged." But it would happen "much the sooner, if those who are convinced of its Unlawfulness continue frequently and firmly to bear their Testimony against it, and to communicate Instruction for promoting the Influence of Truth and Benevolence." There was a risk to the cause and to Black people themselves if the issue were forced. "Unless the Minds of Men in some parts of this State, become more softened than they appear at present to be," he explained to Pemberton, "it is much to be feared, that any Measures by which they might be irritated, would really add to the Distresses of those whom the humane desire to relieve." Dickinson expressed his willingness to work for the cause. He enclosed the bill he had put forward in 1786 and requested the Quakers' help in improving it. When they returned it, he assured them, "it shall be my diligent Endeavour, as much as I am able, to promote its being pass'd into a Law."[52]

Warner Mifflin, for one, did not accept Dickinson's explanation of the political situation. Without Dickinson's long experience as a statesman writing and debating legislation, drafting constitutions, and dealing with partisan or uneducated colleagues, he didn't understand Dickinson's strategy for approaching abolition. Seeing only what was apparent on the surface, he assumed the worst. "I am very strongly suspicious that John Dickinson knew that was our meeting-day, as he then moved that the blacks should be prevented by the constitution from purchasing real property, etc."[53] Mifflin had harsh words for other members of the convention, but Dickinson, as a Quaker fellow traveler, was the focal point of his ire.

As Dickinson stepped down from his post as president of the convention, he was so exhausted that he was confined to his house for several weeks thereafter. Murmurings he heard during this time led him to believe he was not safe from further demands to serve by the public. He feared a second election to the highest office in Delaware and moved to preempt it. "Having understood, that it is intended at the next general Election to vote for me as Governor," he wrote in a statement to the electors of the State of Delaware, "I think myself indispensably bound, for removing entirely and as soon as possible any expectations relating to me."[54] He didn't think he could fulfill the duties of the office.

He avoided that service, but in the fall of 1792, he was on a ticket for the state legislature, to which he was elected to serve as senator for the next year.[55] "I have consented to take a Seat in the Legislature," he told Richard Bassett, "for the sole purpose of rendering at this particular Period to the State any Services that may lye within my Power." He believed that the coming year would be crucial as "Laws were to be passed for commencing the Operations of the new Constitution."[56]

Before the term commenced, on October 22, James Pemberton sent Dickinson a revised version of the abolition bill Dickinson had sent him in June. Pemberton wasn't sure, however, of the best way to introduce the bill to the Assembly. He thought maybe it could be done through one of the Delaware abolition societies. However, although there was one such society in Dover and another in Wilmington, "discouragements have produced a languor with them." Still, he thought that perhaps an address from each would engage the attention of the lawmakers. Or perhaps Dickinson himself would do it.[57]

As soon as the new session of the legislature began in 1793, Dickinson did indeed try again. But the bill died "in embrio."[58] Just as in 1786, when the bill had died the first time and Dickinson had freed his own slaves unconditionally, he again considered what he could do personally and immediately. In February, he wrote to Phil and attempted to convince him to free his slaves. Dickinson appealed to him on both American and Quaker principles, both for the sake of the happiness of the Black people themselves and for the welfare of his brother's immortal soul.

He got nowhere. Phil and John held very different ideas about the world and the good of the nation. During this time, as American institutions were struggling to become established, Phil behaved in other ways that garnered his older brother's disapproval. The practice of speculation, that is, buying land or stock very cheaply, often preying upon the misfortunes of others, and selling it at very high prices, was something Dickinson abhorred. He found that "the greedy sons of Speculation" were "the Pests of Society."[59] Even as the assistant secretary of the Treasury, Tench Coxe, provided his friends with insider tips on stocks, Philemon sought information from him so persistently that Coxe found he exhibited a "Spirit of Speculation which exceeds everything known in this Western World."[60]

On the matter of freeing those he enslaved, Phil resented his brother's interference and the implicit commentary on his behavior. "I endeavor to regulate my Conduct," he replied curtly, "by the Principles of justice, & humanity, & I am strongly inclined to believe, you are not particularly acquainted with my conduct towards those persons who you deem so unhappy." He then preceded to enumerate the "facts" that proved his slaves' contentment in his possession. Ultimately, Phil was neither a Quaker nor an abolitionist. "Not being influenced by the same motives that you are," he concluded, "& my situation not permitting me to make so great a sacrifice as you request, I hope, I shall stand excused, even in your mind— I am greatly obliged, by your fraternal wishes for my future happiness, which, I am under no apprehensions will be endanger'd, by my holding that species of property, you so much reprobate."[61] Philemon's response was a sound rebuke to his older brother's meddling.

Dickinson struggled through the first session of the legislature. After preparing vigorously to begin just after the new year, his exertions brought on another bout of illness. Nevertheless, he attended almost every day, contributing to the debates and serving on five committees to prepare various bills.[62] Come March when the Senate adjourned, he drafted another resignation letter.[63] But the mild spring weather and spending time with his family did wonders.

Back home in Wilmington during the recess, he gradually recuperated.[64] When health permitted, he and Polly flourished, enjoying family, one another, and their respective pastimes. They would rise early, and after breakfast, while Dickinson retreated to his study, Polly would work in the garden, directing the hired help—they no longer enslaved people—to execute her vision for the landscape. She tried to ride out on horseback each day for exercise, sometimes joined by John or Debby.[65] In the afternoons, they would take tea using their little teapot, which announced that it belonged to "John and Mary Dickinson." And in the evenings, they enjoyed the fruits of Polly's labors by dining luxuriously on strawberries and milk. Their asceticism prohibited them from consuming the cream, though Dickinson knew that Phil's family, whom Sally and Maria occasionally visited, would consider this "Table Herecy." "We do not envy them their Enjoyments," he said amiably, "and We hope, they will not laugh at our Errors."[66]

When the Senate reconvened at the end of May, Dickinson was well enough to finish the session. He served on two more committees and made significant contributions to two other laws. One likely displeased the Quakers. He motioned that instead of passing a law exempting pacifists from military service, the law should channel the fines against them for not serving to the use of the poor. Surely Quakers would have preferred the exemption and giving to the poor voluntarily. The other bill was a renewal of a law he had passed in the Delaware Assembly in 1760, to punish those who enslaved free Blacks and mixed-race persons. First, he attempted to have feminine pronouns removed from the bill, presumably to prevent guilty women being stripped and publicly whipped. The motion failed. Second, he motioned for a paragraph that freed any enslaved person whom masters attempted to sell out of the state. That one passed, as did the bill. It was the best he could do for them. Then on June 19, Dickinson resigned his seat in a legislative body for the last time.[67]

It was good to be home for good, both for his own sake and for Polly's. These days, she frequently suffered from long bouts of illness. Sally, ever the dutiful daughter, would curtail her activities with friends to stay by her mamma's side.[68] Beginning in August, the family's movements were limited even further when an outbreak of yellow fever that swept Philadelphia lasted through November and took the lives of five thousand people. With bodies piled up in the streets, all who could flee did so, including government officials, many heading south to Delaware. "One of the most painful circumstances attending this disorder," observed Sally to her cousin, "is the seperation of friends, often of most Tender connections, during illness, and even preventing the sad comfort of a last farewell."[69] Because they heard that "the air seems to be infected," the Dickinsons wished Cousin Hannah Griffitts would come for a visit from Philadelphia.[70] Happily, the fever didn't take any family, and the only health scare Dickinson suffered that season was a bite on his left hand from a grey squirrel, possibly the pet of ten-year-old Maria. It was a potentially serious wound. His forefinger became infected and "very distressing," making it difficult to write.[71] By mid-October, he was nearly healed, but, reported Sally, "he has suffered a vast deal of pain, and has lost the tendons, so that the finger will be of but little use."[72] Luckily, although he could no longer extend the finger, he could still grasp his pen.

Although he no longer had the stamina to serve in office, Dickinson was far from finished working or serving the public as a private citizen. He continued to manage his many tenant properties, he kept his hand in the law, and he continued his usual benevolent projects large and small, such as donating to the Presbyterian Church in Dover in June 1794.[73] His main efforts, however, concerned two matters: public education and the country's foreign relations. Both were motivated by his understanding of the Divine will and the well-being of the country.

Under the current federal administration and a new political landscape, there was no shortage of causes he could take on. The ratification of the Constitution had made clear the division between the Federalists, who were in favor, and the Anti-Federalists, who were opposed. Since ratification, the political scenery had changed drastically, as those battle lines dissolved and new ones formed along the fissures of governmental philosophy, economy, foreign relations, and religion. Now the Federalists favored a strong executive, an economy based on manufacturing, close ties with Britain in trade, and more traditional, conservative forms of religious expression, such as Episcopalianism, as American Anglicanism had become known. On the other side were the Democratic-Republicans, who sought more popular power; an agrarian economy; closer ties with France, including support for her revolution; and dissenting religions, such as evangelicalism and deism, as opposite as those were. Over the course of the 1790s as the new United States struggled to find her footing, citizens gravitated towards one faction or another, gradually forming what came to be called "the First Party System," although these were neither parties nor a system as Americans would later understand them.

Dickinson despised factions and had friends and family on both sides. But he was at heart a Republican, while the ruling faction, with Washington at its head, was Federalist. Although he had nothing against Washington personally, Dickinson did not share the ardor of many for the man. "I disliked several parts of General Washington's Conduct as a Commander, and as a Statesman," Dickinson later admitted. "They were, in my Opinion, Errors, committed not for Want of Abilities, but for Want of that Information, which a more extensive Acquaintance with History would have afforded."[74] It was generally known that Washington was neither widely read nor well versed in political philosophy or history. He was first and foremost a planter, utilizing more than three hundred enslaved humans. To bolster his reputation and remedy his deficiencies in education, he surrounded himself with advisors. It was clear to Dickinson that Washington took his cues from Alexander Hamilton, whom Republicans saw as the architect of a new American aristocracy of manufacturers. For the Federalists, a robust trade with Britain was the cornerstone of that edifice. They also saw the French Revolution as a threat to a social hierarchy that they—and their British counterparts—wanted to preserve, believing that it would unleash upon the world not only radical egalitarianism but atheism.

Dickinson, whose Francophilia had grown over the years since France's aid had allowed America to defeat the British in the Revolutionary War, was a solid supporter of France and its revolution, which had been inspired by America's. Dickinson's own *Farmer's Letters*, many believed, "added to the Seeds of liberty planted in that Country," as Benjamin Rush put it.[75] Dickinson believed a revolution in France was appropriate because, unlike America under Britain, the French had no constitution to which they could resort for protection of their rights. But without careful tending and pruning, the tree of liberty could quickly grow wild. Such accelerated growth led to "internal discord" in America; in France, this wildness became the Terror, which lasted from 1793 to 1794 and involved the execution of more than sixteen thousand persons deemed counterrevolutionaries. Dickinson abhorred the violence and especially the execution of the king and queen, whose support had facilitated the creation of the American Republic.[76] But he also said,

"FRENCHMEN fought, bled, and died for us."[77] Americans owed it to them to honor their alliance with them. He was a supporter of the French people rather than any French regime.

As tensions increased between Britain and France in the early 1790s, America proclaimed her neutrality. Britain was anxious to maintain the United States as its primary trading partner but demonstrated its affections aggressively, such as by capturing nearly three hundred American vessels laden with goods from the West Indies. In March 1794, discussions in Congress ensued about sending an "Envoy Extraordinary" to Britain to negotiate a treaty of amity and commerce. The Federalists contemplated Hamilton for the job, but in a letter to Thomas Jefferson, Senator James Monroe wrote, "I should think it more suitable to employ John Dickinson, who I believe drew the last petition of Congress to the king, in the course of the late revolution."[78] But, as Monroe predicted, his party did not have the votes, and John Jay, currently chief justice of the Supreme Court, was sent, which Monroe feared would "bind the aristocracy of this country stronger and closer to that of the other."[79]

Designed by Hamilton, the treaty attempted to resolve the remaining tensions between the two countries after the 1783 Treaty of Paris. Although it did avert war, the language of the new treaty enraged France by violating the terms of the 1778 Treaty of Alliance with the United States. France's friends in America, who saw it as a struggling republic and Britain as the seat of decayed aristocracy, were also enraged.

Battle lines between the Federalists and Republicans hardened, as became evident in the press. Over recent years, the number of newspapers published in the United States had exploded, and they had become more bitterly partisan than Americans could have imagined. Since Dickinson was still considered a leading figure in Delaware, friends and foes alike kept their eyes on him. "In celebrating the Anniversary of the memorable 4th of July 1776, in the State of Delaware," a Federalist newspaper in Connecticut reported, "some persons at the convivial boards drank *Purogatory* and *Damnation* to *John Jay*, one of the heroic band who signed the Declaration of Independence." The correspondent added that they paid "particular respect to, and shouting on the *4th July*, John Dickinson the celebrated Farmer; and for benevolence and every virtue an honor to his Country, but, the strenuous *opposer* of the Declaration of Independence!"[80] Eager to sneer at Republicans, this Federalist seemed to have forgotten that John Jay did not, in fact, sign the Declaration.

Dickinson was deeply troubled by the betrayal of America's ally, as were many other Americans, who were mobilizing against the treaty. On August 4, 1795, the leading citizens of Wilmington called a town meeting, convened at Upper Market House on High and Market Streets. Dr. James Tilton assumed the chair and promptly adjourned the meeting so it could reconvene at the larger Presbyterian meeting house. The turnout was astounding. Never in the history of the city had so large a crowd gathered about a political matter. Many had to stand outside. Caesar A. Rodney opened the meeting by resolving that "it is the constitutional right of freemen to assemble together, & express their opinions of public measures," which was immediately adopted. After attempting some favorable observations on the Jay Treaty, he gave up and confessed he could find no good in it.[81]

Dickinson then rose and said that, though not feeling strong, "as the hand of age and infirmity was upon him," it was his duty to appear at the meeting to make his thoughts against the Jay Treaty public. Still, he hoped that someone younger "would take the laboring oar, and break the way, in order that the elder might the more easily follow."[82] He then sat down and waited for that person to step forward. No one did. "Mr. Dickinson," reported the *Political Gazette*, "rose, and in a strain of dignified eloquence, above our praise, exposed the defects of that instrument." He spoke for around two hours, expressing "patriotic sentiments which inspired the persons present with the love and admiration of this illustrious and venerable patriot."[83]

From his speech came the makings of a memorial. Among the fifteen or so reasons he gave for objecting to the treaty were that it in several ways put the United States and its citizens at a disadvantage in relation to other nations; it favored Britain over France in commerce and in general, thereby violating the treaty the United States had signed with France in 1778; and it abandoned the United States' commitment to neutrality. It did all of these things and more without the approval of the people through a legislative process, thereby placing too much power in the hands of the executive. In sum, Dickinson believed it would be disastrous for the country.

When he finished, there was silence. So the question was soon put, "Does the treaty meet the approbation of this meeting?" The meeting was unanimous that it did not. A committee of nine was then appointed to draft a memorial to President Washington that contained the resolutions, fifteen in all. It was clear who the draftsman would be. Dickinson then got to work to produce the documents, which were published on August 8.[84]

Reports appeared in papers around the country of this and other such meetings against the Jay Treaty. They frequently remarked on the workings of deliberative democracy in action. Citizens of all ranks and occupations attended, from quasi-aristocratic planters to laborers and merchants. Committees were appointed that then "reported their opinions, deliberately formed, to the people; that when the report was made, the reasons for the opinions expressed in it were fully given, and each citizen had an opportunity of judging for himself; that instead of the meetings being composed of factious and designing men, of the 'giddy multitude,' as they have been called, among them were seen some of the oldest and most distinguished patriots of the revolution."[85] They would mention that "among them, it is remarkable, appeared Mr. John Dickinson of Delaware, better known by the name of the *Pennsylvania Farmer*, a man who, by his writings, at a time when most of the supporters of these measures were in *their cradles, first roused* his countrymen to an opposition to the attempts to raise a revenue in America, which ultimately led to the establishment of their independence."[86] It was leaders such as these who gave their "*disinterested opinions*" on the treaty. This was democracy in action.

Washington responded to Delaware's memorial by sending a letter he had written to the selectmen of Boston on the same subject. He assured them that he believed he was doing what was best for the country and within the proper bounds of his office.[87] Dickinson suspected that the treaty would have profoundly unfavorable ramifications for the young United States.

Although the treaty continued to be debated well after it was ratified, the Dickinsons returned their attentions to their philanthropic works, particularly educational, religious, and scientific endeavors. Although they gave the most to Quakers, Dickinson had always supported other religious denominations, including the Presbyterians and German Lutherans. Now John and Polly gave to a newly formed religion, deeding land to the Methodists. This was the most significant donation Francis Asbury and his brethren had yet received, allowing them to provide for ministers traveling westward, establish a fund to support orphans and widows, and found Cokesbury College.[88] The Dickinsons also gave to scientific causes. The *Pennsylvania Gazette* reported in 1792 "that Mr. Dickinson's late donation of Fifty Pounds, to the premium offered by the Medical Society of the State of Delaware, while it demonstrates the liberality of that gentleman, is, at the same time, a proof of the rising importance of science in our American Republicks."[89] Over the years, Dickinson had also provided funds to educate the children of his friends, relatives, neighbors, tenants, and employees. According to his wishes, most of the recipients and amounts will never be known.

By the mid-1790s, the Dickinsons and the Quakers seemed to have resolved their curricular differences and reached a compromise on the boarding school. "A proposed alteration in the form of the trust" between them read, "to have the children instructed in the most advantageous branches of literature, and in such a practical knowledge of agriculture gardening, mechanics, manufactures, preparation of medicines and Household management, as may be useful to them afterwards, in their several stations in life."[90] The Dickinsons' gift of a lot in Philadelphia enabled Friends to purchase "a very handsome property" for the establishment of the school in Westtown Township in Chester County.[91] It would be called Westtown School.

Thinking so much about education caused Dickinson's mind to turn to the relationship between the will of the Divine Author and science as the basis for his philosophy of education. He believed that certain European philosophers, such as Voltaire, had "done Mischief" with writings that made "degrading Representations" of mankind.[92] Seeking to counter the "metaphysical ballooners," he began a treatise he entitled "On the Religious Education of Youth."[93] Although he had clear ideas, he told Benjamin Rush, "I cannot hit it off."[94] Instead, in late 1795, he sent a much-abbreviated draft to Rush for his review. "Though I never aimed at the Character of an Author," he confided, "yet, whenever peculiar Circumstances have compelled Me by a Sense of Duty, to publish my Sentiments, all my Labors have been dedicated to the Interests of Liberty—which allways imply a Connection with Virtue and Piety."[95]

Calling his little piece *A Fragment* of his planned essay, Dickinson was part of a growing movement in the new nation to marry natural science and religion in the popular mind with the goal of creating an informed and virtuous citizenry.[96] Everything depended on educating the youth. "There is a Candor and Integrity in Young Persons," he explained, "exceedingly favourable to the Investigation and Advancement of Truth. To mislead or impair these Dispositions, are Offences of the deepest Dye."[97] Rush replied enthusiastically, happy to have something that would "counteract the infidel writers of the age" such as Thomas Paine's heretical *Age of Reason*, which especially targeted Quakers.[98]

Atheist writers were not the only ones who troubled Dickinson. At the very beginning of what historians would call the Second Great Awakening, heirs of revivalist ministers such as George Whitefield continued and intensified his message of the detriment of learning and reason to an individual's faith. Dickinson believed the religion of these evangelicals was "mix'd with a great Deal of Error." He longed for rationality to be a core tenet of Christianity. "What must be the Effects of the Christian System, divested of the Creeds of Bigots and of the Reveries of Enthusiasts?" he asked. They would be wonderful. "Reason would then no longer be displaced to make Way for Faith, nor the Testimony of Nature be degraded by the Evidence of Revelation. An harmonious Relationship among all the Gifts of Heaven, would be seen, confest, and felt." The errors of evangelical enthusiasm had opposite results: "What Infidelity has been caused by Attempts to make Men believe too much— What Confusion by the Efforts of Zeal without Knowledge."[99] Confusion was only one danger. The other was the potential oppression of some citizens by others in the name of religion. "As for those, who in their overweening Zeal for Religion," he said, "would direct the Governor of the Universe, and suppose a possibility of advancing it by injuring the Cause of Liberty, I lament their Error."[100] His *Fragment* was designed to restore balance between reason and religion.

After Dickinson finished revising his essay, Rush sent it to the printer, and it appeared before the end of 1796. Upon hearing of Dickinson's work, Joseph Priestley, the English scientist and theologian, asked Rush for an introduction, which pleased Dickinson immensely, notwithstanding a number of "gigantic" errors Dickinson found in Priestley's opinions. "My objection," explained Dickinson to Rush," is that he decides peremptorily on subjects that lye beyond the limits of <u>human</u>, perhaps of all finite understanding. Within these limits, I am for unbounded freedom of enquiry."[101]

Dickinson's work on education was also part of a larger debate about the purpose of education, one that had been growing over the last decades. With America now independent and seeking the best future for its citizens, many more joined in. The trend was to reject impractical or abstract intellectual exercises in favor of "useful knowledge." For some, such as Benjamin Franklin and Benjamin Rush, this meant dispensing with ancient languages such as Greek and Latin. While Dickinson was certainly in favor of practical skills and knowledge that had application to daily life, he counted those languages and the literatures they provided as valuable and useful for many branches of knowledge indispensable to a democratic republic. History, for example, could teach citizens about governments, laws, and peoples, both of their virtues and their mistakes. To understand the worlds of Cicero, Tacitus, and Sallust was to learn how to be an American. It could well be that even as he and Rush agreed strongly on religion and science as part of the curriculum, because the doctor shunned classical education, Dickinson lost interest in the college that bore his name and on whose board he served as permanent president.[102] Rush was surely disappointed when Dickinson omitted the college in his will.[103] Instead, the Dickinsons' resources went towards schools such as the Brandywine Academy, for which they donated land, for instruction in both advanced sciences and the Classics.[104]

Private life agreed with Dickinson very much. He ended 1796 writing to Polly from Kent, "I am as hearty as You have seen me at any Time for several Years past." But still, he was unable to disengage entirely from politics. Only now his influence was indirect, itself a form of education, namely continuing to mentor and advise junior lawyers and politicians in high office. Such activity had long been part of his law practice, and many of his clerks went on to distinguished careers, including James Wilson, Jacob Rush, Peter Z. Lloyd, and John Armstrong Jr. Now his most promising protégé was George Logan.

George and Debby Logan's religious preferences were like John and Polly's—Debby was a Quaker, George a disowned Friend and less strict in certain Quaker principles. Though he had studied medicine, he had given up practicing to cultivate the land on the family estate, Stenton, located not far from Fairhill. Dickinson's and Logan's political philosophies were also very similar. Both Democratic-Republicans, they were deeply opposed to the aristocratic tendencies of the Federalists. In particular, they hated their schemes to make America a nation of manufacturers and their disregard of America's best ally, France. Three years after Logan founded the Philadelphia Society for Promoting Agriculture in 1785, he formed the first democratic-agrarian society, consisting only of working farmers, called the Philadelphia County Society for the Promotion of Agriculture and Domestic Manufactures, and engaged in experiments to improve agricultural production and animal husbandry.[105] Dickinson joined him in this interest, writing frequently to the botanist Humphrey Marshall requesting seeds and plants for himself and others.[106] In the 1790s, as the sun rose on Logan's political career and set on Dickinson's, Dickinson's mentoring role to Logan intensified.

In 1790, already disillusioned with the new federal government under the Washington administration and thinking about how he could best serve his country, Logan took two steps. First, he joined the militia. It was a short-lived experiment; he resigned when his unit was called up during the Whiskey Rebellion, which took place from 1791 to 1794. Logan later came around to Dickinson's position that only defensive war was lawful. But this was enough to get him disowned from the Quaker meeting.[107]

Logan also alienated himself from Quaker elite by publishing a series of "Letters to the Yeomanry" in 1790, which were reproduced as a pamphlet the following year in 1792. He chose as his pen name "A Farmer," a tribute to Dickinson, who had captured the fledgling nation's imagination from the first words, "I am a Farmer." Dickinson remained America's first "Farmer," and in retirement his interest in agricultural methods was known.[108] He did not reject manufacturing and commerce; he had always supported them as essential to America's domestic and foreign policy. He had great respect for merchants and their enterprises, "But however estimable very many of them are, however excellent their Characters," he clarified, "I do not look to the Body of them, for the soundest Maxims of Policy, nor to them . . . as promoting, as they ought to do, the Practice of Morality."[109] Logan built on Dickinson's ideas as well as those of the French physiocrats, who themselves had recognized a kindred spirit in the Pennsylvania Farmer.[110] The physiocrats advocated the "rule of nature," believed that economic wealth was tied to agriculture, and argued that the government should not interfere with agricultural production or markets. Now Logan advocated this approach as an alternative to Hamilton's aristocracy of manufacturers.

In 1797, Dickinson resumed publishing on political topics. A few years earlier, he had started a tenth Fabius letter, commenting on the worrisome health of the young nation, but it had never advanced beyond drafts.[111] Now at what appeared to be a looming national crisis with France, he moved to the topic of foreign relations. "The latter part of General Washington's Administration was the weakest Scene of political Character that ever was acted," wrote Dickinson to Charles Thomson. "And wretched as it was, it has become the Tone of our Country." He meant the anti-French sentiment. "Unless his Errors can be corrected, our Posterity will lament in Ages of Misery, that ever such a Man existed." Dickinson equated Washington's poor political decisions with his leadership of the Continental Army. "He twice, at least, in the Course of our late War prest us into a Cul de Sac." Dickinson meant his stunning loss of Fort Washington in New York in 1776 and his defeat at the Battle of Brandywine in 1777. "But luckily, without his Care, the upper End of the sack was left open. Now," with the Jay Treaty, "he has put Us into another—and has tyed the Top as closely as he could."[112] With France in the throes of her own revolution, Dickinson did not trust the Federalist administration. For the first time in many years, he tried his hand again at verse. Celebrating the French people with an "Ode" in classical imagery, he proclaimed, "The cause of FRANCE is Freedom's cause."[113]

Despite his harsh words, Dickinson did not dislike Washington personally. The same cannot be said for his successor. John Adams was sworn in on March 4. On May 15, he took the extraordinary step of calling Congress back into session to deliberate on the deterioration of the nation's relations with France. Adams's action "rouzed" Dickinson, and he again heard the call of duty. "Laden with Years, full of Infirmities, estranged from Public Engagements, Sensible of my Weaknesses," he said, "I once against have ventured to take a Pen into my trembling Hand."[114] Although it was difficult for him even to hold books, in merely thirty days he completed a second set of fifteen *Fabius Letters* "on the present situation of public affairs."[115] They concerned the course of the French Revolution and the country's resistance to the combined European powers set out to conquer it. He emphasized the importance of America's maintaining good relations with France as it succeeded Britain as the next great European state.

Although one undoubtedly Federalist reviewer called them "a feeble effort . . . by a dull writer," the essays were quickly picked up by newspapers from New Hampshire to Virginia. Benjamin Rush predicted that their impression on the public mind was such that Dickinson would not be able to conceal his name for long. Joseph Priestley found them to be "written with so much force, and yet with so much moderation" that he wished Dickinson would reveal his identity. He added that America's friends in England had greatly enjoyed the *Farmer's Letters*.[116] The next year, Dickinson obliged by allowing Thomas McKean to draft a preface for the French version containing both sets of *Fabius Letters* that revealed Dickinson's identity.[117] Rush then sent several copies overseas.[118] McKean reported to Dickinson that Vice President Thomas Jefferson "spoke to me of this Pamphlet & of you in very pleasing terms," and years later, readers were still noting Dickinson's "good sense and humanity" as Fabius.[119]

At the end of October 1797, the Dickinsons went to see the progress on the building of Westtown School for themselves. On the twentieth, the whole Dickinson family made the seventeen-mile journey from Wilmington up to Chester County for a tour of the site. The drive was one that Dickinson had made many times over four decades of traveling the court circuit. Compared to his early years of practice, there were perhaps a few more houses along the way, and tiny villages had grown into towns. The landscape echoed with other memories as well, such as that of the eleven-hour battle fought along the Brandywine Creek, in which several thousand men had died and the Americans had ceded Philadelphia to the British.

They met with the builder, Owen Biddle, in Concord and traveled the rest of the way with him, bumping along the rocky and hilly terrain. The fresh autumn air and foliage, almost at peak color, compensated for the discomfort. Biddle showed the family Westtown's buildings and the farm, which had progressed nicely. They toured the barn first, then the mansion house with student apartments and the many outbuildings. They made their way through the woods and fields as well. Dickinson was extremely pleased and declared that he felt like the "Queen of the South"—the Queen of Sheba from the New Testament, who traveled to Jerusalem to determine if King Solomon was truly wise. Indeed, he was very pleased with how Friends were managing the project. Although there was still much to be done, Westtown School opened in May 1799 with three teachers and two hundred students.[120] Friends complained that the Pennsylvania Assembly did not grant Westtown tax-exempt status, as it did for the schools of other societies.[121]

Dickinson spent time at the end of the year in Kent, enjoying the solitude, but hardly alone. He passed cold and rainy days indoors by the fire with "very little living Company, but, some excellent dead Company." He conversed with St. Paul about a new translation of the Bible. "He animates, soothes, and directs me," John told Polly. "I strive to pursue the Course which the Apostle triumphantly trod." A number of theologians "and some other excellent Friends are in the Room; and I find them to be most instructive and delightful Associates."

The joys and benefits of study never ceased to amaze him. With childlike wonder, he marveled, "How bright a Blessing is conferred by the use of Letters!" In these golden moments he was overwhelmed by optimism about the future. "The Effects are so great, that sometimes I indulge Myself in a pleasing prospect, that human Affairs are flowing in a gradual Amelioration, and that Truth of every kind, physical, moral, and revealed, will be diffused over Earth with satisfactory Evidence, and the production of abundant Happiness to Mankind."[122]

Dickinson wrote to the Polish general and American Revolution hero Tadeusz Kościuszko, who had recently returned from Europe. There was great understanding between them. The general responded, "In my heart I am a kwaker too, will do anything for the hapiness of Human kind." He was an ebullient correspondent, effusive in his admiration. "In Poland," he said, "you have many friends, amongst whom your Character is in very high estymation." He wanted "to shake you by the hand, and convers with you; whoes habilities and good heart renderd so many Services to the Public—you inproved Sir their mind to vertue, love of the Country and Humanity."[123] Dickinson could look forward to a visit from him soon. Meanwhile, Kościuszko chided Dickinson for not having sent him a copy of his *Fabius Letters*. "What come's from your pen, I must have in my library," he insisted.[124]

At the end of 1797, when Dickinson returned to Wilmington from his sojourn with the deceased, the behavior of his fellow citizens dampened his optimism, and a national crisis became personal. The economy of the fledgling United States had always been unstable, with panics large and small rippling through the states. Dickinson had urged the creation of banks for stability, but there was resistance, and the country couldn't be insulated from financial shocks in Europe, especially during wartime. A panic had begun in 1796, taking down land speculators as the real estate market evaporated. The biggest figure to fall was Robert Morris, the man who more than any other had ensured the nation's financial survival during the Revolution. At one time the wealthiest man in America, he was now in desperate financial straits and had borrowed money from friends—a usual practice without stable banks—which he was unable to pay back, despite owning more land than anyone else. Morris was proof that landownership did not equate to virtue. Among his creditors was Dickinson, from whom he had borrowed £14,000 in 1791 and still owed $7,000, which Dickinson's lawyer, Moses Levy, was now attempting to collect. After the sheriff sold Morris's unfinished mansion on Chestnut Street, Morris promised to pay the interest as it came due, but he begged Dickinson not to demand the principal for at least a year and preferably more than three. "You formerly ever shewed a Friendly disposition towards me," he implored, "& now, when I am under the pressure of misfortune and disappointments I hope it will not be withdrawn."[125]

Dickinson and Morris shared a special relationship. Not only had they worked together for decades, but Morris was the only other Pennsylvania delegate who had abstained from the vote on independence, though he later signed the Declaration. Dickinson was highly displeased about the debt, not hiding his feelings in curt letters. He had little choice but to show Morris compassion and accede to his plea. In allowing Morris's interests to prevail, he said, "My own shall pause." He made it clear that Morris's irresponsibility was injurious. Dickinson was indeed wealthy, but he was exceedingly careful with his money, and even he would suffer by the loss of such a considerable sum.[126] Morris's debt to Dickinson was miniscule compared to what he owed others. The month after he and Dickinson corresponded, Morris was remanded to debtors' prison, where he spent three and a half years. When he died in 1806, Philadelphians ignored his unmarked grave.[127]

In early 1798, national affairs hardly looked better. As relations with France deteriorated, first with the so-called XYZ Affair, in which the French government refused to see three American diplomats on a peace mission unless they paid a bribe, and then the Quasi War, Dickinson thought, "never was the Happiness of a People more wantonly exposed to Hazard."[128]

George Logan shared both Dickinson's fears and his affection for France. What he did next had Dickinson's approbation and his assistance. Believing that "as a citizen of a free independent Republic it is my right and I have ever considered it as my duty to promote the good of my Country under all circumstances & in every situation in which my exertions could be useful," Logan decided to travel to France to negotiate peace where Adams's ministers had failed.[129] It was a very Quakerly thing to do. From their inception, Friends, impelled by the Light in their consciences, had traveled as individuals to meet with heads of state to discuss urgent spiritual matters.[130] For Dickinson, at least, and likely Logan as well, war and peace were most definitely spiritual concerns. Of course, when Quakers sought audiences with heads of state, they had permission from their meetings. Logan had only a certificate from Vice President Thomas Jefferson attesting to his good character and another confirming his credentials from Chief Justice of Pennsylvania Thomas McKean. He nonetheless set sail.[131] President Adams was not informed.

Logan was a great success in Paris for much of the reason Benjamin Franklin had been before him—he fit the French idea of the good Quaker. In this case, he actually was—or had been—a real Quaker; Franklin had merely dressed the part and let assumptions stand. Logan gained an audience with the right people in the government and made his case. As it happened, the French had already sent a message to the United States indicating a desire for reconciliation. Logan was able to convince them that for their assertion to be believed, they would need to lift the embargo on American goods and release imprisoned sailors. As Logan departed with decrees in hand granting the United States' wishes, the French toasted to Franco-American amity.[132] The mission at least gave reason for hope in the short term.

Upon his return in early November, however, Logan found that he was being painted as an enemy of the United States by the Federalists.[133] He personally informed President Adams of his trip. His next visit was to his mentor. An unsigned letter in a Federalist newspaper reported that Logan stayed "at the Old Jacobin and piddling genius's Dickinson's house."[134] The letter was likely written by Allen McLane, a collector of customs at the Port of Wilmington and Dickinson's former partner in 1786 abolition efforts. As Logan traveled and reported on his trip, he was predictably skewered and celebrated by the Federalist and Republican presses, respectively. The Federalists accused him of maligning President Adams, which could mean prosecution under the newly passed Sedition Act, a law that surely reminded Dickinson of the William Smith libel trial three decades earlier and caused him to reflect on the purpose of the First Amendment.[135]

So he decided to test it. In January 1798, in solidarity with Logan, Dickinson published a pamphlet entitled *A Caution; Or, Reflections on the Present Contest between France and Britain*, which contained an "Ode, On the French Revolution." Advertisements for the pamphlet ran almost every day from February to September in Pennsylvania's *Aurora General Advertiser*. He began by blaming the administrations of Washington and Adams for provoking France. Then, with arguments steeped in the histories of England and ancient Rome, he made a case for avoiding war. In striking contrast to his essay on the flag-of-truce trade forty years earlier, he extolled France's commercial prowess and armed forces, with the "caution" being that it should not be underestimated in a military contest. In the contemplation of two questions, whether France could dominate the sea and whether it could successfully invade Britain, he suggested that both were likely enough that America should not be overly confident in winning a war with her.[136]

Although Dickinson's work escaped notice by the administration, the Federalist-controlled Congress wasted no time in passing legislation to prevent any such Quaker meddling as Logan's in the future. On January 30, 1799, President Adams signed the so-called Logan Act, which criminalized the involvement of private citizens with foreign governments, into law.

During these years as Dickinson looked to Quakers to help him realize his charitable ambitions, Friends, "knowing Thy truely Christian & Amiable disposition for doing goode in many ways, especially in acts of Charity & Benevolence," turned to him to advance their causes as well.[137] In 1799, James Bringhurst, a fervent abolitionist, considered Dickinson's "superior abilitys & eminent Qualifications for allmost every service with thy pen" and thought this "would ensure thy Influence with some Effect over thy Cotemporarys, & with our beloved President G. Washington and some in exhalted stations respecting the Abolition of Slavery in their own family." He encouraged Dickinson again to use his pen in the cause.[138]

Dickinson's response was not exactly what Bringhurst had hoped, though not entirely disappointing either. Now sixty-six years old and deeply engrossed in the study of theology, Dickinson wrote passionately about the ability of God's Light to penetrate "mental foggs" and also marveled at the "intellectual darkness" of someone such as Washington who would, despite being "a person of large understanding and many good qualities," nevertheless continue "holding members of his fellow men, at this time in severe Bondage." Yet he demurred. "I fear," he lamented, "that thy Opinion is too favorable of me, in imagining that any Efforts of mine could be of use on that occasion. I know by experience the horrid Infatuation" of owning slaves. "Allmost miraculously I escaped out of the thick clay and the lured Atmosphere, and was in that Instance favored to turn my back on the Tents of Abomination." He also knew Washington's stubborn personality and was probably aware that earlier efforts by Quaker Robert Pleasants had failed.[139] Perhaps Dickinson also had an earlier failure of his own in mind, when he tried unsuccessfully in 1793 to convince Phil to free his slaves. Thus Dickinson declined Bringhurst's request to appeal to Washington but gave his permission for his words to be used if they "might be an encouragement to slave owners to set theirs free."[140]

Down in Kent towards the end of the year 1799 to look after Poplar Hall, Dickinson was contented with his life. Writing to Polly on November 13, his birthday, he took stock of his previous year. "This Day completes my sixty sixth Year." Thinking of his "Republican Family," he added, "For how many and how great Blessings am I indebted."[141] His blessings were all well enough. Nathaniel Luff stopped by his house in Wilmington and reported that Maria had a slight cold and Sally a toothache. Polly was out riding, so Dickinson knew she was better than usual. His niece, Molly, the spitting image of Phil, was also there.[142]

Soon Dickinson was back in Wilmington when reports of George Washington's death on December 14 arrived. In this tense political climate, Dickinson was perhaps too free with his thoughts, and a minor scandal erupted. "Tories," claimed Thomas Rodney, were reporting "that Dickinson (Pennsylvania Farmer) has said that Washington, aught to have died Ten years ago." It is not improbable that Rodney ensured this rumor sprouted wings. For years, he had harbored an abiding jealously of Dickinson for his celebrity, frequently recording in his diary dreams in which honors were bestowed upon him while Dickinson humbly paid him tribute. Smiling to Dickinson's face and claiming to love him like a brother, Rodney confided derogatory remarks about his neighbor to his diary. Had Dickinson known Rodney's true feelings, or that Rodney also recorded his recurring dreams of preying upon and raping his friends' daughters—which he likewise tried to act upon—Dickinson might have watched both his back and his children in Rodney's presence.[143] Up in Trenton, Phil heard of his brother's alleged slight against Washington and condemned the remark. John had to tread lightly; Phil had once served as second to their cousin, General John Cadwalader, when he fought a duel against another American general for slighting Washington.[144]

"What I said was this," Dickinson clarified artlessly: "that his Life would have been more beneficial to his Country, if it had terminated before he made the British Treaty." He truly could not dissemble, even when doing so would hurt no one and would keep peace with a brother. He went on to explain that "my Esteem for General Washington's Person and my Respect for his Character, have allways been perfectly sincere." Although Dickinson confessed, "I cannot with a wild Enthusiasm call him a consummate Statesman or General, Yet it is true, that his Integrity and Firmness have been eminently serviceable to The United States." There was plenty of evidence of Dickinson's respect for Washington. As a trustee of the University of Pennsylvania, he had put his name to the honorary degree that institution conferred on Washington.[145] "I allways considered him as a great and good Man," he later wrote to George Logan.[146] To commemorate his life, Dickinson had even written and published a seventeen-line poem in the newspaper and marched in a funeral procession held in Wilmington.[147] Dickinson surely recognized that the death of Washington was the end of the Revolutionary-era unity that the Farmer had cultivated three decades earlier.

15

"A constant Watchman for
the public Interest"

A Politician behind the Scenes, 1800–1804

The new year, 1800, was an election year. The first two presidential elections in American history had been remarkably calm affairs. Washington had been elected almost unanimously and the unpopular John Adams rode Washington's Federalist coattails into office. This one promised to be nothing like what most Americans could have imagined when they declared themselves to be a unified and sovereign nation just twenty-four years earlier. Although the Federalists did what they could to damage Thomas Jefferson and members of his party, including referencing his relations with his deceased wife's enslaved half-sister, Sally Hemings, they did not prevail.[1] The contest was so brutal that Republicans felt they needed every advantage, and this increased their determination to bring Dickinson back into office.

Over Dickinson's protests, he had been put forward for the Senate in 1795, and now the calls were harder to ignore.[2] A newspaper in Carlisle, home of Dickinson College, wrote that the Republicans of Delaware "have now fixed upon the venerable American Farmer, one of the surviving patriarchs of our revolution, John Dickinson . . . to come forward once more to lend his wisdom in aid of those, who are solicitous to heal the wounds with which British influence, corruption, and domestic faction and ambition, have afflicted our country for a few years past."[3] Others in Philadelphia hoped that the "*noble spirited* John Dickinson, will resume his station!!"[4]

When other retired statesmen, such as Thomas McKean, recently elected governor of Pennsylvania, returned "to save their country from impending ruin," Virginians challenged Dickinson to do the same. "Are not the republican citizens of Delaware just," they queried, "in looking to you for that assistance which *you alone* are able to afford?" They insisted, "The eyes of the Republicans throughout the continent have selected you, to aid their generous exertions: The hearts of the republicans of Delaware are centered in

You, as the only person who can rescue the state from contempt, and place it in that rank in the union which it deserves, but which has been unfortunately forfeited."[5] Dickinson seriously considered running, but he ultimately had to decline. "We are sorry," reported a Philadelphia paper, "to say that the debilitated state of Mr. Dickinson's health will not permit him to meet the wishes of his fellow-citizens in representing them in the Congress of the United States."[6]

But the country, if not Delaware, had a surrogate for Dickinson. George Logan's mission to France had only bolstered his reputation among Republicans, who elected him to represent Pennsylvania in the Senate. In his first service at the national level, Logan turned to his mentor even more. "While Dr. Logan was a Senator of the United States," wrote Debby, "he was in the habit of submitting every measure of importance which came before that body to the judgment of Mr. Dickinson."[7] And Dickinson put matters before Logan that he wished to see taken up by the Senate, including punishing counterfeiters, ensuring nonimportation of British goods, and maintaining militias, among other things. Tellingly, when Phil represented New Jersey in the Senate from 1790 to 1793, Dickinson did not work with him; Phil was much more conservative than his older brother.

Logan's election was just a small part of what Jefferson called the "Revolution of 1800." It was a wave that engulfed the entire federal government and signaled the end of the party of Washington, Hamilton, and Adams and the ascendance of Jeffersonianism. Most extraordinarily, of all those whom Adams could have blamed for his being a one-term president, he looked at the Dickinsons, John and Polly both. Reflecting on the First and Second Continental Congresses, Adams said, "The Quaker and Proprietary Interests in Pennsilvania now addressed themselves to Mr. Dickinson, who as well as his Wife were Quakers, and in various Ways stimulated him to oppose my designs and the Independence of the Country." They had done this so effectively, Adams believed, that "although they could not finally prevent any one of my Measures from being carried into compleat Execution, they made him and his Cousin Charles Thompson, and many others of their Friends, my Ennemies from that time to this," Adams concluded bitterly. "Hence one of the most considerable Causes of Mr. Jefferson's Success in 1801."[8] Had the Dickinsons an inkling that this was true, surely they would have enjoyed taking credit for such an accomplishment.

Dickinson, heartened and relieved at the change in America's leadership, wrote to express his congratulations to James Madison on his advancement to the office of secretary of state: "The late Changes open a cheerful Prospect to those who love their Country."[9] He likewise sent effusive congratulations and well wishes to Jefferson: "My Heart impells Me to congratulate our Country and of Course thyself, on thy Promotion to the high Office of presiding over her Wellfare." In case the president harbored any doubts about Dickinson's views concerning independence, Dickinson reassured him, "As to the past, as far as I am enabled to form a Judgment, I believe, that our Minds have been in perfect Unison."[10]

Jefferson responded in kind. Speaking of the outgoing administration, he said, "Our fellow citizens have been led hoodwinked from their principles by a most extraordinary combination of circumstances." But, he assured Dickinson, "nothing shall be spared on my part, short of the abandonment of the principles of our revolution."[11] They had never had more than a cordial working relationship, and they could hardly be more different in their personal qualities and private lives. Jefferson lived extravagantly beyond his means, racking up debt to keep himself in luxuries such as books and French wine; Dickinson, one of the wealthiest men in America, lived frugally and plainly, preferring to spend his fortune on public causes. Jefferson enslaved hundreds of Black people and made no secret of his fear and disgust at the color of their skin; Dickinson, having freed those he enslaved, had a few paid servants and advocated liberation for the enslaved and aid for freed Black people. Jefferson disregarded women; Dickinson valued and uplifted them. Jefferson kept God at a distance; Dickinson's life was centered on his faith. Jefferson's true opinions and principles were difficult to discern; Dickinson was transparent to a fault. But the two men shared a vision for the new country as mainly an agrarian nation, which stimulated an unlikely friendship between the forthright, Quakerly Dickinson and the mercurial deist Jefferson. The republican virtues of hard work, frugality, simplicity, and self-sacrifice for the common good were founded in a connection with the land.

Because Jefferson recognized that "the purity & perspicuity of your views are respected by all parties," Dickinson became something of an advisor to him.[12] More likely, however, is that Jefferson couldn't deny the utility of Dickinson's deep experience and connections. "It is extremely important to the administration of the public affairs," he said to Dickinson, "for me to be on terms of confidence with some persons of dispassionate judgment & integrity in every state, through whom I can obtain a knoledge of such matters within their state." In one instance, Jefferson sought Dickinson's opinion on the matter of Allen McLane, the collector of customs at the Port of Wilmington, who had been accused of electioneering. "It is to satisfy my own conscience I ask it," said Jefferson, "fearful of being led astray by the opinions of others not so well known to me as you are."[13]

Dickinson replied enthusiastically that he would "cheerfully express" his opinions. But before he responded to Jefferson's query on McLane, he took the opportunity to "let my Thoughts flow from my Pen without Reserve" on the matter of governance during this time of debilitating partisanship. First and foremost, Dickinson counseled tolerance of diverse political opinions, even when opponents "wander from salutary Truths, to which you wish to bring them back, for their own Wellfare as well as for the general Benefit." Republicans "cannot in any Consistency with the Principles of their system, proscribe any of their Fellow Citizens, merely for a Difference of political Opinion." The good of the whole must be considered. "Real Republicans," he explained, "are not governed by Reasonings only. They discover in them-selves Sensations superior to Arguments. Their Benignity is not completely gratified, unless their Adversaries share in their Satisfactions."[14]

Later Dickinson went further. "I look upon Republicanism," he said to Caesar A. Rodney, "to be the Gospel of Policy." To Rodney he conveyed ideas that might have fallen flat with Jefferson. "In primitive Times the Heathens used to say—'Behold! how these Christians love one another.'" Now Americans would behave in the same way. "Let the Heathens—I mean the Enemies of Truth—in our own Days, be forced to exclaim—"Behold! how these Republicans love one another."[15] Yet Dickinson agreed with Jefferson when he said all Americans were both Republicans and Federalists.[16]

But partisan realities had to be dealt with. Dickinson prescribed two methods for Jefferson to bring the Federalists around to working produc-tively with the Republicans: first, by working together on small measures on which there was general approval, and second, "by turning the Countenance of Government with Respect and Kindness upon those who differ from the Rulers in Opinion." Jefferson could accomplish this by his appointments, and Dickinson had a specific suggestion. "I should like to see the son of our Enemy, John Adams, appointed Minister to the Court of Petersburgh. The more unexpected such an Act, the greater will be its Effect." And there was another reason for such an appointment—pity. "This honorable Regard to a falling Family, will be soothing to them."[17] Appointing John Quincy Adams was also part of a foreign and economic strategy Dickinson had in mind, that of making Russia and France the two main trading partners of the United

States. He didn't recommend only the sons of his enemies for posts with the new administration. Dickinson also suggested that Jefferson retain George Read Jr., the son of his old friend, in the position of United States attorney for the District of Delaware.[18]

As to the matter of McLane's electioneering, Dickinson said, "I question, whether any Man in these States has been more zealous in that Way."[19] Perhaps Dickinson was aware of McLane's opinion of him as an "old Jacobin and piddling genius," because he gave glowing recommendations for two men who could replace him. Jefferson must have decided that electioneering was not sufficient grounds for removal. And neither did he heed Dickinson's counsel on John Quincy Adams, who would have to wait for the Madison administration in 1809 for the appointment. But he did retain Read.

With the Republicans looking to press their advantage with the public, it must have seemed a likely moment to John Vaughan, an avid promoter of Republican writings, to market a new publication. He approached Dickinson about collecting and publishing a two-volume set of his best-known pamphlets and political documents. The edition, which appeared in 1801, was one of the earliest such publications in America of the writings of a public figure. And Dickinson himself took the lead as chief editor of them, collecting and annotating the documents. The edition contained only fourteen items, a tiny fraction of the hundreds he had produced on public affairs throughout his long career, but the new nation had no archives and few repositories where such works might be housed. Dickinson's own library had suffered from being plundered during the war, so he had trouble finding even an edition of his *Farmer's Letters*.

His more recent writings were easier to come by. He republished his 1797 set of *Fabius Letters* together with the first set from 1788. He annotated them by quoting long passages from Thomas Paine's *Rights of Man*, "containing similar sentiments, expressed with a remarkable resemblance of language" to his 1788 "Fabius Letters," "especially on the two great subjects—the OR-GANIZATION of a CONSTITUTION from *original* rights, and the FORMATION of GOVERNMENT from contributed rights, both of so much importance in laying regular FOUNDATIONS of civil society, and consequently in securing the advancement of HUMAN HAPPINESS." Dickinson was unconcerned with Paine's plagiarism of his work. Rather, it was a mark of sound thinking to imitate one's predecessors, when those predecessors were greatly admired. Dickinson accepted Paine's compliment. He dedicated his edition "To the American People." In marketing the volumes, the publisher "offered no encomium"; Dickinson's "uniform labors in defence of the *rights of the people*" were panegyric enough.[20]

At the close of 1801, a tragedy compelled Dickinson to put into practice his nonpartisan sentiments. Alexander Hamilton's nineteen-year-old son Philip was killed in a duel on November 24. Dickinson deplored Hamilton's "Aberrations," as he discretely referred to Hamilton's public scandals, especially if his untoward behavior might infect others.[21] But upon learning the news of Philip's death, Dickinson was overwhelmed by a sense of pity for his father, the talented young man who, it seemed to Dickinson, persisted in struggling mightily against God. He thus wrote a heartfelt letter of condolence. Although the men had opposed one another, furiously at times, and could hardly have been more different in personal traits, political style, or governing philosophy, Dickinson wrote for a couple of reasons—first, because of his appreciation of Hamilton's service to the country they both loved and, he said, "the satisfaction I have received from our Acquaintance." But also, he had a strong and Quakerly desire to offer a hint towards happiness. "Yet, amidst the Calamities of this fleeting Life," he suggested, "there is one Source of Consolation allways open." Dickinson meant religion, but he did not dwell on it.[22]

He did not expect a response; but a few months later, one arrived. "Be assured," wrote Hamilton, "that consolation from you on such an occasion was particularly welcome to me, and that I shall always remember it with a grateful sense." Then he confessed his youthful dismissals of Dickinson. "The friendship of the wise and good rises in value, in proportion as we learn to form a just estimate of human character and opinion."[23] Dickinson found it to be a very affectionate answer, but he had hoped for more of an opening to discuss religion with him. Not finding it, he decided not to press the matter. When Hamilton himself was killed in a duel less than three years later and Dickinson heard rumors that Hamilton had been deeply touched by the condolence letter, he "much regretted" not encouraging him to profess some religion. "Poor Hamilton!" he thought.[24]

Living in retirement in Wilmington, Delaware, Dickinson was slightly off the beaten path. Still, strangers went out of their way, looking to meet "the celebrated author of the Farmer's Letters." When a visitor from New York spent an afternoon and the next morning with him, he provided a vivid portrait of Dickinson for curious readers (Fig. 22). "His countenance," began the narrator, is "adorned with locks of the purest silver, exhibits the marks of advanced years, yet is heightened by a tempered spirit and vivacity of eyes and feature that denotes a mind still in the possession of its vigor. His features are frank and open, bespeaking confidence while they convey intelligence. In his person he is above the middle size, erect, and inclined to slender."

Dickinson's visitor found him "of the most gentlemanly manners, and charitable in the highest extreme." In his face you could trace the "patriotic proofs of integrity and talent by which his life has been distinguished. I found him, easy of access, and his conversation cheerful, affable and interesting." The visitor added, "He appears to take the highest interest in the welfare of his country, and the same patriotism . . . burns with a flame as clear and as steady at this as at any former moment."[25]

Sometimes Dickinson actively looked for visitors. In retirement, he didn't miss the incessant work, partisan battles, or the glare of popularity; but he did miss debating public affairs. Standing in his front doorway one midday, he saw his friend Hezekiah Niles, a struggling young Quaker printer, passing by and hailed him to come in for a bit of wine. After a couple of glasses, Dickinson asked, "What is thy opinion of the discussion in Congress on the great question of the judiciary?" It was 1801, and Congress had just passed and President Adams signed the Judiciary Act. It would reduce the number of Supreme Court justices from six to five and, instead of the justices riding circuit, it created six new districts with sixteen new judgeships. Republicans were outraged at what they considered an innovation that would weaken the rights of the states. That Adams rushed to fill these vacancies just as he left office seemed a way for Federalists to cling to power despite losing the election. Republicans' resistance to it would lead to the case of *Marbury v. Madison* in the Supreme Court in 1803.

After Niles briefly gave his opinion, Dickinson eagerly offered, "I'll tell thee mine." It was not exactly what Dickinson said—like other Democratic-Republicans, he was opposed to the act and wanted it repealed—but rather how he said it that captured Niles's attention. He began calmly enough but gradually became more animated. As though forgetting where he was, he rose slowly from his seat and transformed before Niles's eyes. Now Dickinson was in a legislative assembly addressing Niles as the chairman of the body. As the Farmer held forth, Niles knew he was bearing witness to the same energy, the same spark that ignited a revolution. "I never heard a discourse," Niles later said, "that was comparable to his *speech* for its fire and spirit, poured forth in a torrent, and clothed in the most beautiful and persuasive language." For half an hour, he was "rivetted" watching "the graceful gestures of the orator."

Then it was over as suddenly as it had begun. A family member entered the room, breaking the spell. Dickinson stopped mid-word and dropped into his seat. Appearing confused to be transported back to his drawing room, he apologize for his strange behavior. But Niles didn't mind. On the contrary, he thought surely Dickinson could never have delivered a speech "so eloquent, so chaste, and so beautiful." Niles could see that "it was his *soul* rather than his person that acted on the occasion, and a *master-spirit* it was."[26]

It was these fires of patriotism that caused Dickinson to monitor public affairs closely in Delaware, Pennsylvania, and the nation. Through trusted friends such as George Logan, Thomas McKean, Benjamin Rush, Caesar A. Rodney, and Tench Coxe, he learned of policies and legislation that were under consideration. His attention shifted from one to the other as developments dictated. As he had done before he took his seat in the Frist Continental Congress, he continued to exert influence indirectly from the sidelines. Now he acted as mentor to a new generation of politicians, several of them sons of old friends. He not only proposed policy and secured passage of legislation he deemed crucial to the young nation; he even continued to write it. In Delaware, for example, he was nearly successful in securing the passage of an amendment to a Delaware inheritance law. State Senator John Vining, the flamboyant and profligate son of his old friend, informed him that not only did it pass unanimously in the Senate, but as of that time, "Not a Bill has Passed either House but the one, which is emphatically called yours." But it died in the House, perhaps because Vining himself expired in the middle of the legislative session, likely from excessive alcohol consumption.[27]

On the national level, issues of interest or concern continued to arise, drawing him back into deliberations behind the scenes. He had been concerned for some time about the manner in which public functionaries—both senators and cabinet positions—were chosen. He thus wrote a lengthy letter to Logan suggesting points that ought to be clarified to prevent misbehavior and detriment to the nation, including how senators were chosen in the state legislatures so that a minority could not prevent senators from being seated, how long senators should serve, and that senators ought not be empowered to interfere with the president's appointment of cabinet officials.[28] He also urged Logan in the Senate to curb the "Demands of the Union against those called the debtor States." The present policy was, he said, "utterly inconsistent with Justice" and was adversely affecting property values in Delaware.

He believed that renunciation of the demands would "evidence a fraternal Liberality of Sentiment."[29]

Other developments boded well for the enlightenment of the republic. Upon learning that a joint committee of Congress to establish a library was formed on January 26, 1802, Dickinson "scratched out" a list of books for inclusion and sent it to Logan.[30] It was over one page in two tightly written columns, containing works of history, law, and political thought; travel and geography; botany, husbandry and agriculture; and literature, poetry, and fables. Specifically, in addition to the requisite histories and accounts of America and western European nations, ancient and modern, he also wanted works on Russia, Poland, Africa, Greenland, the Jews, the Five Nations Indians, and the French dominions in North and South America, which also included detailed accounts of Indigenous peoples. His favorite authors were represented, including Harrington, Montesquieu, Grotius, and Pufendorf, as well as Catharine Macaulay, Lady Rachel Russell, and Catherine II. And he was sure to include a couple of his favorite Quaker writers, William Penn and Dr. John Fothergill. The scientific topics included bees, fruit trees, carrots, hydraulics and hydrostatics, and silkworms. Americans should be a well-rounded people, and the library should reflect that.

Despite not living in Pennsylvania, Dickinson likewise had difficulty abstaining from the politics of that state. When Thomas McKean was elected governor, Dickinson had declared his hope "that many thousands of the deluded Inhabitants of Pennsylvania will become sincere Converts to Republicanism; when they find the Government of Republicans uniting sound Policy, Firmness, Justice, and Mercy in its Administration, and faithfully aiming at the promotion of general Happiness."[31] But even after McKean was re-elected governor in the fall of 1802, the scene grew increasingly troubled. Although the commonwealth was controlled by Democratic-Republicans, any consensus surrounding the election of Jefferson to the presidency disintegrated quickly. Three main factions coalesced that bore a resemblance to the factions during the Revolution. The Federalist elites were on the one extreme, representing the conservative element, including many Quakers; the Democrats, on the other, were radical laborers who resented the wealthy; and representing a "third way" between the two were the moderate Tertium Quids. The Quids included many of Dickinson's friends and allies—McKean, of course; but also the political economist, erstwhile Federalist, and former secretary of the Pennsylvania Abolition Society Tench Coxe; the jurist Alexander Dallas; and the publisher Matthew Carey—and, by extension,

Dickinson. While the Federalists looked on with amusement, the Democrats grew increasingly restive, threatening to tear down the structures that they believed were working against them to enforce inequality. They wanted pure democracy and simple majority rule. By contrast, the Quids sought to preserve these structures, which they believed protected individual and property rights.

Dickinson believed that McKean's election was laudable proof of the "inestimable Whiggism of that State." But, he warned his friend, "The History of Mankind" proves "that there has ever been an unceasing Struggle of the few for obtaining Aggrandisement at the Expence of the many." He held up the Greek goddess Minerva as representing their ideals. She was the goddess of justice and law and the sponsor of the arts and trade. These represented the demands of the Democrats. Dickinson believed that they had valid claims that must be addressed if the commonwealth were to flourish. He thus sent McKean drafts of five bills he hoped would pass in Pennsylvania, each of which promoted republicanism by securing property of one sort or another to ordinary citizens and limiting entails, that is, inheritances, to prevent the accumulation of wealth by a few individuals. They were much like the laws he had written in the 1760s to aid ordinary people with little time, education, or legal assistance to navigate the complexities of the law. He fervently hoped that McKean would advocate their passage, which would "be happy Examples to other States."[32]

Minerva was also the patron of defensive war, so Dickinson repeated his belief in the necessity of "a well-organized, a well-equipped, and a well-disciplined militia," which was the only way to protect themselves and posterity against "internal Confusions" and "foreign Invasions." He had in mind three main things: insurrections by citizens, slave revolts, and the army of Napoleon. "Yet—What have We done on this momentous Business?" he queried. "Prattled—and trifled. The Love of Money and the Love of Ease are conspiring against our national Happiness."[33] He waited in vain for a response.

Dickinson's longtime interest in foreign affairs drew his gaze beyond American shores. The United States continued to be caught between France and Britain, and its policy should be clear and careful. "Some well written publication should be made," wrote Dickinson to Coxe, "manifesting the Disposition of The United States to cultivate the most friendly Intercourse with France" to prove that trade would benefit both countries. Americans' esteem for France, he said, was not "cancelled by any Novelties introduced into their Form of Government," by which he meant the advent of a dictator. "For whatever that Form may be, <u>the people</u> of France are the Objects of our Regard."[34]

In 1803, writing as "Anticipation," Dickinson thus took up his pen for what would be his last publication. He wrote it as though he were delivering a speech to the nation. Recounting the recent history of the two nations, as both struggled since their respective revolutions, he found that "*France, however ardent her love of liberty, may not, perhaps, be yet prepared for a government of the best form*," namely a republic. Worse than that, "A gigantic Power seems animated by the devastating spirit of conquest, and glares with a fierce aspect on all around." That "gigantic power" was Napoleon.

Since he had written to Coxe on the matter, his views had evolved. While in the past, Dickinson had urged friendly relations with and loyalty to France because it had been America's staunch ally during the Revolution, now he urged a prudent amity with her as security from the rapacious Napoleon, or the "Corsican Adventurer," as Dickinson called him.[35] In addition to relegating much of Europe to French provinces, Napoleon had attempted to reinstate "the direful traffic in human flesh" in Haiti, which had been fighting for independence from France since 1791.[36] Dickinson feared he would soon turn his eyes to America and begin his march in that direction. After depriving Americans of their arms and pressing them into military engagements beyond seas "to consummate your woes," Dickinson warned, "*religious establishments*, violating the rights of conscience, and soul-racking *definitions of heresy*, are to be expected; so that the generations of your posterity, condemned to an ignorance of the holy truths."[37] Napoleon's acquisition of the Louisiana territory from Spain told Dickinson all he needed to know. "We cannot entertain the least doubt," he warned, "but that the *French* government means to acquire the dominion of all America, and that the possession of *Louisiana* is to be the first act of the tragedy."[38] To counteract the compact between France and Spain, Dickinson now proposed a closer relationship with Britain, something most Republicans wanted to avoid. As ever, he believed that this relationship should be based on free trade, but before that could happen, first, "let her for ever abolish the *African* slave-trade, that enormous sin," which persists "in defiance of the clearest light that ever shone upon a people, and menaces to sink her into perdition."[39]

Perhaps because *A Caution* had garnered little response, Dickinson sent this pamphlet, titled *An Address on the Past, Present, and Eventual Relations of the United States to France*, to his friend Samuel Miller in New York to have it published there.[40] The advertisements for the piece appeared in the New York papers on February 12, and some reviews shortly thereafter. One was negative and dismissive, but others found it written in "a strain of interesting eloquence" and containing "much force and spirit."[41] "I shall be satisfied," Dickinson confessed, "if I come off tolerably from the Critics. Should they be angry, they never can deprive Me of the Pleasure arising from the Purity of my Motives, and from the Usefulness of my Labors."[42] Unfortunately, the pamphlet didn't sell enough to cover the cost of the printing.[43]

The year Dickinson's last pamphlet appeared, he suffered a loss from which he would never recover. Over the last fifteen years, Polly had slowly declined until this spring, of 1803, when the doctors saw that bleeding no longer worked. On July 23, at the age of sixty-three, she went to the waiting arms of the All-Gracious Maker and the family members she had mourned so long— her parents, her beloved Sally, and her three babies. Her obituary was simple, as she wanted it: "A woman not surpassed by any in the virtues of the female character, or in piety."[44] Although Dickinson tried to resign himself to the Divine Will in all things, this one was impossible to overcome. Feelings of helplessness turned into "indigent Grief" and anger at a new generation of physicians whose cures seemed worse than the diseases they treated.[45]

Receiving condolences from friends and relations, near and far, eased him through his bereavement. "I am sure," said Benjamin Rush, "you believe, the beloved friend, and companion of your life is 'not lost, but gone before.' "[46] He thanked Rush for "thy Sympathy with my afflicted Mind. My heart is indeed deeply wounded. She is gone, who gave to Life its highest value."[47] His old friend Thomas McKean wrote, "You have the comfortible reflection, from the purity & piety of her whole life whom death has torn from you, that she was not unprepared for the change and that she is happy."[48] Newer friends as well, such as Thomas Jefferson, wrote promptly to extend sympathy for his "wounded Heart."[49] He appreciated the kind words, but, "At present," he admitted, "I am stunned by the Blow that has struck Me down." He turned to God in "humble submission to his holy Will. I grieve and adore."[50] As he remembered Polly, he thought, "I am every where, allways, and entirely thy affectionate John Dickinson"[51]

Life was hard to fathom without Polly. She had exerted a profound influence on him for nearly forty years, from even before they were married. What woman could have suited him better, himself having been raised by a self-possessed and erudite Quaker woman? Although Polly may not have joined him in reading his law books like his mother, she was as conversant as he with *belles lettres*. She could discourse with him on politics and was not afraid to press her views. And she did what her mother-in-law did not: she gradually brought him around to embracing religion and living his faith in ways to which he could only aspire as a young man. She was his helpmeet and soul mate and his partner in benevolent endeavors. Their last charitable act together, completed a few months before she died, was the donation of a lot to the Quaker-run Philadelphia Society for the Establishment and Support of Charity Schools.[52]

Although Dickinson certainly learned about the abilities of women from his mother, when he met and then joined the Rural Circle, the Quaker poets' sorority, his education advanced. Surrounded by strong, highly literate, and outspoken Quaker women who jealously guarded their independence from men, Dickinson was made to see that women and girls were not highly valued for the contributions they could make; and they were disadvantaged in a society dominated by men.[53] Accordingly, he paid them special attention in his law practice, his public offices, his charity work, and his aid to those whom he had formerly enslaved. He represented women in difficult situations peculiar to women who struggled as mothers, wives, and widows.

Raising two daughters with Polly only heightened Dickinson's concern to advocate for the interests and rights of women and girls. He wrote a clause in the Articles of Confederation protecting women's religious liberty and freedom of public speech. Grace Galloway and Elizabeth Graeme Fergusson could attest that when fleeing Loyalists abandoned their wives during the Revolutionary War, Dickinson offered those wives friendship and support. He pressed for the marriage law in Pennsylvania to include a provision for divorce and alimony to allow women to escape abuse and poverty. And the educational opportunities he provided for children always included girls.

Dickinson valued women's contributions to causes dear to him and encouraged the publication of works by and about women to further political, civic, and religious ends. He admired, encouraged, and befriended such women over the course of his adult life—members of the Rural Circle as well as Susanna Wright, Debby Norris Logan, Catharine Macaulay, Patience Wright, and others—who were as valuable to him as his male friends. He likewise eagerly purchased books about the lives of strong women and urged the reprinting of works on women "who have been eminently distinguished by Talents or Strength of Mind, where these Qualities have been dedicated to laudable purposes."[54] He wrote to Philadelphia printers Birch and Small that he valued virtuous women for what they could contribute as moral human beings. He therefore trusted that the printers would publish *Female Biography, or Memoirs of Illustrious Women of All Ages and Countries* (1803) out of a "Desire . . . to promote a Love of Virtue and Religion" rather than "to gratify the Curiosity" of an audience unused to reading about extraordinary women. He recommended it especially because the genre of biography allows the accounts to be "adorned with some Points of the persons described which, is a pleasing addition to such kind of Writing, as it forms a sort of Acquaintance between the Reader and the subject." He even offered to lend the printers his volumes of Daniel Dana's *Memoirs of Eminently Pious Women* (1803), "tho, such is my Estimation of those that on no other Consideration would I let them go out of my Hands."[55]

Thinking about the future well-being of his daughters and their daughters, and the difficulties women faced under the laws of primogeniture and coverture, he added specific language to his own will. First, to prevent all their property by default from devising to a first-born son, "it is my Advice," he said, "that in Case of their having Children they respectively from Time to Time make such Settlements for the Division of their Estates among their several Children." The will "also enjoined each of my Daughters never to make over her Estate or any part of it to a Husband."[56]

Dickinson knew well that his efforts—and women's roles and rights—were limited by the times. His provision in the Articles of Confederation was immediately struck by the committee. And as erudite, as savvy in business, as courageous on the battlefield, and as virtuous in their morals as women could be, they were denied the privileges of citizenship, to vote and hold office. When Benjamin Rush pleaded with Dickinson to write the "Memoirs of his Life relating to your political Opinions and Conduct," Dickinson demurred. A main purpose of that literary genre was to serve as an instruction manual for sons coming up in the world and going into politics. Dickinson reminded Rush, "my Children are Daughters."[57]

In raising their daughters, the Dickinsons felt they had been successful in producing virtuous Quakerly women. "Sally," he observed in a letter to John Lloyd, "is all we wish her to be." Now almost thirty, she was a true daughter of the Rural Circle—they did not believe she would marry, "unless it be to a Man of a well-cultivated Mind, and an uncommonly amiable Character." Maria, who took after her tall and slender father, was almost eighteen and "a Girl of fine Understanding." She possessed "a cheerful Disposition, balanced by a strong sense of Religious Truth." It looked as though she would marry her distant cousin, Albanus Logan, son of George and Debby Logan. Although they were "both brought up Friends," only Sally held formal membership in the Society.[58] But both John and Polly took care that their daughters were "taught to regard other Societies with Liberality and Benevolence."[59]

Although Dickinson found "my Mind is continually engaged in contemplating" Polly's death, he soldiered on as a widower with her memory his "constant Companion," reminding him to love his Adorable Creator and to venerate virtue.[60] With Sally and Maria dutifully at his side, he continued his life and work, managing his properties, doing a little legal work, and riding to meeting. Benevolent causes remained foremost in his mind. He gave land to Merion Friends Meeting in Pennsylvania and the Claymont School in New Castle County, money to Wilmington Monthly Meeting for the poor, shares of stock in the Spring-Water Company to the Library Company of Wilmington, and 150 bushels of corn to the citizens of Kent County when their crops failed. He also extended aid to individuals. Sometimes he let his identity be known, as when he paid for the schooling of an aspiring school-master named Thomas Mason. But other times, he was a secret benefactor, as when he requested that Francis Gallet, a Frenchman living in Philadelphia whom Dickinson had helped settle, seek out "eminently deserving and help-less persons" for whom Dickinson could "exercise his beneficence."[61] "I love Mankind," Dickinson declared, "and I ardently wish their Wellfare. It is a glo-rious Thing to contribute to their Felicity. It is a Cause worth laboring for— worth dying for."[62]

The year 1803 ended eventfully on several fronts. Dickinson was a party to several lawsuits during this period, at least one of which concluded favorably.[63] He was sued in the Delaware Supreme Court concerning a tract of land by fellow Delaware politicians Gunning Bedford Jr., Nicholas Vandyke Jr., and David Hall, the governor of Delaware at the time, who were represented by James Ashton Bayard, a Federalist lawyer. Dickinson asked his attorney, George Read Jr., to subpoena witnesses for him.[64]

On November 8, the verdict came down. Dickinson informed Caesar A. Rodney that "the Court expressed their Detestation of the Plaintiffs, in the strongest language, animated by a sensation of the meditated Injustice."

Indeed, Bayard seemed chagrined by his own clients. When Dickinson made his closing arguments, the plaintiffs moved for a nonsuit, admitting they had failed to prove their case. Bedford then stormed out of the court; Vandyke thought they should only demur, which was effectively the same as a nonsuit; and Hall continued to argue his nonsensical case. Bayard exclaimed, "there was not a man in the U.S. bearing the name of lawyer but Hall who would have been stupid and impudent enough to deny that an Estate in general tail descended from a Parent to a Child in preference to a second cousin."[65] Dickinson observed with satisfaction that "the Countenances of some persons were truly pitiable."

Dickinson's elation at his victory was not lessened even by a near catastrophe later the same day—he took "the most dreadful Fall I ever experienced in my Life." His entire right side from his lower leg to his torso was badly bruised. "My escape from Death and from broken Limbs was," he believed, "wonderful." Although he could only with difficulty sit up to write letters, he stoically "rejected all medical Aid and all friendly Sollicitations," which, he noted, "as I am within three Days of being Seventy-one, is somewhat remarkable."[66] By his birthday, however, he had contracted a bad cold.

Traveling to Poplar Hall a few days later, he had improved. He was as comfortable in his carriage as if he had been sitting in his dining room, hardly feeling his bruises at all, and the licorice he had taken for his cold had relieved it neatly.[67] When happily ensconced in his beloved home, he conducted his business as the sun shone into his room all day long. "As powerful as his Rays are, I find his humble auxiliary, a Hickory Fire, of great Importance for obtaining a Victory over Cold."[68] Age had crept into his bones like the chill, and thoughts of his own demise were never far from his mind. He did not fear death for himself; he wished only that his children would be prepared for his and their own. "You have lost one Parent, and may expect soon to lose another."[69] He never missed an opportunity to remind them to take care of their physical and spiritual health, "as that excellent Woman, Lady Rachel Russel expressed herself, 'in dressing up the Soul, to meet is Maker.' "[70]

Dickinson was not home from Kent long when he was compelled to return. On March 7, 1804, he learned that Poplar Hall, then leased, had burned from a fire that started on the roof. Only the walls of his childhood home remained. This news came almost a year after another terrible loss by fire. In April 1803, John Montgomery had informed Dickinson of a devastating fire at Dickinson College. A new dormitory to house all the students had burned to the ground. Happily, the library and "philosophical apparatus" had not yet been moved into the building. And "before the Smoaking ruins had time to Cool," they had received $16,000 in donations and loans to rebuild an even larger building than the one they'd lost.[71] This was fortunate, since Dickinson felt unable to donate to the college at that time.[72]

Perhaps Dickinson had that catastrophe in mind when, on December 29 of the previous year, he had taken out a policy on the house with the Insurance Company of North America.[73] But the company offered him only $2,000, which he did not believe covered the value of his loss. He wrote to Charles Petit, the president, asking him to deposit the funds in his account in the Bank of North America, which Petit did.[74] He then hired Polly's cousin David Evans to do the work of rebuilding but oversaw every detail himself. "You cannot imagine, what an accumulation of Labors it is to build a large House in the Country," he wrote to Sally and Maria. "Building in Town is a mere play in comparison."[75] More than two years and thousands of dollars later, although rebuilding more simply than before, with only two stories instead of three, Dickinson was still wrangling with the insurance company to persuade it to cover his expenses.[76] In the midst of this ordeal, a missive arrived from Tench Coxe in early May informing him of a fire raging in Philadelphia that had begun on Dock Street and consumed fifteen or twenty buildings and several ships at the docks. Although it spread as far as Third Street, opposite the Bank of the United States, it had not reached any of Dickinson's property. "Providence has exempted you from any share in this calamity," Coxe observed.[77]

Coxe admired Dickinson tremendously and had in recent years become a close friend. Now that Coxe had renounced the Federalist party and turned Republican, the two men shared very similar political philosophies and had developed "an intimate and confidential" correspondence that ranged over topics including foreign affairs, the military, religion, slavery, and medicine.[78] Of late, they had been corresponding about the value of Dickinson's properties in Pennsylvania, with Coxe acting as an advisor and agent. Dickinson was looking to sell several large tracts of land north of the city worth tens of thousands of dollars. He was also seeking a buyer for a couple of valuable lots in Philadelphia, for which he and Coxe had an exciting idea. The Philadelphia Board of Brokers—the group of merchants who met at the Merchants' Coffee-House, more commonly known as City Tavern— had begun discussing the building of a Merchants' Exchange in the city as a more proper place to conduct their business. When Coxe sent Dickinson the preliminary plan, Dickinson excitedly imagined all the various uses for the building, saying, "Whenever an Exchange shall be erected, it is to be hoped, that it will be in a Taste and Spirit becoming the Athens of America," as Philadelphia was known.[79] He very much hoped that the merchants would buy his property on Second Street for the building and offered it at fair price and favorable terms. The neoclassical architect Benjamin Latrobe, who had recently established his offices in Philadelphia and been hired as the architect of the Capitol in the District of Columbia, had indicated that he favored Dickinson's lots for the building.[80] But as the months wore on without a decision, it looked increasingly unlikely that the merchants would buy his property. No movement, indeed, would happen during the lifetimes of Dickinson, Coxe, or Latrobe. The Merchants' Exchange, designed in neoclassical splendor by Latrobe's student William Strickland, opened in 1834, a block away from Dickinson's lots.

In retirement, Dickinson had plenty to fill his time agreeably. Between managing his various properties, traveling to and from Kent, considering various philanthropic ventures, and working on various writings he had in mind, it seemed as though he could be satisfied enough with monitoring public affairs from the wings, mentoring junior politicians, and offering advice from afar. Such, however, was not his way.

16

"To bear my public Testimony"

Once More into Politics, 1804–1808

In the waning years of Dickinson's life, few could have been surprised that he was again drawn into an active role in national affairs. He had one primary concern: to preserve the Union, against which there were two principal and related threats, one internal, the other external. Both had been a long time coming. First, keeping his eye on the federal government through George Logan, he became increasingly aware of the growing menace of slavery to the Union. It was, he believed, a central problem in two areas: the recent purchase of the Louisiana territory, which had been announced on July 4, 1803, and trade with the newly independent nation of Haiti. Second, tensions between Britain and France, with the United States caught in between, had escalated and threatened to erupt in open hostilities. As these matters demanded Dickinson's attention, so did affairs in Pennsylvania threaten the stability of that state's government.

At the end of January 1804, the Senate debated a bill for the government of Louisiana, much of which centered on whether to allow slavery there. Logan had read a petition from the American Convention for Promoting the Abolition of Slavery praying that slavery would not be introduced into the new territory.[1] Dickinson followed the debate as closely as he could from afar. On January 30, he sent his opinions to Logan. "As Congress is now to legislate for our extensive Territory lately acquired," he said, "I pray to Heaven, that they may build up the system of the Government, on the broad and sacred Principles of Freedom. Curse not the Inhabitants of those Regions of The United States in General, with a permission to introduce Bondage." He returned to a belief he had held his entire life. "Slaves are deeply, deeply injurious to the Morals of the Masters and their Families," he explained. But since the revolution in Saint Domingue, as Haiti was known, the danger was no longer just to individuals; it threatened the United States as a whole, and on various levels. Americans in all regions of the country feared a contagion of slave rebellion in the United States. Indeed, it seemed already to be happening. Gabriel's Conspiracy in Virginia during the spring and summer of 1800 had threatened the city of Richmond, and the Easter Plot in 1802, spanning several counties in Virginia and North Carolina, could have grown much bigger.

Dickinson was unafraid of Black people, and unlike some, including Jefferson and Coxe, he was not opposed to Black people and white people living together in society. Slaves, however, "are internal Enemies," Dickinson insisted, "allways to be watched and guarded against." Short of abolishing slavery altogether, there were two ways the United States should preserve itself. First, "our Liberty must depend on our being an <u>armed</u> Nation." And second, "considering the power of those with whom We may have to contend, We must be a <u>populous</u> Nation." It wasn't only violence that Dickinson feared; he believed that slavery deprived Americans of the virtues of democratic agrarianism. "The Labor of Slaves," he argued, "must in a certain proportion exclude the Cultivation of the Earth by Freemen, and thereby diminish our internal safety and external Security." Although some in the Senate agreed with his antislavery sentiments and most shared his fear of slave rebellions, others believed that white men were incapable of the hard labor in unfavorable conditions of the sort slaves were compelled to undertake. For his part, Dickinson was clear: "Let the pernicious project, the detestable precedent, never be sanctioned by Votes of the Sons of Liberty."[2]

Over much of 1804, Americans received a steady stream of horrifying news from Haiti. The rebels were systematically torturing and massacring families of white people who remained on the island, even those who had sympathized with the Black population. In a proclamation entitled "Liberty or Death," Governor General of Haiti Jean-Jacques Dessalines justified the violence against white people, the "true cannibals," as "war for war, crime for crime, outrage for outrage."[3] In December, Dickinson expressed concern for the weak state of the militias, reiterating, "With all my abhorance for War, I hold it to be guilt of the deepest dye not to defend to the 'ultima conata' "— last attempt—"the Blessings which our adorable Creator has bestowed upon us. It is part of a Freeman's Religion."[4]

Beginning with the Adams administration, the United States had developed a close trading relationship with Haiti. Adams had seen it as a way to weaken France. Under Jefferson, the United States' neutral stance had benefited Haiti and American merchants. But as Southern enslavers' anxieties increased and the French pressured Jefferson to halt the trade that was arming the rebels, Jefferson's policy towards Haitian trade evolved. In his fourth annual message to Congress on November 8, 1804, he made it clear that he wanted the trade restrained.[5] Agreeing with him, in early 1805 Dickinson began an energetic campaign to push Logan to act in the Senate to halt all trade with Haiti. Warning that there was "an appearance of Duplicity in the proceedings of Congress on this subject," he wanted the language of their acts to clarify that the legislation could not serve as cover for the arms trade. In February, he reiterated his desire for the United States to behave as a "neutral Nation."[6] By now, Logan was planning on introducing a bill of his own.

At the same time, Dickinson also alerted Logan that American slave traffickers had devised a scheme not only to skirt the penalties levied by Congress but actually to profit from them. They enlisted informants to report on traffickers, and when "property" was forfeited to an informant, that person simply divided it with his accomplices. Dickinson was so disgusted by the scheme that he didn't even have a word to describe these despicable men. He proposed that half of the forfeitures go to the United States as a deterrent.[7] With slavery still such a booming business, abolition of the practice seemed a long way off.

In 1805, Pennsylvania seemed to be devolving into chaos under McKean's leadership. In a very real sense, the radical Democrats in Philadelphia were still fighting the American Revolution, seeking to displace the Philadelphia oligarchy, which they identified with the British aristocracy, and raise up the working man. In their minds, the moderate Tertium Quids were no better than conservative Federalists. So they sought to tear down the institutions that they perceived gave cover to the wealthy to maintain their hegemony. The Quids recognized, however, that these institutions were the republican checks and balances that protected all people. Thus the same danger threatened now as before—that majority rule would trample on minority rights.

One catalyst for the unrest was a seemingly minor law that actually represented the hopes of one faction and the fears of another. Called the $100 Act, it was designed to allow litigants with less than $100 at stake to bypass the expensive and convoluted court system and enter into arbitration instead. At first, McKean vetoed the bill twice in December 1802. When it came before him again in March 1804, he allowed it to pass by ignoring it.[8] Like McKean, most Quids were opposed to this law, believing that it was designed to undermine the judicial branch and ultimately destroy the independence of the judiciary, one of the bedrocks of republicanism, and replace it with majority rule. But an important minority of Quids believed that the court system had become so byzantine that ordinary citizens were denied justice. Reform was essential, but it was not forthcoming.

The courts were only one problem. Taxes were another. By chance in August 1805, Dickinson realized another danger for all citizens, especially the most vulnerable. He happened to see an advertisement in the newspaper for some land he owned near Philadelphia being sold to pay taxes he was entirely unaware he owed. He was incredulous and outraged. "To a vast Extent," he wrote to Coxe, these direct taxes "will be more destructive to Property than the Devastations of our revolutionary War." The tax laws had all the hallmarks of poorly written legislation: "Descriptions so vague as to be indefinite and unintelligible, and Ignorance or Inattention of Owners or Tenants, to say no more, may snatch from Families very valuable Estates, the Inheritance of Generations, and vest them for a few Dollars in greedy Speculators watching to prey on Innocence and Honesty."[9] It was bad enough that he was a victim of this policy, but he was less concerned for himself than for others. He had advantages most did not—experience with land ownership, an agent living near the property, and considerable knowledge of the laws and taxation policy. If this could happen to him, he reasoned, "woe—woe—woe—to Women, Children, and the Uninformed."[10] This gave him all the reason he needed, when the time was right, to press Governor McKean to enact reforms in Pennsylvania.

That moment came after the October 1805 election, in which McKean was returned to office by only the slimmest victory. It was a sign that he finally needed to take the views of his opponents seriously if he wanted to preserve Pennsylvania institutions that served to check the power of the majority. Dickinson wrote to his friend of nearly half a century, both to congratulate him on his return to office and to plead with him to enact changes. Although he believed that the Revolutionists, as he called the Democrats, "meditated Innovations, which seemed to Me likely to produce ruinous Consequences," whether the Constitutionalists, as he called the Tertium Quids, could maintain their power would all depend on the exertion of their "Wisdom and Virtue." For Dickinson, both history and his own experience had taught him that "Moderation is a Law of our Nature"; because he and McKean had "studied in the same School," he believed this was a principle they shared.

Dickinson argued that moderation should compel McKean to recognize that the "Malcontents," as some Quids dismissively referred to the Democrats, were driven to extremes by the "<u>actual Feeling</u> of the Distresses caused by Delays and Expenses in the Administration of Justice." He then effectively repeated the very arguments the Democrats employed against the Quids, asking, "Is it not an alarming Circumstance, that these Delays and Expenses are more Oppressive in the Infancy of our republican Institutions, than the judicial Evils experienced by the British in the advanced Age of their Monarchy?" In other words, Dickinson agreed with the Democrats that they were being oppressed by a quasi-aristocratical system. The only point on which he disagreed with them was their methods. Their complaints, he believed, "could be remedied, without overturning the Constitution." Once again, Dickinson advocated radical reforms through moderate means, the hallmark of his Quakerly political style.

Using the freedom of their long friendship, Dickinson called on McKean, "by the Love for they Fellow Citizens . . . by Commiseration for Widows, Orphans, the weak and uninformed, and by thy Veneration for sacred Justice," to use his position "for redressing Grievances, and promoting the general Wellfare." Specifically, he wanted new laws written and old ones revised that would halt the sources of animosity. Because McKean seemed to have ignored the five laws he had sent in 1802, Dickinson reminded the governor of those and added another that would give landholders valid title to their land against all individuals and the state after legal possession for twenty or twenty-five years.[11]

McKean's response was not encouraging. After mirroring Dickinson's affectionate sentiments, he went on to accuse his opponents of pushing a "conspiracy hatched in hell and propogated by the imps of darkness." God, he believed, "would frustrate the nefarious attempt" to overthrow the Pennsylvania constitution. After claiming to "pant after moderation & conciliation," McKean described the Democrats as "demons in human shape," concluding that "such wretches must be controlled by fear and by force." He then proceeded to hand out political favors to his supporters and punishments to his opponents.[12] Had he taken the persuasive approach Dickinson had used in 1764 to preserve the 1701 Pennsylvania constitution, perhaps he would not have faced the impeachment proceedings that dogged him through 1807. During that period, Dickinson continued to work for the welfare of the people of Pennsylvania by collecting materials so that Tench Coxe could revise and improve the $100 Act—not to overturn the judiciary but to provide an easier path to justice.[13] The Democrats may have gotten wind of Dickinson's advocacy of their causes. In a fictitious dialogue between a Democrat and a Quid in the *Aurora General Advertiser*, the Democrat invoked Dickinson as one of a few statesmen who "will long ornament the page of history" as one of Pennsylvania's leaders.[14]

Against the backdrop of these national and state crises, a new history of the Founding appeared. In 1805, Mercy Otis Warren, sister of Dickinson's late friend James Otis and fellow Democratic-Republican, published her three-volume history of the American Revolution.[15] Hers was not the first; the ink was hardly dry on the Constitution when David Ramsay's history appeared. A South Carolina politician and physician, he described Dickinson as "a worthy citizen" who "may be said to have sown the seeds of the revolution."[16] At this point, the "celebrated Dickinson" may have come to accept this unintended consequence of his actions as his legacy. It was rumored that he called Ramsay the "Polybius of America."[17] By contrast, when Chief Justice of the Supreme Court John Marshall began publishing a multi-volume biography of George Washington in 1804, Dickinson found a problem. Contrary to all evidence, Marshall credited Richard Henry Lee with writing the 1774 Petition to the King in the First Continental Congress.[18] Receiving credit for writing the petition was "of little Moment" to Dickinson. "Of vast Importance," however, was that Marshall's work, coming shortly after the appearance of Dickinson's edition of his writings, in which he included the First Petition, made him look like a liar.[19] He wrote to George Logan, asking of him two things. First, he asked that Logan convey a letter to Marshall alerting him to the mistake and requesting a correction. Marshall immediately agreed, providing it in the fourth volume of the work, which appeared in 1805.[20] Second, Dickinson asked Logan to direct the clerk of Congress to search for the draft of this and other congressional documents in his handwriting. These original drafts, said Dickinson, "may defend Me against future Misrepresentations."[21] Or so he hoped.

Warren's account of Dickinson's role in the Revolution was most gratifying. She explained that "no man was more strenuous in support of the rights of the colonies" than he and described his stance against independence as one intended to protect American rights and liberties.[22] This was exactly right. She could not have been trying to please him; she did not know that Dickinson was still alive until shortly after she had delivered her manuscript to the press.[23] Then she wrote to him, initiating a long-distance friendship that Dickinson cherished until the end of his life. He considered her good opinion of him a "real Honor" and took great pleasure in their "Communion of Minds" despite never having met. Like with Catharine Macaulay, he encouraged her, writing, "Thy generous Exertions to inform thy fellow citizens, and to present thy Country before the World in a justly favorable Light, will be, I firmly believe, attended with the desired Success."[24] The following year, he received two sets of her history.[25]

At the end of 1805, Dickinson was impatient for progress in the Senate concerning "the impolitic and dishonourable Trade to St. Domingo. Renew," he beseeched Logan, "thy motion to prohibit that Trade entirely. Our Rapacity in that Respect, and our Ambition in acquiring Territory, will destroy our Peace, our wellfare, our Reputation." He had been rereading his second set of *Fabius Letters* and thought a reprinting of certain sections of them would be seasonable, specifically those "in which a just value for the Blessings of Peace is contrasted with the blind Rage for War."[26] Logan was one step ahead of him; the previous day he had requested permission to bring in a bill, which he did with a long speech on the twentieth.[27] "Is it sound policy," he asked, "to cherish the black population of St. Domingo whilst we have a similar population in our Southern States, in which should an insurrection take place, the Government of the United States is bound to render effectual aid to our fellow-citizens in that part of the Union?" Ultimately, however, the goal of the bill was not to please France or Britain or punish the Haitians but "to preserve the immediate honor and future peace of the United States."[28]

But peace, as Dickinson envisioned it, was not exactly why the bill gained momentum. Support came predominantly from the Southern planters, who sought to dominate the enslaved population. Thus the strange bedfellows of this political climate were a Quakerly Union-supporting abolitionist and rapacious Southern slaveholders.

By January 25, 1806, Logan was so confident that his bill would pass that, at a dinner party held by the French minister, he boasted that it would pass the Senate 21–7.[29] Logan reported his confidence to Dickinson, who replied, "I rejoice that the advocates for thy Bill are increasing."[30] Eager for more news, he wrote again before the end of the week to ask "whether thy Bill was Strong enough to make a total prohibition of the infamous traffic it was designed to prevent." Dickinson could see that it was not and "supposed the thirst of gain should tempt men to carry it on without clearances," which prompted him to enquire "what Laws of these States would they thereby violate, and to what penalties would they be liable?" He hoped any further amendments on the bill could be introduced in the House of Representatives.[31]

But Logan actually did not want to make such adjustments. The bill, which passed the Senate and which Jefferson signed into law on February 28, prohibited trade with the portions of the island held by the Black revolutionaries and required compliance on penalty of forfeiture of ship and cargo. It then became the basis for the Embargo Act of 1807. Whether Logan actually agreed with Dickinson's purposes for the bill, he was not entirely Dickinson's tool. In a conversation with Republican Senator William Plumer of New Hampshire, Logan admitted that he had no intention of prohibiting the trade with Haiti but "only to pass a bill that would please the French . . . and not injure our own traders."[32]

Dickinson's own motives for desiring the trade embargo against Haiti were, first, to protect America from a devastating slave revolt and, second, to secure peace with the major Atlantic powers. "Our business is to treat," he told Logan, "and strive together upon some plan of accommodation."[33] But his stance necessitated his holding double standards concerning rights and liberties and their protections for white and Black populations. Despite the Haitian Revolution being the only one of the era in which the people were not just metaphorically but *actually* enslaved by their oppressors, Dickinson refused to allow that the Haitian Revolution was legitimate. Whereas Americans and the French should defend their rights and liberties with arms, he was not willing that arms should be traded to provide Haitians with the same opportunity. It was an unfortunate coincidence that Dickinson's calls for America to be an "armed nation" became the ideology of the Southern planter class to defend white hegemony. After all, Dickinson was pro-Union and not just antislavery but pro-abolition. He had demonstrated a genuine concern to improve the lives of Black people by providing education and support to those he formerly enslaved. While Jefferson was driven by racial animus in his policy towards Haiti, Dickinson shared neither Jefferson's hatred of Black people nor his conviction that the races must remain separate. Rather, his motive for nonimportation was the same as his motive for writing the *Farmer's Letters*.

From the early years of the contest with Britain, Dickinson had consistently and vigorously argued that unity was America's salvation. It must come before all else. Had he lived to see the American Civil War, he would have agreed with President Lincoln, who wrote in a letter to Horace Greeley, "My paramount object in this struggle *is* to save the Union, and is *not* either to save or to destroy slavery." He added, "What I do about slavery, and the colored race, I do because I believe it helps to save the Union."[34] Likewise, in the Haitian Revolution, Dickinson saw "the horrors of a total dissolution of the Union."[35] For Dickinson as the principled trimmer, national unity took precedence.

Over the years, Dickinson had become very clear about his hatred of slavery. During the ratification debates in 1788, when he could not risk alienating Southerners, he allowed that slavery might remain to preserve the Union. "Whatever regions may be destined for servitude," he said, "let us hope, that some portions of this land may be blessed with liberty; let us be convinced, that nothing short of such an union as has been proposed, can preserve the blessing."[36] By 1804, Dickinson's condemnation of the institution of slavery remained unequivocal: "The sanctions of Law, the most solemn national Acts, and the eternal Distinction between Right and Wrong," he proclaimed, "all forbid property to spring from such a source." As outrageous as it was that the British had still not prohibited the trade and "with a deplorable Inconsistency, are continually employed, under public Authority too, in enslaving their Fellowcreatures in other parts of the World," what was happening in America was much worse. "Too many of our Countrymen exceed them in Folly and Wickedness; for not satisfied, as the British Depredators are, with carrying their Fellowcreatures into Captivity in other parts of the World, they are striving to pour a Deluge of Slavery over their Own Country."[37]

Yet even this most enlightened of the American Founders—the only one of the major figures to free those he enslaved during his lifetime and work for abolition—could look the other way when opportunities to help Black people presented themselves. On the subject of slavery, Dickinson was slipping behind the times. Whereas once his thinking on the welfare of Black people had been ahead of most in America, now a few had caught up and surpassed him in their work for racial justice. These people not only wanted abolition but made the obvious argument that Haiti was a sovereign nation that should be accorded the same privileges as others. In explaining why he had voted against the Logan-Dickinson trade bill, Samuel White, a young Federalist senator, also from Kent County in Delaware, made a long and impassioned speech arguing that the people of Haiti had the right to liberty and sovereignty on the same principles as the Americans had fought for and gained their independence. Basing his argument on the law of nations, he found that "in their commercial relations" America ought to treat France and Haiti "with like civility."[38] It was the kind of speech Dickinson might have given when he was thirty-five.

At every moment, Dickinson felt the burden of his public stature greatly and attempted to do the right thing. "I esteem it my Duty," he explained, "to seek for Information on every Side, that I may be enabled the better to discharge the accepted Trust. It is a very serious Reflection in Business that concerns thousands, to know that if I err, I may also cause others to err, and thus injure Multitudes, if not Ages."[39] Unfortunately, injury is arguably what his final political contribution achieved for Black people in Haiti.

By 1807, keeping up with current events was increasingly overwhelming for Dickinson. Though his health had fluctuated his entire life as a result of overwork—the one area of life in which he did not practice moderation—since retirement, generally, it was quite good. In his seventy-fifth year, "excepting a pain in the small of my Back at times severe, my Health is good, considering my Age," he wrote Mercy Otis Warren. "I see, and hear, and walk, and ride, as well as I did in my Youth. Such an old Age could hardly be expected by a Man born in the Middle part of Maryland."[40] But the increasing discord between his patriotic fervor and physical limitations frustrated him. In addition to the "lumbago," or lower back pain, he suffered from gout, rheumatic pains, and the occasional "bilious complaint." Sometimes he "broke through Obstructions that seem'd to condemn Me to Silence and Inactivity" of advanced age and "manifold Infirmities." Since Polly's death, he had come to distrust younger physicians and their methods. "I abhorr the Revolution in Physick," he exclaimed to Coxe. He missed the days when medicine was guided by the common-sense practices of seventeenth-century physicians Thomas Sydenham and Herman Boerhaave. So he trusted in his own remedies or recommendations from friends. For stomach ailments, if eating less food did not suffice, he found that bleeding along with a cathartic to encourage elimination did the trick. Magnolia twigs reduced the pain of his arthritis. On recommendation from Coxe, he found that a carriage ride eased his lumbago, as did taking bark, soaking in mineral springs, or taking a cold bath. In general, the best medicines he knew were exercise, temperance, fresh air, and cheerfulness, which was also a duty to God.[41] Happily for Dickinson, as Debby Logan said, "his natural disposition was exceedingly cheerful."[42] The efficacy of his approach was vindicated when in the autumn of 1807 he escaped the influenza that afflicted Sally and Maria.[43]

Still, he was slowing down just as the world seemed to be speeding up. "Human Affairs are now pouring along in a vast Torrent," proclaimed

Dickinson to Warren. "It will not continue." He was thinking about his country's road to salvation and the great changes required to succeed. It would happen, he believed, but it was still "two or three Centuries remote."[44] Contemplating a future America without him and his own end of days, he was increasingly fascinated by theological explorations. History, political thought, and theology were all connected for him, and he spent many days and weeks laboring over essays and attempting to pull the various strands together on paper. He now spoke about religion as he had about political matters in the past. Cousin Debby found that "when he spoke of divine things, he implored an Holy Awe upon those that heard him that even reprobates felt, and were by it silenced."[45]

His intense interest gained him a new sort of acolyte in Samuel Miller, a Presbyterian minister in New York. Originally from Dover, Samuel's father, John Miller, also a Presbyterian minister, had been Dickinson's friend. The younger Miller had studied at Dickinson College.[46] In 1803, he dedicated *A Brief Retrospective of the Eighteenth Century*—a work celebrating and elucidating the confluence of religion and science—to Dickinson, knowing that he would approve of his discussion of "the progress of elegant letters and substantial science, as tending to promote the dignity and happiness of man." Among other qualities, Dickinson was "an elegant Scholar," "a Master of so many of its literary and scientific improvements," and "a munificent Patron of American literature."[47]

Their letters were rich with discussion about various points of theology and religious controversies. Miller often sent works by others and himself for Dickinson to read. Although they agreed about some things, Dickinson objected to the hierarchy he found in Presbyterianism. Reading one of Miller's treatises, he replied, "I was highly gratified for a considerable Time, by observing, as I thought, a singularity respecting the Appointment or Admission of Ministers, among Presbyterians and Quakers, till I found . . . a Rejection of 'Lay ordinations', and a Claim to 'a Succession of ordinations, by Ministers of some Kind.' To this exclusive Derivation of Ministry," he objected, "I cannot assent."[48] It was too unlike the spiritual democracy that Dickinson appreciated in Quakerism. But Miller esteemed Dickinson so much as a theologian that, he proclaimed, "I make it a rule to publish nothing, without submitting it to your inspection."[49]

Dickinson also spent time reflecting on his personal theological beliefs. For decades, especially after he had begun to resemble Quakers outwardly and share their commitment to the same benevolent causes, Friends had hoped he would join with them in formal membership. Indeed, many who knew Dickinson well, or thought they did, from friends such as Benjamin Rush to enemies such as John Adams, believed he was a Quaker. But in the waning months of his life, Dickinson was clear. "I am not," he said to Miller, "and probably never shall be united to any religious Society, because each of them as a Society, holds Principles I cannot adopt." Anyone who knew him well also knew the main reason he could not join with Friends in particular. "I am on all proper Occasions," he clarified to Tench Coxe, "an advocate for the lawfulness of defensive War. This Principle has prevented me from Union with Friends."[50]

Dickinson never gained traction on his theological treatise. To Albanus Logan, he wrote, "I have never been a Volunteer Writer; but have only taken up my Pen occasionally, to defend, as well as I could, my Country, against the Strokes aimed by Tyranny and Folly at her Vitals."[51] Perhaps his leading on this topic was not strong enough. For the countless pages Dickinson filled with notes and ideas, he did not succeed in publishing anything out of them. He never managed to produce a legible draft. Perhaps he even found that he was happier riding his horse, on his birthday, singing "Where all thy Mercies, O my God," his preferred birthday ode.[52]

In the first years of the new century, mentions of Dickinson in the press had been fewer and farther between, which suited him just fine. He was pleased to bid adieu to Pheme, whose vindictiveness was as intense as her affections. Yet she had not wholly relinquished her claim on him. Even the dismissals of some scribblers signaled her hold. "However great might have been the celebriety of a Bolingbroke or a Dickinson, as political writers," wrote one in 1803, "yet who is it that recollects much of . . . the elegant language of the American patriot, animating his countrymen to a noble and just defence of their lives, their property and their liberty? Compositions of this kind may be aptly compared to a distant comet, which astonishes for a while, by its luminous appearance and then flies off, perhaps never more to be seen."[53]

This assessment of Dickinson's work was unfounded. The same year, the words of Richard Rush, son of Benjamin, belied that analogy when he described Dickinson as "The eminent patriot of the Revolution; the fine Scholar and accomplished Speaker; author of the celebrated and classic Productions that made their appearance in 1767 under the signature of 'Farmers Letters;' and various other and later Productions against the system of British taxation and government in America."[54] Dickinson was still, on occasion, toasted on the Fourth of July for his "private virtues and public merits."[55] In 1805, the Republican paper *True American* updated its readers with a report that "John Dickinson, Esquire, the celebrated author of the Pennsylvania 'Farmer,' Letters of Fabius, &c. still lives, and enjoys health of body and sanity of mind uncommon at his advanced stage of life," which they followed with a poem in his honor.[56] To these tributes the Federalists replied with a generous dose of snark: "We have no objection to Mr. John Dickinson's enjoying good health and length of days; but if history speaks truth, that gentleman, 'was not a *planner* of American Independence.'" Of course, the opposite was true—he had planned for independence more than any other delegate, strategizing to keep Americans unified, drafting the Articles of Confederation, laying the foundations for American foreign policy, and working to strengthen the nation's military and financial health.[57] For the other side, Thomas Paine wrote that while men such as Dickinson and Charles Thomson had gone into "honourable and peaceable retirement," Federalists such as John Adams and John Jay had gone "into obscurity and oblivion."[58] In March 1807, an article on the Massachusetts gubernatorial election quoted extensively from Dickinson's 1774 *Essay on the Constitutional Power of Great Britain* as evidence of the "principles we at first pursued, and which procured us Independence, Honour, Prosperity, and Happiness." An article signed "A Farmer" in the same paper reminded voters "that virtue is the only foundation of a republican government."[59]

Not only were Dickinson's past contributions guiding Americans almost forty years later, when the country appeared again to be in crisis, but his admirers looked to him for leadership. In June 1807, the USS *Chesapeake*, caught unprepared, suffered an unprovoked attack by the HMS *Leopard*, which had been lurking off the Virginia coast to blockade French vessels. After being denied permission to board the *Chesapeake* to search for British seamen, the crew of the *Leopard* fired upon the American ship, wounding several seamen and carrying off four alleged British deserters. "I did not think it probable," said Dickinson to Attorney General Caesar A. Rodney, "that during the short remnant of my life a time would come, when I should find myself pressed by a sense of duty again to bear my public testimony to the rights and liberties of my injured and insulted country." But British actions against America could not stand. "The time is come," Dickinson declared, "and I cheerfully commit my family my connections, all that can be dear to man, to every hazard that may occur in the vindication of her sacred cause."[60]

Shortly thereafter, the people of Wilmington "so earnestly and respect-fully" requested his presence at a town meeting that he could not "without Pain, reject the invitation." He attended but abstained from authoring the resolutions they put forward.[61] That summer, the state Republicans approached him about putting his name on the ballot for the October con-gressional election.[62] Although he told the committee "in the plainest, strongest Expressions, that if I should be chosen, my Infirmities would not, could not admit of my Attendance," the committee members nonetheless forced the nomination upon him.[63] Americans as far away as Pittsburgh cel-ebrated the move and exclaimed, "Respected for his talents, revered for his virtues, venerated for his experience, and grown old in the practice of re-publican efforts and principles, this sacrifice of public wishes for the general good, must receive the plaudits of his countrymen."[64]

As he awaited the fall election, Dickinson's thoughts returned to that mo-ment of independence thirty-one years earlier. Warren had requested his opinion of her treatment of the events in her *History*. With his admittedly "fading memory," he was unaware of her inaccuracies; indeed, he was un-aware of his own. The broad contours were still within his grasp, but the timeline failed him. He recalled the parts played by Richard Henry Lee and John Adams, and he recalled, though imperfectly, the reasons he had sought a delay—in hopes Great Britain would see reason and to gain French sup-port. But he misremembered the progression of his own views. "After the re-jection of the Olive Branch Petition, not a syllable to my recollection was ever uttered in favour of a reconciliation with Great Britain." Actually, he had continued working for reconciliation until almost the eve of independence, only setting it aside during his speech on July 1. But after the Declaration passed, on the most important point he could not be mistaken. Despite "apprehension of great Calamities" attending independence, "dreadful as those Calamities might be, they were to be firmly encountered whatever the consequences."[65] It was the credo he had declared for himself as he departed the Middle Temple in 1757—with no self-regard, to stand against any force for what was right.

Delaware was a Federalist state, and Dickinson could not have been sur-prised when that party prevailed, to the outrage of the Republicans. "The candidate for member of Congress, at this election, *who was opposed by the federalists*," they fumed, "was the venerable compatriot and friend of Washington, the celebrated revolutionary patriot John Dickinson, so well known for the conspicuous figure he made in 'times that tried men's souls,' by the side of *Franklin, Adams, Hancock* and *Washington*—and for his valuable political writings, entitled the *'Pennsylvania Farmer'*—which had so much agency in inculcating the principles of liberty.—This was the man whom federalists, to a man, opposed."[66] Clearly, even Dickinson's own party had an interest in bending the truth to make their hero agree with Washington, Franklin, and Adams when it suited them. Now, they believed, "Aristocracy has gained the ascendancy over the state of Delaware." John Dickinson would "remain a private citizen, while his virtue and patriotism are essentially necessary to be called forth in order to shield us from oppressions."[67] With his loss, throughout Delaware, people lamented the demise of democracy in their "tory-ridden" state.[68] Their consolation now was that "memory of his former services will remain to encourage his friends in the duties they owe their country."[69]

To Dickinson, however, his loss was a "blessed Disappointment."[70] He was relieved to retain his position just off stage, giving advice to the players in their prime. To this end, he recommended to Rodney that the maritime defenses of the nation be enhanced. "Let us prepare as well and as quietly as We can against the most imminent Dangers," he said, recommending that fifteen or twenty gunboats be deployed in the Delaware River. Their own state was the most vulnerable. "A single Vessel might plunder and burn New Castle and this Town," he warned. This fortification against the British would serve a dual purpose, as Dickinson was also convinced "that France aims at universal Empire."[71]

It was indeed for the best that he did not win; he likely would not have relished the work had he been equal to the demands. The last mentions of Dickinson in the public papers during his lifetime suggested the troubling lack of principle his fellow citizens displayed. Appearing around the country from mid-January to February 1808 and true to the era in their polarization, their purpose was to dupe readers with false information. Several papers reported that the United States attorney general had sought Dickinson's opinion on the British proclamation issued in October 1807 concerning the *Chesapeake–Leopard* affair in which the British announced they had a right to board any American vessels to retrieve their deserted seamen. "We are told, that Cæsar A. Rodney, Esquire," they said conspiratorially, "has addressed a letter to the celebrated John Dickinson, Esq. (an eminent Republican Lawyer, and author of the *Farmer's Letters*) requesting his opinion of the ground, which Great Britain has taken, regarding her Seamen; and that Mr. Dickinson, in his answer has stated, that the ground, which she had taken, *was proper.*[72] Of course, the opposite was true. At the same time, another jab appeared that may have perplexed Dickinson's friends and enemies alike. In a little blurb on Major Andrew Jackson, one paper proclaimed that "his *good nature* towards John Dickinson, is as unfortunate as his enmity towards Mr. Jefferson."[73] It seems unlikely Dickinson would have been heartened by the new breed of politician coming up in the world.

In the second week of February, Dickinson began feeling unwell. Knowing from the onset of a "violent fever" that he was "just about to step from Time into Eternity," his mind was serene and composed.[74] As he descended quickly into delirium, he was attended by Dr. Tilton, who had stood with him against the Jay Treaty almost fifteen years ago. But his illness, sepsis, stemming perhaps from pneumonia, "baffled the power of medicine."[75] Drifting in and out of consciousness, he fretted about Napoleon, before whom all of Europe was falling, and imagined him invading America from the west. His last worry was his perennial concern, the welfare of his beloved nation. From his deathbed, he gave one last moving address to the American people.

Finally, as Dickinson had recorded the birth of Debby Logan in his almanac in 1761, so did she record his last moments in her diary. "It was affecting to the Bystanders," she wrote, "to hear the effusions of his benevolent Spirit for the Prosperity of his Country and the happiness of Mankind pourd out in a sublime & pathetic address to the sovereign of the Universe."[76] The Pennsylvania Farmer died on First Day morning, the fourteenth day of the second month, at around seven o'clock. Though not a Quaker, that people was nevertheless proud to claim him, allowing him to be laid to rest beside his beloved Polly in Wilmington Friends Burial Ground on February 17.[77] Committing her fond recollections of her cousin to paper, Debby wrote, "Of his Public Life I shall say nothing. History will do Justice to his Patriotism & talents."[78]

Epilogue

"My Name remembered by Posterity":
The Dismantling of a Legacy, 1808–2024

As the members of Congress in both houses reflected on Dickinson's contributions to the Founding in February 1808, they were guided by the obituaries—initially a trickle, then a deluge. The first papers reported his death on February 16, and as the news spread, his passing was an occasion for national mourning from Georgia to Maine. The early accounts of his life were brief; longer ones appeared later, and several papers from North to South, Federalist and Republican, ran multiple announcements.[1] These included not merely the news of his passing and accomplishments, but also the resolutions of both houses of Congress and the board of trustees of Dickinson College to wear black crepe arm bands in his honor.[2] Before that time, only the death of George Washington in 1799 had received such widespread demonstrations of bipartisan public grief.

As one would expect, the obituaries reminded readers of Dickinson's *Farmer's Letters* and his efforts on behalf of the American cause. They also informed the public of his life since the Revolution and extolled his virtues. "Refined morality, and great powers of research," wrote one Philadelphia paper, took Dickinson "into the most enlightened paths of true religion." He "anxiously searched after truth, practised its dictates and was particularly bounteous to institutions for youthful instruction, for the reformation of vice, for the protection of the weak and helpless, for well-directed charities and benevolence, and for the promotion of that religion, in which he firmly believed."[3] A South Carolina paper added, "John Dickinson was a republican in his manners and his sentiments—in public life the powerful advocate of his fellow citizens, and in a private station, *the friend of the poor*, . . . he distributed vast sums to works of charity and literature. . . . He treated all men with great gravity of manners, and knew no distinction in society but virtue."[4]

Even these effusive tributes couldn't do justice to all Dickinson had accomplished for the Founding. There was hardly an aspect of the new nation that

Dickinson did not touch. He was much more than merely a "penman of the Revolution"; he was the draftsman for the Founding as an architect drafts the plans of a building. His earliest writings for the American cause had educated the colonists about their rights—concerning not only property but also religious liberty—and how to protect them using the Quaker method of civil disobedience, much later used by Martin Luther King Jr. From there, he taught them that unity was the only way America would prevail against Britain or any other challenge and gave his countrymen their first national motto: "By *uniting* We stand, by *dividing* We fall." The delays he caused in declaring independence allowed critical preparations to take place—many of which he undertook himself, including building up the military and fortifications, drafting the basis for America's foreign policy, and drafting America's first constitution. After independence, he continued enhancing the country's foreign policy, including drafting the basis for the peace settlement with Britain, working for fiscal reform, and planning for a Board of Admiralty to govern the navy. He transformed Delaware from a failing state into a model state and created a militia that anticipated the National Guard. In Pennsylvania, he averted a mutiny of Continental soldiers, put down a civil war, and managed a diplomatic incident that led to a clause in the forthcoming Federal Constitution. He was instrumental to the calling of the Federal Convention, where he provided, among other things, the solution for representation in the legislature—and the solar system metaphor to explain it—and limited the spread of slavery. As a private citizen, in an era in which philanthropy by the wealthy was seen as a duty, he was perhaps the greatest benefactor to the needy of the era, giving freely yet quietly to countless individuals and organizations, three of which still survive—Dickinson College, Westtown School, and the Pennsylvania Prison Society.

As remarkable as what Dickinson did accomplish is what he failed to do. Most notably, he was unable to convince Americans to realize the principles of liberty and equality in the Declaration of Independence by ending slavery, securing women's rights, dealing honorably with Indians, and lifting Americans out of poverty and ignorance. But he was also the only one of the leading figures who tried to do so. These offerings, and perhaps others yet to be realized, were "the stones the builders rejected" that became the cornerstones of the nation.[5]

Dickinson's contemporaries believed that his name would be remembered for all time. "Over the ashes of such a man, we may weep without the indulgence of immoderate grief," said one New York obituary. "Having passed a long and illustrious life, he has left a name, which will, in future times, be often invoked on the side of principle and virtue."[6] Tench Coxe planned a biography of Dickinson, believing that it would "reflect credit upon the middle states and honor upon our country at large." He was convinced that reading about Dickinson's life could be beneficial for "the character of mankind."[7] As Dickinson himself said to Coxe, "There is a Vibration in Virtue, and some of its energies reach far."[8]

In the years after his death, Dickinson's name continued to appear in various tributes. Children were named after him, as were more ships.[9] Beginning in 1813, and possibly again in 1819, "John Dickinson" was used as a pseudonym for someone writing a series of letters on history, law, politics, and war.[10] That James Wilkinson, a frontier governor and general who was suspected of treason, sang his praises in 1816 might have caused chagrin.[11] How he would have viewed his words being enlisted in disapproval of the Supreme Court's decision in *McCulloch v. Maryland* (1819), which denied Maryland the power to tax the Second Bank of the United States, can't be known.[12] In the 1820s, he was associated with Jefferson and also prison reform, which would have pleased him.[13] Possibly as late as 1840, a ship sailed with a carving of Dickinson as her figurehead, holding a copy of his *Farmer's Letters* (Fig. 23).

His own writings lived on. A second edition of his *Writings* was published in 1814, and *A Fragment*, on the education of youth, was advertised again in 1820.[14] Unsurprisingly, his *Farmer's Letters* have endured the longest. In 1899, the *Philadelphia Inquirer* called them "a revelation to the American people." Moreover, "they prepared the public mind for the great step which the colonies were about to take." Dickinson's work "was as necessary to the Declaration of Independence as the subsequent labors of WASHINGTON upon the Battlefield."[15] Glimpses of his influence are evident even today, with political commentary bearing titles such as the 2011 *Letters from an Ohio Farmer* and historian Heather Cox Richardson's daily newsletter, "Letters from an American," begun in 2019, though it's likely the authors are ignorant of the origin of their pen names. The Ohio Farmer claims inspiration from, among others, Richard Henry Lee's Federal Farmer, while Richardson attributes hers to Crèvecoeur writing as an "American Farmer."[16] Both Lee and Crèvecoeur were consciously following Dickinson.

Few could have imagined that, within a few short decades, he would be almost entirely forgotten, his contributions to the Founding erased, attributed to others, or twisted into contemptible caricatures of the truth. The inevitable question is why Dickinson was so well known and admired in his day yet virtually unknown in ours. There are three main, related reasons: politics, the availability and accessibility of his papers, and Quakerism. The first led to misrepresentations of his actions and character; the second allowed those misrepresentations to stand unchallenged; and the third caused confusion, even among those inclined to do him justice.[17]

Although short biographical sketches appeared in the years immediately after Dickinson's death, Coxe or others who might have attempted a biography simply did not have the sources necessary to write one. Dickinson did not keep a journal, and he had explicitly declined a request by Benjamin Rush to write his memoir. "As to the Remembrance of my Name, and if it is remembered, as to the Character of my Conduct," he said to Rush in 1797, "with humble Submission I commit Myself to that adorable Being from whom I received my Existence, and the situation I have had among his Works."[18] His papers remained in possession of his elder daughter, Sally Norris Dickinson, until after her death, when they went to descendants of her sister Maria's family, the Logans. Tragically, in the name of privacy, Sally had also burned most of her parents' letters to one another, as well as correspondence between her mother and her closest friends.[19] It wasn't until the late 1930s and early 1940s that Robert R. Logan donated one of the largest collections of Dickinson's papers to the Library Company of Philadelphia and the Historical Society of Pennsylvania. Not only were these documents in disarray, but many of them were effectively illegible. Among the most complex of any Founder, they contained not only heavily edited manuscripts with idiosyncratic shorthand but also Latin and legal terminology. To be legible at the most basic level, they would require transcription by trained paleographers. Many of his most valuable drafts of state papers and essays were submerged in reams of ink-covered pages without dates or titles. With chaos at all levels, they were fundamentally inaccessible.

Other manuscripts were scattered around the country in archives from New York to Los Angeles. Because Dickinson was so little known by the time the major historical repositories had been founded—the Library of Congress Manuscript Division, for example, was established in 1897—archivists had no reason to prioritize his documents, which meant that rather than building collections of Dickinson papers or at least cataloging them under his name, they frequently scattered the documents throughout collections under the names of Dickinson's correspondents. Only when a document had politically significant content did it rise to the surface, but frequently Dickinson's name wasn't associated with it.

Just over a decade after Dickinson's death, Thomas Jefferson contributed to the destruction of Dickinson's legacy with his account of the creation of the 1775 Declaration on Taking Up Arms, one of Congress's most important publications, widely seen as the precursor to the Declaration of Independence. According to Jefferson's autobiography, written in 1821 when he was seventy-seven, the version he had drafted "was too strong for Mr. Dickinson. He still retained the hope of reconciliation with the mother country, and was unwilling it should be lessened by offensive statements. He was so honest a man, & so able a one that he was greatly indulged even by those who could not feel his scruples."[20] In suggesting that Dickinson was timid, meek, and someone who needed to be *indulged* rather than followed, he echoed similar comments by Dickinson's enemy, John Adams. In Jefferson's telling, the belligerent and provocative language came from his own pen, not Dickinson's. Of course, he had it exactly reversed. Dickinson had written the "offensive statements." This misrepresentation of the creation of one of the most significant documents of the American Revolution bolstered Jefferson's legacy at the expense of Dickinson's. As is frequently the case with Jefferson, his motives are difficult to discern. Whatever they were, his interpretation in 1821 of Dickinson's position conveniently aligned with what would soon be the prevailing view of him. It was not until Julian Boyd, editor of the *The Papers of Thomas Jefferson*, undertook a forensic analysis of the two versions of the Declaration on Taking Up Arms that the record was set straight. But by then the damage had been done.[21]

While the papers of other leading Founders were collected and published multiple times beginning in the early nineteenth century, enabling biographies and studies, the first of many abortive attempts to publish Dickinson's hundreds of writings was made by Paul L. Ford in 1895. But he only produced one volume. He was murdered before he could produce the second.[22] When the project of creating modern documentary editions of the Founders' papers was established in the 1950s, several of the leading figures already had at least one edition of their papers or other writings published. At this time, Congress officially designated who was a "Founder" and allocated funding for the publication of their papers. Dickinson was not among them. A series of individuals attempted editions of his papers in the mid-twentieth century, but with neither funds, staff, nor collegiality, their efforts were doomed to fail.

The dearth of sources notwithstanding, in 1827, the *American Quarterly Review*, noticing that Dickinson's "life has not been written; nor, indeed, is there extant concerning him any thing more than mere brief dictionary sketches," undertook a brief but able tribute. While suggesting that his stance against the Declaration of Independence "has, perhaps, affected the degree in which he would and should have been known and revered by the present generation of Americans," the tribute went on to describe not just "the firmness and warmth of his patriotism" but also a surprising number of his key writings for the cause, including the 1774 Petition to the King, which Richard Henry Lee's biographer was claiming for Lee based on Marshall's misattribution in his *Life of Washington*, as well as the Declaration on Taking Up Arms, now claimed by Jefferson.

Politics going back well over a century played a key role in the lack of interest in Dickinson and his writings. With the groundwork laid by John Adams in 1775, the dismantling of his legacy began in earnest in nineteenth-century New England. Historian George Bancroft surely had both Adams's papers and Jefferson's autobiography before him when he wrote his ten-volume *History of the United States, from the Discovery of the American Continent*, which became the definitive treatment of the American Founding. Bancroft was the most visible of the so-called whig historians who, seeking to solidify and define America's national identity, wrote unapologetically and uncritically patriotic history. The story they told was unabashedly celebratory. Men (and it was only men) of the Founding generation were either patriots or traitors. Everything for these historians hinged on the position the man took on the Declaration of Independence, which was only just rising to the level of American scripture.[23] Since Dickinson, though appearing frequently in volumes 7 through 9 of Bancroft's *History*, did not vote on or sign the Declaration, he didn't merely lose his status as a leading Founder—he became an archenemy of the cause.

Bancroft hardly let an opportunity pass to skewer Dickinson, who argued "with chilling erudition," which had the effect of "allaying the impassioned enthusiasm of patriotism."[24] He was "[d]eficient in [energy,] that great element of character which forms the junction between intelligence and action."[25] Rather than attributing Pennsylvania's "languor" before independence to the Quakers, who controlled the provincial government, Bancroft blames Dickinson, who "[f]rom the first . . . acted in concert with the proprietary government."[26] Like Dickinson's enemies in Pennsylvania, Bancroft did not understand that the 1701 Charter that Dickinson supported actually nullified the power of the proprietors. According to Bancroft, Dickinson only "claimed to lead the patriot party of Pennsylvania."[27] The Battles of Lexington and Concord left Dickinson unmoved.[28] Unsurprisingly, Jefferson receives sole credit for "the most decisive measure" adopted by Congress in 1775, the Declaration on Taking Up Arms.[29]

Meanwhile, Bancroft's fellow New Englander John Adams, whose "nature was robust and manly," "had justly thrown blame on 'the piddling genius'" of Dickinson. "Wounded in his self-love and vexed by the ridicule thrown on his system, from this time [Dickinson] resisted independence with a morbid fixedness."[30] His instructions to the Pennsylvania delegates in November 1775 had the effect of "preparing for Dickinson a life of regrets."[31]

When Dickinson was about to give his speech against independence on July 1, his "excessively sensitive nature was writhing under the agonies of wounded self-love."[32] "The logical contradiction in the mind of Dickinson," explains Bancroft, "still perplexed his conduct. His narrow breast had no room for the large counsels of true wisdom; and he urged upon every individual and every body of men over whom he had any influence, the necessity of making terms of accommodation with Great Britain. In this way he dulled the resentment of the people, and paralyzed the manly impulse of self-sacrificing courage."[33]

Even Dickinson's service to the cause, such as his authorship of the Articles of Confederation, is reason for denigration in Bancroft's account. "Dickinson, from his timidity, his nice refining, his want of mastery over his erudition, his hostility to independence, his inconsolable grief at the overthrow of the proprietary government in Pennsylvania," claims Bancroft, "was particularly unfit to be the architect of a permanent national constitution; and in his zeal to guard against the future predominance of congress, he exaggerated the imperfections, which had their deep root in the history of the states."[34] Bancroft concludes that this was an "anarchical scheme," which, placing all the power in the states, was "reminiscent of the war-cries of former times, not a creation for the coming age."[35] In reality, Dickinson's draft provided for a strong central government, which is why it was rejected.

One might expect Bancroft to give Dickinson at least a little credit for his military activities. But the historian can't even allow him this rare achievement for a member of Congress. "He never took part in hard fighting," complains Bancroft—which is true enough; no officers did—"and making an excuse about rank, he left the army in the moment of his country's greatest danger."[36] With that claim, and his parting shots, Bancroft thoroughly adopts the libels printed by Dickinson's enemies, the radicals in Pennsylvania: he "discredited the continental currency" and refused to serve as a delegate from Delaware to Congress because he was "so thoroughly convinced of the necessity of returning to the old state of dependence."[37] It's no wonder that almost nothing was written about Dickinson for several decades following what can only be called a literary assassination. The first biography of him, by Charles J. Stille, appeared in 1891, prompting reviews marveling how "John Dickinson's name to-day is unknown" but "once it was a household word." The reviewer continued, "It is only now, after a century of defamation, that the honor of Dickinson has been conclusively vindicated."[38] The next biography wouldn't appear for ninety-two years.

The third cause of Dickinson's present obscurity is due to his being a Quaker "fellow traveler"—adopting much of Quakerism but not being a formal member of the Society of Friends. Refusing to be categorized, Dickinson has confused scholars, especially those inclined to ignore religion. Thoroughly perplexed by his energetic leadership of the resistance to Britain yet his refusal to vote on or sign the Declaration of Independence, Dickinson scholar John H. Powell wondered, "Where in hell did Dickinson learn the complicated way of politics he tried to put into practice?"[39] Powell, a professional historian, labored a lifetime on Dickinson with only a few articles to show for it. Only Quaker historian Frederick B. Tolles sensed that Quakerism was the source of his political theory. But no one followed up on the start he made in 1956 to articulate the Quaker influence on Dickinson until the next century.[40] Instead, the prevailing explanation of Dickinson came from political scientist Milton E. Flower's 1983 biography, *John Dickinson, Conservative Revolutionary*. Calling Dickinson "conservative" is not only confusing to modern readers who associate the term with today's Republican Party, but it also makes no sense for Dickinson. In the eighteenth century, a "conservative," might oppose revolution, as did Edmund Burke, but, unlike Burke, Dickinson supported the French Revolution. He also held the then-radical positions of supporting the abolition of slavery and advocating women's rights. Everything that infuriated Bancroft and puzzled later scholars, namely Dickinson's refusal to vote on or sign the Declaration of Independence, makes sense within the context of Quaker political thought—protest vigorously but peacefully for individual rights, but preserve unity. But even when the explanation of this theory was available, some remained determined to ignore it.

With some exceptions, treatments of Dickinson in the late twentieth and early twenty-first centuries have merely reheated Bancroft's old, faulty narrative or repeated Flower's confusion. These approaches became especially prevalent with the advent of "Founders chic" at the turn of this century. This fad, suggests historian David Waldstreicher, revives the whig history of the antebellum period, serving some of the same political purposes. Founders chic belongs to the "culture wars" of our times, with the entertainment industry capitalizing on the renewed public interest in the period.[41] Not only do these works present facile patriotic narratives, but their authors universally eschew archival research that could complicate their stories. The most notable example of the neo-whig approach is David McCullough's *John Adams* (2001) and the resulting HBO miniseries of the same name. In these we see the same heroic portrayal of Adams, with Dickinson as his villainous foil. The statue of Dickinson at the National Constitution Center (est. 2000) is only marginally kinder.

Some authors in the Founders chic genre have melded Bancroft's and Flower's interpretations for one purpose or another. In John Ferling's *Independence: The Struggle to Set America Free* (2011), for example, religion is absent from the struggle. He does not mention Dickinson's Quaker ties and presents no analysis of his position beyond a few glancing remarks. Echoing Flower's anemic interpretation, Ferling's Dickinson "was haunted by a conservative's fear of the forces of change." In a familiar refrain for authors who avoid original research, Ferling claims, "Dickinson never offered an explanation for his abstention" from the vote on independence. This is an astounding claim, as Dickinson explained his abstention repeatedly. "A cynic might argue," he muses, "that Dickinson, who remained politically ambitious and enjoyed the taste of power, was merely seeking to avoid the ruin of his career." No one who has read Dickinson's writings would make such a suggestion. He was, as he himself explained repeatedly, "governed by the Dictates of his Conscience & Judgment in public Affairs" and perfectly aware of the political disadvantage inherent in taking the course he did: "Any man not more than half an Ideot," said Dickinson, understood the danger in which he placed himself.[42]

As it happens, even the creators of a cartoon have a better understanding of Dickinson's position at the moment of independence than most. One of the most accurate representations came in 2003 from Comedy Central's

South Park, which depicts Dickinson in the July 1, 1776, debate taking a principled and pragmatic stand for pacifism.[43]

In 2013, the conservative political journalist William Murchison published a biography of Dickinson entitled *The Cost of Liberty*, in which he calls Dickinson an "American Burke," even while admitting that the comparison "is not easy to sustain." Indeed, while Burke earned his conservative credentials because of his opposition to the French Revolution, Dickinson supported it wholeheartedly. Murchison's version of Dickinson is principled and virtuous, but, like the others, this work only skims the surface of his life, especially in the latter half. Since the secondary sources on Dickinson in the 1790s are scant, Murchison concludes that "Dickinson scarcely spoke up" during this period.[44] The historical record proves otherwise.

Also in 2013, award-winning historian Richard Beeman published *Our Lives, Our Fortunes and Our Sacred Honor* in which he laments that Dickinson was "never very self-revelatory in his writings."[45] Had Beeman read even the primary sources available online, he would have found Dickinson very forthcoming. Like others before him, Beeman finds that "Dickinson never explained his failure to vote that day and never attempted a public defense of it."[46] Except that he did, fully, in 1783.[47] According to Beeman, Dickinson was erudite and eloquent but ultimately a victim of his own emotions, too "moderate in temperament" and "mild-mannered" to win the debate.[48]

Most recently, in 2021, award-winning historian Joseph J. Ellis published *The Cause: The American Revolution and its Discontents, 1773–1783*. Here Dickinson is an "enlightened conservative," with Murchison credited with "rescuing" Dickinson "from marginalization." Ellis finds that after the Olive Branch Petition was rejected, "Dickinson was understandably silent, since the diplomatic path forward he had hoped to blaze had become a dead end." He continues, "By the late fall of 1775, Dickinson had become the chief spokesman for those reluctant American patriots who did not know what to do."[49] In fact, Dickinson continued tirelessly on the same tracks, working to put America on a solid footing for war, keeping the colonies united, and writing extensively for the third phase of the plan Congress approved—negotiations with Britain. He continued to give public speeches on these matters not just in Congress, but also to the New Jersey legislature and the officers of the Pennsylvania Associators. And, most significantly, he wrote the 1775 instructions to the Pennsylvania delegates that prevented America from declaring independence until July 1776.

An additional misrepresentation requires correction. Dickinson is singled out for being overly sensitive to slights—"his excessively sensitive nature," as Bancroft puts it—and then criticized for defending himself. These authors fail to consider what historian Joanne Freeman demonstrates amply in her work *Affairs of Honor*: that this was an age when gentlemen were exquisitely delicate about their honor, in part because it was like today's credit score; one's ability to do business was at risk if one's honor were besmirched. There is a blatant double standard at work. Hamilton's feelings were so fragile that he repeatedly fought duels until he died in one. Washington was known for having a "thin-skinned aversion to criticism," flying into rages when he felt slighted.[50] Adams, with a "volcanic temper set on a hair-trigger," complained incessantly that he wasn't treated fairly, alienating those around him.[51] Gordon Wood has shown that to a significant degree, Franklin's devotion to the American cause was not selfless patriotism but a personal vendetta: "He was hurt and bitter over the way the British ministers had treated him."[52] Even Sphinx-like Jefferson, to use Ellis's expression, "took all criticism personally."[53]

Dickinson's long career in which he frequently took highly visible and controversial stances gave him abundant opportunity to win enemies. While it is true that the other leading Founders had legions of enemies who struck at every opportunity, of these, none was targeted as violently as Dickinson— none had his home looted or burned, or was pursued as an enemy of the very state he served, suffering not just libels but distraint of his property. Yet after challenging Joseph Galloway to a duel as a young man, Dickinson bore the slings and arrows of public life stoically. He defended his honor in print, but confided his hurt and anger only to close friends. He never understood why he was a target, that he had spent his "whole Life Seeking, solely seeking Americans' Good in my various public Functions, and greatly impairing instead of improving my Fortune in their Service, yet what Loads of Obloquy mix'd with the rankest Malignity have been thrown upon Me?"[54]

If Dickinson is painted as a thin-skinned whiner because he responded publicly to libels that had the potential to thwart his work in executive office, he is also depicted as a timorous coward, lacking in either the deep feeling or energy to engage in conflict. But time and again he risked reputation, fortune, life, and limb by speaking truth to any power placed over him and by fully enacting his principles in his public and private life.

To the extent Dickinson sacrificed his celebrity for his beliefs, he was entirely satisfied with that result. As much as he loved his fellow citizens, he was aware that they were susceptible to party rage that might blind them to the benevolent intent of his actions and motives. Instead, he placed his faith in cool-headed posterity. "If I shall ever occurr to the Thoughts of any who come after Us," he mused to Rush,

> I have a pleasing Hope, that I shall be considered as a Man that with all his Frailties, was from early Youth to the End of a long Life an ardent Lover of Liberty, and a disinterested Friend to his Country—and to Mankind— that, according to the best of his Abilities was a constant Watchman for the public Interest upon all great Emergencies, and in performing what he deem'd his Duty, sought no Profits, and dared all Dangers. Perhaps upon a closer Examination it may be acknowledged, that he never hated any Man, and never treated unkindly any Man by whom he was hated.

Only Galloway might dispute his last claim. Finally, in keeping with his wish for anonymity, he begged Rush not to publish any extracts from their correspondence.[55]

At this particular moment in American history, when patriotism is distorted into nationalism by some and rejected completely by others, John Dickinson offers us something we desperately need: a model of a public figure who stood on principle rather than popularity; who put not merely his constituents but his country before his own self-interest; who was loyal to no party; who made peace a central component of his public policy; whose deep religious belief demanded respect for other faiths as well as for science and liberal learning; who considered the most vulnerable in society and not only gave liberally of his own wealth but tried to implement policies to mitigate their misfortunes; who recognized his own privilege and the injustice of inequality; who saw education as a basic necessity for all people; who followed his conscience, regardless of the consequences; and who owned and acknowledged his own failings and sought to learn from them.

For Dickinson, this is what it means to be an American. With unbounded faith in his countrymen he said, "I trust, that the Principles that have been my political guides, will diffuse their blissful Influences on Ages, yet unborn."[56]

Notes

Introduction

1. Moses Coit Tyler, *The Literary History of the American Revolution, 1763–1783* (New York: G. P. Putnam's Sons, 1897), 21–34.
2. Hezekiah Niles, "A Speech in a Dream!" *Niles' Weekly Register* 8 (1818): 300–1.
3. For Dickinson's political Quakerism explained, see Jane E. Calvert, *Quaker Constitutionalism and the Political Thought of John Dickinson* (New York: Cambridge University Press, 2009).
4. Richard Striner, "Political Newtonianism: The Cosmic Model of Politics in Europe and America," *WMQ* 52, no. 4 (1995): 583–608.
5. George Savile, *The Character of a Trimmer* (London, 1688), preface.
6. JD to Robert Edge Pine, July 6, 1785. RRL, HSP.

Prologue

1. The description of Washington, DC, is drawn from the following sources: Constance M. Greene, *Washington: A History of the Capital: 1800–1950*, vol. 1 (Princeton: Princeton University Press, 1962–1963), esp. ch. 2, "The 'Seat of Empire': 1800–1812," 23–55; *Coming into the City: Essays on Early Washington, D.C.: Commemorating the Bicentennial of The Federal Government's Arrival in 1800*, ed. Jane Freundel Levey et al. (Washington, DC: The Historical Society of Washington, D.C., 2000); Daniel Sewall, *Hutchins Revived. An Almanac, for the Year of Our Lord, 1808* (New York: Smith Forman, 1807).
2. Third Census of the United States, 1810 (NARA microfilm publication M252, 71 rolls). Bureau of the Census, Record Group 29. National Archives, Washington, DC.
3. *Journal of the House of Representatives* (Washington: Gales and Seaton, 1826), 6:187.
4. *Debates and Proceedings in the Congress of the United States . . . Tenth Congress—First Session. Comprising the Period from October 26, 1807, to April 25, 1808, Inclusive* (Washington: Gales and Seaton, 1852), 133–4.
5. Ibid.
6. George Read Jr., in William Thomson Read, *The Life and Correspondence of George Read* (Philadelphia: J. B. Lippincott & Co., 1870), 570; the estimate of Dickinson's landholdings was provided by the John Dickinson Mansion in Dover, Delaware, [March 2011]; Diary of DNL, 1808–1814, p. 88. LCP.
7. JD to Charles Thomson, August 10, 1776. CTP, LOC.

8. Copy of JD to Caesar A. Rodney, July 22, 1807. N-YHS.

9. Thomas Jefferson, "First Inaugural Address," March 4, 1801, *PTJ*, Main Series, 33:149.

10. Diary of DNL, 1808–1814, p. 87.

11. Ibid.

12. Ibid.

13. John Adams to Thomas Jefferson, November 12, 1813. *PTJ*, Retirement Series, 6:612–14.

14. *New-York Gazette*, October 8, 1769. Adams's remark appears in at least two places: John Adams, *Twenty-Six Letters, Upon Interesting Subjects, Respecting the Revolution of America* (New York, 1780), 32; and John Adams to Hendrik Calkoen, October 10, 1780, *PJA*, 10:216.

15. JD, "Arguments against the Independance of these Colonies," [July 1, 1776]. Gratz, HSP; JD to unknown, August 25, 1776. RRL, HSP.

16. Thomas Jefferson to Joseph Bringhurst, February 16, 1808. Rockwood, UDSC.

Chapter 1

1. Paul G. E. Clemens, "From Tobacco to Grain: Economic Development on Maryland's Eastern Shore, 1660–1750," *The Journal of Economic History* 35, no. 1 (1975): 256–9; Mary McKinney Schweitzer, "Economic Regulation and the Colonial Economy: The Maryland Tobacco Inspection Act of 1747," *The Journal of Economic History* 40, no. 3 (1980): 551–69.

2. John Martin Hammond, *Colonial Mansions of Maryland and Delaware* (Philadelphia: J. B. Lippencott Co., 1914), 252. See also Michael Bourne, "Inventory For State Historic Site Survey: Crosia-doré," Maryland Historic Trust, May 1977. "The Maryland Room. Historic Sites: Crosiadore," *Talbot County Free Library*, accessed February 29, 2024, https://www.tcfl.org/mdroom/sites/display.php. This evaluation found Crosia-doré to be in good condition and that it architecturally "represent[ed] the tastes of several generations of the Dickinson family," before it was demolished by an Ohio-based real estate development firm.

3. DNL quoted in "Biography of the Lives of the Signers of the Declaration of Independence," *American Quarterly Review* 1 (March & June 1827): 416–17.

4. Dickinson family Bible. Logan, HSP.

5. Finding aid for the Cadwalader Family Papers. HSP.

6. "John Cadwalader," in *Lawmaking and Legislators in Pennsylvania: A Biographical Dictionary, Volume 2: 1710–1756*, ed. Craig W. Horle et al. (Philadelphia: University of Pennsylvania Press, 1997), 249–53; Paul Crawford, "A Footnote on Courts for Trial of Negroes in Colonial Pennsylvania," *Journal of Black Studies* 5, no. 2 (1974): 167–74.

7. DNL quoted in "Biography of the Lives of the Signers," 416–17.

8. The British Empire was functioning under the Julian calendar, but after Parliament decreed in 1750 that England and her plantations should take up the Gregorian calendar, and the transition was made in 1752, Dickinson thenceforth considered his birthdate to be November 13. See below at p.44.

9. For the colonial American socio-political order, see Gordon S. Wood, *The Radicalism of the American Revolution* (New York: Vintage Books, 1993).

10. T. H. Breen, *The Marketplace of Revolution: How Consumer Politics Shaped American Independence* (New York: Oxford University Press, 2005).

11. Capper Nichols, "Tobacco and the Rise of Writing in Colonial Maryland," *The Mississippi Quarterly* 50, no. 1 (1996–1997): 5–18.

12. In present-day Easton, MD.

13. John Faldo, *Quakerism No Christianity: Or, a Throw Quaker No Christian Proved by the Quakers Principles, Detected out of Their Chief Writers . . . with . . . an Account of Their Foundation Laid in Popery* (London, 1675), 120.

14. Marcus Rediker, *The Fearless Benjamin Lay: The Quaker Dwarf Who Became the First Revolutionary Abolitionist* (Boston: Beacon Press, 2017).

15. Minutes of the Men's Meeting (1676–1746), Third Haven Monthly Meeting. Quaker Meeting Records, FHL.

16. Dickinson family Bible. Logan, HSP; Samuel Troth to JD, December 17, 1798. Logan, HSP.

17. Charles Pettit to JD, April 13, 1804. Mf, HSP.

18. *PG*, January 5, 1764.

19. MCD, ledger, 1758–1764. RRL, HSP; *WJD*, 2:296; JD, manumission deed, May 12, 1777. RRL, HSP.

20. John Macpherson, *A Pennsylvania Sailor's Letters, Alias the Farmer's Fall* (Philadelphia: printed for the author, 1771), 12.

21. *Minutes of the House of Assembly of the Three Lower Counties upon Delaware, 1741–52* (1929), 46–7.

22. See JD, "Commonplace Book III," [n.d.], *WJD*, 2:322–33.

23. JD to MCD, August 15, 1754, *WJD*, 1:57.

24. Max Skjönsberg, "Lord Bolingbroke's Theory of Party and Opposition," *Historical Journal* (2015): 1–39.

25. JD's reading materials have been gleaned from his citations in his writings. See Volumes 1 and 2 of *WJD*.

26. DNL quoted in "Biography of the Lives of the Signers," 416–17.

27. JD to MCD, September 6, 1754, *WJD*, 1:62.

28. Dudley Cammett Lunt, *Tales of the Delaware Bench and Bar* (Newark: University of Delaware Press, 1963), 76; *PG*, June 6, 1754.

29. *PG*, December 14, 1752.

30. Alexander Hamilton, *Itinerarium: Being a Narrative of a Journey . . . 1744* (St. Louis: W. K. Bixby, 1907), 37.

31. Gottlieb Mittelberger, *Journey to Pennsylvania in the Year 1750, and Return to Germany in the Year 1754* (Philadelphia: John Jos. McVey, 1898), 49.

32. Alan Tully, *Forming American Politics: Ideals, Interests, and Institutions in Colonial New York and Pennsylvania* (Baltimore: Johns Hopkins University Press, 1994).

33. *Votes* (1751), 46.

34. *SALP*, 5:128.

35. Voltaire, *Letters on the English Nation* (London: C. Davis, 1733), 30.

36. Joshua Evans, Journal of Joshua Evans, 310–11a. FHL.

37. Billy G. Smith, *The "Lower Sort": Philadelphia's Laboring People, 1750–1800* (Ithaca: Cornell University Press, 1990), 217.

38. Hamilton, *Itinerarium*, 19–36; Jessica C. Roney, *Governed by a Spirit of Opposition: The Origins of American Political Practice in Colonial Philadelphia* (Philadelphia: University of Pennsylvania Press, 2014), 60; J. Thomas Scharf and Thompson Wescott, *History of Philadelphia, 1609–1884* (Philadelphia: L. H. Everts, 1884), 174–219.

39. Frank Lambert, *Inventing the "Great Awakening"* (Princeton: Princeton University Press, 2001).

40. JD, "Commonplace Book II," [c. 1760], in *WJD*, 2:112.

41. Perhaps the first time by Christopher Sauer. See "An Early Description of Pennsylvania: Letter of Christopher Sauer Written in 1724, Describing Conditions in Philadelphia and Vicinity, and the Sea Voyage from Europe," ed. Rayner W. Kelsey, trans. Adolph Gerber, *PMHB* 45 (1921): 249.

42. *SALP*, 5:77.

43. Scharf and Westcott, *History of Philadelphia*, 1:186, 208; John F. Watson, *Annals of Philadelphia and Pennsylvania* (Philadelphia, 1856), 1:62; *SALP*, 5:108.

44. *SALP*, 5:111.

45. Jack D. Marrietta and G. S. Rowe, *Troubled Experiment: Crime and Punishment in Pennsylvania, 1682–1800* (Philadelphia: University of Pennsylvania Press, 2006), esp. ch. 2.

46. JD to a young gentleman, [n.d.], *WJD*, 2:392.

47. Lunt, *Tales of the Delaware Bench*, 75.

48. Robert Earle Graham, "The Taverns of Colonial Philadelphia," *Transactions of the American Philosophical Society* 43, no. 1 (1953): 320.

49. JD to MCD, October 29, 1754, *WJD*, 1:67.

50. JD to SD, January 24, 1755, *WJD*, 1:72.

51. *WJD*, 1:328, 334; 2:168.

52. JD, "Draft Transcript of Opening Arguments in the Smith Libel Trial," [January 17, 1758], *WJD*, 1:182.

53. JD, "Notes on a Libel in the Admiralty on Behalf of Some Danish Sailors," [1759], *WJD*, 2:81, n. 42.

54. JD, "Draft Speech of a Debate on the Validity of American Court Proceedings upon the Death of George II," [c. February–August 1761], *WJD*, 2:194.

55. JD, "Deposition for *Paxton v. Van Dyke*," [February 1759], *WJD*, 2:19.

56. JD, "Arguments for *John Campbell v. The Owners of The Spry*," [1761], *WJD*, 1:348, 359.

57. Ibid., 1:348. Emphasis added.

58. JD, "Notes on a Flag-of-Truce Case," [n.d.], *WJD*, 1:297.

59. JD to SD, August 2, 1756, *WJD*, 1:137.

60. JD to SD, September 6, 1754, *WJD*, 1:65.

61. Robert Poole, "'Give Us Our Eleven Days!': Calendar Reform in Eighteenth-Century England," *Past & Present*, no. 149 (1995): 95–139.

62. Gary B. Nash, *The Liberty Bell* (New Haven: Yale University Press, 2011), 8.

63. John Hill Martin, *Martin's Bench and Bar of Philadelphia* (Clark, NJ: Lawbook Exchange, 2006), 237.

64. JD to SD, January 18, 1754, *WJD*, 1:8. This sum would be around $28,000 in today's dollars. See Ian Webster, "£100 in 1753 → 2024 | UK Inflation Calculator," Official Inflation Data, Alioth Finance, accessed February 22, 2024, https://www.officialdata. org/uk/inflation/1753?amount=100.

65. JD to George Read and Samuel Wharton, [October 1753], *WJD*, 1:2.

Chapter 2

1. JD to SD, April 22, 1754, *WJD*, 1:30.

2. Details of London are drawn from Emily Cockayne, *Hubbub: Filth, Noise, & Stench in England* (New Haven: Yale University Press, 2007); and "The London Letters," in *WJD*, 1:3–140.

3. Wilfrid Prest, "The Unreformed Middle Temple," in *History of the Middle Temple*, ed. R. O. Havery (Oxford, OR: Hart Publishing, 2011), 229, 237.

4. Ibid., 215.

5. JD to MCD, September 6, 1754, *WJD*, 1:63.

6. JD to SD, April 22, 1754, *WJD*, 1:30.

7. Details about Middle Temple Hall come from a conversation with Middle Temple archivist Lesley Whitelaw, London, July 17, 2019.

8. JD to SD, January 18, 1754, *WJD*, 1:9.

9. JD to a young gentleman, [n.d.], *WJD*, 2:390.

10. William Blackstone, *Commentary on the Laws of England*, 4 vols. (Oxford: Clarendon Press, 1765–69), 1:33.

11. JD to MCD, January 22, 1755, *WJD*, 1:74.

12. Ibid., January 19, 1754, *WJD*, 1:13.

13. JD to SD, March 8, 1754, *WJD*, 1:20.

14. JD to MCD, January 19, 1754, *WJD*, 1:11.

15. *The American Mock-Bird, or Songster's Delight: Being a Choice Collection of Entire New Songs* (New York: S. Brown, 1764), 96–7.

16. JD to MCD, January 19, 1754, *WJD*, 1:12.

17. Douglas Hay, "The Courts of Westminster Hall in the Eighteenth Century," in *The Supreme Court of Nova Scotia 1754–2004: From Imperial Bastion to Provincial Oracle*, ed. P. Girard, J. Phillips, and B. Cahill (Toronto: Osgoode Society for Canadian Legal History and University of Toronto Press, 2004), 13–29 at 14.

18. Sally Hadden and Patricia Hagler Minter, "A Legal Tourist Visits Eighteenth-Century Britain: Henry Marchant's Observations on British Courts, 1771 to 1772," *Law and History Review* 29, no. 1 (2011): 133–79 at 151.

19. JD, legal notebook, 1754–1755, John Dickinson Coll., DHS.

20. JD to SD, March 8, 1754, *WJD*, 1:22.

21. Ibid., 1:21.

22. Ibid.

23. Cockayne, *Hubbub*, 71–2, 158–9; JD to SD, March 8, 1754, *WJD*, 1:21.

24. JD to MCD, January 19, 1754, *WJD*, 1:12.

25. Ibid., March 8, 1754, *WJD*, 1:18.

26. Anonymous, *The Tricks of the Town Laid Open: Or, A Companion for Country Gentlemen* (London: H. Slater, 1746), 65.

27. JD to MCD, March 8, 1754, *WJD*, 1:17.

28. JD to SD, March 8, 1754, *WJD*, 1:20.

29. JD to MCD, March 8, 1754, *WJD*, 1:16.

30. Ibid., 1:16.

31. Ibid., January 19, 1754, *WJD*, 1:10.

32. Sarah Wise, "Meat—An Interlude," in *The Italian Boy: A Tale of Murder and Body Snatching in 1830s London* (New York: Metropolitan Books, 2004), 131–47.

33. Marietta and Rowe, *Troubled Experiment*, 161.

34. JD to SD, April 22, 1754, *WJD*, 1:31.

35. Howard M. Jenkins, "The Family of William Penn (continued). IX. Thomas Penn," *PMHB* 21, no. 3 (1897): 339.

36. JD to MCD, May 25, 1754, *WJD*, 1:36.

37. On Quaker Pennsylvania and the relationship between the Assembly and Thomas Penn during the French and Indian War, see James H. Hutson, *Pennsylvania Politics, 1746-1770: The Movement for Royal Government and Its Consequences* (Princeton: Princeton University Press, 1972).

38. Jenkins, "Family of William Penn," 339.

39. Theodore Thayer, *Israel Pemberton: King of the Quakers* (Philadelphia: Historical Society of Pennsylvania, 1943), 38, n. 55.

40. JD to MCD, May 25, 1754, *WJD*, 1:36.

41. JD to SD, April 22, 1754, *WJD*, 1:32.

42. Ibid., February 19, 1755, *WJD*, 1:81.

43. Ibid., January 21, 1755, *WJD*, 1:72.

44. "Bond of JD," May 3, 1754; *WJD*, 1:33–5; "Bond for William Hicks," June 12, 1754, *WJD*, 1:49–51.

45. JD to SD, March 8, 1754, *WJD*, 1:20.

46. JD, "Commonplace Book III," [n.d.], *WJD*, 2:324.

47. JD to SD, January 21, 1755, *WJD*, 1:71.

48. Ibid., September 6, 1754, *WJD*, 1:66.

49. Ibid., August 15, 1754, *WJD*, 1:60.

50. Ibid., September 6, 1754, *WJD*, 1:65.

51. JD, "Commonplace Book III," [n.d.], *WJD*, 2:323.

52. JD to SD, September 6, 1754, *WJD*, 1:66.

53. JD to MCD, March 17, 1756, WJD, 1:121; JD to SD, March 8, 1754, *WJD*, 1:22.

54. JD to SD, March 8, 1754, *WJD*, 1:22.

55. Ibid., March 29, 1754, *WJD*, 1:28.

56. JD to MCD, August 1, 1754, *WJD*, 1:53–4.

57. Ibid., 1:53.

58. JD to SD, August 15, 1754, *WJD*, 1:60.

59. Ibid., February 19, 1755, *WJD*, 1:82.

60. Ibid., August 15, 1754, *WJD*, 1:61.

61. Ibid., 1:60.

62. Ibid., March 8, 1754, *WJD*, 1:20.

63. JD to MCD, May 25, 1754, *WJD*, 1:36.

64. Ibid.

65. Ibid., 1:36.

66. Ibid., 1:37.

67. Ibid., August 15, 1754, *WJD*, 1:57.

68. Alexander Pope, *An Essay on Man. In Epistles to a Friend. Epistle I* (London: J. and P. Knapton, 1753), 6.

69. JD to MCD, August 15, 1754, *WJD*, 1:57.

70. JD to SD, September 6, 1754, *WJD*, 1:65.

71. Ibid.

72. Ibid., 1:66.

73. JD to MCD, February 19, 1755, *WJD*, 1:78.

74. Alexander Pope, *The Dunciad, in Four Books* (London: M. Cooper, 1743), 77.

75. JD to MCD, February 19, 1755, *WJD*, 1:79.

76. Ibid.

77. Ibid.

78. JD to MCD, August 12, 1755. *WJD*, 1:86.

79. Ibid., August 1, 1754, *WJD*, 1:52–3.

80. JD to SD, January 21, 1755, *WJD*, 1:71.

81. Ibid., February 19, 1755, *WJD*, 1:82.

82. Ibid.

83. Ibid.

84. JD to MCD, January 22, 1755, *WJD*, 1:73–4.

85. Ibid., February 19, 1755, *WJD*, 1:77.

86. Ibid., August 12, 1755, *WJD*, 1:87.

87. Ibid.

88. Ibid., April 8, 1755, *WJD*, 1:84.

89. Ibid., August 12, 1755, *WJD*, 1:88.

90. JD to SD, August 12, 1755, 1:89.

91. Ibid., 1:88.

92. JD to MCD, March 17, 1756, *WJD*, 1:118.

93. JD to SD, January 8, 1756, *WJD*, 1:92; *ODNB*.

94. Ibid., 1:92; Jean-Yves Guillain, *Badminton: An Illustrated History—From Ancient Pastime to Olympic Sport* (Paris: Publibook, 2012).

95. Hutson, *Pennsylvania Politics*, 15–16.

96. Herman Wellenreuther, "The Political Dilemma of the Quakers in Pennsylvania, 1681–1748," *PMHB* 94 (1970): 135–72; Calvert, *Quaker Constitutionalism*, ch. 4, esp. 162–5.

97. Hutson, *Pennsylvania Politics*, 24–6.

98. Ibid., 14–17.

99. JD, "Transcription of a Hearing 'Before the Lords of Trade & Plantations,'" February 26, [1756], *WJD*, 1:97.

100. Ibid., 1:97–8.

101. Ibid., 1:104.

102. JD to MCD, March 17, 1756, *WJD*, 1:118.

103. Ibid., June 6, 1756, *WJD*, 1:127–8.

104. Ibid.; JD to SD, June 6, 1756, *WJD*, 1:131.

105. *Votes* (1756), 101; *PG*, June 10, 1756.

106. See Jack D. Marietta, *The Reformation of American Quakerism, 1748–1783* (Philadelphia: University of Pennsylvania Press, 1984).

107. *PG*, May 20, 1756; JD to MCD, August 2, 1756, *WJD*, 1:135.

108. JD to MCD, March 17, 1756, *WJD*, 1:120.

109. Ibid., June 6, 1755, *WJD*, 1:126.

110. Ibid., 1:126.

111. JD to SD, August 2, 1756, *WJD*, 1:137.

112. John Spelman, "Certificate of John Dickinson's Call to the Bar at the Middle Temple," March 14, 1757, *WJD*, 1:140.

Chapter 3

1. Violet Brown's recollections, white notebook of SND, [c. 1837]. Logan, HSP.

2. Ibid.

3. Matthias Harris, *A Sermon, Preached in the Church of St. Peters in Lewis, in Sussex County on Delaware, on July 8, 1757* (Philadelphia: J. Chattin, 1757), v.

4. JD to MCD, March 17, 1756, *WJD*, 1:121.

5. Andrew Burnaby, *Travels through the Middle Settlements in North-America. In the Years 1759 and 1760* (London: T. Payne, 1775), 44..

6. Robert Earle Graham, "The Taverns of Colonial Philadelphia," *Transactions of the American Philosophical Society* 43, no. 1 (1953): 320–1.

7. Thomas G. Morton and Frank Woodbury, *The History of the Pennsylvania Hospital, 1751–1895* (Philadelphia: Times Printing House, 1879), 32.

8. *ANBO*.

9. *At the Instance of Benjamin Franklin: A Brief History of the Library Company of Philadelphia* (Philadelphia: Library Company of Philadelphia, 2015).

10. Diary of DNL, 1808–1814, p. 88.

11. JD to Thomas McKean, October 20, 1757, *WJD*, 1:140.

12. JD, "Notes for *Lesee of Daniel Weston and Mary Weston v. Stammers and Paul*," [1759], *WJD*, 2:55.

13. Ibid., 2:62, n. 8.

14. Ibid., 2:58.

15. JD, "Intention the Guide—the Pole Star in Construing Wills," [n.d.]. Logan, HSP.

16. JD, "Private Advantage to Yield to the Public Good," [n.d.], *WJD*, 2:388.

17. JD, "Intention the Guide." [n.d.].

18. JD, "Notes for *Benjamin Enoch & Mary Enoch v. George Crowe et al.* and *Benjamin Enoch & Mary Enoch v. John Eccles et al.*," [n.d.], *WJD*, 2:341.

19. JD, "Notes for *Uriah Blue & William McKnight v. William Clark, William McAllan, & Mary Forsythe*," [n.d.], *WJD*, 2:378.

20. Ibid., 2:374, 378.

21. JD, "Intention the Guide," [n.d.].

22. Ibid.

23. Robert Barclay, *The Anarchy of the Ranters and Other Libertines* (London, 1676), 37.

24. JD, "Set Two of Notes for *Paxton v. Van Dyke*," [February–May 1759], *WJD*, 2:19–20.

25. Ibid., 2:21.

26. JD, "Set One of Notes for *Paxton v. Van Dyke*," [February 1759], *WJD*, 2:14; JD, "Set Two of Notes for *Paxton v. Van Dyke*," [February–May 1759], *WJD*, 1:22.

27. JD, "Set Two," *WJD*, 2:21, 24.

28. Ibid., 2:25.

29. "Proposed Order of the Court in *Paxton v. Van Dyke*," August 25, 1759, *WJD*, 2:45.

30. JD, "Notes on *Ruth Mendenhall v. Samuel Broom*," February 1759, *WJD*, 2:34–7.

31. *PG*, October 6, 1758.

32. *PG*, December 1, 1757.

33. *Votes* (1758), 18.

34. JD to MCD, June 6, 1756, *WJD*, 1:127.

35. JD, "Draft Transcript of Opening Arguments in the Smith Libel Trial," [January 17, 1758], *WJD*, 1:177.

36. Ibid., 1:177–8.

37. Ibid., 1:178.

38. Ibid., 1:179.

39. Ibid., 1:180.

40. Ibid., 1:181.

41. Ibid.

42. Ibid., 1:181–2.

43. Ibid., 1:182–3.

44. Ibid., 1:185.

45. JD, "Draft Closing Arguments in the Smith Libel Trial," [January 20, 1758], *WJD*, 1:274; JD, "Fragment of Draft Transcript of David Hall's Deposition in the Smith Libel Trial," [January 21, 1758], *WJD*, 1:274.

46. JD, "Notes on Depositions in the Smith Libel Trial," [January 18–19, 1758], *WJD*, 1:200–1.

47. JD expressed this portion thusly: "The Eyes of the Young Gentleman who spoke, applied these words where they were intended, in a manner that coud not be observd by them who were at a Distance" (*WJD*, 1:271).

48. JD, "Fragment of Draft Transcript," *WJD*, 1:269–72.

49. *Votes* (1758), 27–8.

50. JD, "Draft Closing Arguments," *WJD*, 1:211.

51. JD, "Draft Transcript of Closing Arguments for the Smith Libel Trial," [January 21, 1758], *WJD*, 1:234–5.

52. Ibid., 1:237.

53. JD, "Draft Closing Arguments," *WJD*, 1:217.
54. JD, "Draft Transcript of Closing Arguments," *WJD*, 1:249.
55. Ibid., 1:250–1.
56. Ibid., 1:251.
57. Ibid., 1:252.
58. JD, "Draft Closing Arguments," *WJD*, 1:221.
59. Ibid., 1:221, 223, 221.
60. JD, "Draft Transcript of Closing Arguments," *WJD*, 1:254.
61. Ibid., 1:254–5.
62. Ibid., 1:255.
63. JD, "Legal and Political Notes on Pennsylvania," [n.d.], *WJD*, 2:291.
64. JD, "Draft Transcript of Closing Arguments," *WJD*, 1:256.
65. Ibid., 1:260.
66. Ibid., 1:261.
67. Ibid., 1:263.
68. JD, "Draft Closing Arguments," *WJD*, 1:229. JD left the last thought only partially completed, so it has been filled in here.
69. JD, "Edited Summary of the Smith Libel Trial," [January 25, 1758], *WJD*, 1:288.
70. *Votes* (1758), 32–3.
71. *Votes* (1758), 33. The language has been rendered in the first person here.
72. *Votes* (1758), 33.
73. Peter C. Hoffer, "Law and Liberty: In the Matter of Provost William Smith of Philadelphia, 1758," *WMQ* 38, no. 4 (1981): 681–701 at 683.
74. Isaac Norris to Benjamin Franklin, February 21, 1758, *PBF*, 7:385.
75. JD, "Draft Summary of the Smith Libel Trial," [January 25, 1758], *WJD*, 1:279.
76. Ralph Ketcham, "Benjamin Franklin and William Smith: New Light on an Old Philadelphia Quarrel," *PMHB* 88, no. 2 (1964): 142–63 at 159.
77. *MPCP*, 8:445–6.
78. JD, "Notes on a Libel in the Admiralty on Behalf of Some Danish Sailors," [1759], *WJD*, 2:66.
79. Diary of DNL, 1808–1814, p. 88; JD to MCD, September 14, 1763, *WJD*, 2:297.
80. JD, "Notes on a Libel," *WJD*, 2:68–9.
81. JD, "Interrogatories in the Vice Admiralty Court on Behalf of Captain John Macpherson et al.," [1758], *WJD*, 1:362–4.
82. See four documents related to *Campbell v. Owners of The Spry*, *WJD*, 1:335–61.
83. On the flag-of-truce trade, see *WJD*, 1:292–3.
84. *Read's Weekly Journal, or, British-Gazetteer* (London), September 6, 1760.
85. *PG*, July 1759.
86. JD, "Draft Two of Notes for *Spring & Kemp v. Ospray & Elizabeth*," [c. 1758], *WJD*, 1:320.
87. JD, "Notes on a Flag-of-Truce Case," [n.d.], *WJD*, 1:304.
88. JD, "Draft One of Notes for *Spring & Kemp v. Ospray & Elizabeth*," [c. 1758], *WJD*, 1:313.
89. An English Merchant, [JD], "Reflections on the Flag of Truce Trade in America," [c. 1761], *WJD*, 2:164.

90. Ibid., 2:167.

91. Ibid., 2:169.

92. Solomon Eccles, "Signs Are from the Lord to a People or Nation to Forewarn Them," [1663], in *Quaker Tracts*, vol. 6 (London, 1663–1664). This item is a foldout in the middle of the volume with no page number.

93. [JD], "Reflections," *WJD*, 2:140–1.

94. Ibid., 2:153.

95. JD, "Draft Two of Notes for *Spring & Kemp*," *WJD*, 1:319.

96. [JD], "Reflections," *WJD*, 2:160.

97. Montesquieu, *The Spirit of the Laws*, bk. XX, c. 6.

98. [JD], "Reflections," *WJD*, 2:127–8.

99. Ibid., 2:128.

100. Ibid., 2:160.

101. Ibid., 2:131.

Chapter 4

1. "Election Returns for Kent County, Delaware," [c. October 1–11, 1759], *WJD*, 2:47–50.

2. Burnaby, *Travels*, 42–5.

3. *LSD*, 1:373–4.

4. *PG*, October 25, 1759.

5. *PA*, 3:688–9.

6. "The Assembly of the Three Lower Counties to the Trustees of the Loan Office for Kent County," October 27, 1759, *WJD*, 2:51.

7. JD, "To the Public," January 21, 1777. RRL, HSP.

8. *PA*, 3:723.

9. Ibid., 3:724.

10. *LSD*, 1:374.

11. Ibid., 1:374–80.

12. JD et al., "Report of the Committee Appointed to Settle the Campeign Accounts in the year 1759," April 29, 1760, *WJD*, 2:94–7.

13. [JD?], "Obituary for Samuel Dickinson," *PG*, July 24, 1760, *WJD*, 2:98–9.

14. Ledger of MCD, 1758–1764.

15. *WJD*, 2:98–9; Violet Brown's recollections, white notebook of SND [c. 1837].

16. *LSD*, 1:384.

17. "A Further Supplement to the Act, Intituled, 'An Act for the Better Regulation of Servants and Slaves within this Government,'" in *LSD*, 1:380–1.

18. [JD], "Reflections on the Flag of the Truce Trade in America," *WJD*, 2:134.

19. *LSD*, 1:383–4.

20. JD to George Read, October 1, 1762, *WJD*, 2:247–8.

21. [JD?], "Obituary for John Moland," *PG*, January 8, 1761, *WJD*, 2:170.

22. *The Diary of Elizabeth Drinker: Volume One: 1758–1795*, ed. Elaine F. Crane, 3 vols. (Boston: Northeastern University Press, 1991), 87.

23. JD, "Notes on Judicial Tenure," [c. February 1761], *WJD*, 2:170–202; JD, "Draft Speech of a Debate on the Validity of American Court Proceedings upon the Death of George II," [c. February–August], *WJD*, 2:189–202.

24. JD to George Read, October 1, 1762, *WJD*, 2:248; *PG*, May 13, 1762; *WJD*, 2:237.

25. *Votes* (1762), 53.

26. JD to John Hall, May 3, 1762, *WJD*, 2:235–6.

27. Ibid.

28. JD to MCD, June 14, 1762, *WJD*, 2:240.

29. JD to Thomas McKean, June 8, 1762, *WJD*, 2:239.

30. Ibid., 1762, *WJD*, 2:241–2.

31. *ANBO*; DNL, "Some Memorandums respecting Charles Thomson," Diary of DNL, 1817–1819. Logan, HSP.

32. Steven C. Harper, "The Map That Reveals the Deception of the 1737 Walking Purchase," *PMHB* 136, no. 4 (2012), 457–60.

33. JD to MCD, June 14, 1762, *WJD*, 2:240.

34. JD to Israel Pemberton, September 11, 1762; Israel Pemberton to JD, October 30, December 6, December 21, 1762, *WJD*, 2:245, 251–2.

35. JD, "Three Questions [on a Murder]" [n.d., post-1769]. RRL, HSP.

36. JD, "Notes for *Dominus Rex v. Joseph Jordan*," [c. September 1761], *WJD*, 2:215–28.

37. Thomas G. Morton, *The History of the Pennsylvania Hospital, 1751–1895* (Philadelphia: Times Printing House, 1895), 128–9, 131.

38. JD to George Read, October 1, 1762, *WJD*, 2:248.

39. JD to MCD, January 16, 1763, *WJD*, 2:258–9.

40. *Votes* (1763), 8, 14, 17, 18.

41. Library Company of Philadelphia Minute Books, vol. 1, 1731–1742, p. 207. LCP.

42. JD to MCD, March 7, 1763, *WJD*, 2:276.

43. "John Dickinson," in Whitfield J. Bell, *Patriot-Improvers: Biographical Sketches of the Members of the American Philosophical Society* (Philadelphia: American Philosophical Society, 1997), 1:383.

44. "Memoirs of the Gloucester Fox Hunting Club" in *History of the Schuylkill Fishing Company* (Philadelphia, 1889), 407, 410.

45. *Votes* (1763), 34–35.

46. JD to MCD, March 7, 1763, *WJD*, 2:276.

47. *Diary of Elizabeth Drinker*, 1:99.

48. *WJD*, 2:298, n. 6.

49. JD, "Account of Negroes for Thomas Wilson's Estate," [n.d.]. Logan, HSP.

50. JD to a young gentleman, [n.d.], *WJD*, 2:390.

51. *PJ*, April 28, 1763.

52. *Votes* (1763), 43–4.

53. JD to MCD, September 14, 1763, *WJD*, 2:297.

54. JD, "Commonplace Book III," [n.d.], *WJD*, 2:328, 332.

55. JD to unknown, August 24, 1763, *WJD*, 2:293.

56. JD to MCD, August 26, 1763, *WJD*, 2:293–5.

57. They married on July 14, 1767. *ANBO*.

58. JD to George Read, January 23, 1763, *WJD*, 2:260.

59. JD, "A Song," December 1759, *WJD*, 2:53–4.

60. To a young gentleman, [n.d.], *WDJ*, 1:391.

61. "Invoice from David Hall," September 6, 1763, *WJD*, 2:296.

62. JD to MCD, September 14, 1763, *WJD*, 2:297.

63. *Votes* (1763), 49.

64. JD to MCD, September 14, 1763, *WJD*, 2:297.

Chapter 5

1. *Votes* (1764), 5.

2. "Fragments of a Journal Kept by Samuel Foulke, of Bucks County," *PMHB* 5, no. 1 (1881): 69.

3. For details about the Paxton Riots, see Kevin Kenny, *Peaceable Kingdom Lost: The Paxton Boys and the Destruction of William Penn's Holy Experiment* (New York: Oxford University Press, 2009).

4. John Gottlieb Ernestus Heckewelder, *A Narrative of the Mission of the United Brethren among the Delaware and Mohegan Indians from Its Commencement in the Year 1740 to the Close of the Year 1808* (Cleveland: Burrows Bros. Co., 1907), 195.

5. *MPCP*, 9:126.

6. Ibid., 9:132. On the house, where JD spent much time during his married life, and its inhabitants, see Susan Stabile, *Memory's Daughters: The Material Culture of Remembrance in Eighteenth-Century America* (Ithaca: Cornell University Press, 2004).

7. *Votes* (1764), 40.

8. Ibid., 41; "Fragments of a Journal Kept by Samuel Foulke"; *The Journals of Henry Melchior Mühlenberg*, trans. T. G. Tappert and J. W. Doberstein, 3 vols. (Madison: University of Wisconsin Press, 1942), 2:18.

9. *Votes* (1764), 42–3.

10. Marietta, *Reformation*, 190.

11. [David Dove], *The Quaker Unmask'd* (Philadelphia: A. Stueart, 1764), 9–10.

12. Lewis Weiss to Frederick Marshall, March 2, 1764, documents on murder trial of the Indian Renatus. Moravian Archives, Bethlehem, PA.

13. *Votes* (1764), 40.

14. JD, "A Letter to the Inhabitants of the Frontiers on Their Intended Expedition against the Indians under the Protection of the Government," [February 3–7, 1764], *WJD*, 3:21–8.

15. [JD], "Draft of "Protest in the Assembly against the Clause for Making Paper Bills of Credit a Legal Tender in Payment of All Contracts 'Proprietary Sterling Rents Only Excepted,'" March [10–13], 1764, *WJD*, 3:43–5; JD, "Draft Notes for Debate in the Assembly over Ways and Means of Raising Funds," [January 12–February 1, 1764], *WJD*, 3:8.

16. "Fragments of a Journal Kept by Samuel Foulke," 69.

17. On the royal government controversy, see Hutson, *Pennsylvania Politics*.

18. JD, *A Reply to a Piece Called the Speech of Joseph Galloway* (Philadelphia: W. Bradford, September 17, 1764), *WJD*, 3:178; Hannah Moland to JD, April 9, 1764, *WJD*, 3:46.

19. *PG*, May 10, 1764.

20. Isaac Norris, August 30, 1760, quoted in Hutson, *Pennsylvania Politics*, 156.

21. Elbert Russell, *The History of Quakerism* (New York: Macmillan Company, 1942), 215–16.

22. *Votes* (1764), 80–1.

23. JD, *A Speech, Delivered in the House of Assembly in the Province of Pennsylvania* (Philadelphia: W. Bradford, 1764), *WJD*, 3:51.

24. Benjamin Franklin, "Argument for Making the Bills of Credit Bear Interest," [January? 13–14, 1764], *PBF*, 11:7–18.

25. George Savile, *The Character of a Trimmer* (London, 1688), 10.

26. JD, *Speech*, *WJD*, 3:59.

27. Ibid.

28. Ibid., 3:61.

29. Ibid., 3:63

30. Ibid., 3:64.

31. Ibid., 3:70.

32. Ibid., 3:67.

33. Adapted from Isaac Norris to William Penn, September 23, 1710, in *Correspondence between William Penn and James Logan, Secretary of the Province and Others*, ed. E. Armstrong, 2 vols. (Philadelphia: Historical Society of Pennsylvania, 1870–72), 2:431.

34. Ibid., 3:68.

35. Savile, *Character of a Trimmer*, 10.

36. JD, *Speech*, *WJD*, 3:76.

37. JD, "Last Tuesday Morning . . ." (Philadelphia: W. Bradford, October 1, 1764), *WJD*, 3:203.

38. JD, *To the King's Most Excellent Majesty* (Philadelphia: [H. Miller?], [July] 1764, *WJD*, 3:87–9.

39. David Hall letterbook, 1759–1764. David Hall Papers, APS.

40. JD, *Reply*, 3:155.

41. *Votes* (1764), 87.

42. JD, *Reply*, *WJD*, 3:153–94. All information about publishing the *Speech* came from here.

43. *PG*, June 14, 1764.

44. [Joseph Galloway?], *The Maybe, Or Some Observations Occasion'd by Reading a Speech Deliver'd in the House of Assembly, the 24th of May* (Philadelphia: A. Armbruster, 1764), *WJD*, 3:80–3.

45. Hutson, *Pennsylvania Politics*, 157–8.

46. Joseph Galloway and Benjamin Franklin, *The Speech of Joseph Galloway, Esq;* (Philadelphia: W. Dunlap, 1764), *WJD*, 3:91–151.

47. Benjamin Franklin to Richard Jackson, September 1, 1764, *PBF*, 11:326.

48. JD, *Reply*, *WJD*, 3:155.

49. Ibid.

50. Ibid., 3:158.

51. Ibid., 3:184, 172.

52. Ibid., 3:184.

53. JD, *A Receipt to Make a Speech. By J——- G———, Esquire* ([Philadelphia: W. Bradford, 1764)] and "The Kennel Raker" [c. September 1764], *WJD*, 3:195–8.

54. *Votes* (1764), 94.

55. Ibid., 95.

56. *PJ*, September 27, 1764.

57. Benjamin Franklin to Richard Jackson, October 11, 1764, *PBF*, 11:397–8.

58. *Votes* (1765), 14–16.

59. Ibid.

60. JD, *A Protest Presented to the House of Assembly . . .* (Philadelphia: W. Bradford, October 26, 1764), *WJD*, 3:209–13.

61. *Votes* (1764), 52, 54, 57–58; JD, essay on transparency in the Pennsylvania Assembly, [October 17–18, 1770]. Logan, HSP.

62. [Benjamin Franklin], *Remarks on a Late Protest Against the Appointment of Mr. Franklin an Agent for this Province* (Philadelphia: B. Franklin and D. Hall, November 7, 1764), *WJD*, 3:223.

63. JD, "Observations on Mr. Franklin's Remarks on a Late Protest," [post–November 22, 1764], *WJD*, 3:230–6.

64. [Benjamin Franklin], *Remarks on a Late Protest against the Appointment of Mr. Franklin an Agent for This Province* [Philadelphia: B. Franklin and D. Hall, November 7, 1764], *WJD*, 3:219.

65. Samuel Wharton to Benjamin Franklin, December 19, 1764, *PBF*, 11:525–9.

66. Ibid.

67. Karin Wulf, "A Marginal Independence: Unmarried Women in Colonial Philadelphia" (PhD diss., Johns Hopkins University, 1993), 319.

68. Diary of DNL, 1808–1814, p. 30; Mark Reinberger and Elizabeth McLean, "Isaac Norris's Fairhill: Architecture, Landscape, and Quaker Ideals in a Philadelphia Colonial Country Seat," *Winterthur Portfolio* 32, no. 4 (1997): 243–74.

69. MND et al., "The Rural-Circle, or Band of Friendship, in familiar Letters between Several Young Ladies, Interspers'd with a variety of Valuable Characters," [c. 1760–1768]. JDP, LCP.

70. Sarah E. Fatherly, "'The Sweet Recourse of Reason': Elite Women's Education in Colonial Philadelphia," *PMHB* 128, no. 3 (2004): 249.

71. MND et al., "Rural-Circle," 9.

72. Ibid., 11, 19, 9.

73. Ibid., 21, 11.

74. Ibid.,13, 14, 20, 8.

75. David Yosifon and Peter N. Stearns. "The Rise and Fall of American Posture," *The American Historical Review* 103, no. 4 (1998): 1057–95.

76. *PG*, October 26, 1752.

77. MND et al., "Rural-Circle," 14–15.

78. Ibid., 14.

79. JD's copy of R. Saunders, *A Pocket Almanac for the Year 1760* (Philadelphia: B. Franklin and D. Hall, 1760. RRL, HSP.

Chapter 6

1. Anonymous, *Nosum Nosorum: Or, a New Treaise on Large Noses* (Philadelphia: [A. Steuart, 1764]), *WJD*, 3:243–50.

2. *Votes* (1765), 17–47.

3. JD, "Notes for *Dominus Rex v. Andrew Yeatman*," February 1765; *WJD*, 3:295–7; JD, "Notes for *Winter v. Erskine*," [n.d.], *WJD*, 2:386–8.

4. JD, "Set Three of Notes for *Overseers of Newtown Township v. Overseers of Marple Township*," February 1765, *WJD*, 3:589–93.

5. JD, "Notes for *Lessee of Peter Sigfreidus Alricks v. David Stewart*," [c. 1765], *WJD*, 3:427.

6. JD, "Notes for *Proprietary v. Ralston*," [n.d.]. Logan, HSP; JD, "Notes for *London Land Company v. Joseph Campbell*," [c. April–December 1761]; and JD, "Notes for *London Land Company v. Several Tenants*," [c. April–December 1761], *WJD*, 2:203–11; JD, "Notes on *Baltimore v. Vining*," [n.d.], *WJD*, 3:310, 312–13.

7. On the Stamp Act, see Edmund S. Morgan and Helen M. Morgan, *The Stamp Act Crisis: Prologue to Revolution* (Williamsburg: University of North Carolina Press for the Omohundro Institute, 1962); C. A. Weslager, *The Stamp Act Congress: With an Exact Copy of the Compete Journal* (Newark: University of Delaware Press, 1976).

8. JD, *The Late Regulations Respecting the British Colonies . . .* (Philadelphia: W. Bradford, December 7, 1765), *WJD*, 3:392.

9. Ibid., 3:392.

10. JD to MCD, January 16, 1763, *WJD*, 2:258–9.

11. Edwin G. Burrows and Mike Wallace, *Gotham: A History of New York City to 1898* (New York: Oxford University Press, 1998) , 170.

12. *PG*, August 22, 1765.

13. JD to MCD, July 15, 1765, *WJD*, 3:340.

14. Susanna Wright, "To Eliza Norris—at Fairhill," in Pattie Cowell, "'Womankind Call Reason to Their Aid': Susanna Wright's Verse Epistle on the Status of Women in Eighteenth-Century America," *Signs* 6, no. 4 (1981): 799, 800.

15. Susanna Wright to JD, November 3, 1772. RRL, HSP.

16. William T. Parsons, "The Brief Married Life of Isaac and Sarah Norris," *Quaker History* 57, no. 2 (1968): 67–83.

17. See "Documents Related to the Stamp Act Congress," *WJD*, 3:343–405.

18. JD to MCD, October 7, 1765. *WJD*, 3:356–8.

19. *ANBO*.

20. John Jones to JD, November 23, 1761, *WJD*, 2:230.

21. JD, "To the Electors of Philadelphia County," *PG*, August 8, 1765, *WJD*, 3:342; Samuel Purviance Jr. to Ezra Stiles, November 1, 1766, *Extracts from the Itineraries and Other Miscellanies of Ezra Stiles* (New Haven: Yale University Press, 1916), 557.

22. *New-York Mercury*, October 10, 1765.

23. Weslager, *Stamp Act Congress*, 220, 224, 148.

24. JD, "Friends and Countrymen" (Philadelphia: B. Franklin and D. Hall, [November], 1765), *WJD*, 3:376. For the fullest statement of Quaker civil disobedience, see Martin

Luther King Jr., *Letter from a Birmingham City Jail* (Philadelphia: American Friends Service Committee, 1963).

25. JD, *Late Regulations, WJD*, 3:378–405.
26. Ibid., 3:385.
27. JD to William Pitt, December 21, 1765, *WJD*, 3:419.
28. Ibid., 3:416.
29. *PJ*, February 27, 1766.
30. JD, "Essay on a Report Concerning the Petition for a Change of Government," [March 1766], *WJD*, 3:443.
31. Hutson, *Pennsylvania Politics*, 204–7.
32. *PG*, April 3, 1765.
33. *PG*, May 1, 1766.
34. A North-American [JD], *An Address to the Committee of Correspondence in Barbados. Occasioned by a Late Letter from Them to Their Agent in London* (Philadelphia: W. Bradford, 1766), *WJD*, 3:476–92.
35. Sir Robert Filmer, *Patriarcha: Or, the Natural Power of Kings* (London: W. Davis, 1680).
36. [JD], *Barbados Address, WJD*, 3:483.
37. Ibid., 3:485, 483.
38. Ibid., 3:482, 483, 488.
39. A Barbadian [Kenneth Morrison], *An Essay towards the Vindication of the Committee of Correspondence in Barbados* (Barbados: G. Esmand, June–August 1766), *WJD*, 3:507.
40. A Native of Barbados, *Candid Observation on Two Pamphlets Lately Published* (Barbados: G. Esmand, July–August 1766), *WJD*, 3:527.
41. William Knox, *The Controversy between Great-Britain and Her Colonies Reviewed* (London: J. Almon, January 1769), 11.
42. JD to John Jay, July 22, 1779. HSP, RRL.
43. Hannah Griffitts, "An Anecdote—Recommended to the Serious Attention of every Member of the Convention," November 1787. Hannah Griffitts Papers LCP.
44. MND, untitled essay beginning with "Surely Gloom is not the Characteristick of a Christian." MND et al., Poems, 1764–1768. JDP, LCP.
45. JD to [Sally Norris], [1768]. RRL, HSP.
46. Wulf, "A Marginal Independence," 313–17.
47. On the relationship between Hannah Griffitts and Susanna Wright, see Angela Vietto, *Women and Authorship in Revolutionary America* (New York: Routledge, 2016), 24–6.
48. Anne M. Ousterhout, *The Most Learned Woman in America: A Life of Elizabeth Graeme Fergusson* (University Park: Penn State University Press, 2004).

Chapter 7

1. On Lloyd, see Isaac Norris's copy of *Poor Richard's Almanac*, January 28, 1765. Rosenbach Library; *Martin's Bench and Bar*, 242, 287.

2. JD to a young gentleman, *WJD*, 2:391.

3. Susan E. Klepp, *Revolutionary Conceptions: Women, Fertility, and Family Limitation in America, 1760–1820* (Chapel Hill: University of North Carolina Press, 2009), 226.

4. *PG*, March 15, 1759.

5. Although there is no definitive evidence that Francisco escaped execution, this seems the most likely outcome. JD, notes for *Dominus Rex v. Rachel Francisco*, [March 1767]. Logan, HSP; John Vining to Benjamin Chew, April 13, 1767. Supreme Court of Pennsylvania, Gratz, HSP. Some language has been reconstructed from partial notes.

6. Although Henry Brooke published six "Farmer's letters" in Ireland in 1745, there is no evidence in JD's papers that he was influenced by them. Moreover, their anti-Caltholic fear-mongering and advocacy of violence was antithetical to JD's ecumenical approach to religion and the peaceful message of his Farmer. See Henry Brooke, *The Farmer's Letters to the Protestants of Ireland* (Dublin: G. Faulkner, 1745).

7. A Farmer [JD], "Letters from a Farmer in Pennsylvania," *PG*, December 3, 10, 17, 24, 1767; January 7, 14, 21, 28; February 4, 11, 18, 1768.

8. Ibid., "No. VII," *PG*, January 21, 1768; and "No. I," *PG*, December 3, 1767.

9. Ibid., "No. III," *PG*, December 17, 1767.

10. Ibid.

11. Savile, *Character of a Trimmer*, 13.

12. A Farmer, "No. IV," January 28, 1768.

13. JD to MCD, February 19, 1755, *WJD*, 1:77.

14. Ibid., "No. III," *PG*, December 17, 1767.

15. Calvert, *Quaker Constitutionalism*, esp. 300–1.

16. American Philosophical Society, *Early Proceedings of the American Philosophical Society for the Promotion of Useful Knowledge* (Philadelphia: McCalla & Stavely, 1884), 4, 7, 9; Bell, *Patriot-Improvers*, 383.

17. *Speeches of the Governors of Massachusetts from 1765 to 1775* (Boston: Russell and Gardner, 1818), 134–6.

18. *Boston Gazette*, March 21, 1768.

19. Ibid, March 28, 1768.

20. *PG*, March 31, 1768.

21. John Devotion to Ezra Stiles, February 8, 1768, *Extracts from the Itineraries . . . of Ezra Stiles* (New Haven: Yale University Press, 1814), 471.

22. *PC*, December 18–25, 1769.

23. William Franklin to Benjamin Franklin, May 10, 1768, *PBF*, 15:121.

24. N. P., "Letters in Answer to the Farmer's. No. II," *Boston Evening-Post*, February 13, 1769.

25. A Citizen [William Hicks], "The Nature and Extent of Parliamentary Power Considered," *PJ*, January 28–February 25, 1768.

26. See correspondence between JD and Hicks, March 31, 1768, and [n.d]. RRL, HSP.

27. N. P., "Letters in Answer to the Farmer's. No. II," *Boston Evening-Post*, February 13, 1769.

28. Benjamin Franklin to William Franklin, March 13, 1768, *PBF*, 15:74–8.

29. N. N. [Benjamin Franklin], "The British Editor to the Reader," *Letters from a Farmer in Pennsylvania* (London: J. Almon, [May] 1768); Carl F. Kaestle, "The Public Reaction

to John Dickinson's Farmer's Letters," *Proceedings of the American Antiquarian Society* (Worcester, MA: American Antiquarian Society, 1969), 328.

30. JD to Matthew Carey, January 6, 1789. Emmet, NYPL.

31. A. B. [JD], "The Centinel. Nos. VI, VII, VIII, [XVI?]," *PJ*, April 28; May 5, 12; [July 7?], 1768.

32. [JD], "The Centinel. No. VIII," May 12, 1768.

33. Pacificus [JD], *To the Public* Philadelphia: W. Goddard, July 16, 1768.

34. JD, "Copy of a Letter from a Gentleman in Virginia, to a Merchant in Philadelphia," *PG*, July 22, 1768.

35. William Penn, *Some Fruits of Solitude: In Reflections and Maxims Relating to the Conduct of Human Life* (London: T. Northcott, 1693), 103–4.

36. JD, draft fragment of "To the Public" [July 1768]. RRL, HSP.

37. JD to James Otis, July 4, 1768. RRL, HSP.

38. *DJA*, 1:341–2

39. *Boston Post-Boy*, August 22, 1768.

40. JD, "An Address Read at a Meeting of the Merchants," *PJ*, April 28, 1768.

41. [JD and Charles Thomson], "An Address at the Pennsylvania State House on July 30," *PG*, August 4, 1768; "The Instructions to the Representatives of the City and County of Philadelphia," *PC*, August 8, 1768.

42. A Countryman, "To the Printer of the Pennsylvania Chronicle," *PC*, August 1, 1768.

43. Machiavel, "'Latet anguis in herba.' A Snake in the Grass," *PC*, August 22, 1768. A Miller, "To the Printer of the Pennsylvania Chronicle," *PC*, August 15, 1768. Thomas Peaceable, "To the Worshipful Company of Epigram Writers," *PC*, August 29, 1768.

44. An American, "Quid de quoque viro, dicas; saepe videto. Be Not Hasty to Condemn," *Boston Gazette*, October 17, 1768.

45. JD to Thomas Barton, August 29, 1768, in William Barton, *Memoirs of the Life of David Rittenhouse* (Philadelphia: E. Parker, 1813), 227.

46. EGF, "The Dream. A Poem. The Philosophical Farmer," October 15, 1768. Poemata Juvenilia, LCP.

47. *Votes* (1768), 128–34; Hutson, *Pennsylvania Politics*, 225–6.

48. Letter of Philadelphia Merchants' Committee to London Merchants' Committee, November 1, 1768, *London Chronicle*, June 10, 1769.

49. JD to [Sally Norris], [1768]. RRL, HSP.

50. Ibid.

51. JD to MCD, August 12, 1755, *WJD*, 1:88.

52. JD to [Sally Norris], [1768].

53. JD to [Hannah Harrison], August 24, 1769. CTP, LOC; JD to [Sally Norris], [1768].

54. Ibid.

55. JD to [Hannah Harrison], August 24, 1769.

56. MND, "To the Young Gentlemen," [1768]. MND et al., Poems, 1764–1768.

Chapter 8

1. Copy of Richard Henry Lee to JD, November 26, 1768. RHLP, APS.

2. For details of the resistance in Pennsylvania, see Richard Alan Ryerson, *The Revolution Is Now Begun: The Radical Committees of Philadelphia, 1765-1776* (Philadelphia: University of Pennsylvania Press, 1978); and Arthur M. Schlesinger, *Colonial Merchants and the American Revolution* (New York: Atheneum, 1968).

3. Copy of JD to Richard Henry Lee, January 16, 1769. RHLP, APS.

4. *His Majesty's Most Gracious Speech before Both Houses of Parliament, on Tuesday, the Eighth Day of November, 1768* (London: M. Baskett, 1768).

5. Excerpt from "A Letter from a Gentleman in London," *PJ*, April 27, 1769.

6. Schlesinger, *Colonial Merchants*, 128; *PBF*, 4:210-11.

7. "Early Days of the Revolution in Philadelphia: Charles Thomson's Account of the Opposition to the Boston Port Bill," *PMHB* 2, no. 4 (1878): 411-23.

8. *Georgia Gazette*, April 27, 1768; *New-Hampshire Gazette*, March 26 and June 3, 1768.

9. *PJ*, April 6, 1769.

10. *PJ*, March 30, 1769.

11. *New-York Gazette*, October 9, 1769.

12. Voltaire, *Letters Concerning the English Nation* (London: C. Davis, 1733), 30.

13. Benjamin Rush to JD, October 11, 1797, *LBR*, 2:792-3.

14. *Ephémérides du citoyen ou Bibliotheque Raisonee des Sciences Morales et Politiques*, Dixieme Tome, ed. Pierre Samuel du Pont (Paris: Lacombe, 1769), 44-9.

15. *Wienerisches Diarium*, December 21, 1776.

16. Jonathan Singerton, "'Some of Distinction Here Are Warm for the Part of America': Knowledge of and Sympathy for the American Cause in the Habsburg Monarchy, 1763-1783," *Journal of Austrian-American History* 1, no. 2 (2017): 148.

17. Zofia Libiszowska, "Polish Opinion of the American Revolution," *Polish American Studies* 34, no. 1 (1977): 11.

18. Excerpt from "Extract of a Letter, dated Nov. 18, from a Gentleman in London," *Providence* (RI) *Gazette*, March 4, 1769.

19. Schlesinger, *Colonial Merchants*, 130.

20. JD, notes on *Dominus Rex v. John Holland*, [1769]. RRL and Logan, HSP.

21. JD to [Hannah Harrison], August 24, 1769. CTP, LOC.

22. Sara Stidstone Gronim, "Imagining Inoculation: Smallpox, the Body, and Social Relations of Healing in the Eighteenth Century," *Bulletin of the History of Medicine* 80, no. 2 (2006): 247-68.

23. MND, untitled poem in the letter copy from Sally Norris to MND, July 30, 1768, [1769]. MND et al., Poems, 1764-1768.

24. Hannah Griffitts, "To the Memory of Sally Norris who Died of the Small Pox in the 23d year of her Age," 1768, in *Milcah Martha Moore's Book: A Commonplace Book from Revolutionary America*, ed. Catherine La Courreye Blecki and Karin Wulf (University Park: Pennsylvania State University Press, 1997), 186.

25. MND, untitled poem in the letter copy from Sally Norris to MND, July 30, 1768, [1769].

26. JD to Arthur Lee, June 26, 1769. ALP, HL.

27. David Hay to JD, June 26, [1769]. Logan, HSP.

28. *Newport* (RI) *Mercury*, July 17, 1769.

29. JD to David Hay, June 27, 1769. RRL, HSP.

30. JD to unknown, [n.d.]. Logan, HSP.

31. Hannah Moland Hay to JD, [June 27, 1769]. Logan, HSP.

32. *Gentleman's Magazine*, August 1772.

33. Patricia C. O'Donnell, "This Side of the Grave: Navigating the Quaker Plainness Testimony in London and Philadelphia in the Eighteenth Century," *Winterthur Portfolio* 49, no. 1 (2015): 29–54.

34. Griffitts, "To the Memory of Sally Norris," 186.

35. Copy of Sally Norris to MND, July 30, 1768. MND et al., Poems, 1764–1768. JDP, LCP.

36. MND, untitled poem in the letter copy from Sally Norris to MND, July 30, 1768, [1769].

37. JD to [Hannah Harrison], August 24, 1769. CTP, LOC.

38. MND, untitled poem in the letter copy from Sally Norris to MND, July 30, 1768, [1769].

39. MND, "A Pastoral, Autumn 1768." MND Poems, 1764–1768.

40. Marriage certificate of JD and MND, July 19, 1770. JDP, LCP.

41. *PC*, March 19, 1770.

42. [Alexander McDougall], *To the Betrayed Inhabitants of the City and Colony of New York* (New York: J. Parker, 1769).

43. JD to Arthur Lee, March 31, 1770. ALP, HL.

44. *Boston Gazette*, April 4, 1770.

45. *PG*, May 10, 1770.

46. Marriage certificate of JD and MND, July 19, 1770; Henry Mühlenberg to JD, July 20, 1770. Copy in SMC, DPA; The Workmen to JD, July 20, 1770. RRL, HSP.

47. JD to Mary Parker Norris, September 20, 1770. Logan, HSP.

48. Ibid.

49. Alexander McDougall to JD, April [1], 1771. JDP, LCP.

50. Correspondence with Osgood Hanbury, 1770, 1771. Logan, HSP; correspondence with Hannah Griffitts. RRL and Logan, HSP.

51. JD to Arthur Lee, October 31, 1770, *The Life of Arthur Lee*, ed. R. H. Lee, 2 vols. (Boston: Wells and Lilly, 1829), 2:302–3; JD to Catharine Macaulay, October 31, 1770. Correspondence of Catherine Macaulay, Gilder-Lehrman Coll., Gilder Lehrman Institute of American History.

52. JD, note on public service, [c. 1775]. Logan, HSP.

53. William Goddard, *The Partnership, Or the History of the Rise and Progress of the Pennsylvania Chronicle* (Philadelphia: W. Goddard, 1770).

54. *Votes* (1771), 208–10; JD, essay on transparency in the Pennsylvania Assembly, [October 17–18, 1770]. Logan, HSP.

55. *SCP*, vol. 5; Charles Miner, *History of Wyoming, In a Series of Letters, from Charles Miner, to his Son, William Penn Miner, Esq.* (Philadelphia: J. Crissy, 1845), 114–24.

56. *Votes* (1771), 237–8, 240–1; JD, draft "A Message to the Governor from the Assembly," [1771]. Logan, HSP.

57. JD to the Overseers of the Poor, [1771]. RRL, HSP.

58. *Votes* (1771), 245.

59. *Rules, Minutes, &c. of the Society of the Friendly Sons of St. Patrick, 1843, 1771–1793* (1771). Falvey Library, Villanova University, Villanova, PA ; John Hugh Campbell, *History of the Friendly Sons of St. Patrick and of the Hibernian Society for the Relief of Emigrants from Ireland* (Philadelphia: Hibernian Society, 1892), 143.

60. The Sons of St. Tammany, invitation to John Dickinson (Philadelphia: R. Aitkin, April 28, 1773).

61. JD to Arthur Lee, September 21, 1771, *The Life of Arthur Lee*, ed. R. H. Lee, 2 vols. (Boston: Wells and Lilly, 1829), 2:303–4.

62. *Votes* (1765), 14–16.

63. JD, "Notes and Drafts of a Speech in Assembly on Two Bills," [February 1771]. JDP, LCP.

64. JD, draft "To The King's most Excellent Majesty, The humble Petition of the Representatives of the Freemen of Pennsylvania in General Assembly met," February 12, 1771. JDP, LCP; *Votes* (1771), 258.

65. James Pemberton to JD, October 4, 1771. JDP, LCP.

66. It's not clear when or why MCD moved to Fairhill, only that she was there in the years 1772 and 1774. Mary Parker Norris to JD, January 27, 1772. Mf, HSP; Copy of paper drawn up by Joseph Reed for William Henry Drayton. MDL, HSP.

67. Nicholas B. Wainwright, *Colonial Grandeur in Philadelphia* (Philadelphia: Historical Society of Pennsylvania, 1954), 142–8; William Logan to John Smith, February 23 and 27, 1771. John Smith Papers, LCP.

68. JD to James Wilson, December 28, 1771. Gratz, HSP.

69. Francis Alison to JD, January 4, 1772. JDP, LCP.

70. *WJD*, 2:298, n. 6.

71. See estate papers of William Hicks. Logan, HSP.

72. JD to unknown, August 25, 1776. RRL, HSP.

73. Jacob Rush to JD, February 8, 1772. RRL, HSP.

74. William M. Wiecek, "Somerset: Lord Mansfield and the Legitimacy of Slavery in the Anglo-American World," *The University of Chicago Law Review* 42, no. 1 (1974): 86–146.

75. Granville Sharp, *An Essay on Slavery, Proving from Scripture Its Inconsistency with Humanity and Reason* (Burlington, NJ: I. Collins, 1773), vii–viii.

76. Bill of sale for Dinah and child, June 22, 1772. Logan, HSP.

77. Bill of sale for Nanny, November 13, 1772. 54/7, Rose Cottage, Dover, DE.

78. Josiah Quincy's "Opening for the Defense," November 29, 1770, *Legal Papers of John Adams*, ed. L. Kinvin Wroth et al., 3 vols. (Cambridge: Belknap Press of Harvard University Press, 1965), 3:158–69.

79. *PG*, June 25, 1772.

80. Darius Sessions et al. to JD, January 1773. JDP, LCP.

81. Ibid.

82. Richard Henry Lee to JD, April 4, 1773. RHLP, APS.

83. Copy of JD to Richard Henry Lee, May 30, 1773. RHLP, APS.

84. Abraham Yates to JD, August 24, 1772. See Thomas J. Humphrey, "'Extravagant Claims' and 'Hard Labour': Perceptions of Property in the Hudson Valley, 1751–1801," *Pennsylvania History: A Journal of Mid-Atlantic Studies* 65 (1998): 141–66.

85. John Montgomery to JD, August 20, 1773. RRL, HSP.

86. John Montgomery to JD, October 1, 1773. RRL, HSP; William Smith to JD, November 23, 1773. JDP, LCP; William Smith to JD, November 23, 1773. MDL, HSP; Rodney K. Miller, "The Influence of the Socio-Economic Status of the Anglican Clergy of Revolutionary Maryland On Their Political Orientation," *Historical Magazine of the Protestant Episcopal Church* 47, no. 2 (1978): 197–210.

87. JD, draft "Opinion on 40 [per] Poll Act in Maryland," October 1, 1773. JDP, LCP; Charles Thomson to JD, October 14, 1773. JDP, LCP.

88. *PG*, October 24, 1771; *PG*, April 5, 1775.

89. *Massachusetts Spy*, September 5, 1771; *Censor* (MA), May 2, 1772.

90. Abigail Adams to Thomas Jefferson, July 25, 1784, *AFC*, 5:376.

91. Charles Coleman Sellers, *Patience Wright: American Artist and Spy in George III's London* (Middletown, CT: Wesleyan University Press, 1976).

92. *PG*, May 30, 1771.

93. *PG*, August 2, 1775.

94. *Poulson's*, August 15, 1825.

95. Catharine Macaulay to JD, July 18, 1771. Catharine Graham Macaulay Papers, Gilder Lehrman Coll., Gilder Lehrman Institute of American History.

96. Francis Alison to JD, January 4, 1772.

97. A Farmer, "No. II," *PG*, December 10, 1767.

98. Ibid., "No. VII," *PG*, January 14, 1768.

99. Frederick William Hunter, *Stiegel Glass* (Boston: Houghton Mifflin Company, 1914). JD's papers related to Elizabeth Furnace are in Logan, HSP.

100. John Macpherson Jr. to William Patterson, February 24, 1768. W. H. Harnor Collection, HSP.

101. John Macpherson, *Macpherson's Letters, &c* (Philadelphia, 1770); Pennsylvania Sailor [John Macpherson], *A Pennsylvania Sailor's Letters, Alias the Farmer's Fall* (Philadelphia, 1771).

102. EGF to JD, October 15, 1772. JDP, LCP; Ousterhout, *The Most Learned Woman in America*, 145.

103. William Killen to JD, September 19, 1772. Logan, HSP.

104. Election circular, October 1, 1772, [n.p.].

105. Samuel Adams to JD, March 27, 1773. Papers of Samuel Adams, NYPL.

106. JD to Samuel Adams, April 10, 1773. Papers of Samuel Adams, NYPL.

107. Josiah Quincy Jr., "Journal of Josiah Quincy, Jr.," *Proceedings of the Massachusetts Historical Society*, 3rd ser., 49 (1916): 471.

108. Ibid., 471–2.

109. Ibid., 473.

110. JD draft to Archibald Stewart & Son, December 16, 1771; Archibald Stewart & Son to JD, September 23, 1773. Logan, HSP; Bartholomew Alston to JD, February 22, 1772. RRL, HSP.

111. Quincy, "Journal of Josiah Quincy, Jr.," 473.

112. Ibid.

113. Ryerson, *Revolution*, 34.

114. Ibid., 36.

115. *PJ*, November 3, 1773.

116. Rusticus [JD], *A Letter from the Country to a Gentleman in Philadelphia* (Philadelphia: November 27, 1773).

117. The Committee of the Association, "To the Friends of Liberty and Trade, of the City and County of New-York" (New York: December 4, 1773).

118. Ryerson, *Revolution*, 34.

119. *PP*, January 31, 1774.

Chapter 9

1. Samuel Adams to JD, April 21, 1774. Samuel Adams Papers, NYPL.

2. For details on the Philadelphia resistance in the spring and summer of 1774, see Ryerson, *Revolution* , esp. ch. 3. Arthur Lee to JD, April 2, 1774. JDP, LCP; From Josiah Quincy Jr., May 27, 1774. RRL, HSP.

3. Circular Letter of the Boston Committee of Correspondence, May 13, 1774, *The Writings of Samuel Adams*, ed. Harry Alonzo Cushing, 4 vols. (New York: G. P. Putnam's Sons, 1904–1908), 3:107–9.

4. "Copy of a Paper drawn up by Joseph Reed for W. Henry Drayton," [n.d.]. MDL, HSP.

5. Details of the following episode were drawn from two sometimes-conflicting sources: "Copy of a Paper Drawn up by Joseph Reed to W. Henry Drayton"; and Charles Thomson, "Early Days of the Revolution in Philadelphia," *PMHB* 2, no. 4 (1878): 411–23.

6. JD to Charles Morrison, May 1774. Bancroft Coll., NYPL.

7. Paul Revere's report on the May 20 Philadelphia meeting, *Essex* (MA) *Gazette*, May 31, 1774.

8. Ibid.

9. P. P. [JD], "Letter I: To the Inhabitants of the British Colonies," *PJ*, May 25, June 1, 8, 15, 1774.

10. P. P. [JD], "Letter II: To the Inhabitants of the British Colonies," *PJ*, June 1, 1774.

11. *Boston Gazette*, June 20, 1774.

12. *PJ*, June 22, 1774.

13. The mechanics' address to John Dickinson, June 27 and July 4, 1774. JDP, LCP.

14. JD, *An Essay on the Constitutional Power of Great-Britain over the Colonies in America; with the Resolves of the Committee for the Province of Pennsylvania, and Their Instructions to Their Representatives in Assembly* (Philadelphia: W. and T. Bradford, 1774).

15. JD, notes [1774]. RRL, HSP.

16. Camillus, "A serious and extensive view of the Gubernatorial Election," *New-England Palladium* (Boston), March 31, 1807.

17. JD, "Instructions," in *Constitutional Power*, 9–32.

18. Arthur Lee to JD, August 19, 1774. Loudoun, HSP.

19. Force, 1:607–8.

20. Thomas Mason to JD, August 25, 1774. RRL, HSP.

21. [DNL] quoted in "*Biography of the Lives of the Signers*," 416–17.

22. *DJA*, 2:132, 137.

23. JD, "A Singular Dream of J. Dickinson." MDL, HSP.

24. DNL, "Some Memorandums," p. 160.

25. *JCC*, 1:31–9.

26. DNL, "Some Memorandums," p. 162.

27. Several drafts of the First Petition of Congress to the King, [October 1774]. RRL, HSP; JD, Draft of "To the Inhabitants of the Colonies," [October 1774]. RRL, HSP; JD, Draft of "A Letter to the Inhabitants of the Province of Quebec," [October 26, 1774]. JDP, LCP; JD, draft "Heads of Grievances and Rights," [October 14, 1774]. John Adams Papers, MHS. On the creation of these documents, see *A Decent Respect to the Opinions of Mankind: Congressional State Papers, 1774–1776,* ed. James H. Hutson (Washington, DC: Library of Congress, 1975).

28. [JD], *A Letter to the Inhabitants of the Province of Quebec* (Philadelphia: W. and T. Bradford, 1774), 42.

29. DNL, "Some Memorandums," pp. 161–2.

30. JD, reflections on John Marshall's history in the hand of SND, [1804]. RRL, HSP.

31. *DJA*, 2:156.

32. John Adams to François Adriaan van der Kemp, April 8, 1815. John Adams Papers, MHS.

33. Josiah Quincy, *Figures of the Past: From the Leaves of Old Journals* (Boston: Roberts Brothers, 1888), 80.

34. *DJA*, 3:316.

35. Ibid., 3:311–13.

36. Ryerson, *Revolution*, 94–7.

37. JD to Patience Wright, January 30, 1775, *Journal of the Friends Historical Society* 20, nos. 1/2 (1923): 95–6.

38. JD, note on public service, [c. 1775]. Logan, HSP.

39. Ibid.

40. *PJ*, February 8, 1775.

41. *New-York Rivington's Gazette*, February 2 and 23, 1775; Ryerson, *Revolution*, 100–6.

42. *PEP*, February 9, 1775.

43. JD to Patience Wright, January 30, 1775.

44. *PEP*, April 15, 1775.

45. JD to Arthur Lee, April 29, 1775. ALP, HL.

46. Ibid.

47. Philadelphia Monthly Meeting, Northern District, *Record of Births and Deaths, 1772–1806*, p. 64. Quaker and Special Collections, Haverford College, Haverford, PA.

48. Dickinson family Bible. Logan, HSP; Hannah Griffitts, "On the Death of a Child of P. Dickinson who Died of ye Small-Pox, May 5th 1775." Hannah Griffitts Papers, LCP.

49. Susanna Wright to JD, April 1775 and May 18, 1775. RRL, HSP. That Wright described JD in her will as "the able & never failing friend of our whole family the Benevolent

John Dickinson" suggests that she was not disappointed. See Wulf, "A Marginal Independence," 214, n. 33.

50. George Read to Gertrude Reed, [May 23, 1775], *LDC*, 1:400.

51. JD to Arthur Lee, April 29, 1775. ARP, HL. For the best scholarly treatment of JD in the 1775 Congress, see David L. Jacobson, *John Dickinson and the Revolution in Pennsylvania, 1764–1776* (Berkeley: University of California Press, 1965), 86–102.

52. *JCC*, 2:22.

53. JD to Arthur Lee, April 29, 1775. ALP, HL.

54. JD to Tench Coxe, January 24, 1807. Coxe, HSP.

55. JD, notes [May 23–25]. Gratz, HSP.

56. *JCC*, 2:52.

57. Silas Deane's Diary, *LDC*, 1:352.

58. JD, "We may act in any of these 3 Ways," [May 16–25, 1775]. Gratz, HSP.

59. Ibid.

60. "Arguments in Congress in Favour of Treating, rather than inflaming the Contest," [May 16–25, 1775]. Gratz, HSP.

61. *JCC*, 2:64–6.

62. Samuel Adams to James Warren, June 10, 1775, *Adams-Warren Letters: Being Chiefly a Correspondence between John Adams, Samuel Adams, and John Warren*, 2 vols. Boston: Massachusetts Historical Society), 1:54.

63. John Adams to James Warren, May 21, 1775, *PJA*, 3:11. He repeated the same sentiments to Abigail on May 29, 1775, *AFC*, 1:207.

64. John Adams to Moses McGill, June 10, 1775, *PJA*, 3:20–1.

65. John Adams to Abigail Adams, June 17, 1775, *AFC*, 1:216.

66. *Votes* (1775), 645.

67. Patience Wright to JD, April 6, 1775. Transcription from Leon de Valinger's John Dickinson Project, HSP.

68. JD, "Instructions for enlisting Rifle Men in the Service of the Colony of Pennsylvania," [June 1775]. RRL, HSP.

69. Ibid., 648.

70. JD, "To My Opponents," *PG*, January 15, 1783.

71. *PEP*, May 11, 1775.

72. *Journal of Nathaniel Luff, M.D. of the State of Delaware* (New-York: Clark & Sickels, 1848), 15.

73. John Adams to James Warren, June 20, 1775. *PJA*, 3:34.

74. Thomson, "Early Days of the Revolution," 423.

75. John Adams to James Warren, [July] 6, 1775, *PJA*, 3:61–2

76. John Adams to Joseph Palmer, [July] 6, 1775, *PJA*, 3:54.

77. John Adams to James Warren, [July] 6, 1775, *PJA*, 3:61–2.

78. Julian P. Boyd, "The Disputed Authorship of the Declaration on the Causes and Necessity for Taking Up Arms, 1775," *PMHB* 74, no. 1 (1950): 51–73.

79. JD, Draft of the Declaration on Taking Up Arms, [June–July 1775]. N-YHS; JD and Thomas Jefferson, *A Declaration by the Representatives of the United Colonies of North-America, Now Met in Congress at Philadelphia, Setting Forth the Causes and Necessity of Their Taking Up Arms* (Philadelphia: W. and T. Bradford, [July 6], 1775).

80. *Essex Gazette*, September 7–14, 1775.

81. *Wienerisches Diarium*, no. 80, 2–3, October 7, 1775.

82. JD to Mercy Otis Warren, September 9, 1801. MDL, HSP; JD, notes [May 23–25]. Gratz, HSP.

83. John Adams to William Tudor, July 6, 1775, *PJA*, 3:54.

84. *PBF*, 22:120–5.

85. See John Adams to James Warren, July 23, 1775. *PJA*, 3:86–88.

86. John Adams to James Warren, July 23, 1775, *PJA*, 3:87

87. John Adams to Abigail Adams, July 23, 1775. *AFC*, 1:253.

88. John Adams to James Warren, July 24, 1775, *PJA*, 3:89.

89. *DJA*, 3:318.

90. Charles Lee to JD, January 18, 1776. JDP, LCP. Thirty years hence, Adams found other ways to justify the "unfortunate Accident" of his published letter. First, he wrote it in a hurry so he could give a messenger boy some business. Next, he had grown irritated by Dickinson's "unpoliteness" and "mortified with his Success in Congress." And, finally, "[t]he printers made it worse, than it was in the Original," a claim the editors of his papers disbelieve (*DJA*, 3:317–19, 321).

91. *DJA*, 2:173.

92. R. B. Bernstein, *The Education of John Adams* (New York: Oxford University Press, 2020), 78.

93. *DJA*, 2:176.

94. Ibid., 2:182; *LDC*, 2:50.

95. MND, "1775." Logan, LCP.

96. Force, 3:873, 864; *Votes* (1775), 658–9.

97. Ibid., 3:173–4.

98. Ibid., 3:985–6.

99. Ibid., 3:1819.

100. Ibid., 3:497, 872.

101. Ibid., 3:861–2.

102. Ibid., 3:862–3.

103. Ibid., 3:861.

104. *PJ*, September 13, 1775; Ryerson, *Revolution*, 136.

105. *Votes* (1777), 626, 628.

106. Richard Alan Ryerson, *John Adams's Republic: The One, the Few, and the Many* (Baltimore: Johns Hopkins University Press, 2016), 166.

107. *Votes* (1777), 660.

108. Ibid., 659.

109. Ibid., 635.

110. Ibid., 636.

111. Ibid., 638.

112. Ryerson, *Revolution*, 144.

113. *Votes* (1777), 633.

114. JD, draft instructions to the Pennsylvania delegates to Congress, [November 9, 1775]. Gratz, HSP.

115. JD, instructions to the Pennsylvania delegates to Congress, *PG*, November 15.

116. *PJ*, November 22, 1775; *PL*, November 25, 1775; *PJ*, December 6, 1775.

117. Force, 3:1874–5, 1871.

118. *PJ*, December 27, 1775.

Chapter 10

1. Craig Nelson, "Thomas Paine and the Making of *Common Sense*," *New England Review* 27, no. 3 (2006): 249.

2. Thomas Paine, *Common Sense*, in *Selected Writings of Thomas Paine*, ed. Ian Shapiro and Jane E. Calvert. Rethinking the Western Tradition Series (New Haven: Yale University Press, 2014), 24.

3. JD, "Arguments in Congress in Favor of Reconciliation," [May 16–25, 1775]. Gratz, HSP.

4. A Farmer, "No. III," *PG*, December 17, 1767.

5. JD, "2 Points Recommended & Enjoined by Our Constituents," [January 16, 1776]. Gratz, HSP.

6. JD, "To My Opponents," *FJ*, January 15, 1783.

7. Philadelphia Yearly Meeting, *Ancient Testimony and Principles of the People Called Quakers* (Philadelphia, January 20, 1776); Jane E. Calvert, "Thomas Paine, Quakerism, and the Limits of Religious Liberty during the American Revolution," in Shapiro and Calvert, 602–29.

8. Paine, "Appendix," in Shapiro and Calvert, 41–52.

9. Charles Lee to JD, January 1, 3, 18, February 9, 1776. JDP, LCP; *JCC*, 4:151.

10. JD, "To My Opponents," *FJ*, January 15, 1783.

11. *PP*, February 19, 1776.

12. DNL, "Some Memorandums," pp. 162–3.

13. JD, "Arguments in Congress in Favour of Treating, rather than inflaming the Contest."

14. *PG*, March 27, 1776.

15. Philemon Dickinson to JD, March 22, 1776. Originals, SMC, DPA.

16. Hermann Wellenreuther, "White Eyes and the Delawares' Vision of an Indian State," *Pennsylvania History: A Journal of Mid-Atlantic Studies* 68, no. 2 (2001): 139–61.

17. JD to John Pemberton, [April 10, 1776]. High Court of Errors, Gratz, HSP (misdated as 1774; see *JCC*, 4:268).

18. Ryerson, *John Adams*, 167–81.

19. *PJ*, June 5, 1776.

20. [Thomas Paine], "Forester Letter," *PJ*, May 8, 1776; Jane E. Calvert, "Thomas Paine," in Shapiro and Calvert, 612.

21. Thomas Paine, "The Crisis. No. III," April 19, 1777, in Shapiro and Calvert, 82.

22. *JCC*, 4:342.

23. John Adams to Benjamin Hichborn, May 29, 1776. *PJA*, 4:218.

24. Committee of Inspection and Observation, "In Committee Chamber . . ." (Philadelphia: W. and T. Bradford, May 16, 1776).

25. Thomas Rodney to Caesar Rodney, May 29, 1776. Rodney Correspondence, DHS.

26. For a detailed account of this moment, see Ryerson, *Revolution*, 211–16.

27. DNL, "Some Memorandums," p. 163.

28. *Votes* (1777), 741.

29. William Bradford, "A Memorandum Book and Register, for the Months of May & June 1776." Bradford Family Papers, HSP.

30. *PG*, June 26, 1776.

31. JD, "To My Opponents," *FJ*, January 15, 1783.

32. *JCC*, 5:433.

33. *DJA*, 3:338. In 1980, the editors of *PJA* identified the work on this treaty to be solely that of Adams (*PJA*, 4:260–65). Shortly before the publication of the present biography, however, the John Dickinson Writings Project discovered a manuscript that complicates this interpretation. As is typical of JD's papers, this document is heavily edited with partial thoughts and has no title or date, but it is clearly a draft of the Model Treaty. Adams's draft, by contrast, is clean, containing only minor edits. Although it seems probable that JD's is the earlier draft on which Adams based his, the final determination on that point must wait until the editors of the Adams and Dickinson papers conduct a forensic analysis similar to Julian Boyd's work on JD's and Jefferson's drafts of the Declaration on Taking Up Arms. For JD's draft, see RRL [4], HSP. For the Adams draft with analysis, see *PJA*, 4: 260–78. See also Boyd, "Disputed Authorship."

34. JD's draft of the Articles of Confederation, "Hints of a Confederation," and miscellaneous notes for the Articles are in RRL, HSP.

35. JD, "To My Opponents," *PG*, December 24, 1782; *Votes* (1777), 736; *JCC*, 5:433.

36. Abigail Adams to John Adams, March 31, 1776, *AFC*, 1:370.

37. John Adams to Abigail Adams, April 14, 1776, ibid., 1:382.

38. Jane E. Calvert, "The Friendly Jurisprudence and Early Feminism of John Dickinson," in *Great Christian Jurists in American History*, ed. Daniel L. Dreisbach and Mark David Hall (New York: Oxford University Press, 2019), 133–59.

39. *Votes* (1777), 739.

40. *PEP*, June 8, 1776.

41. Edward Rutledge to John Jay, June 29, 1776, *John Jay: Unpublished Papers*, ed. Richard B. Morris et al. (New York: Harper & Row, 1975), 2:280–1.

42. Robert L. Brunhouse, *The Counter-Revolution in Pennsylvania* (Harrisburg: Pennsylvania Historical and Museum Commission, 1971), 7, 13.

43. *JCC*, 5:503–6.

44. The following reconstruction has been taken from two imperfect sources: JD's notes in Gratz, HSP, and a version published by John H. Powell in 1941. When comparing the two versions, it is clear that the manuscript source is missing at least one page that is, however, present in the Powell version. Conversely, the Powell version omits portions of the manuscript, including some smaller scraps with notes probably written at the same time. In 1822, Hezekiah Niles published a speech alleged to be Dickinson's, but, because it bears no resemblance to his notes except in general being against independence, the editors of his papers do not consider it to be JD's work. See JD, "Arguments against the Independence of These Colonies," [July 1, 1776]. Gratz, HSP; J. H. Powell, "Notes and Documents," *PMHB* 65, no. 4 (1941): 458–81; Hezekiah

Niles, *Principles and Acts of the Revolution in America* (Baltimore: W. O. Stiles 1822), 493–5.

45. The Address, Petition, and Remonstrance of the City of London, to the King, in Favour of the Americans, and their Resolves, presented to his Majesty, July 5, 1775 (London, 1775).

46. "Arguments in Congress in Favour of Treating, rather than inflaming the Contest," [May 16–25, 1775].

47. Savile, *Character of a Trimmer*, 43.

48. Thomas McKean to A. J. Dallas, September 26, 1796, *LDC*, 1:533–4; *Washington Review*, August 19, 1826.

49. Calvert, *Quaker Constitutionalism*, 241–4.

50. JD, "To My Opponents," *FJ*, January 1, 1783.

51. Thomas McKean to Caesar A. Rodney, August 22, 1813, *Letters of the Members of the Continental Congress* (Washington, DC: Carnegie Institution of Washington, 1921), 1:534–5.

52. DNL, "Some Memorandums," p. 163.

53. John Adams to Abigail Adams, July 3, 1776, *AFC*, 2:30.

54. Thomas Jefferson, "To the Editor of the *Journal de Paris*," August 29, 1787, *PTJ*, Main Series, 12:64.

55. *JCC*, 5:516; "To My Opponents," *FJ*, January 15, 1783.

56. JD, "To My Opponents," *FJ*, January 15, 1783.

57. JD, "To My Opponents," *FJ*, January 8, 1783.

58. MND to JD, July 30, 1776. Logan, HSP; MND to JD, July 29, 1776. Logan, HSP.

59. JD to Charles Lee, July 25, 1776. DCA.

60. JD to Charles Thomson, August 7, 1776. N-YHS.

61. Paul L. Ford, "The Adoption of the Pennsylvania First Constitution of 1776," *Political Science Quarterly* 10, no. 3 (1895): 426–59 at 451.

62. JD, *Essay on a Frame of Government for Pennsylvania* (Philadelphia: J. Humphreys Jr., 1776).

63. John Adams to Abigail Adams, July 10, 1776, *AFC*, 2:42.

64. Charles Thomson to JD, August 16, 1776. Logan, HSP.

65. Savile, *Character of a Trimmer*, 1.

66. William Livingston to JD, August 1, 1776. JDP, LCP.

67. *Minutes of the Proceedings of the Convention of the State of Pennsylvania* (Philadelphia: H. Miller, 1776), 27.

68. JD, donation of pay to families of Associators, [August 1776]. RRL, HSP.

69. *The Papers of William Livingston*, ed. Carl E. Prince et al., 5 vols. (Trenton: New Jersey Historical Commission, 1979), 1:55–6.

70. James Morris Jr., [August 1776]. JDP, LCP.

71. The following episode is drawn from JD to unknown, August 25, 1776. RRL, HSP.

72. JD, "To My Opponents," *FJ*, January 15, 1783.

73. *Minutes of the Proceedings of the Convention of the State of Pennsylvania* (Philadelphia: H. Miller, 1776), 37.

74. JD, "To My Opponents," *FJ*, January 15, 1783.

75. Ibid., *PG*, January 8, 1783.

76. JD's edits on the Declaration of Rights in *The Constitution of the Common-Wealth of Pennsylvania* (Philadelphia: J. Dunlap, 1776).

77. JD, notes for a publication on British–American relations, [1774]. RRL, HSP.

78. Samuel Chase to JD, September 29, 1776. RRL, HSP; Thomas Stone to JD, [September 1776]. RRL, HSP; Samuel Chase to JD, [October 12, 1776]. RRL, HSP; Samuel Chase to JD, October 19, 1776. RRL, HSP.

79. *PG*, October 23, 1776.

80. John Adams to Benjamin Rush, October 12, 1779, *LBR*, 1:240.

81. *PG*, November 13, 1776; *MCDS*, 26.

82. JD to the Delaware Assembly, November 14, 1776. Logan, HSP.

83. JD, proposal to amend the Pennsylvania Constitution, November 27, 1776. JDP, LCP.

84. JD to the Council of Safety, January 21, 1777. RRL, HSP.

85. JD, "To My Opponents," *FJ*, January 15, 1783.

86. *PG*, February 12, 1777.

87. "December 2, [1776]," *Extracts from the Diary of Christopher Marshall* (Albany: Joel Munsell, 1877), 105.

88. Benjamin Rush to JD, December 1, 1776. Logan, HSP.

89. JD, "To My Opponents," *FJ*, January 22, 1783. JD specified only that it was a cousin of Polly's; most of the Dickinsons' interactions were with James Pemberton.

90. *PP*, December 27, 1776; *PEP*, December 28, 1776.

91. JD to the Council of Safety, January 21, 1777. RRL, HSP.

92. JD, "To the Public," February 27, 1777. RRL, HSP.

93. JD, "To My Opponents," *FJ*, January 22, 1783.

94. MND to Sally Fisher, January 22, 1777. Logan, HSP.

95. Samuel Adams to James Warren, September 12, 1776, *Adams–Warren Letters*, 1:280.

96. JD, "To My Opponents," *FJ*, January 15, 1783; JD, "To the Public," February 27, 1777. RRL, HSP.

97. *PG*, March 19, 1777.

98. JD to the Council of Safety, January 21, 1777. RRL, HSP.

99. Ibid.

100. JD to George Read, January 20, 1777. RSR, DHS.

101. There are three drafts of what appear to be the same document, dated December 30, 1776, January 21, 1777, and February 27, 1777. Although a letter from Thomas Cadwalader indicates it may have been published, if it was, that version is likely no longer extant. These drafts do, however, form the basis for JD's defense against the same charges that appeared in the *FJ* in 1783 after his election to the Pennsylvania presidency.

102. JD, "To the Public," February 27, 1777, p. 8. RRL, HSP.

103. Ibid., p. 10.

104. Ibid., p. 12.

105. Ibid., p. 11.

106. From George Washington to the Pennsylvania Council of Safety, December 19, 1776, *PGW*, Revolutionary War Series, 7:380–1.

107. JD to the Council of Safety, January 21, 1777. RRL, HSP.

108. JD, "To the Public," February 27, 1777, p. 7. RRL, HSP.

109. Ibid., p. 13. RRL, HSP.

110. Ibid., p. 14. RRL, HSP.

111. Ibid., p. 11. RRL, HSP.

112. JD to the Council of Safety, January 21, 1777. RRL, HSP.

113. Thomas Cadwalader to JD, [1777]. Logan, HSP.

114. Phocion [JD], *PJ*, March 12, 1777; *PP*, March 25, 1777.

115. Alexander Douglas's affidavit of use of Continental currency, March 6, 1777. MDL, HSP; Francis Gurney's affidavit of use of Continental currency, March 7, 1777. MDL, HSP; *PJ*, March 12, 1777.

116. JD to Israel Pemberton, April 27, 1777. Gratz, HSP.

117. JD to Benjamin Rush, June 14, 1777. DCA.

118. Warner Mifflin to JD, August 11, 1786. RRL, HSP. Portions of the discussions of JD, slavery, and abolition are adapted from Jane E. Calvert, "An Expansive Conception of Rights: The Abolitionism of John Dickinson," in *When in the Course of Human Events: 1776 at Home, Abroad, and in American Memory*, ed. William R. Jordan (Macon, GA: Mercer University Press, 2018), 21–54.

119. JD, draft petition to the king, February 12, 1771. JDP, LCP.

120. JD, *Constitutional Power*, 51–2.

121. JD, "Notes on a Libel," *WJD*, 2:74.

122. JD, "To Be Lett," *PG*, January 5, 1764.

123. Rebecca J. Siders and Pamela C. Edwards, *The Changing Landscape of the St. Jones Neck under the Influence of the Dickinson Family, 1680–1850: An Exhibit Script* (University of Delaware: Center for Historic Architecture and Public Policy, 1994), 16.

124. James Bringhurst to Elizabeth Coggeshall, October 8, 1799. JBL, FHL. Emphasis added. On Quaker abolitionism, see Gary B. Nash and Jean Soderlund, *Freedom by Degrees: Emancipation in Pennsylvania and Its Aftermath* (New York: Oxford University Press, 1991); Brycchan Carey, *From Peace to Freedom: Quaker Rhetoric and the Birth of American Anti-slavery, 1657–1761* (New Haven: Yale University Press, 2012).

125. Alfred W. Blumrosen and Ruth G. Blumrosen, *Slave Nation: How Slavery United the Colonies and Sparked the Revolution* (Naperville, IL: Sourcebooks, 2005), 147–50.

126. JD, manumission deed, May 12, 1777. RRL, HSP.

127. JD, "To My Opponents," *FJ*, January 22, 1783.

128. Thomas McKean, JD's commission for brigadier general in the Delaware militia, September 26, 1777. RSR, DHS.

129. JD, "To My Opponents," *FJ*, January 22, 1783.

130. Calvert, "Thomas Paine," 618–20.

131. Thomas Gilpin, *Exiles in Virginia: With Observation on the Conduct of the Society of Friends during the Revolutionary War* (Philadelphia, 1848); and Norman E. Donoghue II, *Prisoners of Congress: Philadelphia's Quakers in Exile, 1777–1778* (University Park: Penn State University Press, 2023).

132. Thomas McKean to John Adams, September 19, 1777. TMP, HSP.

133. Robert F. Oaks, "Philadelphians in Exile: The Problem of Loyalty during the American Revolution," *PMHB* 96, no. 3 (1972): 298–325.

134. John Adams to Abigail Adams, September 8, 1777, *AFC*, 2:338.

135. JD to MND, October 30, 1777. Logan, HSP.

136. Blue notebook of SND. [n.d.]. Logan, HSP.

137. John Adams, *Twenty-Six Letters upon Interesting Subjects Respecting the Revolution of America* ([London], [1786?]), 32.

138. JD to the Council of Safety, January 21, 1777. RRL, HSP.

139. DNL, *Memoir*, 40–1.

140. White notebook of SND, [c. 1837]. Logan, HSP.

141. Grace Growden Galloway and Raymond C. Werner, "Diary of Grace Growden Galloway," *PMHB* 55, no. 1 (1931): 40–1.

Chapter 11

1. Susanna Wright to MND, February 17, 1778. SMC, DPA.

2. Benjamin Rush to JD, March 20, 1778. JDP, LCP.

3. See Calvert, "Thomas Paine," 620.

4. Samuel Adams to Peter Thacher, August 11, 1778, *LDC*, 10:421.

5. JD, "Arguments to Prove the Dependance of these Colonies—in Congress," [July 2, 1776]. Gratz, HSP.

6. JD, "Plan to Engage Great Britain to Acknowledge Our Independance," [c. June 1778]. It is unclear whether Dickinson actually met with the Commission.

7. *JCC*, 11:615.

8. JD, "Plan to Engage Great Britain."

9. Anthony Gregory, "'Formed for Empire': The Continental Congress Responds to the Carlisle Peace Commission," *Journal of the Early Republic* 38, no. 4 (2018): 643–72.

10. MND to JD, August 18, 1778. MDL, HSP; JD to MND, August 10, 1778. Originals, SMC, DPA.

11. Mary Parker Norris to JD, August 21, 1778. MDL, HSP.

12. Dickinson family Bible. Logan, HSP.

13. MND and JD to Mary Parker Norris, December 26, 1778. MDL, HSP.

14. JD's certificate of fidelity to the State of Delaware (Lancaster: F. Bailey, June 29, 1778). RRL, HSP.

15. *MCDS*, 261, 269, 270.

16. MND to Mary Parker Norris, March 23, 1779. JDP, LCP.

17. MND, June 11, [1779?]. Loudoun, HSP.

18. JD to MND, May 19, 1781. Logan, HSP.

19. Philemon Dickinson to JD, March 27, 1779. Loudoun, HSP.

20. John Jones to JD, March 12, 1779. JDP, LCP

21. Jack N. Rakove, *The Beginnings of National Politics: An Interpretive History of the Continental Congress* (Baltimore: Johns Hopkins University Press, 1979), 255–74.
22. *JCC*, 14:501, 548.
23. *Secret Journals of Congress* (Boston: T. B. Wait, 1821), 426.
24. JD to Thomas Rodney, July 22, 1779. Gratz, HSP.
25. JD, *To the Inhabitants of the United States of America* (Philadelphia: D. Claypoole, May 26, 1779).
26. JD to Thomas Rodney, July 22, 1779; JD, "Plan for Putting a Stop to Emissions of Bills of Credit," July 23, 1779. RRL, HSP.
27. Caesar Rodney to JD, April 29, 1779. JDP, LCP.
28. *JCC*, 14:661–2.
29. JD, "Questions Proposed by the Committee to Col. Coxe Regarding the Quarter Master General," June 12, 1779. RRL, HSP; JD, notes on wagons for the Continental Army, June 11, 1779. RRL, HSP; JD, "Quarter Master General: 3 Divisions of the Continent," [c. June 1779]. RRL, HSP; JD, notes in Congress on the quarter master general, [c. June 1779]. RRL, HSP; JD, draft resolves in Congress for supply commissioners, [May 28–June 14, 1779]. JDP, LCP.
30. *JCC*, 14:812.
31. John Jay to George Washington, April 26, 1779, *PGW*, Revolutionary War Series, 20:224–5.
32. *JCC*, 14:708.
33. JD, "Plan for a Commission of Marine," [June 1779]. RRL, HSP.
34. JD to Arthur Lee, March 30, 1780. J. Pierpont Morgan Collection, NYPL; Arthur Lee to JD, September 19, 1779. Logan, HSP.
35. Arthur Lee to JD, September 19, 1779. Logan, HSP.
36. William Lee to Arthur Lee, September 28, 1779, *Letters of William Lee*, ed. W. C. Ford (Brooklyn, NY, 1891), 3:753.
37. *JCC*, 14:744.
38. *Secret Journals*, 123–4.
39. JD to Caesar Rodney, May 10, 1779. Thomas Rodney Papers, LOC.
40. JD to John Jay, July 22, 1779. RRL, HSP.
41. *DJA*, 4:247.
42. *JCC*, 14:1003; JD, resolutions on Paulus Hook, [September 4, 1779]. RRL, HSP.
43. *JCC*, 14:805; "Corbin, Margaret Cochran," in *Notable American Women, 1607–1950: A Biographical Dictionary*, ed. Edward T. James et al., 3 vols. (Cambridge: Belknap Press of Harvard University Press), 1:385–6.
44. [MND], account of Elizabeth Norris's death. Logan, LCP.
45. Dickinson family Bible. Logan, HSP.
46. MND to JD, September 24, 1781. MDL, HSP.
47. EGF to JD, September 10, 1779. JDP, LCP.
48. JD to EGF, September 18, 1779. Rosenbach Library.
49. *PG*, January 11, 1780; JD to the Delaware Assembly, April 12, 1780. Logan, HSP.
50. *JCC*, 15:1287
51. *ANBO*.

52. JD to MND, September 30, 1780. Logan, HSP.

53. JD to John Parrish, April 25, 1780. Parrish Family Papers, FHL.

54. JD to SND, October 12, 1780. Rockwood, UDSC.

55. *PG*, December 13, 1780.

56. George Read to JD, December 2, 1780. JDP, LCP.

57. Thomas McKean to JD, December 25, 1780. RRL, HSP.

58. Charles Thomson to JD, December 25, 1780. JDP, LCP.

59. Ibid.

60. Charles Ridgely to JD, April 4, 1781. RRL, HSP.

61. *PJ*, August 15, 1781.

62. William Molleston to JD, August 11, 1781. JDP, LCP; *PJ*, August 15, 1781; *PP*, August 16, 1781; *New-Jersey Gazette*, August 29, 1781; Eleazar McComb to JD, August 11, 1781. RRL, HSP.

63. JD, manumission deed, September 27–29, 1781. Logan, HSP.

64. See indenture forms in Logan, HSP.

65. MCD to JD, September 24, 1781. MDL, HSP.

66. *PP*, October 9, 1781; JD's affirmation of office, October 25, 1781, *MCDS*, 654.

67. Peter Z. Lloyd to JD, October 22, 1781. RRL, HSP.

68. *Acts of the General Assembly of the Delaware State* (Wilmington, DE: J. Adams, 1782), 3–22.

69. JD to MND, November 7, 1781. Logan, HSP.

70. *MCDS*, 679.

71. J. H. Powell, "John Dickinson, President of the Delaware State, 1781–1782," *Delaware History* 1, no. 1 (1946): 8–9.

72. JD, acceptance speech for the presidency of Delaware, [n.p.], November 13, 1781. Gilbert, LOC.

73. See, for example, from the Delaware Regiment with answer, *PP*, December 8, 1781; from the Corporation of Wilmington with answer, *PJ*, December 29, 1781; from St. George's congregation, New Castle County with answer, *PG*, May 22, 1782.

74. JD, *A Proclamation* (Wilmington, DE: J. Adams, November 19, 1781).

75. JD to James Booth, August 1, 1782. RRL, HSP.

76. *PJ*, January 6, 1782.

77. "Diary of the Transactions of the Government, State of Delaware," November 15, 1781–December 30, 1782, p. 2. Gilbert, LOC.

78. JD to Samuel Miller, January 19, 1782. SMP, PUL.

79. *MCDS*, 679; "Diary," p. 1.

80. JD, *A Proclamation* (Wilmington, DE: J. Adams, November 20, 1781).

81. George Washington to JD, December 3, 1781. Gratz, HSP.

82. JD to George Washington, December 4, 1781. GW Papers, LOC.

83. Receipt from Edward Wright for wood and straw for Wilmington Hospital, December 13, 1781. Gratz, HSP.

84. White notebook of SND, [c. 1837].

85. JD to MND, January 12, 1782. Originals, SMC, DPA.

86. An Act for the Protection of the Trade of this State on the River and Bay of Delaware, February 5, 1782. RRL, HSP.

87. JD, draft of "Instructions to Chas. Pope Esqr. Commander of the State-Schooner Vigilant," November 19, 1781. Gilbert, LOC.

88. JD, *An Act for Establishing a Militia within this State* (n.p., February 5, 1782), 1.

89. JD to the brigadier generals of each county, February 5, 1782. RRL, HSP.

90. Charles H. Fithian, "'A System, concise, easy and efficient': John Dickinson's Version of von Steuben's Regulations for the Delaware Militia, 1782" (unpublished manuscript, 2022), 46–7.

91. JD, *An Act for Establishing a Militia*, 7.

92. [JD], *For the Use of the Militia of the Delaware State, An Abstract of the Regulations for the Order and Discipline of the Troops of the United States* (Philadelphia: C. Cist, 1782).

93. JD to the members of the Legislative Council and of the House of Assembly in each county, February 5, 1782. RRL, HSP.

94. JD to the brigadier generals of each county, February 5, 1782. RRL, HSP.

95. Samuel Patterson to JD, October 28, 1782. Gratz, HSP.

96. William Killen to the Delaware Assembly, [n.d.]. JDP, LCP.

97. David Finney to JD, January 15, 1782. JDP, LCP.

98. An Act for Increasing the Powers of the Justices of the Supreme Court, February 5, 1782, *LSD*, 2:769.

99. JD, draft "Act to Exclude the Members of the General Assembly from Places of Profit," February 1, 1802. Legislative Series, DPA.

100. John Hanson to JD, November 15, 1781. JDP, LCP.

101. From Robert Morris, November 17, 1781. JDP, LCP.

102. JD, "Message from the President of the State of Delaware to the General Assembly," *PP*, November 7, 1782.

103. JD, draft message to the Assembly, June 17, 1782. RRL, HSP.

104. *MCDS*, 715–16.

105. *PJ*, April 6, 1782.

106. Charles Ridgely to JD, April 1, 1782. RRL, HSP.

107. *MCDS*, 725.

108. JD to George Read, May 24, 1782. Correspondence, DHS; JD to James Booth, May 31, 1782. Gilbert, LOC.

109. JD to George Washington, May 30, 1782. GW Papers, LOC.

110. William M. Fowler, *American Crisis: George Washington and the Dangerous Two Years after Yorktown, 1781–1783* (New York: Walker & Company, 2011), 64–5.

111. *PP*, July 4, 1782.

112. JD, "An Account of the Rejoicings on the Birth of The Dauphin," June 22, 1782. JDP, LCP.

113. JD to Chevalier de la Luzerne, June 29–July 2, 1782. RRL, HSP; Chevalier de la Luzerne to JD, July 1, 1872. RRL, HSP.

114. *IG*, July 20, 1782.

115. *Poulson's*, May 6, 1826.

116. JD to John Stanwick, June 6, 1782. Logan, HSP; JD to Samuel Patterson, June 19, 1782. JDP, LCP. JD requested that Delaware finish repaying the loan to Morris in 1789. See JD to George Read, May 7, 1789. Gilbert, LOC.

117. JD to public officials of Delaware on safety of public records, August 15, 1782. Gilbert, LOC; *PEP*, July 4, 1778; JD to Nathanael Greene, July 5, 1782. RRL, HSP.

118. William H. Williams, *Slavery and Freedom in Delaware, 1693–1865* (Wilmington, DE: Scholarly Resources, 1996), 171–2.

119. JD, "Message from the President," *PP*, November 7, 1782.

120. See Hugh Durborow to JD, July 19, 1782. Logan, HSP; indenture for the purchase of Abigail (wife of Nathan), Joshua (8), Nancy (6), Curtis (4), Reuben (2), and Sally (7 mos.), January 14, 1783. Logan, HSP.

121. JD, *A Proclamation* (Wilmington, DE: J. Adams, October 31, 1782).

122. *PP*, October 12, 1782.

123. JD to John Coke, November 4, 1782. Legislative Papers, DPA.

124. *Martin's Bench and Bar*, 64.

125. JD, farewell address, January 11, 1783. Gilbert, LOC.

126. "Diary," p. 17.

127. JD, farewell address, January 11, 1783. Gilbert, LOC.

128. JD to Samuel Miller, January 19, 1782. SMP, PUL.

129. JD "To My Opponents," *FJ*, January 15, 1783.

130. *PG*, November 27, 1782.

Chapter 12

1. An Enemy to Injustice [JD], "To a Friend to Justice," *PJ*, February 19, 1793.

2. *PJ*, November 6, 1782; *IG*, November 9.

3. "Address to His Excellency by the Officers of the Troops of Pennsylvania in the Continental Army and Answer," *PG*, December 18, 1782.

4. JD, acceptance speech to the Pennsylvania General Assembly, *PG*, November 12, 1783; JD, draft acceptance speech to the Pennsylvania General Assembly, [n.d.]. RRL, HSP.

5. Benjamin Rush to John Armstrong Jr., March 19, 1783, *PBR*, 1:296, 300; John Witherspoon to JD, September 26, 1782. JDP, LCP; Thomas Willing to JD, November 25, 1782. RRL, HSP.

6. John Jay to JD, March 11, 1783. Logan, HSP.

7. John Jay to John Vaughan, February 15, 1783, *The Selected Papers of John Jay*, ed. E. M. Nuxoll et al. (Charlottesville: University of Virginia Press, 2010–), 3:317.

8. *FJ*, October 2, 1782.

9. "Aug. 31st, 1814," Diary of DNL, 1808–1814, [unnumbered page].

10. *FJ*, January 15, 1783.

11. JD, "Letters to Printers," October 2, 1782. Logan, HSP; *PP*, November 7, 1782.

12. *IG*, February 18, 1783.

13. *PG*, December 18, 1782; *PP*, January 9, 1783; *PG*, February 12, 1783; *PG*, May 21, 1783; *FJ*, April 30, 1783.

14. *PG*, February 5, 1783.

15. Ibid.

16. JD, receipt for loan to the State of Pennsylvania, January 4, 1783. JDP, LCP.

17. JD, *A Proclamation* (Philadelphia: F. Bailey, January 6, 1783).

18. JD, "A Message from the President and Supreme Executive Council to the General Assembly," February 28, 1783, *MSEC*, 13:518; JD, *A Proclamation* (Philadelphia: F. Bailey, March 26, 1783).

19. JD, "A Message from the President and Supreme Executive Council to the General Assembly," November 15, 1782, *MSEC*, 13:426; JD to delegates in Congress, April 4, 1783, *PA*, 10:25

20. JD to delegates in Congress, April 29, 1783, *PA*, 10:45.

21. *PA*, 10:46. Daniel K. Richter, *Trade, Land, Power: The Struggle for Eastern North America* (Philadelphia: University of Pennsylvania Press, 2013), 210.

22. "Correspondence of Rev. James Finley," *PA*, 10:40–4; JD, "Instructions to Rev. James Finley," February 6, 1783, *PA*, 10:163–5.

23. Ellis, *His Excellency, George Washington* (New York: Knopf, 2004), 141–4.

24. Edward Swain et al., petition to Governor Dickinson from the poor soldiers, March 11, 1783. RRL, HSP.

25. Samuel Smith et al., petition to His Excellency John Dickinson, [February 1783]. JDP, LCP.

26. JD, "A Message from the President to the General Assembly," *IG*, February 8, 1783; *Newport Mercury*, May 3, 1783.

27. JD, "A Message from The President and The Supreme Executive Council to The General Assembly," [1783]. JDP, LCP.

28. JD, "Rough Draft of Clauses for Act to relieve Officers and Soldiers," [1783]. JDP, LCP.

29. *PP*, September 25, 1783.

30. James Madison, notes on debates, June 21, 1783, *The Papers of James Madison*, ed. William T. Hutchinson et al., 17 vols. (Charlottesville: University of Virginia Press, 1962–), 7:177.

31. Alexander Hamilton to George Clinton, June 29, 1783, *PAH*, 3:408.

32. Kenneth R. Bowling, "New Light on the Philadelphia Mutiny of 1783: Federal-State Confrontation at the Close of the War for Independence," *PMHB* 101, no. 4 (1977): 438–9.

33. Ibid., 332–33, 342.

34. Ibid., 444; Benjamin Rush to John Adams, April 1812. Rush Family Papers, LCP; *MSEC*, 13:665.

35. Bowling, "Mutiny," 432, n. 27.

36. JD, "Message from the President—An Account of the Mutiny," *PG*, September 24, 1783.

37. Charles Thomson to Hannah Harrison Thomson, June 30, 1783, *LDC*, 20:385.

38. Benjamin Rush to John Montgomery, June 27, 1783, *PBR*, 1:302.

39. JD, "Message from the President and Supreme Executive Council to the General Assembly," October 31, 1783, *MSEC*, 13:733; JD, "Message from the President and Supreme Executive Council to the General Assembly," September 9, 1783, *MSEC*, 13:682.

40. *PG*, October 29, 1783.

41. Benjamin Rush to John Armstrong Jr., March 19, 1783, *PBR*, 1:296, 300; Maria Elena Korey, *The Books of Isaac Norris (1701–1766) at Dickinson College* (Carlisle: Dickinson College, 1976).

42. Dickinson family Bible.

43. JD, Pennsylvania presidential acceptance speech, *PG*, November 12, 1783.

44. JD to Assembly, December 2, 1783. RRL, HSP; *PP*, January 17, 1784; *FJ*, May 12, 1784.

45. *PP*, December 9, 1783.

46. *PP*, December 16, 1783.

47. *Newport Mercury*, January 31, 1784.

48. *Independent Journal* (NY), February 4, 1784.

49. *PP*, January 24, 1784

50. Philip Freneau, "Occasioned by Rejoicings in Philadelphia on the Acknowledgment of the National Independence," May 10, 1784, in *Poems Relating to the American Revolution* (New York: W. J. Widdleton, 1865), 271–4.

51. Megan Walsh, "The Politics of Vision: Charles Willson Peale in Print," *Early American Literature* 46, no. 1 (2011): 69–92.

52. JD to Thomas Mifflin, March 28, 1785. Emmet, NYPL.

53. JD to the president and directors of the Bank of Pennsylvania, February 9, 1784. JDP, LCP.

54. *PG*, April 6, 1785.

55. See Janet Wilson, "The Bank of North America and Pennsylvania Politics: 1781–1787," *PMHB* vol. 66, no. 1 (1942), 3–28.

56. JD, draft address to the trustees of Dickinson College, April 8, 1784. JDP, LCP.

57. Benjamin Rush with L. H. Butterfield, "Dr. Benjamin Rush's Journal of a Trip to Carlisle in 1784," *PMHB* 74, no. 4 (1950): 443–56 at 454.

58. "Proposals by Messieurs Donaldson & Hollingsworth for removing the Chevaux de Frize," April 20, 1784. RRL, HSP.

59. *IG*, April 10, 1784.

60. Aedanus Burke, *Considerations on the Society or Order of the Cincinnati* (Charleston, SC: A. Timothy, 1783); Minor Myers, *Liberty without Anarchy: A History of the Society of the Cincinnati* (Charlottesville: University Press of Virginia, 1983).

61. JD, Richard Henry Lee, and David Humphries, *A Circular Letter Addressed to the State Societies of the Cincinnati, by the General Meeting, Convened at Philadelphia, May 3, 1784. Together with the Institutions, as Altered and Amended* (Philadelphia: E. Oswald and D. Humphries, 1784).

62. *SCP*, esp. vols. 7 & 8; *Documents Relating to the Connecticut Settlement in the Wyoming Valley*, ed. William Henry Engle (Harrisburg: E. K. Myers, 1893), 629–30; JD, *A Proclamation* (Philadelphia: F. Bailey, January 6, 1783); *MSEC*, 14:116, 167–8, 222; John Armstrong Jr. to Sheriff of Northumberland Co., July 24, 1784, *PA*, 10:295; Terry Boulton, *Taming Democracy: "The People," the Founders, and the Troubled Ending of the American Revolution* (New York: Oxford University Press, 2009), 164; Thomas Hewitt, Robert Martin, and David Mead to JD and the Executive Council, August 6, 1784, Miner, *History of Wyoming*, 352–3; JD to Boyd and Armstrong, August 10, 1784, *PA*, 10:307; Robert Martin to James Potter and William Montgomery, August 14, 1784, Miner, *History of Wyoming*, 358; JD to John Armstrong, August 27, 1784,

PA, 10:317; JD to John Armstrong, August 30, 1784, *PA*, 10:319; *Minutes of the First Session of the Eighth General Assembly of the Commonwealth of Pennsylvania* (Philadelphia: D. Hall and W. Sellers, 1783), 319, 336; JD to the Vice President and the Supreme Executive Council, October 5, 1784, *MSEC*, 14:219–20; JD, *A Proclamation* (Philadelphia: F. Bailey, October 5, 1784); JD to John Buyers et al., October 6, 1784, *PA*, 10:347.

63. G. S. Rowe and Alexander W. Knott, "The Longchamps Affair (1784–86), the Law of Nations, and the Shaping of Early American Foreign Policy," *Diplomatic History* 10, no. 3 (1986): 218, 207.

64. JD to Thomas McKean, May 25, 1784. TMP, HSP.

65. JD to François Barbé-Marbois, October 30, 1784. Emmet, NYPL.

66. Rowe and Knott, "The Longchamps Affair," 219.

67. *FJ*, November 3, 1784.

68. Frederick B. Tolles, *George Logan of Philadelphia* (New York: Oxford University Press, 1953), 56.

69. Aaron Doan to JD, October 17, 1784. Stauffer Coll., HSP.

70. G. S. Rowe, "Outlawry in Pennsylvania, 1782–1788, and the Achievement of an Independent State Judiciary," *The American Journal of Legal History* 20, no. 3 (1976), 227–44.

71. JD draft to judges in *Respublica v. Doan*, November 22, 1784. Logan, HSP.

72. See G. S. Rowe, *Thomas McKean: The Shaping of an American Republicanism* (Boulder: Colorado Associate University Press, 1978), 181–2.

73. Rowe, "Outlawry," 240.

74. JD, "A Message from the President and Supreme Executive Council to the General Assembly," February 1, 1785, *MSEC*, 14:330.

75. Ibid., 338.

76. Ibid., 349.

77. Ibid., 350.

78. See Negley K. Teeters, *They Were in Prison: A History of the Pennsylvania Prison Society, 1787–1937* (Philadelphia: John C. Winston Co., 1937).

79. JD, "Heads of Regulations for Prisons," *MSEC*, 14:358.

80. JD to the Commissioners for the City and County of Philadelphia, February 14, 1785, *MSEC*, 14:352.

81. *MSEC*, 14:261–2.

82. JD, "A Message from the President and Supreme Executive Council to the General Assembly," February 24, 1785, *MSEC*, 14:366–7.

83. JD, "Indian Letters," [n.d.]. RRL, HSP.

84. JD to the Pennsylvania delegates to Congress, October 4, 1783. JDP, LCP.

85. JD to Samuel Atlee, William Maclay, and Francis Johnston, August 31, 1784, *PA*, 10:321.

86. William J. Campbell, *Negotiating at the Oneida Carry: Fort Stanwix National Monument Historic Resource Study* (Organization of American Historians / National Park Service, 2017), 99–120.

87. Samuel Adams to JD, April 14, 1785. JDP, LCP.

88. *PP*, May 4, 1785.

89. *IG*, July 9, 1785.

90. JD to Robert Edge Pine, July 6, 1785. RRL, HSP.

91. JD, "A Message from the President and Supreme Executive Council to the General Assembly," August 18, 1785, *MSEC*, 13:648.

92. *PG*, June 22, 1785.

93. Fred S. Rolater, "Charles Thomson, 'Prime Minister' of the United States," *PMHB* 101, no. 3 (1977): 322–48 at 338.

94. Charles Thomson to JD, July 19, 1785. JDP, LCP. A draft portion of this message appears in a letter from JD to Charles Thomson. In Bowling's article, "New Light on the Philadelphia Mutiny of 1783," this letter is misdated as June 12, 1783, and Bowling cites it in the context of the mutiny, which occurred that month (426). But that date was written much later at the top of the letter by a cataloguer. The actual date is July 12, 1785. The confusion comes from JD's having first written 1783 and then changing the 3 to a 5.

95. JD, "Message from the President and the Supreme Executive Council to the General Assembly," *PP*, August 27, 1785.

96. JD to the chief justice and judges of the Supreme Court, October 8, 1785. Pennsylvania Misc. Papers, NYPL.

97. Thomas Hartley to JD, April 16, 1785. JDP, LCP.

Chapter 13

1. JD to Benjamin Rush, August 10, 1803. DCA.

2. *Poulson's*, November 22, 1822. Kent Street is now Eighth Street. *Philadelphia Inquirer*, October 7, 1831. See also Claudia L. Bushman, *So Laudable an Undertaking: The Wilmington Library, 1788–1988* (Wilmington: Delaware Heritage Press, 1988), 29–30.

3. J. Thomas Scharf, *History of Delaware, 1609–1888*, 2 vols. (Philadelphia: L. J. Richards & Co., 1888), 2:651.

4. JD to Benjamin Rush, August 10, 1803. DCA.

5. SND to DNL, April 16, 1788. Logan, HSP; SND to DNL, January 31, 1790. Logan, HSP.

6. SND to DNL, April 9, 1790. Logan, HSP.

7. Ibid., April 16, 1788. Logan, HSP.

8. MND to Hannah Griffitts, October 19, 1785. JDP, LCP; Marbled notebook of SND, [c. 1821]. Logan, HSP.

9. Susanna Dillwyn Emlen to William Dillwyn, March 23, 1809. Dillwyn Papers, HSP.

10. MND to Hannah Griffitts, October 19, 1785.

11. Diary of DNL, 1808–1814, p. 89.

12. JD to James Pemberton, March 13, 1786. Etting, HSP.

13. Ibid., December 20, 1786. Logan, HSP.

14. JD to [James] Pemberton, July 21, 1792. Old Congress Coll., Gratz, HSP.

15. JD, notes for the Delaware abolition bill, [1786]. RRL, HSP.

16. Woolman, *Some Considerations on the Keeping of Negroes*.

17. JD, notes on the Pennsylvania Act for Abolishing Slavery, [n.d.]. RRL, HSP.

18. Ibid.

19. Gary B. Nash, *Warner Mifflin: Unflinching Quaker Abolitionist* (Philadelphia: University of Pennsylvania Press, 2017), 135; JD to [James] Pemberton, June 21, 1792.

20. James Pemberton to JD, March 10, 1786. JDP, LCP.

21. SND, "Extracts from several old Wills of my dear Father, and his wish for the establishment of a School in Kent," [n.d.]. JDP, LCP.

22. Warner Mifflin to JD, August 11, 1786. RRL, HSP.

23. James Bringhurst to Elizabeth Coggeshall, October 8, 1799. JBL, FHL.

24. JD to [John Lloyd], August 15, 1801. JDP, LCP.

25. SND, "Extracts from several old Wills." She noted that this codicil was later cancelled, presumably by an updated will, but she did not indicate if any provision replaced it.

26. JD, "Memorandum for My Wife & Executors," October 17, 1787. JDP, LCP.

27. See, for example, receipts to JD from Smith & Stevenson, October 8, 1790, and March-May 1791. RRL, HSP; receipt to JD from King Dougal, November 15, 1792. RRL, HSP; receipt to JD from Ephraim Stevenson, June-September 1793. RRL, HSP.

28. Nash, *Warner Mifflin*, 136.

29. Williams, *Slavery and Freedom*, 172.

30. JD to [James] Pemberton, June 21, 1792.

31. Nash, *Warner Mifflin*, 139.

32. JD to Benjamin Rush, February 14, 1791, quoted in Milton E. Flower, *John Dickinson, Conservative Revolutionary* (Charlottesville: University Press of Virginia, 1983), 266-7.

33. JD to James Pemberton, March 13, 1786. Etting, HSP.

34. JD to James Pemberton, December 20, 1786. Logan, HSP; Samuel Pleasants to JD, January 10, 1788. Mf, HSP.

35. *Draught of a Plan of Education for the Wilmington Academy* (Wilmington: J. Adams, 1786), [1], 7; E. Miriam Lewis, ed., "The Minutes of the Wilmington Academy, 1777–1802," *Delaware History* 3 (1949): 181–226. See also "Copy of a Plan of Education to be proposed to the Board of Trustees for the Wilmington Academy," May 1786. RRL, HSP.

36. JD to James Pemberton, March 13, 1786. Etting, HSP.

37. JD to Noah Webster, February 18, 1786. John Dickinson Misc. Papers, NYPL.

38. *Daily Advertiser* (New York), April 5, 1786.

39. George Churchman to JD, July 20, 1786. RRL, HSP.

40. JD to George Read, August 27, 1786. RSR, DHS.

41. JD, Report of the Annapolis Convention, September 14, 1786. Emmet, NYPL; *JCC*, 32:71.

42. JD to Charles Thomson, November 21, 1786. JDP, LCP; *Daily Advertiser* (New York), May 1, 1787.

43. Charles Thomson to JD, November 29, 1786. JDP, LCP.

44. R. S. Cotterill, "The South Carolina Land Decision," *The Mississippi Valley Historical Review* 12, no. 3 (1925): 380.

45. JD to James Pemberton, March 29, 1787. Etting, HSP.

46. Ibid.

47. See Negley K. Teeters, *They Were in Prison: A History of the Pennsylvania Prison Society, 1787-1937* (Philadelphia: John C. Winston Co., 1937), 126-9.

48. JD to James Pemberton, December 20, 1786. Logan, HSP; James Pemberton to JD, February 7, 1787. Pemberton Papers, HSP; JD to James Pemberton, March 29, 1787.

49. Michael Vinson, "The Society for Political Inquiries: The Limits of Republican Discourse in Philadelphia on the Eve of the Constitutional Convention," *PMHB* 113, no. 2 (1989): 185-205.

50. *PG*, August 22, 1787.

51. George Fox to JD, May 11, 1787. JDP, LCP.

52. Benjamin Rush to JD, April 5, 1787. Logan, HSP.

53. JD to Benjamin Rush, February 27, 1786. DCA.

54. James Duane to JD, May 4, 1787. Logan, HSP.

55. JD to the Delaware Assembly, January 19, 1787. Misc. Mss., LOC.

56. George Read to JD, January 4, 1787. RSR, DHS.

57. William Thomson Read, *The Life and Correspondence of George Read* (Philadelphia: J. B. Lippincott & Co., 1870), 440.

58. JD to George Read, January 6, 1787. RRL, HSP.

59. JD, *Fragments on the Confederation of the American States* (Philadelphia: T. Dobson, 1787), [first unnumbered page].

60. Jacob Broom to JD, May 13, 1787. JDP, LCP; George Read to JD, May 21, 1788, Read, *Life and Correspondence*, 443-4.

61. JD to Maria Dickinson, May 16, 1787. MDL, HSP.

62. JD to Maria Dickinson, [n.d.]. Loudoun, HSP.

63. *Supplement to Max Farrand's Records of the Federal Convention of 1787*, ed. James H. Hutson. New Haven: Yale University Press, 1987, [328].

64. Farrand, 4:92, 237.

65. JD to MND, May [29], 1787. Logan, HSP.

66. JD to unknown, [June 1787]. Logan, HSP.

67. JD, "Plan for a Federal Government," [May 30, 1787]. JDP, LCP. See also Hutson, *Supplement*, 84-8.

68. Farrand, 1:86.

69. Ibid., 1:87.

70. Ibid.

71. Forrest McDonald, *Novus Ordo Seclorum: The Intellectual Origins of the Constitution* (Lawrence: University of Kansas Press, 1985), 215.

72. Ibid., 1:153; JD, notes, [n.d.]. RRL, HSP.

73. Farrand, 1:196.

74. Ibid., 1:509.

75. Ibid., 4:242.

76. Hezekiah Niles, "A Speech in a Dream!" *Niles' Weekly Register* 8 (1818): 300-1; [DNL] quoted in "*Biography of the Lives of the Signers*," 416-17; William Pierce, "Character Sketches of Delegates to the Federal Convention," Farrand, 3:92.

77. Farrand, 1:304–11. Hutson, *Supplement*, [330].

78. Farrand, 1:327.

79. Farrand, 1:588.

80. JD to Samuel Dickinson, August 15, 1754, *WJD*, 1:61.

81. JD, "Acting before the World" [1787]. JDP, LCP. See also Hutson, *Supplement*, 158–9.

82. Farrand, 1:597. Because the voting on the three-fifths provision took place from July 11 through July 14 and was bound up with related issues such as western expansion, it is difficult to follow. For a clear timeline, see Staughton Lynd, "The Compromise of 1787," *Political Science Quarterly* 81, no. 2 (1966): 225–50 at 238.

83. Farrand, 2:15–16.

84. Fabius, "No. VIII," *PM*, April 29, 1788. Quotation marks added on "compromise" for emphasis.

85. *Life, Journals and Correspondence of Rev. Manasseh Cutler* (Cincinnati: Robert Clarke & Co., 1888), 1:268–9.

86. Farrand, 2:318; 1:167–8; 2:299; 2:298; 2:465.

87. JD, "Acting before the World" [1787].

88. Farrand, 2:372–3, 416.

89. Ibid., 2:357.

90. Ibid., 2:396.

91. Ibid. 2:415.

92. Ibid., 2:416.

93. JD, "Acting before the World" [1787].

94. A Countryman [Hugh Hughes], "Letters from a Gentleman in Dutchess County to His Friend in New York. No. I," *New-York Journal*, November 21, 1787.

95. Ibid., "No. II," *New-York Journal*, November 23, 1787.

96. JD to [John Lloyd], August 15, 1801. JDP, LCP.

97. "An Anecdote," *Federal Gazette and Pennsylvania Evening Post*, January 7, 1789.

98. Farrand, 2:123, 1:360, 2:292–3, 2:316, 2:448, 2:278.

99. For US Const. Art. 1 sect. 8, cl. 10; *Respublica v. De Longchamps* (1784), see *WJD*, 1:lvi; Richard Tuck, *The Rights of War and Peace: Political Thought and the International Order from Grotius to Kant* (Oxford: Oxford University Press, 1999).

100. James Russell Lowell, "The Place of the Independent in Politics," in *Political Essays* (Boston: Houghton Mifflin, and Co., 1888), 295–326.

101. Fabius, "No. III," *PM*, April 17, 1788.

102. Ibid., "No. IV," *PM*, April 19, 1788.

103. Farrand, 2:114–15.

104. Ibid., 1:87; 2:69

105. Fabius, "No. II," *PM*, April 15, 1788.

106. JD, note on the Constitution, [n.d.]. RRL, HSP.

107. Fabius, "No. VIII," *PM*, April 29, 1788.

108. Ibid., "No. IV," *PM*, April 19, 1788.

109. Ibid., "No. VIII," *PM*, April 29, 1788.

110. Ibid..

111. Fabius, "Nos. V, VIII, and I," *PM*, April 22, 29, and 12, 1788.

112. JD, "Amendments of The Constitution," [n.d.]. RRL, HSP.
113. Farrand, 2:278.
114. Ibid., 2:335, 342, 461, 468.
115. Fabius, "No. V," *PM*, April 22, 1788.
116. MND et al., Poems [1764–1768].
117. JD to MND, August 30, 1787. Logan, HSP.
118. JD, *A Fragment* (Philadelphia: T. Dobson, 1796), 11.
119. See Farrand, 2:628; Calvert, "Expansive Rights," 43.
120. JD, *Constitutional Power*, 51.
121. JD to [John Lloyd], August 15, 1801. JDP, LCP.
122. Erica Armstrong Dunbar, *Never Caught: The Washingtons' Relentless Pursuit of Their Runaway Slave, Ona Judge* (New York: Simon & Schuster, 2017).
123. *Dred Scott, Plaintiff in Error, v. John F. A. Sandford*, 60 U.S. 393 (1856).
124. James Wilson, "Speech to the Pennsylvania Convention," December 4, 1787, *Friends of the Constitution: Writings of the "Other" Federalists, 1787-1788*, ed. Colleen A. Sheehan and Gary L. McDowell (Indianapolis: Liberty Fund, 1998), 211.
125. JD to Eleazar McCombe, November 29, 1787. Logan, HSP; Eleazar McCombe to JD, December 5, 1781. Logan, HSP.
126. JD to Tench Coxe, May 4, 1797. Coxe, HSP.
127. Fabius [JD], "Observations on the Constitution Proposed by the Federal Convention," *PM*, April 12, 15, 17, 19, 22, 24, 26, 29, May 1, 1788. For a detailed account of the origin of the 1788 "Fabius Letters," see *DHRC*, 17:74–80.
128. Fabius, "No. I," *PM*, April 12, 1788.
129. Ibid..
130. Ibid., "No. VI," *PM*, April 24, 1788.
131. JD, scrap with addition to the *The Letters of Fabius in 1788* (Wilmington: W. C. Smyth, 1797), 18. The scrap is in RRL, HSP; the book is in LCP.
132. Fabius, "No. VIII," *PM*, April 29, 1788.
133. Ibid., "No. II," *PM*, April 15, 1788.
134. Ibid., "No. VII," *PM*, April 26, 1788.
135. Ibid.
136. Ibid., "No. VIII," *PM*, April 29, 1788.
137. M. J. D. Roberts, "The Society for the Suppression of Vice and Its Early Critics, 1802–1812," *The Historical Journal* 26, no. 1 (1983): 160; Fabius, "No. III," *PM*, April 17, 1788.
138. JD, "The Centinel. No. VIII," *PJ*, May 12, 1768; JD, miscellaneous notes, [n.d.]. Logan, HSP.
139. JD, notes in the Federal Convention, [1787]. JDP, LCP; see also Hutson, *Supplement*, 138; JD to SND and Maria Dickinson, March 28, 1804. Originals, SMC, DPA.
140. Fabius, "No. III," *PM*, April 17, 1788.
141. JD, *Barbados Address*, *WJD*, 3:482.
142. Fabius, "No. IV," *PM*, April 19, 1788.
143. John Vaughan to JD, April 17, 1788. JDP, LCP.
144. *DHRC*, 17:180.

145. *DHRC*, 17:79.

146. George Washington to John Vaughan, April 27, 1788. *PGW*, Confederation Series, 6:241–2.

147. Caesar A. Rodney, inscription to Thomas Erskine in *The Letters of Fabius, in 1788, On the Federal Constitution; and On the Present Situation of Public Affairs* (Wilmington: W. C. Smyth, 1797). LCP copy.

148. John Vaughan to JD, June 11, 1788. JDP, LCP.

149. Matthew Carey to JD, January 5, 1789. JDP, LCP; JD to Matthew Carey, January 6, 1789. Emmet, NYPL.

150. Philip Freneau, "Epistle to the Patriotic Farmer," 1788, *The Miscellaneous Works of Mr. Philip Freneau* (Philadelphia: F. Bailey, 1795), 324.

151. JD, "Ten Quæries on Moving the Capital to the Potomack," [1790]. JDP, LCP.

Chapter 14

1. JD to Tench Coxe, July 14, 1788. DCA.

2. *Constitution, By-Laws, and Catalogue of the Wilmington Library* (Wilmington: R. Porter, 1815).

3. James Bringhurst to Elizabeth Coggeshall, October 8, 1799.

4. Anne Emlen to JD, December 21, 1787. Society Coll., HSP.

5. Nathaniel Luff Jr., April 23, 1799. JDP, LCP.

6. JD to Samuel Miller, August 10, 1807. RRL, HSP.

7. Samuel Troth to John Dickinson, December 17, 1798. Logan, HSP.

8. JD, religious notes, [n.d.]. RRL, HSP; Calvert, *Quaker Constitutionalism*, 284.

9. JD to Samuel Pleasants, January 22, 1788. Logan, HSP and OBP, EDA. In September 1787, George Dillwyn, who was then in England, informed George Churchman that John Pemberton had mentioned Churchman's wish to "have a particular account of the institution and regulations of Ackworth school." Dillwyn had already "taken some pains . . . to obtain it." See *Friends' Miscellany*, ed. John Comly and Isaac Comly (Philadelphia, 1839), 12:95–6.

10. DNL, *Memoir*, 24.

11. Anne Emlen to JD, December 21, 1787. Society Coll., HSP.

12. JD to Samuel Pleasants, January 22, 1788. Logan, HSP and OBP, EDA.

13. Heb. 11:1.

14. 2 Tim. 1:10.

15. JD to Samuel Pleasants, January 22, 1788. Logan, HSP and OBP, EDA.

16. Ibid.; JD to Samuel Pleasants (SND copy), January 22, 1788. Logan, HSP.

17. Owen Biddle to JD, July 4, 1789. Biddle Family Papers, HSP.

18. Samuel Pleasants to JD, March 16, 1788. Mf, HSP.

19. JD to Owen Biddle, July 20, 1789. OBP, EDA.

20. Minutes of the trustees of an estate granted by John and Mary Dickinson, August 20, 1790–January 31, 1791. OBP, EDA.

21. JD to Owen Biddle, August 2, 1790. OBP, EDA.

22. JD to Maria Dickinson, January 7, 1793. Loudoun, HSP.

23. JD, last will, October 17, 1787. JDP, LCP. "Cancelled" is written in JD's hand under the docketing.

24. JD to Benjamin Rush, October 21, 1790. DCA.

25. JD to James Pemberton, December 6, 1791. Duyckinck Family Papers, NYPL.

26. JD to George Read, December 15, 1791. RRL, HSP.

27. JD to James Pemberton and Owen Jones, December 27, 1791. RRL, HSP.

28. JD to Philemon Dickinson, August 15, 1791. Emmet, NYPL.

29. *ANBO.*

30. White notebook of SND, [c. 1837].

31. A. J. Dallas, *Reports of Cases Rules and Adjudged in the Several Courts of the United States and of Pennsylvania*, vol. 4 (Philadelphia: Fry and Kammerer, 1807); JD, resignation as judge on the Delaware Court of Appeals, October 10, 1791. Originals, SMC, DPA.

32. JD to MND, November 11, 1791. Loudoun, HSP.

33. *Votes and Proceedings of the House of Assembly of the Delaware State* (Wilmington: P. Brynberg and S. Andrews, 1791), 9.

34. Ibid., 10.

35. JD to the electors of New Castle County, September 19, 1791. RRL, HSP.

36. *Minutes of the Grand Committee of the Whole Convention of the Delaware State* (Wilmington: J. Adams, 1792).

37. *Minutes of the Convention of the Delaware State* in *Proceedings of the House of Assembly of the Delaware State 1781–1792 and of the Constitutional Convention of 1792*, ed. Claudia L. Bushman et al. (Newark: University of Delaware Press, 1988), 842.

38. Ibid., 844–6.

39. JD to [James] Pemberton, June 21, 1792.

40. Warner Mifflin to Henry Drinker, June 27, 1702, *Life and Ancestry of Warner Mifflin: Friend—Philanthropist—Patriot*, comp. by Hilda Justice (Philadelphia: Ferris & Leach, 1905), 104.

41. Warner Mifflin, "To the Citizens of the Delaware State, and More Particularly to the Members of the Convention Now Sitting at Dover," *Minutes of the Convention of the Delaware State, at the Second Session thereof . . .* (Wilmington: P. Brynberg and S. Andrews, 1792), 5–7.

42. JD, "Memorandums of public Business in Pennsylvania," [c. 1785]. JDP, LCP.

43. Julie Winch, "Free Men and 'Freemen': Black Voting Rights in Pennsylvania, 1790–1870," *Pennsylvania Legacies* 8, no. 2 (2008): 14–19.

44. JD, religious notes, [n.d.]. RRL, HSP.

45. Ibid., 37.

46. Warner Mifflin to Henry Drinker, June 27, 1702, *Life and Ancestry*, 104.

47. *Minutes of the Convention, Second Session*, 38. Given the gaps in the historical record, a certain amount of speculative reconstruction of events and motives is required. Here we should keep in mind the words of Senator William Plumer in a similar vote on the matter of slavery in 1805, which may shed light on Dickinson's. He agreed with the principle, but not with the motives or party of the person who made the

motion: "The journals are imperfect notes of our proceedings—they are true—but do not contain the whole truth. If my name should appear agt. this motion, its obvious import to readers would be that I was a supporter of *slavery*—This would be false, I will therefore never suffer my fame to be attacked by these records—I will always vote when by ayes & nays for or agt. a measure according as the question appears on the journal without any reference to the subject itself. I will never consent that, that brief loose & imperfect journal shall be used with the people against me" (William Plumer, *Memorandum of Proceedings in the United States Senate, 1803–1807*, ed. E. S. Brown [New York: MacMillan Co., 1923], 354).

48. *Minutes of the Convention, Second Session*, 39.

49. James Pemberton to JD, June 6, 1792. JDP, LCP.

50. Warner Mifflin to Henry Drinker, June 27, 1702, *Life and Ancestry*, 104.

51. JD to [James] Pemberton, June 21, 1792.

52. Ibid.

53. Mifflin to Drinker, June 27, 1792, *Life and Ancestry*, 104.

54. JD, "To the Electors of the State of Delaware," June 21, 1792. Logan, HSP; *Delaware Gazette*, July 7, 1792.

55. *Delaware Gazette*, September 15, 1792.

56. JD to Richard Bassett, December 31, 1792. Dreer Auto. Coll., HSP.

57. James Pemberton to JD, October 22, 1792. JDP, LCP.

58. Warner Mifflin to John Parrish, January 21, 1793. Cox Parrish Wharton Papers, HSP.

59. JD to Tench Coxe, April 11, 1806. Coxe, HSP.

60. Coxe quoted in Justin Ernest, *Tench Coxe and the Early Republic* (Chapel Hill: University of North Carolina Press for the Omohundro Institute of Early American History and Culture, 1978), 177.

61. JD's letter to Philemon is not extant. Philemon Dickinson to JD, February 16, 1793. JDP, LCP.

62. *Journal of the Senate of the State of Delaware* [January 1–February 2, 1793] (Wilmington: S. and J. Adams, 1793).

63. JD to the freemen of New Castle County, March 1793. JDP, LCP.

64. JD to George Read, March 19, 1793. RSR, DHS.

65. JD to MND, January 7, 1793. Loudoun, HSP.

66. JD to SND and Maria Dickinson, June 4, 1794. Originals, SMC, DPA.

67. *Journal of the Senate of the State of Delaware* [May 27–June 19, 1793] (Wilmington: S. and J. Adams, 1793), 16, 14, 40.

68. SND to DNL, April 4, 1791. Logan, HSP.

69. SND to DNL, October 6, 1793. Logan, HSP.

70. Ibid.; JD to Hannah Griffitts, November 16, 1793. MDL, HSP.

71. JD to Deborah Ferris Bringhurst, September 1793. Rockwood, UDSC; JD to George Read, September 18, 1793. RSR, DHS.

72. SND to DNL, October 6, 1793.

73. JD to George Read, June 19, 1793. RRI., HSP.

74. JD to George Logan, January 1, 1806. Logan, HSP.

75. Benjamin Rush to JD, October 11, 1797. *LBR*, 2:792–3.

76. JD, *The Letters of Fabius in 1797* (n.p., [1797]), 147; JD, note on Marie Antoinette, [n.d.]. RRL, HSP.

77. JD, *Fabius in 1797*, 143.

78. James Monroe to Thomas Jefferson, March 16, 1794, *PTJ*, Main Series, 28:42.

79. Ibid., March 31, 1794, *PTJ*, Main Series, 28:46.

80. *Connecticut Courant*, July 20, 1795.

81. *Gazette of the United States* (Philadelphia), August 11, 1795.

82. *The American Remembrancer; or an Impartial Collection of Essays, Resolves, Speeches, &c. Relative, or Having Affinity, to the Treaty with Great Britain* (Philadelphia: M. Carey, 1795), 29.

83. *Political Gazette* (Newberryport, MA), September 20, 1795.

84. JD et al., "To George Washington, President of the United States, The Memorial of the citizens of Wilington and its vicinity, in the State of Delaware," *Delaware Gazette*, August 8, 1795.

85. *City Gazette* (Charleston, SC), November 13, 1795.

86. Ibid.

87. "From George Washington to Boston Selectmen, July 28, 1795," *PGW*, Presidential Series, 18:441–3.

88. Francis Asbury and Thomas Coke to JD, November 17, 1796, and JD to Francis Asbury and Thomas Coke, January 12, 1797. Logan, HSP. See also *The Journal and Letters of Francis Asbury*, ed. E. T. Clark et al., 3 vols. (London: Epworth Press, 1958), 3:47–8, 154–5.

89. *PG*, August 29, 1792.

90. "A proposed alteration in the form of the Trust &c—so far as relates to the Meeting of Friends," [n.d.]. Logan, HSP.

91. Anne Mifflin to Dorothy, May 31, 1804. Small Ms. Coll., Chicago History Museum. See also JD, draft grant from John and Mary Dickinson to Philadelphia Yearly Meeting for Westtown School, June 10, 1795. Logan, HSP. This grant refers to a 1790 deed, which has not yet been located, but is mentioned in Watson DeWees and Sarah B. DeWees, *Centennial History of Westtown Boarding School, 1799–1899* (Philadelphia: Sherman & Co., 1899), 40–1, 23.

92. JD to Benjamin Rush, January 27, 1796. Logan, HSP.

93. JD, *Fabius in 1797*, 156.

94. JD to Benjamin Rush, [1796]. Dickinson–Rush Corresp., DHS.

95. JD to Benjamin Rush, December 29, 1796. DCA.

96. See Lily Santoro, "Promoting the Book of Nature: Philadelphia's Role in Popularizing Science for Christian Citizens in the Early Republic," *Pennsylvania History: A Journal of Mid-Atlantic Studies* 84, no. 1 (2017), 30–59.

97. JD, *A Fragment* (Philadelphia: T. Dobson, 1796), 6, 7.

98. Benjamin Rush to JD, February 16, 1796, *LBR*, 2:770–1.

99. JD to Benjamin Rush, October 21, 1790. DCA.

100. Ibid., November 6, 1797. DCA.

101. Benjamin Rush to JD, April 5, 1796, *LBR*, 2:773–4; JD to Benjamin Rush, April 25, 1796. Logan, HSP.

102. See Meyer Reinhold, "The Quest for 'Useful Knowledge' in Eighteenth-Century America," *Proceedings of the American Philosophical Society* 119, no. 2 (1975), 108–32. *Poulson's*, March 10, 1808.

103. "Letters Testamentary & Copy of John Dickinson's Will & Codicils, 1808," April 9, 1807. RRL, HSP.

104. Scharf, *History of Delaware*, 2:686; Carol E. Hoffecker, *Brandywine Village: The Story of a Milling Community* (Wilmington: Old Brandywine Village, 1974), 62.

105. Tolles, *George Logan*, 88–9.

106. See, for example, JD correspondence with Humphrey Marshall, November 1, 1796, July 31, 1797, and November 7, 1797. Humphry and Moses Marshall Papers, Clements Library, University of Michigan.

107. Tolles, *George Logan*, 106–8.

108. *PG*, July 16, 1788.

109. JD to Tench Coxe, June 8, 1807. Coxe, HSP.

110. *Lettres d'un Fermier de Pensylvanie, aux Habitans de L'Amèrique Septentrionale*, trans. and preface by Jacques Barbue du Bourg (Amsterdam: aux dèpens de la Compagnie, 1769).

111. JD, multiple drafts of "Fabius, No. 10," May 15, 1794, [n.d.]. RRL, HSP.

112. JD to Charles Thomson, October 13, 1797. Originals, SMC, DPA.

113. JD, "Ode on France," *New World* (Philadelphia), January 21, 1797.

114. JD to Benjamin Rush, April 15, 1797. DCA.

115. Ibid., April 27, 1797. Dickinson–Rush Corresp., DHS; JD to Thomas McKean, April 14, 1797. TMP, HSP.

116. Benjamin Rush to JD, May 2, 179[7], *LBR*, 2:786. Joseph Priestley to JD, November 30, 1797. Loudoun, HSP.

117. *Gazette of the United States*, April 22, 1797; Thomas McKean, draft "Preface" to the *Fabius Letters*, January 1798. TMP, HSP; *Boston Gazette*, May 29, 1797. See advertisement in *New-York Commercial Advertiser*, October 23, 1797.

118. JD to Benjamin Rush, September 30, 1797. DCA; Benjamin Rush to JD, October 11, 1797, *LBR*, 2:292–3.

119. Thomas McKean to JD, January 20, 1789. TMP, HSP; *Farmer's Museum, or Literary Gazette*, November 30, 1802.

120. DeWees and DeWees, *Westtown*, 48; J. Smith Futhey and Gilbert Cope, *History of Chester County, Pennsylvania* (Philadelphia: L. H. Everts, 1881), 303.

121. Anne Mifflin to Dorothy, May 31, 1804. Small Ms. Coll., Chicago History Museum.

122. JD to MND, November 25, 1797. Loudoun, HSP.

123. Tadeusz Kościuszko to JD, November 24, [1797]. Gratz, HSP.

124. Tadeusz Kościuszko to JD, [1798]. Gratz, HSP.

125. Robert Morris Bond to JD, March 7, 1791. Logan, HSP; Robert Morris to JD, January 15, 1798. Gratz, HSP.

126. JD to Robert Morris, January 18, 1798. JDP, LCP.

127. *ANBO*.

128. JD to Thomas McKean, May 3, 1798. TMP, HSP.

129. George Logan to fellow citizens, September 9, 1798. Logan, HSP. It is clear from Logan's letters to DNL that JD was well aware of Logan's plans and DNL was to turn to JD for any help she needed in his absence.

130. Hugh Barbour, *Quakers in Puritan England* (New Haven: Yale University Press, 1964), 127.

131. Thomas Jefferson, George Logan's credentials, June 4, 1798. Logan, HSP.

132. Tolles, *George Logan*, 153–73.

133. Ibid., 156–8.

134. Ibid., 179–80; *Gazette of the United States*, December 11, 1798.

135. Tolles, *George Logan*, 181.

136. JD, *A Caution; Or, Reflections on the Present Contest between France and Britain* (Philadelphia: B. F. Bache, 1798).

137. James Bringhurst to JD, January 1, 1803. JBL, FHL.

138. Ibid., July 9, 1799. JBL, FHL.

139. Ellis, *His Excellency*, 160–1.

140. James Bringhurst to Elizabeth Coggeshall, October 8, 1799.

141. JD to George Logan, March 8, 1802. JDP, LCP; JD to MND, November 13, 1799. Loudoun, HSP.

142. Nathaniel Luff, December 8, 1797. Logan, HSP. For SND's observations on her, see SND to DNL, January 1, 1791. Logan, HSP.

143. JD to Thomas Rodney, September 27, 1803. Gratz, HSP; Thomas Rodney diary, [December?], 27, 1799. Thomas Rodney Papers, LOC. For Rodney's dreams and sexual predation, see his diaries generally.

144. *ANBO.*

145. Mandamus granting degrees including an honorary doctorate of laws to General George Washington, July 1, 1783. General Administration Coll. pre-1820, University of Pennsylvania.

146. JD to George Logan, January 1, 1806. Logan, HSP.

147. JD to Philemon Dickinson, January 11, 1800. Loudoun, HSP.

Chapter 15

1. See, for example, the *Richmond* (VA) *Recorder*, September 1, 1800.

2. *Hampshire Berkshire Chronicle*, March 2, 1795.

3. *Kline's Carlisle* (PA) *Weekly Gazette*, June 25, 1800.

4. *Philadelphia Gazette*, June 4, 1800.

5. *Times* (VA), June 21, 1800.

6. *Claypoole's American Daily* (PA), June 24, 1800.

7. DNL, *Memoir*, 145.

8. *DJA*, 3:316.

9. JD to James Madison, April 7, 1801, *The Papers of James Madison*, Secretary of State Series, ed. Robert J. Brugger et al. 13 vols (Charlottesville: University Press of Virginia, 1986–), 1:72.

10. JD to Thomas Jefferson, February 21, 1801, *PTJ*, Main Series, 33:32.

11. Thomas Jefferson to JD, March 6, 801, *PTJ*, Main Series, 33:197.

12. Ibid., July 23, 1801, *PTJ*, Main Series, 34:617.

13. Thomas Jefferson to JD, June 21, 1801, *PTJ*, Main Series 34:401–2.

14. JD to Thomas Jefferson, June 27, 1801, *PTJ*, Main Series, 34:464–7.

15. JD to Caesar A. Rodney, November 9, 1803. Gratz, HSP.

16. Thomas Jefferson, "First Inaugural Address," *PTJ*, Main Series, 33:149.

17. JD to Thomas Jefferson, June 27, 1801, *PTJ*, Main Series, 34:464–7.

18. George Read Jr. to JD, April 8, 1802. RSR, DHS.

19. JD to Thomas Jefferson, June 27, 1801, *PTJ*, Main Series, 34:466.

20. *Mirror of the Times* (Wilmington, DE), March 18, 1801.

21. JD to Tench Coxe, October 18, 1806. Coxe, HSP.

22. JD to Alexander Hamilton, November 30, 1801, *PAH*, 25:438–9.

23. Alexander Hamilton to JD, March 29, 1802, *PAH*, 25:583.

24. JD to Tench Coxe, October 18, 1806. Coxe, HSP.

25. *Salem* (MA) *Gazette*, December 10, 1802.

26. Niles, "A Speech in a Dream!" 301.

27. John Vining to JD, January 15, 1802. JDP, LCP; JD to John Vining, January 18, 1802. Caesar Rodney Papers, NYPL; *Journal of the House of Representatives of the State of Delaware* (Dover: W. Black, 1802), 66.

28. Ibid., January 11, 1802. JDP, LCP.

29. Ibid., March 8, 1802. JDP, LCP.

30. Ibid., April 20, 1802. Mf, HSP.

31. JD to Thomas McKean, July 9, 1800. TMP, HSP.

32. Ibid., December 9, 1802. TMP, HSP.

33. Ibid., November 22, 1802. TMP, HSP.

34. JD to Tench Coxe, August 2, 1802. Coxe, HSP.

35. Ibid., June 23, 1806. Coxe, HSP.

36. JD, *An Address on the Past, Present, and Eventual Relations of the United States to France* (New York: T. and J. Swords, 1803), 9.

37. Ibid., 11.

38. Ibid., 13. See also two letters from "J.D." to unknown, not in JD's hand, on this pamphlet. RRL, HSP.

39. Ibid., 18–19.

40. T. and J. Swords to Samuel Miller, June 7, 1813. Logan, HSP; Samuel Miller to the executors of the late John Dickinson, Esqr., June 29, 1813. Logan, HSP.

41. *Morning Chronicle* (New York), February 12, 1803; *New-York Herald*, February 19, 1803; *Federal Republican* (Elizabethtown, NJ), February 22, 1803; *New-York Commercial Advertiser*, February 14, 1803.

42. JD to Albanus Charles Logan, March 3, 1804. Logan, HSP.

43. Samuel Miller to the executors of the late John Dickinson, Esq., June 29, 1813. Logan, HSP.

44. *Poulson's*, July 29, 1803.

45. JD to Tench Coxe, December 11, 1806. Coxe, HSP.

46. Benjamin Rush to JD, August 6, 1803. *LBR*, 2:874.

47. JD to Benjamin Rush, August 10, 1803. Logan, HSP.

48. Thomas McKean to JD, August 2, 1803. TMP, HSP.

49. JD to Thomas Jefferson, August 1, 1803. TJ Papers, LOC.

50. JD to Thomas McKean, August 8, 1803. TMP, HSP.

51. JD to MND, April 20, 1799. Loudoun, HSP.

52. *Constitution and Laws of the Philadelphia Society for the Establishment and Support of Charity Schools* (Philadelphia: 1860), 53–4.

53. The following paragraphs on women are adapted from Jane E. Calvert, "The Friendly Jurisprudence and Early Feminism of John Dickinson," in *Great Christian Jurists in American History*, ed. Daniel L. Dreisbach and Mark David Hall (New York: Oxford University Press, 2019), 133–59.

54. JD to William Y. Birch and Abraham Small, January 7, 1807. JDP, LCP. For a discussion of early Quaker writers on women and attributing their strength to God, see Amanda Herbert, "Companions in Preaching and Suffering: Itinerate Female Quakers in the Seventeenth- and Eighteenth-Century British Atlantic World," *Early American Studies* 9, no. 1 (2011), 73–113.

55. JD to William Y. Birch and Abraham Small, January 7, 1807.

56. "Letters Testamentary & Copy of John Dickinson's Will & Codicils, 1808." RRL, HSP.

57. JD to Benjamin Rush, April 27, 1797. Dickinson–Rush Corresp., DHS.

58. See Wilmington Monthly Meeting Membership List, 1807– 1812. FHL.

59. JD to [John Lloyd], August 15, 1801. JDP, LCP. Williamina Ridgely to Ann Moore Ridgely, December 20, 1802; July 8, 1803. *A Calendar of Ridgely Family Letters, 1742– 1899*, 3 vols. (Dover: Delaware Archives Commission, 1961), 1:238.

60. JD to Tench Coxe, May 22, 1804. Coxe, HSP; JD to SND and Maria Dickinson, November 15, 1803. Originals, SMC, DPA.

61. Claymont School deed, August 9, 1805. New Castle County, Recorder of Deeds, Deed Books, Book E, vol. 3, pp. 317–19, DPA; Scharf, *History of Delaware*, 2:834; JD to John Bellach, March 30, 1805. Originals, SMC, DPA; JD to John Bellach, April 11, 1805. Originals, SMC, DPA; JD to Thomas McKean, February 2, 1799. TMP, HSP; Francis Gallet to JD, January 25, [n.d.]. JDP, LCP; Thomas Mason to JD, August 13, 1804. Mf, HSP.

62. JD to Caesar A. Rodney, December 8, 1803. Mf, HSP.

63. Records of these suits are sparse, usually with only cryptic mentions in JD's correspondence. He was sued in the Circuit Court of the United States in c. 1805–1806 by Henry Stidham's lessee, for which, see George Read Jr. to JD, October 14, 1805 and case notes in Logan, HSP.

64. JD to George Read Jr., November 1, 1803. Literary and Historical Manuscripts, Morgan Library and Museum, New York.

65. "Letters of James Ashton Bayard, 1802–1805," *Bulletin of the New York Public Library* vol. 4 (1900): 229.

66. JD to Caesar A. Rodney, November 9, 1803. Logan, HSP

67. JD to SND and Maria Dickinson, November 15, 1803. Originals, SMC, DPA.

68. Ibid., November 22, 1803. Originals, SMC, DPA.

69. Ibid., November 15, 1803. Originals, SMC, DPA.

70. Ibid., November 22, 1803. Originals, SMC, DPA.

71. John Montgomery to JD, April 25, 1803. MDL, HSP; JD to John Montgomery, May 23, 1803. MDL, HSP. See also "An Act for the Relief of Dickinson College," *SALP*, 17:352–3.

72. JD to John Montgomery, May 23, 1803. MDL, HSP.

73. JD to the president and directors of the Insurance Company of North America, March 7, 1804. Mf, HSP.

74. JD to Charles Petit, April 30, 1804. Mf, HSP; Charles Petit to JD, May 2, 1804. Mf, HSP.

75. JD to SND and Maria Dickinson, April 4, 1804. Originals, SMC, DPA.

76. JD to Charles Petit, February 22, 1806. Mf, HSP; JD to Charles Pettit, July 30, 1806. Logan, HSP.

77. Tench Coxe to JD, May 9, 1806. RRL, HSP; *Philadelphia Gazette*, May 10, 1806.

78. JD to Thomas Jefferson, September 30, 1807. Letters of Application and Recommendation, TJ Papers, National Archives, Washington, DC.

79. JD to Tench Coxe, March 31, 1806. Coxe, HSP.

80. JD to Tench Coxe, December 20, 1806. Coxe, HSP.

Chapter 16

1. *The Debates and Proceedings in the Congress of the United States . . . Ninth Congress . . . December 2, 1805, to March 3, 1807* (Washington: Gales & Seaton, 1852), 238.

2. JD George Logan, January 30, 1804. Logan, HSP.

3. *PEP*, June 5, 1804.

4. JD to George Logan, December 13, 1804, DNL, *Memoir*, 148.

5. *A Compilation of the Messages and Papers of the Presidents, 1789–1902*, ed. J. D. Richardson, 11 vols. (n.p.: Bureau of National Literature and Art, 1894), 1:370.

6. JD to George Logan, January 23, 1805, DNL, *Memoir*, 150; JD to George Logan, February 7, 1805. Logan, HSP.

7. JD to George Logan, January 21, 1805. RRL, HSP.

8. "An Act for the Recovery of Debts and Demands Not Exceeding $100 before a Justice of the Peace, for the Election of Constables and for Other Purposes," *SALP*, 17:782–97.

9. JD to Tench Coxe, August [27], 1805. Coxe, HSP.

10. Ibid.

11. JD to Thomas McKean, October 28, 1805. RRL, HSP.

12. Thomas McKean to JD, November 28, 1805. RRL, HSP. See also G. S. Rowe, *Thomas McKean and the Shaping of American Republicanism* (Boulder: Colorado Associated University Press, 1978), 363.

13. JD to Tench Coxe, April 3, 1807. Coxe, HSP.

14. *Aurora General Advertiser*, May 9, 1805.

15. Mercy Otis Warren, *History of the Rise, Progress and Termination of the American Revolution*, 3 vols. (Boston: Manning and Loring, 1805), 1:307–8.
16. David Ramsay, *The History of the American Revolution*, 2 vols. (Philadelphia: Aitkin & Sons, 1789), 1:212; 2:[appendix no. 4].
17. *Essex* (MA) *Register*, October 14, 1807.
18. John Marshall, *The Life of Washington*, 5 vols. (Philadelphia: C. P. Wayne, 1804–[1807]), 2:180.
19. JD, reflections on Marshall's history in the hand of SND, [1804]. RRL, HSP
20. Marshall, *Life of Washington*, 4:627.
21. JD to George Logan, January 12, 1805. Logan, HSP.
22. Warren, *History*, 1:307–8.
23. Mercy Otis Warren to JD, September 18, 1805. RRL, HSP.
24. JD to Mercy Otis Warren, September 25, 1805, *Adams–Warren Letters*, 2:347.
25. JD to Mercy Otis Warren, December 22, 1806, *Adams–Warren Letters*, 2:350.
26. JD to George Logan, December 19, 1805, MDL, HSP.
27. *Journal of the Senate of the United States of America, 1789–1873* (Washington: Gales & Seaton, 1821), 13.
28. *Debates and Proceedings in the Congress*, 26–9.
29. Plumer, *Memorandum*, 390.
30. JD to George Logan, January 30, 1806, DNL, *Memoir*, 155.
31. JD to George Logan, [January 31–February 1, 1806], DNL, *Memoir*, 156.
32. Plumer, *Memorandum*, 387.
33. JD to George Logan, February 6, 1806, DNL, *Memoir*, 157.
34. Abraham Lincoln to Horace Greeley, August 22, 1862, *The Collected Works of Abraham Lincoln*, ed. R. P. Basler et al., 9 vols. (New Brunswick, NJ: Rutgers University Press, 1953), 5:388.
35. Fabius, "No. 1," *PM*, April 12, 1788.
36. Fabius, "No. VIII," *PM*, April 29, 1788.
37. JD to Tench Coxe, May 22, 1804. Coxe, HSP.
38. *Debates and Proceedings in the Congress*, 117–38.
39. JD to Richard Bassett, December 31, 1792. Dreer Auto. Coll., HSP.
40. JD to Mercy Otis Warren, December 22, 1806, *Adams–Warren Letters*, 2:348.
41. JD to Tench Coxe, October 21, 1805; JD to Tench Coxe, July 3, 1806; JD to Tench Coxe, October 7, 1806; JD to Tench Coxe, December 11, 1806. Coxe, HSP.
42. Diary of DNL, 1808–1814, p. 87.
43. JD to Tench Coxe, September 16, 1807. Coxe, HSP.
44. JD to Mercy Otis Warren, December 22, 1806. Adams–Warren Letters, MHS.
45. Diary of DNL, 1808–1814, p. 87.
46. *ANBO*.
47. Samuel Miller, *A Brief Retrospect of the Eighteenth Century* (New York: T. and J. Swords, 1803).
48. JD to Samuel Miller, August 10, 1807. SMP, PUL.
49. Samuel Miller to JD, July 16, 1807. JDP, LCP.
50. JD to Samuel Miller, August 10, 1807; JD to Tench Coxe, January 24, 1807. Coxe, HSP.
51. JD to Albanus Charles Logan, March 3, 1804. Logan, HSP.

52. JD to MND, November 13, 1799. Loudoun, HSP.

53. *Hive* (Lancaster, PA), September 21, 1803.

54. Richard Rush, on the envelope of a letter from JD, June 6, 1803. Rush Family Papers, PUL.

55. *National Intelligencer and Washington Advertiser*, July 11, 1804.

56. *True American* (Leesburg, VA), April 22, 1805.

57. *Trenton* (NJ) *Federalist*, April 29, 1805.

58. *Providence* (RI) *Phoenix*, June 15, 1805.

59. Camillus, "A Serious and Extensive View of the Gubernatorial Election," *New-England Palladium*, March 31, 1807.

60. Copy of JD to Caesar A. Rodney, July 22, 1807. John Dickinson Coll., N-YHS.

61. JD to Tench Coxe, July 7, 1807. Coxe, HSP.

62. "Meeting of the Democratic Republican Conferees, of the State of Delaware," [Dover: n.p.], August 4, 1807.

63. JD to Tench Coxe, October 17, 1807. Coxe, HSP.

64. *Commonwealth* (Pittsburgh, PA), September 23, 1807.

65. JD to Mercy Otis Warren, September 9, 1807. Adams–Warren Letters, MHS.

66. *Democratic Press* (Philadelphia), October 30, 1807.

67. *Aurora General Advertiser*, October 14, 1807.

68. Ibid., October 15, 1807.

69. *Essex Register*, November 2, 1807.

70. JD to Tench Coxe, October 17, 1807. Coxe, HSP.

71. JD to Caesar A. Rodney, November 16, 1807. DCA.

72. *Connecticut Herald*, January 25, 1808. See also *Poulson's*, January 15, 1808; *New-York Commercial Advertiser*, January 15, 1808; *New-York Evening Post*, January 15, 1808; *Trenton Federalist*, *Mercantile Advertiser* (New York), *L'Oracle and Daily Advertiser* (New York), January 18, 1808; *New-York Herald, New-York Spectator*, January 20, 1808; *Connecticut Journal*, January 21, 1808; *New-England Palladium* (Boston), January 22, 1808; *Newburyport* (MA) *Herald*, January 26, 1808; *Portland Gazette, and Maine Advertizer*, February 1, 1808.

73. *Public Advertiser* (New York), January 16, 1808.

74. Marbled notebook of SND, [c. 1821]; JD to Thomas McKean, October 10, 1805. TMP, HSP.

75. DNL to Charles Thomson, February 16, 1808. CTP, LOC.

76. Ibid. This description is repeated almost verbatim from DNL's diary, which said: "He died at a Period when the best Interests of his Country, and indeed of the civilized world, appeard to be in imminent Hazard from the Power of Buonaparte— in his last illness his mind was deeply engaged for the prosperity of the one and the safeguard of the other, and a most pathetic address to the divine Being on their behalf, fell from his dying lips, which deeply affected all who heard it" (Diary of DNL, 1808–1814, p. 90).

77. Marbled notebook of SND, [c. 1821].

78. Diary of DNL, 1808–1814, p. 88–9.

Epilogue

1. *Poulson's*, February 16, 1808; *New-York Commercial Advertiser, Public Advertiser*, February 17, 1808; *Republican Watch-Tower* (New York), February 19, 1808; *New-York Spectator, New-York Weekly Museum*, February 20, 1808; *National Intelligencer and Washington Advertiser, Trenton Federalist*, February 22, 1808; *New-Jersey Journal*, February 23, 1808; *Alexandria* (VA) *Daily Advertiser, National Intelligencer and Washington Advertiser*, February 24, 1808; *Enquirer* (VA), *Kline's Carlisle Weekly Gazette, New-England Palladium*, February 26, 1808; *Alexandria Daily Advertiser, Columbian Phenix* (Providence, RI), *Democrat* (Boston), *New-York Herald, Providence* (RI) *Gazette, Public Advertiser*, February 27, 1808; *Portland Gazette, and Maine Advertiser, Political Observatory* (Walpole, NH), *Public Advertiser*, February 29, 1808; *Sentinel of Freedom* (Newark, NJ), *New-York Gazette & General Advertiser, Republican Star or Eastern Shore General Advertiser* (Easton, MD), March 1, 1808; *Commonwealth* (Pittsburgh), March 2, 1808; *American Mercury* (Hartford, CT), *Independent Chronicle* (Boston), *Eastern Argus* (Maine), March 3, 1808; *Albany* (NY) *Register, City Gazette and Daily Advertiser* (Charleston, SC), March 4, 1808; *Essex Register, Sun* (Pittsfield, MA), March 5, 1808; *Independent Chronicle, Trenton Federalist*, March 7, 1808; *New-Hampshire Gazette*, March 8, 1808; *Commonwealth, City Gazette and Daily Advertiser, Democrat, Essex Register*, March 9, 1808; *Carolina Gazette* (Charleston, SC), March 11, 1808; *Columbian Phenix*, March 12, 1808; *Political Observatory, World* (Bennington, VT), March 14, 1808; *Albany Register, Norfolk Repository* (Dedham, MA), March 15, 1808.

2. On the resolutions of Congress: *Alexandria Daily Advertiser, Columbian Centinel* (Boston), *Essex Register, New-York Evening Post, Public Advertiser, New-York Commercial Advertiser*, February 24, 1808; *Pennsylvania Correspondent and Farmers' Advertiser*, March 1, 1808; *Poulson's*, March 2, 1808; *Relfs Philadelphia Gazette, L'Oracle and Daily Advertiser*, February 25, 1808; *New-York Spectator*, February 27, 1808; *City Gazette and Daily Advertiser*, March 7, 1808; *Commonwealth*, March 9, 1808; *Albany Register, Carolina Gazette*, March 11, 1808; *Columbian Phenix, Sun*, March 12, 1808; *Norfolk Repository*, March 15, 1808; *Republican Spy* (Northampton, MA), March 16, 1808; *Miller's Weekly Messenger* (Pendleton, SC), March 26, 1808); *Farmers' Cabinet* (Amherst, MA), March 29, 1808. On the Dickinson College board of trustees: *Poulson's*, March 10, 1808; *Essex Register*, March 23, 1808.

3. *Democratic Press*, February 19, 1808.

4. *City Gazette and Daily Advertiser*, March 4, 1808.

5. Psalm 118:22.

6. *Albany Register*, March 4, 1808.

7. Tench Coxe to Charles Thomson, September 26, 1808. Andre deCoppet Collection, PUL.

8. JD to Tench Coxe, November 19, 1806. Coxe, HSP.

9. *Philadelphia Inquirer*, June 22, 1829.

10. *Democratic Press*, October 4 and 14, 1813; February 1, November 25, 1814. *True American* (Bedford, PA), April 6, 1815. See also October 22, 1813; *Poulson's*, August 19, 1819.

11. "[T]he sage, the patriot, and the Christian, John Dickinson, a citizen as eminent for wisdom, as he was conspicuous for private and social virtues," James Wilkinson, *Memoirs of My Own Times* (Philadelphia: A. Small, 1816), xiv.

12. *Reporter* (Washington, PA), May 10, 1819.

13. *Poulson's*, October 29, 1829; *Berks and Schuylkill Journal* (Reading, PA), June 17, 1826.

14. By Miller Dunott of Wilmington; *Poulson's*, September 9, 1820.

15. *Philadelphia Inquirer*, December 25, 1899.

16. See Zachary McLeod Hutchins, "The Slave Narrative and the Stamp Act, or Letters from Two American Farmers in Pennsylvania," *Early American Literature* 50, no. 3 (2015): 645–80.

17. For more detailed discussions of JD's present obscurity, on which the following paragraphs draw, see Jane E. Calvert, "Myth-Making and Myth-Breaking in the Historiography on John Dickinson," *The Journal of the Early Republic* 34, no. 3 (2014): 467–80; and "Introduction," *WJD*, 1:xvii–xli.

18. JD to Benjamin Rush, April 27, 1797.

19. Marbled [c. 1821] and white [c. 1837] notebooks of SND. Logan, HSP.

20. *Memoir, Correspondence, and Miscellanies, from the Papers of Thomas Jefferson*, ed. Thomas Jefferson Randolph, 4 vols. (Charlottesville: F. Carr and Co., 1829), 1:9.

21. Boyd, "Disputed Authorship."

22. Paul L. Ford, *The Writings of John Dickinson* (Philadelphia: Historical Society of Pennsylvania, 1895); "Paul L. Ford Slain by His Brother," *New York Times*, May 9, 1902.

23. For the history of the creation and sanctification of the Declaration of Independence, see Pauline Maier, *American Scripture: The Making of the Declaration of Independence* (New York: Alfred A. Knopf, 1997).

24. George Bancroft, *History of the United States, from the Discovery of the American Continent*, 10 vols. (Boston, 1844–1891), 7:45, 82.

25. Ibid., 7:377.

26. Ibid., 8:72.

27. Ibid., 8:74.

28. Ibid., 8:73.

29. Ibid., 8:56.

30. Ibid., 8:308, 109.

31. Ibid., 8:140.

32. Ibid., 8:452.

33. Ibid., 8:324.

34. Ibid., 9:47–8.

35. Ibid., 9:50.

36. Ibid., 9:47.

37. Ibid., 9:199.

38. *Patriot* (Harrisburg, PA), May 25, 1891.

39. John H. Powell, undated notes. J. H. Powell Papers, APS.

40. Fredrick B. Tolles, "John Dickinson and the Quakers," in *"John and Mary's College": The Boyd Lee Spahr Lectures, 1951–1956* (Carlisle, PA: Fleming H. Revell Co., 1956), 67–88. For a complete chronological bibliography of secondary sources on JD, see "Appendix: Secondary Works on John Dickinson," *WJD*, 1:367–72.

41. David Waldstreicher, "Founders Chic as a Culture War," *Radical History Review* 84 (2002): 185–94.

42. John Ferling, *Independence: The Struggle to Set America Free* (New York: Bloomsbury Press, 2011), 136–7, 330, 331. JD to unknown, August 25, 1776. RRL, HSP.

43. Comedy Central, "I'm a Little Bit Country," *South Park*, S7, E3, 2003.

44. William Murchison, *The Cost of Liberty: The Life of John Dickinson* (Wilmington: Intercollegiate Studies Institute, 2013), 84, 206.

45. Richard Beeman, *Our Lives, Our Fortunes and Our Sacred Honor: The Forging of American Independence, 1774–1776* (New York: Basic Books, 2013), 471, n. 3.

46. Ibid., 380.

47. JD, "To My Opponents," *FJ*, December 24, 1782, which also appears in full in Charles J. Stillé, *The Life and Times of John Dickinson, 1732–1808* (Philadelphia: HSP, 1891), 364–414. Manuscript drafts of this explanation and other writing on the topic can be found in RRL, HSP.

48. Beeman, *Our Lives, Our Fortunes*, 64, 77, 78.

49. Joseph J. Ellis, *The Cause: The American Revolution and Its Discontents, 1773–1783* (Liveright, 2021), Kindle edition, 72, 335, 64–5.

50. Ellis, *His Excellency*, 29, 57.

51. Bernstein, *Education of John Adams*, 180.

52. Gordon S. Wood, *The Americanization of Benjamin Franklin* (New York: Penguin Press, 2004), 158.

53. Joseph J. Ellis, *American Sphinx: The Character of Thomas Jefferson* (New York: Alfred A. Knopf, 1997), 62.

54. JD to Benjamin Rush, October 17, 1797. DCA.

55. Ibid., April 27, 1797.

56. JD to Albanus Charles Logan, March 3, 1804. Logan, HSP.

Index

For the benefit of digital users: indexed terms that span two pages (e.g., 52–53) may, on occasion, appear on only one of those pages.